Shake Rattle & Roll

ROCK & ROLL

Reference Series
Tom Schultheiss, Series Editor

Available only through Popular Culture, Ink., P.O. Box 1839, Ann Arbor, Michigan 48106
Phone 1(800) 678-8828 or (313) 973-1460.

**Available only through Popular Culture, Ink., P.O. Box 1839, Ann Arbor, Michigan 48106
Phone 1(800) 678-8828 or (313) 973-1460.**

Shake Rattle & Roll

THE GOLDEN AGE OF AMERICAN ROCK 'N ROLL, VOLUME 1: 1952-1955

by
Lee Cotten

Popular Culture, Ink.
1989

Book design and layout by Tom Schultheiss.
Graphic arts direction by Carol Jennet.
Cover design by Diane Bareis.
Text preparation by Tonya White and Gloria Thompson.
All cover art is copyright © 1989 by Popular Culture, Ink.
All Rights Reserved.

ISBN 1-56075-017-0
LC 87-63455

Published by Popular Culture, Ink., P.O. Box 1839,
Ann Arbor, Michigan 48106 U.S.A.

"The best rock-and-roll books in the world!"

Contents

Artists Of The Month, 1952-1955

This book is dedicated to
the memory
of
JOE TURNER
The Boss of the Blues

"ROCK 'N ROLL IS JUST RHYTHM AND BLUES UP-TEMPO."

Little Richard

(On the occasion of the 50th anniversary
of the birth of Elvis Presley)

Preface

The year 1986 marked the official beginning of the Rock And Roll Hall Of Fame. On January 23, the first ten performers were honored at an induction ceremony, and in May, Cleveland was chosen as the permanent site for the hall of fame museum. The elite ten, chosen from a list forty-one nominees by 200 rock music experts, were Chuck Berry, James Brown, Ray Charles, Sam Cooke, Fats Domino, the Everly Brothers, Buddy Holly, Jerry Lee Lewis, Little Richard, and Elvis Presley. Special awards were also presented to acknowledge the contributions of several nonperformers as well as early blues, country and gospel artists. Initial recipients in these secondary categories were the founder of Memphis' Sun Records Sam Phillips, deejay Alan Freed, country singer Jimmie Rodgers, and bluesmen Robert Johnson and Jimmy Yancey. A year later, an additional fifteen performers were inducted into the Hall of Fame: Bo Diddley, Bill Haley, Aretha Franklin, Rick Nelson, Smokey Robinson, B.B. King, Roy Orbison, Eddie Cochran, Clyde McPhatter, Marvin Gaye, the Coasters, Carl Perkins, Joe Turner, Muddy Waters, and Jackie Wilson. Also honored at the 1987 induction were blues artist T-Bone Walker, country artist Hank Williams, r&b/pop artist Louis Jordan, Atlantic Records founders Ahmet Ertegun and Jerry Wexler, and Leonard Chess, founder of Chess Records. Those inducted in the third year, January 1988, were The Beatles, The Beach Boys, The Drifters, Bob Dylan, and Diana Ross and The Supremes. Other 1988 honorees were folk singer Woody Guthrie, blues singer Leadbelly, pop/jazz guitarist Les Paul, and Berry Gordy, Jr., founder of the Motown Records empire. Recently the Hall of Fame 1989 inductees and honorees were named. The first group is comprised of The Rolling Stones, The Temptations, Stevie Wonder, Dion, and Otis Redding; the second includes blues singer Bessie Smith, r&b/pop vocal group The Ink Spots, gospel group The Soul Stirrers, and producer/record company owner Phil Spector. Of the fifty-four names mentioned above, twenty-one play an important part in the four years covered in this, the first volume of a chronological history of American rock 'n roll's earliest days . . . 1952-1955.

No one would contradict me if I said that rock 'n roll music in the 1980s is vastly different from its predecessor in the 1950s. Thirty years ago, many independent record companies were operated by ex-musicians, record collectors, and music store owners. There were a few entrepreneurs, but the vast majority of rhythm and blues (and later rock 'n roll) labels were operated by people who, first of all, understood and loved the music and the musicians for aesthetic reasons. Unfortunately, today there is an unbalanced emphasis in the record industry on commercial success. Owners frequently have no direct connection with the music, being primarily accountants or professional businessmen. There is much less patience in the 1980s than there was in the 1950s in every facet of our daily life. In music, this translates into pressure on the artist to have a hit record with the first release. Artists are not given the luxury of time to develop an audience. New talent that cannot produce an immediate profit for the company is discarded.

The sound of today's rock music is also far removed from that generated in the fifties. Advances in the ability to generate music electronically are responsible in large part for the current "sound" of modern rock music. But the biggest single change for all recorded musicians has been the expanding use of the multi-track tape recorder, which has freed musicians from the requirement of having to interact with their fellow players. Music can be layered, rerecorded, and overdubbed. The lead singer is not required to coexist with the backing vocal group; the guitarist often never sees the drummer; the string section can be recorded in New York on Monday and the horn section can be recorded in Memphis a week or more later. The deep-rooted result has been that rock 'n roll today is packaged for the masses. There are no mistakes on the record, and there is often no excitement. Whether or not the rock 'n roll of the 1950s was "better" than its 1980s offspring could be debated for years. But, it most certainly was different.

Writing this book has been a rebirth of sorts for me. As a hobby that started in 1954 actually became a business fifteen years ago, my personal study of the music decreased. In the beginning of my addiction to rock 'n roll, I obsessively made complicated catalogues of artists and songs, "top ten" lists, biographies, and discographies. I was forever cross-checking and indexing the information in countless formats. Over the years, as I talked "music" with thousands of other rock 'n roll collectors, I came to realize that the need for tangible inventories is a common occurrence. Fortunately, I retained many of my files, some dating back to the 1950s, and their existence is the nucleus of this book.

Upon completion of the first manuscript for *All Shook Up: Elvis Day-By-Day, 1954-1977* in December 1983, I began to organize this material with the idea of someday publishing it in a usable format for other collectors. With the green light from Pierian Press in 1984, I found myself in the grips of yet another addiction: collecting and checking mountains of facts. The result is the first of a planned multi-part chronological history of American rock 'n roll music, from its beginnings through to the end of its "golden age" in the 1960s. It is expected that each book will encompass approximately four years (it's nice that the musical trends that go together to make up rock 'n roll fit neatly into four-year time spans). Volume 2 will start with Elvis Presley's first national televised performance (January 1956) and end with his title of "King of Rock 'n Roll" being challenged by Frankie, Ricky, Fabian, Paul, and a whole host of Bobbys as he languishes in West Germany (compliments of the U.S. Army). Volume 3 will start just before Elvis's triumphant return to civilian life (and rock 'n roll) and end with the years of dance-crazes and girl groups. The final volume will begin with the Beatles' descent on an unsuspecting America (February

1964) and end just after the celebration of Woodstock. It promises to be a long, fascinating, and ultimately rewarding journey.

The sources for this book are truly countless. So much has been read and absorbed by me over the last thirty years that specific credit often cannot be given. Each of the forty-eight biographies that conclude the monthly chapters in this first volume is the result of research that often included more than a dozen sources. The information on individual performances in theaters and clubs came primarily from Black-oriented newspapers serving those cities which I chose to represent the United States during the period covered by this book: Los Angeles, Baltimore, New York, Detroit, Philadelphia, New Orleans, Washington, and Chicago. These cities were chosen both for their contribution to rhythm and blues as well as their geographical location. The importance of the Northeastern theater circuit (the Apollo, Howard, Royal, Regal, Earle, and the Uptown) was balanced by the Midwestern clubs in Chicago and Detroit and the ballrooms in Los Angeles and New Orleans. It would have been nearly impossible and very repetitious to cover the entire country more completely.

This book is broken down into as many daily entries as possible. Where a specific date could not be determined, then the item appears under one of the "Early," "Mid-," or "Late" monthly entries. Record releases appear on Monday of each week and are listed under the "first week of January," etc. The date of individual record releases represents the actual week that the record was *distributed* by the record company as close as can be determinded, since in some cases, independent companies were forced by economics to distribute their records on a piecemeal basis across the country.

LEE COTTEN
Sacramento, California

Introduction

**You Ain't Heard Rock 'N Roll Until You've Heard
The Ames Brothers' "So Will I" (Victor)**

**Rock 'N Roll With a Cha-Cha Beat
(Alan Dales's "Rockin' The Cha-Cha" on Coral)**

**A Rockin' Big Band Sound
(Ray Anthony's "Flip Flop" on Capitol)**

**Perry Como In Action On A Great 'Rock-And-Roll' Record
("Ko-Ko-Mo" on Victor)**

All of the above headlines ran in advertisements in 1955.

Rock 'n roll defies easy definition. I have been listening to rock 'n roll music for more than thirty years, and I still am not certain what specific ingredients must be present to qualify one song and not another. The fine line between rock 'n roll, rhythm and blues, and rockabilly is smeared beyond all hope of restoration.

But, I am certain *not one* of the above four songs are rock 'n roll.

I also know that to adequately study such a long-term and ongoing phenomenon, the reader must look at as many specific points as possible, preferably in a chronological context, noting that each step is built upon the preceding advancements. Of the hundreds of books written on the subject of rock 'n roll, not one attempts to cover the subject in such minute detail. And, it is only through poring over the day-by-day activities of many artists, agents, record companies, theaters, and night clubs that the trends that came together to form rock 'n roll become increasingly apparent.

THE FIRST ROCK 'N ROLL RECORD

During the normal course of this book, the reader might well ask, "Which *was* the first record that can be pointed to as the 'missing link,' the one that first truly qualifies as rock 'n roll?"

This is a legitimate question, and I feel it should be answered up front. Most authors on the subject cite "Gee" by the Crows, which was a top-selling r&b record in the spring of 1954. Others have picked "Sh-Boom" by the Chords from the summer of that same year. Neither one actually fits the correct time frame upon closer scrutiny. Forgotten are "Money Honey" by the Drifters and "Crazy Man Crazy" by Bill Haley from 1953, or "60 Minute Man" by the Dominoes and "Rocket 88" by Jackie Brenston from 1951. Or the hits by Fats Domino that began appearing in 1950. And, what about "Drinkin' Wine Spo-Dee-O-Dee" by Stick McGhee from 1949? Then there are Louis Jordan's records from the mid-1940s. Arguments have been made for, and against, all of the above.

Of those just mentioned, Brenston's record has the fastest and most frantic delivery, but there is no back beat taking the front line. Fats Domino's early songs were more a cross between the popular boogie-woogie styles of Joe Turner and Amos Milburn and the blues of Charles Brown and T-Bone Walker. The Dominoes and the Drifters come close, but they are only the forerunners of rock 'n roll. Haley had the right idea if only he would really "cut loose" one time. McGhee's classic is too restrained. And Jordan is more of a bridge between big band boogie and rhythm and blues.

The first record that I would tag as rock 'n roll was the biggest r&b hit of 1952, "Lawdy Miss Clawdy" by Lloyd Price on the small Specialty label. The recording has all of the earmarks of classic rock 'n roll: the vocal is in a strained posture; the loose arrangement allows instrumental freedom; but, most of all, there is the pounding drum punctuating the second (or "back") beat. One thing is certain, the sound of rock 'n roll has that beat out front. In an interview, the late Bumps Blackwell, artist and repertoire chief for Specialty Records (Price's label at the time), agreed. And "Lawdy Miss Clawdy" is a record that he did *not* produce.

TRENDS IN RHYTHM AND BLUES MUSIC

Certainly, there were recordings that qualified as "modern" rhythm and blues before 1952. But, my choice to start this series of books with 1952 is not based on an arbitrary need to begin at a specific time. In 1952, the forces that were finally brought together to form rock 'n roll were at that moment coming into full play.

The history of any musical form is liquid. Ideas continually flow from tributaries into the mainstream. Rhythm and blues did not start in 1954, or 1952, or 1949, or with any one artist or any one record. And rock 'n roll did not emerge newborn from rhythm and blues on a specific date. These changes took many years, as record companies and recording artists probed to find musical styles that would please the postwar audience. At the same time, social upheaval had a two-pronged effect of bringing Blacks into the central flow of the nation and widening the rift between teen-agers and their parents. Rock 'n roll music would prove to be both the surest gauge of age and the focal point for an enormous amount of pent-up rage.

As 1952 opens, the music called rhythm and blues represents a blending of the styles that have gone before: boogie and blues. Boogie represented the "jump" side of the coin and the blues the "ballad" side.

Boogie-woogie came to prominence in the late 1930s, and it has maintained its stronghold as one branch of rhythm and blues music ever since. The rolling rhythms of boogie called New Orleans and St. Louis home, and they could be heard in the tunes of Amos Milburn, Roy Brown, Fats Domino, and Joe Turner.

Blues in 1952, on the other hand, has to be divided into two distinct categories. Country blues (or Delta blues or Mississippi blues) was uncomplicated and born of the hardships of farming land that could never be owned in a region of the country that suppressed every iota of personal freedom for Black people. Urban (or city) blues sang of a different form of suppression: economic ghettos, lost dreams, displacement, factory work. But the universal themes of the blues ran through both: lost love and bad whiskey. And, there were more than just the regional differences. Country blues was a solo voice wailing against the backdrop of a flattop guitar punctuated by the moaning of a hand-me-down harmonica. It was relegated to the street corner and front porch. City blues had pianos and saxophones and amplifiers so that the music could be heard in the back of crowded night clubs. It could jump with electricity and still tell its woeful tale. City blues romped on 50,000-watt radio waves heard halfway across the country. Country blues wafted across the fields from the cramped quarters of a radio station above the feed store. In the city, the blues was slick and smooth. In the country, the blues was gritty and gutsy.

Behind both boogie and blues, there was gospel. Virtually every performer highlighted in this book came from a church choir background. The music in Black churches was pervasive, and the fervor with which it was sung was of equal importance. The division within the Black community on the matter of gospel *vs* blues ran as deep as any other single issue. A singer who dared to cross the line from gospel to blues risked condemnation within his own family. Yet, it was not until the blues singers infused their performances with gospel emotions that rhythm and blues finally became a national music.

Before that time came, there had to be a mixture of boogie and blues. No artist could hope to extend their musical lifespan without variety in their stage act. Joe Turner constantly crossed the line, combining rhythm and blues in a manner that suited his needs at the time. So did Charles Brown and T-Bone Walker. And, as country blues became amplified (Muddy Waters and B. B. King are the best known examples), the musical divisions quickly lost the specific edges that had made them unique.

The most important trend unfolding in 1952 was the increased influence of the country blues singers in the national market. Record companies were taking these artists and imposing on them fuller musical arrangements, dressing them up for the Northern buyers. The result would eventually influence the "pop" market itself.

RHYTHM AND BLUES BEFORE 1952

There were a few rhythm and blues hits in each of the years just preceding 1952 that I feel qualify for inclusion in this book:

1949

Spring
"Ain't Nobody's Business" - Jimmy Witherspoon
"Drinkin' Wine Spo-Dee-O-Dee" - Stick McGhee
"Hucklebuck" - Paul Williams

Summer
"Blue And Lonesome" - Memphis Slim
"D'Natural Blues" - Lucky Millinder
"Drinkin' Wine Spo-Dee-O-Dee" - Wynonie Harris
"Hold Me Baby" - Amos Milburn
"Hucklebuck" - Roy Milton
"Little Girl Don't Cry" - Bull Moose Jackson
"Tell Me So" - Orioles

Fall
"All She Wants To Do Is Rock" - Wynonie Harris
"Baby Get Lost" - Dinah Washington
"Numbers Boogie" - Sugar Chile Robinson
"Rooming House Boogie" - Amos Milburn
"So Long" - Ruth Brown

Early Winter
"Blues For My Baby" - Billy Wright
"Boogie At Midnight" - Roy Brown
"Guess Who" - Ivory Joe Hunter
"I'll Get Along Somehow" - Larry Darnell
"No Rollin' Blues" - Jimmy Witherspoon
"Why Don't You Haul Off And Love Me" - Bull Moose Jackson

1950

Late Winter
"Anytime, Any Place, Any Where" - Joe Morris (with Laurie Tate)
"Double Crossin' Blues" - Johnny Otis (with Little Esther and
    the Robins)
"Forgive And Forget" - Orioles
"For You My Love" - Larry Darnell
"I Almost Lost My Mind" - Ivory Joe Hunter
"Information Blues" - Roy Milton
"Rag Mop" - Lionel Hampton

Spring
"I Need You So" - Ivory Joe Hunter
"Mistrustin' Blues" - Johnny Otis (with the Robins, Little Esther
    & Mel Walker)
"Rag Mop" - Joe Liggins and his Honeydrippers

Summer
"Every Day I Have The Blues" - Lowell Fulson
"The Fat Man" - Fats Domino
"Hard Luck Blues" - Roy Brown
"I Almost Lost My Mind" - Nat "King" Cole
"I Wanna Be Loved" - Dinah Washington

Fall
"Blood Shot Eyes" - Wynonie Harris
"Blue Shadow" - Lowell Fulson
"Deceivin' Blues" - Johnny Otis (with Little Esther and Mel Walker)
"Love Don't Love Nobody" - Roy Brown

Early Winter

"Every Night About This Time" - Fats Domino
"Lovin' Machine" - Wynonie Harris

1951

Late Winter

"Bad, Bad Whiskey" - Amos Milburn
"Red's Boogie" - Piano Red
"Rockin' Blues" - Johnny Otis (with Mel Walker)
"Telephone Blues" - Floyd Dixon

Spring

"Don't Take Your Love From Me" - Joe Morris (with Laurie Tate)
"I Apologize" - Billy Eckstine

Summer

"Don't You Know I Love You So" - Clovers
"Gee Baby" - Johnny Otis (with Mel Walker)
"I'm Waiting Just For You" - Lucky Millinder
"Rocket 88" - Jackie Brenston (with Ike Turner's band)

Fall

"Chains Of Love" - Joe Turner
"Cold Cold Heart" - Dinah Washington
"The Glory Of Love" - Five Keys
"I Got Loaded" - Peppermint Harris
"60 Minute Man" - The Dominoes
"'T' 99 Blues" - Jimmy Nelson

Early Winter

"Best Wishes" - Roy Milton
"Cry" - Johnny Ray
"Little Red Rooster" - The Griffin Brothers (with Margie Day)
"Weepin' And Cryin'" - The Griffin Brothers (with Tommy Brown)

TOP RHYTHM AND BLUES ARTISTS BEFORE 1952

Louis Armstrong [1]	Rosco Gordon	Lucky Millinder
Charles Brown	The Griffin Brothers	The Mills Brothers[1]
Roy Brown	Lionel Hampton [1]	Roy Milton
Ruth Brown	Peppermint Harris	Joe Morris
The Cardinals	Wynonie Harris	The Orioles
Savanah Churchill	John Lee Hooker	Johnny Otis
The Clovers	Lightnin' Hopkins	The Ravens
Nat "King" Cole [1]	The Ink Spots [1]	Joe Turner
Varetta Dillard	Louis Jordan	Sarah Vaughan [1]
Fats Domino	The Larks	Mel Walker
The Dominoes	Joe Liggins	T-Bone Walker
Billy Eckstine [1]	Little Esther	Dinah Washington
H-Bomb Ferguson	Buddy Lucas	Sonny Boy Williamson
Ella Fitzgerald [1]	Percy Mayfield	Jimmy Witherspoon
Lowell Fulson	Amos Milburn	

([1] - denotes Black artists generally regarded to be in the "pop" market)

THE TOUR CIRCUITS

Commercial music has at its very center a cycle that perpetuates and feeds on itself. The artist strives for that elusive hit record that will make him an important personality and lead to club and theater bookings, which in turn lead to ever higher sales of his recordings. The very large number of r&b acts that were constantly on the road is an indication of the great interest that rhythm and blues records held in the national marketplace. To keep this conglomeration of talent on the move, a half dozen booking agents toiled full time keeping their clients performing in a variety of settings.

THE NORTHEAST THEATERS

Every major urban center had at least one movie theater that catered exclusively to the Black audience. In New York's district of Harlem it was the Apollo. In Washington it was the Howard. In Philadelphia it was the Earle and later the Uptown. In Chicago it was the Regal. These theaters, being firstly movie houses, to a varying degree also presented live entertainment between the feature films. This entertainment, by 1952, consisted of a variety revue booked into each theater on a weekly basis, opening in a new town each Friday night, closing the following Thursday, and then moving on to the next stop. Acts were booked on these circuits in package tours which consisted of an instrumental combo or orchestra, a comedian, a tap dance team, maybe an acrobatic team, and one or two rhythm and blues vocalists or groups. The Theater Booking Association at one time kept forty theaters, the majority of which were located in the northeastern quarter of the country, on a never-ending tour circuit. "TBA" also came to be known as "tough on Black asses" due to the low wages, poor working conditions, and substandard hotels and restaurants which were the norm for the entertainers. In 1952 the number of active Black theaters had dwindled to maybe a dozen, and of these, only the Apollo and the Howard offered entertainment on a regular basis.

THE SOUTHERN CLUBS AND THE WEST COAST BALLROOMS

Outside the urbanized Northeast, entertainment for the rhythm and blues audience could usually be found in a loose-knit trail of night clubs, saloons, and ballrooms. The term "chitlin circuit" is often used to describe these road houses where entertainers vied with the smell of barbecued ribs, collard greens, and chitlins. Club work was much rougher here than on the theater tours. The longest stand usually ran to three days, Friday through Sunday. During the week, it was one night here and the next night a hundred miles down the road. Crowds in the saloons were loud and unrestrained. In the ballrooms, patrons came to dance the night away. The music heard ran to the raucous and not the polished. Entertainers who made their home on these endless one-night stands were a special breed: Charles Brown, Roy Milton, the Midnighters, Little Richard, Ray Charles, the "5" Royales, Jimmy McCracklin, Pee Wee Crayton, Smiley Lewis, and Fats Domino. Few of these performers were asked to spend a week in one town, and they were forced to develop an onstage act that was more explosive than the theater regulars. When you have only four hours to make a name for yourself, you have to bring the house down every night.

RECORD COMPANIES

Just as with the venue for entertainment, the specific location of the various companies that issued records for the rhythm and blues audience had a determining factor in the "sound" of the music. The phonograph record industry, like so many other businesses in this country, had its commercial start in New York City. It is only natural that the independent rhythm and blues record companies should spring up here, too. New York was the center for the booking agencies and the record distributors. This was the home of the trade papers, the critics - the movers and shakers. It was also the home of a large Black population. But, rhythm and blues music, as noted above, was fractured into various forms, each with a different audience depending as much on location as any other single factor. So, in areas far removed from New York, record companies evolved to serve the local and, if they were fortunate, the national audience. Los Angeles, Chicago, New Orleans, Detroit, Cincinnati, and Philadelphia all had r&b companies. So did Houston, Nashville, Gary, Newark, Jackson, and Memphis.

The music issued by these various companies generally ran in specific patterns. New York's Atlantic, Rama, and Jubilee hired professional studio musicians, arrangers, and songwriters the same way that the major "pop" record companies had done for years. Chicago's Chess issued basic blues numbers sung by displaced Mississippians who had traveled north in search of a better life. The West Coast companies RPM/Flair/Modern, Imperial, and Aladdin, feeling that there was a market but no local talent, began issuing records recorded in New Orleans or Memphis, thereby imparting a "Southern" feel to their records. In Memphis (Sun/Flip), Houston (Peacock), and Nashville (Excello/ Nashboro), the records had even more of this country sound, as befits the background of both the owners and artists. Cincinnati's King and Newark's Savoy Records issued mixtures of styles that sounded at times like New York and at times like New Orleans.

In the rhythm and blues field, unlike the "pop" and country fields, the independent record company was much more likely to have a hit record than were the "top five" major companies. This is a reflection of the personal involvement that the owners of these companies took in their artists and in the distribution of the records. Often, the owner was the sole employee of the record company with the exception of a secretary. He searched out the talent, worked the tape machines in the studio, plugged the records with deejays, and distributed his records by lugging them from store to store in the trunk of his car. Such dedication brought results in the form of closer contact with his clientele both inside and outside the industry.

The most active record companies issuing rhythm and blues *before 1952* included:

Aladdin	Federal
Aristocrat (soon to be Chess)	Freedom
Atlantic	Imperial
Bethlehem	Jubilee
Capitol [2]	King
Chess	M-G-M
Dot	Mercury [2]
Duke	Miracle

Modern
National
Natural
Okeh (subsidiary of Columbia [2])
Peacock
Rainbow
Regal
Rockin'

RPM
Savoy
Sittin' In With
Specialty
Supreme
Swing Time
Victor [2] (also known as R.C.A. Victor)

([2] - denotes the major companies regarded as members of the "top 5" [along with Decca])

THE R&B DEEJAY

After World War II, the number of radio stations in the country committed to playing the blues was very small, and the few r&b markets were located mainly in the major northeastern cities and in an occasional southern city. By the end of 1951 this pattern had changed; across the country, almost every independent station had a deejay programming either exclusively r&b or a combination of "pop" and r&b. The South was particularly strong in this field, with several stations owned and operated by Blacks. As the number of hours devoted to r&b programming grew, the importance of the deejay increased proportionally.

At the sametime, the dividing line separating "pop" and r&b was becoming invisible, and the r&b deejay's biggest problem was whether or not to include any "pop" material in his rhythm and blues format. The r&b deejay could more easily "break" new releases than his "pop" counterpart because most r&b deejays were completely autonomous in their programming. The high turnover of new rhythm and blues acts resulting from the failure of the act to "click" with its second or third release meant that "the latest" became the r&b deejay's battle cry.

COVER RECORDS

Over the past thirty years, one of the most maligned practices in the music industry has been the cover record, which became a major trend in music during the period from 1952 into the mid 1950s. As rhythm and blues songs took an increasingly large share of the "pop" market, the major record companies, whose revenues depended on selling their product to a primarily White audience, took the r&b song, and in many cases the specific musical arrangement, and had it "covered" by one of their top-selling "pop" artists. The "majors" justified this practice in a variety of ways: covers opened up a wider market for the r&b song, artist, and label; covers made money for the r&b artist, who was himself frequently the composer of the song for the r&b label, which even more often self-published the song. And, covers, in one form or another, dated back to the very beginning of the song publishing business and were not limited to "pop" covers of r&b material.

The practice reached a pre-1952 peak with covers of the songs of country and western star Hank Williams. "Cold, Cold Heart" was very successful in a 1951 cover version by Tony Bennett. After Williams' untimely death on January 1, 1953, there was an increase in the number of covers of more of Williams's songs and many were hits for "pop" artists: "Jambalaya," "Your Cheatin' Heart," "Settin' The Woods on Fire," and "Hey Good Lookin'."

The inner workings of the music industry created the climate for cover records. An interview with Columbia Records' artist and repertoire chief Mitch Miller, published in *Audio* magazine (November and December 1985), sheds some light on this matter. According to Miller, in the years before rhythm and blues became a factor in the "pop" field, publishers, in an effort to reap higher profits, would line up as many artists as possible to record a new song. Exclusive rights for a singer were unknown, and specific release dates for records were arranged so that all versions were issued at the same time. It was the *song* that was important because each time a song was performed live, played over the radio or on a jukebox, or sold on a record, the publisher made money.

By the early 1950s, most independent r&b companies often initiated deals between the r&b and "pop" record companies *before* the original record was released. And, since the r&b record company and publisher were the same entity, money was made no matter which version of the record sold. By 1954, the "cover" record had turned into an industry of its own.

The following is a partial list of 150 "covers" of r&b songs by "pop" artists from just two years, 1954 and 1955:

Cover Artist /Record Label	Song Title	Original Artist
Louis Armstrong (Decca)	Only You	Cues, Platters
Louis Armstrong (Decca)	Sincerely	Moonglows
Les Baxter (Capitol)	Earth Angel	Penguins
Les Baxter (Capitol)	Happy Baby	Bill Haley
Pat Boone (Dot)	Ain't That A Shame	Fats Domino
Pat Boone (Dot)	At My Front Door	El Dorados
Pat Boone (Dot)	Gee Whittakers	Five Keys
Pat Boone (Dot)	Tra-La-La	Fats Domino
Pat Boone (Dot)	Tutti Frutti	Little Richard
Pat Boone (Dot)	Two Hearts	Charms
Bop-A-Loos (Mercury)	Hearts Of Stone	Jewels, Charms
Teresa Brewer (Coral)	Pledging My Love	Johnny Ace
Burton Sisters (Victor)	Piddily Patter	Nappy Brown
Cab Calloway (Bell)	Such A Night	Drifters
Cheers (Capitol)	Bazoom (I Need Your Lovin')	Charms
Cheers (Capitol)	Whadya Want	Charms
Dorothy Collins (Coral)	My Boy Flat-Top	Boyd Bennett
Perry Como (Victor)	Ko-Ko-Mo	Gene and Eunice
Dolly Cooper (Victor)	I Wanna Know	DuDroppers
Don Cornell (Coral)	Most Of All	Moonglows
Crew-Cuts (Mercury)	Chop Chop Boom	Danderliers, Savoys
Crew-Cuts (Mercury)	Don't Be Angry	Nappy Brown
Crew-Cuts (Mercury)	Earth Angel	Penguins
Crew-Cuts (Mercury)	Gum Drop	Otis Williams (Charms)
Crew-Cuts (Mercury)	Ko-Ko-Mo	Gene and Eunice
Crew-Cuts (Mercury)	Sh-Boom	Chords
Crew-Cuts (Mercury)	Oop Shoop	Shirley Gunter
Crew-Cuts (Mercury)	Story Untold	Nutmegs

Crew-Cuts (Mercury)	Two Hearts	Charms
Crew-Cuts (Mercury)	Unchained Melody	Al Hibbler, Roy Hamilton
Gary Crosby and Louis Armstrong (Decca)	Ko-Ko-Mo	Gene and Eunice
Bill Darnell and Betty Clooney ("X")	Ko-Ko-Mo	Gene and Eunice
DeCastro Sisters (Abbott)	Teach Me Tonight	Dinah Washington
Lola Dee (Mercury)	Only You	Cues, Platters
Lola Dee (Mercury)	Ookey Ook	Penguins
Helene Dixon (Epic)	Piddily Patter	Nappy Brown
Rusty Draper (Mercury)	Seventeen	Boyd Bennett
Les Elgart (Columbia)	Bazoom (I Need Your Lovin')	Charms
Esquire Boys (Guyden)	Rock A-Beatin' Boogie	Treniers, Bill Haley
Billy Fields (M-G-M)	Sincerely	Moonglows
Eddie Fisher (Victor)	Dungaree Doll	Rock Brothers
Eddie Fisher (Victor)	Song Of The Dreamer	Billy Brooks
5 DeMarco Sisters (Decca)	Love Me	Willie and Ruth
Ralph Flanigan (Victor)	Sh-Boom	Chords
Fontane Sisters (Dot)	Hearts Of Stone	Jewels, Charms
Fontane Sisters (Dot)	Most Of All	Moonglows
Fontane Sisters (Dot)	Rollin' Stone	Marigolds
Fontane Sisters (Dot)	Seventeen	Boyd Bennett
Four Aces (Decca)	(It's No) Sin	Savannah Churchill
Four Coins (Epic)	I Love You Madly	Charlie and Ray
Four Coins (Epic)	Story Untold	Nutmegs
Four Escorts (Victor)	Love Me	Willie and Ruth
Four Lads (Columbia)	Pledging My Love	Johnny Ace
Stan Freberg (Capitol)	Great Pretender	Platters
Stan Freberg (Capitol)	Sh-Boom	Chords
Gadabouts (Wing)	Two Things I Love	Cardinals
Sunny Gale (Victor)	Goodnight Sweetheart Goodnight	Spaniels
Sunny Gale (Victor)	Soldier Boy	Four Fellows
Sunny Gale (Victor)	Teardrops On My Pillow	Orioles
Ronnie Gaylord (Mercury)	Ain't That A Shame	Fats Domino
Ronnie Gaylord (Mercury)	Pledging My Love	Johnny Ace
Gaylords (Mercury)	My Babe	Little Walter
Georgia Gibbs (Mercury)	Dance With Me Henry (The Wallflower)	Etta James
Georgia Gibbs (Mercury)	I Want You To Be My Baby	Lillian Briggs
Georgia Gibbs (Mercury)	Love Me	Willie and Ruth
Georgia Gibbs (Mercury)	Mambo Baby	Ruth Brown
Georgia Gibbs (Mercury)	Tweedle Dee	LaVern Baker
Goofers (Coral)	Flip, Flop And Fly	Joe Turner
Goofers (Coral)	Hearts Of Stone	Jewels, Charms
Goofers (Coral)	My Babe	Little Walter
Rudy Gray (Capitol)	Hearts Of Stone	Jewels, Charms
Helen Grayco ("X")	Oop Shoop	Shirley Gunter
Hamilton Sisters (Columbia)	Oop Shoop	Shirley Gunter
Jack Haskell (Camden)	Hearts Of Stone	Jewels, Charms

Hilltoppers (Dot)	Only You	Cues, Platters
Hilltoppers (Dot)	Teardrops From My Eyes	Five Keys
Eddie Howard (Mercury)	(It's No) Sin	Savannah Churchill
June Hutton (Capitol)	Gee	Crows
Hutton Sisters (Capitol)	Ko-Ko-Mo	Gene and Eunice
Mickey Katz (Capitol)	Tweedle Dee	LaVern Baker
Lancers (Coral)	Tweedle Dee	LaVern Baker
Lancers (Coral)	Two Hearts	Charms
Snooky Lanson (Camden)	Earth Angel	Penguins
Snooky Lanson (Dot)	Why Don't You Write Me	Jacks
Steve Lawrence (Coral)	The Chicken And The Hawk	Joe Turner
Steve Lawrence (Coral)	Speedo	Cadillacs
Johnny Long (Coral)	Maybellene	Chuck Berry
Jim Lowe (Dot)	Maybellene	Chuck Berry
McGuire Sisters (Coral)	Goodnight Sweetheart Goodnight	Spaniels
McGuire Sisters (Coral)	Sincerely	Moonglows
Tommy Mara (M-G-M)	Pledging My Love	Johnny Ace
Ralph Marterie (Mercury)	Crazy Man Crazy	Bill Haley
Ralph Marterie (Mercury)	Maybellene	Chuck Berry
Ralph Marterie (Mercury)	Ring Dang Doo	Chuck Willis
M-G-M Studio Orch (M-G-M)	Rock Around The Clock	Bill Haley, Sonny Dae
Mills Brothers (Decca)	Gum Drop	Otis Williams
Modernaires (Coral)	At My Front Door	El Dorados
Lou Monte (Victor)	Dance With Me Henry (The Wallflower)	Etta James
Buddy Morrow (Mercury)	Greyhound	Amos Milburn
Buddy Morrow (Mercury)	I Don't Know	Willie Mabon
Buddy Morrow (Mercury)	Night Train	Jimmy Forrest
Buddy Morrow (Mercury)	Rock And Roll	Red Prysock
Buddy Morrow (Mercury)	Rock A-Beatin' Boogie	Treniers, Bill Haley
Ella Mae Morse (Capitol)	Big Mamau	Smiley Lewis
Ella Mae Morse (Capitol)	Forty Cups Of Coffee	Danny Overbea
Ella Mae Morse (Capitol)	Goodnight, Sweetheart Goodnight	Spaniels
Ella Mae Morse (Capitol)	Lovey Dovey	Clovers
Ella Mae Morse (Capitol)	Money Honey	Drifters
Ella Mae Morse (Capitol)	Razzle-Dazzle	Bill Haley
Ella Mae Morse (Capitol)	Seventeen	Boyd Bennett
Pat O'Day (M-G-M)	Earth Angel	Penguins
Pat O'Day (M-G-M)	Soldier Boy	Four Fellows
Patti Page (Mercury)	Everyday	Count Basie with Joe Williams
Patti Page (Mercury)	I Cried	Velvets
Patti Page (Mercury)	I Went To Your Wedding	Steve Gibson with Damita Joe, Little Sylvia
Patti Page (Mercury)	Oh What A Dream	Ruth Brown
Patti Page (Mercury)	Piddily Patter	Nappy Brown
Bunny Paul (Capitol)	Honey Love	Drifters
Bunny Paul (Capitol)	Lovey Dovey	Clovers
Bunny Paul (Capitol)	Song Of The Drummer	Billy Brooks
Bunny Paul (Essex)	Such A Night	Drifters

Mike Pedicin (Victor)	Mambo Rock	Bill Haley
Perez Prado (Victor)	Such A Night	Drifters
Johnny Ray (Columbia)	Flip Flop And Fly	Joe Turner
Johnny Ray (Columbia)	Song Of The Drummer	Billy Brooks
Johnny Ray (Columbia)	Such A Night	Drifters
Joe Reisman (Victor)	Bo Diddley	Bo Diddley
Rhythmettes (Victor)	Only You	Cues, Platters
Jackie Riggs (Media)	Great Pretender	Platters
Tito Rodriguez (Tico)	Ko-Ko-Mo	Gene and Eunice
Something Smith and the the Redheads (Epic)	Gee	Crows
Jo Stafford (Columbia)	I Got A Sweetie [Woman]	Ray Charles
Jo Stafford (Columbia)	Teach Me Tonight	Dinah Washington
Kay Starr (Capitol)	Fool Fool Fool	Clovers
Kay Starr (Capitol)	Wheel Of Fortune	Eddie Wilcox and Sunny Gale
Gale Storm (Dot)	I Hear You Knocking	Smiley Lewis
Gale Storm (Dot)	Teenage Prayer	Gloria Mann
Three Rays (Coral)	The Wallflower	Etta James
Tophatters (Cadence)	Dim, Dim The Lights	Bill Haley
Turtles (Victor)	Mystery Train	Elvis Presley, Junior Parker's Blue Flames
Jane Turzy (Decca)	Such A Night	Drifters
June Valli (Victor)	I Understand	Four Tunes
June Valli (Victor)	Unchained Melody	Al Hibbler, Roy Hamilton
Billy Williams (Coral)	Sh-Boom	Chords
Vicki Young (Capitol)	Hearts Of Stone	Jewels, Charms
Vicki Young (Capitol)	Honey Love	Drifters
Vicki Young (Capitol)	Riot In Cell Block #9	Robins
Vicki Young (Capitol)	Tears On My Pillow	Chimes
Vicki Young (Capitol)	Tweedle Dee	Lavern Baker

"Pop" Record Companies That Covered (number of records/percentage of above list)

(Total 150)

Abbott 1 / 0.6%
Bell 1 / 0.6%
Cadence 1 / 0.6%
Camden (Victor) 2/ 1.3%
Capitol 27 / 18%
Columbia 7 / 4.6% [with affiliates: 12 / 8%]
Coral (Decca) 17 /11.3%
Decca 7 / 4.6% [with affiliates: 24 / 16%]
Dot 16 / 10.6%
Epic (Columbia) 4 / 2.6%
Essex 1 / 0.6%
Guyden 1 / 0.6%
M-G-M 4 / 2.6%
Media 1 / 0.6%
Mercury 36 / 24% [with affiliates: 37 / 24.6%]
Tico 1 / 0.6%

Victor 18 / 12% [with affiliates: 22 / 14.6%]
Wing (Mercury) 1 / 0.6%
"X" (Victor) 2 / 1.3%

　　　As the reader can quickly see from the above chart, four major "pop" companies accounted for over 60 percent of the total number of cover records during the period of 1954-1955.

　　　"Pop" companies and artists were not the only ones covering r&b in the early 1950s. There were several country artists (Red Foley, Elvis Presley, and Marty Robbins are the best known) who issued a series of records which were popular in their own field. "Hearts Of Stone" by Foley, "Baby Let's Play House" and "Mystery Train" by Elvis, and "Maybellene" and "That's All Right" by Robbins were all major c&w releases. Country singer Bonnie Lou built an early career by covering r&b and rock 'n roll with "Seventeen" and "Tweedle Dee."

　　　And, rhythm and blues songs were covered by other r&b and rock 'n roll artists.

　　　The following is a short list:

Cover Artist/ Record Label	Song Title	Original Artist
Boyd Bennett (King)	Poison Ivy	Willie Mabon
Cardinals (Atlantic)	Wheel Of Fortune	Eddie Wilcox, Sunny Gale
Charms (DeLuxe)	Hearts Of Stone	Jewels
Charms (DeLuxe)	Ko-Ko-Mo	Gene and Eunice
Charms (DeLuxe)	Ling Ting Tong	Five Keys
Savannah Churchill (Decca)	Shake A Hand	Faye Adams
Billy Duke (Duke)	Flip, Flop And Fly	Joe Turner
Billy Eckstine (M-G-M)	Only You	Cues, Platters
Flamingos (Parrot)	Ko-Ko-Mo	Gene and Eunice
Bill Haley (Decca)	Burn That Candle	Cues
Bill Haley (Decca)	Forty Cups Of Coffee	Danny Overbea
Bill Haley (Essex)	I'll Be True	Faye Adams
Bill Haley (Decca)	Rock A-Beatin' Boogie	Treniers
Bill Haley (Decca)	Rock Around The Clock	Sonny Dae
Bill Haley (Decca)	See You Later Alligator	Bobby Charles
Bill Haley (Decca)	Shake Rattle And Roll	Joe Turner
Roy Hamilton (Epic)	Unchained Melody	Al Hibbler [3]
Jacks (RPM)	Why Don't You Write Me	Feathers
Gloria Mann (Sound)	Earth Angel	Penguins
Gloria Mann (Sound)	Goodnight, Sweetheart, Goodnight	Spaniels
Marvin and Johnny (Specialty)	Ko-Ko-Mo	Gene and Eunice
Midnighters (Federal)	It's You Baby	Louis Brooks
Johnny Moore (Recorded In Hollywood)	Johnny Ace's Last Letter	Johnny Fuller
Platters (Federal/ Mercury)	Only You	Cues
Savoys (Savoy)	Chop Chop Boom	Danderliers
Squires (Combo)	Sindy	Tenderfoots

Thunderbirds (DeLuxe)	Baby Let's Play House	Arthur Gunter
Thunderbirds (DeLuxe)	Pledging My Love	Johnny Ace
Milt Trenier (Victor)	Rock Bottom	Rams
Titus Turner (Wing)	All Around The World	Little Willie John
Billy Ward & His Dominoes (Federal)	When The Swallows Come Back To Capistrano	Ray-O-Vacs
Chuck Willis (Okeh)	Going To The River	Fats Domino

([3]-Hibbler was a "crossover" artist himself, frequenting both the r&b and "pop" fields)

And, "pop" songs were not immune from being covered by rhythm and blues artists.

The following is a brief list:

Cover Artist/ Record Company	Song Title	Original Artist
Chords (Cat)	Cross Over The Bridge	Patti Page
Counts (Dot)	Let Me Go Lover	Joan Weber
Dominoes (King)	Three Coins In The Fountain	Four Aces
Flamingos (Chance)	Cross Over The Bridge	Patti Page
Four Tunes (Victor)	Come What May	Patti Page
Buddy Lucas (Jubilee)	You Belong To Me	Patti Page
Moonglows (Chance)	Secret Love	Doris Day
Orioles (Jubilee)	Crying In The Chapel	June Valli
Orioles (Jubilee)	In The Chapel In The Moonlight	Kitty Kalen
Orioles (Jubilee)	You Belong To Me	Patti Page

ANSWER RECORDS

Another major trend in rhythm and blues music that began in early 1953 and ran into 1955 was the "answer" record. It all began with Linda Hayes's "Yes I Know" which answered Willie Mabon's "I Don't Know." Mabon's recording was a novelty song that revolved around the phrase, "What did I say to make you mad this time, baby?" (A popular version of the song can be heard on the Blues Brothers first album, "Briefcase Full of Blues.") With the Hayes disk becoming almost as big a hit as the Mabon original, it was inevitable that other records would become the target for answers.

"Mama (He Treats Your Daughter Mean," by Ruth Brown and "Hound Dog" by Willie May Thornton were the first after "I Don't Know" to receive the treatment. But, it was an early 1954 hit by the Royals/Midnighters which set the chain reaction into perpetual motion as answers began answering answers.

Here's a close look at the "Annie Series":

Song Title	Artist	Month Released
Work With Me Annie	Royals (Midnighters)	Feb. 54
Sexy Ways	Midnighters	Jun. 54
Annie Had A Baby	Midnighters	Aug. 54
Annie's Answer	Hazel McCollum and the El Dorados	Oct. 54
My Name Ain't Annie	Linda Hayes	Oct. 54
Annie's Aunt Fannie	Midnighters	Oct. 54
Annie Kicked The Bucket	Nu Tones	Dec. 54
The Wall Flower (Dance With Me Henry)	Etta James	Jan. 55
Tired Of Your Sexy Ways	Mac Burney and the Four Jacks	Feb. 55
Hey Henry	Etta James	May 55
Henry's Got Flat Feet	Midnighters	May 55
Annie Met Henry	Cadets	Jun. 55

THE CROSSOVER

Louis Jordan's novelties were among the precursors of 1950s rhythm and blues, and they were regularly as popular among White audiences as Black. In large measure, artists such as Louis Armstrong, Nat Cole, and Ella Fitzgerald helped break down the stereotypical racial barriers in music. By 1949, the ancient terms "race" and "sepia" had been dropped in favor of rhythm and blues. But, there was still an uncharted line over which most other r&b songs could not pass. These songs were the more "Negro" tunes that White promoters felt displayed feelings too base to inflict upon the ears of the more genteel White audience. Novelties that made fun of "coloreds" were okay (Jordan's "Saturday Night Fish Fry" is the most famous) in much the same way that everyone could have a good laugh at "Amos And Andy" on radio and television, while the idea of two Blacks kissing on screen would be going too far.

I believe it is safe to say that the years following World War II brought about serious economic, social, sexual, moral, and religious changes at a more rapid rate than any previous era. The nation was quite literally on the move, and old ties and mores were dropped as easily as changing addresses. Hundreds of years of subservience suffered by the Blacks in America were rapidly coming to an end. Along with this change, more and more White teen-agers were eager to experience new cultures other than their own. Thus, it was teens who first to accept the sounds of rhythm and blues music in the White market. Justification for forsaking their parents' music was readily available. After all, weren't teen-agers and Blacks kindred spirits? Both slaves to the past?

The first truly rhythm and blues record to make the jump from the r&b market to the "pop" field was "60 Minute Man" by the Dominoes in 1951. The impact of this record went far beyond its titillation with suggestive lyrics. Here was a song which was sung by Blacks who sounded like Blacks. These weren't Blacks singing to a White audience. To insulated White teen-agers, this was a revelation. By the thousands, they started tuning in to the blues radio stations to hear more of the same. The door was swinging open.

It was over a year before another r&b song crossed into the "pop" market, and this time it was the smooth ballad "Crying In The Chapel" by the Orioles. Other versions of the song were already popular before the Orioles released their record, but theirs sold enough copies and received enough airplay and jukebox spins to vie with June Valli and Rex Allen. Another ballad, "Marie" by the Four Tunes, also sold well in the "pop" market in 1953, but it was "Gee" by the Crows in April 1954 that really told of things to come. Another novelty jump number, "Gee" didn't have enough push to stay more than a week on the "pop" charts, but the song was well received among teens. Summer 1954 brought "Sh-Boom" by the Chords, the first rhythm and blues record to crack the *top ten* on the "pop" charts. The impact of this record was widespread. Even though it was covered by the Crew-Cuts (who had the number one hit), the version by the Chords sold impressively well, leading to both a general increase in cover versions and an increase in airplay for original r&b songs. Suddenly, radio stations that had aired only smooth "pop" sounds were playing records by the Charms, the Penguins, the Five Keys, and Bill Haley. Admittedly, Haley wasn't from a rhythm and blues background, but his music was a far cry from the usual "pop" fare. In fact, Haley's records were criss-crossing back and forth from "pop" to r&b with little regard to heritage. By the end of 1955, Chuck Berry's "Maybellene" was the biggest selling rhythm and blues record in both the "pop" and r&b markets, and the top record of the year was Haley's "Rock Around The Clock," which beat out such favorites as "The Yellow Rose Of Texas" and "The Ballad Of Davy Crockett." At the same time, Little Richard's "Tutti Frutti" was inching its way across the land. An otherwise unknown hillbilly named Elvis Presley had been scheduled for four prime time Saturday night television appearances that would begin on January 28, 1956.

In the span of only four short years, a fundamental social change had taken place that would alter the course of American society.

Now it's time to look at those four years beginning with New Year's Day 1952 . . .

Shake Rattle & Roll

THE GOLDEN AGE
OF
AMERICAN ROCK 'N ROLL

1952

1952
A Look Ahead

"THE BLUES START TO FALLING OUT THE CEILING"
Arthur "Big Boy" Crudup

As the year opens, Johnnie Ray's "Cry" is riding high in both the "pop" and rhythm and blues fields, and will go on to be the top-selling record of the year in both areas. The significance of the impact of this record can readily be seen in light of the fact that Johnnie Ray was the *only* White male vocalist up to that time to have a record which sold well enough in the Black market to make the rhythm and blues record sales charts. In fact, only two other White male artists had *ever* been on the rhythm and blues charts: band leader Johnny Otis, whose records featured vocals by the Robins, Little Esther, and Mel Walker; and guitarist Les Paul, whose "How High The Moon" in 1951 featured the gimmicked vocals of wife Mary Ford. This acceptance by Blacks of Johnnie Ray's impassioned style (a major part of his stage act featured a feigned emotional breakdown as he wept to the lyrics of "Cry" and "Little White Cloud That Cried," a stunt that preceded James Browns' similar act by several years) was evidence that racial color lines were drawn by politicians. The average listener and record buyer enjoyed the music with little regard to race.

Nevertheless, the top-selling recording artists of the day are Eddie Fisher, Perry Como, Frankie Laine, Peggy Lee, Rosemary Clooney, Teresa Brewer, Vic Damone, Dinah Shore, Tony Bennett, Doris Day, Eddy Howard, and Les Paul and Mary Ford. The top vocal groups are the Ames Brothers, the Weavers, and the Four Aces. The top bands are lead by Les Baxter and Ray Anthony. Typical record buyers are in their early twenties. In 1952, jukebox owners will buy fifty million 78 rpm records, accounting for fifteen percent of the total number of 78's manufactured. The 45 rpm record had been introduced in June 1949 by RCA Victor as an alternative to the 78, and by 1952 the 45 rpm single had increased its share of the market to thirty percent of all records pressed.

The year will see "Wheel Of Fortune" by Eddie Wilcox and Sunny Gale become the most imitated record, with versions by Dinah Washington, the Cardinals, and Maurice King and his Wolverines in the r&b field, Bobby Wayne in country music, and Kay Starr for the "pop" audience. The immediate upshot of the large number of successful

3

cover versions of "Wheel Of Fortune" is that song publishers start submitting more and better songs to independent rhythm and blues companies for consideration.

Although 1952 will be a transitional year, trends started as early as 1949 continue to have an influence on the records issued this year. The biggest surprise, as well as the biggest r&b record of the year, will come from an unknown New Orleans teen-ager, Lloyd Price, and it will signal another dramatic change in the course of rhythm and blues music. Price will be discovered by West Coast record company executives who are searching through New Orleans for another Fats Domino (who also records for a Los Angeles record company). Instead, they will find an artist who will have an even more drastic effect on r&b than Domino, at least in the short run.

Constant touring is the name of the game for all rhythm and blues artists in 1952. B. B. King will be on the road over 300 days. So will Fats Domino, Amos Milburn, Roy Milton, Joe Liggins, and Louis Jordan. These tours are vital as to the artist's popularity as they are largely responsible for providing the artists with income; royalties from record sales are virtually nonexistent for Black performers.

As evidence of the strength and continued growth of rhythm and blues music in 1952, the independent r&b record companies themselves will work feverishly to acquire new affiliates: Peacock will take over Duke, Modern/RPM starts Flair and Rhythm and Blues, and Chess initiates Checker.

NATIONAL NEWS

Dwight Eisenhower, "Ike," is elected to his first term as President in November, just after America's first H-bomb test on Eniwetok Atoll in the Marshall Islands. The summer presidential conventions are the first covered by television . . . Walter Cronkite, CBS-TV's convention anchorman, is criticized by his bosses for talking too much. "Bwana Devil" is the first commercial 3-D movie, a gimmick that Hollywood hopes will lure television viewers back to the theaters. Chlorophyll is America's newest product, and it promises to make us all more socially acceptable if we will use any of the ninety "green" products containing the substance . . . the American Medical Association is skeptical, noting that goats live on a diet of chlorophyll and still smell bad. Hypnotist Morey Bernstein leads us on a "Search For Bridey Murphy" as Colorado housewife Ruth Simmons recalls her past lives. Vice President Nixon makes his "Checkers" speech, throwing himself on the mercy of the TV audience. The best-selling book of fiction is "The Silver Chalice" by Thomas B. Costain, with over 200,000 copies sold . . . In non-fiction the Revised Standard Version of the Bible sells two million copies. Academy Awards go to "The Greatest Show On Earth," Gary Cooper, and Shirley Booth. "Your Show Of Shows" takes home the Emmy as Best Variety Program, while "I Love Lucy" is voted the Best Situation Comedy. England crowns Queen Elizabeth II, but in America Uncle Miltie is the King of Tuesday Night. The war continues in Korea. Senator McCarthy continues hunting for Communists in the government. There will be over 600 UFO sightings. Suburbs, shopping malls, and outdoor barbecues are becoming the norm . . . so are the terms "baby boom" and "cultural wasteland" . . . .

January 1952

THE RAVENS
The most distinguishing feature of the Ravens was the deep bass voice of Jimmy Ricks (1924-74). The Ravens got together to sing in Harlem in 1945, and during a 1946 appearance at the Apollo Theater they brought the house down with their version of "My Sugar Is So Refined," soon leading to a contract with Hub Records.

JAN 1   New Year's Day 1952 finds the **Ravens** and Erroll Garner in the middle of a three-week booking at the Cafe Society in New York. Also in town, Tiny Bradshaw is currently at the Savoy Ballroom.

Dinah Washington with Cootie Williams and his orchestra are touring the South and the West Coast. The tour started December 24th and will wind up in Oakland on February 11th.

Ruth Brown and Willis Jackson's orchestra are completing two weeks on the road through Indiana, Ohio, New Jersey, Pennsylvania, New York, and Washington, DC.

Joe Liggins and Jimmy Witherspoon headline a New Year's Day show at the Oakland Auditorium in California.

The Howard Theater in Washington is hosting the Lionel Hampton combo through January 3rd.

Sarah Vaughan and Billy Ward and his Dominoes are in the middle of a week's stay at the Regal Theater in Chicago.

Peppermint Harris is currently on a tour of one-nighters in West Virginia.

In Los Angeles, Willie Mae Thornton is in her tenth and final week at the Club Oasis.

Earl Bostic is presently hospitalized in New York City following a December auto accident in Tifton, Georgia, while he was enroute to an engagement in Phoenix City, Alabama. During his six-month recovery, Bostic's combo will be led by Burnie Peacock.

Al Hibbler and Ivory Joe Hunter are at the Frolic Showbar in Detroit, while across town at the Flame Showbar, **LaVern "Little Miss Sharecropper" Baker** will be sharing the bill with any number of other artists over the next six months.

Philadelphia's Club Harlem hosts Chris Powell and his Five Blue Flames.

In New Orleans, Professor Longhair and his Shuffling Hungarians are in their third week of an extended engagement at the Hi-Hat Club.

LaVern Baker was born November 11, 1949, in Chicago. Her first recordings were made in 1949 for Columbia Records as "Little Miss Sharecropper."

JAN 4   At the Apollo Theater in New York City, the headliners for this week's revue are Cab Calloway and the Four Tunes.

Johnny Otis and **Little Esther** start a three-day appearance at the Club Alabam in Los Angeles. They are currently touring the West Coast.

Jimmy Lewis, guitar playing balladeer, begins a two-day stay at New Orleans' Dew Drop Inn.

Esther Mae Jones ("Little Esther" Phillips) was only sixteen in early 1952, but she had already been performing for three years. Her "Double Crossin' Blues" backed by the Johnny Otis Orchestra on Savoy was an r&b hit in 1950.

JAN 7   Roy Milton and his Solid Senders open at the Show Boat Club in Philadelphia.

New releases for the first week of January include "Blue Moon" by Ivory Joe Hunter on M-G-M; "Tell Me Why" by the Swallows and

"Heartache Blues" by Big Tom Collins, both on King; "Ride Daddy Ride" by Fats Noel on DeLuxe; "Careless Love" by Fats Domino on Imperial, and "Best Wishes" by **Lowell Fulson** on Swing Time.

EARLY JANUARY

Jubilee Records signs the Enchanters, a female group, to a contract. Their first record will be "Today Is My Birthday."

Steve Gibson and his Red Caps have been extended at the Copa Room in Miami until April 11th, making a total of sixteen weeks.

JAN 8   The Griffin Brothers start a week at the Trocaveria Club in Columbus, Ohio.

JAN 10   In Los Angeles, **T-Bone Walker** begins a three-day stint at the Club Alabam, while the Treniers open for four days at the Club Oasis.

JAN 11   "Cry" by Johnny Ray passes the million mark in singles sales.
          The Four Buddies join Errol Garner, Bette McLaurin, and Sonny Stitt as headliners of the weekly show at the Howard Theater in Washington.
          The Cabineers join the Dizzy Gillespie show at the Apollo Theater in New York for a week.
          In New Orleans, Willie Mae Thornton entertains at the Dew Drop Inn.

JAN 12   **Jewel King** returns to the West Coast after eight months of club dates. She is scheduled for a recording session with Imperial Records that will produce at least two new singles.
          Following a tour that included Texas, Mississippi, and northern Louisiana, Fats Domino returns to his hometown of New Orleans to play a one-nighter at the Pentagon Ballroom.
          Peacock Records purchases a record pressing plant in the company's hometown of Houston, Texas. Previously, the company had used plants on both the East and West coasts.
          Billy Eckstine and Spike Jones headline the "All Star Revue" at Detroit's Frolic Theater.

JAN 13   Eddie "Cleanhead" Vinson and his orchestra start a series of one-nighters with a show in Nashville.
          Ivory Joe Hunter opens at the Cotton Club in Cincinnati for a week.
          Dinah Washington is the headliner at the Sunday night dance at the Elks Ballroom in Los Angeles.

New releases for the second week of January include two on Savoy: Paul Williams's "Blowin' The Blues" and H-Bomb Ferguson's "Slowly Goin' Crazy"; the Four Tunes' "I'll See You In My Dreams" on Victor; "Mellow Blues" by Sonny Thompson on King; "Sposin'" by Velma Middleton on Dootone; "Laughin' On The Outside, Cryin' On The Inside" by the Majors on Derby; and "Wheel Of Fortune" by Eddie Wilcox and Sunny Gale, both on Derby.

Lowell Fulson's long career spans the 1940s through the 1980s. His most powerful contribution to the legacy of the blues lies with "Every Day I Have The Blues" (Swing Time, 1950) and "Reconsider Baby" (Checker, 1954).

Aaron Thibeaux "T-Bone" Walker was a major influence on all r&b guitarists. His biggest-selling record was the classic "Call It Stormy Monday" (also known as "Stormy Monday Blues"), recorded in 1947.

Jewel King's 1949 recording of "3 x 7 = 21" on Imperial was waxed at the same session which produced "The Fat Man" for Fats Domino, and though it appeared "3 x 7 = 21" would be the big seller, it faded quickly.

Ivory Joe Hunter's two biggest hits came on variations of the same theme. In 1950 "I Almost Lost My Mind" topped the r&b charts; and in the winter of 1956-57, "Since I Met You Baby" crossed into the "pop" field.

JAN 15   The owners of Modern Records, Jules and Joe Bihari, leave
the West Coast for a trek through the South in search of both
r&b and country talent.

MID-JANUARY

New York's Billy Shaw of the Shaw Agency, one of the most influential
promoters of rhythm and blues acts, opens a West Coast office. Prior
to this, Shaw had been working with other promoters via split
commissions.

Little Richard is currently on tour in Kentucky.

Louis Jordan establishes a fund in his name to loan money to
underprivileged students in Arizona.

JAN 16   The new show at the Paramount Theater in New York City
features Sarah Vaughan and the Erskine Hawkins orchestra for
the week.

JAN 17   The Four Tunes open at Montreal's Maroon Club for three
weeks.
Jimmy Witherspoon starts a two-week stay at the Club Alabam
in Los Angeles, while Joe Liggins is at the Club Oasis for the
weekend.

JAN 18   **Roy Milton** travels to the Apollo Theater in New York City
for a week-long stay.
Ruth Brown, backed by Willis Jackson's band, opens for ten
days at the Celebrity Club in Providence, Rhode Island.
Sarah Vaughan receives the "Most Popular Female Vocalist"
award from New Jersey's Upsala College, edging out both Doris
Day and Patti Page. Miss Vaughan is currently on stage at the
Paramount Theater in New York.
T-Bone Walker, Savannah Churchill, and the Striders start
a week-long engagement at the Howard Theater in Washington.

JAN 19   Roy Brown opens at the Circle Theater in Cleveland.
In New Orleans, **Ernie Fields** plays a double date, entertaining
from 8:00 to 10:00 p.m. at the Booker T. Washington Auditorium
and from 10:00 "'til" at the San Jacinto Club.
Ivory Joe Hunter starts two days at the W. C. Handy Theater
in Memphis.

JAN 20   Pee Wee Crayton heads the bill at the Elks Ballroom in Los
Angeles.

New releases for the third week of January include "My Lost Love"
by the Larks on Apollo, and Aladdin's first three releases for the new
year: **Charles Brown's** "Hard Times," the Five Keys' "Yes Sir, That's
My Baby," and Peppermint Harris's "P.H. Blues." Also new for the week
is "Where Are You" by the Mello-Moods on Robin (soon to be Red
Robin) Records; "Brown Boy" by Clarence Palmer and the Jive Bombers
on Citation; "When The Swallows Come Back To Capistrano" by the
Ray-O-Vacs on Decca; "TNT" Tribble's "I Get My Kicks In The Country"

"Little" Richard Penniman was
born December 5, 1932, not
Christmas Day 1935, as his
early biographies state. As a
teen-ager, he toured with
medicine shows and won an
Atlanta talent contest in 1951
which led to a two-year
contract with Victor Records.

Roy Milton had a series of
hits in Los Angeles (starting
in 1946 with "R.M. Blues" on
Jukebox) before he established
his own Roy Milton Records.
He moved on to Specialty in
1948, where he had a big hit
a year later with "The
Hucklebuck."

Bandleader Ernie Fields had
an instrumental hit in late
1959 with a romping combo
version of "In The Mood" on
Rendezvous Records. Although
he made the Los Angeles area
his home, he was born in
Nagadoces, Texas.

Charles Brown was born in
1920 in Texas City, Texas.
Most of his pre-1952
recordings were made as
vocalist/pianist with the
legendary Johnny Moore's
Three Blazers, including
the big hit "Drifting Blues"
in 1946.

on Victor; and Johnny Otis's "Oopy Doo" on Mercury.

IVORY JOE HUNTER

JAN 23   **Ivory Joe Hunter** is playing at the Liberty Theater in Chattanooga.

JAN 25   Todd Rhodes's orchestra moves into the Midtown Club in St. Louis.
          T-Bone Walter and the Tab Smith combo open at the Apollo Theater in New York.
          Ivory Joe Hunter starts a four-night run at Atlanta's Royal Peacock Club.
          The Howard Theater in Washington presents Roy Milton and his orchestra, with "TNT" Tribble, the Heartbreakers, and Jimmy Nelson for the week.
          The Ravens headline the Earle Theater revue in Philadelphia this week.

JAN 27   The Elks Ballroom in Los Angeles plays host to Johnny Otis, Little Esther, and Mel Walker for the evening.

JAN 28   Tiny Bradshaw and his orchestra follow Ruth Brown into the Celebrity Room in Providence.
          The Dominoes, backed by Paul Gayton's orchestra, start a series of one-nighters with a show in Washington, DC.
          In New Orleans, Roy Brown teams with Professor Longhair for a one-night stand at the L. B. Landry High School gym.

Pianist and vocalist Albert "Sunnyland Slim" Luandrew's recording career began in 1947 for Hytone Records, and continued with Tempo, Tone, Sunny, Mercury, Aristocrat, Apollo, J.O.B., Regal and any number of other small rhythm and blues labels. Sunnyland Slim is credited as the man who first brought Muddy Waters into a recording studio.

Neither the Flamingos nor Harris ever recorded for Savoy, although Harris had previously had a January 1951 session for Regent, a subsidiary of Savoy.

New releases for the fourth week of January include "Baby Mine" by the Cabineers on Prestige, "Carolina Blues" by Brownie McGhee and Sonny Terry on Savoy, "Hit The Road Again" by **Sunnyland Slim** on Mercury, and two releases from H-Bomb Ferguson: "Rock H-Bomb, Rock" on Atlas and "Feel Like I Do" on Prestige.

LATE JANUARY

Wynonie Harris plays at Turner's Arena in Washington, DC.

Savoy Records announces the signing of blues singers **"Dimples" Harris** and Columbus Perry, the **Flamingos**, and the re-signing of Varetta Dillard.

Atlantic Records reports signing nineteen-year-old Odelle Turner, a female blues singer, and Oscar "Big Blues" Black, both from Richmond, Virginia.

Allen Bunn, lead singer with the Larks, records his first solo disk, "The Guy With The '45,'" for Apollo.

THE TOP TEN ROCK 'N ROLL RECORDS FOR JANUARY 1952

1. Flamingo - Earl Bostic
2. Cold, Cold Heart - Dinah Washington
3. Weeping And Crying - The Griffin Brothers
4. Fool, Fool, Fool - The Clovers
5. Three O'Clock Blues - B. B. King
6. Cry - Johnnie Ray
7. I Got Loaded - Peppermint Harris
8. Best Wishes - Roy Milton
9. Because Of You - Tab Smith
10. Lovin' Machine - Wynonie Harris

January 1952
ARTIST OF THE MONTH

EARL BOSTIC
(Earl Eugene Bostic, b. April 25, 1913; d. October 28, 1965)

It is fitting that Earl Bostic is the first "Artist of the Month" in this history of rock 'n roll, for he is representative of the major change within the Black jazz community which would result in the establishment of separate pools of music for "jazz" and "rhythm and blues." Bostic clearly straddled both fields.

The year 1952 brought about significant changes in the field of jazz as it was related to rhythm and blues music. Prior to the late 1940s, most of the music generally referred to as jazz that was performed by American Blacks was classified first as race music and later as rhythm and blues. This included such diverse styles as be-bop or cool jazz, hot jazz (a form of Dixieland), big band jazz, urban jazz, and jump. Practically the only Black jazz musicians who were not lumped the rhythm and blues category were Nat Cole, Louis Armstrong, Duke Ellington, and Erroll Garner.

Born in Tulsa, Bostic was an accomplished musician on the alto saxophone by the time he enrolled in Creighton University in Omaha. He stayed only his freshman year before switching to New Orleans' Xavier University. During his three years as a student at Xavier, Bostic caught the attention of the faculty and administration to such an extent that he was asked to stay on after graduation and become the director of the university's symphony orchestra. During his college years in New Orleans, Bostic had also been an active member of the local music scene, frequently sitting in as a sideman with bands' (including the Fred Marabel combo), in night clubs all over the city.

After a few successful years as director of the orchestra at Xavier, Bostic packed his saxophone and moved to New York City by 1938, determined to make his mark. He started his own small combo and played the night club circuit in Harlem for three years before landing major jobs with Don Redman, Cab Calloway, and Lena Horne. Bostic worked with Lionel Hampton's band in 1942 as an arranger. He stayed with Hampton for two years before moving on to arrange for Paul Whiteman and then to play first with Louis Prima and then with Jack

EARL BOSTIC

Teagarden for several years. Also in 1944, he recorded with the Buck Ram All Stars on Savoy.

In 1945 he made his first records under his own name with the Majestic label. Bostic joined Gotham Records a year later with a nine-piece band. His popularity increased steadily as he combined a heavy rhythm backing underneath his own smooth saxophone style which, although it featured an improvisational form similar to other jazz artists of the day, was decidedly more bluesy than most other sax instrumentalists. In fact, although his improvisations stayed close to the written melody line, the overall sound that he created was reminiscent of that heard in many of the late-night clubs. The listener could almost see the thick cigarette smoke and smell the sweat in Bostic's recordings.

Bostic's continued success led to his signing with King Records of Cincinnati, a stronger, more diverse company than Gotham which could more completely exploit Bostic's rising popularity. Bostic's recording of "Flamingo," released in 1951, reportedly sold more than a million copies, and was Bostic's only gold record.

On stage Bostic was a virtuoso on the alto saxophone, blowing raw and wild with his band wailing behind. He was a fine maestro and master of ceremonies when he played the revues in the theater circuit, emceeing as though he sincerely wanted each new act to make good.

By 1960 Bostic had retired from the music scene. But in 1965, in the middle of a well-received comeback, he died of a heart attack following a performance in Richmond, New York.

There is no question about Bostic's enormous influence on the rhythm and blues saxophone players who followed him. His style can readily be heard in the later recordings of Red Prysock, Boots Brown, Rusty Bryant, and King Curtis.

February 1952

FEB 1   Ella Fitzgerald and the Gene Ammons Combo start a week's engagement at New York's Apollo Theater.

Ruth Brown is robbed of an estimated $10,000 in jewelry and furs when her car is broken into while she is eating at the Bailey Hotel's cafe in Pittsburgh. She is enroute to Elizabeth, New Jersey, for a show this evening.

FEB 2   Roy Brown remains in New Orleans for a show at the San Jacinto Club before setting off on a series of one-night stands through Ohio. Also in town, sax-man **Lee Allen** joins Professor Longhair at the Hi-Hat Club for a week.

Derby Records is moving into the "pop" music field based on the strength of "Wheel Of Fortune" by Eddie Wilcox and Sunny Gale. The record eventually reached number 14 on *Billboard's* "pop" charts.

Roy Milton stops for a weekend layover at Braggs' Club in Detroit.

One of New Orleans most sought-after tenor sax players, Lee Allen was born on July 2, 1926. His biggest hit came in 1958 with the instrumental, "Walking With Mr. Lee" on Ember Records.

FEB 3   Little Willie Littlefield, who is currently on a Pacific coast tour, plays a one-night stand at the Elks Ballroom in Los Angeles.

FEB 4   Ruth Brown headlines a one-week appearance at Callaway's in Providence, Rhode Island.

Roy Milton and his orchestra are at Gleason's Casino in Cleveland for a two-week stay.

New releases for the first week of February include two versions of "Wheel Of Fortune" by Dinah Washington on Mercury and by the **Cardinals** on Atlantic. Also out this week are "'Cause I Lost My Helping Hand" by Lil Miss Cornshucks on Coral; "Ida Red" by Bumble Bee Slim on Fidelity; "Wee Wee Hours" by Stick McGhee on Atlantic; "Naturally Too Weak For You" by the Victorians and "Gonna Need My Help Someday" by Memphis Slim, both on Specialty; "You're Not Going To Worry My Life Anymore" by Lightnin' Hopkins on Aladdin; Oscar "Big" Black's "Troubled Mind Blues" and Willis "Gator Tail" Jackson's "Wine-O-Wine", both on Atlantic; and "I Need A Shoulder To Cry On" by Billy Bunn and his Buddies on Victor.

The members of the Cardinals came from Baltimore and signed with Atlantic in 1951. Their first release, "Shouldn't I Know," sold well regionally. The group was first known as the Mellotones, but they are not connected to the Mellotones who recorded for Columbia in 1950-51.

EARLY FEBRUARY

Wynonie Harris and Larry Darnell play Turner's Arena in Washington.

New Orleans radio station WMRY hires Daddy-O to deejay the daily r&b show.

FEB 8   Billy Eckstine and Count Basie take in $2,500 against sixty

Wynonie Harris began his career as a drummer, and it wasn't until 1940 at age twenty-five that he started fronting bands as a singer. His popularity soared when he fronted Lucky Millender's Band for recordings in 1944.

percent of the gross in Houston. They are on a thirty-five date tour of the South until March 21.

The Orioles, the Paul Williams Orchestra, and **Peppermint Harris** start a week-long tour of Virginia with a show tonight in Newport News. Other shows include Portsmouth (9), Norfolk (10-11), Richmond (12-13), and Roanoke (14).

FEB 9   Jules Bihari of RPM/Modern Records is served with a $1 million lawsuit by Diamond Records of Jackson, Mississippi, that contends that Bihari signed and recorded Leroy Holmes and his Darktown Boys while they were under contract to Diamond.

The Clovers and Lynn Hope's combo share the spotlight for the evening at New Orleans' Place Theater. Also in town, Jesse Allen starts a nightly engagement at the Tijuana Club and Little Miss Sharecropper (LaVern Baker) is booked into the Hi-Hat Club.

FEB 10   Amos Milburn is at the Elks Ballroom in Los Angeles for the evening.

FEB 11   **Buddy Johnson** and his sister, Ella, along with vocalist Arthur Prysock, play a one-nighter in Detroit at the Graystone Gardens Ballroom.

New releases for the second week of February include "Jukebox Cannonball" by Bill Haley and the Saddlemen on Holiday, "Bookie's Blues" by H-Bomb Ferguson on Savoy, "I'm Gonna Jump In The River" by the Buddy Johnson Orchestra with Ella Johnson on Decca, Charles Brown's "Tender Heart" on Aladdin, and "Groove Station" by the Al Sears Orchestra on King.

FEB 14   The Joe Morris Cavalcade opens in Erie, PA.
Joe Turner plays the CIO Hall in Muskegon, MI.
The Treniers are at Los Angeles' Club Oasis, while the Club Alabam hosts Dinah Washington in a record-breaking engagement. Also in Los Angeles, **Jimmy Witherspoon** is the guest performer at the grand opening of the Cotton Club.

FEB 15   Sonny Thompson joins Arnett Cobb for a week at Washington's Howard Theater.
Professor Longhair moves into the Caldonia Club in New Orleans for three nights. His stay is extended to four consecutive weekends.
Pee Wee Crayton opens at the 5-4 Ballroom in Los Angeles for the weekend.

MID-FEBRUARY

Recent record companies signing new talent include Peacock Records' contract with **Lafayette Thomas** and Savoy Records' acquisition of Melvin Evans of Atlanta. Also, Okeh Records is overjoyed in announcing their newest acquisition, Hadda Brooks, who had previously recorded for Modern and Victor.

The Griffin Brothers and Peppermint Harris play sixty one-nighters throughout the West and Texas starting in February.

FEB 16   The Orioles move into the Holiday Inn in Newark, New Jersey, for the week.

FEB 17   Charles Brown plays the Sunday night dance at the Elks Ballroom in Los Angeles.
    Johnny Otis, Little Esther, and Willie Mae Thornton appear at the Rosenwald Gym in New Orleans with Gatemouth Brown and **Marie Adams**.

FEB 18   Roy Milton and his Solid Senders start a two-week layover in Atlanta at the Royal Peacock.

New releases for the third week of February include "Chocolate Blonde" by Joe Hill Louis and "Wind Is Blowin'" by Jimmy Witherspoon, both on Modern; "It Rocks! It Rolls! It Swings!" by the Treniers on Okeh; "Train Kept A-Rollin'" by **Tiny Bradshaw** on King; Johnny Greer's "Strong Red Whiskey" and "Come What May" by the Four Tunes, both on Victor; Billy Wright's "Married Woman's Boogie" and Varetta Dillard's "Please Tell Me Why," both on Savoy; and three releases on Swing Time: "Kissa Me Baby" by Ray Charles, "Three O'Clock In The Morning" by Lowell Fulson and "Movin' On Down The Line" by Jimmy McCracklin.

FEB 20   Billy Eckstine and Count Basie split the bill for one show at New Orleans' Booker T. Washington Auditorium.

FEB 22   **Sarah Vaughan** shares the bill with Bull Moose Jackson's band for a week at the Apollo Theater in New York.
    Ivory Joe Hunter entertains for a week at Speedie's New Musical Room in Philadelphia.
    The Orioles, Hal "Cornbread" Singer, and Lowell Fulson open for a week at the Howard Theater in Washington.
    Billy Bunn and his Buddies with comedian Pigmeat Markham start a week-long tour of Virginia with a show in Newport News. Other performances include Portsmouth (23), Norfolk (24-25), Richmond (26-27), and Roanoke (28).
    In Los Angeles, the 5-4 Ballroom presents Charles Brown for the weekend.

FEB 24   The Elks Ballroom in Los Angeles plays host to Percy Mayfield for the evening.
    In New Orleans, the three-day weekend finds Smiley Lewis fronting the **Dave Bartholomew** band at the Hi-Hat Club.

FEB 25   Todd Rhodes and his combo start four weeks at the Cotton Club in Cincinnati.

New releases for the fourth week of February include "Bad Neighborhood" by Floyd Dixon with Johnny Moore's Three Blazers on Aladdin; "Dig These Blues" by the Four Clefs and "I'm Only Fooling My Heart" by the **Heartbreakers**, both on Victor; "Delta Blues" by Joe Williams on Trumpet; and "Lawdy, Lawdy, Lord" by Dave Bartholomew on King.

FEB 27   Roy Milton opens at the Royal Peacock in Atlanta.

FEB 28   Birdland in New York City presents Ivory Joe Hunter for

Marie Adams reportedly weighed more than 250 pounds. In 1957, together with two other female vocalists, she formed the Three Tons Of Joy. They had a British hit record with the oldie "Ma, He's Making Eyes At Me."

Tiny Bradshaw's "Train Kept A-Rollin'" was revived by Johnny Burnette and the Rock 'N Roll Trio (1956) and the Yardbirds (1965).

Born March 27, 1924, in Newark, New Jersey, Sarah Vaughan began her illustrious career singing bebop with Charlie Parker and Dizzy Gillespie. Her first hit on the "pop" charts came in 1948 with "It's Magic" on Champion Records.

After playing trumpet with a variety of bands in the 1940s, Dave Bartholomew first recorded on Deluxe in 1949, but switched to Imperial as a New Orleans talent scout later that same year. He was born in Edgard, Louisiana, in 1920.

The Heartbreakers first single was "Heartbreaker" on the small DC label in Washington. They re-recorded the song for Victor, but the group released only three additional Vicot singles. This Heartbreakers is not related to other vocal groups of the same name that recorded for Vik, Brent, and Atco.

SARAH VAUGHN

a two-week stay.

FEB 29   Lowell Fulson starts a week-long stint at the Apollo Theater in New York. Also booked on the show is Hal "Corn Bread" Singer's orchestra.

LATE FEBRUARY

Sarah Vaughan opens at the Rendezvous Room in Philadelphia.

Okeh Records, reactivated only six months ago as a subsidiary for Columbia Records to promote rhythm and blues artists, is made a full-fledged operation by the parent company. The latest acquisition for the label is the pop group the Four Lads.

THE TOP TEN ROCK 'N ROLL RECORDS FOR FEBRUARY 1952

1. 3 O'Clock Blues - B. B. King
2. Cry - Johnnie Ray
3. Best Wishes - Roy Milton
4. Flamingo - Earl Bostic
5. Weeping And Crying - The Griffin Brothers
6. Fool, Fool, Fool - The Clovers
7. Wheel Of Fortune - Eddie Wilcox and Sunny Gale
8. I Didn't Sleep A Wink Last Night - Arthur Prysock
9. Booted - Rosco Gordon
10. Because Of You - Tab Smith

February 1952
ARTIST OF THE MONTH

B.B. KING

B. B. KING
(Riley B. King, b. September 16, 1925)

Just as with Earl Bostic, January 1952's Artist Of The Month, B. B. King represents a significant change in the musical stream of rhythm and blues music. His influence in the somewhat narrow vocal blues field cannot be overstated. In short, King literally, and single-handedly, created another branch in the blues.

But King's well-deserved fame did not come without more than its share of personal set-backs. He was born in Itta Bona, Mississippi, on what has been described as a cotton plantation, but what probably was little more than a large Mississippi Delta cotton farm near Indianola, fifteen miles from the Mississippi River. His parents separated when he was only four, and his mother took him with her to work the cotton fields in a neighboring town. She died when King was nine, but the boy remained to work in the fields of his new home until he was fourteen, at which time his father located him and brought him back to the farm where he was born. During this time King had little formal education, although he showed an interest in playing the guitar, and he subsequently bought one for eight dollars when he was about fifteen. King was taught to play by an uncle who was a Baptist minister. In

14

fact, King's family was very religious, and King's first organized musical work was with a gospel quartet that he formed, and with which he played guitar.

King was drafted into the Army in 1944, and following basic training he was stationed at Ft. Benning, Georgia. It was in the Army that he first became aware of his talent for singing the blues, and he probably performed for the soldiers in the barracks at night. However, his service in the Army was cut short so that he could return to the Mississippi cotton farm where he was needed as a tractor driver. The deep religious background of his relatives forbade any interest in the secular blues, but King's interest could not be dissuaded. On weekends he would take his guitar and travel to one of the neighboring towns where he would sing on street corners. Although this smacks of a Quixotic fable, in reality it was the economics involved that brought King to realize that his talents for singing the blues outweighed his future in the cotton business. He would be paid thirty-five cents for picking a hundred pounds of cotton, a dollar-and-a-half a day chopping down the cotton stalks, and two-and-a-half dollars a day driving the tractor. On those street corners, singing music to passers-by, he could make ten to fifteen dollars on an average Saturday. His mind was made up, and he secured his first regular singing job on WGRM radio in Greenwood, Mississippi, where he hosted a fifteen-minute show and sang his songs.

About 1947 King traveled the 125 miles north to Memphis, where he stayed with his cousin and fellow blues singer, Bukka White. At this time, he was also influenced by another blues singer, Rice Miller, who performed under the pseudonym of Sonny Boy Williamson. Miller was employed by a Memphis radio station, and it was through his help that King got his first night club job, at the 16th Street Grill, which led to his being hired by radio station WDIA to sing commercials. Very shortly, King was again hosting his own daily fifteen-minute radio show, spinning records, singing his songs and guiding his audience to the 16th Street Grill where he played six nights a week for room and board. It was while with WDIA that he was tagged with the nickname "The Boy From Beale Street" or "The Beale Street Blues Boy," which later was shortened to "Blues Boy" and, finally, simply to "B. B."

King made his first recordings for the small Bullet label in 1949, but the two releases were successful only in bringing him to the attention of the Bihari brothers of Los Angeles who owned RPM Records. In 1950 King started what developed into a sixteen-year association with the company that produced almost thirty hit singles (for RPM and its successor, Kent Records). In 1952, as his first hit for RPM, "3 O'Clock Blues," was beginning to reach a national audience, he stopped his radio work to concentrate on night club dates. He worked with the Beale Streeters Band that had been founded the previous year by pianist Rosco Gordon, and which featured King on guitar, John Alexander ("Johnny Ace") on piano, Earl Forrest on drums, with Bobby Bland sharing the vocals. Even so, national fame outside of the Black community eluded him until the late 1960s, when blues bands from England and the United States brought well-deserved attention to the founding fathers of the idiom.

King has often said that his style is a direct result of not being able to sing and play his guitar (a Gibson model, affectionately named "Lucille") at the same time. He would sing a line, and then the guitar would take a brief lead while he thought of the next vocal line. It was this alternating between the vocal and the instrumental that set him apart from other urban blues artists of the early 1950s. Another interesting development in King's style that came more from a mistake than from design was his stretching of a 12-bar musical passage out to thirteen or fourteen bars. This creates a tension in the music which is conveyed in King's demanding vocals and expressive facial contortions. Although King possesses only a modest voice, he has a style that pleases his audience coupled with a strong sense of rhythm and an upbeat personality on stage.

B. B. King has influenced an entire generation of blues-oriented guitarists including Eric Clapton and Mike Bloomfield. In turn King was influenced by jazz guitar greats such as Charlie Christian and Django Reinhardt, and by veteran blues artist T-Bone Walker.

Today B. B. King is the undisputed "King Of The Blues," but success has not caused any lessening of the dedication on his part. Just as he has in the past, King still devotes most of his time to playing an average of 300 dates a year, having an all-time personal high of 342 one-nighters in 1956.

March 1952

MAR 1   It is reported in the music press that song publishers are now more willing to submit tunes to independent record companies following the success of "Cry" by Johnnie Ray on Okeh and "Wheel of Fortune" by Eddie Wilcox and Sunny Gale on Derby. Companies likely to benefit from this move include King, Jubilee, and Okeh, as well as a number of West Coast labels including Imperial, **Aladdin**, and RPM/Modern.

MAR 2   Sonny Thompson opens at the Ebony Lounge in Cleveland for two days.

        T-Bone Walker plays a one-nighter at the Elks Ballroom in Los Angeles.

New releases for the first week of March include "Night Train" by Jimmy Forrest on United; "Hambone" by the Red Saunders Orchestra on Okeh; "The Big Question" by Percy Mayfield, and "Wheel Of Fortune" by the **Four Flames**, both on Specialty; "My Playful Baby's Gone" by Wynonie Harris and "Your Daddy's Doggin' Around" by Todd Rhodes, both on King; "Solitude" by Tiny Grimes on United; "Summertime" by Little Esther on Federal; and "Thinkin' And Drinkin'" by Amos Milburn on Aladdin.

MAR 4   Bull Moose Jackson is in Philadelphia at the Club Harlem.

MAR 6   Ivory Joe Hunter plays a one-night stand in Richmond, Virginia.

MAR 7   Sonny Thompson and his orchestra, with Lulu Reed and the Ravens open for a week at the Apollo Theater in New York.

        Dave Bartholomew is back at the Hi-Hat in New Orleans sharing the stage for two weeks with **Tommy Ridgely**.

        The Tiny Bradshaw orchestra and the Tab Smith combo entertain for the week at the Howard Theater in Washington.

MAR 9   Roy Milton is the evening's entertainment at Los Angeles' Elks Ballroom.

        The Rosenwald Gym in New Orleans is the scene of a show featuring Buddy Johnson's orchestra with sister Ella and **Arthur Prysock**.

New releases for the second week of March include "5-10-15 Hours" by Ruth Brown, "One Mint Julep" by the Clovers, and "Sweet Sixteen" by Joe Turner, all on Atlantic; "When The Swallows Come Back To Capistrano" by Billy Ward and his Dominoes on Federal; "Voodoo Magic" by Jimmy Cook on Modern; and "I've Got The Last Laugh Now" by Roy Brown on DeLuxe.

MAR 12   In New York City, Ella Fitzgerald opens at the Paramount

Aladdin Records was founded in Los Angeles in 1945 by Eddie and Leo Meisner. Early hits were by Charles Brown, the Five Keys, and Peppermint Harris.

The Four Flames also recorded as the Hollywood Four Flames (1951-54) and the Hollywood Flames (1954-60) for various companies. The most famous alumnus of the group is Bobby Day ("Rock-In Robin," 1958).

Tommy Ridgely is a veteran of the New Orleans scene. In 1949, he recorded "Shrewsbury Blues" for Imperial just before Fats Domino was discovered by the same company. In the ensuing fame of "The Fat Man," Ridgely was lost in the shuffle. Early Ridgely recordings feature the band of R.C. Robinson (better known as Ray Charles).

Arthur Prysock's resounding baritone kept him working on the supper club circuit for twenty years, but his records generally went unsold. He did have a minor hit with "I Didn't Sleep A Wink Last Night" on Decca in early 1952.

Theater, while Sarah Vaughan is the headliner at Birdland. Miss Vaughan will be heard live over the ABC radio network during her Birdland engagement.

MAR 14   Charles Brown starts a tour of forty-one playdates throughout Texas.

The **Cardinals** join Bull Moose Jackson and Maxine Sullivan for a week at the Earle Theater in Philadelphia.

Washington's Howard Theater offers patrons the talents of the Ravens for this week's entertainment.

MAR 15   Pee Wee Crayton plays the Flame Club in Detroit. Also on the bill is LaVern Baker, resident vocalist at the club.

MID-MARCH

Arthur Prysock continues on the road with a series of one-nighters and theater dates backed by the Buddy Johnson orchestra. Engagements include Philadelphia, Cleveland, Boston, and New York City. The tour will run through May.

Talent scouts from New York's Apollo Records, in Memphis searching for another Rosco Gordon or B. B. King, sign two artists: Bill Harvey, formerly with Peacock Records, and Bonita Cole.

MAR 16   Roy Milton moves into the Lincoln Theater in Los Angeles for the week. Also in town, **Eddie "Cleanhead" Vinson** is at the Elks Ballroom for the evening.

MAR 17   Ruth Brown entertains at the Hi-Hat Club in Boston for one week.

New releases for the third week of March include "Are You Lonesome Tonight" by Dream Man on Regent, "Count The Days I'm Gone" by **Piano Red** on Victor, "Guy With The '45'" by Allen Bunn on Apollo, "Juke Box Cannonball" by Red Stone and his Grave Diggers on Oscar, and "I Found A New Love" by Little Donna Hightower on Decca.

MAR 20   Dave Bartholomew and Tommy Ridgely take their show to New Orleans' Tijuana Club for the night.

MAR 21   Dinah Washington with Cootie Williams's combo open at the War Memorial Auditorium in Trenton, New Jersey.

The Ravens and Wini Brown start a week-long tour of Virginia with a show tonight at Newport News. Other dates on the tour are Portsmouth (22), Norfolk (23-24), Richmond (25-26) and Roanoke (27).

Philadelphia's Earle Theater presents Johnnie Ray and the Swallows for the week.

The Eddie Wilcox band featuring vocalist Sunny Gale and the Blenders start a week's stay at the Apollo Theater in New York.

The Cardinals, Lil Green, and Odelle Turner are on the bill with Charlie Parker at the Howard Theater for a week in Washington.

THE CARDINALS

Eddie Vinson was born in Houston, December 18, 1917, and his premature baldness earned him the obvious nickname "Cleanhead." In 1942, Vinson's searing alto sax got him hired by the Cootie Williams Band, but it was his superb blues vocals that sold records in the late 1940s with songs such as "Cherry Red Blues."

"Piano Red" was an original rhythm and blues wildman. Born Willie Lee Perryman, October 19, 1911, he started singing and playing piano in Atlanta nightclubs in the 1930s. He and his brother, Rufus "Speckled Red" Perryman, were nicknamed for their skin pigmentation: they were albino Negroes.

The Ravens left Hub Records after three releases and briefly recorded for King before joining National label. Here, their second release, "Old Man River," featuring the incredible bass voice of Jimmy Ricks, was an immediate hit in 1947.

During a stage show in Cleveland promoted by Alan Freed, local deejay on WJW, a riot breaks out. The show is cancelled.

MAR 22   Joe Medlin goes into the Flame Club in Detroit.

Ivory Joe Hunter opens in Columbus, Ohio, at the Trocaveria Club.

In New Orleans, Larry Darnell entertains at the Palace Theater for the evening.

MAR 23   Pee Wee Crayton performs at Los Angeles' Lincoln Theater.

New releases for the fourth week of March include "Come On Back Home" by Sonny Boy Williamson on Trumpet; "Goin' Back To Georgia" by **Big Boy Crudup** and "Get Rich Quick" by Little Richard, both on Victor; and "Stolen Love" by Jimmy Liggins on Specialty.

Arthur "Big Boy" Crudup was a successful blues singer in the 1940s, and is best known today as the composer of "That's All Right," the A-side of Elvis Presley's first single. Crudup was born in 1905 in Forest, Mississippi.

MAR 28   The Apollo Theater presents the Clovers, the James Moody Combo, and pianist Eddie Heywood's band for the week.

MAR 30   Floyd Dixon plays a one-nighter at the Elks Ballroom in Los Angeles. Also in town, Roy Milton starts three days at the Lincoln Theater with Pee Wee Crayton.

New releases for the fifth week of March include "Down At The Depot" by John Lee on Federal, "Boogie Woogie Lou" by **Joe Liggins** and his Honey Drippers on Specialty, "Born On The 13th" by Smokey Hogg on Fidelity, and "I Can't Lose With The Stuff I Use" by Lester Williams on Specialty.

Saxophonist Joe Liggins's first year as a recording artist saw the release of his enormously popular dance tune, "The Honeydripper," on Exclusive Records. His immediate success encouraged his brother, Jimmy, to give up boxing for a career as a singer/guitarist.

LATE MARCH

Amos Milburn opens at Pep's Musical Lounge in Philadelphia.

Mercury Records signs Lightnin' Hopkins and L. C. Williams.

It is reported that promoter Hal Waller of Los Angeles recently booked blues singer **Floyd Dixon** into Phoenix on a special three-day trial promotion where Dixon played to White, Mexican, and Black audiences on separate nights. The White audience was by far the biggest of the three.

Pianist and blues vocalist Floyd Dixon made his first records in 1947 for the Supreme label in Los Angeles. He later replaced Charles Brown (with whom he is often compared) in Johnny Moore's Three Blazers.

THE TOP TEN ROCK 'N ROLL RECORDS FOR MARCH 1952

1. 3 O'Clock Blues - B. B. King
2. Booted - Rosco Gordon
3. Night Train - Jimmy Forest
4. Wheel Of Fortune - Dinah Washington
5. Wheel Of Fortune - Eddie Wilcox and Sunny Gale
6. Cry - Johnny Ray
7. Best Wishes - Roy Milton
8. Flamingo - Earl Bostic
9. Wheel Of Fortune - The Cardinals
10. I Got Loaded - Peppermint Harris

March 1952
ARTIST OF THE MONTH

ROSCO GORDON
(b. 1934)

ROSCO GORDON

In 1951, after one release ("Hey Fat Girl") on the local Duke label, Gordon's piano shuffle rhythm became a mainstay in the records that he made starting in 1950. In the late 1940s Gordon associated himself with the Beale Streeters, arguably the richest collection of rhythm and blues talent in the Memphis area. The group, at one time or another, boasted B. B. King, Johnny Ace, Bobby "Blue" Bland, Earl Forrest, and, of course, Rosco Gordon. It was Gordon who by 1950 had become one of the best-known singers in the clubs that lined dockside Beale Street. He, along with B. B. King, was discovered by the Bihari brothers of Los Angeles' RPM Records on one of their talent searching trips through the South. Gordon's earliest sessions were produced by Sam Phillips, the legendary Memphis record executive who was several years away from his own Sun Record Company. One of their first sessions produced Gordon's first hit record, "Booted."

Much confusion surrounds the release of "Booted." Although Gordon was signed to RPM Records, the song was first issued by Chess Records of Chicago. It is apparent that Phillips sent a demonstration disk to Chess Records to see if the Chess would be interested in having one of their artists record the song. Instead, Chess released the master "as-is" without anyone's approval. Needless to say, the song was an immediate hit. In the ensuing legal entanglement, the Bihari's had Gordon re-record the song for release on RPM and the Chess version was withdrawn from the market. However, time being one of the biggest factors in deciding which record will be the hit version of a song, it was the Chess release that garnered the initial honors. But it was Gordon's career that really flourished. Imagine his surprise and delight at having two of the most powerful independent record companies in the land both pushing his records.

In 1952 Joe Bihari and his newly acquired talent scout of the area, Ike Turner, set up a session for Gordon at the studios of WMAC radio in Memphis. This was a wise move for Bihari, for the tie-in insured airplay over one of the most powerful radio stations in the South. The resulting record, "No More Doggin'," was another smash hit for Gordon and appeared on the national rhythm and blues charts alongside "Booted." At this time Gordon found himself caught between the powers of RPM Records and another independent record company. This time it was Memphis-based Duke Records, which had been acquired by Don Robey, owner of Peacock Records of Houston. Gordon re-signed with Duke in 1952, and the Biharis immediately sued to retain their artist, but Gordon remained with Duke through 1954, recording four singles.

By 1955 Gordon's recording popularity had been surpassed by artists whose records were aimed at the fledgling rock 'n roll audience. He signed with Phillips's Sun label for a few sides then had a regional hit with "The Chicken" released on Phillips's Flip subsidiary. By 1959 he was signed with Vee-Jay Records, and it was here that he found his biggest commercial success with "Just A Little Bit." The song went on to have a life of its own as one of the era's most performed pieces for aspiring rock 'n roll bands.

Gordon has recorded for many companies since his 1959 hit,

including ABC, Old Town, Jomada, Rae-Cox, Calla, and Ref-O-Ree. In the 1970s he continued to tour wherever he could find a booking, and in 1982 he completed a successful round of European performances. Today he is semi-retired, living in New York.

Gordon's early recordings feature a heavy beat characteristic of the times with a boogie bass line under a twin saxophone lead. He was one of the first recording artists to place the beat up front in his recordings, with the drum being very prominent while the guitar and piano remained in the background. His recordings are not as frantic as those of, say, Louis Jordan, but Gordon's influence was widely felt.

April 1952

APR 1   **Steve Gibson** and his Red Caps are at the Club Harlem in Philadelphia.

APR 2   During his swing through the Southwest, Charles Brown plays a one-nighter in Houston.

APR 4   B. B. King rocks the crowd at Trenton's War Memorial Auditorium.

APR 7   Louis Jordan begins a two-week stand at New York's Warner Theater with his new orchestra. This is his first appearance following a December 1951 announcement of indefinite retirement due to illness.
    The Celebrity Club hosts Tiny Grimes in Providence, Rhode Island.

New releases for the first week of April include "Wheel Of Fortune" by Maurice King and his Wolverines on Okeh; "Heavenly Father" by Edna McGriff on Jubilee; "Smokin' and Dreamin'" by the Street Singers on Comet; and "Rock The Joint" by Bill Haley and the Saddlemen on Essex.

EARLY APRIL

Sax-man Joe Houston, lately with Modern, has been signed by **Imperial Records** of Los Angeles.

Atlantic Records is releasing the first platter from their new female singing sensation, Odelle Turner. She has recorded "Alarm Clock Boogie," a song she recently premiered at the Apollo Theater.

M-G-M Records has branched into the rhythm and blues market by adding blues shouter Johnny King, a protege of Leonard Feather. His first recording session is backed by the Buddy Johnson Orchestra.

APR 8   Chris Powell and his Five Blue Flames begin a series of club dates in Pennsylvania that will last through April 26th and include a week at Philadelphia's Showboat starting on the 14th.

APR 11   Jimmy Witherspoon travels to the Royale Peacock in Atlanta.
    The Swallows perform at the Howard Theater in Washington.
    Dinah Washington starts a week at New York's Apollo Theater with Jimmy McPhail and Arnett Cobb.
    Al Hibbler is at Detroit's Flame Club for the week.
    The Regal Theater in Philadelphia presents Lowell Fulson, Hal "Cornbread" Singer, Lil Green, and Sugar Chile Robinson for patrons this week.

APR 12   In New Orleans, Paul Monday, Peacock Records' piano playing
blues singer, headlines at the Dew Drop Inn. Nearby, **Jesse Hill**
starts a series of weekend stands at the Corine Club in Mereaux,
Louisiana.

APR 13   The Orioles perform before a crowd of 2,000 teen-agers at
the Pershing Ballroom in Chicago.
Big Jay McNeeley headlines the show at South Park in Los
Angeles. Also in town, Lloyd Glenn is at the Elks Ballroom for
the evening.
Joe Turner and Gatemouth Brown entertain dancers for the
evening at New Orleans' Rosenwald Gym.
Roy Milton entertains for the Easter Dance at the Oakland
Auditorium.

APR 14   The Club Harlem in Philadelphia plays host to Steve Gibson
and his Red Caps for the week.
In New Orleans, Dave Bartholomew and his combo perform
at the Labor Union Hall.
Wini Brown is at George's Bar in Indianapolis. Tiny Bradshaw
starts an engagement at the Club Trocaveria in Columbus, Ohio.

New releases for the second week of April include **"Every Beat Of
My Heart"** by the Royals, **"Better Beware"** by Little Esther, and **"Louisiana
Hop"** by Pete "Guitar" Lewis, all on Federal; "Red Sails In The Sunset"
by the Five Keys and "Waiting In Vain" by Lil Miss "Cornshucks," both
on Aladdin; "Don't Blame Her" by Lonnie Johnson on Aladdin; "My Heart
Is Yours" by the Marveltones on Regent; "Rock 'N Roll Blues" by Anita
O'Day on Mercury; "Screamin' In My Sleep" by Gene Parris on Victor;
and Jimmy Scott's "When You Surrender" on Coral.

MID-APRIL

Jubilee Records signs Billy Paul, the sixteen-year old winner of the
Apollo Theater's weekly amateur contest, and the Marylanders from
Baltimore. Other recent signings include the Dreamers with Mercury,
and Eddie Mack with Savoy. Tempo Records inks its first r&b artist,
Little Billy Big. Specialty Records' chief, Art Rupe, has returned from
a talent search in the South. He has signed bandleader and singer Lloyd
Price, **Peter McKinney**, and Little Sonny Houston.

Record industry sources report that 78 rpm records still maintain
approximately eighty percent of the market. This figure is expected
to be reduced to seventy percent by the end of 1953. In a related
report, almost one-half of all the new needles sold for record players
are for the RCA 45 rpm models.

Fats Domino opens for a month at Grady's Supper Club in Nashville.
He and his six-man band will split $2,500 a week.

Atlantic Records promotes Jesse Stone to the position of musical director.
Stone has previously had several combos and has composed many r&b
songs.

Jesse Hill remained an obscure
New Orleans club singer until
1960 when his novelty song,
"Ooh Poo Pah Doo" on Minit
Records, became a major hit.

"Every Beat Of My Heart," a
composition by Johnny Otis, was
revived in 1961 to launch the
career of Gladys Knight and The
Pips.

Peter McKinney, a nephew of the
late blues great Bessie Smith,
was from Shreveport, Louisiana.

Hal "Cornbread" Singer appears at the Regal Theater in Chicago before embarking on a tour through the Midwest. (See May 31st.)

APR 16   Jimmy Witherspoon and Tab Smith share the bill for the Sunday night dance at the Elks Ballroom in Los Angeles.

APR 17   Al Hibbler travels to New Orleans for a two-week engagement. Charles Brown and Joe Turner pack the Paradise Garden Club in Biloxi, Mississippi.

APR 18   Little Esther, backed by the Johnny Otis band, opens at the War Memorial Auditorium in Trenton, New Jersey.
The Clovers play the Howard Theater in Washington. Also on the bill are Charlie Parker, Lil Green, and the Billy Ford orchestra.
On the Virginia circuit this week, the **Five Keys** share the bill with Varetta Dillard. Shows are at Newport News tonight, Portsmouth (19), Norfolk (20-21), Richmond (22-23) and Roanoke (24).
The Swallows share the stage with Pearl Bailey at New York's Apollo Theater for the week.

APR 19   Winners at the Seventh Annual *Pittsburgh Courier* Theatrical Awards perform at New York's Carnegie Hall. The line-up includes the Dominoes, Billy Eckstine, blues singer Lester Williams, Lionel Hampton's big band, and Nat Cole's trio. Billy Ward and his Dominoes are winners of the vocal group division.

APR 20   The Elks Ballroom in Los Angeles hosts a "Blues Jamboree" featuring **Little Willie Littlefield** and Floyd Dixon.
New York's Birdland presents Billy Ward and his Dominoes for two weeks.
There is a "Battle Of The Blues" at New Orleans' San Jacinto Club featuring Joe Turner and Gatemouth Brown.

APR 21   Big John Greer, Victor blues singer, opens at the Regal in Columbus, Ohio, for two weeks. Also in town, Tiny Bradshaw and his combo entertain at the Cotton Club.
WWRL radio in New York initiates an hour-long r&b show in an after-midnight slot. George Woods, formerly from Chicago, is the deejay. WOV radio, also in New York, counters by announcing that it will air an hour of r&b every afternoon featuring two of their most popular personalities, Willie Bryant and Ray Caroll.

New releases for the third week of April include "Beside You" by the **Swallows**, "I'll Drown In My Tears" by Sonny Thompson and Lulu Reed, and "Keep On Churnin'" by Wynonie Harris, all on King; "Have Mercy, Baby" by the Dominoes on Federal; "I Got The Blues Again" by T-Bone Walker and "Goin' Home" by Fats Domino, both on Imperial; "I'd Be A Fool Again" by the Blenders on Decca; "I'm A Sentimental Fool" by the Marylanders on Jubilee; "Sowing Love And Reaping Tears" by the Three Baritones on Derby; "So Tired" by Roy Milton, "Lawdy Miss Clawdy" by Lloyd Price, and "Dripper's Boogie" by Joe Liggins, all on Specialty; "I've Lost" by the Enchanters on Jubilee; and "You Took My Heart" by Damita Jo on Recorded In Hollywood.

The Five Keys originally called themselves the Sentimental Four when two sets of brothers, Raphael and Ripley Ingram and Bernie and Rudy West, got together in the late 1940s. They added Dickie Smith, then Raphael went into the Army and was replaced by Maryland Pierce. The lineup of Ripley Ingram, Pierce, the West brothers and Smith recorded for the Aladdin label from February 1951 to September 1953.

Little Willie Littlefield was born in Houston on September 16, 1931. At age fifteen he first recorded for Eddie's Records in Los Angeles. In 1949, still only eighteen, he switched to Modern where he found immediate success with "It's Midnight."

The Swallows started recording for King Records in 1951 and their first release, "Dearest," was their biggest seller. In 1946, they formed in Baltimore as a sextet of thirteen-year olds calling themselves The Oakleers. Their idols were the Orioles, the neighborhood's first professional vocal group.

24

APR 22   Louis Jordan closes at the Warner Theater in New York. He is booked solid through late November with dates in theaters in Washington and Philadelphia, as well as clubs in San Franciso and Los Angeles.

APR 24   Lionel Hampton and his orchestra start a week's engagement at Toronto's Casino Theater.

APR 25   The Orioles begin a series of one-nighters.
          Following a one-week tour of Louisiana, **Gatemouth Brown** joins Paul Monday at New Orleans' Dew Drop Inn for the weekend.
          The Earle Theater in Philadelphia hosts the Griffin Brothers, Sugar Chile Robinson, Joe Turner, and Margie Day for a week's engagement.
          At the Apollo Theater in New York, Johnny Otis and his orchestra headline for the week. Vocalists include Little Esther, Willie Mae Thornton, and Mel Walker.
          Savannah Churchill starts a week's stay at the Flame Club in Detroit.

Clarence Brown's smile was as wide as a garden gate, hence the nickname, "Gatemouth." He was born in Orange, Texas, April 18, 1924, and although he started his performing career as a drummer, it was as a virtuoso on the guitar that he found fame in the late 1940s.

APR 27   **Joe Morris** and his orchestra with vocalist Laurie Tate are the featured attractions at this Sunday night's dance at the Elks Ballroom in Los Angeles.
          Charles Brown and Amos Milburn join forces for the evening at New Orleans' Coliseum Arena.

Joe Morris' "Blues Cavalcade" was one of the first and most successful of the multi-artist rhythm and blues traveling shows. After having worked with Lionel Hampton from 1942-46, he joined Atlantic Records in 1947 just as the company was starting up.

New releases for the fourth week of April include "That's When Your Heartaches Begin" by Billy Bunn and his Buddies on Victor; "Mailman's Sack" by Tiny Bradshaw and "Ram-Bunk-Shush" by Lucky Millinder, both on King; "Rock This Morning" by Jesse Allen and "My Last Affair" by Charles Brown, both on Aladdin; "They Raided The Joint" by Helen Humes on Decca; and "Goomp Blues" by Johnny Otis on Mercury.

APR 28   Charles Brown and Amos Milburn play New Iberia, Louisiana, as the first date on a one-nighter tour.

APR 29   Amos Milburn takes to the road for thirty-nine one-nighters in Texas.

LATE APRIL

Billy Eckstine is currently at the Copacabana in New York.

Billy Eckstine's rakish looks dazzled women from coast to coast. Although born in Pittsburgh in 1914, he looked years younger than his true age. His handsome features were only part of the reason he was America's first Black r&b star. The other was his scintillating baritone voice.

BILLY ECKSTINE

THE TOP TEN ROCK 'N ROLL RECORDS FOR APRIL 1952

1. Night Train - Jimmy Forest
2. Booted - Rosco Gordon
3. 5-10-15 Hours - Ruth Brown
4. Heavenly Father - Edna McGriff
5. No More Doggin' - Rosco Gordon
6. 3 O'Clock Blues - B. B. King
7. Trouble In Mind - Dinah Washington
8. Wheel Of Fortune - Dinah Washington
9. Wind Is Blowin' - Jimmy Witherspoon
10. Middle Of The Night - The Clovers

April 1952
ARTIST OF THE MONTH

JIMMY FORREST
(James Robert Forrest, b. June 24, 1920; d. August 26, 1980)

Jimmy Forrest was a product of the St. Louis music scene that spawned so many other jazz artists. Located midway up the length of the Mississippi River, St. Louis seemed perfectly placed to represent an accumulation of musical styles that started in New Orleans and worked its way up river through the bayous of Louisiana, the farm lands of Mississippi, and the streets of Memphis.

Forrest's parents were musicians, so it was natural that he would follow their example. At the tender age of twelve, Jimmy, already proficient on the saxophone, joined his mother's band, The Eva Forrest Stompers, to work the riverboats up and down the Mississippi. Early in life he was also a frequent musician at the many roadhouses in the St. Louis area. Among the many other musicians that Forrest worked with through his career were Duke Ellington, Charlie Byrd, and Jay McShan. In 1942 Forrest joined the Andy Kirk Band, which featured as its vocalist a young LaVern Baker. The band garnered a recording contract with the prestigious Decca label, but World War II intervened and the first sessions for the group were not held until December 1943. By 1947 the Kirk combo had called it quits and Forrest found himself back in St. Louis playing small clubs. In 1949 Ellington called him to replace Al Sears, whom Forrest had replaced in the Kirk unit. The Ellington band was in chaos at the time, and even though Forrest stuck for a while, he was back in St. Louis by 1950.

Here he formed his own combo, and in November of 1951 they traveled to Chicago to record for the new United Records Company, which had only been in business since the previous July. That first session produced the enormously popular version of "Night Train" that Forrest co-wrote and which became a major rhythm and blues hit during the first half of 1952. As happened to so many rhythm and blues artists during this time, Forrest's recording did not make a dent in the popular music field even though the song has become one of the most performed instrumental pieces of music in the history of rock 'n roll.

Forrest had only one other minor hit, "Hey Mrs. Jones," also in

1952. But it wasn't the hit records that brought in the money for a rhythm and blues artist in the early 1950s, it was touring. And Forrest was now on the road constantly.

By 1953, Forrest's life was a shambles as the result of an ever-increasing dependency on drugs. It took three years to beat the many habits he had acquired, but in 1957 he was back on the road with a very successful stint at New York City's jazz mecca, Birdland. The years from 1958 through 1962 were the best of his life, he later recalled, as he toured with the Sweets Edison band. Following that period, he moved to Los Angeles, but jazz had changed through the years, and steady work was very difficult to find. By 1970, when things must have looked very bleak indeed, he was called again, this time by Count Basie, to join another touring unit. Throughout the 1970s he was able to work whenever it suited him.

Forrest's main contribution to the history of rock 'n roll must rest on the single release of "Night Train." The record is a natural extension of the sound that Earl Bostic had been developing since the late 1940s. The beat represented by the bass and drums is very much in the forefront of the sound, definitely competing with the lead of the saxophone for attention. The sax, on the other hand is wailing, shrieking, and moaning, mimicking that of the train in the title. This definitely was not jazz in any of its various forms. It is the blues played instrumentally, but with all the power of a vocal. The record was a revelation in its day, a harbinger of things to come. Its influence is most apparent in the stylings of Red Prysock, who was playing with the Tiny Bradshaw Orchestra at this time, and Rusty Bryant, whose "All Night Long" is a virtual copy of "Night Train."

JOHNNIE RAY

Myron "Tiny" Bradshaw was born in Youngstown, Ohio in 1905. He played piano, sang, and was a featured recording artist with King Records from 1949-58. Among the many members of his numerous bands were brothers Arthur and Red Prysock.

Damita Jo (DuBlanc) was born August 5, 1940, in Austin, Texas. She possessed a sultry beauty and was an excellent vocalist. She left Gibson in 1958 and scored a big hit two years later with "I'll Save The Last Dance For You," her answer to the Drifter's smash.

Granville "Stick" McGhee was the younger brother of blues great, Brownie McGhee. Born in Knoxville in 1918, his 1948 recording of "Drinking Wine Spo-dee-o-dee" was Atlantic Records' first hit.

May 1952

MAY 1   Charles Brown and Amos Milburn play a one-nighter in Houston.

Johnnie Ray and Billy Ward and his Dominoes begin a two-week run at Chicago's Oriental Theater.

MAY 2   Philadelphia's Earle Theater presents Tiny Grimes, Edna McGriff, and the Charioteers for a week.

Louis Jordan starts a weeklong stint at the Howard Theater in Washington.

Tiny Bradshaw brings his orchestra to the Apollo Theater in New York for the week.

MAY 3   The Palace Theater in New Orleans offers the Orioles for tonight's ticket holders.

New releases for the first week of May include Joe Houston's "Jump The Blues" on Imperial; "(Let Me Love You) All Night Long" by Bull Moose Jackson, "In The Alley" by Dave Bartholomew, and "Rocket 69" by Todd Rhodes, all on King; "I Wonder" by the Four Tunes and "I May Hate Myself In The Morning" by Steve Gibson and his Red Caps, both on Victor; "Flying Home" by Amos Milburn on Aladdin; "Loud Mouth Lucy" by Chuck Willis on Okeh; and "It's Funny" by the Serenaders on Coral.

MAY 6   Steve Gibson and his Red Caps begin a two-week layover at the Riviera in Las Vegas. Featured vocalist with the combo is Gibson's wife, Damita Jo.

MAY 7   Billy Eckstine opens at his new club, the Savoy, on the Sunset Strip, Hollywood.

EARLY MAY

Ruth Brown is highlighted in the May issue of *Ebony* magazine. She also starts a twenty-date tour with Charles Brown's orchestra that will travel throughout the South.

Gatemouth Brown and Paul Monday are touring the South in a series of one-nighters.

Decca recording artists Larry Cummings and the Rhythm Aces are booked at the Trocadero in Kansas City.

Annie Laurie and Stick McGhee are touring the South through May.

The Larry Darnell, Wynonie Harris, Eddie Duram package is presently playing a series of one-night stands in the Midwest.

28

MAY 8   B. B. King and H-Bomb Ferguson bring their brand of blues to the Virginia circuit this week starting in Roanoke tonight. Other dates include Newport News (9), Portsmouth (10), Norfolk (11-12), and Richmond (13-14).

May 9   Joe Turner and the **Five Keys** front the Count Basie band for a week at the Apollo Theater in New York.
Louis Jordan opens for a week at Philadelphia's Earle Theater.
Paul Monday plays a two-day stand at New Orleans' Dew Drop Inn.

MAY 10   Lionel Hampton plays a one-nighter at the Mosque Theater in Newark before returning to Canada for a week at Montreal's Seville Theater on the 15th.
Chess Records of Chicago announces the formation of a new subsidiary, Checker Records.

MAY 11   Roy Milton performs for the Sunday night crowd at the Elks Ballroom in Los Angeles.
In New Orleans, the San Jacinto Ballroom offers **Jackie Brenston** and Rosco Gordon for the Mother's Day Dance.

MAY 12   Tiny Bradshaw is at the Sky Bar in Cleveland, Ohio.

New releases for the second week of May include "Mistakes" by the Five Keys and "Right Back On" by Peppermint Harris, both on Aladdin, "Why Don't I" by the Heartbreakers and "Lonesome And Blue" by John Greer, both on Victor; "Big Dog" by Bill Doggett on King; "Bip Bop" by Jimmy Forrest on United; "Feed My Body To The Fishes" by Willie Love and his Three Aces on Trumpet; "Hadacol, That's All" by the Treniers and "Ida Red" by Chris Powell and his Five Flames, both on Okeh; "Money Ain't Everything" by Sonny Parker on Peacock; "You're Part Of Me" by the Four Buddies on Savoy; "Gone So Long" by **Roy "Bald Head" Byrd** on Federal; and "Proud Of You" by Sonny Til, "It's Over Because We're Through" by the Orioles, both on Jubilee.

MID-MAY

While on tour the Orioles are involved in an auto accident as they travel between engagements in Memphis and Shreveport. A tire on Sonny Til's 1947 sedan suffers a blowout as bass singer Johnny Reed is driving. Fortunately, no one is hurt.

Sonny Thompson is currently on a one-nighter tour until the 28th.

Ike Turner, of Clarksville, Mississippi, and Jay Franks of Texarkana, Arkansas, have been signed to RPM Records of Los Angeles.

Peacock Records, one of the most active independent r&b and gospel record companies, announces that all future releases will be issued on both 45 and 78 rpm speeds. Previously, all issues had been 78 rpm only.

MAY 16   The Four Tunes open at the Blue Mirror in Washington.
Joe Turner and the Five Keys move into the Howard Theater

THE FIVE KEYS

Jackie Brenston played baritone saxophone in Ike Turner's band, and sang lead on the 1951 hit "Rocket 88" on Chess. He later drove a truck in his hometown of Clarksdale, Mississippi, and died after a heart attack, December 15, 1979.

Louisiana born and bred, Henry Roeland (Roy) Byrd first recorded in 1949 for Star Talent Records using his better known alias, "Professor Longhair." In 1950, he hit with "Bald Head" on Mercury, leading to a new nickname.

Ike Turner's Kings Of Rhythm were among the most prolific studio groups working out of Memphis. Ike played guitar but did not vocalize, preferring to hire others to front his band.

Billy Wright had a long career as a New Orleans vocalist. His two biggest records came on Savoy with "Blues For My Baby" and "You Satisfy" in 1949.

TOMMY EDWARDS

King Pleasure (Clarence Beeks) was a professor at Hartford. A hobbyist's interest in jazz led him to compose lyrics to James Moody's improvised version of "I'm In The Mood For Love," which Beeks retitled "Moody Mood For Love."

Baltimore's Four Buddies were on Savoy Records from 1950-53. Lead singer Greg Carroll left the group in 1954 to join the Orioles, and the remaining members recorded for Glory (as the Buddies) and Decca (as the Barons). In 1963, Carroll was producer for Doris Troy's "Just One Look" on Atlantic.

in Washington for a week with Count Basie's orchestra. Following this week, the Five Keys are off on a one-nighter tour through Virginia.

Louis Jordan and his Tympany Five headline the revue at the Apollo Theater in New York for the week.

Billy Wright performs the first of a pair of three-day weekends at New Orleans' Dew Drop Inn.

Pearl Bailey shares the stage with Chris Powell and his Five Blue Flames this week at Philadelphia's Earle Theater.

MAY 17   M-G-M Records announces a major move into the rhythm and blues field. Henceforth, the company plans to issue at least one r&b record a week. Up to this time in 1952, the company had only issued a total of three r&b titles.

In New Orleans, the Palace Theater welcomes Lowell Fulson and the Cardinals for the evening.

MAY 18   Dinah Washington and **Tommy Edwards** entertain this evening at the Philadelphia Armory as part of the "Caravan Of Stars."

Lloyd Glenn is at the Elks Ballroom in Los Angeles for the night.

New releases for the third week of May include "I Only Have Eyes For You" by the Swallows on King; "Harmonica Boogie" by Pete "Guitar" Lewis on Federal; Why, Oh Why" by Lloyd "The Fat Man" Smith on Peacock; "Mary Jo" by the Four Blazes on United; and "Easy, Easy Baby" by Varetta Dillard on Savoy.

MAY 20   **King Pleasure** moves into the Club Harlem in Philadelphia.

MAY 21   Dinah Washington, the Mills Brothers, and Tommy Edwards star on a one-nighter at Baltimore's Coliseum. A near riot breaks out when white "zoot suiters" start to dance during Washington's rendition of "Wheel Of Fortune."

MAY 23   The **Four Buddies** join Illinois Jacquet at the Earle Theater in Philadelphia. Also on stage is vocalist Wini Brown.

Buddy Johnson's orchestra, featuring his sister Ella and her husband Arthur Prysock, headline the show at the Apollo Theater in New York for the week.

Al Hibbler, Edna McGriff, Chris Powell and his Five Blue Flames, and Jimmy Tyler headline the revue this week at Washington's Howard Theater.

MAY 24   A survey published in Los Angeles reports that the major portion of rhythm and blues records are purchased by Spanish and mixed-nationality buyers. As many as forty percent of the buyers are reported to be White where previously the buyers for r&b were almost all Blacks.

Louis Jordan makes a guest appearance on the "Songs For Sale" television show.

MAY 25   The Elks Ballroom in Los Angeles plays host to Roy Brown. Across town at the Shriner's Club Ball, Earl Bostic is entertaining the crowd.

The San Jacinto Club in New Orleans offers a "Double Battle Of The Blues" with **Dave Bartholomew** *vs* Joe Phillips and Fats Domino *vs* Professor Longhair. Across town, Joe Turner plays a one-nighter at the Dew Drop Inn.

MAY 26 The Griffin Brothers spend the evening at the Farmdell Club in Dayton.

Billy Wright fills out the rest of the weekend at New Orleans' Dew Drop Inn.

Earl Bostic performs at the Shrine Auditorium in Los Angeles.

New releases for the fourth week of May include "After 'While You'll Be Sorry" by Joe Turner on Fidelity; "Aged And Mellow" by Little Esther and "Sure Cure For The Blues" by Shirley Haven and the Four Jacks, both on Federal; "I'm Gonna Put You Down" by Tampa Red on Victor; "Stripped Gears" by Jay Franks on RPM; "Louisiana" by **Percy Mayfield** on Specialty; and "You're Driving Me Insane" by Ike Turner on RPM.

MAY 28 Sonny Thompson opens for ten days at the Farmdell Club in Dayton.

MAY 29 Cleveland's Savoy Club hosts the Tiny Bradshaw Orchestra as they begin a three-week engagement.

MAY 30 New York's Apollo Theater welcomes the Lionel Hampton orchestra for a week's stay.

Joe Turner returns to the Dew Drop Inn in New Orleans for the evening. Billy Wright fills out the remainder of the weekend.

Dinah Washington along with Arnett Cobb and the Ravens opens at the Earle Theater in Philadelphia for the Memorial Day weekend.

MAY 31 Ray Charles, Joe Turner, and Hal "Cornbread" Singer start a month-long Texas tour.

The **Swallows** are welcomed to New Orleans' Palace Theater for the evening.

Lloyd Price hits the road on his first tour, covering three states in two weeks. Tonight he plays LaPlace, Louisiana.

LATE MAY

Starting the end of the month, the Clovers and Rosco Gordon play one-nighters through Texas.

Wynonie Harris is back in New York following his Midwest tour.

Ruth Brown and Hot Lips Page are in Virginia for a series of one night stands.

Rainbow Records has signed Joe Bailey and sax-man Lloyd Williams.

Dave Bartholomew first met Fats Domino in December 1949 when he was club-hopping with Imperial Records owner Lew Chudd in New Orleans looking for talent to record. The same night that they met Domino, Bartholomew supervised the recording session for "The Fat Man."

Percy Mayfield, a native of Minden, Louisiana, was discovered in New Orleans by Supreme Records of Los Angeles. He soon moved across town to the hot Specialty label; his first release, "Please Send Me Someone To Love," sold well in 1950.

The Swallows recorded for King Records from June 1951 until November 1953. A year later, they had one record on After Hours and then broke up. A newly formed group of Swallows returned to the King company, recording four releases for Federal Records in 1958.

THE TOP TEN ROCK 'N ROLL RECORDS FOR MAY 1952

1. 5-10-15 Hours - Ruth Brown
2. One Mint Julep - The Clovers
3. Night Train - Jimmy Forrest
4. No More Doggin' - Rosco Gordon
5. Middle Of The Night - The Clovers
6. Heavenly Father - Edna McGriff
7. Goin' Home - Fats Domino
8. Sweet Sixteen - B. B. King
9. That's What You're Doing To Me - Billy Ward and his Dominoes
10. Have Mercy, Baby - Billy Ward and his Dominoes

May 1952
ARTIST OF THE MONTH

RUTH BROWN
(Ruth Weston, b. January 30, 1928*)

RUTH BROWN

Is this the Ruth Brown whose initial desire was only to become a big-band vocalist? Could this be the same Ruth Brown who for many years unashamedly imitated Billie Holiday, Sarah Vaughan, and Dinah Washington? Yes, this is the same Ruth Brown who was also the first female star of rhythm and blues - whose powerful style can be credited with aiding in the formation of the music that would soon be called rock 'n roll.

Her father, a Methodist choir director, never approved of Ruth's blues singing. During World War II, underage and without telling her family, Ruth Weston sneaked away to the USO clubs in her native Portsmouth, Virginia, to entertain the troops with a singing style that was uncannily close to that of Billie Holiday. She quickly found work in local Virginia clubs, which led to a trip to Detroit and a meeting with bandleader Lucky Millinder. She was hired to front Millinder's band, but then she was fired within a month while the band was in Washington, DC. She auditioned and was hired to sing at the Crystal Caverns Club managed by Cab Calloway's sister, Blanche Calloway. Her initial engagement ran to sixteen weeks and Miss Calloway became her manager. Based on the overwhelming recommendation by Blanche Calloway, as well as Washington deejay Willis Conover, and the owner of Quality Record Store next door to the Howard Theater, Atlantic Records signed Ruth Brown to a contract. On October 29, 1948, enroute to New York for her first recording session and an opening engagement at the Apollo Theater, she was badly hurt in an auto accident. She remained hospitalized for several months, but by April 1949 she was ready to start what turned out to be a long-term association with Atlantic Records.

Her first recordings in 1949, "Rockin' Blues," "So Long," and "I'll Get Along Somehow," were based on the big band style of blues, but pressure from Atlantic worked to mold her voice to fit rhythm tunes.

(*Date of birth also given as January 12, 1928)

It took a long time - "5-10-15 Hours" was her eleventh release for Atlantic. However, her "new" energetic singing style soon earned her the nickname of "Miss Rhythm," first applied by Frankie Laine when they shared the bill at the Earle Theater in Philadelphia in October 1952. It stuck, and by 1962 Ruth Brown had released over eighty songs for Atlantic, more than any other artist, and she had become Atlantic's top-selling performer throughout the 1950s. She was consistently named by the music trade magazines as the top female vocalist in the rhythm and blues field. She had three records that each sold more than a million copies: "5-10-15 Hours" and "Mama (He Treats Your Daughter Mean)" in 1952, and "Lucky Lips" in 1957. For six years she toured with sax-man Willis "Gatortail" Jackson's orchestra, eventually marrying him and bearing him a son in 1955. Jackson became one of Atlantic's foremost house musicians based on his association with Miss Brown.

Her stage performances were something to behold! She came into the spotlight dressed in a skintight, low-cut gown designed to accent her well-developed bosom. She was vigorous and vibrant, shouting in a dramatic style, and her voice could jump from a "throaty alto to a tremulous soprano." She possessed an unlimited personal electricity and a voice that easily reached to the back of the largest theaters. Her songs were intended to be sexy, with a bedroom flavor featuring slightly "blue" lyrics, and she knew how to get the most out of each number. She was a "sure audience pleaser."

In 1962 she moved on to Phillips Records, but rock 'n roll music had passed her by. In the 1970s she recorded for Cobblestone and President but, although the albums received critical acclaim, sales were disappointing. Ruth Brown is no longer an active singer, preferring to stay home in Deer Park, Long Island, and raise her son when she is not making television appearances as an actress. She has attempted several comebacks but they have been short-lived, though she still appears occasionally at jazz and blues festivals.

Today, Ruth Brown is credited with developing a rock 'n roll style that was enjoyed equally by both Blacks and Whites. Her influence can be seen most immediately in the style of LaVern Baker, who was her only contemporary rival, and in the early hit recordings of Brenda Lee and Connie Francis.

June 1952

JUN 1   Louis Jordan, Roy Brown, and Jimmy Witherspoon are the featured artists at the Eighth Cavalcade of Jazz held at Wrigley Field in Los Angeles.

Lloyd Price continues on his first tour with a show in Hattiesburg, Mississippi. Tomorrow he travels to Pensacola, Florida.

JUN 2   Wini Brown opens in Cleveland for a week following her successful engagement at the Earle Theater in Philadelphia.

New releases for the first week of June include "Help Me Blues" by **Joe Williams** on Trumpet; "Heartache, Here I Come" by Mel Walker on Savoy; "Roll, Mr. Jelly" by Amos Milburn on Aladdin; "Break Thru" by John "Schoolboy" Porter and "That's All Right" by Little Walter, both on Chance; "Wait Down At The Bottom Of The Hill" by Johnny King on M-G-M; and "Sposin'" by the Charioteers on Keystone.

JUN 6   Ruth Brown fronts the Erskine Hawkins band for her week's stay at the Apollo Theater in New York.

In Louisiana, Lloyd Price makes a stopover at Donaldson tonight and Port Allen on the 7th.

JUN 7   **Capitol Records** reports that 45 rpm disk sales are up fifty-two percent in the first four months of 1952 as compared to the previous year. RCA Victor, on the other hand, reports that total sales for all records are down ten percent for the same period.

EARLY JUNE

Alan "Moondog" Freed, Cleveland's well-known r&b disk jockey, is in New York to set up talent for several forthcoming dance programs in the Cleveland area in June. Among those signed are the Swallows, Edna McGriff, and Buddy Lucas's orchestra.

Little Esther, Willie Mae "Big Mama" Thornton, and Johnny Otis and his combo are touring the Pacific Northwest before returning to Otis's home base of California.

Roy Brown is reportedly bringing in the crowds on his swing through the West Coast. Also currently on tour, Jimmy Forrest is traveling throughout the South for most of the month.

JUN 8   Louis Jordan performs at the Shrine Auditorium in Los Angeles.

JUN 9   In Cleveland, Earl Bostic entertains at the Club Ebony.
Percy Mayfield starts a tour of the Eastern Seaboard.

New releases for the second week of June include "Don't You Think

The Joe Williams who recorded blues for Trumpet Records is not to be confused with the Joe Williams (real name: Joseph Goreed) who worked for years with the Count Basie Orchestra. This singer, commonly referred to as Big Joe Williams, recorded often for forty years starting in the 1930s.

Capitol Records was founded in Hollywood in 1942 and a year later signed Nat "King" Cole, one of the first major Black stars of the day. The company dabbled in r&b, recording the Five Keys in 1954.

ROY BROWN

I Ought To Know" by Little Donna Hightower on Decca; "Blackout" by Paul Bascomb on States; "Don't Marry Too Soon" by Lil Miss Cornshucks on Coral; "Steady Eddie" by Al Sears on King; "Worried 'Bout You Baby" by Big Boy Crudup on Victor; and "Why Did You Leave Me?" by the Ravens on Mercury.

JUN 11   The Swallows are off on a one-nighter tour.

JUN 12   **Sonny Thompson** opens at the Farmdell Club in Dayton.
          Louis Jordan takes to the road on his tour of the West Coast.

JUN 13   Edna McGriff and Buddy Lucas's orchestra begin a series of one-night stands in the bay area of Virginia with a show in Petersburg.
          Ruth Brown headlines for a week at the Howard Theater in Washington.
          Savannah Churchill and the Striders front the Dizzy Gillespie combo for a week at the Earle Theater in Philadelphia.
          In New Orleans, Lloyd Price is scheduled for a three-day weekend at the Dew Drop Inn. He is held over for an additional three weekends. A local newspaper calls Price "the biggest drawing card since Roy Brown."
          Sarah Vaughan is the featured attraction in Philadelphia at the Club Harlem. Also in town, **Bill Doggett** is at Lawson's Nite Club.

JUN 14   Billy Ward and his Dominoes play a double date in New Orleans. There is an afternoon show at the Booker T. Washington Auditorium followed by an evening performance at the Coliseum Arena. The crowd for the Arena show is reported to be "frenzied."

JUN 15   The Clovers, backed by the Billy Ford band, hit the road for a month of one-nighters through the South and West.
          Johnny Otis, Little Esther, and Willie Mae Thornton are the headliners for the Sunday night dance at the Elks Ballroom in Los Angeles.
          The Orioles stop in New Orleans for a one-night stand at the Booker T. Washington Auditorium.

MID-JUNE

The **Ravens** are sued by their parent recording company, National Records, for $100,000 as the result of their failure to show up for a recording session. The lawsuit names Columbia Records as having allegedly induced the singers into a breach of contract. The Raven's latest release, "Mam'selle" is on Columbia's Okeh subsidiary. The Ravens countersue National for $7,615 in back royalties.

The Bihari brothers, owners of RPM Records, are seeking an injunction against Duke Records for releasing disks by Rosco Gordon.

Specialty Records, one of the top independent rhythm and blues record companies, announces that they are entering the country and western field with four initial releases.

Sonny Thompson led a popular r&b orchestra/dance band in the 1940s and '50s. His hits were many, including 1948's "Long Gone" on Miracle, and "Fast Freight" on Premium. He started a long association with King Records in 1952.

William Ballard (Bill) Doggett, born February 16, 1916, in Philadelphia, started as an $18-a-week pianist in 1935. By 1949, after years with Lucky Millinder, the Ink Spots, and Lionel Hampton, he joined Louis Jordan's Tympany Five. He began fronting his own combo in 1952, playing the Hammond organ.

The Ravens issued twenty-one records for National, starting in 1947. By 1952, the personnel in the group were changing constantly, and within two years every original member of the quartet would be replaced.

Specialty Records was founded by Art Rupe in Los Angeles in 1946 after he folded his Juke Box label. Roy Milton and Joe Liggins provided the necessary early hits, and Lloyd Price's "Lawdy Miss Clawdy" made Specialty a national contender.

Arthur Prysock quits the Buddy Johnson Orchestra after eight years to embark on a solo career. Johnson will remain as Prysock's personal manager.

Mercury Records signs Mel Walker, previously with Savoy, and the Freddie Mitchell orchestra, formerly with Derby Records.

Louis Jordan takes his Tympany Five to Honolulu for the week.

Austin Powell, former lead singer with the Cats and a Fiddle, signs with Atlantic Records.

JUN 16   The Four Tunes begin a twelve-week engagement at the Club Harlem in Atlantic City.
　　　　　The Griffin Brothers start a week's run at the Trocaveria Club in Columbus, Ohio.
　　　　　Ella Fitzgerald is playing the Harlem Club in Philadelphia for a week.
　　　　　T-Bone Walker starts a two-week stay at the Club Oasis in Los Angeles.

New releases for the third week of June include "Call Operator 210" by Floyd Dixon on Aladdin; "I Get That Lonesome Feeling" by Ivory Joe Hunter on M-G-M; "Discouraged" by Allen Bunn on Apollo; "I Like Barbeque" by the Guy Brothers on States; "What'cha Gonna Do For Me" by Titus Turner on Okeh; "Let's Call It A Day" by Sonny Thompson and Lulu Reed on King; and "Walkin' The Boogie" by **John Lee Hooker** on Chess.

JUN 19   The Swallows, Edna McGriff, and Buddy Lucas's orchestra embark on a series of one-nighters in Ohio promoted by Cleveland deejay Alan Freed. This night, the performers entertain at the Crystal Beach Ballroom in Lorraine. On the 20th they are at the Summit Beach Ballroom in Akron, and on the 21st they entertain at the Avon Oaks Ballroom in Youngstown. Total attendance is over 5,000 for all three shows.
　　　　　Joe Liggins starts a tour of the Southwest.
　　　　　Roy Brown plays a one-nighter at the Cobra Club in San Diego.

JUN 20   Roy Milton sets off on a one-nighter tour of the South that will include a few club dates.
　　　　　Ivory Joe Hunter travels to the Apollo Theater in New York City for the week.
　　　　　Dinah Washington, Bill Harris's All Stars, and Joe Holiday's orchestra open at Birdland.
　　　　　Sarah Vaughan and **Timmie Rogers** share the stage for a week at Washington's Howard Theater.
　　　　　Louis Jordan plays a one-nighter in Yakima, Washington. He follows this date with a show on the 21st in Spokane and on the 22nd at the Trianon Ballroom in Tacoma.
　　　　　Chicago's Regal Theater presents the Count Basie Orchestra and the Ravens this week.
　　　　　The new show at the Earle Theater in Philadelphia features the orchestra of Tiny Bradshaw.

JOHN LEE HOOKER

In blues music, John Lee Hooker is the "King Of The Boogie." His style of rolling guitar was derived from listening to Charlie Patton, a close family friend. In turn, Hooker greatly influenced any number of guitarists and groups (notably Canned Heat), play the blues with a boogie beat.

Timmie "Oh Yeah" Rogers' long career as band vocalist yielded only one hit, 1957's "Back To School Again" on Cameo, sung so that teens could dance the "stroll."

JUN 22   In New Orleans, one-night stands are the norm this evening for the r&b audience: Roy Milton, Pee Wee Crayton, and Lil Greenwood are at the Coliseum Arena; Gatemouth Brown, Lloyd Price, and **Gene Ammons** are at the Rosenwald Gym; and Lowell Fulson is at the Club Desire.

New **releases** for the fourth week of June include "Starting From Tonight" by the Royals and "Monday Morning" by Lil Greenwood and Little Willie, both on Federal; "(I'm A) Sentimental Fool" by Arthur Prysock on Decca; and "Mother's Letter" by Andrew Tibbs on Peacock.

JUN 23   The package tour of Ray Charles, Joe Turner, and Hal "Cornbread" Singer winds up its month-long trek with a show in Little Rock.
     Tiny Bradshaw is featured for three days in Philadelphia at Pep's Musical Bar.
     Bill Doggett's combo opens at the Carver Bar in the Glen Hotel in Philadelphia.

JUN 24   Louis Jordan continues his tour of the Northwest with a show in Vancouver. This is followed by shows in the Century Ballroom in Tacoma (25) and McElroy's Ballroom in Portland (26).

JUN 25   The **Griffin Brothers** come off of a well-deserved three-week vacation by starting a series of one-night stands with a show in Milwaukee.

JUN 26   The Four Tunes begin a summer engagement at the Harlem Club in Atlantic City.
     Tenor saxman Frank "Floorshow" Culley starts at the Farmdell Club in Dayton for two weeks. Culley played tenor sax on the 1949 Atlantic hit, "Cole Salw."
     In Los Angeles, Joe Liggins is the evening's attraction at the Elks Ballroom.

JUN 27   Lynn Hope's Orchestra with Amos Milburn kicks off the summer season at Weeke's Cafe in Atlantic City with a week's engagement.
     Following his stand in Philadelphia, Tiny Bradshaw opens for a week in Washington's Howard Theater.
     New York's Apollo Theater welcomes Joe Turner to this week's revue.

JUN 28   The Buddy Johnson Orchestra is off on a one-nighter tour through the North, East Coast, and Midwest until July 11 after closing a successful stint in Boston.

New **releases** for the fifth week of June include "Walking And Crying" by Sonny Boy Holmes on Recorded In Hollywood; "Lay It On The Line" by Tiny Bradshaw's Orchestra and "Puddin' Head Jones" by Freddie Hall, both on King; "Mam'selle" by the Ravens on Okeh; and "The Question" by **Memphis Slim** on Mercury.

Gene Ammons was the son Albert Ammons, the father of boogie woogie piano. Gene took up saxophone and played in the bands of Billy Eckstine and Woody Herman. He joined Sonny Stitt in 1950 in a twin-lead combo playing raucous, "party" rhythm and blues. Ammons died in 1974 at age 49.

The Griffin Brothers Orchestra was one of Dot Records' earliest successes. With vocalist Margie Day, they hit with the classic "Little Red Rooster" in 1951.

MEMPHIS SLIM

Memphis Slim was born Peter Chatman in Memphis in 1915 or 1916. He was a proficient barrelhouse pianist/vocalist. In 1939, he was part of the migration of Blacks to Chicago. He has been on the record scene since 1940, when his "Beer Drinking Women" caused a sensation.

Dinah Washington opens at Birdland in New York City.

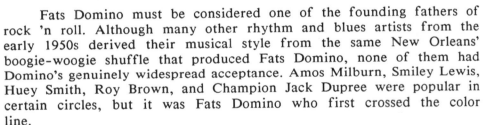

THE TOP TEN ROCK 'N ROLL RECORDS FOR JUNE 1952

1. Goin' Home - Fats Domino
2. 5-10-15 Hours - Ruth Brown
3. Have Mercy, Baby - The Dominos
4. One Mint Julep - The Clovers
5. Lawdy, Miss Clawdy - Lloyd Price
6. So Tired - Roy Milton
7. Night Train - Jimmy Forrest
8. No More Doggin' - Rosco Gordon
9. Moody Mood For Love - King Pleasure
10. Heavenly Father - Edna McGriff

June 1952
ARTIST OF THE MONTH

FATS DOMINO
(Antoine Domino, Jr., b. February 26, 1928*)

FATS DOMINO

Fats Domino must be considered one of the founding fathers of rock 'n roll. Although many other rhythm and blues artists from the early 1950s derived their musical style from the same New Orleans' boogie-woogie shuffle that produced Fats Domino, none of them had Domino's genuinely widespread acceptance. Amos Milburn, Smiley Lewis, Huey Smith, Roy Brown, and Champion Jack Dupree were popular in certain circles, but it was Fats Domino who first crossed the color line.

Antoine Domino was born in New Orleans into a large family of six brothers and three sisters. He grew up in a musical environment and began playing piano at the age of five. His fine boogie woogie piano stylings were first learned from an uncle, Harrison Verrett, a well known New Orleans violinist. Fats also listened attentively to the recordings of Albert Ammons, the premier boogie woogie pianist, who, incidently, died in 1949, the same year that Fats recorded his first hit single, "The Fat Man." After quitting school at age fourteen, Fats got a day job working on an ice delivery truck. Another job in a factory that manufactured bedsprings almost stopped his career as a pianist before it really had a chance to begin when he suffered a badly cut hand. Fortunately, the hand healed, and he continued to perform for rent parties and in small night clubs.

In 1949, while he was playing at the Hideaway Club for three dollars a week, he met Dave Bartholomew, a local trumpet player and a talent scout for Imperial Records, who coaxed Fats into eventually signing with Imperial. His first record, the autobiographical "The Fat Man," was an immediate success with the blues audience in early 1950,

(*Official BMI biography and early interviews often give May 10, 1929 as date of birth.)

and the recording reportedly went on to become the first of a long string of million sellers for Fats.

By 1952 "Goin' Home" was his eleventh release and his first number one record on the r&b charts. Although he was in constant demand on the circuit of southern Black night clubs, Fats found time to play on many other artists' records, including providing the distinctive piano backing on Lloyd Price's "Lawdy, Miss Clawdy," which topped the rhythm and blues charts just after his own "Goin' Home."

Domino absorbed much of the New Orleans rhythm and blues heritage which was a direct descendent of pre-World War II jazz. His recordings featured good-humored, self-penned lyrics with tightly arranged backings by Bartholomew. Much of his success lies with the local session musicians that he used extensively, many of whom became almost legends in their own right. Most of Domino's releases were recorded in New Orleans under the direction of Cosimo Matassa at his J&M Studios. This friendship among the musicians comes across in the off-the-cuff, house party atmosphere in the music. Even the blues songs recorded by Domino have little of the bitterness found in the recordings of artist such as B. B. King, thereby giving them a wider appeal.

(More about Fats Domino in the next volume of *The Golden Age of American Rock 'N Roll.*)

July 1952

JUL 2   Following one-night stands in Eugene, Oregon, and Sacramento and Redwood City in California, Louis Jordan performs at the Del Monte Gardens in Monterey. The following two nights find him in on stage in San Francisco and Oakland.

JUL 3   Jimmy Weatherspoon headlines the dance at the Oro Ballroom in Los Angeles tonight and also on the Fourth of July. Also in Los Angeles for the weekend are Hal "Cornbread" Singer with Joe Turner, who are appearing for three days at the 5-4 Ballroom.
         Roy Brown travels to the Club DeLisa in Portland, Oregon.

The Five Keys, from Newport News, had their first hit with "The Glory Of Love" on Aladdin in 1951. They also achieved national prominence with "Ling Ting Tong" and "Close Your Eyes" on Capitol in 1955.

JUL 4   Weeke's Cafe in Atlantic City hosts the **Five Keys**, Wini Brown, and Piney Brown for the week.
         Dinah Washington is scheduled to perform in Trenton, New Jersey, but she does not show up. Legal action against her is settled in September with the scheduling of another show.
         Ruth Brown entertains for a week at the Royal Theater in Baltimore.
         Wynonie Harris, along with Larry Darnell and Annie Laurie, opens at the Howard Theater in Washington for a week.
         Billy Eckstine entertains at the Chicago Theater for a week.

JUL 5   **Big Jay McNeeley** starts an extended engagement at the Waldorf Center in Los Angeles.

Cecil "Big Jay" McNeely is credited with being one of the first sax-men to play the horn while laying on his back, a staple in the acts of wild r&b sax players ever since. He was born April 29, 1928, and first recorded in 1946 for Exclusive.

JUL 6   Roy Brown plays the Sunday night dance at the Elks Ballroom in Los Angeles.

JUL 7   Arthur Prysock moves into the Regal Theater in Columbus, Ohio, for three weeks.

New releases for the first week of July include "I Hadn't Anyone 'Til You" by the Five Keys and "Two Faced Daddy" by Mickey Champion, both on Aladdin; "Ting-A-Ling" by the Clovers, "Don't You Cry" by Joe Turner, and "Rock, Rock, Rock" by Willis "Gator Tail" Jackson, all on Atlantic; "The Sales Tax Boogie" by Piano Red on Victor; "The Bells Are Ringing" by Smiley Lewis on Imperial; "Get Mad Baby" by the Gaylords on Savoy; and five releases from Jubilee: "Barfly" by the Orioles, "I Can't Get Started With You" by Frank "Fat Man" Humphries and the Four Notes, "Hustlin' Family Blues" by Buddy Lucas, "It's Raining" by Edna McGriff, and "You Didn't Know" by Billy Paul. The last two releases also feature the Lucas Band.

EARLY JULY

Rainbow Records, continuing to add to its stable of r&b acts, signs the **Five Crowns** and the Miller Sisters.

THE FIVE CROWNS

The Five Crowns featured Bobby Hendricks and Benny Nelson. Hendricks had a 1958 hit with "Itchy Twitchy Feeling" for Sue. Soon thereafter, the Five Crowns and Nelson were picked to replace the Drifters. At that time, Nelson changed his name to Ben E. King.

40

Okeh Records, a subsidiary of New York's Columbia Records, reports that its scouts are off to the West Coast and the South in search of new talent.

The Paul Williams Orchestra opens for a week at Cleveland's Ebony Club.

JUL 8   Tiny Bradshaw's orchestra starts a four-week run in Cincinnati.

JUL 9   As part of a month-long tour of California, Louis Jordan returns for a week-long stand at the Clayton Club in Sacramento, California.

JUL 11   The Buddy Johnson Orchestra starts a week at the Regal Theater in Chicago.
         Charles Brown shares the bill with the Orioles at Weeke's Cafe in Atlantic City for a week.
         Ivory Joe Hunter starts at the Glass Bar in St. Louis.
         Ruth Brown plays a one-nighter in Birmingham, Alabama, followed the next night by a show in Alexandria, Virginia.
         Dinah Washington, the Ravens, and comedians **Redd Foxx** and Slappy White are the stars this week at the Howard Theater in Washington.
         Varetta Dillard plays the Flame Show Bar in Detroit for a week as the opener for her Midwest tour.

JUL 12   A package consisting of Edna McGriff, Tab Smith, and Lynn Hope's Orchestra embarks on a tour of twenty-two one-nighters through the South.

JUL 13   Earl Bostic is at the Elks Ballroom in Los Angeles for the evening.

JUL 14   Amos Milburn starts a week's stay at the Ebony Club in Cleveland.

New releases for the second week of July include "Strictly Cash" by Preston Love and "Please Open Your Heart" by Danny Sutton, both on Federal; "I Got Eyes For You" by John Lee Hooker and **Little Eddie Kirkland** on Modern; and three releases from Swing Time: "Baby I'm Losing You" by Cecil Gant, "Baby, Let Me Hear You Call My Name" by Ray Charles, and "Wake Up, Baby" by Felix Gross.

JUL 15   On the "Ted Mack Amateur Hour" television program, the annual run-off winner is eight-year-old **Gladys Knight** of Atlanta. She takes home $2,000 and a gold cup.

MID-JULY

Bull Moose Jackson is finishing up his tour on the West Coast.

In the resort city of Wildwood, New Jersey, Sarah Vaughan is entertaining at the Beachcomber, the Treniers and the **Jive Bombers** are at the Riptide, Steve Gibson and his Redcaps featuring Damita Jo are at the Martinique, and the Golden Dragon plays host to the

Comedian Redd Foxx's real name is John Sanford. The character he portrayed on his hit TV series was Fred Sanford.

Eddie Kirkland was born in Jamaica in 1928. His only recording session for R.P.M./Modern featured John Lee Hooker on guitar. Many years later, Kirkland surfaced again, playing guitar behind Otis Redding and Joe Tex, and had a regional hit in 1965 with "The Hawg" on Volt.

Gladys Knight turned pro in 1957, joining her brother, two cousins and a sister to form the Pips, one of the most successful soul groups of the 1960s and 1970s. Their first hit was a 1961 remake of the Royals' "Every Beat Of My Heart," written by Johnny Otis.

The Jive Bombers, lead by Clarence Palmer, had a novelty hit with "Bad Boy" on Savoy in 1957, a song which featured Palmer's intense vocal waverings.

ARTHUR PRYSOCK

Singer/pianist Jimmy McCracklin was born in St. Louis in 1931. He first recorded in Los Angeles in the late 1940s for Globe Records before signing with Modern in 1949 and Swing Time in 1951.

Clarence "Gatemouth" Brown was born in Orange, Texas, on April 18, 1924. He first recorded in 1947 for Aladdin Records before moving to Houston, where his popularity impressed Don Robey, owner of the Bronze Peacock club since the 1940s. Finding "Gate" without a manager or recording contract, Robey stepped in.

In 1947, Don Robey started Peacock Records as an outlet for Gatemouth Brown's music. Don Robey was the first Black to own a record company in the South or Southwest. At this time, the Duke label was owned by Memphis deejay James Mattis.

Five Barons.

New Orleans radio station WJMR sets aside two hours every afternoon for its "Poppa Stoppa" deejay show dedicated to r&b.

JUL 16   Louis Jordan starts a stand at the Say When Club in San Francisco that will run through the 27th.

JUL 18   Ruth Brown with Willis Jackson's band starts a week's engagement at Weeke's Cafe in Atlantic City.
          T-Bone Walker opens for the three-day weekend at Los Angeles' 5-4 Ballroom.
          The Howard Theater in Washington plays host to the Paul Williams Orchestra and the Orioles for a week.
          Arthur Prysock begins a two-week engagement at the Flame Show Bar in Detroit.

JUL 20   **Jimmy McCracklin** and Jimmy Witherspoon engage in a "Battle Of The Blues Bands" at the Elks Ballroom in Los Angeles.

JUL 21   Ivory Joe Hunter opens at the Ebony Club in Cleveland for a week.
          Dinah Washington is at the Blue Mirror in Washington.

New releases for the third week of July include "Ain't Nothin' Happenin'" by Little Richard and "They Don't Understand" by the Four Tunes, both on Victor; "Strickly Gone" (sic) by Nature Boy Brown on United; "Baby Don't Go" by Jesse Belvin, "Brown Skin Baby" by Jimmy Liggins, and "Old Baldy Boogie" by Camile Howard, all on Specialty; "Call Operator 210" by Johnny Otis on Mercury; "I'll Be Home Again" by the Four Jacks on Federal; "Just Got Lucky" by **Clarence "Gatemouth" Brown** on Peacock; and "Tab's Purple Heart" by Tab Smith on King.

JUL 24   Bull Moose Jackson goes into the Savoy Ballroom in New York for a week.

JUL 25   Billie Holiday and the Wild Bill Davis Trio start a week in Atlantic City at Weeke's Cafe. Also working this date, except on the 26th, is Hal "Cornbread" Singer.
          Joe Turner, coming off of a California tour, opens at the Dew Drop Inn in New Orleans for three weeks.

JUL 26   Sarah Vaughan and Hal "Cornbread" Singer perform for the inauguration of the Saturday night Chesapeake River cruises out of Washington, DC.
          Roy Brown stops at the San Jacinto Club in New Orleans for the evening.
          The "Third Annual Blues Jubilee" at the Shrine Auditorium in Los Angeles features many local favorites including T-Bone Walker, Jimmy Witherspoon, Al Hibbler, Big Jay McNeeley, Peppermint Harris, Joe Houston, and Floyd Dixon.
          Peacock Records, based in Houston, takes over Duke Records of Memphis.

JUL 27   Bette McLauren starts a ten-day engagement at the Regal in Columbus, Ohio.

In Los Angeles, the Sunday night dance at the Elks Ballroom features Little Willie Littlefield and Joe Houston.

JUL 28   Atlanta's Club Poinciana plays host to Varetta Dillard.

The new releases for the fourth week of July include two from Mercury: "Forget If You Can" by Bubber Johnson and "I Know You Will" by Big Bill Broonzy; "Five Long Years" by Eddie Boyd on J.O.B.; three from Savoy: "Key Hole Blues" by Eddie Mack, "Gonna Take A Train" by Johnny Otis, and "Georgia Woman" by Lazy Slim Jim; two from Apollo: "Hold Me" by the **Larks** and "Honey's Lovin' Arms" by the Bobby Smith Orchestra; "I Went To Your Wedding" by Steve Gibson and his Redcaps with Damita Jo on Victor; "Moonrise" by the Royals on Federal; three from King: "Trying" by Todd Rhodes with LaVern Baker, "Two Little Girls" by Jimmy Witherspoon, and Wynonie Harris's "Night Train"; and Duke Bayou's "Rub A Little Boogie" on Apollo.

The original Larks, from Durham, North Carolina, had a short recording career (1951-53) on Apollo. Lead singer Eugene Mumford briefly formed another group of Larks that recorded for Lloyds (1954) before he joined Billy Ward and his Dominoes (with fellow Lark David McNeil). Mumford sang lead on "Stardust" and "Deep Purple" in 1957.

JUL 29   Earl Bostic stops by the Blackhawk Club in San Francisco for a two-week stand as part of his West Coast swing.

LATE JULY

Leo "Mad Lad" Parker and his orchestra become the first r&b group to play the Latin Quarter in St. Louis. They were booked as a result of the response during their six-week stay at the Boulevard Room in Kansas City.

Savannah Churchill is at Chubby's Cafe in Camden, New Jersey.

Savannah Churchill (born Savannah Valentine in Colfax, Louisiana, August 21, 1920) recorded frequently with the Sentimentalists, soon to be known as the Four Tunes - starting in 1948. Seventeen of the group's thirty-two releases on Manor/Arco Records feature Miss Churchill.

It is reported by the recording industry that for the first half of 1952, 78 rpm records made up fifty percent of all sales down from eighty percent in April, followed by 45 rpm at thirty percent and 33 1/3 rpm at sixteen percent of all units sold.

THE TOP TEN ROCK 'N ROLL RECORDS FOR JULY 1952

1. Have Mercy, Baby - The Dominoes
2. Lawdy Miss Clawdy - Lloyd Price
3. Goin' Home - Fats Domino
4. One Mint Julep - The Clovers
5. Moody Mood For Love - King Pleasure
6. I'll Drown In My Tears - Sonny Thompson with Lulu Reed
7. Mary Jo - The Four Blazes
8. No More Doggin' - Rosco Gordon
9. Ting-A-Ling - The Clovers
10. Night Train - Jimmy Forrest

July 1952
ARTIST OF THE MONTH

BILLY WARD AND HIS DOMINOES

THE DOMINOES

The Dominoes were the extension of the personal dream of a single individual, Billy Ward. Throughout the ten years that the group was performing, it was Ward's vision that remained constant, even though the personnel within the group changed constantly.

Billy Ward was born September 19, 1921, in Los Angeles, but early in his life the family moved to Philadelphia where his father was the preacher at the Wayland Baptist Church. Ward studied piano and voice, and starting at the age six he sang in the church choir. At fourteen he won a contest with his classical piano composition, "Dejection." During World War II Ward was an officer at Ft. Eustis, Virginia, where he led the Coast Artillery Choir. He also excelled as an amateur boxer and was a Golden Gloves division champion. After the war Ward studied at the Chicago Art Institute and the Juilliard School of Music in New York City. He then found time to be the East Coast sports editor for the *Transradio Press* and a vocal coach at Carnegie Hall, as well as acting as a talent agent.

The Dominoes were started by Ward in the late 1940s from the headquarters of his music studio on Broadway in New York City. Originally, the group was named the Ques and was formed as a gospel quintet. They made their debut in popular music at the Wednesday night amateur contest at the Apollo Theater in Harlem. This led to an appearance on Arthur Godfrey's "Talent Scouts" in October 1950, which resulted in a contract with Federal Records, a new subsidiary of the Cincinnati-based independent, King Records. At this time the group consisted of seventeen-year-old Clyde McPhatter (first tenor), Charles White (second tenor), William Joseph Lamont (also spelled Lamount) (baritone), Bill Brown (bass), and Ward, who played piano and filled in vocally where needed. The group's first release, "Do Something For Me," hit the record stores in early 1951.

The first major hit for the Dominoes was not long in coming. "Sixty Minute Man," issued in the spring of 1951, was the top r&b record of the year, reportedly selling over two million copies. It was also the first rhythm and blues song strong enough to enter the field of "pop" music. In 1952 White and Brown left the group and were replaced by James Van Loan (brother of Joe Van Loan, lead tenor with the Ravens) and David McNeil (previously with the Larks). In May 1953 McPhatter left the group to form the Drifters for Atlantic Records. His place was taken by Sonny "Jackie" Wilson. The Dominoes (officially known by this time as Billy Ward and his Dominoes) stayed with Federal for several years before moving on to Decca and then to Liberty Records. In 1956 Wilson's distinctive vocal led the group on the hit "St. Theresa Of The Roses" before he went off on a successful solo career. The groups' last hits were for Liberty and included "Stardust" and "Deep Purple" in 1957.

On stage the Dominoes performed as a four man vocal group with piano and guitar accompaniment. Although at least one reviewer in 1952 thought their harmonies were of only average quality, it was noted that the Dominoes had a loyal following of teen-agers who shrieked and screamed at every note the group sang. When Clyde McPhatter was the lead tenor the Dominoes were a formidable stage presence.

The live versions of "Have Mercy, Baby" or "The Bells" stopped the show every night, which was a problem early in their career for headline performers who had the misfortune to be scheduled to follow the Dominoes on stage. Later, when the Dominoes were placed last on the bill, their frantic stage act was a sure-fire crowd-pleaser. This loyalty followed the group wherever they played and their popularity at this time cannot be overestimated. When McPhatter left the group he was replaced by a performer who may have been even more dramatic and was certainly more acrobatic, Jackie Wilson. The Dominoes alternated between the finest hotels and night clubs from Las Vegas to New York where they entertained mostly White audiences, and the theater circuit along the East Coast where their audiences were made up largely of the same yelping Black teen-agers that bought their records. consequently, the Dominoes were one of the first purely rhythm and blues groups to cross these barriers.

August 1952

AUG 1   Wynonie Harris is booked into the Royal Theater in Baltimore for the week.

AUG 2   The Clovers and Charles Brown headline the talent on the Chesapeake River Saturday night cruise sailing from Washington.

AUG 3   In Los Angeles, Al Hibbler plays the Elks Ballroom.
The "Battle Of The Blues" at the Rosenwald Gym in New Orleans features Joe Turner *vs* Guitar Slim.

New releases for the first week of August include four from Atlantic: "Western Rider Blues" by Soldier Boy Houston, "The Bump" by the Cardinals, Ruth Brown's "Daddy Daddy," and "Bald Head Woman" by Joe Morris' Blues Cavalcade with Billy Mitchell on vocals; three from Aladdin: "There's A Dead Cat On The Line" by **Peppermint Harris**, "Without Your Love" by Charles Brown, and "How Could You Be So Mean" by Johnny Moore's Three Blazers; two from Checker: "Juke" by Little Walter and "Baby Please No No" by Al "Fats" Thomas; "There Is Time" by the Heartbreakers on Victor; "Sittin' Here Drinkin'" by Christine Kittrell on Tennessee; "You Played Your Part In Breaking My Heart" by Little David on Zig-Zag; Sonny Simms's "Tears Falling, Hearts Breaking" on Republic; "There Is No Greater Love" by Bull Moose Jackson on King; and "Night Train" by the Four Blazes on United.

AUG 4   Joe Turner and Guitar Slim take their blues battle on the road with a show in Plaguamine, Louisiana, followed by Biloxi, Mississippi (5th), and Thibodaux (6th), and New Iberia in Louisiana (7th).

AUG 5   Joe Turner moves into the Orchid Room in Kansas City.

AUG 7   The Orioles open at the Farmdell Club in Dayton for four days.

EARLY AUGUST

The Tiny Bradshaw Orchestra starts a two-week gig in Dayton.

Universal Attractions is sending out "The Greatest Show Of '52," which includes **Wini Brown**, the Swallows, H-Bomb Ferguson, LaVern "Little Miss Sharecropper" Baker, and the Todd Rhodes Orchestra for up to seven weeks in the South and East.

Roy Brown and Tab Smith are currently touring the South on separate one-nighter circuits.

AUG 8   James Moody and Sonny Thompson are the featured attractions

Hits for Peppermint Harris came with "Rainin' In My Heart" on Sittin' in With (1950) and "I Got Loaded" on Aladdin (1951). In all, he recorded for six labels in six years (1950-55), the two mentioned above, plus Modern, Money, Cash and "X" (the Victor subsidiary).

Wini Brown and the Boyfriends issued only two records on Mercury in 1952, including her hit version of "Be Anything (But Be Mine)." The Boyfriends had earlier recorded on Jubilee (1951) and Mercury (1952) as The Dreamers.

46

at the Howard Theater in Washington for the week.

Lloyd Glenn opens for three nights at the 5-4 Ballroom in Los Angeles with the Four Flames. They remain at the 5-4 for the next weekend.

AUG 9   Ruth Brown and Amos Milburn perform on the Chesapeake River Saturday night cruise sailing out of Washington.

Wynonie Harris shares the bill with the Five Keys and Annie Laurie at the Royale Theater in Baltimore.

Following a performance at the Steel Beach, in Atlantic City, Charlie Fuqua, guitarist with the Ink Spots, announces that he is leaving the group and will form a "New Ink Spots."

AUG 10   Jimmy Nelson, Peppermint Harris, and **Bumps Blackwell's** Harlem Revue are the featured entertainers at the Elks Ballroom in Los Angeles.

AUG 11   Charles Brown opens for a week at the Farmdell Club in Dayton, Ohio.

Amos Milburn starts a week at Pep's Musical Bar in Philadelphia.

New **releases** for the second week of August include three from the new Chance label: "Fire Dome" by School Boy Porter, "Lonesome Ole Train" by the James Williams Trio, and "Josie Jones" by Johnny Sellers; "(Going Down To) The River" by **Little Caesar** on Recorded In Hollywood; two from Swing Time: "Harlem Blues" by Little Son Willis and "Highway Is My Home" by Lowell Fulson; Little Esther's "Ramblin' Blues" on Federal; "Rockin' Chair On The Moon" by Bill Haley and the Saddlemen on Essex; and "He's My Man" by Marie Adams on Peacock.

AUG 12   The Orioles front the Paul Williams Orchestra for a week at the Apollo Theater in New York City.

Gatemouth Brown plays the Orchid Room in Kansas City following a two-month tour of Alabama, Florida, Georgia, Kentucky, Texas, Mississippi, and Ohio.

Louis Jordan travels to the Beachcomber in Wildwood, New Jersey, for the week. He is joined by singer Dottie Smith.

AUG 14   The Griffin Brothers return to New York following a successful Southern tour.

AUG 15   Billy Ward and his Dominoes headline this week's revue at New York's Apollo Theater.

On the Virginia circuit, the Dreamers and James Moody's combo start with a show in Newport News tonight. Other dates include Portsmouth (16), Norfolk (17), Richmond (18), and Petersburg (19).

MID-AUGUST

Ray Charles, **Laurie Tate**, and the Joe Morris Orchestra complete a successful engagement at the Royal Peacock in Atlanta.

New York City hosts the music trade show, which includes a large

Robert A. "Bumps" Blackwell is better known as the producer of Little Richard's hits on Specialty Records, 1955-57. He also co-wrote several of Little Richard's hits, including "Good Golly Miss Molly" and "Rip It Up."

Harry "Little" Caesar is not the same as Carl "Little Caesar" Burnett, who released "Those Oldies But Goodies" in 1961. Harry Caesar was born in 1928, in Pennsylvania and moved to Los Angeles in 1945. Caesar often played saxophone with Joe Liggins' Honeydrippers when not appearing as a solo artist. He became a Hollywood actor in 1955, appearing in ten movies and over a dozen TV shows.

Laurie Tate had an infectious nasal voice, and sang lead on Joe Morris' top ranked 1950 hit, "Anytime, Anyplace, Anywhere" on Atlantic. Miss Tate left the band to raise a family after their second hit, "Don't Take Your Love From Me." Her place on the "Joe Morris Blues Cavalcade" was taken by Fay Scruggs (Faye Adams).

BULL MOOSE JACKSON

The drummer added by Gibson was New Orleans session man Earl Palmer, famous for his work on the early hits by Fats Domino.

M-G-M Records was formed by its movie-making parent company to release soundtracks and records by actor/singers, but it found widespread acceptance after signing Hank Williams in 1947. M-G-M's r&b lineup was always small, and in the early 1950s consisted almost entirely of Ivory Joe Hunter and the Crickets.

New Orleans-born Roy Brown (September 10, 1925) was the first to record "Good Rockin' Tonight," for Deluxe in 1947. The song was soon covered by Wynonie Harris (1948), and later became Elvis Presley's second release for Sun Records (1954).

turnout from the r&b manufacturers. Among those present are the owners of Imperial, Specialty, Peacock/Duke, Modern/RPM, Atlantic, Aladdin, Savoy, Sittin' In, Derby, United, and States, as well as most of the r&b men from the major labels. Performers include newcomer Johnny Ace, whose first release on Duke will be out in a week.

Roy Brown is on tour in Little Rock, Arkansas.

Bull Moose Jackson is playing the Country Club in New York City for ten days.

Ivory Joe Hunter is off on a one-nighter tour in Florida for most of the month.

Steve Gibson has added a **drummer** to his Red Caps for the first time.

An in-person promotion by Alan "Moondog" Freed, Cleveland deejay, featuring the Clovers and Charles Brown at the Summit Beach Ballroom in Akron, brings in over 3,000 paid attendance, with more than 2,000 turned away at the door.

Earl Bostic is at the Blackhawk Club in San Francisco.

Owners of various rhythm and blues record companies join in a move to leave the American Federation of Musicians and set up their own union.

RCA Victor introduces the Extended Play (EP). Also, **M-G-M Records** brings out its first 12-inch long-play album. Previous M-G-M LP's had been 10-inch issues.

AUG 16   The Orioles and Lynn Hope perform on the Saturday night Chesapeake River cruise leaving from the docks of Washington.
　　　　　Charles Brown plays a tonight in Philadelphia, then he will be off on a string of one-night stands through the Southwest until the 29th.
　　　　　Roy Brown and Roy Milton with the Illinois Jacquet Combo appear at Carr's Beach Club in Annapolis, Maryland.

AUG 17   T-Bone Walker plays a one-nighter at the Elks Ballroom in Los Angeles.
　　　　　The "Greatest Show Of '52" plays a double date in New Orleans with a concert at the Booker T. Washington Auditorium in the afternoon and a dance at the Labor Union Hall in the evening. (See Early August.)

New releases for the third week of August include "Each Time" by Delores Hawkins and the Four Lads on Okeh; "Tell Me So" by John Greer on Victor; "Naggin' Woman Blues" by Poppa Treetop on ART; "Going Away Walkin'" by Harmonica Frank on Chess; "Red Cherries" by Floyd Dixon and "I Don't Know Any Better" by Patty Anne, both on Aladdin; "My Days Are Limited" by Jimmy McCracklin on Peacock; and "Lost My Head" by Dossie Terry on Victor.

AUG 21   The Sunday night dance at Los Angeles' Elks Ballroom features

48

the Johnny Otis Orchestra with vocalists **Mel Walker** and Little Esther.

AUG 22   Dinah Washington, the Dreamers, and the Cootie Williams Orchestra start a week's stay at the Apollo Theater in New York as the first stop on a theater tour.

AUG 23   The Griffin Brothers and the Five Keys are the Saturday night entertainment on the Chesapeake River cruise departing from Washington.

Due to increased demand, Lew Chudd of Imperial Records announces that he has set up distribution for his label in Canada and Europe.

AUG 24   Earl Bostic appears for the evening at the Elks Ballroom in Los Angeles, while across town another sax-man, Joe Houston, is at the 5-4 Club.

New releases for the fourth week of August include Roy Milton's "Night And Day" and "Flying Saucer" by the Solid Senders, both on Specialty; "You Know I Love You" by B. B. King and "Looking For My Baby" by **Bonnie and Ike Turner**, both on RPM; "My Song" by Johnny Moore's Three Blazers and "Monkey Motion" by Houston Boines, both on Modern; "Hey Now" by Ray Charles on Swing Time; "Let's Roll" by J. B. Lenoir on J.O.B.; "Courage To Love" by the "5" Royales on Apollo; "Moonglow" by Earl Bostic on King; "Stop Now, Baby" by Sonny Boy Williamson on Trumpet, and "Tryin'" by Todd Rhodes with LaVern Baker on King.

AUG 29   Charles Brown and the Clovers, just off a string of one-nighters from Ohio through Texas, New Mexico, and Arizona, set off on a West Coast tour with a show in San Diego. Filling the bill is Rosco Gordon.

Florence Williams opens at the Howard Theater in Washington. She recently switched labels from National to Savoy. Along with Miss Williams are the Five Keys, Bull Moose Jackson, and Varetta Dillard.

Billy Ward and his Dominoes appear at the Michigan State Fair.

Billy Eckstine and Buddy Rich's combo headline the revue at the Apollo in New York this week.

AUG 30   **Paul Williams** and Danny Cobb go head-to-head with Ray Charles and Joe Morris in a battle of the bands, while Laurie Tate joins on vocals, as they close out the Saturday night Chesapeake River cruise season in Washington.

AUG 31   In a pre-Labor Day midnight dance in Atlanta's Auditorium, Ruth Brown, Amos Milburn, and Willis Jackson gross $10,000.

Louis Jordan, fronting a full-size orchestra with two female vocalists, plays a double-header in New Orleans at the Booker T. Washington Auditorium (afternoon) and the Coliseum Arena (evening).

Mel Walker's fine baritone was a mainstay on the Johnny Otis blues caravans for several years. Walker was a vocalist on several of Otis's 1950 hits for Savoy: "Mistrustin' Blues," "Deceiving' Blues," "Dreamin' Blues," and "Rockin' Blues."

Yes, Bonnie was Ike Turner's wife. But no, she wasn't to become as famous as Tina Turner. Tina (real name Anna Mae Bullock) wasn't discovered by Ike for several more years.

Paul Williams had the original hit version of "The Hucklebuck" on Savoy in 1949. Roy Milton had a cover version on the blues charts, while "pop" artists issuing the dance song inluded Tommy Dorsey and Frank Sinatra.

Marie Adams was one of the first female vocalists to tour extensively as a major part of the Johnny Otis review. She had but one regional hit, "I'm Gonna Play The Honky Tonks" on Peacock in 1952.

Johnny Ace's version of "My Song" has produced a bumper crop of "cover" versions, including those by Hadda Brooks, Dinah Washington, and **Marie Adams**. This is the first time that an r&b song has been covered by this many versions in many years.

In Philadelphia, Tiny Grimes is at Bill & Lou's club and Bill Doggett opens at Pep's Musical Lounge.

The "Biggest Show Of '52" plays a one-night stand at the Shrine Auditorium in Waterloo, Iowa. (See Early August.)

Al Hibbler is currently performing in St. Louis at the Glass Bar.

Savoy Records announces several new acquisitions to its r&b roster: Hal "Cornbread" Singer who started on Savoy several years previous, Dolly Cooper from Philadelphia, blues singer Carleton Coleman from Tampa, and singer-guitarist Calvin Frazier from Detroit.

THE TOP TEN ROCK 'N ROLL RECORDS FOR AUGUST 1952

1. Lawdy Miss Clawdy - Lloyd Price
2 Have Mercy, Baby - Billy Ward and his Dominoes
3. Ting-A-Ling - The Clovers
4. Mary Jo - The Four Blazes
5. Call Operator 210 - Floyd Dixon
6. My Song - Johnny Ace
7. Goin' Home - Fats Domino
8. My Heart's Desire - Jimmy Lee
9. One Mint Julep - The Clovers
10. Moody Mood For Love - King Pleasure

August 1952
ARTIST OF THE MONTH

LLOYD PRICE
(b. March 9, 1933*)

LLOYD PRICE

In 1952 Lloyd Price was a frantic entertainer. He sang uninhibited rhythm and blues. On stage he preferred to wear orange trousers with green shoes, and he pounded the piano wildly and exhibited a maximum of motion to cover his lack of a distinctive singing voice. No matter, this was the year of change, and if Lloyd Price is remembered for only one record, "Lawdy Miss Clawdy" should be recalled as one of the very first records to reach toward a sound that would soon be tagged "rock 'n roll."

He was born in the New Orleans suburb of Kenner, Louisiana, to a family with ten other brothers and sisters. His earliest musical training was in the local church choir. As a high school freshman he

(*Date of birth also listed as 1932 and 1934.)

took up the trumpet and started a five-piece band to play school dances. While still a teen-ager he signed with WBOK radio in New Orleans to do a fifteen-minute live show for which he wrote original material and advertising jingles. It was one of the jingles that brought Price to the attention of Art Rupe, owner of the West Coast-based Specialty Records, who was in town interviewing musicians in hopes of finding a new performer comparable to Fats Domino. Rupe, in turn, was interviewed by a local disk jockey, which led to a meeting with Price, not yet nineteen at the time. Rupe was impressed enough to schedule an immediate recording date, and the outcome was the million-selling "Lawdy Miss Clawdy."

Lloyd Price's musical influences parallel those of other New Orleans artists of the time including Fats Domino. His choir work led to the inevitable gospel phrasing, while the sounds of the city prompted him to use an undercurrent of boogie and big band. "Lawdy Miss Clawdy" was one of the first of the rhythm and blues recordings to bridge the color line between Black and White listeners. The song has a definite gospel feel in Price's shouting delivery, but the lyrics are absolutely secular. This song was recorded during a session which was so rushed that Price did not have time to fully work out any arrangements with the band. It was the radio jingle that formed the basis for "Lawdy Miss Clawdy," and the song was completed in only three takes. The instrumental backing on the record, which features the piano stylings of Fats Domino and production by Domino's session man Dave Bartholomew, is sparse, especially in light of Price's later big band arrangements. The "B" side, "Mailman Blues," is a fine example of an up-tempo boogie-blues featuring excellent support from Domino's rolling piano.

Price's follow-up singles, "Oooh, Oooh, Oooh," "Restless Heart," and "I Wish Your Picture Was You," were not nearly as successful as "Lawdy Miss Clawdy," but he remained in demand on the club circuit until he was drafted into the Army in early 1954. He was assigned to the Special Services, which allowed him to form a swing band to tour the Far East, including Japan and Korea, providing backing for USO shows starring Debbie Reynolds, Jimmie Durante, and actress Terry Moore.

Unfortunately, upon his return to civilian life in December 1955 he discovered that he no longer had a contract with Specialty Records.

Among those directly influenced by Lloyd Price was Larry Williams, one-time valet to Price whose first release, also on Specialty, was a cover of "Just Because," and who had several raucous rock 'n roll hits for Specialty starting in 1957.

(More about Lloyd Price in future volumes of *The Golden Age of American Rock 'N Roll*.)

JIMMIE McCRACKLIN

Indianapolis-born Bobby Lewis (February 9, 1933) went on to hit Number One on the "pop" charts in 1961 with "Tossin' and Turnin'" for Beltone.

September 1952

SEP 1   Little Esther and Mel Walker with Johnny Otis's Orchestra continue breaking records in Texas, the Deep South, and the eastern states following the conclusion of their West Coast dates.

Lowell Fulson and Joe Turner start a thirteen-day Georgia/Florida tour with a show in Augusta, Georgia.

Philadelphia's Labor Day Dance features Joe Morris's Orchestra and the Orioles.

New releases for the first week of September include "Glasgow Kentucky Blues" by Johnny Wick's Orchestra on United; "Sweet Talking Daddy" by Marie Adams on Peacock; Rosco Gordon's "What You Got On Your Mind?" on RPM; Little Son Willis's "Skin and Bones" on Swing Time; the Marylanders' "Make Me Thrill Again" and the Orioles' "Don't Cry Baby," both on Jubilee; "Mumbles' Blues" by Bobby Lewis on Chess; and "Stop Fooling Around" by Shirley Haven and the Four Jacks on King.

SEP 4   Tiny Bradshaw and Mabel Scott start a Midwest tour that runs through September 19th.

Little Caesar and Little Willie Littlefield play a one-nighter at the Elks Ballroom in Los Angeles.

SEP 5   Jimmy Forrest and Roy Brown share the spotlight in Washington at the Howard Theater for the week.

The Clovers with Rosco Gordon open for three days at Los Angeles' 5-4 Ballroom.

Sarah Vaughan is featured for a week at New York's Apollo Theater.

SEP 6   Thelma Carpenter is in Detroit at the Flame Club.

SEP 7   Jimmy McCracklin and Pee Wee Crayton are at the Elks Ballroom in Los Angeles for the night.

EARLY SEPTEMBER

The Ray-O-Vacs, who formerly recorded for Decca Records, sign a contract with Jubilee Records. Jubilee also has signed Little Sylvia, whose first release will be "I Went To Your Wedding," a song recently recorded by several r&b thrushes, including Damita Jo with Steve Gibson's Red Caps.

SEP 8   Joe Morris and his orchestra begin a week's engagement in Youngstown's Spodoree Club.

New releases for the second week of September include "Oooh, Oooh, Oooh" by Lloyd Price on Specialty; "Flame In My Heart" by the Checkers

Little Sylvia (Vanderpool) would soon achieve fame as the female half of the duo Mickey and Sylvia.

After the Dominoes had such a success with the bass lead on "60 Minute Man," King Records took Charlie White out of the group and formed the Checkers to record "Don't Stop Dan," an answer to the earlier record.

52

on King; "She's My Baby" by Jimmy Huff and "That's All Right" by Little Eddie Kirkland, both on RPM; Piney "Kokomo" Brown's "You Made Me This Way" on Atlas; and "Goodbye Baby" by Little Caesar on Recorded In Hollywood.

SEP 9 Tiny Grimes opens in Philadelphia at the Red Rooster Club.

SEP 12 Buddy Johnson and Erroll Garner share the spotlight for a week at the Howard Theater in Washington.

Ray Charles is booked for two weeks at the Flame Club in Detroit with LaVern Baker, who is just back home from a national tour. She remains at the Flame for the next four weeks.

The Orioles headline the revue featuring **Edna McGriff** and the Paul Williams Orchestra at the Apollo Theater in New York this week.

Lloyd Glenn and the **Four Flames** are at the 5-4 Ballroom in Los Angeles for three days. Also in town, Billy Eckstine starts a West Coast tour with a show at the Shrine Auditorium.

SEP 14 Lowell Fulson stops at the San Jacinto Club in New Orleans for the evening.

SEP 15 Atlanta's Club Poinciana plays host to Larry Darnell for a week.

New releases for the third week of September include Earl Brown's "Dust My Broom" on Swing Time; "Look A There, Look A There" by Tampa Red on Victor; Country Paul's "I'll Never Walk In Your Door" on King; "Bye Bye Baby Blues" by Johnny Giles and the **Jive Five** on Movieland; "Blue Boy" by Chris Powell and his Five Blue Flames on Okeh; Jimmy Scott's "You Never Miss The Water ('Til The Well Runs Dry)" on Coral; "You Belong To Me" by the Buddy Lucas Orchestra on Jubilee; Dinah Washington's "Double Dealing Daddy" on Mercury; and "Boudoir Boogie" by Johnny Sparrow and his Bows and Arrows on Gotham.

MID-SEPTEMBER

Bull Moose Jackson is booked for a week at Cleveland's Ebony Club.

Billy Eckstine is presented with a gold record by the Harlem Record Dealers Association. He is touted as being the "biggest boon to the record business in a decade."

SEP 18 The **Ink Spots** start a Canadian tour with a show in Toronto's Casino Theater.

SEP 19 The Orioles move into Storyville in New Haven, Connecticut. Illinois Jacquet is the week's entertainment at the Fox Theater in Detroit.

The Five Keys grace the stage for the week at New York's Apollo Theater.

Billy Ward is feted at a surprise birthday party in Cincinnati, home of Federal Records. Guests include boxers **Joe Louis** and Ezzard Charles, band leader Lucky Millinder, and Ward's manager

EDNA McGRIFF

The Four Flames (later known as the Hollywood Four Flames) were among the most frequently recorded of all the Los Angeles rhythm and blues groups. Lead vocals on most recordings were handled by Earl Nelson, who had a big dance record under the name Jackie Lee in 1965 with "The Duck" (Mirwood). On Ebb Records, the Hollywood Flames hit in 1957 with "Buzz-Buzz-Buzz."

This Jive Five is apparently not related to the group of the same name that had a 1961 hit with "My True Story" on Beltone.

The Ink Spots began recording in 1935. With the addition of Bill Kenny (tenor) in 1939, the Ink Spots established a style of harmony imitated by rhythm and blues groups ever since.

Joe Louis, "The Brown Bomber," was heavyweight champ from 1937 to 1949 before stepping down. His title was eventually won by Ezzard Charles after a series of elimination bouts. Charles held the championship belt for two years.

Rose Marks, who presents Ward with a Cadillac.

Arthur Prysock headlines a one-nighter tour through the South and East Coast. The tour is billed as the "Number One Blues And Jazz Show," and other performers include Peppermint Harris, Varetta Dillard, Joan Shaw, and Bill "88" Hutchins's Blues Express Orchestra. The tour will run for a month.

Ivory Joe Hunter is the star at the Royal Peacock in Atlanta for four days.

SEP 20 The Dominoes break the one-day record at the Lyric Theater in Louisville, Kentucky. They are just beginning a Midwest tour that is scheduled to run through October 5th.

Professor Longhair starts an extended engagement at the Graystone Club in New Orleans. Across town, Tiny Bradshaw and Mabel Scott play the Palace Theater on a one-night stand.

SEP 21 Lloyd Price plays the Elks Ballroom for one night in Los Angeles.

Tommy Ridgely fronts the **Dave Bartholomew** Combo at the Pelican Club in New Orleans. The duo remains at the Pelican for the next two and a half months. They share the bill with Christine Kittrell the first two weeks.

SEP 22 Floyd Dixon travels to the Orchid Room in Kansas City for the week.

Lynn Hope opens the fall season at the Showboat in Philadelphia for a week's stay.

New releases for the fourth week of September include "My Story" by Chuck Willis and "Rocking On Sunday Night" by the **Treniers**, both on Okeh; Jimmy Lewis's "Dark And Lonely Room" on Victor; "Lonesome Highway" by Percy Mayfield on Specialty; "Flirtin' Blues" by Ray Agee on Modern; and "Everyday I Have The Blues" by Joe Williams on Checker.

SEP 23 Ruth Brown, Willis Jackson, and Joe Turner have a one-nighter in Youngstown, Ohio.

SEP 25 The Ink Spots continue their Canadian tour with a week at the Seville Club in Montreal.

SEP 26 In Philadelphia, the Earle Theater reopens following a summertime renovation with Duke Ellington's 1953 Revue.

The Ravens and Betty Carter split the bill at the Apollo Theater in New York for the week.

The Clovers, Rosco Gordon, and **Charles Brown** play a three-day weekend at the 5-4 Ballroom in Los Angeles. Brown follows this date with a tour of Texas.

Savoy Records sues Mercury Records for $100,000 over the contract of Mel Williams. Savoy claims to have an exclusive contract as of March 23, 1951.

SEP 27 The Griffin Brothers start a four-day stint at the Sportsman's Club in Newport, Kentucky.

SEP 29 Louis Jordan and his Tympany Five embark on a tour of

Aside from discovering Fats Domino, Dave Bartholomew was also instrumental in launching the careers of Lloyd Price, the Spiders, and Shirley and Lee.

The Treniers featured twin brothers Claude and Clifford Trenier, who were accomplished singer/dancer/acrobats. They got their big break with Jimmie Lunceford's Orchestra in the 1940s. In 1951, the twins were joined by two more brothers, Buddy and Milt, for a series of wild jump records on Okeh.

CHARLES BROWN

one-night stands throughout the Southeast.

    Earl Bostic shares the stage with Johnny Ray for the evening at the Municipal Auditorium in New Orleans.

    Illinois Jacquet plays a week-long engagement at the Trocaveria Club in Columbus, Ohio.

New releases for the fifth week of September include Amos Milburn's "Greyhound" and Clayton Love's "Chained To Your Love," both on Aladdin; Smokey Hogg's "Baby, Don't You Tear My Clothes" on Modern; "Love In My Heart" by the Royals on Federal; "Blue Serenade" by Baby Face Turner on Modern; **"Jivin' With Dr. Jive"** by Charles Singleton on Atlas; and two by Hal Singer: "Frog Hop" on Savoy and "Please Dr. Jive" on Coral.

Tommy "Dr. Jive" Smalls was a very popular disk jockey in New York. In the fall of 1955, his "Dr. Jive's Rhythm and Blues Show" at the Apollo Theater rivaled the revues of Alan Freed in popularity.

SEP 30   Billy Ford, Mr. Sad Head, Charles Brown and his orchestra, and Shirley Haven start a one-nighter tour with a show in San Antonio. They will be on the road for a month.

    The Clovers and Rosco Gordon appear at the Club Alabam in Los Angeles for a week.

LATE SEPTEMBER

Atlanta's Royal Peacock Club plays host to Edna McGriff for four days.

Atlantic Records, in a surprise move, is asking deejays to send in suggestions for an as-yet-unnamed five-man vocal group recently signed to the label.

One of the first small independent radio stations in the South or Southwest, KDET in Center, Texas, has started an hour-long r&b show each day called "Melvin's Jive."

THE TOP TEN ROCK 'N ROLL RECORDS FOR SEPTEMBER 1952

1. Lawdy Miss Clawdy - Lloyd Price
2. Ting-A-Ling - The Clovers
3. My Song - Johnny Ace
4. Have Mercy, Baby - Billy Ward and his Dominoes
5. Mary Jo - The Four Blazes
6. I'll Drown In My Tears - Sonny Thompson with Lulu Reed
7. Daddy, Daddy - Ruth Brown
8. You Know I Love You - B. B. King
9. Call Operator 210 - Floyd Dixon
10. Goin' Home - Fats Domino

September 1952
ARTIST OF THE MONTH

THE CLOVERS

THE CLOVERS

Considered one of the first rhythm and blues groups to cross over into rock 'n roll, the Clovers were certainly central in forming both styles of music. Their easily identifiable sound was based on a combination of blues and gospel. With credit to the staff at Atlantic Records, the recordings of the Clovers did not follow the "pop" singing style of the Ink Spots or Mills Brothers, which had been the strongest influence on the group in their beginning. The Clovers also sound distinctly different from the Orioles and the Larks, rhythm and blues music's first role models. Also breaking the earlier mold, the Clovers had their greatest success with up-tempo songs, although several ballads were also hits; and they were not named after a bird, as so many of the early rhythm and blues groups had been.

The Clovers started as a trio of Armstrong High School students in 1946, all of which had grown up in the same neighborhood near 7th and T Streets in Washington, DC. The leader of the group was Harold "Hal" Lucas, who sang baritone. From 1946 through 1949 there were many personnel changes in the group as they performed in several of the area's small nightclubs. In 1950 they were heard by Lou Krefetz, a local music dealer, during an engagement at the Rose Club. He negotiated a contract with Rainbow Records, a small New York label, but only one record was released in 1950. In February 1951 the group signed with Atlantic Records, where they stayed for seven years. Their first Atlantic release, "Don't You Know I Love You So," sold an impressive quarter of a million copies. The follow-up, "Fool, Fool, Fool," did even better with sales reaching half a million, and "One Mint Julep" almost went gold. Of their first nine singles on Atlantic, three topped the rhythm and blues charts, three went as high as number 2, and two stopped at number 3. This is a remarkable accomplishment for any artist.

In 1952 the group consisted of Lucas, John "Buddy" Bailey (first tenor), Matthew McQuater (2nd tenor), Harold Jerome Winley (bass), and Bill Harris (guitar). In September 1952 Bailey was drafted, and he was replaced first by John Phillip and then by Charlie White, who had been an original member of the Dominoes and the Checkers. In 1953 Billy Mitchell, who had been a solo artist with Atlantic, took over lead tenor. When Bailey returned from Korea in May 1954 he alternated with Mitchell and the group expanded to six members, and the personnel remained constant for the next six years.

Their peak year was 1952 with five songs in the national r&b top ten, but the Clovers continued having hits for Atlantic until 1957. Their last hit was "Love Potion #9" for United Artists in 1959. By the early 1960s the group had disbanded with two new groups of Clovers, one led by Bailey and one by Lucas, touring the country. The Lucas congregation continued to perform in clubs into the 1970s.

The sound of the Clovers is heavy on the bottom. Both the vocal group and the instrumental backing employ an accentuated bass line. No distinctive lead tenor carries the group; rather, it is a blending of all the voices over a varied mixture of drums, saxophone, and piano that gives the recordings by the group the feel of warmth even on the up-tempo numbers.

There are few rhythm and blues groups in this period that can claim the immense popularity and longevity of the Clovers. This, by itself, does not begin to do this group justice. While the Dominoes and the Orioles opted for the "better" clubs and hotels, the Clovers stayed within the Black community, becoming "their" vocal group more than any other at this time.

October 1952

OCT 2   The Buddy Johnson Orchestra is currently off on a tour of the West Coast.
         The Louis Jordan tour makes a stop in Atlanta.

OCT 3   The Orioles, following a successful engagement in New Haven, open at the Earle Theater in Philadelphia. Other entertainers on the bill include Bette McLaurin and Erskine Hawkins's Orchestra.
         In New Orleans, Johnny Ace starts the first of two weekend stands at the Dew Drop Inn.
         Steve Gibson and his Red Caps are at Chubby's Bar in Camden, New Jersey.

OCT 4   The **Rock-Ola** Juke Box Corporation introduces its 120-selection 45 rpm "Fireball" model that is destined to revolutionize the industry.
         The Palace Theater in New Orleans presents Billy Ward and his Dominoes for the evening.

OCT 6   Savannah Churchill stars for a week in York, Pennsylvania.
         Johnny Otis, Little Esther, and Mel Walker, currently on tour, stop for the evening at New Orleans' Rosenwald Gym.
         Wynonie Harris opens at Lawson's Palace in Philadelphia for a week. Also in Philadelphia, **WFIL-TV** premiers a television show featuring teen-agers dancing to records. Hosts for "**Bandstand**" are Bob Horn and Lee Stewart.

New releases for the first week of October include three from Atlantic: Ray Charles's first for the label, "Roll With Me Baby," "Hey, Miss Fannie" backed with "I Played The Fool" by the Clovers, and "Three Letters" by Ruth Brown. Other releases include "Blues Is A Woman" by T-Bone Walker on Imperial; "My Nights Are Long And Sleepless" by Willie Mae Thornton on Peacock; the Four Blazes' "Please Send Her Back To Me" on United, and "Rock Me All Night Long" by the **Ravens** on Mercury.

EARLY OCTOBER

The "Biggest Show Of '52" is currently playing dates in Florida. (See Early August.)

Little Walter is appearing in Chicago at the Hollywood Rendezvous Club.

OCT 10   Bull Moose Jackson, the Four Tunes, and Wini Brown open at New York's Apollo Theater for a week's run.
         Ivory Joe Hunter, the Four Blazes, Thelma Carpenter, and Larry Darnell start for a week at the Earle Theater in Philadelphia.
         Roy Brown sets off on a one-nighter tour of the Midwest.

Rock-ola wasn't the first company to virtually abandon 78s in favor of the smaller 45s. Seeburg had issued its "Select-O-Matic" MB-100B in 1950. The other major jukebox company, Wurlitzer, was frantically trying to figure out new ways to squeeze more 78 rpm records into existing boxes.

WFIL-TV's experiment with "Bandstand" went on to become a television institution as the immensely popular "American Bandstand." When the show was broadcast nationally over ABC-TV beginning August 5, 1957, the host of the afternoon dance party was Dick Clark.

"Rock Me All Night Long" would be the last hit record for the Ravens even though the group continued to record some fine sides for Mercury, Jubilee and Argo into 1956, more than eleven years after they started.

OCT 13   Amos Milburn is scheduled for a week's stay at the Trocaveria Club in Columbus, Ohio.

New releases for the second week of October include "I Can't Do No More" by Ray Charles on Sittin' In With; Brownie McGhee's "Key To The Highway" on Jax; Joe Liggins' "Going Back To New Orleans" on Specialty; "Voo Doopee Do" by Piano Red and "My Heart Belongs To You" by Arbee Stidham, both on Victor; "Sittin' And Thinkin'" by Memphis Slim on Peacock; **Mickey Baker**'s "Mambola" on Savoy; and Willie Mae Thornton's second release on Peacock in as many weeks, "Mischievous Boogie."

MID OCTOBER

Okeh Records signs blues singer **Big Maybelle** Smith.

Joe Bihari of RPM Records is off on a talent search of the South with his talent representative, Ike Turner.

Atlantic Records will record Doctor Willie Jones, former lead singer with the Joe Morris Orchestra. Morris's new lead singer will be Lowell Fulson, who has disbanded his own combo.

OCT 16   The Five Keys open for four days at Dayton's Farmdell Club.

OCT 17   Earl Bostic and Roy Milton headline the week at the Howard Theater in Washington.
The Four Blazes and the Freddy Mitchell Combo entertain patrons for a week at the Apollo Theater in New York.

OCT 18   Louis Jordan plays the Sixth Annual CIAA National Classic Dance in Washington, DC.

OCT 19   At the Elks Ballroom in Los Angeles, the night's featured attraction is Buddy Johnson's Orchestra featuring Ella Johnson.
Charles Brown stops for the evening at the Labor Union Hall in New Orleans.

New releases for the third week of October include "Evilest Woman In Town" by Rock Heart Johnson on Victor; "I'm Gone" by **Shirley and Lee** on Aladdin; "Nelson Street Blues" by Willie Love and his Three Aces on Trumpet; "I've Tried" by King Porter on Four Star; "Damp Rag" by Stomp Gordon on Decca; and two by Billy Ward and his Dominoes: "Yours Forever" and "No Room," both on Federal.

OCT 22   The Ravens are booked for the week at New York's Paramount Theater in the show celebrating Duke Ellington's twenty-fifth anniversary in show business.

OCT 23   Dinah Washington plays the Pasadena Civic Auditorium in California.

OCT 24   The Four Tunes open at Uncle Tom's Plantation in Detroit.
At the Howard Theater in Washington, the week's headliners are Ivory Joe Hunter, the **Four Blazes**, and Mabel Scott.

McHouston "Mickey" Baker was born in Louisville, Kentucky, October 15, 1925. A guitarist of great accomplishment and a leading New York session musician, he would achieve fame as the male half of the duo Mickey and Sylvia, who recording "Love Is Strange" in 1956.

Big Maybelle was born in 1926 in Jackson, Tennessee. She first recorded at age eighteen with Christine Chatman's Orchestra.

BIG MAYBELLE

Shirley (Goodman) and (Leonard) Lee were New Orleans youngsters, ages fourteen and fifteen respectively, when they recorded "I'm Gone." They continued to issue songs describing their "pretend" romance for several years, earning the title "Sweethearts Of The Blues."

"Mary Jo" was the only record by the Four Blazes that sold well nationally. It was also their first release for United, where they continued to work, issuing six more singles into 1954.

Pianist/vocalist Floyd Dixon was born February 8, 1929, near Marshall, Texas. His recording career started with Eddie Williams and the Brown Buddies on Supreme Records in 1949. He recorded under his own name for Aladdin, Specialty, Cat, Cash, Ebb and Checker.

Pete "Guitar" Lewis (real first name, Carl) had only two recording sessions for Federal and one for Peacock, all in Los Angeles in 1952, before fading from the scene with a total of five singles to his credit.

Little Willie Littlefield starts three days at the 5-4 Ballroom in Los Angeles.

OCT 25   Charles Brown completes his one-month tour of the Southwest only to start another set of one-nighters through the Deep South on the 27th with Mr. Sad Head and Shirley Haven.

OCT 26   **Floyd Dixon** and Margie Day perform in New Orleans at the San Jacinto Club.

OCT 27   The Orioles return to Philadelphia for an engagement at Pep's Musical Bar.

New releases for the fourth week of October include "You're My Inspiration" by the Five Crowns on Rainbow; "Saturday Evening Blues" by Sammy Cotton on Derby; "Please Be Careful" by Lucky Millinder on King; "Boogie Woogie On St. Louis Blues" by Lloyd Glenn and "Jeronimo" (sic) by Jay McShann on Swing Time; "No Time At All" by Larry Darnell on Okeh, "Scratchin' Boogie" by **Pete Lewis** on Federal; "I'll Always Be A Fool" by the Hollywood Four Flames on Recorded In Hollywood; and "It's So Peaceful" by Smiley Lewis on Imperial.

OCT 28   Lloyd Price plays a one-nighter in Philadelphia at Reynold's Hall and Tropical Garden.

OCT 31   Ruth Brown and Frankie Laine share top billing at the Earle Theater in Philadelphia for a week. Her new contract with Atlantic Records calls for a minimum of $100,000 in record royalties over the next five years.
          Lloyd Price and the Earl Bostic Combo are featured for a week at the Apollo Theater in New York City.
          Buddy Lucas's Orchestra and Edna McGriff start a month-long string of one-nighters with a show in Dayton, Ohio.
          Rose Murphy starts an engagement at Angelo's Club in Omaha, Nebraska.
          Buddy Johnson's Orchestra sets off on a one-nighter tour through the Southwest.

LATE OCTOBER

Amos Milburn follows Charles Brown into Texas for a month of one-night stands.

Bette McLaurin opens at Birdland for two weeks.

BETTE McLAURIN

60

THE TOP ROCK 'N' ROLL RECORDS FOR OCTOBER 1952

1. My Song - Johnny Ace
2. You Know I Love You - B. B. King
3. Juke - Little Walter
4. Daddy, Daddy - Ruth Brown
5. Lawdy, Miss Clawdy - Lloyd Price
6. Five Long Years - Eddie Boyd
7. Ting-A-Ling - The Clovers
8. Mary Jo - The Four Blazes
9. Goodbye Baby - Little Caesar
10. Have Mercy, Baby - Billy Ward and his Dominoes

October 1952
ARTIST OF THE MONTH

JOHNNY ACE
(John Marshall Alexander, Jr., b. June 9, 1929*,
d. December 25, 1954)

JOHNNY ACE

Johnny Ace died too soon. Of that there can be no doubt. His career had skyrocketed to the very pinnacle of success in the short span of two-and-a-half years. And then it ended. Foolishly. Tragically. Of that there can be no doubt.

John Alexander was born in Memphis, where he spent an undistinguished childhood before joining the Navy near the end of World War II. He was stationed in Virginia and returned home to Memphis in 1947. Although he had not been musically motivated up to that time, he started practicing on his mother's new piano and by 1949 was playing well enough to join a fledgling band led by Adolph Duncan. This band, which evolved into the Beale Streeters, at one time or another featured Rosco Gordon, B. B. King, Bobby "Blue" Bland, and Earl Forrest. When B. B. King left his job at WDIA radio in 1952 to pursue a career more oriented to nightclub performing, the rest of the band auditioned to fill King's spot with Alexander eventually taking most of the vocals.

With the success of B. B. King, it was not long before record company talent scouts were combing through Memphis in search of raw talent. Memphis-based Duke Records was acquired in July 1952 by Don Roby, owner of Peacock Records of Houston, Texas, and Roby was in need of recording artists for his new label. After hearing the work of B. B. King and Rosco Gordon who were signed to the West Coast label, RPM, it did not take him long to sign the remainder of the Beale Streeters band to Duke. Within three weeks Johnny Ace (as he was now billed) had written and recorded "My Song," which became the second release for the "new" Duke Records. Before it was officially released Roby and Ace traveled to New York, where Ace appeared at the convention of the National Record Merchandisers Association. This performance led to advance orders for 50,000 copies of the record.

Although he had been a member of one of Memphis' foremost

(*Date of birth also listed as June 29.)

club bands, most of the recordings done by Johnny Ace were backed by the orchestra of Johnny Otis, an accomplished musician and arranger whose credits include many of the finest rhythm and blues hits of the period. "My Song," on the other hand, sounds as though it might have been rushed into production. The feel of the arrangement is relaxed and there is a "home recording" quality to the song.

Ace's career was an immediate success, and he was signed to a series of one-nighters with Willie Mae "Big Mama" Thornton. His earliest appearances were marked by a stiffness in his delivery that was not commensurate with his voice. He frequently sang to the microphone while seated at the piano, virtually ignoring his audience. Nevertheless, over the next two years, every record released by Johnny Ace was a major rhythm and blues hit.

Johnny Ace was more of a Black "pop" balladeer than a rhythm and blues stylist. He possessed a smooth baritone, and he confined his songs mostly to ballads, which appealed a wider audience. It is obvious that he aspired to a career parallel to Nat Cole or Billy Eckstine: acceptance in both the Black and White communities simultaneously. His vocal phrasing directly influenced the later recordings of Sam Cooke, Jesse Blevin, and Eddie Floyd.

And then on Christmas Eve 1954, backstage at the Houston City Auditorium before a performance, Johnny Ace was playing "Russian roulette" with a loaded pistol in an attempt to impress a girl. The gun discharged, and Ace was pronounced dead within hours. His then-current single, "Pledging My Love," became his biggest-selling record, and it went on to become the biggest-selling rhythm and blues record of 1955. As with so many other rock 'n roll artists who would die in their youth, the legend of Johnny Ace increased dramatically after his death.

November 1952

NOV 1   Charles Brown and **Billy Ford** start a mid-Atlantic tour with a show in Fayetteville, North Carolina. Other dates this week include the following cities in Virginia: Danville (2); Newport News (3); Portsmouth (4); Petersburg (5); Virginia Beach (6); and Charleston, South Carolina (7).

In Detroit, Billy Eckstine appears at the Broadway-Capitol Theater for a one-nighter.

NOV 2   Bumps Blackwell plays Los Angeles' 5-4 Ballroom for one night.

New releases for the first week of November include "Rollin' Like A Pebble In The Sand" by Charles Brown and "I Cried For You" by the Five Keys, both on Aladdin; Rosco Gordon's "Dream Baby" and Drifting Sam's "What's The Matter With Me?," both on RPM; "Them There Eyes" by Varetta Dillard and "Sweet Tooth For My Baby" by the Four Buddies, both on Savoy; the Jackson Brothers' "We're Gonna Rock This Joint" on Victor; "Rockin' And Rollin' #2" by **Lil Son Jackson** on Imperial"; and What Can I Say" by the Ray-O-Vacs and "Good" by Edna McGriff and Sonny Til, both on Jubilee.

NOV 6   The Clovers travel to New Orleans for an evening's performance at the Palace Theater.

NOV 7   Lloyd Price headlines the live show at the Howard Theater in Washington.

NOV 9   Buddy Johnson with sister Ella play the Labor Union Hall in New Orleans.

EARLY NOVEMBER

Presently on separate one-nighter tours are the **"new" Ink Spots** and the Five Crowns.

Gatemouth Brown is touring the Southwest with the Al Grey Orchestra.

Johnny Ace is currently at the Orchard Room in Kansas City.

Billy Ward buys up the personal appearance contract between his group the Dominoes and Universal Attractions, which had been booking the unit.

Leo and Eddie Meisner of Aladdin Records start a new label, 7-11 Records. Songwriter Rudolph Toombs, composer of such hits as "One Mint Julep," "5-10-15 Hours," "Greyhound," and "Daddy, Daddy," will head the operation.

Billy Ford, born March 9, 1925, Bloomfield, New Jersey, was a solo artist on United (1953-54) and Josie (1955) before forming the Thunderbirds. One member of the group was Lillie Bryant, with whome he teamed as Billy and Lillie for 1957's "La Dee Dah" on Swan.

Melvin "Lil Son" Jackson was a Texas singer/guitarist, born August 17, 1916, near Tyler. He first recorded for Gold Star in the late 1940s, and Imperial from 1950-53. He died in Dallas in June 1976.

The "new" Ink Spots featured Charlie Fuqua and Deek Watson of the old group. Fuqua was an uncle to Harvey Fuqua of the Moonglows. Watson later composed "(I Love You) For Sentimental Reasons."

63

Lowell Fulson was born in Tulsa in 1921, but he was brought up on the Choctaw Strip on the Oklahoma-Texas border. There he was exposed to a conglomeration of blues, hillbilly, and Mexican music, although he said that he was influenced most by Blind Lemon Jefferson.

JOE MORRIS

Lil Green died of bronchial pneumonia on May 1, 1954, age 40, in her Chicago home.

In 1945, Sid Nathan formed King Records in Cincinnati as a country and western label, and was very successful in this field before moving on to r&b two years later. King Records subsidiaries included Deluxe (r&b), Bethlehem (jazz) and Starday (c&w).

NOV 10   **Lowell Fulson** fronts the Joe Morris Orchestra at the Sportsman's Club in Newport, Kentucky. They are currently on a tour of sixty one-nighters.

New releases for the second week of November include Little Sylvia's "A Million Tears" on Jubilee; "Blues Train" by Browley Guy and the Skyscrapers on States; Country Paul's "Sidewalk Boogie" on King; "Sugaree" by Lazy Boy Slim and "Tortured Love" by H-Bomb Ferguson both on Savoy; Lynn Hope's "Move It" on Aladdin; "Standing Around Crying" by Muddy Waters on Chess; and "Real Rock Drive" by Bill Haley with Haley's Comets on Essex.

NOV 11   The Orioles and Fats Domino share the spotlight for a two-day stand in Pittsburgh.
Billy Ward and his Dominoes backed by the Joe Morris Combo start a three-week tour of the West Coast.

NOV 14   Pee Wee Crayton and Lloyd Glenn are featured in Los Angeles for three days at the 5-4 Ballroom.
The Five Keys headline the "Smart Affairs of '52" revue at the Earle Theater in Philadelphia. During the week they are each presented with gold keys from Aladdin Records in appreciation for their record sales in 1952.
Lloyd Price headlines the show at the Regal Theater in Chicago for the week.

NOV 15   Lowell Fulson and **Joe Morris** are at the Belmont Club in Toledo, Ohio, for four days.
Buddy Lucas and Edna McGriff share the spotlight for the evening at the Palace Theater in New Orleans.
Charles Brown, currently on tour, wires his manager in New York to buy him a $2,500 wardrobe including imported plaid jackets and fifteen pairs of shoes.

MID-NOVEMBER

Savoy Records signs three blues artists, Willie Johnson, Dollie Cooper, and Henry Manse. Other recent record company signings include **Lil Green** with Victor and Memphis Slim, formerly with Mercury and Peacock, with United.

Sonny Thompson and his orchestra are back at the Show Boat in Philadelphia.

King Records' president, **Sydney Nathan**, and his a&r chief, Henry Glover, start a talent-searching trip through the South.

NOV 16   In Los Angeles, T-Bone Walker entertains at the Elks Ballroom's Sunday dance.

NOV 17   Lynn Hope plays the Sportoree Club in Youngstown, Ohio.
Steve Gibson and his Red Caps start a four-week lay-over at Chubby's in North Collingswood, New Jersey.

New releases for the third week of November include Marvin Phillips'

"Old Man's Blues" and the Royal Kings' "Teachin' And Preachin'," both on Specialty; "Where Do I Go From Here" by the Swallows, "Soft" by Tiny Bradshaw, and "Night Curtains" by the Checkers, all on King; "You Belong To Me" by the Orioles on Jubilee; "Last Laugh Blues" by Little Esther and **Little Willie** on Federal; and two on Victor: Little Richard's "Please Have Mercy On Me" and John Greer's "I'm The Fat Man."

NOV 18   Johnny Ace starts an engagement at the Club Alabam in Los Angeles.

NOV 19   Lowell Fulson and Joe Morris's Orchestra play a one-nighter at the Belmont Club in Toledo.

NOV 20   The Lowell Fulson-Joe Morris Blues Cavalcade plays the first of a two-night engagement at the Top Hatter in Dayton.

NOV 21   The Apollo Theater in New York hosts Illinois Jacquet and Bette McLauren for the week.
The Heartbreakers appear at the Howard Theater in Washington for the next week.
Mabel Scott starts a two-week engagement at the Flame Show Bar in Detroit.
Little Caesar opens for three days at the 5-4 Ballroom in Los Angeles.
The Earle Theater in Philadelphia presents Dinah Washington and the Royals this week.
Wini Brown headlines the "Smart Affairs Of '52" revue at Chicago's Regal Theater.

NOV 22   Billy Eckstine holds court at the Shubert Theater in Philadelphia.
Coral Records announces that it is starting a rhythm and blues department to issue songs on its Brunswick label.

NOV 24   The Sportsman's Club in Newport, Kentucky, offers the talents of the Five Keys for a week-long engagement.
Bull Moose Jackson travels to Uncle Tom's Plantation in Detroit for the week.

New releases for the fourth week of November include two seasonal releases on Swing Time: "Lonesome Christmas" by Lowell Fulson and "How I Hate To See Christmas Come Around" by Jimmy Witherspoon; "Whoopin' And Hollerin'" by **Earl Forrest** and the Beale Streeters, "Lovin' Blues" by **Bobby "Blue" Bland**, and "Too Many Women" by **Rosco Gordon**, all on Duke; and "Hey, Little School Girl" by Peppermint Harris and Maxwell Davis on Aladdin.

NOV 27   Amos Milburn hits the road for a six-week tour of California.
The Apollo Theater presents the Johnny Otis Revue featuring Little Esther, Willie Mae Thornton, and Mel Walker for ticket holders this week in New York.
In Philadelphia, the Earle Theater presents its first week-long **amateur show**. Thirty-one contestants compete nightly for up to $60 in prizes and a place on the Christmas Week Lionel

"Little Willie" was born William John Woods in Camden, Arkansas, November 17, 1937. He had just celebrated his fifteenth birthday when this single was released. He had previously recorded for Prize Records with the Paul Williams combo. He went on to become famous as Little Willie John.

Wini Brown took over the spotlight with Lionel Hampton's band after Dinah Washington decided to go solo in 1946.

In Memphis, Earl Forrest, Rosco Gordon, and Bobby Bland had all been members of the Beale Streeters along with B.B. King and Johnny Ace.

Amateur shows were a very important part of the weekly schedule of every inner city theater, nightclub and ballroom. Performers were encouraged to bring along as many of their friends and family as possible, inasmuch as the winner was determined by audience reaction.

Hampton Revue.

NOV 29   Ruth Brown fronts the Willis Jackson Orchestra at the Riviera Club in St. Louis.

NOV 30   The Buddy Lucas-Edna McGriff tour winds up with a show in Minneapolis.
        In New Orleans, the Labor Union Hall hosts a "Battle Of The Blues" between Chuck Willis and Papa Lightfoot.

LATE NOVEMBER

Charles Brown and his orchestra start a two-week engagement at Gleason's in Cleveland.

THE TOP TEN ROCK 'N' ROLL RECORDS FOR NOVEMBER 1952

1. My Song - Johnny Ace
2. You Know I Love You - B. B. King
3. Juke - Little Walter
4. Five Long Years - Eddie Boyd
5. Oooh, Oooh, Oooh - Lloyd Price
6. Goodbye Baby - Little Caesar
7. Lawdy, Miss Clawdy - Lloyd Price
8. Hey, Miss Fannie - The Clovers
9. My Story - Chuck Willis
10. Rock Me All Night Long - The Ravens

November 1952
ARTIST OF THE MONTH

LITTLE WALTER
(Marion Walter Jacobs, b. May 1, 1930; d. February 15, 1968)

LITTLE WALTER

Little Walter was a pioneer in the use of the electronically amplified harmonica in rhythm and blues recordings. His style so widely influenced other bluesmen that it has become an integral part of the mainstream of blues and rock music. The harmonica is well suited for blues music. It is both inexpensive and expressive. The soulful sound of the "mouth organ" has been a part of America's musical heritage since its invention in the late 1700s by none other than Benjamin Franklin. Walter Jacobs certainly was not the first man to play harmonica in a blues band, and he was greatly influenced by Sonny Boy Williamson (Rice Miller). But it is Little Walter who gained attention by playing his "harp" through a microphone, thereby increasing its amplification which allowed the lowly harmonica to be brought into the modern blues band along with other amplified instruments such as the guitar, piano, saxophone, and, of course, the voice.

Walter Jacobs was born in Marksville, near Alexandria, Louisiana, in the Mississippi Delta, and by his teenage years he was considered an expert on the harmonica, a natural instrument, of the region that was used unamplified by many blues musicians. It has been written that Walter only chose to play the harmonica because he could not afford his first choice in musical instruments, a saxophone. As a result he played his harp as lyrically as though it were a sax.

Although only a teen-ager, he left the Delta in the late 1940s, along with many other Blacks, and migrated north to Chicago. In 1947 Walter recorded "I Just Keep Loving Her," which was issued first on Ora-Nelle Records and later reissued on Chance. By 1948 he had joined the Headcutters, who backed Muddy Waters, the foremost "electric" bluesman of the day. Little Walter worked regularly with Waters during this time even though it meant many nights in ghetto clubs with little or no pay. Studio work in 1950 included "Muskadine Blues" for Regal Records. He also recorded several sides with Waters in June 1950 for Chicago's Chess Records, owned by Leonard and Phil Chess. Musicians in Muddy Waters's band were given free rein to improvise, and Little Walter took immediate advantage of this freedom to invent a series of stunning solos that highlight the Muddy Waters records of this period.

Little Walter's biggest big break after joining Muddy Waters's band came with an instrumental, "Juke," which was released under his nickname for Checker Records, a subsidiary of Chess, in May 1952. Originally titled "Your Cat Will Play," the music had a driving rhythm with a boogie beat that caught the record-buying public's ear as soon as it was released. Instrumentals usually have a longer "hit" life than vocal records, and "Juke" was no exception. Little Walter continued to record with Muddy Waters while issuing singles under his own name, and in 1955 he came up with another major hit in "My Babe," which featured Walter's fine vocal as well. In all, Walter recorded more than one hundred songs for Checker Records.

Although Walter's recordings give the impression of spontaneous interplay among the musicians, each tune was meticulously worked out in advance through long hours of rehearsal. Yet, to a man, the musicians who worked with Walter attest to his fairness as well as his talent.

Little Walter has been called "the single most original instrumentalist ever to come out of Chicago." His influence has been felt throughout the past thirty years of rhythm and blues and rock 'n roll music. He has been directly responsible for the styles of Paul Butterfield, Junior Wells, and the rock group Cream. His harmonica styles can be heard in the playing of such diverse artists as John Sebastian (of the Lovin' Spoonful) and James Cotton.

His popularity as a recording artist waned in the late 1950s, although he continued to work for Chess Records up through 1967's "Super Blues" session with his old studio mates Muddy Waters, Bo Diddley, and Otis Spann. By the time of his death in 1968 (he was stabbed, possibly after suffering a cerebral hemorrhage during a beating), he had been largely forgotten except by other musicians, who applauded his triumph with that lowly instrument, the harmonica.

December 1952

DEC 1   Amos Milburn is the star this week at Cleveland's Ebony Club.

The Orioles headline the show at Detroit's Uncle Tom's Plantation.

New releases for the first week of December include two on Savoy: "Oh, Happy Day" by Mickey "Guitar Baker" and "Bad News" by **Brownie McGhee**; Willie Mabon's "I Don't Know" on Chess; "Sad Hour" by Little Walter on Checker; Big Maybelle's "Gabbin' Blues" on Okeh; "Rock, Rock, Rock" by Amos Milburn on M-G-M; "Corn Whiskey" by Jimmy Witherspoon on Federal; "Who Drank The Beer While I Was In The Rear" by Dave Bartholomew and "Early Morning Blues" by Archibald, both on Imperial; and Dave Bartholomew's "High Flying Woman" on King.

DEC 5   The "5" Royales begin six weeks of one-nighters through New Jersey, New York, and Pennsylvania.

Billie Holiday, the Checkers, and Johnny Hodges' band open at the New York Apollo Theater for the week.

Arthur Prysock starts his engagement at Detroit's Flame Show Bar.

Joe Lutcher and Smokey Hogg split the bill for three days at the 5-4 Ballroom in Los Angeles.

DEC 7   Joe Liggins plays one night in Los Angeles at the Elks Ballroom.

Roy Brown pleases the patrons at the San Jacinto Club in New Orleans.

EARLY DECEMBER

A new record company, Southern Records, reports that they have signed the Buccaneers and the Ford Brothers.

TNT Tribble is appearing at the Top Hat in Philadelphia.

Earl Palmer, recently drummer with Steve Gibson and his Red Caps, opens at Spider Kelly's in Philadelphia.

Gatemouth Brown plays a one-night stand in Tulsa sporting his new $1,200 Fender model guitar.

Jimmy McCracklin signs with Peacock Records.

Coral Records announces the signing of the McGuire Sisters.

Brownie McGhee (guitar) performed and recorded with blind Sonny Terry (harmonica), an association which began in 1941 and lasted forty years. McGhee and Terry were later rediscovered in the 1960s by folk music audiences after the popularity of blues declined in the 1950s.

BILLIE HOLIDAY

Earl Palmer's steady drumming was as integral a part of the New Orleans sound as the sax breaks by Lee Allen and Herb Herdesty. He was a regular member of Dave Bartholomew's band and, besides Fats Domino, he backed Little Richard, Larry Williams, Eddie Cochran and Bobby Vee.

New releases for the second week of December include "New Boogie Chillin'" by John Lee Hooker on Modern; "Bambalya" by the Bayou Boys on Checker; B. B. King's "Story From My Heart And Soul" on RPM; Dinah Washington's "Gambler's Blues" on Mercury; Stomp Gordon's "Ooh Yes" on Decca; "You Go To My Head" by Earl Bostic and "Lonesome Train" by **Eddie "Cleanhead" Vinson**, both on King.

DEC 12   The Apollo Theater hosts the Fifteenth Annual *Amsterdam News* Benefit Show. Appearing are Milton Berle, Bill Kenny and his Ink Spots, the Enchanters, Bette McLaurin, and many others.

Ray Charles breaks the house record during his three-day stand at the Pelican Club in New Orleans.

Hadda Brooks and LaVern Baker star for a week at the Flame Show Bar in Detroit.

In Los Angeles, Amos Milburn plays one night at the Oro Ballroom, while Jimmy Forrest and his combo start three days at the 5-4 Ballroom.

Dinah Washington and the Swallows with Cootie Williams's Orchestra open for a week at the Regal Theater in Chicago.

DEC 13   M-G-M Records announces that it will actively push into the rhythm and blues market in January 1953.

Lester Bihari starts Meteor Records in Memphis apart from his brothers who own RPM, Modern, and Flair Records in Los Angeles.

DEC 14   At the Elks Ballroom Sunday night dance in Los Angeles the featured attraction is Roy Milton.

MID-DECEMBER

The Five Keys, Edna McGriff and Buddy Lucas's Orchestra are touring around New England.

Varetta Dillard is appearing in the Philadelphia area on a set of one-nighters.

New releases for the third week of December include the Royals' "Are You Forgetting?" on Federal; a reissue of "Found Me A Sugar Daddy" by the **Nic Nacs** on RPM; Titus Turner's "Christmas Morning" on Okeh; the Diamonds' "A Beggar For Your Kisses" on Atlantic; "Sonny Boy's Christmas Blues" by Sonny Boy Williamson and "Gonna Find My Baby" by Elmore James, both on Trumpet; and Big Boy Crudup's "Lookin' For My Baby" on Victor.

DEC 19   Earl Bostic, currently on a series of one-night stands, plays Wilmington, North Carolina. Other dates this week include New Bern, North Carolina (20); Charleston, South Carolina (21); and Wilson, North Carolina (22).

Ray Charles returns to the Pelican Club in New Orleans for another three-day layover. Across town, his old labelmate Lowell Fulson holds forth at the Dew Drop Inn for the weekend.

DEC 20   Archie Bleyer, musical director for Arthur Godfrey's radio and television shows, starts **Cadence Records** in New York City.

Vocalist/saxophonist Eddie Vinson's career spans nearly fifty years beginning in the 1930s, yet it wasn't until a European tour with Johnny Otis in 1969 that he gained the widespread popularity accorded such blues artists such as Joe Turner, B.B. King, and Bobby "Blue" Bland. Vinson died in Los Angeles on July 2, 1988.

The Nic Nacs were actually the Robins, who were moonlighting for a little extra session money. The song "Found Me A Sugar Daddy" was released three separate times by RPM (No. 313, 316, and 342) twice with different flip-sides.

The top artists on Cadence were the Everly Brothers, who had their first hit with "Bye Bye Love" in 1957. Other performers on the label included the Chordettes, Link Wray, Johnny Tillotsen, and Andy Williams.

69

DEC 21   Jimmy Forrest plays the Sunday night dance at the Elks Ballroom in Los Angeles.

New releases for the fourth week of December include "The Bells" by Billy Ward and his Dominoes on Federal; "Still In Love" by Joe Turner on Atlantic; "Believe Me Baby" by Roy Milton and "Dream Girl" by **Jesse and Marvin**, both on Specialty; Smokey Hogg's "Do It No More" on Federal; and Johnny Otis's "Wedding Boogie" on Savoy.

DEC 24   The Five Keys front the Charlie Barnett Orchestra at the Arcadia Club in Providence, Rhode Island.
          In New Orleans, the Dew Drop Inn offers the talents of Al Hibbler for Christmas week.
          Earl Bostic plays a Christmas Eve show in Orlando. Other dates on the Florida leg of his tour include Miami (25), Sanford (26), Key West (27), Lake City (29), Florenceville (30), and St. Petersburg for New Year's Eve.
          The Paramount Theater in New York presents Sarah Vaughan, the Four Tunes, and Illinois Jacquet for the next two weeks.

DEC 25   Lloyd Price plays a Christmas dance at the Coliseum in Baltimore.
          Christmas finds Billy Ward and his Dominoes in Los Angeles at the Elks Ballroom.
          In Louisiana, Jimmy McCracklin plays the high school auditorium in Shrewsbury on his one-nighter tour. In New Orleans, Al Hibbler takes time off from his Dew Drop Inn stand to guest star at the early show at the Labor Union Hall.

DEC 26   In Baltimore, the Royal Theater offers holiday entertainment with the Ink Spots and the **James Moody** Combo.
          Lionel Hampton is booked into the Earle Theater in Philadelphia this week.
          Joe Morris's Blues Cavalcade is booked for the week at Uncle Tom's Plantation in Detroit.
          The Regal Theater in Chicago presents Dinah Washington, the Swallows and the Cootie Williams band for the week.
          The Stanley Theater in Pittsburgh hosts the Billy Eckstine show for a week.
          In Washington, the Checkers headline the "Larry Steele Revue" at the Howard Theater this week.

DEC 28   Louis Jordan is on tour in Texas. Tonight finds him in Ft. Worth. He plays Dallas on the 29th, and on New Year's Eve he opens for two weeks at the Golden Hotel in Reno.
          In New Orleans, **Gatemouth Brown** performs for dancers at the Labor Union Hall.

DEC 29   Fats Domino plays one night in Detroit at the Graystone Garden Ballroom.

New releases for the fifth week of December include "Salty Tears" by Chuck Willis on Okeh, "Baby Don't Do It" by the "5" Royales on Apollo, and Ray Charles's "Walkin' And Talkin' To Myself" on Rockin'.

DEC 31   Charles Brown finishes his lengthy Florida tour. Next week, he's off on a month-long series of one-nighters on the West Coast.

In Los Angeles, Percy Mayfield and the Four Blazes close out the year with a show at Armory Hall, while Amos Milburn starts three days at the 5-4 Ballroom.

LATE DECEMBER

The Orioles, Edna McGriff, and the Buddy Lucas Orchestra are playing one-night stands around New York and New Jersey over the holidays.

Ivory Joe Hunter returns to Pep's Musical Bar in Philadelphia.

THE TOP TEN ROCK 'N' ROLL RECORDS FOR DECEMBER 1952

1. Five Long Years - Eddie Boyd
2. Juke - Little Walter
3. My Story - Chuck Willis
4. You Know I Love You - B. B. King
5. I Don't Know - Willie Mabon
6. My Song - Johnny Ace
7. Hey, Miss Fannie - The Clovers
8. I Played The Fool - The Clovers
9. Oooh, Oooh, Oooh - Lloyd Price
10. Port Of Rico - Illinois Jacquet

December 1952
ARTIST OF THE MONTH

EDDIE BOYD
(Edward Riley Boyd, b. November 25, 1914)

EDDIE BOYD

Eddie Boyd once rivaled his first cousin, Muddy Waters, as Chicago's most popular blues artist. In the early- to mid-1950s Boyd was the leader of one of the finest combos in the area. By the end of his career he had retired to Europe, where he is still considered a legend.

Boyd was another product of the Mississippi Delta. Born in Stovall, near Clarksdale, Mississippi, his earliest influence was his father, a part-time entertainer. Eddie tried playing the guitar and the trumpet with little success. He even attempted the kazoo. Finally he settled on the piano, playing with a style influenced by Roosevelt Sykes and Leroy Carr. After a possible run-in with the law, Eddie left home at fourteen to move to Arkansas. In the early 1930s he was already working juke joints in the area bounded by Mississippi, Arkansas, Missouri, and Tennessee. In 1936 he married and moved his permanent residence to Memphis. Here he formed a two-man band, and eventually found work in the many clubs that lined Beale Street. He worked twelve-hour days for a dollar a day, playing the clubs seven days a week. In 1937 Boyd formed the Dixie Rhythm Boys and continued to work the Memphis bars for four more years.

In 1941, along with many other southern Blacks, Boyd moved his family to Chicago in search of higher wages. He found work in a defense plant and, more importantly, caught up with Memphis Slim, one of the legendary blues pianists and Eddie's half-brother. Shortly thereafter, Boyd was playing with Memphis Slim, Johnny Shines, Big Bill Broonzy, and John Lee "Sunny Boy" Williamson at the Triangle Inn in Chicago. In 1945 he first recorded on Williamson's "Elevator Woman" for Victor's Bluebird label, which became a major r&b hit at the time. Boyd's first record under his own name came in 1947 with "I Had To Let Her Go" on the Flyright label. Also in 1947, he had a session with Chess Records that produced a minor hit in "Rosa Lee Swing" backed with "Blue Monday Blues." In 1947-48 he recorded with J. T. Brown's Boogie Band on Victor. His own recordings for Aristocrat (a Chess subsidary) and Victor remained unissued at this time. In 1950 he recorded three songs for Regal Records.

It was during this time that his personal life fell apart. He was divorced, then re-married. He was working for eighty cents an hour in a steel mill, and his music seemed to be taking him nowhere. Boyd saved what money he could to hire musicians for his recording of "Five Long Years," which was released on J.O.B. Records in 1952. The record was not immediately successful, but it did bring him to the attention of Chess Records once again. He re-recorded "Five Long Years," and it was an instant hit. Follow-up releases, "24 Hours" and "Third Degree," while not quite as successful as "Five Long Years," sold well enough to make the national r&b charts.

Boyd's popularity within the blues community was now firmly established. Although he did not have another national hit after "Third Degree," he continued to record and, more importantly, he continued to tour, and it was the continuous one-night stands that brought in money on which to live. It was in 1957 during just such a long tour that he was injured in an automobile accident outside of Waukegan, Illinois, which left him in a cast for ninety-five days. Still he came back, touring as frequently as ever. In 1965 he was part of the historic American Folk Blues Festival tour of Europe with Willie Mae Thornton and Buddy Guy that led to a recording session with English blues artist John Mayall in 1967.

Boyd continued to tour Europe through the 1970s, and he finally settled in Paris. He worked almost exclusively in European theaters and clubs thereafter. Today, he is virtually forgotten in America, but among blues buffs in Europe, he is best remembered as a solid piano player and fine writer of r&b songs.

Shake Rattle & Roll

THE GOLDEN AGE
OF
AMERICAN ROCK 'N ROLL

1953

1953
A Look Ahead

"WE GONNA RUB A LITTLE BOOGIE"
Champion Jack Dupree

The new year will bring a revolution in the musical tastes of many Americans. The traditional ratio of Black to White record buyers is changing. Previously, a "hit" in the rhythm and blues field meant sales of a quarter of a million records. This year it will not be at all unusual for top-selling r&b disks to go gold. Rhythm and blues can no longer be considered just a stepchild of the "pop" record business.

Independent record companies still have the strongest hold on the r&b market, but labels affiliated with major record companies are making some inroads. Columbia's Okeh, with Chuck Willis and Big Maybelle, and Mercury, with Dinah Washington and Buddy Johnson's orchestra featuring Ella Johnson, are the two major labels with consistent best sellers. RCA Victor can boast Piano Red, John Greer, Steve Gibson and his Red Caps, and the Four Tunes, all of whom will make their presence known during the coming year. Decca, Capitol, and M-G-M still trail far behind, even with the talents of Savannah Churchill (Decca) and the Crickets (M-G-M). On the other hand, new independent labels are popping up with increasing regularity. Baton, Bruce, Central, Crown, Herald, Jay-Dee, Rama, Red Robin, Sun, and Vee-Jay will all begin releasing records during 1953.

An offshoot of the surge in the number of independent record companies is the growing importance of the independent record distributor. Small labels normally have no means for getting their records to distant markets without this loose chain of distributors. The distributor also plays the role of promoter for the independent label, since it is definitely to the distributors' advantage to have a hit record to market.

As in the previous year, the dominant form of rhythm and blues music continues to be by the newer male vocalists. Lloyd Price, Fats Domino, Chuck Willis, Johnny Ace, B. B. King, and Little Junior Parker control the charts. On the tour circuit veterans Johnny Otis, Amos Milburn, Roy Milton, Louis Jordan, Floyd Dixon, and Percy Mayfield continue to draw the crowds.

Female vocalists, led by the veterans Dinah Washington and Ruth Brown, are heard more frequently in 1953 than previously. The biggest-selling record of the year will be Willie Mae "Big Mama" Thornton's

"Hound Dog." Other women making a name for themselves include Faye Adams, Linda Hayes, and Varetta Dillard.

The vocal group sound also is showing renewed popularity. The big news here is the formation of the Drifters by Clyde McPhatter, ex-member of Billy Ward and his Dominoes. Other groups with hit records this year include the Spiders, the Royals, the Flamingos, the Flairs, and the Dominoes. Only the Orioles are holdovers from previous years, attesting to the shift in the rhythm and blues group sound away from that pioneered by the Mills Brothers and the Ink Spots in the 1940s and the Orioles and the Ravens in the early 1950s.

The major rhythm and blues trend in 1953 is the "answer" record. It all starts innocently enough with Linda Hayes's "Yes, I Know," a cute reply to Willie Mabon's hit "I Don't Know." Before long there is "I Don't Know, Yes I Know" (Johnny Moore's Three Blazers) and the race is on. "Hound Dog" brings "Bear Cat" by Rufus Thomas, Jr., which is followed "Mr. Hound Dog Is In Town" by Roy Brown. But the record that garners the most answers is Ruth Brown's "Mama (He Treats Your Daughter Mean)". The answers to the record literally flood the market, and include "Papa (I Don't Treat That Little Girl Mean)" by Scatman Crothers, "Papa (She Treats Your Son So Mean)" by Benny Brown, and "Mama, Your Daughter Told A Lie On Me" by the Five Keys.

Overall, rhythm and blues records in 1953 will continue to account for only a five percent portion of the total gross record sales in the country. But that will soon change.

NATIONAL NEWS

In October, Senator McCarthy begins to investigate the Army concerning alleged subversive operations. The mambo dance craze filters across the land, making Arthur Murray a national hero. In June, Ethyl Merman and Mary Martin highlight the "Ford Anniversary Show" on television, which is aired simultaneously on NBC and CBS, proving that even TV can offer quality entertainment . . . "Hamlet" on TV is seen by more people than in all of its revivals over the past 350 years. In March, Dr. Jonas Salk, Professor of Research Bacteriology at the University of Pittsburgh, announces that the first tests of a polio vaccine are successful. Billy Martin's ninth-inning home run in the seventh game of the World Series makes the Yankees the champs for the fifth time in a row. Academy Award winners are "From Here To Eternity," William Holden, and Audrey Hepburn. Emmys go to the "U.S. Steel Hour," "I Love Lucy," and "Omnibus." Ben Hogan is named Athlete of the Year. The best-selling work of fiction is "The Robe" by Lloyd C. Douglas (188,000 copies), while the Revised Standard Version of the Bible continues to be the top nonfiction book, selling 1.1 million copies. The fad of the year is started by Roger Price, who first presents his amusing "Droodles" on Garry Moore's TV show.

January 1953

JAN 1   Savannah Churchill appears at the Offbeat Club in Omaha.

In Detroit, King Pleasure starts one week at the Flame with club regular LaVern Baker. Across town, Joe Morris and Laurie Tate are at Uncle Tom's Cabin through the 4th.

Willie Mabon and Big Maybelle front the Gene Ammons Combo for a week at the Earle Theater in Philadelphia. Mabon's current hit, "I Don't Know," has recently been covered by Buddy Morrow (pop) and Ernie Ford (c&w).

JAN 2   **Sarah Vaughan** and the Four Tunes headline the revue at New York's Paramount Theater for the week.

Little Richard makes his first New Orleans stop with a two-week appearance at the Dew Drop Inn. He is in the middle of a record-breaking coast-to-coast tour with his combo, the Famous Six.

JAN 5   Joe Morris is at the Sportoree Club in Youngstown, Ohio.

Chuck Willis entertains in Detroit at Uncle Tom's Cabin for three days.

New releases for the first week of January include "Block Buster" by Boots Brown and his Blockbusters on Victor; "I Believe" by Elmore James on Meteor; **Little Willie Littlefield**'s "K. C. Loving" on Federal; The Treniers' "Poon-Tang" on Okeh; "Mistreater" by the Bill Doggett Orchestra on King; and "Old Fashioned Blues" by the Blues Chasers and "Cold Mama" by Gabriel Brown, both on M-G-M.

JAN 7   The Royals are hit with a $10,000 lawsuit while on tour in Columbus, Georgia, which alleges that advertisements for the group show pictures of the "5" Royales. The Royals are permanently enjoined against "impersonating" the "5" Royales.

JAN 8   Earl Bostic plays a benefit at Douglas High School in Thomasville, Georgia, to help raise funds to build an annex for Archibald Memorial Hospital, which admits only Black patients.

In Philadelphia, **Big Maybelle** moves across town from the Earle Theater to play Emerson's Cafe for the evening.

EARLY JANUARY

Charles Brown is currently on the West Coast for a series of one-night stands. It is rumored that he will disband his trio at the end of the month and start over with a full orchestra.

Aladdin Records announces that they will reactivate the firm's other r&b label, Score Records.

Sarah Vaughan's vocal style was strongly influenced by the phrasing of Billy Eckstine. Combining this with the "scat" style she had picked up during her days singing bebop, she put together a solid string of Columbia recordings during the early 1950s, including "These Things I Offer You" in 1951.

Little Willie Littlefield's original version of "K.C. Loving" (written by Jerry Leiber and Mike Stoller) was re-recorded in 1959 by Wilbert Harrison and became a gigantic hit on Fury as "Kansas City."

Big Maybelle Smith's first solo recordings were made for King Records in 1946, and her first hit came in 1953 with "Gabbin' Blues" on the Okeh label.

M-G-M Records is actively acquiring new r&b talent. Signed recently are Boots Green, Teddy Williams, the **Crickets**, Al King, Paula Watson, and Beula Bryant.

JAN 9   Bill Kenney and his Ink Spots open in Brooklyn at the Country Club.
The "new" Ink Spots backed by Johnny Otis's Orchestra open at the Earle Theater in Philadelphia.
LaVern Baker is held over at the Flame Club in Detroit.
Willie Mabon starts a week's engagement at Emerson's in Philadelphia.

JAN 11   Dinah Washington is the guest performer for the Sunday night dance at the Elks Ballroom in Los Angeles.

New releases for the second week of January include Wynonie Harris's "Bad News Baby" and Lucky Millinder's "Old Spice," both on King; Johnny Otis's "The Love Bug Boogie" and **Jay McShann**'s "Reach," both on Mercury; and "Just Crazy" by Big Jay McNeeley on Federal.

JAN 15   Fats Domino and the Clovers embark on a two-week tour of the Virginia area with a show in Roanoke.

MID-JANUARY

New York has a new night spot featuring r&b and jazz talent, the Bandbox, located next door to Birdland on the former site of the Iceland Restaurant.

The **Delta Rhythm Boys** are currently on a successful tour of Canada and the Midwest.

JAN 16   The "5" Royales, Willie Mabon, and Gene Ammons start a one-week engagement at New York's Apollo Theater.
The Griffin Brothers begin a southern tour in Miami. They will then work their way back up the East Coast.
LaVern Baker entertains at the Booker T. Washington Restaurant in Washington for two weeks.
Rose Murphy plays a ten-day engagement in Rochester at Williams' Club.
Louis Jordan's Combo is on hand for three days at Billy Berg's 5-4 club in Los Angeles.
The Five Keys open for a week at the Royal Theater in Baltimore. After this engagement, they are off on a tour of the Southeast.
The "new" Ink Spots and the Johnny Otis Orchestra open for the week at Washington's Howard Theater.
Big Maybelle shares the bill at Detroit's Flame Club with Varetta Dillard.

JAN 17   "Hi Yo Silver," the original "B" side of the Trenier's "Poon-Tang" has been withdrawn due to copyright infringement claimed by the interests of the masked man. The new "B" side will be "Moon Dog."

JAN 18   **Shirley and Lee** and the Four Blazes play the Elks Ballroom in Los Angeles.

JAN 19   Ivory Joe Hunter starts at the Warren Grill in Worchester, Massachusetts.
Earl Bostic opens at Pep's Musical Bar in Philadelphia.

SHIRLEY AND LEE

New releases for the third week of January include "Ain't It A Shame?" by Lloyd Price, "The River's Invitation" by Percy Mayfield, and "Freight Train Blues" by Joe Liggins, all on Specialty; "Cross My Heart" by Johnny Ace on Duke; "Keep It A Secret" by the Five Crowns on Rainbow; and "Teardrops On My Pillow" by the Orioles on Jubilee.

JAN 23   Following their successful week at the Apollo in New York, the "5" Royales are off on an extended tour of the South. Following the "5" Royales into the Apollo are Ruth Brown and Tiny Bradshaw's Combo.
Louis Jordan is back at the 5-4 Club in Hollywood for the next three days.
Lionel Hampton graces the stage at the Howard Theater in Washington for the week.
The Earle Theater in Philadelphia offers patrons the talents of the "new" Ink Spots and Johnny Otis's orchestra.

JAN 26   **Bull Moose Jackson** starts a week at the Showboat in Philadelphia.
Big Maybelle begins a two-month-long tour with a week at the Top Hat in Dayton, Ohio. She will play club dates in Columbus and Youngstown before taking her show to Baltimore on February 20th.
In Detroit, Uncle Tom's Cabin hosts Lynn Hope for an extended stay.

Benjamin Clarence "Bull Moose" Jackson was the most successful of the original rhythm and blues artists on King Records. Beginning in 1945, he stayed with the label for over ten years, and his booming voice hit with "I Love You, Yes I Do," as well as the splendidly wicked "I Want A Bowlegged Woman" and "Big Ten Inch Record."

New releases for the fourth week of January include Amos Milburn's "Let Me Go Home Whiskey" on King; "Train, Train, Train" by Danny Overbea on Checker; "Nobody Loves Me" by Fats Domino on Imperial; "Yes I Know" by Linda Hayes on Recorded In Hollywood; "Slow Your Speed" by Jimmy Witherspoon and Smokey Hogg's "River Hip Mama," both on Modern; "Mama (He Treats Your Daughter Mean)" by Ruth Brown and "Jumpin' In The Morning" by Ray Charles, both on Atlantic; Rosco Gordon's "Just In From Texas" on RPM; Little Son Willis's "Operator Blues" on Swing Time; "Another Fool In Town" by Lightnin' Hopkins on RPM; and "That's What Makes My Baby Fat" by the Joe Morris Blues Cavalcade featuring **Fay Scruggs** on Atlantic.

When Joe Morris left Atlantic, later in 1953, Fay Scruggs would move with him to Herald Records. After she changed her name to Faye Adams, they would have a major 1953 hit with "Shake A Hand."

JAN 30   Willie Mabon, Illinois Jacquet, and Bette McLaurin share the bill at the Regal Theater in Chicago for this week. Jacquet's recording of "Port Of Rico" has gone over the 100,000 mark in sales.

JAN 31   Ivory Joe Hunter starts a one-nighter tour through Texas that will run until March 1st.

Modern Records was the foundation for one of Los Angeles' most successful rhythm and blues record companies. Started by the Bihari brothers in 1945, in only a few years the company was busy launching new labels such as RPM, Flair, and Crown.

The Bihari brothers, Les and Saul, have moved the headquarters of **Modern and RPM Records** into new offices in Beverly Hills.

Amos Milburn, scheduled to open a tour of the East with a show in Philadelphia, has been extended on his current tour of the West Coast for the next three months.

Currently on the one-nighter circuits are Gatemouth Brown and Al Grey in the Southwest, B. B. King (who recently signed a new three-year contract with RPM Records) in the South and Texas with the Bill Harvey Orchestra, Jesse Belvin from Arizona through Texas, and Marie Adams joining Arthur Prysock in the Midwest.

THE TOP TEN ROCK 'N' ROLL RECORDS FOR JANUARY 1953

1. I Don't Know - Willie Mabon
2. I'm Gone - Shirley and Lee
3. Sad Hours - Little Walter
4. I Played The Fool - The Clovers
5. Soft - Tiny Bradshaw
6. The Bells - Billy Ward and his Dominoes
7. Baby Don't Do It - The "5" Royales
8. My Story - Chuck Willis
9. Five Long Years - Eddie Boyd
10. Juke - Little Walter

January 1953
ARTIST OF THE MONTH

WILLIE MABON
(b. October 24, 1925; d. April 19, 1985)

WILLIE MABON

Willie Mabon had a smile that could send even the strongest female heart into palpitations. In every colloquial sense of the word, he was "smooth." To his credit, and possibly to his eternal damnation, he popularized the rhythm and blues style that is most evident in the song "Riot In Cell Block #9," a hit for the Robins in 1955. He built a career on the format of that opening riff.

Although Willie Mabon was born into a Memphis family where music was a major part of their everyday life, he was little influenced by the indigenous musical makeup of the city. Rather, he only agreed to participate in the boy's choir at his church at his mother's insistence. As a teen-ager Willie participated as a member of the family's gospel quartet. He did take up the harmonica and became quite proficient by his teen years. By his own admission he was never allowed to go near Beale Street, but rather, for musical diversion the family listened to the local country and western radio broadcasts.

In 1942, following the death of his mother, Willie's father moved the family to Chicago in search of employment. Willie took day-jobs as a baker, mechanic, plumber, and newsboy while studying jazz piano whenever possible, all the while attending DuSable High School. In 1944 he joined the Marines, but by 1946 he was back in Chicago playing at the Tuxedo Lounge while working days in a steel mill. Chicago was a hotbed of blues activity at the time, sporting the names of Big Maceo Merriweather, Sunnyland Slim, Memphis Slim, Big Bill Broonzy, and Muddy Waters. Mabon followed their lead into the recording studio, and in 1949 "Bogey Man" was released on the Apollo label under the pseudonym "Big Willie." In 1950 he formed the Blues Rockers, also known as Earl and his Blues Rockers for guitarist Earl Draines, and recorded six sides for Aristocrat Records and one release for Chess, "Little Boy, Little Boy." Not much happened with the records except that Mabon was able to obtain steady local club work.

In 1952 he returned to the studio and recorded "I Don't Know," a novelty blues number learned from Cripple Clarence Lofton, for Parrot Records. The master was picked up by Chess and subsequently became one of 1953's biggest hits. Although the song had been around since the 1930s under the title of "Strut That Thing," it was Mabon's urbane sense of comedic timing that made the song so popular. In addition, Mabon also wrote and recorded "Seventh Son," a 1960s hit for Mose Allison and Johnny Rivers, and "Poison Ivy," identified with Buddy Guy.

After nine singles with Chess, Mabon moved on to Federal in 1957 for one session, and then to Mad Records in 1960 and Formal/USA in 1962. By 1966, convinced that he had been cheated of most of the royalties due him, he retired from the music business to start a nightclub that subsequently failed. This forced him to take a job as a truck driver. A short return to recording in 1969 on the Blues on Blue label also proved unsuccessful.

Willie Mabon's early Memphis country and western influences, coupled with his Chicago jazz piano training and the influence of the local Chicago blues scene, resulted in a mixture of musical styles that was more of a West Coast sound than that usually identified with either Chicago or Memphis. Mabon was a sensitive artist who wrote witty lyrics in a jump blues style that, among other things, prompted 1953's "answer" song craze by influencing other artists to pen a reply to his recording of "I Don't Know."

But it was his insistence on staying with the musical format popularized in "I Don't Know" that certainly doomed any long-term popularity. It is easy to understand why an artist sticks with the same style; after all, this is the style that brought him the audience in the first place. But to stick rigidly to such a limiting sound can only bring a reduction in his audience in the long term. So it was with Willie Mabon.

Willie Mabon continued to perform on the blues festival circuit until his death in 1985 in Paris, Texas, following a long illness.

February 1953

LYNN HOPE

Bobby Marchan was one of the most outrageous acts in rhythm and blues. He was raised in Youngstown, Ohio, where he entered show business as a female impersonator. Seeking wider acceptance, he moved to New Orleans with his "Powder Box Review" of six drag queens about 1952.

The Emitt Slay Trio was composed of Slay (guitar and vocals), Bob White (organ and vocals) and Lawrence Jackson (drums). They had only two Savoy sessions which produced just three singles.

FEB 1   The Fats Domino/Clovers tour ends its Virginia circuit with a show in Virginia Beach.
Louis Jordan takes the "Biggest Show Of 1953" to the West Coast through January 10th.

New releases for the first week of February include "Getting Ready For My Daddy" by Varetta Dillard on Savoy; "Blues For Anna Bacoa" by **Lynn Hope** on Aladdin; Roy Brown's "Hurry Baby" on King; Winie Brown's "Can't Stand No More" on Mercury; and "Fine Brown Frame" by the Buccaneers on Southern.

FEB 6   The Earle Theater in Philadelphia plays host to the Clovers for a week.
Bill Kenney and his Ink Spots start a week's club date at the Stanley Theater in Pittsburgh. Sharing the headline is Ella Fitzgerald.
The Howard Theater in Washington presents the Orioles, Ruth Brown, and the Paul Williams' Orchestra for the week.
In New York, the Apollo Theater offers the talents of Billy Ward and his Dominoes and Arnett Cobb's Orchestra for the week.
At the Graystone Club in New Orleans, **Bobby Marchan**, "the Bronze Balladeer," performs as the supporting act for Wiggles, "the Acrobatic Dancer." Also in town, Joe Turner is at the Dew Drop Inn for the next two weekends.

FEB 7   Willie Mabon starts a week at the Riviera Club in St. Louis with Bette McLaurin.

EARLY FEBRUARY

United Records signs Billy Ford, the Dozier Boys, and Debbie Andrews. Ford was most recently with RCA Victor.

The Bihari brothers, owners of RPM and Modern Records, have started a new label, Music Masters, which will specialize in extended-play releases with four songs instead of the usual two per record.

The **Emitt Slay Trio** is currently at the Plantation Room in Detroit. The group is a recent acquisition of Savoy Records, which released their first record this week.

FEB 9   Varetta Dillard spends the week at the Cavakas Club in Washington.

New releases for the second week of February include John Greer's "You Played On My Piano" and Tampa Red's "Too Late Too Long," both on Victor; "My Kind Of Woman" by the Emitt Slay Trio on Savoy;

"Til I Waltz Again With You" by the Five Bills on Brunswick; The Ravens' "Don't Mention My Name," Elmore Nixon's "Playboy Blues" and Memphis Slim's "Drivin' Me Mad, all on Mercury; "Come Go My Bail Louise" by the Five Keys on Aladdin; "Hollerin' And Screamin'" by **Little Esther** on Federal; and the Orioles' "I Miss You So" on Jubilee.

FEB 11   Little Walter and Eddie Boyd wrap up their tour of Texas. They are scheduled for two weeks of one-night stands through the South and then two weeks in Chicago.

FEB 12   Buddy Johnson, sister Ella, and his orchestra entertain at New York's Savoy Ballroom.

FEB 13   The Ink Spots, featuring Bill Kenney, are at the Town Casino in Cleveland.
          The Clovers are the headliners for a week at the Howard Theater in Washington. Also on the bill are Red Saunders and Big Jay McNeeley.
          Billy Ward and his Dominoes with Eddie "Cleanhead" Vinson open at the Earle Theater in Philadelphia for the week.
          Charles Brown is the featured attraction at the 5-4 Ballroom in Los Angeles this weekend.
          The Apollo Theater offers patrons the talents of the Orioles with Betty Carter and the Paul Williams Orchestra for the week's entertainment in New York.

FEB 14   Marie Adams, Arthur Prysock, and Edgar Blanchard's Orchestra start a string of play dates.
          In New Orleans, Lloyd Price is featured at the Palace Theater before embarking on a tour of the Northeast. Across town, Guitar Slim returns to the Club Desire for two days.
          Billy Eckstine performs at the Sands Hotel in Las Vegas for two weeks.

FEB 15   Brothers **Joe and Jimmy Liggins** perform for the Sunday night dance at the Elks Ballroom in Los Angeles.

MID-FEBRUARY

Bill Doggett is playing Pep's Musical Bar in Philadelphia.

New releases for the third week of February include "Crawlin'" by the Clovers on Atlantic; Big Boy Crudup's "Keep On Drinkin'" on Victor; "Nine Below Zero" by Sonny Boy Williamson on Trumpet; "Broken Hearted Traveler" by Floyd Dixon with Johnny Moore's Three Blazers and "Pachuko Hop" by Ike Carpenter, both on Aladdin; and a cover of both Willie Mabon's hit and Linda Hayes' answer: **Annisteen Allen's** "Yes I Know" on King.

FEB 19   Bull Moose Jackson and his orchestra open at the Savoy Ballroom in New York.

FEB 20   Big Maybelle is the headliner at the Royal Theater in Baltimore.
          Mabel Scott starts a week in Philadelphia at the Earle Theater.

"Little Esther" Phillips was born in Galveston on December 23, 1935. She was discovered by Johnny Otis. A performer who mimicked in the style of Dinah Washington, she occupied the spot of lead female vocalist on his caravan tours until 1954.

Charles Brown, still going strong in the 1980s, sang in a quietly smooth blues vein. His own greatest influence can be heard in the earliest sides by Ray Charles.

Both Joe and Jimmy Liggins recorded for Specialty. Jimmy signed in 1947, and Joe moved over to the label from Exclusive in 1950. Joe had an immediate best seller in "Pink Champagne" from his very first Specialty session.

Annisteen Allen's professional career began in 1949 as the featured vocalist with Lucky Millinder's Orchestra.

Also on the bill are comedian George Kirby and the Tiny Bradshaw Combo.

Roy Milton opens for the weekend at the 5-4 Ballroom in Los Angeles.

Billy Ward and his Dominoes, boxer-turned-singer Sugar Ray Robinson, and Louis Armstrong star in the "Blue Ribbon of Stage Shows" at the Detroit Fox Theater for the week.

Earl Bostic and Lloyd Price start a week's engagement at the Regal Theater in Chicago.

FEB 21   RCA Victor Records announces the signing of one of the premier acts in the rhythm and blues field, the **Robins**. Also signed are Boots Brown and Milt Trenier of the Treniers vocal group.

FEB 22   Linda Hayes and Amos Milburn share the bill at Los Angeles' Elks Ballroom for the evening.

New releases for the fourth week of February include "You're Mine" by the Crickets on M-G-M; "Misery In My Heart" by Ray Charles on Swing Time; "Have You Heard" by Sonny Til and "Why, Oh Why" by Edna McGriff with the Buddy Lucas Orchestra, both on Jubilee; Titus Turner's "My Plea" on Okeh; Smokey Hogg's "Your Little Wagon" on Federal; and "Lost Child" by the Todd Rhodes Orchestra with **LaVern Baker** on King.

FEB 26   Savannah Churchill is at the Club Alabam in Los Angeles for two weeks.

FEB 27   Ruth Brown, Billy Eckstine, and Count Basie, billed as the "Biggest Show Of '53," start a long tour in Greensboro, North Carolina. The package will be on the road for six weeks.

In Los Angeles, Charles Brown plays a weekend date at the 5-4 Ballroom.

Billy Ward and his Dominoes headline the bill at the Howard Theater in Washington. Sharing the spotlight are Eddie "Cleanhead" Vinson and Bette McLaurin.

The week's entertainment at New York's Apollo Theater is headlined by Wynonie Harris. Also on the bill are Larry Darnell and the Red Saunders Orchestra.

FEB 28   Sarah Vaughan is at the Au Drap Dior Club in Paris for two weeks as she begins her European tour.

LATE FEBRUARY

Chance Records announces that they have signed the **Flamingos** and several other rhythm and blues hopefuls.

"If It's So Baby" by the Robins (originally spelled Robbins) was a 1950 hit on Savoy before the group joined bandleader Johnny Otis for a series of top-ranked blues records issued by Peacock Records later that same year.

"Lost Child" is the last of the four singles that LaVern Baker recorded with the Todd Rhodes band for King before she went on to Atlantic and stardom with such hits as "Tweedle Dee" (1955), "Jim Dandy" (1956), and "I Cried A Tear" (1958).

THE FLAMINGOS

The Flamingos were formed in 1952 in Chicago. Original members included brothers Zeke and Jake Casey, Solly McElroy, Johnny Carter and Paul Wilson. Carter later became a member of the Dells.

1. Baby Don't Do It - The "5" Royales
2. I Don't Know - Willie Mabon
3. Cross My Heart - Johnny Ace
4. Yes I Know - Linda Hayes
5. Soft - Tiny Bradshaw
6. Mama (He Treats Your Daughter Mean) - Ruth Brown
7. Dream Girl - Jesse and Marvin
8. I'm Gone - Shirley and Lee
9. The Bells - The Dominoes
10. Ain't It A Shame? - Lloyd Price

February 1953
ARTIST OF THE MONTH

THE "5" ROYALES

THE "5" ROYALES

The "5" Royales stayed with their gospel roots more than almost any other rhythm and blues vocal group. But, throughout a twenty-year career, it was the influence of the courts, not the pulpit, that continued to plague the group.

The "5" Royales began as the Royal Suns in 1942, a locally popular gospel quintet based in Winston-Salem, North Carolina. The original members of the Royal Suns included brothers Lowman, Curtis, and Clarence Pauling, along with William Samuels and Otto Jefferies. In 1943 Jimmy Moore replaced Clarence Pauling just as the quintet was gaining a regional reputation in the Carolinas. By 1950 Obediah Carter and Johnny Tanner had replaced William Samuels and Curtis Pauling. This is the makeup of the group that decided, in April 1952, to send a demonstration tape to New York City's Apollo Records, which had a fine reputation for its gospel records. Apollo was interested in the group, but not for gospel recordings. The company was searching for a vocal group that could compete with the Dominoes, the Orioles, and the Cardinals. At first the group was reluctant to change from their gospel heritage because of fear of a severe backlash when the religious community learned that they were recording secular material. It was decided that a new name was in order, hence the "5" Royales.

Their first sessions for Apollo in 1952 produced two singles: "Too Much Of A Little Bit" and "Courage To Love." The next year brought forth their biggest hits as "Baby Don't Do It" and "Help Me Somebody" both topped the national rhythm and blues record sales charts. Following the group's initial success, Otto Jefferies decided to stop touring and concentrate on being the manager of the "5" Royales. His place was taken by Eugene Tanner, although Jefferies continued to record with the group.

From 1952 thru 1954, the "5" Royales were involved in several legal conflicts with another rhythm and blues group, the Royals, who recorded for King/Federal Records. First it was contended that the Royals were making appearances billing themselves as the "5" Royales then, as the popularity of the Royals started to gain momentum, it was the "5" Royales who were on the defensive. To make matters more confusing, the "5" Royales were at this time negotiating to switch labels to King Records. Everything was smoothed over by mid-1954 when the Royals changed their names to the Midnighters, but in August problems between the "5" Royales and Apollo Records still had not been cleared, and Lowman Pauling was in court suing Apollo for back royalties.

The group that recorded for King consisted of Lowman Pauling (bass), Johnny and Eugene Tanner (alternate lead tenors), and Jimmy Moore, Obediah Carter, and Otto Jefferies (harmony). Add to this mixture the stinging guitar licks added by Pauling in a call-and-response fashion that mimicked the gospel style, and the "5" Royales were a natural combination, sure to please.

The years of work on the gospel circuit had been a fine training ground for the "5" Royales. Johnny Tanner's strong lead vocals expressed an overpowering conviction, and the singles by the "5" Royales retain the feel of revival night in a small Black church in the Deep South. In fact, following their initial switch from gospel to secular music, the "5" Royales did issue several singles on Apollo's gospel series, including the popular "Bedside Of A Neighbor" and "Journey's End." It was on King that the group finally found its widest audience, with "Think" in 1957 and "Dedicated To The One I Love." The latter was written by Lowman Pauling, who wrote most of the material for the group, and it is the same song that became an even bigger hit, first for the Shirelles and then for the Mamas and the Papas.

In 1960 the "5" Royales found themselves in another lawsuit, this time over a disagreement with fellow King Records artist James Brown concerning the song "Think." A lawsuit forced the group to leave King, and for a time they recorded for Home Of The Blues in Memphis, which leased the masters to Vee-Jay and ABC Records. By 1964, when the group finally disbanded, they had recorded over one hundred songs.

More than most other rhythm and blues vocal groups of this period, the sound of the "5" Royales never completely divested itself of its gospel background. This in turn opened the door for other Black artists to sing the lyrics of rhythm and blues with the open feeling of gospel, a crossover of styles that was to have monumental impact on such artists as Clyde McPhatter of the Drifters, Hank Ballard of the Royals/Midnighters, and the aforementioned James Brown.

March 1953

MAR 2   Ruth Brown and Billy Eckstine play Charleston, South Carolina. As they continue to tour during the week, they will be in Kinston, North Carolina (3), Roanoke, Virginia (4), Charlotte, North Carolina (5), Norfolk, Virginia (6), Charleston, West Virginia (7), and Nashville (8).

New releases for the first week of March include an answer to both Willie Mabon's "I Don't Know" and Linda Hayes's "Yes I Know" with "I Don't Know, Yes I Know" by Johnny Moore's Three Blazers on Rhythm & Blues Records. Miss Hayes's latest is "Atomic Baby" on Recorded In Hollywood. Other releases for the week include B. B. King's "Woke Up This Morning" on RPM; "You Can't Bring Me Down" by Oscar McLollie on Class; the Five Budds' "I Was Such A Fool" on Rama; **Jimmy Witherspoon**'s "Jay's Blues" on Federal; "Do Right Blues" by Little Caesar on Recorded In Hollywood; Earl Bostic's "Steamwhistle Jump" on King; and two on Swing Time: "It Moves Me" by Lloyd Glenn and "Let Me Ride" by Lowell Fulson.

MAR 4   Big Jay McNeeley and **Erroll Garner** are featured at Birdland in New York for the month.

MAR 5   Savannah Churchill opens at the Club Alabam in Los Angeles.

MAR 6   Bette McLaurin is scheduled for a week's engagement at the Royal Theater in Baltimore.
          In New Orleans, Smiley Lewis shares the stage with Dave Bartholomew's band for the first of two weekend stands at the Pelican Club.
          Johnny Otis and his orchestra headline for the weekend at the 5-4 Club in Los Angeles.
          Lloyd Price plays Reynolds Hall in Philadelphia on his one-nighter tour.
          Big Maybelle is booked into New York's Apollo Theater for the week.

MAR 7   Wynonie Harris, Larry Darnell, Varetta Dillard, and Frank Humphries's Orchestra embark on a series of one-nighters that will continue until April 15th.

EARLY MARCH

Johnny Ace and Willie Mae Thornton are currently on tour as part of a Peacock/Duke Records package.

MAR 8   **T-Bone Walker** and Pee Wee Crayton entertain at the Elks Ballroom in Los Angeles.

Witherspoon's interpretation of such classic blues numbers as "How Long Blues," coupled with his 1949 number one version of "Ain't Nobody's Business" on Supreme, ensured his lasting presence on the blues scene.

ERROLL GARNER

T-Bone Walker was born in Lindin, Texas, in 1909 or 1910. He first recorded in 1929 and is said to have started playing an electric guitar by 1935. In the 1950s he headed one of the most respected rhythm and blues dance bands in the country.

MAR 9   The Ruth Brown/Billy Eckstine tour continues with a performance in Atlanta this evening. Other shows this week include Greensville, South Carolina (10), Jacksonville, Florida (11), New Orleans (13), and Memphis (14). The show in Atlanta is so successful that over 2,000 are turned away at the door.

New releases for the second week of March include "So Long" by Lloyd Price and "Don't You Remember, Baby?" by Roy Milton, both on Specialty; "Hound Dog" by Willie Mae Thornton on Peacock; "24 Hours" by Eddie Boyd on Chess; "My Best Friend" by Carl Green on Meteor; and "Someday, Someway" by the Flamingos on Chance.

MAR 13   The Clovers with Choker Campbell's Orchestra are off on a tour of the Midwest. This will be followed by a southern tour, then dates in Texas and California.
   Linda Hayes joins the Swallows on stage at the Apollo Theater this week in New York. On opening night she is robbed of $5,000 in jewels and musical arrangements from her dressing room. Later that night, thieves break into her car.
   Floyd Dixon and Margie Day appear at the Northwest Casino in Washington, D.C., for two days. Also in Washington, Big Maybelle appears as part of the "Broadway Revels" revue at the Howard Theater this week.
   Johnny Otis returns to Los Angeles' 5-4 Club for the weekend.
   The Palace Theater in New Orleans presents Johnny Ace and Willie Mae Thornton for four performances today.

MAR 15   Earl Bostic plays for the Sunday night dance at the Elks Ballroom in Los Angeles.

MID-MARCH

At Detroit's Fox Theater, Billy Ward and his Dominoes' rendition of "The Bells," featuring Clyde McPhatter, steals the show from such seasoned performers as Louis Armstrong and **Sugar Ray Robinson**, and leads to a TV appearance on Ed Sullivan's show.

Marie Adams and Arthur Prysock are booked through the South. She will soon join the Johnny Otis Orchestra for more touring.

Little Richard, the Tempo Toppers, and the Duce of Rhythm have signed with the Peacock Records.

The six largest record companies (Capitol, Columbia, Decca, Mercury, M-G-M, and RCA Victor) report that their combined output of pop singles has decreased thirty-seven percent over a year ago, while the number of rhythm and blues singles has increased by fifteen percent.

MAR 16   The Ruth Brown/Billy Eckstine tour picks up in Houston for the evening. The one-nighters continue in Texas with shows in Galveston (18), Beaumont (20), and Austin (21) during the week.
   The Orioles start a three-week tour through the Northeast and the South.

New releases for the third week of March include "My Hat's On The

Linda Hayes was an Elizabeth, New Jersey, teen-ager whose only hit record was "Yes, I Know." But, on the basis of that record, she decided to leave her hometown and move to the West Coast, bringing along her brother, Tony, who would soon be joining a new group, the Platters, as Tony Williams.

Sugar Ray Robinson was boxing's welterweight champion from 1946 to 1950. He held the belt as a middleweight twice in 1951 before abandoning his title. After a less than spectacular attempt at a singing and acting career, he returned to the ring and was middleweight champion again, off and on, 1955 to 1959.

Side Of My Head" by the Four Blazes and "Mrs. Jones' Daughter" by Jimmy Forrest, both on United; Shirley and Lee's "Shirley, Come Back To Me" and Papa Lightfoot's "P. L. Blues," both on Aladdin; Piano Red's "I'm Gonna Tell Everybody" and **Otis Blackwell**'s "Number 000," both on Victor; the Royals' "I Feel So Blue" on Federal; and the Jets' "Volcano" on 7-11 Records.

MAR 20   Eddie Boyd and Little Walter open for four nights at Atlanta's Royal Peacock Club.

Fats Domino concludes his swing through Texas.

Buddy Johnson brings his orchestra and sister Ella to the Apollo Theater in New York for the week.

Charles Brown is the weekend's entertainment at Los Angeles' 5-4 Club.

Mabel Scott plays the first of two weekend stands at the Pelican Club in New Orleans.

MAR 21   The Orioles' one-nighter at the Audubon Ballroom in New York is so successful that they gross $1,000 above their guaranteed percentage.

Floyd Dixon and Margie Day headline the Carolina Ball at the Huntspoint Palace in New York.

MAR 23   Ruth Brown and Billy Eckstine wrap up their tour of the Southwest this week, with a performance tonight in Dallas. Other dates this week are San Antonio (24), Ft. Worth (25), Amarillo (26), Oklahoma City (27), Tulsa (28), Kansas City (29), and Wichita, Kansas (30).

Amos Milburn opens at Pep's Musical Bar in Philadelphia following a successful eleven-state tour of the West Coast, Midwest, and Eastern Seaboard.

New releases for the fourth week of March include three "answer" songs: "Bear Cat" by Rufus Thomas, Jr. on Sun; "Papa (She Treats Your Son So Mean)" by Benny Brown on Gotham; and "Daughter (That's Your Red Wagon)" by Sax Kari with Gloria Irving on States. Other releases include "One Room Country Shack" by Mercy Dee on Specialty, and "I Wanna Know" by the **Du Droppers** on Victor.

MAR 26   Charles Brown entertains at the El Sombrero Club in Los Angeles.

In Philadelphia, the Earle Theater closes its doors. Eventually it will be torn down.

MAR 27   Dinah Washington fronts the Joe Morris Orchestra for the weekend at the 5-4 Club in Los Angeles.

MAR 28   **Wynonie Harris**, Larry Darnell, and Varetta Dillard stop in New Orleans for a show at the Palace Theater while on tour in the South.

MAR 29   Roy Milton is the houseguest for the Sunday night dance at the Elks Ballroom in Los Angeles.

MAR 30   Charles Brown is off on a tour of the Southwest starting in Lubbock, Texas. The tour is completely booked through the

Otis Blackwell is best known as the composer of some of the greatest hits in rock 'n roll music, including "Great Balls Of Fire," "All Shook Up," "Don't Be Cruel," "Fever," "Handy Man" and "Return To Sender."

THE DU DROPPERS

The Du Droppers' first single release was "Can't Do Sixty No More" on Red Robin, a belated 1952 answer to the Dominoes' big hit the previous year.

Omaha-born Wynonie Harris joined King Records in 1947. He had moderate hits in the late 1940s with his own versions of "Good Rockin' Tonight" and "Drinking Wine Spo-Dee-O-Dee."

closing date in Tulsa, Oklahoma on April 25th.

New releases for the fifth week of March include the Swallows' "Laugh (Though You Want To Cry)" and **Roy Brown**'s "Grandpa Stole My Baby," both on King; "Big Mamou" by Smiley Lewis on Imperial; "Saturday Night" by Timmie Rogers on Capitol; "One More Drink" by Lazy Slim Jim on Savoy; and "Seems Like A Million Years" by Willie Nix and "She May Be Yours" by Joe Hill Louis, both on Sun.

LATE MARCH

Specialty Records buys out Champion Records of Jackson, Mississippi. Specialty sets up a Jackson office with **John Vincent**, previous owner of Champion, as the district manager.

The Marylanders are booked into the Royal Theater in Baltimore for the week.

After several years without a hit, Roy Brown's career received an enormous boost in 1957 with his Imperial release, "Let The Four Winds Blow."

Johnny Vincent started the successful independent company Ace Records in Jackson in 1955. Big hits on Ace came after a few years, with the singles by Huey Smith and the Clowns and Jimmy Clanton.

THE TOP TEN ROCK 'N' ROLL RECORDS FOR MARCH 1953

1. Mama (He Treats Your Daughter Mean) - Ruth Brown
2. Baby Don't Do It - The "5" Royales
3. Let Me Go Home Whiskey - Amos Milburn
4. I Don't Know - Willie Mabon
5. Soft - Tiny Bradshaw
6. Cross My Heart - Johnny Ace
7. Yes I Know - Linda Hayes
8. Crawlin' - The Clovers
9. Dream Girl - Jesse and Marvin
10. Woke Up This Morning - B. B. King

March 1953
ARTIST OF THE MONTH

AMOS MILBURN
(b. April 1, 1926; d. January 3, 1980*)

AMOS MILBURN

Amos Milburn played driving boogie. Although he was a founding father, along with Fats Domino, of the piano-playing rhythm artist, he was unable to make the transition when the music became rock 'n roll.

Born into a large family in Houston, Milburn quit school in the seventh grade. His taste for music had been whetted on a family piano, and his early influences were the pioneers of the boogie woogie style including Pete Johnson, who backed the legendary Big Joe Turner. His earliest musical idol was Louis Jordan, who was a master of the jump style popular during the early 1940s.

Underage, in 1942 he joined the Navy as a cook and subsequently saw action in the Pacific theater. Following the war he returned to Houston, where he formed a band to play local clubs. His first major

---

(*Date of birth also given as 1927.)

engagement was in San Antonio's Keyhole Club. It was here that he crossed paths with many of the important Black artists of the late 1940s, including Duke Ellington, Lionel Hampton, Slam Stewart, and Louis Jordan. Milburn was prompted by the wife of a Houston doctor to make several demonstration disks of his songs. She subsequently became his manager and financed a trip to Los Angeles, where they hoped to secure a recording contract. Their first meeting was with the Bihari brothers of Modern/RPM Records, but the two parties were unable to come to terms. Another meeting, with the Menser family, owners of Aladdin Records, proved more fruitful, and Milburn was signed on the spot.

Milburn's first session in September 1946 resulted in three immediate releases including "After Midnight," which went on to sell 50,000 copies, a certain hit in the "race" music field. In 1947 Milburn recorded the song that would become his signature tune, "Chicken Shack Boogie." Its success was immediate and overwhelming. He had five charted singles in 1949, leading to his being voted the Top R&B Artist for both 1949 and 1950 by *Billboard* magazine. He was on tour constantly. In 1950 his number one hit of "Bad, Bad Whiskey" led to a succession of drinking songs that culminated with "Let Me Go Whiskey" and "One Scotch, One Bourbon, One Beer" in 1953, his last year with major hit records. By 1954 he had disbanded his seven-piece group, the "Aladdin Chickenshackers," and he signed on as a solo artist with many of the fledgling rock 'n roll packaged tours. In 1959 he recorded a duet album with Charles Brown, and he was on the Motown label in 1963 as that company was just beginning to taste success. But success was over for Amos Milburn. In the 1960s he retired to his home town of Houston, although he continued to perform at blues festivals and to record occasionally for a succession of small labels until a stroke in 1970, brought on in part by years of heavy drinking, took away the use of his left hand. Milburn died in 1980.

Amos Milburn's records are universally recognized as one of the strongest bonds between the 1940s jump style epitomized by Louis Jordan and the pounding boogie beat that would become a cornerstone of rock 'n roll. The name most frequently associated with Amos Milburn is an artist who idolized him, Fats Domino. Milburn's sound was synonymous with the driving middle-beat jump music of New Orleans, even though Amos Milburn was Texas-born and bred and Los Angeles nurtured and fed.

April 1953

APR 3   Eddie Boyd starts his first bookings in the Northeast with a show in Boston. He is co-starring with Linda Hayes on a tour that will continue through April 26th.

Ruth Brown plays the Northwest Casino in Washington, D.C., for the weekend.

Erroll Garner and Big Maybelle headline the Regal Theater revue in Chicago.

New York's Apollo Theater presents the Ravens for patrons this week.

The Robins are the featured performers at the 5-4 Ballroom in Los Angeles for the weekend.

Buddy and Ella Johnson with the Du Droppers open for a week at Washington's Howard Theater.

APR 4   Louis Jordan joins the "Biggest Show Of '53" at Los Angeles' Olympia Arena to kickoff a tour that will be on the road through mid-May.

APR 5   Ruth Brown plays a one-night stand in Newark, New Jersey.

Eddie Boyd and Linda Hayes with the Lynn Hope Orchestra start three nights of play dates in the Washington-Baltimore area.

In Los Angeles, a day-long Easter Sunday show in South Park features Little Caesar, the Robins, **Bumps Blackwell** and others. Also, in Los Angeles that evening, T-Bone Walker and Lowell Fulson perform at the Elks Ballroom.

Billy Wright and Gatemouth Brown play for Sunday dancers at the Labor Union Hall in New Orleans.

APR 6   Following her show in Paterson, New Jersey, Ruth Brown takes a well-deserved three-week vacation.

LaVern Baker opens at the Palace Theater in Harrisburg, Pennsylvania.

Bette McLaurin is at Powelton's Club in Philadelphia.

The **new releases** for the first week of April include more "answer" songs: Scatman Crothers's "Papa (I Don't Treat That Little Girl Mean)" on Recorded In Hollywood; "Mama, Your Daughter Plays It Cool" by Little Mr. Blues on Rainbow; and "I Wanna Know" by Dolly Cooper with Hal Singer's Orchestra on Savoy. Other releases include Little Esther's "Street Lights" on Federal; "No One To Love Me" by the Sha-Weez on Aladdin; "Easy" by Jimmy and Walter on Sun; the Five Crown's "Alone Again" on Rainbow; the Marylanders' "Good Old 99" on Jubilee; **Ivory Joe Hunter**'s "If You See My Baby" on M-G-M; and Sonny Thompson's "Insulated Sugar" featuring Rufus Thomas, Jr. on King.

APR 8   Billy Eckstine starts a two-week layover at the Bandbox in New York with the Count Basie Band.

Bumps Blackwell produced Sam Cooke's first non-gospel records for Specialty. Art Rupe, company founder, wasn't interested in Cooke as a "pop" star, so Cooke and Blackwell went to Keen Records and immediate national success.

Ivory Joe Hunter was born in Kirbyville, Texas, in 1911. His first recordings were made in 1933 for the Library of Congress by Alan Lomax, the musical researcher who also first recorded Muddy Waters.

APR 10   Savannah Churchill starts a two-week engagement at the Flame Show Bar in Detroit.

Boxing champ Joe Louis, the Five Keys, and the Hal Singer Combo entertain ticket holders at the Apollo Theater in New York for the week.

In New Orleans, Annie Laurie opens with **Professor Longhair** for two weekends at the Pelican Club.

APR 11   Amos Milburn, Linda Hayes, and the Orioles bring in $2,500 for one show in Newark, New Jersey.

APR 12   The "Big Show Of '53" featuring Louis Jordan plays a one-nighter in Minneapolis, followed the next night by a show in South Bend, Indiana.

Floyd Dixon and Margie Day stop for a show in New Orleans at the San Jacinto Club.

Steve Gibson and his Redcaps with singer Damita Jo play a date at the Social Club in Erie, Pennsylvania. The next night they open at the Rendezvous in Philadelphia.

Pianist/vocalist Henry Roeland "Roy" Byrd, better known as Professor Longhair, was born December 18, 1918, in Bogalusa, Louisiana. His influence among New Orleans' musicians was overwhelming. He passed away on January 30, 1980, only a few days before the annual Mardi Gras celebration in which he always played a large part.

New releases for the second week of April include two of "Going To The River," by Fats Domino on Imperial and by Chuck Willis on Columbia. Also new this week are "Help Me Somebody" by the "5" Royales on Apollo; "You Let My Love Grow Cold" by Dinah Washington and "Come A Little Bit Closer" by the Ravens, both on Mercury; "I Love To Ride" by Paula Watson and "I Got A Letter" by Lem Johnson, both on M-G-M; "Devil's Daughter" by Stomp Gordon on Decca; "Crazy She Calls Me" by Larry Darnell on Okeh; and two more answers/covers: to Ruth Brown's hit, Wynonie Harris's "Mama, You Daughter's Done Lied To Me" on King; and to Willie Mae Thornton's smash - Little Esther's "Hound Dog."

MID-APRIL

As the current glut of "answer" songs continues unabated, the copyright holders of the original songs are starting to question the practice on legal grounds. Record companies, in a rush to jump on this latest fad, have been neglecting to obtain a license from many of the original publishers that would allow them to release all of the parodies.

Recent record company signings include the Blenders with M-G-M, southern blues singer James Allen with Brunswick, the Cincinnatians with Coral, and Jubilee Records' signing of twelve-year-old blues singer Andrew Wideman, who was discovered on NBC-TV's "Star Time" show.

Philadelphia's popular rhythm and blues disk jockey Douglas "Jocko" Henderson of WHAT radio is guesting on WLIP in New York every Saturday.

The Buccaneers' recording of "Fine Brown Frame" on Southern Records has been purchased by Rainbow Records.

APR 16   Amos Milburn, Linda Hayes, and the Orioles are on stage at the Laurel Gardens in Newark, New Jersey.

APR 17   Fats Domino holds forth at the 5-4 Ballroom in Los Angeles for the weekend before leaving the West Coast to tour Louisiana, Georgia, and Florida.

There is a "Battle Of The Blues" show featuring Wynonie Harris, Larry Darnell, and Varetta Dillard this week at the Howard Theater in Washington.

New York's Apollo Theater offers King Pleasure and Betty Carter fronting the Count Basie orchestra.

APR 19   Percy Mayfield and **Mercy Dee** perform for the Sunday crowd at the Elks Ballroom in Los Angeles.

Charles Brown brings his tour to New Orleans' Labor Union Hall.

Joe Houston opens at the Rainbow Club in Denver.

APR 20   Bette McLaurin travels to Lawson's Place in Harrisburg, Pennsylvania.

New releases for the third week of April include "I'm Mad" by Willie Mabon on Chess; "Off The Wall" by Little Walter on Checker; the Orioles' "Dem Days" on Jubilee; Stick McGhee's "Meet You In The Morning" and "Big Leg Mama" by Van Walls and the Rockets, both on Atlantic; "Hittin' On Me" by Buddy and Ella Johnson on Mercury; Ike Carpenter's "Crazy Crazy" on Decca; "Till Dawn And Tomorrow" by the Five Bills on Brunswick; "She Felt Good To Me" by Jimmy McCracklin on Peacock; and two answer records: first, to Ruth Brown's hit - the Five Keys' "Mama, Your Daughter Told A Lie On Me" on Aladdin; and to Willie Mae Thornton's record - "Mr. Hound Dog's In Town" by Roy Brown on King.

APR 23   Louis Jordan and the "Big Show Of '53" are in Buffalo for the evening, followed by a performance on the 25th in Rochester.

APR 24   Earl Bostic starts a weekend stint at the 5-4 Club in Los Angeles.

Little Esther and the "5" Royales perform with **Arnett Cobb's** orchestra for a week at the Regal Theater in Chicago.

At New York's Apollo Theater, the entertainment for this week includes Sarah Vaughan and the Erskine Hawkins Orchestra.

Charlie Fuqua and the "new" Ink Spots perform at the Mocombe Club in Hollywood.

Smiley Lewis and Dave Bartholomew's combo, both just returned to New Orleans from a tour of Texas, Mississippi, and Louisiana, open for the weekend at the Pelican Club. They are held over for the next weekend.

APR 25   Charles Brown, Amos Milburn, Chuck Willis, Guitar Slim, Margie Day, and the Paul Williams Combo bring in $5,700 for a single performance in Kansas City.

APR 26   Ruth Brown, along with **Billy Eckstine**, Timmie Rogers, and Johnny Hodges, opens for a week at the YMCA Circus in St. Louis. Proceeds go to local underprivileged children.

Oscar McLollie, Effie Smith, and Pee Wee Crayton are the evening's entertainment at the Elks Ballroom in Los Angeles.

Mercy Dee (Walton) was a self-taught pianist, born in Waco, Texas, August 3, 1915. He moved to the West Coast in the late 1930s. He first recorded for the Spire label of Fresno in 1949, followed by Imperial, Bayou, Colony, Flair, Rhythm, and Specialty in the 1950s.

In 1933, Houston-born Arnett Cobb started in music at age fifteen as a drummer. By 1942, he switched to tenor sax and joined Lionel Hampton's outfit, where he replaced Illinois Jacquet. His 1947 recordings on Apollo with his own combo are considered the turning point in his long and varied career.

While Billy Eckstine is best known for his M-G-M recordings of "My Foolish Heart" (1950) and "I Apologize" (1951), his career really started in 1942 with Earl "Fatha" Hines' band. He broke away to form his own superb orchestra, one that featured Dizzy Gillispie, Miles Davis, Charlie Parker, Sonny Stitt, Gene Ammons and Art Blakey.

APR 27   The Emitt Slay Trio is at the Farm Dell Club in Dayton, Ohio.

New releases for the fourth week of April include "Crazy Man, Crazy" by Bill Haley with Haley's Comets on Essex; George Green's "Finance Man" on Chance; "Hey Fine Mama" by the Five Notes on Specialty; "I've Learned My Lesson" by the Emitt Slay Trio on Savoy; "Just Want Your Love" by Big Maybelle on Okeh; and five records from Victor: "Got A Mind To Leave This Town" by Tampa Red, "All Night Baby" by the Robins, "Rock Bottom" by Milt Trenier, "Ride, Pretty Baby" by John Greer, and "Oo-Shoo-Be-Do-Be" by the Deep River Boys.

APR 30   Lowell Fulson, T-Bone Walker, and **Lloyd Glenn** open a month-long southwestern tour with a show in Houston that takes in $5,600.

Pianist/bandleader Lloyd Glenn was born in San Antonio in 1909. He started touring in 1928, moved to Los Angeles in 1942, and was a mainstay of the 1940s West Coast style of blues. Glenn's combo backed up T-Bone Walker on the original recording of "Call It Stormy Monday." Glenn passed away on May 23, 1985, after spending 57 years in the music business.

THE TOP TEN ROCK 'N' ROLL RECORDS FOR APRIL 1953

1. Hound Dog - Willie Mae Thornton
2. Mama (He Treats Your Daughter Mean) - Ruth Brown
3. Crawlin' - The Clovers
4. Let Me Go Home Whiskey - Amos Milburn
5. Red Top - King Pleasure
6. Baby Don't Do It - The "5" Royales
7. Woke Up This Morning - B. B. King
8. Bear Cat - Rufus Thomas, Jr.
9. I Wanna Know - The Du Droppers
10. Daughter (That's Your Red Wagon) - Sax Kari with Gloria Irving

April 1953
ARTIST OF THE MONTH

WILLIE MAE THORNTON
(b. December 11, 1926; d. July 25, 1984)

Willie Mae Thornton wasn't called "Big Mama" for nothing. She was a behemoth of a woman, high at the waist and big at the hip. On stage she was raucous, almost primitive. Her gyrations were excessively sexy for the time, and she possesed a voice that was almost beyond description. She panted, moaned, grunted, and wailed in a manner more fit for the revival tent. She wore overalls and men's shoes. She topped the scale at 275 pounds, and she knew how to use every ounce. Her performances were sizzling and controversial. Once, while performing, a man bashed her over the head with a chair only to find himself hurtling out the door the next instant. If she'd had more than one hit, she might have brought on the rock 'n roll revolution all by herself.

Willie Mae Thornton is one of only a very small handful of recording artists to have the dubious distinction of having her first charted record reach number one (on the rhythm and blues charts), and then to never have another charted record. She also felt a double injustice when that very same song sent the career of a young rock 'n roll singer out of earthly orbit barely three years later. The song,

WILLIE MAE THORNTON

of course, was "Hound Dog."

Willie Mae came by her singing ability naturally enough. Her father was a local minister and both he and her mother sang in the church choir in their hometown of Montgomery, Alabama. But it appears Willie Mae was destined to follow a more secular path. At the age of fourteen she won an amateur singing contest, and she immediately left home to join the Atlanta-based Hot Harlem Revue. She stayed with the traveling show from 1941 to 1948, playing the drums and harmonica as well as handling some of the vocal chores. Next she settled in Houston, Texas, where she earned a living playing local night clubs as well as rent-raisings and other small functions.

In 1951 Willie Mae made her first recordings with the Harlem Stars on E&W Records; by 1952 she had been discovered by one of the foremost entrepreneurs in early rhythm and blues music, bandleader Johnny Otis. Already billed as "Big Mama" Thornton, she joined the Johnny Otis "Rhythm And Blues Caravan" in Los Angeles. By the time the tour took them to the stage of the Apollo Theater in April of that year, she was well on her way to becoming a legend in the business. Coming on stage early in the evening's revue, she completely dominated the stage with her presence, and thereafter she remained the closing act.

Back in Los Angeles she was given the song "Hound Dog" by its composers, Jerry Leiber and Mike Stoller. Legend has it that the lyrics were scribbled on a brown paper bag. Johnny Otis conducted the combo and received a third of the composer's credit for his arrangement on the record, and Willie Mae's version was released by the Houston-based Peacock Record Company. It was an immediate sensation. Willie Mae's powerful vocal gave homage to her singing idols Bessie Smith and Ma Rainey. Over the guitar bridge in the middle of the song, she started howling as though she was possessed by the hound dog of the title. Then, at the end of the record, the whole band joined in, baying and whooping like bloodhounds on the scent.

The next few years, though hitless, were full of tours, most notably with Johnny Ace and other members of the Peacock/Duke family. Following Ace's untimely death on Christmas Eve 1954, while the tour was playing her hometown of Houston, she gave up the exhausting national tours to settle first in Houston and then in San Francisco so that she could return to playing bars and an occasional blues festival. In 1957 her recording contract with Peacock was not renewed, but she continued to record for other independent companies including Kent, Baytone, and Sotoplay, and she had a short-term contract with Mercury Records. She was a crowd-pleasing hit at the influential Monterey Jazz Festival in 1964. In 1966 she made a well-received album for Arhoolie Records of Berkeley, followed by performances at the Monterey Jazz Festival (1968) and the Newport Jazz Festival (1969, 1973, 1980). She died of a heart attack in Los Angeles at the age of fifty-seven.

Willie Mae "Big Mama" Thornton continued the fine tradition of the female blues shouter as typified by Bessie Smith and Memphis Minnie. In turn she was most influential on the style of Janis Joplin, who witnessed her Monterey performance of "Ball And Chain" and became transfixed. And once again, "Big Mama" watched as the younger, White performer took her material to launch a superstar career.

May 1953

MAY 1   Floyd Dixon begins an engagement at the 5-4 Ballroom in Los Angeles.

Lynn Hope plays his first New York date at Hunts Point Palace in the Bronx.

Savannah Churchill opens at the Stagecoach Club in Hackensack, New Jersey.

Fats Domino has to cancel one-nighters in Louisiana, Alabama, and Georgia due to illness.

Pearl Bailey is the week's attraction at the Howard Theater in Washington.

The Apollo Theater presents Joe Louis and Al Hibbler this week in New York.

MAY 4   Varetta Dillard goes into the Downbeat Club in Providence, Rhode Island.

New releases for the first week of May include "These Foolish Things Remind Me Of You" by Billy Ward and his Dominoes on Federal; Frankie Lee Sims's "Lucy Mae Blues," Henry Pierce's "Hey Fine Mama," and Percy Mayfield's "The Lonely One," all on Specialty; "Baby What's Wrong" by Elmore James on Meteor; "Wasted Love" by **Peppermint Harris** and "Too Much Jellyroll" by Floyd Dixon, both on Aladdin; and "Livin' In Misery" by Titus Turner on Okeh.

MAY 7   Louis Jordan and the "Biggest Show Of '53" play the Philadelphia Arena.

Clyde McPhatter, former lead tenor with Billy Ward and his Dominoes, signs a contract with Atlantic Records. He will form a new group to be named the Drifters, which will record exclusively for Atlantic.

EARLY MAY

The Orioles are currently at Philadelphia's Peps' Musical Bar.

Four Star Records, a West Coast company, buys Big Town Records of New York.

Joe Liggins's Honeydrippers entertain at the Rainbow Ballroom in Denver.

B. B. King and Bill Harvey are currently on a tour of northern Michigan and Ohio.

MAY 8   Arthur Prysock is booked into the Orchid Room in Kansas City, Missouri.

Mabel Scott starts an eight-week run at the DeLisa Club in Chicago.

Savannah Churchill was happily married with two children when her husband was killed in a car crash in 1941. Facing up to her financial responsibilities, she soon wrangled a singing job in Benny Carter's band and cut her first record with Carter for Capitol Records in 1943.

Harrison Nelson originally took the stage name "Peppermint" Nelson in the 1940s so as to avoid bringing any undue scorn down upon his family from their local religious community. In 1950, the moniker was further changed when the owner of Sittin' In With Records couldn't remember the name "Nelson," and issued "Raining In My Heart" as by Peppermint Harris. When the record became a hit, Nelson was stuck with a new name and a blossoming career.

Four Star Records was known at this time as a country label, having issued records by cowboy star Eddie Dean and honky tonk pianist Del Wood.

Roy Milton, both as drummer and vocalist, led one of the West Coast's most popular rhythm and blues dance bands, the Senders. During the years 1948 to 1951, the Specialty label issued twenty-five singles by the Milton aggregation.

"SCREAMIN' JAY" HAWKINS

Screamin' Jay Hawkins had one of the wildest stage acts of the 1950s: to start with, he was wheeled onstage inside a coffin. Hawkin's biggest hit came in 1956 with the bizzare "I Put A Spell On You" on Okeh.

The Falcons originally featured Joe Stubbs, whose brother, Levi, would later lead The Four Tops. The Falcons did not have a hit single until 1959's "You're So Fine." Other lead singers of the Falcons included Wilson Pickett and Eddie Floyd.

Little Walter appears at the 5-4 Ballroom in Los Angeles for the weekend. New York's Apollo Theater presents Earl "Fatha" Hines and his combo with Etta Jones and the Diamonds for the week.

MAY 10   **Roy Milton** and Earl Bostic are the night's attraction at the Elk's Ballroom in Los Angeles.

MAY 11   The "5" Royales, Little Esther, Jimmy Forrest, and Sonny Stitt play a one-nighter at the Graystone Ballroom in Detroit.

New releases for the second week of May include Jimmy Nelson's "Married Men Like Sport" on RPM; "Trying To Live My Life Without You" by Annisteen Allen and "Cherokee" by Earl Bostic, both on King; "Jockey Jump" by Willie Jones on Atlas; Charles Brown's "Take Me" on Aladdin; "Goodbye My Love" by the Chapters on Republic; "No Help Wanted" by the Crows and "I Guess It's All Over Now" by the Five Budds, both on Rama; "Whiskey Drinkin' Woman" by St. Louis Jimmy and "I've Got News For You" by Blind Billy Tate, both on Herald; "Gone, Gone, Gone" by Smokey Hogg on Federal; "(Danger) Soft Shoulders" by Sonny Til on Jubilee; "She's Gotta Go" by Jimmy Ricks on Mercury; and "Beggar For Your Kisses" by the Diamonds on Atlantic.

MAY 15   Amos Milburn, Tiny Grimes, **Screamin' Jay Hawkins**, and comedienne Jackie "Moms" Mabley open at the Howard Theater in Washington for a week.

Louis Jordan and his Tympany Five make a week-long stopover at New York's Apollo Theater.

LaVern Baker opens at the Royal Theater in Baltimore for a week, followed by a week of one-nighters in Virginia.

Oscar McLollie shares the stage with the Four Plaid Throats for the weekend at the 5-4 Ballroom in Los Angeles.

MID-MAY

Savoy Records has recently signed the **Falcons** from New York and the Carols, both from Detroit.

Lou Krefitz, sales manager for Atlantic Records, is leaving the company to manage the Clovers. Meanwhile, Ahmet Ertegun, owner of Atlantic, is in Canada setting up distribution for the label. The label recently signed Hal Paige and Chuck Norris.

H-Bomb Ferguson is at the Whispering Pines Inn near Heightstown, New Jersey.

TNT Tribble is enjoying an indefinite run at the Flamingo Club in Washington.

The Gale Agency is negotiating with the Joe Louis Band for a package tour in July that will include Ruth Brown, the Clovers, Wynonie Harris, and the Erskine Hawkins Band.

The Five Keys are the inaugural act at the El Sambo Club, Jacksonville, Florida's newest night spot.

98

MAY 16   Sax Kari and Gloria Irving start a southern tour that is booked through June 7th.

Sonny Boy Williamson and Wini Brown front Hal Singer's Orchestra for a one-night stand at the Palace Theater in New Orleans.

MAY 18   Ruth Brown entertains at the Town Casino in Buffalo, New York.

Big Maybelle starts at the Orchid Room in Kansas City.

New releases for the third week of May include "Roll 'Em" by Mitzi Mars and "Me And My Chauffeur" by Memphis Minnie, both on Checker; Tiny Bradshaw's "The Blues Came Pouring Down," Stick McGhee's "Whiskey, Women and Loaded Dice," and the Checkers' "Ghost Of My Baby," all on King; the Falcons' "You're The Beating Of My Heart" on Savoy; "Ride 'Til I Die" by John Lee Hooker on Modern; "Red Top" by Gene Ammons on United; "We're All Loaded" by Rosco Gordon on RPM; "I Don't Miss You Anymore" by the Blenders on M-G-M; "Lonely Wall" by Schoolboy Porter on Chance; "Wine Head" by **King Curtis** on Monarch; and the Treniers' "Rockin' Is Our Bizness" on Okeh.

MAY 20   Margie Day joins the Paul Williams Orchestra in Locklin, Ohio.

Ruth Brown opens for a week in New York at the Bandbox Club with Illinois Jacquet's Combo.

MAY 21   Billy Ward and his Dominoes appear at the Fox Theater in Detroit for the third time in as many months. During the week they again stop the show, and headliner Lionel Hampton cannot perform.

MAY 22   Varetta Dillard is welcomed for a week of performances at Weeke's in Atlantic City.

The Ink Spots featuring Bill Kenney are playing a week's worth of one-night stands around Duluth, Minnesota.

MAY 23   **Lowell Fulson**, T-Bone Walker, and Lloyd Glenn close their tour of the Southwest with a performance in Albuquerque.

MAY 24   Roy Brown is the evening's entertainment at the Elks Ballroom in Los Angeles.

New releases for the fourth week of May include Ruth Brown's "Wild, Wild Young Men" and "You Are My Only Love" by the **Cardinals**, both on Atlantic; "I Found Out" by the Du Droppers on Victor; Little Sam Davis' "1958 Blues" on Rockin'; "Love Me 'Til Dawn" by Willie Johnson on Savoy; Mercy Dee's "Please Understand" on Bayou; "Long, Long Day" by Amos Milburn on Aladdin; "Mercy Mr. Percy" by Varetta Dillard on Savoy; "Baby, Don't Turn Your Back On Me" by Lloyd Price on Specialty; Jimmy Wilson's "Call Me A Hound Dog" on Big Town; and two from Joe Houston: "Sabre Jet" on Bayou and "Cornbread And Cabbage" on Recorded In Hollywood.

MAY 28   Ruth Brown, the Orioles, and Sunny Stitt start a series of personal appearances with a performance at Glen Cove, Long Island.

There are three blues singers who called themselves Sonny Boy Williamson. This book deals only with harmonica-wizard Rice Miller, often referred to as Sonny Boy #2, who recorded for the Trumpet label in Jackson, Mississippi, before shifting his home to Chicago. He signed with Checker in 1955.

"King" Cutris Ousley was king of the tenor sax players. His distinctive solos became the backbone of recordings by the Coasters, among others. He was born February 7, 1934, in Fort Worth. In the 1960s, under his own name, he issued a series of r&b/jazz instrumental albums.

Throughout his career, Lowell Fulson had to contend with the misspelling of his last name as either Fulsom or Folsom. In the 1960s, with the growth of soul music, Lowell Fulson continued to have hits for Kent Records. "Black Nights," "Make A Little Love," and "Tramp" even crossed into the rock field.

When the Cardinals signed with Atlantic Records, the vocal phrasing of lead tenor Ernie Warren was very close to that of Clyde McPhatter, who at the time was in the Dominoes. The Cardinal's recording of "Wheel Of Fortune" bears more than a passing resemblance to many of the Dominoes' ballads.

Other shows for this week include the Armory in Troy, New York (29), the St. Nicholas Arena in New York City (30), and Turner's Arena in Washington (31).

MAY 29   T-Bone Walker is scheduled for three days at the 5-4 Club in Los Angeles.
Louis Jordan and LaVern Baker start a week's engagement at the Howard Theater in Washington.
Lionel Hampton and his orchestra entertain patrons at New York's Apollo Theater for the week.
Joe Louis and Hal Singer make the Regal Theater in Chicago their home for the week.

MAY 30   Winnepeg's Don Carlos Club plays host for the week to the Ink Spots featuring Bill Kenney.

MAY 31   **Tiny Grimes** plays for a dance at the Met Ballroom in Philadelphia.

LATE MAY

Jerry Wexler, formerly director of publicity with Big Three Publishers, joins Atlantic Records as a partner to work with Ahmet Ertegun in all areas of the business. Another Atlantic executive officer, Herb Abramson, is currently serving in the U.S. Army as a dentist.

Herald Records has signed the Embers to the label.

Screamin' Jay Hawkins, formerly vocalist with Tiny Grimes, has joined Johnny Sparrow and his Bows and Arrows for an engagement at the Powelton Cafe in Philadelphia.

Lloyd "Tiny" Grimes was born in 1916 (or 1917) in Newport News. He started entertaining as a drummer, pianist, and dancer, but by 1939 he had learned to play the guitar and was working with The Cats And A Fiddle. In 1941/42 he helped form a popular jazz trio with Art Tatum.

THE TOP TEN ROCK 'N' ROLL RECORDS FOR MAY 1953

1. Hound Dog - Willie Mae Thornton
2. I'm Mad - Willie Mabon
3. Mama (He Treats Your Daughter Mean) - Ruth Brown
4. Red Top - King Pleasure
5. I Wanna Know - The Du Droppers
6. Help Me Somebody - The "5" Royales
7. Going To The River - Fats Domino
8. Bear Cat - Rufus Thomas, Jr.
9. Crawlin' - The Clovers
10. Woke Up This Morning - B. B. King

May 1953
ARTIST OF THE MONTH

RUFUS THOMAS, JR.
(b. 1918)

RUFUS THOMAS, JR.

In Memphis, Rufus Thomas holds a distinct place in the musical subculture. His hit records spanned the two most important decades in the emergence of rhythm and blues into rock 'n roll. He was also a long-time deejay on WDIA, which billed itself as "America's Only 50,000-Watt Negro Radio Station." His hours on the radio were filled with high jinks and shenanigans. So were his records.

Thomas was born and raised in Colliersville, Tennessee, near the Mississippi River levies surrounding Memphis. He sang in the church choirs as a youth, but it was the blues that held his attention. In the 1930s the Memphis area was rich with the sounds of traveling Black minstrels. Thomas soon joined them. His home during these times was wherever the Rabbit Foot Show pitched its tent. He also toured with the Royal American Show.

In 1949 he made his first records for the Star Talent Company, which released "I'll Be A Good Boy." In 1951 he was recording in Memphis with Sam Phillips, who was leasing the masters to Chess Records. In a two-year span there were three records issued: "Night Talkin'," "No More Doggin' Around" and "Juanita." In 1952 King released "Insulated Sugar," which featured Thomas fronting the Sonny Thompson Orchestra.

At this time he was working at WDIA with B. B. King, Johnny Ace, and Rosco Gordon. He was featured six days a week on two separate thirty-minute shows playing the latest records from both sides of the rhythm and blues field. WDIA had an impact far beyond the large Black audience reached by its fearsome wattage. White teen-agers also tuned in regularly. Elvis Presley in Memphis; Carl Perkins in Jackson, Tennessee; Jerry Lee Lewis in Ferriday, Louisiana; and Johnny Cash in Kingsland, Arkansas, all took in the music in massive doses.

When not on the air, Thomas was in constant demand on the small club circuit around Memphis. His songs usually ran to the ridiculous, which he delivered with as much enthusiasm as his large frame could muster. He was very familiar with the recording facilities operated by Sam Phillips which was frequently used by the other deejays at WDIA, all of whom had recording contracts by 1953.

In March 1953 Willie Mae Thornton released her version of "Hound Dog," and it became an immediate sensation. Thomas, in a position to see the public's reaction first hand, penned an "answer" to "Hound Dog," and persuaded Sam Phillips to record it and release it on Phillips' fledgling Sun label. Just like "Hound Dog," "Bear Cat" took off, too. Thomas's vocalizing, if one could call it that, was rudimentary. He aped Thornton's howling with grunts and growls of his own. The record became Sun's first bona fide hit, riding the national charts in tandem with the original. Big hit or no, there was little in the way of royalties to show for it following a lawsuit by the publishers of "Hound Dog", who won an out-of-court settlement claiming infringement. A follow-up Sun release, "Tiger Man," also sold well, but there was nothing to follow. For years thereafter, Thomas continued working at WDIA while performing on the side.

When a new record company opened its doors in Memphis in 1960,

Thomas was one of the first to lend his support. The new owners were not very familiar with rhythm and blues, and only consented to record r&b because the theater that they rented as a studio happened to be in the middle of one of Memphis' Black neighborhoods. Because it was named the Capitol Theater, many of the residents thought it was Capitol Records. Nevertheless, Thomas dropped by to audition one day, bringing his seventeen-year-old daughter, Carla. They sang a duet, "'Cause I Love You," which was recorded and released on Satellite. The record sold well enough around Memphis to establish the record company and the studio, which together became known as Stax Records. Rufus and Carla Thomas became the company's main artists, releasing several singles a year.

Then, in 1963, that elusive lightning known as a hit record struck again, when Rufus wrote and recorded, "The Dog," a song built around a local dance step. The record sold well enough to make the top soul and "pop" music charts, and it was followed by Thomas' biggest hit, "Walking The Dog." "Walking The Dog" led to an endless succession of sequels by Thomas: "Somebody Stole My Dog," "Can Your Dog Do The Monkey," "Do The Funky Chicken," and "The Funky Penguin." With "Walking The Dog" being such a major national hit, Thomas was now in demand on performance circuits far afield from Memphis. He toured throughout the United States as well as making several trips to England and the European Continent. No longer was he just another act on the bill, now he was the headliner in such strange locations as Disneyland. In 1970 his string of novelty records had yet to wear thin, and he and James Brown seemed to be trying to outdo each other with their funky dance songs. In 1971 Thomas was honored by the National Association of Recording Arts and Sciences at the Grammy Awards.

In the 1980s he is still going strong, performing for blues revival concerts from coast to coast in front of an endless succession of audiences who crowd the stage to marvel at this man, nearing seventy, who can still walk the dog, dance the funky chicken and tame the bear cat.

June 1953

JUN 1   Wynonie Harris surrenders to Richmond, Virginia, authorities. He has been sought since May 7th when he was indicted as an accessory in an April 13th robbery of $580 from singer Larry Darnell's vault. Harris is released on $1,000 bail and is finally cleared of all charges in late June.

New releases for the first week of June include Eddie Boyd's "Third Degree" on Chess; "For You I Have Eyes" by the Crickets on M-G-M; "My Inspiration" by the Four Plaid Throats on Mercury; "Baby I'm Gonna Throw You Out" by **Allen Bunn** on Apollo; Jimmy Witherspoon's "One Fine Gal" on Federal; and the Carols' "Fifty Million Women" on Savoy.

JUN 5   Willie Mabon headlines the revue this week at New York's Apollo Theater.

In Cleveland, Billy Ward and his Dominoes, Joe Louis, and Bill Haley and his Comets play a one-nighter promoted by Bill Randle.

The Lee Allen Combo is featured as the house band at the Dew Drop Inn for the next month in New Orleans.

JUN 6   Billy Ward starts a two-week stint at Chicago's Regal Theater.

The Four Blazes play a one-nighter at the Palace Theater in New Orleans.

EARLY JUNE

Lynn Hope starts a week of dates in Bermuda, coinciding with the ceremonies surrounding the celebration of the coronation of Queen Elizabeth II. He has signed an exclusive contract with Philadelphia's Showboat Lounge for all of 1954.

Buddy Johnson is in the South for a month of one-nighters that will end in Texas.

The Four Tunes open at the Maroon Club in Montreal for the month of June.

Alan "Moondog" Freed is back at work as deejay at WJW in Cleveland following recovery from an April auto accident.

Flair Records, another West Coast subsidiary of the R.P.M./Modern Company, enters the rhythm and blues field.

New releases for the second week of June include "My Lean Baby" by Dinah Washington and "That's How I Feel About You" by Buddy and Ella Johnson, both on Mercury; B. B. King's "Please Love Me" on

Alden "Allen" Bunn, on top of being a founding member of the Larks on Apollo, also recorded blues as "Tarheel Slim" on Lamp, Red Robin, Fire, and Fury.

In 1954 Buddy Johnson switched labels from Decca to Mercury. His sister Ella did vocals for most releases. Johnson's composition of "Since I Fell For You" became a 1963 hit for Lenny Welch (Cadence).

After little success on his own, Bobby Marchan joined New Orleans' premier vocal group, Huey Smith and the Clowns. He sang lead on most of their hits including "High Blood Pressure" and "Don't You Just Know It." He left the group in 1960 and immediately had a solo hit with "There Is Something On Your Mind" on Fire.

LITTLE RICHARD
The Tempo Toppers were a vocal and instrumental group from New Orleans. The band served as a launching platform for wildman, pianist, singer Little Richard, who's featured on this release.

Huey Smith was one of the most influential performers in 1950s New Orleans. His session work on piano behind Smiley Lewis, Lloyd Price, and Guitar Slim led to his own hit records as Huey Smith and the Clowns on Ace Records, 1957 to 1960.

RPM; T-Bone Walker's "Party Girl" on Imperial; Elmore James's "Early In The Morning" on Flair; Danny Overbea's "Forty Cups Of Coffee" on Checker; "Nobody's Lovin' Me" by the Swallows and Bull Moose Jackson's "Meet Me With Your Black Dress On," both on King; and **Bobby Marchan**'s "Just A Little Walk" on Aladdin.

JUN 9   Ruth Brown returns to New York's Bandbox, the site of her record-breaking engagement last month. Also on the bill are Woody Herman and the Jackie Davis Trio.

JUN 12   Chance Records' Johnny Sellers is at the New Era Club in Nashville.

The Clovers are involved in an auto accident while traveling from Houston to Midland, Texas. Only guitarist Harold Winley requires medical attention.

Floyd Dixon is this weekend's entertainment at the 5-4 Club in Los Angeles.

The Howard Theater in Washington hosts the Joe Louis Revue featuring Hal "Cornbread" Singer and the Nicholas Brothers.

LaVern Baker fronts the Tito Puente Combo for a week at New York's Apollo Theater.

Lionel Hampton is the headliner at the Uptown Theater in Philadelphia for the week. The Uptown is starting a policy of combining live revues with movies to replace the Earle Theater, which closed March 26th and has since been demolished.

JUN 13   Shirley and Lee front Stomp Gordon's Band for the evening at New Orlean's Palace Theater.

JUN 14   Roy Brown plays a one-night stand in Los Angeles at the Elks Ballroom.

The San Jacinto Club in New Orleans offers a blues battle between Guitar Slim and Smiley Lewis.

JUN 15   Ruth Brown performs at the Hi Hat Club in Boston for a week.

The Flamingos start an engagement at Gleason's in Cleveland.

New releases for the third week of June include the Du Droppers' "Come On And Love Me Baby" and "I Want To Love You Baby" by the Serenaders, both on Red Robin; Jimmy Coe's "After Hours Joint" on States; "I Lost Everything" by Charles Brown on Aladdin; and "Fool At The Wheel" by the Duce of Rhythm and the **Tempo Toppers** on Peacock.

MID-JUNE

While on a talent search in New Orleans, Lee Magid of Savoy Records waxes **Huey Smith**, Billy Wright, and Earl and Willie Johnson.

The Treniers are currently headlining at Philadelphia's Sciolla's Cafe.

JUN 19   T-Bone Walker is at the 5-4 Club in Los Angeles for the weekend.

Al Hibbler starts a two-week engagement at Detroit's Flame

Show Bar.

Louis Jordan and his Tympany Five start a week at the Regal Theater in Chicago.

JUN 21   Edna McGriff and the **Crickets** headline the dance at the Bedford YMCA in Brooklyn.

The Clovers and Marvin Phillips entertain at the Elks Ballroom in Los Angeles.

Dinah Washington opens at Carr's Beach Resort in Annapolis, Maryland.

JUN 22   Ruth Brown plays a week at Pep's Musical Bar in Philadelphia.

New releases for the fourth week of June include "The Deacon Don't Like It" by Wynonie Harris, "Whispering Blues" by Piney Brown, and ex-boxing champ Sugar Ray Robinson's debut "Knock Him Down Whiskey," all on King; Dolly Cooper's "Alley Cat" on Savoy; "Get It" by the Royals on Federal; and "Ain't Nothin' Baby" by Ike Carpenter on Decca.

JUN 26   Lloyd Price appears for three days at the 5-4 Club in Los Angeles.

The Vocaleers are on stage at the Apollo Theater in New York for the week.

The Uptown Theater in Philadelphia plays host to the Joe Louis Revue.

New releases for the fifth week of June include Johnny Ace's "The Clock" and Earl Forrest's "Last Night's Dream," both on Duke; "Shirley's Back" by Shirley and Lee on Aladdin; "Decatur Street Boogie" by **Piano Red** on Victor; "Don't Deceive Me" by Chuck Willis on Okeh; Roy Milton's "Let Me Give You All My Love" and Joe Liggins' "Farewell Blues," both on Specialty; "Gee" by the Crows on Rama; Roy Brown's "Old Age Boogie" on King; the Five Willow's "My Dear, Dearest Darling" on Allen; Jimmy Wilson's "Tell Me" on 7-11 Records; "One More Time" by the Orioles on Jubilee; Fats Domino's "Please Don't Leave Me" on Imperial; and the Clovers' "Good Lovin'" on Atlantic.

The Crickets on the M-G-M label should not be confused with the rockabilly band behind Buddy Holly. This rhythm and blues vocal group was discovered by Joe Davis, who was associated at the time with M-G-M Records. When he quit M-G-M to form Jay-Dee Records, the Crickets came along, but after only six months of success, they broke up.

PIANO RED

Piano Red's greatest recording success came under another pseudonym, as Dr. Feelgood and the Interns on Okeh, beginning in 1962. Under his new name, he issued the popular novelty "Dr. Feel-Good," and he re-recorded his own "Right String But The Wrong Yo-Yo."

THE TOP TEN ROCK 'N' ROLL RECORDS FOR JUNE 1953

1. Help Me Somebody - The "5" Royales
2. Going To The River - Fats Domino
3. I Wanna Know - The Du Droppers
4. I'm Mad - Willie Mabon
5. These Foolish Things Remind Me Of You - Billy Ward and his Dominoes
6. Hound Dog - Willie Mae Thornton
7. Wild, Wild Young Men - Ruth Brown
8. Red Top - King Pleasure
9. Is It A Dream - The Vocaleers
10. Crazy Man, Crazy - Bill Haley and his Comets

June 1953
ARTIST OF THE MONTH

JOHNNY OTIS
(John Veliotes, b. December 28, 1921)

JOHNNY OTIS

Although Johnny Otis is not represented on this month's music charts, as are most of the other "Artists Of The Month," he certainly deserves further discussion based on his untiring promotional efforts on behalf of the music that he loved most.

Johnny Otis had no serious interest in music until the age of twenty. He was the son of Greek parents, and he grew up in Vallejo, across the bay from San Francisco. There, in 1941, he happened to attend a concert given by the Count Basie Band. He was impressed enough by Basie's drummer, Joe Jones, to immediately began intensive studying. Within two years he was proficient not only on the drums, but also on the vibraphone and the piano.

He was first enlisted to play in the bands of Harlan Leonard and Count Prince Otis Matthews, who worked the casinos in Reno. In 1943 he formed the Otis-Love Band with Preston Love and they were hired to perform at the Barrelhouse Club in Omaha. Two years later, fronting his own band, he was featured at the Club Alabam in Los Angeles, followed by a trip to Chicago in October 1946 that led to the Otis orchestra backing the Ink Spots on their worldwide tour. His recording of "Harlem Nocturne" that same year on Excelsior was a big enough hit to start him on a series of tours that did not stop for the next twelve years.

As the era of the big band fell into decline, he reformed his unit into a combo featuring twin saxophones, trumpet, trombone, with himself on the vibes. He settled in Los Angeles in 1948 and opened his own Barrelhouse Club. Here he discovered the Robins, Mel Walker, and Little Esther (Phillips). He negotiated a package deal with Savoy Records, and in 1950 he was producer of three of the top records of the year: "Cupid's Boogie" by Little Esther, "Mistrustin' Blues" by the Robins and Mel Walker, and his own "Double Crossing Blues," which also featured the Robins and Little Esther.

During the period of interest to this book, 1952 through 1955, Johnny Otis was instrumental in the discovery of several other important rhythm and blues artists: Willie Mae Thornton, Jackie Wilson, Little Willie John, and Hank Ballard. More often than not, he could be found at the helm of the "Johnny Otis Rhythm And Blues Caravan," which crisscrossed the country featuring many of the talents he had unearthed. He recorded under his own name on Mercury and Peacock. He produced sessions and fronted the studio band for Little Richard, Miss Thornton, and Johnny Ace on Peacock/Duke. He wrote "Every Beat Of My Heart," which was a hit for the Royals featuring Hank Ballard. He wrote "The Wallflower" (also known as "Dance With Me Henry") for Esther Phillips as an answer to Hank Ballard's "Work With Me Annie." He co-authored "Hound Dog," the smash hit for Willie Mae Thornton.

In 1955 he took a job as a deejay at Los Angeles' KFOX radio while still playing local clubs constantly. This led to his promotion of many of the local dances while he was not touring himself. In short, during the 1950s he seemed to be everywhere. In reality, he was a man of extraordinary talents.

His stage shows were something to behold. Otis would first take

106

the spotlight himself for a solo turn at the drums and vibes for ten minutes before the remainder of the band would come onstage. There would always be a female vocalist or two (Little Esther, Willie Mae Thornton, or, later, Marie Adams) who could be politely called plump, but who could shout the blues. This was followed by a male vocalist (usually Mel Walker) who was smooth with the ballads. The show climaxed with a vocal group (maybe the Robins in the early years) followed by a rousing number or two from the Otis band while Johnny frantically switched back and forth from drums to vibes. All the while, his dark Greek complexion fooled most members of the audience into believing he was Black.

His biggest recording success came in 1958 with "Willie And The Hand Jive" on Capitol. A year earlier he had written "So Fine," a hit for the Fiestas. By the mid-1960s he was out of the music business and into California politics, but Frank Zappa convinced him to return to the studio. The result was the fine album "Cold Shot" on Kent, which featured his son, Shuggie, on guitar. He put together an old-time revue for the 1970 Monterey Blues Festival that featured Joe Turner, Little Esther, and Roy Brown. In 1971 he toured the Far East with his revue, followed by a trip to England the next year. He started the Blues Spectrum label in 1974, which recorded some of the founders of rhythm and blues: Joe Turner, Pee Wee Crayton, Joe Liggins, and Charles Brown. He recorded a new Johnny Otis Show album in 1982 for Alligator Records, and he is currently touring the country with his mobile museum dedicated to rhythm and blues music.

Few people connected with rhythm and blues music have given so much of themselves so often as Johnny Otis. He has worked tirelessly to make the music more accessible to the masses, probably because as a White man who frequently passed for Black he knew the culture from the inside. And he loved it. He has been referred to as the "Godfather of Rhythm and Blues," which has the current connotation of gangsterism. I prefer to think of it in the paternal sense. That he loved the music is beyond question. That he profited from it after all these years is less certain.

July 1953

JUL 1   The Four Tunes begin an engagement at the Martinique Club in Wildwood, New Jersey.

JUL 3   Ruth Brown, Sonny Stitt, and the Crickets are currently at the Apollo.
The Orioles start a two-week tour with the Clovers and the Paul Williams band through the Midwest. The first night's show is in Louisville, Kentucky.
Tiny Bradshaw, Wini Brown, and Sarah McLawler are on stage this week at the Howard Theater in Washington.
Sarah Vaughan plays the Three Rivers Inn in Three Rivers, New York.
Arthur Prysock starts a two-week run at the Midtown Hotel in St. Louis.
The Jackson Brothers and Pee Wee Crayton start a three-day engagement at the 5-4 Ballroom in Los Angeles.

JUL 4   Decca Records announces that it is stepping up the number of rhythm and blues records that it will be releasing. Scheduled for immediate release are five, including material from Little Donna Hightower and the Shadows.

JUL 5   Johnny Otis and Marie Adams entertain at the Elks Ballroom in Los Angeles for the regular Sunday night dance.

JUL 6   Fats Domino brings his band to the Showboat in Philadelphia.

New releases for the first week of July include "Foolish One" by the Rocketeers on Herald; "Mess Around" by Ray Charles on Atlantic; "Please Take Me Back" by the **Blenders** on M-G-M; Sonny Thompson's "Low Flame" and Earl Bostic's "Melancholy Serenade," both on King; "The Midnight Hour Was Shining" by Little Willie Littlefield on Federal; "Please Tell It To Me" by the Four Bells on Gem; and Eva Foster's "You'll Never Know" on Atlantic, which is an answer to the Du Droppers' "I Wanna Know."

EARLY JULY

The "5" Royales with Charlie "Little Jazz" Ferguson and his all-girl orchestra are on a summer-long tour beginning with a show in Parksley, West Virginia. They will wind up on the West Coast in September.

Alberta Adams signs with Chess Records.

Herald Records, a new label from New York, reports strong East Coast action for its new release by the Embers, "Paradise Hill."

Throughout the late 1940s and early 1950s, the big dance band of Myron "Tiny" Bradshaw was one of the most popular on the rhythm and blues tour circuit. Bradshaw was born in 1905 in Youngstown, Ohio.

The Blenders featured as second tenor Ollie Jones, who got his start with the Ravens on Hub Records in 1946. The Blender's first release, "I Can Dream Can't I," was issued in 1949 on National, followed by eight singles on Decca Records.

108

JUL 9   "The Biggest Rhythm And Blues Show" starts its record-breaking tour with a concert and dance in Revere, Massachusetts at the Rollaway Ballroom. Featured performers are Joe Louis, Ruth Brown, Wynonie Harris, Lester Young, and Buddy Johnson's Orchestra. Over 2,000 are turned away at the door. The next night in Newark, New Jersey the crowds remain overwhelming. The tour will run for six weeks and will become the largest grossing r&b tour to date. In Cleveland almost 20,000 turn out, and in Detroit the gate is $18,700.

JUL 10   Dinah Washington makes a stopover at the Howard Theater in Washington for the week.

JUL 11   **Bill Doggett** is entertaining at Pep's Musical Bar in Philadelphia.

After years playing piano behind other artists, Bill Doggett's name came to the fore as arranger/organist for Ella Fitzgerald. In 1963, after ten years of popularity, he returned to work with Miss Fitzgerald as an arranger and conductor for a Verve album.

JUL 12   Roy Brown is the featured entertainer at the regular Sunday night dance at the Elks Ballroom in Los Angeles.

JUL 13   The Graystone Ballroom in Detroit hosts a rhythm and blues battle of the vocal groups between the Orioles and the Clovers.

New releases for the second week of July include Browler Guy's "You Look Good To Me" on Checker; "You Can't Keep A Good Man Down" by Billy Ward and his Dominoes on Federal; Jimmy Witherspoon's "Oh Mother, Dear Mother" on Modern; "Gal! You Need A Good Whippin'" by Herbert Beard on Cool; and three new records from Savoy: Billy Wright's "Four Cold, Cold Walls," Brownie McGhee's "Four O'Clock In The Morning," Earl Johnson's "Beggin' Your Mercy,".

JUL 14   The Orioles and the Clovers wind up a successful two weeks on the road with a performance in Cincinnati. The Clovers immediately join the "Biggest Rhythm And Blues Show" tour. The Orioles take a few day's rest before hitting the road again on the 19th.

JUL 15   Billy Eckstine starts a two-week stopover at Birdland in New York.

MID-JULY

A check of the summer season at the vacation resort of Wildwood, New Jersey, finds the **Treniers** at the Riptide, the Four Tunes at the Martinique, and Lionel Hampton at the Surf Club, as well as a fine showing of jazz artists at several of the other nightspots.

Twins Claude and Clifton Trenier had a marvelous stage act. One would come on as a solo dancer. After working up a feverish sweat, tearing off his jacket, and with hair in his eyes, he would exit only to have his twin, wearing a fresh outfit, enter from the same side of the stage. To the audience, it looked like magic.

In Atlantic City, the vacation season has the Five Keys at Weeke's Cocktail Lounge. Also in town are Billy Ford and his Thunderbirds at the Fort Pitt Club, Jimmy Tyler and Wild Bill Davis at the Club Harlem, the Charioteers at the Dude Ranch, and a number of jazz artists booked into other after-hours clubs.

Vivian Carter, deejay on WGRY, Gary, Indiana, starts a new label, **Vee-Jay**, in partnership with Jimmy Bracken. First artists to be signed are Mississippi blues singer **Jimmy Reed and the Spaniels**, a vocal group

The first releases by Jimmy Reed and the Spaniels on Vee-Jay did poorly and were soon leased to Chance Records of Chicago when Vee-Jay's new owner ran short of cash. Vee-Jay did continue to produce sessions and eventually, when Chance folded, Vee-Jay Records became a force in the business.

from Gary, Indiana.

JUL 17   Roy Brown opens for three days at the 5-4 Club in Los Angeles.
         The "Biggest Rhythm And Blues Show" continues its record-breaking tour with a show in Boston tonight. Other dates include Baltimore (19), Cleveland (20), the Olympia Stadium in Detroit (21), Flint, Michigan (22), Evansville, Indiana (24), and St. Louis (25). (See July 9 for artists.)

JUL 18   Charles Brown delights patrons of the San Jacinto Club in New Orleans for the evening.

JUL 19   The Orioles are this week's entertainment in Kansas City at the Orchid Club.

JUL 20   Willie Mabon opens at the Celebrity Club in Providence, Rhode Island.

LIGHTNIN' HOPKINS

Sam "Lightnin'" Hopkins was born in Leon County, Texas, on March 15, 1912. During his long career, he recorded for an almost limitless number of labels starting with Aladdin in 1946. His nickname came as the logical extension of that of his first piano accompanist, Wilson "Thunder" Smith.

Big Jay McNeely is remembered for 1959's "There Is Something On Your Mind" on Swingin' Records, which featured Little Sonny Warner on vocals.

New releases for the third week of July include "No Use" by the Shadows on Decca; "Crying In The Chapel" by the Orioles on Jubilee; **Lightnin' Hopkins's** "Mistreated Blues" on RPM; "Left With A Broken Heart" by Jimmy Rogers and "Tiptoe" by Eddie Johnson, both on Chess; "Your Mouth Got A Hole In It" by Todd Rhodes on King; "Too Much Lovin'" by the "5" Royales on Apollo; "Fractured" by Bill Haley and Haley's Comets on Essex; and John Lee Hooker's "Please Take Me Back" on Modern.

JUL 21   Little Walter begins a two-week engagement at the Royal Peacock in Atlanta.

JUL 24   **Big Jay McNeeley** starts a three-day stint at Los Angeles' 5-4 Club.
         LaVern Baker returns to the Flame Show Bar in Detroit as a headliner.

JUL 26   Percy Mayfield entertains at the Elks Ballroom Sunday night dance in Los Angeles.

JUL 27   Amos Milburn opens in Youngstown, Ohio at, Sportoree's Club.
         Billie Holiday, Tiny Bradshaw, and Roy Milton share the bill at the Graystone Ballroom in Detroit for the evening.
         The "Biggest Rhythm And Blues Show" continues rolling across the land with a show tonight in Kansas City. Other dates this week include Tulsa (28), Oklahoma City (29), and two Texas shows: Amarillo (30) and Austin (31).

New releases for the fourth week of July include Tab Smith's "Cherry" on United; "Dragnet Blues" by Johnny Moore's Three Blazers on Modern; "Big Eyes" by Little Caesar on Big Town; "Break My Bones" by the Four Fellows on Tri-Boro; Mercy Dee's "Rent Man Blues" on Specialty; Floyd Dixon's "Married Woman" on Aladdin; "Oh Baby" by Smiley Lewis on Imperial; Clarence "Gatemouth" Brown's "Hurry Back Good News" on Peacock; and "Baby It's You" by the Spaniels and "That's My Desire"

110

by the Flamingos, both on Chance.

JUL 30   **Champion Jack Dupree** starts a two-day stand at New Orleans'
Dew Drop Inn.

JUL 31   Fats Domino and the Orioles start a tour of the Southwest
with a performance in Oklahoma City.
Chuck Willis and the Griffin Brothers set off on a package
tour with a show in Mobile, Alabama.
Floyd Dixon appears at the 5-4 Club in Los Angeles for
three nights.
T-Bone Walker is booked for a three-week engagement at
Detroit's Flame Show Bar.

LATE JULY

The **Prisonaires**, a vocal group comprised completely of inmates of the
Tennessee State Penitentiary in Nashville, record several sides for Sam
Phillips's Sun Records, of Memphis.

Joe Morris, formerly with Atlantic, has signed with Herald Records.
His first release will be "Shake A Hand" featuring vocalist Faye Adams.

Buddy Lucas, long-time orchestra leader with Jubilee, has gone over
to RCA Victor where his initial release will be "Greedy Pig."

William Thomas "Champion Jack" Dupree was born in New Orleans, July 4, 1910, and made his first records for Okeh in 1940. Throughout his varied career, he recorded for well over a dozen labels under various names including Duke Bayou, Blind Boy Johnson, Meat Head Johnson, Brother Blues, and Willie Jordan.

The Prisonaires were formed in 1940. With the addition of lead tenor Johnny Bragg in 1943, the group became popular with public officials who wanted to show how well the penal system was rehabilitating the inmates. Their first Memphis session, June 1953, was held under armed guard, but produced the beautiful "Just Walking In The Rain." When the members (except Bragg) were released in 1955, they changed their stage name to the Sunbeams, and then as the Marigolds had a minor hit with "Rollin' Stone" on Excello that same year.

THE TOP TEN ROCK 'N' ROLL RECORDS FOR JULY 1953

1. Help Me Somebody - The "5" Royales
2. Please Love Me - B. B. King
3. The Clock - Johnny Ace
4. I Found Out - The Du Droppers
5. Wild, Wild Young Men - Ruth Brown
6. Goin' To The River - Fats Domino
7. I Wanna Know - The Du Droppers
8. Mercy, Mr. Percy - Varetta Dillard
9. Third Degree - Eddie Boyd
10. These Foolish Things Remind Me Of You - Billy Ward and his
Dominoes

July 1953
ARTIST OF THE MONTH

VARETTA DILLARD
(b. February 3, 1933*)

If "pain" of one sort or another can influence a singer to perform
more powerful blues, then Varetta Dillard's childhood certainly should
have led to fame in that field. From the time she was three, and for
the next fifteen years, Varetta was in and out of the hospital with

---

(*BMI bio gives birth as 1928.)

VARETTA DILLARD

a bone deficiency in her right leg. For her, singing was a therapy. She joined glee clubs in Morris High School so that part of her school day could be spent singing. Being a New Yorker, born in Harlem and raised in the Bronx, the Wednesday night amateur show at the Apollo Theater was naturally alluring. It was during just one such performance in 1952 that Varetta was spotted by Lee Magdid, manager of Al Hibbler and Della Reese and session producer at Savoy Records. Magdid arranged for her immediate signing to a contract for both recordings and personal appearances. He hired the top writers and the best musicians for her recordings. Her first session, in September 1951, produced a fine single, "Love and Wine," and her first chart success came with "Easy, Easy Baby," recorded May 6, 1952.

Although Varetta loved to sing ballads, her biggest success came with up-tempo numbers such as "Mercy, Mr. Percy." Magdid planned for her to be the successor to Ruth Brown's popularity, but when it was obvious that Varetta did not have the staying power of Miss Brown, Magdid tried another ploy. Following Johnny Ace's death in December 1954, he had Varetta record "Johnny Has Gone," a tribute to Ace. While this, in and of itself, certainly is not unheard of, Magdid hyped the record by claiming that Varetta was Ace's girlfriend. Varetta was even made to perform wearing a maternity dress to give the impression that she was pregnant with Ace's child. To Magdid's credit, the record did sell reasonably well in the first months of 1955. But, thereafter, Varetta's career plummeted. She was ultimately dropped by Savoy (her last Savoy session was in May 1955), but in the mid-to-late 1950s she was able to land a series of recording contracts with Groove, RCA Victor, and Cub Records, only to be told to move on after a few releases. She toured extensively with the many rhythm and blues packages that crisscrossed the country, including those of Alan Freed. By 1960 she was broke, claiming that she had been cheated out of all royalties due her. Her life was shattered. She was an alcoholic, a divorcee, a has-been at age twenty-seven.

In the 1960s she dropped out of the music scene completely and tried to rebuild her broken life. Varetta is remembered today as a plump songstress with plenty of volume for singing rhythm numbers, although one reviewer in 1953 noted that she was "too mechanical in her delivery and mannerisms" to develop her full potential. It was her clear diction and crowd-pleasing onstage personality that allowed her to remain a staple of the traveling revues long after her records stopped selling.

August 1953

AUG 2   Louis Jordan stops at the Elks Ballroom in Los Angeles for the evening.

In New Orleans, Jack Dupree moves across town to play the San Jacinto Ballroom.

New releases for the first week of August include the Trenier's "This Is It" on Okeh; "Black Diamond" by Mr. Sad Head and "Beginning To Miss You" by John Greer, both on Victor; "Cut That Out" by Junior Wells on States; "Come Back Baby" by Roosevelt Sykes on United; "When I Met You" by the **Crickets** on Jay-Dee; Woo Woo Moore's "Something's Wrong" on Mercury; Rudy Green's "Love Is A Pain" on Chance; and "Rot Gut" by Wynonie Harris on King.

AUG 4   Following his engagement at the Royal Peacock in Atlanta, Little Walter takes to the road for a series of shows in Florida and along the Eastern Seaboard.

AUG 7   Chuck Higgins and his six-piece combo take over the 5-4 Ballroom in Los Angeles for the weekend.

Jack Dupree returns to New Orleans' Dew Drop Inn for another three-day weekend.

EARLY AUGUST

Recent acquisitions by record companies include the Charioteers by Tuxedo; Lightnin' Hopkins and Savannah Churchill by Decca; and **LaVern Baker**, who had previously recorded with Todd Rhodes' Orchestra on King, by Atlantic.

Billy Ward and his Dominoes bring in a full house at the Wolhurst Club in Littleton, Colorado.

AUG 9   Willie Mae Thornton and Johnny Ace play the Elks Ballroom in Los Angeles.

Ray Charles is featured at the San Jacinto Club in New Orleans for the evening. Also, the "Big Rhythm And Blues Show" featuring Joe Louis, Ruth Brown, Wynonie Harris, the Clovers, the Buddy Johnson Orchestra, and the Lester Young Combo are in town for one show at the Municipal Auditorium (over 4,000 attend).

New releases for the second week of August include "Feelin' Good" by Little Junior's Blue Flames on Sun; "Honey Hush" by Joe Turner on Atlantic;, **Pat Valdeler's** "Baby, Rock Me" on Mercury; "Waiting For My Baby" by Blazer Boy and "Cryin' In My Sleep" by Herb Fisher, both on Imperial; Big Maybelle's "Send For Me" on Okeh; "Nervous, Man Nervous" by Big Jay McNeeley on Federal; Margie Day's "String Bean" on Dot; and "Country Boogie" by Elmore James on Checker.

Individuals who passed through the Crickets and who later sang with other groups include Jimmy Bailey (Velvetones, Cadillacs), Bobby Spencer (Chords, Pearls, Harptones, Cadillacs), Harold Johnson (Mellows), Joe Diaz (Chords), and Fred Barksdale (Cadillacs).

Pat Valdeler was an emcee and singer at New Orleans' Dew Drop Inn for nearly twenty years. He was also an "out in the open" transvestite who hosted the annual New Orleans Gay Ball each Halloween.

AUG 12   The Fats Domino/Orioles tour continues its two weeks of one-nighters with a show in Amarillo, Texas.

AUG 13   Charlie Ferguson and his all-girl band are involved in an auto accident in Cleveland that kills the nineteen-year-old bass player. Ferguson is on the critical list. The band has been on tour with the "5" Royales and was enroute to Tyler, Texas, for another show. The "5" Royales, traveling in another vehicle, are not injured. The tour is booked solidly into December.

This group of Five Satins is apparently not related to the group of the same name which had the enormous hit in 1956 with "In The Still Of the Night."

AUG 14   Alan Freed celebrates the second anniversary of his "Moondog" radio show over Cleveland's WJW with a dance at the Armory in Akron, Ohio. Featured attractions of the show, which is broadcast live over WJW, are the **Five Satins** with Rene Hall's band. The next night Freed takes the show to the Stambaugh Auditorium in Youngstown, Ohio.
          The Apollo Theater in New York presents Billie Holiday and the Duke Ellington Orchestra for the week.

AUG 15   The Du Droppers with the Joe Morris Band start a series of one-night stands.
          The Fourth Annual "World Series Of Blues" takes place at the Shrine Auditorium in Los Angeles. Performers include Willie Mae Thornton, Johnny Ace, Roy Milton, Chuck Higgins, the **Flairs**, the Robins, Jimmy Witherspoon, and Helen Humes.

The Flairs were another of the Los Angeles groups that worked using various names. They began professionally in 1953 as the 5 Hollywood Blue Jays on Recorded In Hollywood. The same group recorded for Flair Records as the Hunters, Whips, Chimes, and Rams as well as the Flairs.

MID-AUGUST

The Dominoes start their second engagement at the Bandbox in New York.

LaVern Baker sets sail for Europe, where she is booked on a six-month tour.

AUG 16   Roy Milton entertains at the Sunday night dance at the Elks Ballroom in Los Angeles.

AUG 17   T-Bone Walker, Margie Day, and the Paul Williams Orchestra start a week's engagement at the Celebrity Club in Providence, Rhode Island.
          Dinah Washington, Earl Bostic, the Royals, **Arthur Prysock**, Edna McGriff, and Buddy Lucas's Orchestra play the Graystone Ballroom in Detroit.

After more than twenty years as a solo artist, Arthur Prysock finally had a few regional hits with "It's Too Late, Baby Too Late" (1965), "A Working Man's Prayer" (1968), and "When Love Is New" (1976).

New releases for the third week of August include "Can't Stop Lovin'" by **Elmore James** on Flair; "My Momma Told Me" by Lightnin' Hopkins on Mercury; "Two Lovers Have I" by the Diamonds on Atlantic; "Loving Baby" by the Charms on Rockin'; "Please Don't Go" by Floyd Dixon on Specialty; Amos Milburn's "One Scotch, One Bourbon, One Beer" on Aladdin; "Nadine" by the Coronets on Chess; "I'll Die Trying" by J. B. Lenoir on J.O.B.; and Jimmy Reed's "Roll And Rhumba" on Chance.

Elmore James' main contribution to the legacy of the blues was his slide-guitar technique, which he first made popular on his 1951 classic interpretation of Robert Johnson's "Dust My Broom," recorded for Trumpet.

AUG 18   Fats Domino and the Orioles wind up their tour of the Southwest. Domino is off to the West Coast while the Orioles return East.

114

AUG 21   The Orioles are booked into the Apollo Theater in New York for the week. Also on the bill are Leslie Uggams and the Lucky Millinder combo.

Lynn Hope opens for two weeks at the Royal Peacock in Atlanta.

Willie Mae Thornton and Johnny Ace are at the 5-4 Club in Los Angeles for three days.

Ray Charles entertains at New Orleans' Dew Drop Inn for the three-day weekend.

AUG 22   "Crying In The Chapel" by the Orioles on Jubilee, currently riding high on the r&b charts, enters the pop records chart in *Billboard* magazine.

"Crying In The Chapel" was first recorded by an otherwise unknown country artist, Darrell Glenn, but the biggest-selling version was by "pop" songstress June Valli.

AUG 24   T-Bone Walker goes out on a tour of the East Coast.

New releases for the fourth week of August include "I Wish Your Picture Was You" by Lloyd Price and "Drunk" by Jimmy Liggins, both on Specialty; "Mother-In-Law" by Edward Gates White on States; LaVern Baker's "How Can You Leave A Man Like This" on Atlantic; "When You Talk" by Cliff Butler and the Doves on States; and "Beginning To Miss You" by Patty Anne on Aladdin and by John Greer on Groove.

AUG 29   **Thurston Harris**, the Lamplighters, and Dootsie Williams's Combo inaugurate the new Harlem Nightclub in Los Angeles.

Thurston Harris often sang lead tenor with the Lamplighters on Federal Records (1953-56). He moved on to Aladdin Records where in 1957, he finally had a big hit covering Bobby Day's "Little Bitty Pretty One" on Aladdin.

AUG 30   Fats Domino sets off on a three-week tour of California.

Johnny Otis and Marie Adams are the evening's entertainment at the Elks Ballroom in Los Angeles.

AUG 31   "The Harlem Talent Search" starts a thirteen-week run over WPIX-TV in New York. The show is hosted by Slim Gaillard.

LATE AUGUST

Late summer talent scouts in the field include Ahmet Ertegun and Jerry Wexler of Atlantic Records in New Orleans and Don Roby of Duke Records in California.

The hot new radio show in Memphis is the "Cool Train" show every Saturday over WDIA. Host is Rufus Thomas, Jr., of Sun Records.

The Four Blazes are currently touring in Michigan.

THE TOP TEN ROCK 'N' ROLL RECORDS FOR AUGUST 1953

1. The Clock - Johnny Ace
2. Crying In The Chapel - The Orioles
3. Good Lovin' - The Clovers
4. Please Love Me - B. B. King
5. Please Don't Leave Me - Fats Domino
6. Help Me Somebody - The "5" Royales
7. Too Much Lovin' - The "5" Royales
8. Don't Deceive Me - Chuck Willis
9. Mercy, Mr. Percy - Varetta Dillard
10. Wild, Wild Young Men - Ruth Brown

August 1953
ARTIST OF THE MONTH

CHUCK WILLIS
(b. January 31, 1928; d. April 10, 1958)

CHUCK WILLIS

A native of Atlanta, Chuck began entertaining when he was eighteen years old. By the time he died in 1958 he was known as the "Dream Man of Singers" because of his unerring knack for writing and singing hit songs. He died with a legacy of close to fifty published songs that had been recorded by the cream of the rhythm and blues field: the Five Keys ("Close Your Eyes"), the Cardinals ("The Door Is Still Open"), Ruth Brown ("Oh What A Dream"), the Cadillacs ("Let Me Explain" and "Sugar Sugar"), and the Clovers ("From The Bottom Of My Heart"). His songs were also covered by Eydie Gorme, Steve Lawrence, Don Cornell, Patti Page, Dean Martin, and Wanda Jackson.

Atlanta was a perfect training ground for Chuck Willis. He was able to appear regularly at the teen canteens, the block parties, and the YMCA dances where he usually fronted the Red McAllister band. It was on just such a gig that he was discovered by Zenas "Daddy" Sears, deejay on local WAOK radio, who personally introduced him to a talent scout from Columbia Records in 1951. After his initial release on Columbia, "Can't You See?," he was reassigned to Columbia's blues affiliate, Okeh Records. One of his first singles, "I Tried" backed with "I Rule My House," sold sufficiently well to insure that Chuck would be with the company for an extended stay. In 1952 he had his first national hit with "My Story," a fine example of the smooth vocal style that was as much Willis's trademark as the turban that he always wore on stage. On "My Story," his strong baritone rose in swells over McAllister's combo; the lyrical quality of the song was stunning.

Two years later, after five straight hits, his career was stymied as more and more airplay was devoted to the up-tempo styles of rock 'n roll. He, along with his contemporary balladeers, had trouble changing to fit the times.

A year with Epic Records, another Columbia subsidiary, produced six singles but no hits. In 1956 Atlantic Records took a chance and signed him to the label just as it had done with several artists whose careers seemed destined to oblivion, including Joe Turner, Ray Charles, and Ivory Joe Hunter. In all four cases, Atlantic's production team was able to turn the artist's sound around from the blues to something more lively that would appeal to the new teen market. Willis's first Atlantic releases, "Juanita" and "It's Too Late," were followed by major successes in the "pop" field with "C. C. Rider" and "Betty And Dupree," which earned him yet another nickname, "The King Of The Stroll."

In April 1958 Willis died in an Atlanta hospital after a two-year bout with bleeding stomach ulcers. Ironically, his biggest hit to date had just been released: the prophetic "What Am I Living For" backed with "I'm Gonna Hang Up My Rock & Roll Shoes."

Once, when he was asked what makes a strong rock 'n roll song, Willis replied, "It's the beat . . . the words. People know a lot about hate, fear, and trouble, and they also know a lot about love, peace, joy, and success. It's the songwriter's job to feel the pulse of the people . . . to see what they want and then try to supply it for them." Although he is best known today for his hit records on Okeh and Atlantic, it was as a songwriter that Chuck Willis found his greatest personal success.

September 1953

SEP 4   Percy Mayfield plays the Labor Day weekend dance at the 5-4 Club in Los Angeles.

Willie Mabon, **Bull Moose Jackson**, and Varetta Dillard open for a week at Washington's Howard Theater.

The Apollo Theater presents Arthur Prysock and Bette McLaurin fronting Illinois Jacquet's Combo for the week.

SEP 6   The Ravens and the Joe Houston Combo perform at the Elks Ballroom in Los Angeles.

New releases for the first week of September include "Crying In The Chapel" by the Four Dukes on Duke; the Lamplighters' "Turn Me Loose" and Little Esther's "Cherry Wine," both on Federal; "Don't Make Me Love You" by Lulu Reed, "Oh Why?" by the Orchids, and "No More In My Life" by Bill Doggett, all on King; Savannah Churchill's "Shake A Hand" on Decca; "Perfect Woman" by the Four Blazes on United; and "They Call Me Big Mama" by Willie Mae Thornton on Peacock.

EARLY SEPTEMBER

RCA Victor's r&b chief, Danny Kessler, is in New Orleans on a talent hunt.

SEP 8   Louis Jordan makes a stopover at the Stateline Country Club at Lake Tahoe.

SEP 11   Ruth Brown and **Billy Eckstine** start a short, eight-day tour of the West Coast.

The revue at New York's Apollo Theater features the talents of the Clovers, Edna McGriff, and the Lucky Millinder Combo.

Louis Jordan stops for the weekend at Los Angeles' 5-4 Club.

SEP 14   Duke Ellington, Billy Ward and his Dominoes, and the Royals play a one-night stand at Detroit's Graystone Ballroom.

New releases for the second week of September include "Money Honey" by Clyde McPhatter and the Drifters and "The Tears Keep Tumbling Down" by Ruth Brown, both on Atlantic; "Rose Mary" by Fats Domino and "4-11-44" by **Bobby Mitchell and the Toppers**, both on Imperial; "I Had A Notion" by Joe Morris (with Al Savage) on Herald; "Sweet Talk" by Joe Morris (with Faye Adams) on Atlantic; "The Drunkard" by the Thrillers on Big Town; and "Blues With A Feeling" by Little Walter on Checker.

MID-SEPTEMBER

Earl Bostic is holding down a spot at the Capitol Lounge in Chicago.

With a nickname like "Bull Moose," one might expect the singer to bellow in a bass voice. In fact, Bull Moose Jackson's normal range was baritone, and the nickname referred to his physical size.

Billy Eckstine's bebop vocal style greatly influenced both Sarah Vaughan (who sang for a while with the Eckstine band) and Ella Fitzgerald. Although Eckstine's orchestra featured top jazz musicians, the leader often took the solo spotlight on trombone or trumpet.

Bobby Mitchell recorded for Imperial, both solo and with the Toppers, from 1953-63. He was born August 16, 1935, in Algiers, Louisiana. Several of his records were later turned into hits by other artists, including "I'm Gonna Be A Wheel Someday" (Fats Domino) and "You Always Hurt The One You Love" (Clarence "Frogman" Henry).

118

Also in the Windy City are the **Four Blazes** at the Club Bagdadat at the start of a national tour. A new nightspot, the Toast Of The Town, has opened and has scheduled the following entertainers for the remainder of the year: Arthur Prysock, T-Bone Walker, Wynonie Harris, B. B. King, Eddie Boyd, and Ivory Joe Hunter.

SEP 16   Louis Jordan and his combo start a two-week stand at the Sands Hotel in Las Vegas

SEP 18   The Orioles, Margie Day, T-Bone Walker, and the Paul Williams Orchestra open at the Howard Theater in Washington for the week.
          Fats Domino and his six-piece band wind up a West Coast tour with a three-day weekend performance at the 5-4 Ballroom in Los Angeles.
          Billy Ward and his Dominoes start a week's engagement at New York City's Apollo Theater. Also on the bill are Mabel Scott and the house band of Lucky Millinder.

SEP 20   The Ink Spots and Joe Liggins and his Honeydrippers play for the Sunday night dance at Los Angeles' Elks Ballroom, while across town, Billy Eckstine and Ruth Brown entertain at the Shrine Auditorium.

New releases for the third week of September include "Big Mouth" by Jimmy Nelson on RPM; "You'll Never Be Mine Again" by the Blenders on Jay-Dee; "Midnight Hours Journey" by Johnny Ace on Flair; the Orchids' "I've Been A Fool From The Start" and "Baby, Baby All The Time" by Amos Milburn, both on King; "The Real Thing" by the Spiders on Imperial; "Blue Skies" by the Four Friends on Brunswick; "You're A Fool" by Willie Mabon on Chess; and "Baby Come Back to Me" by the **Five Echoes** on Sabre.

SEP 25   The following artists are part of the Pittsburgh *Courier's* "Operation Music" show held at the Philadelphia Academy of Music: Ruth Brown, Billy Ward and his Dominoes, Dinah Washington, Joe Louis, **Billie Holiday**, the Ray-O-Vacs, and Buddy Johnson. The highlight of the evening is the presentation of the Bessie Smith Award, given by the Pittsburgh *Courier* to Ruth Brown as top blues singer. Proceeds from the show go to the NAACP legal fund.
          The Orioles with Margie Day and the Paul Williams Orchestra open for a week at the Royal Theater in Baltimore.

SEP 26   Ruth Brown headlines the "Tropicana Revue" at the Apollo Theater in New York for the week.
          While on the West Coast, Fats Domino renews his recording contract with Imperial Records for another nine years.
          Chuck Willis is the house guest of the Palace Theater in New Orleans for the evening.

SEP 27   The Elks Ballroom in Los Angeles hosts a "battle of the blues bands" with Jimmy Witherspoon, Pee Wee Crayton, Charles Brown, and Jimmy Wilson entertaining for the evening.

The Four Blazes faced an uphill battle over the spelling of the last name "Blazers." In fact, no r&b vocal group recorded using the name Four Blazers.

The Five Echoes also recorded for Vee Jay Records in 1955. The group featured Johnnie Taylor, who would go on to have a long soul career with hits on Stax Records (e.g., "Who's Making Love," 1968). In 1971, he had a number one record with "Disco Lady" on Columbia.

Billie Holiday (born Elenora Fagen, Baltimore, 1915) has been referred to as the "voice of jazz." Her vocals were a rare combination of emotional, heart-breaking blues and inspired jazz. Her popularity started slowly in the 1930s, and picked up steam into the 1950s until drugs took their toll. In 1959, "Lady Day" died in a New York hospital awaiting arrest for possession of narcotics.

New releases for the fourth week of September include "Please Hurry Home" by B. B. King on RPM; "Heartbreaker" by Ray Charles on Atlantic; "Hodge-Podge" by Bull Moose Jackson, "Ain't No Meat On De Bone" by Jack Dupree, and "Trust Me" by the Swallows all on King; Joe Liggins's "The Big Dipper" and Percy Mayfield's "How Deep Is The Well?," both on Specialty; Lil Son Jackson's "Confession" and Smiley Lewis's "Little Fernandez" both on Imperial; "Teardrops From My Eyes" by the Five Keys on Aladdin; and "Tiger Man" by Rufus Thomas, Jr. and "Take A Little Chance" by Jimmy DeBerry, both on Sun.

Jimmy DeBerry was one of the growing number of virtually unknown blues artists trekking to Memphis to record for Sun. He was one half of the duo Jimmy and Walter, and his guitar is featured on the flip side of their Sun release, "Easy."

SEP 29   Billy Ward and his Dominoes start an engagement at the Bandbox in New York.

SEP 30   Charles Brown and Johnny Moore's Three Blazers begin another tour of Texas and Louisiana, which will run through October 22nd.
Louis Jordan embarks on a tour of the West Coast and western Canada that will include stops in Los Angeles, Seattle, New York City, and Montreal.

THE TOP TEN ROCK 'N' ROLL RECORDS FOR SEPTEMBER 1953

1. Crying In The Chapel - The Orioles
2. Shake A Hand - Faye Adams
3. Good Lovin' - The Clovers
4. Too Much Lovin' - The "5" Royales
5. The Clock - Johnny Ace
6. Please Love Me - B. B. King
7. Please Don't Leave Me - Fats Domino
8. Don't Deceive Me - Chuck Willis
9. Get It - The Royals
10. One Scotch, One Bourbon, One Beer - Amos Milburn

September 1953
ARTIST OF THE MONTH

THE ORIOLES

In this history of the rise of rock 'n roll, the Orioles represent one of the last ties between the Black vocal groups of the 1940s as typified by the Ink Spots and the Mills Brothers, and the emerging vocal group sound of the 1950s as exemplified by the Dominoes and the Drifters.

The history of the Orioles is completely tied to the life of one man, Sonny Til. Born Earlington Tilghman in Baltimore on August 18, 1925, Sonny was not just another voice from the church environment common to most Black youths. Certainly, his parents both sang in church, but Sonny did not join them. He first started singing in high school, where he formed an acappella trio. Following school he was drafted and spent his time during World War II singing with the USO in the European War Theater. He returned to Baltimore in 1947 and won an amateur singing contest at the Avenue Cafe. This led to the formation of the Vibranaires (also spelled Vibra-Naires) with George Nelson (second

THE ORIOLES

tenor), Alexander Sharp (tenor), Johnny Reed (bass), and Tommy Gaither (guitar). Although their primary musical influence at this time was certainly the aforementioned Ink Spots and Mills Brothers, the Vibranaires sang ballads with a flavoring of the blues.

The group was discovered by a saleslady, Deborah Chessler, who became their business manager. It was Miss Chessler who arranged for the group to perform on the Arthur Godfrey "Talent Scouts" radio program, where they boys came in second place to blind pianist George Shearing. Godfrey invited the group to perform on his daytime program which gave them an enormous audience. Godfrey convinced the group to change their name, and they picked the Orioles, the state bird of Maryland. Soon after appearing with Godfrey, the Orioles received a recording contract from It's A Natural Records of New York, which released "It's Too Soon To Know" in July 1948. Almost immediately, the record company changed its name to Jubilee, and "It's Too Soon To Know" was re-released on the new label. Needless to say, the record became an enormous hit. The group's sound gave rise to a new form of scintilating vocal group harmony based primarily on the blues. The popularity of the group was so strong that many aspiring vocal groups changed their names to those of birds, leading to the Flamingos, the Robins, the Crows, the Wrens, the Larks, the Penguins, and the Ravens, among others.

Personnel changes within the group started almost immediately after their first hit. Gaither was killed in an automobile accident in 1950 that injured Reed and Nelson. He was replaced by Ralph Williams. Nelson quit the group in 1953 (and subsequently died in the 1960s), and was replaced by Gregory Carroll of the Four Buddies, who was in turn replaced by Charlie Hayes. In 1954 the group decided to disband, and Til hired the members of the Regents, forming a new group of Orioles. The personnel now included Albert "Diz" Russell, Paul Griffin, Billy Adams, and Jerry Rodriguez. In 1956 Sonny Til and the Orioles severed ties with Jubilee Records and moved on to record for Vee-Jay, but with no success. The second group of Orioles called it quits in 1957. Til continued to perform, hiring new groups of Orioles as they were needed, and as late as 1981 the latest reincarnation of the group released yet another album before Til's untimely death in 1983.

The biggest commercial success for the Orioles came in 1953 with "Crying In The Chapel," the group's thirty-third release for Jubilee. The song was originally a country and western number with spiritual overtones, and in an odd reverse twist on the many cover versions of rhythm and blues tunes that would dominate the charts for the next few years, the Orioles' version crossed over into the "pop" charts on its own merit. The recording features Til's breathy baritone floating above a tight-knit group harmony, the trademark of the group's sound.

On stage, Sonny Til and the Orioles presented a high-powered performance. Til's emotional vocalizing sold each song in a fervent manner and elicited wild excitement from the crowd. The group used exaggerated stage movements, turns and spins, which made them a natural drawing card for the theater tours. The group's sound had a solid rhythm base whether for the slow plaintive ballads or the fast rhythm numbers. Their songs featured intricate arrangements highlighting Til's fine tenor. Female teen-agers swooned and screamed at each dramatic show as the Orioles built their portion of the revue to a sensual climax. Indeed, many music historians credit the Orioles with being the first true rhythm and blues vocal group.

As mentioned, the Orioles were one of the last ties to early rhythm and blues. Within two years, the business would change rapidly. Unable, or unwilling, to change their style, the group's fans moved on to idolize newer artists. Looking back, the Orioles' legacy rests on their biggest hit, "Crying In The Chapel." So great was its impact on both its own time, as well as on the future of the vocal group sound, that the Orioles' version of the song, alone among the dozens that were released in 1953, remains as a reminder of that time.

October 1953

OCT 1   The Clovers, Rosco Gordon, Little Esther, and Chuck Willis set off on a fifteen-day tour of the South.

OCT 2   Louis Jordan opens at the 5-4 Club in Los Angeles for a three-day weekend.

Ruth Brown stars at the Howard Theater in Washington in a revue titled "Atlantic City Follies."

Lloyd Price headlines the revue at New York's Apollo Theater for the week. Also on the bill is Annisteen Allen.

OCT 3   In a press conference in Washington, Ruth Brown announces that she is launching a movement to eliminate **substandard housing** and restaurants regularly provided for Black entertainers who appear on the many one-nighter and theater circuits.

Lowell Fulson plays the Club Paradise in Biloxi, Mississippi, as part of his one-nighter tour.

OCT 4   Tiny Bradshaw entertains the dancers at the Elks Ballroom in Los Angeles.

New releases for the first week of October include "T.V. Is The Thing" by Dinah Washington and "Rough Ridin'" by the Ravens, both on Mercury; "In The Mission Of St. Augustine" by the Orioles on Jubilee; "Get On My Train" by the Lovenotes on Imperial; "I'm Not The One You Love" by the Crickets on Jay-Dee; and "Mr. Sandman" by the **Chordettes** on Cadence.

EARLY OCTOBER

Danny Kessler, r&b chief for RCA Victor, returns to New York with recordings by the Robins and the Jackson Brothers. In addition, during his trip to New Orleans he has signed **Sonny Terry**, Square Walton, and Sam Butters to the label.

Chauncy Westbrook, guitarist with the Orioles, is arrested in Baltimore for possession of marijuana.

OCT 9   The 5-4 Club in Los Angeles hosts Little Willie Littlefield for three days.

Edna McGriff makes a three-day stop at New Orleans' Dew Drop Inn.

Savannah Churchill starts a two-week stand at the Flame Show Bar in Detroit.

Ruth Brown opens for a week at the Royal Theater in Baltimore.

Clyde McPhatter and the Drifters, blind jazz pianist George Shearing, and Lucky Millinder's band are at the Apollo Theater

Working conditions for Black performers in the early 1950s were dismal. Small, dingy hotel rooms that were little better than flophouses were the norm. In northern cities, theater and nightclub owners provided such accommodations for performers in an attempt to cut every financial corner possible. On the southern nightclub circuits, conditions were, if anything, even worse.

The Chordettes (the lineup for their hits was Margie Needham, Lynn Evans, Janet Ertel and Carol Bushman) got together in Sheboygan, Wisconsin. They were discovered on Arthur Godfrey's "Talent Scouts" TV show.

Sonny Terry (born Saunders Terrell in 1911 in Greensboro, Georgia) was blind since early childhood. He learned to play the harmonica, and teamed with guitarist Brownie McGhee in the 1930s. Forty years later, at the end of their relationship, they had become bitter enemies. In the 1980s, Terrell appeared in the movies "Crossroads" and "The Color Purple." He died on March 3, 1986.

for the week in New York.

OCT 10   Joe Turner starts a six-week string of one-nighters through Texas. Following this tour, he will work the Louisiana-Mississippi area into January.

OCT 11   Fats Domino makes his New York debut at the Audubon Ballroom.
Sonny Thompson and Lulu Reed entertain at the Elks Ballroom in Los Angeles.

OCT 12   The "5" Royales, Willie Mabon, and the Flamingos join the big band of Woody Herman at the Graystone Ballroom in Detroit for a one-nighter.

New releases for the second week of October include "Too Much Boogie" by John Lee Hooker on Modern; "Every Day Of The Week" by Christine Kittrell on Republic; "Down At Hayden's" by the Hunters and "I'm Still In Love With You" by **Richard Berry**, both on Flair; Sonny Thompson's "My Heart Needs Someone" and Little Tommy Brown's "'Fore Day Train," both on King; Red Prysock's "Hey! There" on Mercury; "No Blow, No Show" by Bobby "Blue" Bland on Duke; "The White Cliffs Of Dover" by the Blue Jays on Checker; and "Rock Me Baby" by Johnny Otis on Peacock.

OCT 13   Al Hibbler opens for three weeks at Chicago's Toast Of The Town.

MID-OCTOBER

Recent record company signings include **Tommy Ridgely** and Professor Longhair, both from New Orleans, with Atlantic, and the Wanderers and Babs Gonzales with Savoy.

Atlantic Records and Herald Records are feuding over the talents of Faye Adams. Atlantic claims Herald has no right to issue her records since she was under contract to Atlantic using her given name, Fay Scruggs. Herald claims that Atlantic's release of "Sweet Talk" was only meant to capitalize on Herald's success with "Shake A Hand."

OCT 16   Wynonie Harris and Varetta Dillard open at the Apollo in New York for the week.
Mabel Scott and Arthur Prysock are at the Regal Theater in Chicago this week.
Marvin Phillips and the Flairs start a three-day engagement at the 5-4 Ballroom in Los Angeles.
The new show at the Howard Theater in Washington this week features Joe Morris and his orchestra with Faye Adams and Al Savage.
In New Orleans, Ivory Joe Hunter spends the three-day weekend at the Dew Drop Inn.

OCT 17   For the first time in ten months, there is no "answer" record on the r&b charts. This craze started with answers to "I Don't Know" by Willie Mabon, which was released in November 1952.

Richard Berry was born in New Orleans in 1935, but his family relocated in Los Angeles during his childhood. His career is intertwined with several of the West Coast's most notable r&b groups, including the Robins and Flairs.

After several hits in his home of New Orleans for Imperial in 1949-50, Tommy Ridgely moved on to Atlantic in 1953. He played piano for Dave Bartholomew's band on "Jam Up," a pounding instrumental in 1954.

124

OCT 18　　Amos Milburn, Ruth Brown, Fats Domino, Margie Day, and the Paul Williams Band make a one-night stand at the Laurel Gardens in Newark, New Jersey.

　　　　　Charles Brown with Johnny Moore's Three Blazers play for the evening's entertainment at the Labor Union Hall in New Orleans.

OCT 19　　B. B. King, Billy Harvey, and Gladys Hill appear at the Texas State Fair, Dallas.

New releases for the third week of October include "Swing Train" by Lynn Hope and "Cryin' And Driftin' Blues" by Charles Brown, both on Aladdin; "Without A Song" by the Ravens on Mercury; Rosco Gordon's "Ain't No Use" on Duke; Little Hudson's "Rough Treatment" on J.O.B.; "Time For Lovin' To Be Done" by Eddie Kirkland on King; "Jukebox Cannonball" by Bill Haley and his Comets on Essex; **"Golden Teardrops" by the Flamingos** on Chance; and "Overboard" by Sugar Boy on Checker.

"Golden Teardrops" was the biggest-selling record for the Flamingos while they remained at Chance Records (1953-54). The group moved on to Parrot in 1955, and Checker Records in 1956. Here they had another hit with "I'll Be Home."

OCT 22　　Bill Kenney and the Ink Spots are at the Saville Theater in Montreal.

　　　　　Savannah Churchill plays the Farmdell Club in Cleveland.

OCT 23　　Johnny Ace makes his New York debut on the stage of the Apollo Theater for the week. Also on the bill are Willie Mae Thornton, **Little Junior Parker** and the Tab Smith combo.

　　　　　Ruth Brown joins the Five Keys and the Woody Herman band on a ten-day tour of the Midwest.

　　　　　Ray Charles is booked for three days in the New Orleans area.

　　　　　Sugar Ray Robinson, Billy Ward and his Dominoes, T-Bone Walker, and Count Basie's Orchestra play the Baltimore Coliseum. Other dates for this tour include the Mosque in Richmond (27), the Vet in Philadelphia (28), and Uline Arena in Washington (November 1st).

　　　　　The Royal Theater in Baltimore plays host to Faye Adams and the Joe Morris Orchestra for the week.

Herman "Little Junior" Parker was born in West Memphis in 1927. His harmonica stylings were greatly influenced by Sonny Boy Williamson, and he eventually accompanied Williamson on the tour circuit.

OCT 25　　Roy Milton plays the Sunday night dance at the Elks Ballroom in Los Angeles.

New releases for the fourth week of October include "All Righty!" by the "5" Royales on Apollo; "Peace Of Mind" by Savannah Churchill, "Snatchin' It Back" by Margie Day, and "I Want You To Be My Baby" by Louis Jordan, all on Decca; "Daddy Was A Rolling Stone" by Otis Blackwell on Jay-Dee; "Hey Miss Fine" by the Royals on Federal; "We Could Find Happiness" by the Wanderers on Savoy; "Chains Of Love Have Disappeared" by Little Caesar on RPM; "Mad Love" by Muddy Waters on Chess; "Ten Days In Jail" by the Robins on Victor; "Runaround" by the **Three Chuckles** on "X"; "Whistle My Love" by the Moonglows on Chance; and "The Bells Ring Out" by the Spaniels on Vee-Jay.

The Three Chuckles featured Teddy Randazzo on accordion. Their recording of "Runaround" was first issued on Detroit's Boulevard label. It took more than a year before it caught the public's fancy and entered the "pop" charts.

OCT 30　　The Tempo Toppers featuring Little Richard are appearing for two days in Oklahoma City.

　　　　　Jimmy Wilson and Linda Hayes play the weekend at the 5-4 Ballroom in Los Angeles.

OCT 31   Mabel Scott makes a stopover at Detroit's Flame Show Bar for a week.

LATE OCTOBER

In another story on Chance, J.O.B., a former subsidiary of Chance, has been taken over by Joe Brown.

Duke Records signs **Joseph "Mr. Google Eyes" August**, who bills himself as Seattle's only blues singer.

Joseph Augustus was born in New Orleans in 1931. His first record, for the Coleman label of Newark, billed him as the world's youngest blues singer - he was only fifteen at the time. By 1953 he had already recorded for Okeh, Columbia, Lee, and Domino. By 1960, he had earned and spent a small fortune, lived in Newark and Seattle, and returned home to New Orleans.

The Charms' recording of "Heaven Only Knows" is transferred from Rockin' Records to DeLuxe Records. Both companies are owned by Cincinnati's major independent label, King Records.

Johnny Otis and his Orchestra with Marie Adams are currently on tour.

Lee Magdid leaves Savoy Records to start his own label, Central Records. First talent signed with the new company includes Emmett Hobson, Georgia Lane, and the Ray-O-Vacs.

Brothers Leonard and Phil Chess started Aristocrat Records in 1947, and had an early hit with recordings by Muddy Waters. In 1950, they started their Chess label, which became one of the foremost companies in the blues and r&b fields.

Leonard Chess of **Chess Records** is presently on a trip to New Orleans, Atlanta, and Nashville in search of new talent.

THE TOP TEN ROCK 'N' ROLL RECORDS FOR OCTOBER 1953

1. Shake A Hand - Faye Adams
2. Good Lovin' - The Clovers
3. Crying In The Chapel - The Orioles
4. One Scotch, One Bourbon, One Beer - Amos Milburn
5. Too Much Lovin' - The "5" Royales
6. Feelin' Good - Little Junior's Blue Flames
7. T.V. Is The Thing - Dinah Washington
8. Blues With A Feeling - Little Walter
9. Don't Deceive Me - Chuck Willis
10. Please Hurry Home - B. B. King

October 1953
ARTIST OF THE MONTH

FAYE ADAMS
(Fay Scruggs)

FAYE ADAMS

Determination paid off for New Yorker Fay Scruggs. For years she haunted the corridors of the office buildings housing the many small record companies and song publishers in New York City, finding little solace in her quest to be heard by anyone who might lead to a recording contract. Then lightning struck. As she auditioned for promoter Phil Moore in his Carnegie Hall office, three voice teachers dropped by to listen, then to applaud this brash young girl with the superb voice. Moore immediately became Fay's manager and later, after some consternation on Fay's part, changed her name to the more theatrical "Faye Adams," with which she became nationally famous. Such is the stuff of legends.

You see, this audition with Moore was not really happenstance at all. It was her determination again that provided the path to Moore. Miss Adams worked very hard as a singer, taking any job, no matter how small, in order to be on stage. In a small club in Atlanta she was finally noticed by Ruth Brown, who dropped by after one of her own performances with Count Basie and Billy Eckstine. It was Miss Brown's encouragement, not to mention connections, which led eventually to Moore.

But once the connection had been made, Moore did not hesitate. He introduced Miss Scruggs to Joe Morris, popular rhythm and blues bandleader, who at this time was the backbone for Atlantic Records' recording operation, as well as leading his very successful touring company known as the "Joe Morris Blues Cavalcade." Morris was one of the first artists to record for Atlantic, and his subsequent successes had mostly been with female vocalists fronting his band. When his long time vocalist, Laurie Tate, left the band, he hired Fay Scruggs as a replacement. Together they had only one session with Atlantic. Morris felt he had the perfect song for Fay to record. They even spent time rehearsing it, but before a session could be scheduled Morris left Atlantic and signed with another independent company, Herald Records. The first release by the Morris band was the delayed "Shake A Hand," featuring the newly renamed Faye Adams on vocal. Just as Morris had predicted, the song was an immediate hit.

The record streaked to the number one spot on the rhythm and blues charts in the fall of 1953, and it was followed by two more chart toppers during the next twelve months, "I'll Be True" and "Hurts Me To My Heart." By this time Miss Adams had left Morris's band and struck out on her own. She eventually recorded thirty songs for Herald before leaving in 1957 to join, first, Imperial (where she renewed her friendship with Joe Morris), then in quick succession, Lido, Warwick, Savoy, and Prestige. By 1963 she had retired from the music scene to lead the comparatively normal life of a housewife.

The years of dreaming had paid off for Faye Adams in her stage presence. Although one reviewer mentioned that she was "plain-looking," it was her voice that sold records and tickets. Her vocalizing was clean and the lyrics were clear enough to be heard easily over the brass of Morris's combo. But, she had a "free-wheeling set of pipes," and her full-bodied contralto voice was used with gospel sincerity. She often slurred between notes, creating a stimulating sound. One reason for her short time in the limelight as a recording artist can be found in the technique used on all of her hits: she sang duet with another vocalist, either Morris or Al Savage, thereby diluting the impact of hearing her sing solo.

During her remarkable first year of popularity (in her entire career, she only had those three charted singles, and all three topped the r&b charts!), she was billed as "Atomic Adams," a tribute to her showmanship on stage. But she possessed a voice in the same vein as her mentor, Ruth Brown, and this was her undoing. Ruth Brown's career had started in 1949; and she was, first of all, the foremost woman rhythm and blues singer. Secondly, Ruth Brown's popularity brought her the first choice of top songs to record. Faye Adams seemed to be destined to play the role of "catch up."

In a career field dominated by men, Faye Adams took a courageous step. And, if only for a short time, she succeeded far beyond the dreams of Fay Scruggs.

November 1953

NOV 1   Closing out their short tour, Ruth Brown, the Five Keys, and Woody Herman appear in Indianapolis.

NOV 2   The Orioles are booked into Kansas City's Orchid Room for one week.
Ruth Brown, Charles Brown, and Buddy Johnson's Orchestra open for three days at the Flame Show Bar in Detroit. During this engagement Miss Brown collapses from exhaustion and has to be hospitalized for three weeks in Washington.

New releases for the first week of November include "Rags To Riches" by Billy Ward and his Dominoes and "White Cliffs Of Dover," by the Checkers both on King; "The Feeling Is So Good" by the Clovers on Atlantic; **Sonny Knight**'s "Dear Wonderful God" and the Ebonaires' "Baby You're The One," both on Aladdin; the Barons' "Exactly Like You" on Decca; "Marie" by the Four Tunes on Jubilee; and "I'm Gonna Cross That River" by Tommy Ridgely on Atlantic.

NOV 3   The Royals are at the Trocaveria Club in Columbus, Ohio.

NOV 4   Chuck Willis joins Milt Buckner for a series of one-nighters.

NOV 6   Charles Brown and Johnny Moore's Three Blazers with Lucky Millinder's Orchestra headline the week-long show at the Howard Theater in Washington.
Tiny Bradshaw brings his orchestra to the 5-4 Ballroom in Los Angeles for the weekend.
Arthur Prysock starts a week-long engagement at Detroit's Flame Show Bar.

NOV 7   Louis Jordan is currently entertaining at the Cafe Society in New York.

EARLY NOVEMBER

Sonny Wilson, performing with Billy Ward and his Dominoes on tour with Sugar Ray Robinson, collapses during a show in Charlotte, North Carolina. He is rushed back to his hometown of Detroit for major surgery.

Amos Milburn disbands his combo, billed as the Aladdin Chickenshackers, and will appear as a solo act performing with someone else's combo in theaters and on tour.

Roy Hamilton from Jersey City signs a recording contract with Okeh, a subsidiary of Columbia Records. However, he is switched to a "pop" division of Columbia, Epic records, prior to his first release.

Sonny Knight (born Joseph C. Smith) had only two hits, which came eight years apart: "Confidential," first released on Vita in 1956 (but soon picked up by Dot), and "If You Want This Love Of Mine" on Aura in 1964. He has written a novelized expose' of the music business titled The Day The Music Died, and currently he is a successful nightclub entertainer in Hawaii.

Sonny Wilson later achieved enormous fame recording under the name Jackie Wilson. He was first discovered by Johnny Otis at a 1951 talent show in his hometown of Detroit (born June 9, 1936.)

Otis Blackwell appears at the Northeast Ballroom in Washington.

Cozy Cole, jazz drummer, is putting together a new combo to be called the All Stars.

Monte Bruce starts Bruce Records in New York.

The Treniers start a one-month layover at the Club Society in New York.

New releases for the second week of November include "Don't Pass Me By" by the Du Droppers, "Hootin' And Jumpin'" by Sonny Terry, and "Gimmie Your Bankroll" by Square Walton, all on Victor; "Be Bop Wino" by the Lamplighters and "3-D" by Big Jay McNeeley, both on Federal; T-Bone Walker's "I'm About To Lose My Mind" and Little Son Jackson's "Little Girl," both on Imperial; Roy Brown's "Caldonia's Wedding Day," Billy Ward and his Dominoes' "Christmas In Heaven," and Wynonie Harris's "Please Louise," all on King; Stomp Gordon's "What's Her Whimsey, Dr. Kinsey" and Buddy and Ella Johnson's "I'm Just Your Fool," both on Mercury; Lightnin' Hopkins's "Lightnin' Jump" on TNT; and **Little Esther**'s "Stop Cryin'" on Decca.

NOV 13   Joe Morris's Combo with Faye Adams, the Orioles, and Mr. Stringbean appears in Little Rock. The group is booked through to Christmas week on a tour of the South, Texas, Florida, and the East Coast.
In New York, the Five Keys headline the revue at the Apollo Theater for the week.

NOV 14   Guitar Slim is welcomed for one night at the New Orleans' Caffin Theater. In nearby Kenner, Louisiana, Tommy Ridgely appears at Ruby's Inn.

NOV 15   The "Rhapsodies Of '54" tour featuring Billy Ward and his Dominoes and **Count Basie** plays one show at the Booker T. Washington Auditorium in New Orleans.

MID-NOVEMBER

The "new" Ink Spots featuring Charlie Fuqua report that they are booked solid for the next year. The group recently signed a recording deal with King Records.

Lynn Hope is currently at Gleason's in Cleveland following a one-night stand at that city's Paradise Ballroom.

Tab Smith opens at Philadelphia's Pep's Musical Bar, where he will alternate with a nightly deejay show, Jocko Henderson's "Song Train" on WDAS.

Fats Domino is currently playing at the Showboat in Philadelphia.

Johnny Otis signs with Peacock Records as recording artist. He has previously been active with the label as an arranger and songwriter. He has recorded under his own name most recently for Mercury.

William Randolph "Cozy" Cole played drums with many of the biggest names in jazz in the 1940s, including Cab Calloway, Coleman Hawkins, Dizzy Gillespie, and Louis Armstrong. On his own, he had a major instrumental hit with "Topsy, Part 2" on Love Records in 1958.

Little Esther's move from Federal to Decca did not enhance her career. By 1955 she had retired from show business, but in 1962, she was back, recording for Lennox Records where she had her biggest hit, "Release Me." Esther Phillips died August 7, 1984.

Pianist William "Count" Basie was born in 1904 in Red Bank, New Jersey. By 1935, he was leading one of Kansas City's hottest orchestras. In 1937 he hired Billie Holiday as his vocalist, but by the time the band took New York by storm (1938-39), she had moved on.

While previously working with Peacock Records, Johnny Otis arranged and conducted his band on sessions for Willie Mae Thornton and Little Richard, among others.

Starmaker Records, affiliated with WDIA radio in Memphis, is another new label on the scene. Recent releases have been by Danny Day and Moohah.

Jules Bihari announces that he is starting a new label, Crown Records, in Los Angeles. New artists will include saxophonist Joe Houston.

New releases for the third week of November include "Blind Love" by B. B. King and "Mean Poor Girl" by Jimmy Nelson, both on RPM; Eddie Boyd's "Tortured Soul" on Chess; Floyd Dixon's "Hole In The Wall" on Specialty; the Swallows' "It Feels So Good" on King; Little Caesar's "What Kind Of Fool Is He?" on Big Town; **Memphis Minnie's** "Kissing In The Dark" on J.O.B.; "Tell Me You Love Me" by the Flairs on Flair; and "L'amour Tjour L'amour" by the Four Tunes on Jubilee.

NOV 17   Louis Jordan holds forth at Birdland in New York for two weeks.

NOV 18   The Orioles, Faye Adams, and Joe Morris' Combo play Atlanta.

NOV 20   **Gene Ammons**, the Ebonaires and the TNT Tribble Combo start a week at the Howard Theater in Washington.
Al Hibbler opens his two-week stay at the Flame Show Bar in Detroit.
In New York, Lucky Millinder's Combo, normally assigned duty as the house band at the Apollo Theater, is this week's headline attraction, sharing the bill with Sugar Chile Robinson.

NOV 22   Roy Milton headlines a "Battle Of The Blues" featuring Pee Wee Crayton and Lil Greenwood at New Orleans' Labor Union Hall.

NOV 23   Dinah Washington travels to the Cafe Society in New York for a week.

New releases for the fourth week of November include the Platters' "Give Thanks" and Jimmy Witherspoon's "Move Me, Baby," both on Federal; "Dealing' From The Bottom" by Stick McGhee on King; "Strange Love" by Charles Brown with Johnny Moore's Three Blazers on Recorded In Hollywood; "The Letter" by Rudy Greene on Chance; and Tampa Red's "So Crazy 'Bout You Baby" on Victor.

NOV 24   The Five Keys and Chuck Willis join Milt Buckner for another series of one-night stands along the Eastern seaboard.
Recovered after a three-week hospital stay for exhaustion, Ruth Brown joins Margie Day and Paul Williams and his orchestra for a week-long tour through the Midwest and the South. After this tour she plans to rest at home for six weeks.

NOV 25   Johnny Otis and Marie Adams play a five-day engagement at the 5-4 Ballroom in Los Angeles. They return for another three days the following weekend.

NOV 27   Louis Jordan opens at the Uptown Theater in Philadelphia for a week.

Memphis Minnie (born Lizzie Douglas in 1897) has been referred to as the all-time greatest female blues singer. She moved from New Orleans to Memphis' Beale Street bistros in the 1920s. A decade later, she had already recorded for most of the major recording companies: Victor, Okeh, Decca, Bluebird, and Vocallion.

Gene Ammons was born and died in Chicago (1925-1974). With his tenor sax, he turned pro in 1943 and toured until 1947 with the Billy Eckstine Orchestra.

Ella Fitzgerald, born in 1918, broke into music as a teen-ager by winning the amateur contest at the Apollo Theater. She won her first <u>Down Beat</u> poll as top female jazz vocalist at age nineteen. As a vocalist, her styling falls between the raw emotion of Billie Holiday and the playful inventiveness of Sarah Vaughan.

Marvin Phillips and Johnny Dean had their biggest hit with "Tick Tock" for Modern in 1954, although today it is the flip-side of that record, "Cherry Pie," which is still played as an "oldie."

Ella Fitzgerald and the Wanderers headline the revue at New York's Apollo Theater this week.

NOV 28   Billy Ward and his Dominoes, Count Basie, and Sugar Ray Robinson are scheduled to perform for a benefit Thanksgiving Music Festival in Quincy, Illinois. The two shows are scheduled for 8:00 and 10:00 p.m., but the Dominoes show up at 10:30 p.m. Ward is furious when the promoter withholds their share, and inexplicably he pulls a gun on Robinson. He calms down before events can lead to tragedy.

B. B. King and Willie Mae Thornton play a Thanksgiving dance in Houston.

In Meridian, Mississippi, the Thanksgiving dance features Little Richard, the Tempo Toppers, and Raymond Taylor's Duce of Rhythm.

New releases for the fifth week of November include "I'll Be True" by Faye Adams with the Joe Morris Orchestra on Herald; "Something's Wrong" by Fats Domino on Imperial; Varetta Dillard's "I Ain't Gonna Tell" on Savoy; "Baby Doll" by **Marvin and Johnny** on Specialty; "Lollipop" by Oscar McLollie and Joe Houston's "Blowin' Crazy," both on Modern; and the Shadows' "Don't Be Bashful" on Decca.

LATE NOVEMBER

The Griffin Brothers are booked on a tour of West Virginia.

Nellie Lutcher is appearing at the Crown Propeller Lounge in Chicago, where Muddy Waters and Rudy Greene appear on alternate nights as her co-performers.

THE TOP TEN ROCK 'N' ROLL RECORDS FOR NOVEMBER 1953

1. Money Honey - Clyde McPhatter and the Drifters
2. Shake A Hand - Faye Adams
3. Honey Hush - Joe Turner
4. One Scotch, One Bourbon, One Beer - Amos Milburn
5. T.V. Is The Thing - Dinah Washington
6. I Had A Notion - Joe Morris with Al Savage
7. Good Lovin' - The Clovers
8. Blues With A Feeling - Little Walter
9. Drunk - Jimmy Liggins
10. Feelin' Good - Little Junior's Blue Flames

CLYDE MCPHATTER AND THE DRIFTERS
(McPhatter b. November 15, 1933; d. June 13, 1972)

CLYDE McPHATTER

Clyde Lensley McPhatter was yet another "son of a preacher man," but he was much, much more. His singing style was so unique that his voice could easily be distinguished from the other members of the two vocal groups with which he was so closely associated.

Born in Durham, North Carolina, to a Baptist minister's wife, Clyde was steeped in gospel music from the time of his birth, through a subsequent move to the New York City area when he was twelve, to his joining the Mount Lebanon Singers at the age of fourteen. By the time he reached seventeen he had come under the eye of Billy Ward, who hired him as lead tenor for his new rhythm and blues group, the Dominoes. He sang lead on several of the Dominoes' biggest sellers, including "Have Mercy, Baby," "The Bells," and their first hit, "Do Something For Me." Early in his career, he was even billed as Clyde Ward, in an attempt to pass him off as Ward's brother, possibly because of his age.

By 1953 the relationship between the two men had soured, and McPhatter left the group or was fired, depending on which story is to be believed. He was determined to form another group that would more closely mirror his own perceptions of what a rhythm and blues vocal group should be. The result was the Drifters.

In May 1953 Atlantic Records first approached McPhatter with the idea of forming the new group. McPhatter created the first group of Drifters using former friends from the Mount Lebanon Singers. The first recording session, on June 29, 1953, was totally unsuccessful and there were no immediate releases of the songs recorded. At the insistence of Atlantic, McPhatter fired all of the members and set about creating another set of Drifters. This time, those hired represented the best available talent: Bill Pinkney (tenor and bass), formerly with the Jerusalem Stars; and Andrew "Bubba" Thrasher (second tenor and baritone) and Gerhart "Gay" Thrasher (baritone and tenor), both from another gospel group, the Thrasher Wonders. Finally, Willie Ferbie (bass) and Walter Adams (guitar) rounded out the new group. Adams, however, died soon after the group's formation and was replaced by Jimmy Oliver. Ferbie also did not last long, as he became ill following their first recording session and was forced to drop out of the group.

Then there was McPhatter, leader of the group, lead tenor on virtually all of the records made for the next year and a half, and the "sound" of the Drifters. He possessed an almost soprano vocal range and this, coupled with his intense, emotional delivery, quickly set the Drifters a notch above most other rhythm and blues recording groups. The boyish quality in his vocals allowed him to sing lyrics that were quite risque for the time with a sense of innocence. "Money Honey," which hit the stores in October 1953, set the style for the early Drifters recordings. Singing the story of money for love, the song could have very easily have become an anthem for prostitution. In McPhatter's delivery it is playful and full of wonder. The same is true of "Such A Night" and "Honey Love." The group even had the temerity to jazz up their rendition of the classic yuletide opus, "White Christmas." And each record released by the group was a smash.

McPhatter, was drafted into the U.S. Army in May 1954. So recognizable was his contribution to the Drifter's sound, that the group struggled without him. Four singles featuring McPhatter were released while he was in the Army, even though he had not recorded with the group since shortly after entering the service. McPhatter's place on stage was first taken by David Baughn, who had been a member of the original group of hitless Drifters, and whose voice was uncannily close to McPhatter's. However, audiences quickly caught on to the deception, and by the fall of 1954 the Drifters had become another, routine act. One reviewer noted in March 1955 that the Drifters were the poorest r&b group in months, offering a "tasteless group of numbers," which Baughn presented in a "hyper-gimmicked delivery." After his only session with the Drifters, in April 1955, from which no singles were released for six years, Baughn was replaced by Johnny Moore (not the leader of the Three Blazers but a former member of the Hornets), and he led the Drifters on their next few hits, "Adorable" in late 1955, "Ruby Baby" in the spring of 1956, and "Fools Fall In Love" a year later. Bobby Hendricks took the helm for "Drip Drop" in the fall of 1958 before the group finally closed shop. At this time the Drifters consisted of Moore, Gerhart Thrasher, Charlie Hughes (baritone) and Tommy Evans (bass). Pinkney had left to record for Phillips International Records in Memphis.

In person, the Drifters with McPhatter were frantic. His vocals were polished, and the group's stage movements were a definite lure for the teenage females who frequently showered the group with wolf whistles. Emotion was the basis for the act, and McPhatter oozed with emotion. Without him they floundered.

McPhatter continued his career as a solo artist after his return to civilian life, and the Drifters were reincarnated several times again using more than thirty vocalists and five guitarists in all throughout the years. The Drifters remain with Atlantic to this day, having issued over a hundred recordings.

(More about both McPhatter and the Drifters in future volumes of *The Golden Age Of American Rock 'N Roll*.)

December 1953

DEC 2   Johnny Ace, Willie Mae Thornton, and Little Junior's Blue Flames play Hattiesburg, Mississippi, as the first date on their current one-nighter tour.

DEC 4   In Los Angeles, the **Robins** headline an extended engagement of the "Sugar Hill Revue" at the Club Oasis.

       Buddy Johnson and his Orchestra with Ella Johnson and Clyde McPhatter and the Drifters headline the show at New York's Apollo Theater.

       Bull Moose Jackson starts a three-week engagement at the Flame Show Bar In Detroit.

       The Orioles are booked into Washington's Howard Theater for a week.

New releases for the first week of December include the Harptones' "Sunday Kind Of Love" on Bruce; "Just Can't Stay" by Willie Nix on Sabre, "I Ain't No Fool Either" by Willie Mae Thornton on Peacock; "Mystery Train" by Little Junior's Blue Flames on Sun; "The Joe Louis Story Theme" by **Maxwell Davis** on Aladdin; and "My Gal Is Gone" by the Five Blue Notes on Sabre.

DEC 7   The Clovers and Tiny Bradshaw's Combo play a one-night stand at the Graystone Ballroom in Detroit.

EARLY DECEMBER

Amos Milburn joins Charles Brown and Choker Campbell on a tour of the South that is booked through January.

The Bandbox Club in New York switches from r&b and jazz to Latin music with a series of mambo orchestras and acts, giving in to an increasing new fad in music.

Fats Domino continues to play to full houses on his current tour of the South.

DEC 11   The Ravens start the first of four weekend dates at the 5-4 Ballroom in Los Angeles. Thurston Harris and the Lamplighters join the Ravens for the opening weekend.

DEC 14   Ruth Brown holds court during her week-long engagement at Gleason's in Cleveland.

New releases for the second week of December include "Good Good Whiskey" by Amos Milburn and "Oh Babe" by the Five Keys, both on Aladdin; "You're Still My Baby" by Chuck Willis on Okeh; Mercy Dee's "Get To Gettin'" and Guitar Slim's "The Things That I Used To Do,"

Just like the Flairs, their cross-town rival in Los Angeles, the Robins lasted a long time (from 1949-58) and had many members over the years. The group temporarily disbanded in 1955, and original members - Carl Gardner and Bobby Nunn - formed the Coasters.

Maxwell Davis excelled on the saxophone. From 1948 to 1954 he worked behind the scenes at Aladdin Records as a talent scout and record producer, later moving on to Federal, Modern, and Capitol.

Clarence Garlow was born in Welsh, Louisiana, February 27, 1911, and he died in Beaumont, Texas, July 24, 1986. He could play accordion at an early age, but switched to guitar after hearing T-Bone Walker. His "Bon Ton Roula" on Macy's Records (a small Houston label) in 1950 was important in establishing a market for zydeco music. He recorded for Aladdin, Goldband, and Flair, among other labels.

Gatemouth Brown was weaned on Texas swing and big band jazz before he played the blues, which accounts for his unique style. His sphere of influence on upcoming artists was within the confines of Louisiana and Texas, an area he seldom left.

Joe Turner's "TV Mama" features the slashing slide guitar of Elmore James. Although James never achieved widespread popularity, he recorded for several independent labels including Flair, Checker, and Vee Jay.

both on Specialty; "Cool Cool Baby" by the Magic-Tones on King; "Route 90" by **Clarence "Bon Ton" Garlow** and "Strange Kinda' Feeling" by Elmore James, both on Flair; "Love Me Baby" by Bernie Hardison on Excello; "Oo-wee Mr. Jeff" by Georgia Lane on Central; "Gate Walks To Board" by Clarence 'Gatemouth' Brown on Peacock; "I Know" by the Prisonaires on Sun; "Hey Santa Claus" by the Moonglows on Chance; Country Slim's "What Wrong Have I Done" on Recorded In Hollywood; and Willie John's "Mama, What Happened To Our Christmas Tree" on Prize.

MID-DECEMBER

Alan "Moondog" Freed is currently being heard over WNJR in Newark, New Jersey, via tape recording. The station recently switched to eighteen hours of r&b and jazz air-time per day.

Ahmet Ertegun and Jerry Wexler of Atlantic Records are back in New Orleans recording both new and established artists.

Gatemouth Brown and the Al Grey combo are currently touring Florida.

DEC 18   Percy Mayfield joins the Ravens at the 5-4 Ballroom in Los Angeles for the weekend.

DEC 21   Fats Domino starts a tour of Texas with the Clovers, who are just off a two-week vacation.

New releases for the third week of December include Johnny Ace's "Saving My Love For You" and Joseph "Mr. Google Eyes" August's "O What A Fool," both on Duke; **Joe Turner's "TV Mama"** and the Diamonds "Romance In The Dark," both on Atlantic; "That's It" by the Royals and "Until The Real Thing Comes Along" by Billy Ward and his Dominoes, both on Federal; the Hornets' "Lonesome Baby" on States; "I Got To Go" by Willie Mabon on Chess; "You're So Fine" by Little Walter on Checker; "Taxi Taxi 6963" by Piano Red on Victor; and "Cat Hop" by Sonny Boy Williamson and "Vanity Dresser Blues" by Willie Love, both on Trumpet.

DEC 24   Pee Wee Crayton, Little Willie Littlefield, and Linda Hayes play for the Christmas Eve Dance at the Elks Ballroom in Los Angeles.

DEC 25   T-Bone Walker works a Christmas Day dance at the Cosmopolitan Hotel in Los Angeles.
          The Flamingos share the bill with the Duke Ellington Orchestra for the week at Chicago's Regal Theater.
          Sugar Chile Robinson, Annisteen Allen and Lucky Millinder open at the Howard Theater in Washington.

DEC 26   *Billboard* magazine reports that r&b record sales account for less than five percent of all disk business. Atlantic Records is still the biggest label in the field followed by King Records.

DEC 27   T-Bone Walker opens at the Club Alimony in Los Angeles.

DEC 28   The Four Tunes begin a two-week engagement at the Brown
Derby Club in Toronto.
Dinah Washington plays the Graystone Ballroom in Detroit.

New releases for the fourth week of December include "Call Before
You Go Home" by **Memphis Slim** and "Early Morning Blues" by the Dozier
Boys, both on United; Danny "Run Joe" Taylor's "You Look Bad" on
Victor; Roy Milton's "I Stood By" on Specialty; and "I'll Be True" by
Bill Haley and his Comets on Essex.

DEC 31   The Orioles, Dizzy Gillespie, and Wild Bill Davis help bring
in the New Year in New York with a Rockland Palace show.
Billy Ward and his Dominoes are at the Wolhurst Club in
Denver.
Mel Walker and Mabel Scott play for the Elks Ballroom's
New Year's Eve Dance in Los Angeles.

Memphis Slim composed the classic "Every Day I Have The Blues." Of the more important Chicago bluesmen, Memphis Slim undoubtedly recorded for more labels than any other. Starting on Miricle in 1949, he had records issued by at least ten companies during the next ten years, including King, Chess, Vee Jay, and Peacock.

THE TOP TEN ROCK 'N' ROLL RECORDS FOR DECEMBER 1953

1. Money Honey - Clyde McPhatter and the Drifters
2. Honey Hush - Joe Turner
3. Rags To Riches - Billy Ward and his Dominoes
4. I Had A Notion - Joe Morris with Al Savage
5. Shake A Hand - Faye Adams
6. One Scotch, One Bourbon, One Beer - Amos Milburn
7. I'll Be True - Faye Adams
8. Marie - The Four Tunes
9. T.V. Is The Thing - Dinah Washington
10. Something's Wrong - Fats Domino

December 1953
ARTIST OF THE MONTH

JOE TURNER
(Joseph Vernon Turner, b. May 18, 1911; d. November 24, 1985)

Big Joe Turner. The Boss Of The Blues. His presence on the scene
virtually created the up-tempo style of blues shouting single-handedly.
His influence is so great that even he claimed to have been the man
who invented singing the blues with a beat.

A product of the fertile Kansas City, Missouri, blues scene, Joe
Turner received his initiation into the blues at the age of thirteen
by leading a blind guitarist through the streets as he played for pennies.
Soon thereafter he was working in the Kingfish Club as a singing waiter.
In the crowded, noisy clubs, it was necessary to develop a big voice
to cut through the din. Turner developed the biggest. By the 1930s
he and pianist Pete Johnson were a mainstay on the Kansas City club
scene, playing niteries with such picturesque names as the Back Biters'
Club, but most notably at the Sunset Club, where Turner alternated
between jobs on stage and behind the bar. Working their way across
country, the duo played the Apollo Theater in New York off and on
from 1936 to 1938. Jazz promoter John Hammond brought them to

JOE TURNER

Carnegie Hall in December 1938 for a special series of concerts billed as "From Spirituals To Swing." Turner stole the show and virtually created the craze for boogie woogie overnight. He stayed in New York four years at the Cafe Society while recording for Vocallion, Decca, and Varsity. He joined Duke Ellington's "Jump For Joy" revue in 1941 and sang with Ellington and Count Basie throughout the early 1940s before settling in the Los Angeles area with the Art Tatum band. By 1947 he was back on the road with Pete Johnson as well as with Meade Lux Lewis and Albert Ammons, having recorded with Ammons in 1946.

In 1950 his recording of "Still In The Dark" on the Freedom label brought him to the attention of the Ahmet Ertegun, owner of the newly formed Atlantic Records. In April 1951 Turner signed a three-year contract with Atlantic, and his first big hit followed that summer as "Chains Of Love" nearly topped the rhythm and blues charts. "Sweet Sixteen" in the summer of 1952 and "Honey Hush" a year later firmly established the Turner style. Strong support from the instrumental group often featuring Johnson's superb boogie piano stylings only laid the groundwork for Turner's exciting vocals. He sang in a rush, barely taking time to breathe, yet his diction was clear and his baritone was strong. Turner had no formal vocal training so he let his instincts carry him. He really did not shout the blues so much as he sang with a full voice. The intensity of his singing, especially on the slower blues numbers, can be almost unbearable. But, as has been noted, it was the jump numbers, the rolling boogie tunes, that made Turner so popular.

And when it comes to Joe Turner, the mind naturally jumps to his biggest hits, starting with "Honey Hush" in late 1953, through "Shake, Rattle And Roll" in the summer of 1954, and "Flip, Flop And Fly" in the summer of 1955. The last two became embroiled in the controversy surrounding the common practice at the time of "covering" rhythm and blues hits by "pop" artists, allowing the song to have a wider appeal, but at the same time robbing the r&b artist of both royalties and popularity. "Shake, Rattle And Roll" became a major "pop" hit for Bill Haley and his Comets after the lyrics had been sanitized, and "Flip, Flop And Fly" was recorded by a number of "pop" artists, including Johnnie Ray.

Turner's popularity waned in mid-1956 following "Corrina Corrina." He continued to be a major draw on the circuit of rock 'n roll tours in the late 1950s and at the numerous blues festivals for nearly thirty more years until his health finally failed in late 1985. He was still rocking at age seventy-four!

Turner is credited with fusing jazz and blues styles, coming up with a hybrid that had a musical life of its own. No doubt he was there in the middle. After all, he's not called "Big Joe" for nothing.

Shake Rattle & Roll

THE GOLDEN AGE
OF
AMERICAN ROCK 'N ROLL

1954

1954
A Look Ahead

"GET TOGETHER AND LET THE GOOD TIMES ROLL"
Louis Jordan

By the end of 1954, twenty percent of all "pop" records will have a rhythm and blues beat, sound, or arrangement. Obviously, this is the year that the mainstream of popular music takes closer notice of its wayward fledgling, rhythm and blues.

The increase in the national acceptance of rhythm and blues quickly leads to a division among the members of the music community. The clearest result of this division is the dramatic increase in the number of the "pop" covers of r&b records. "Pop" record producers are quick to note that the excitement inherent in the arrangement, style, lyrics, and performance of a rhythm and blues record can be adapted for the "pop" audience. Owners of the independent r&b labels, on the other hand, are caught in a crossfire of their own making. Since most r&b labels own the publishing rights to their records, it is to their distinct advantage to have the song recorded by as many artists as possible. Conversely, if a "pop" artist takes an r&b song and duplicates the original musical arrangement and style, and then proceeds to sell enough records to eclipse the popularity of the original, the small label loses money in national record sales. Many indie owners attempt to justify this polarity in positions by claiming that the r&b record sells just as many copies as always, and that the "pop" cover is able to spread the influence of rhythm and blues into listeners' circles which would never have heard the original, much less have been motivated to plunk down eighty-nine cents to own a copy of the record. After all, isn't imitation the sincerest form of flattery? In reality, the owner of the r&b record company is the only one in his field reaping any profits as his artists have crossover hits. Another growing reality of the situation is that cover records have to share their "pop" audience with the rhythm and blues originals as more and more radio stations are airing r&b disks. In addition, rhythm and blues pioneers in 1954 will get the chance to play TV as well as the usual theaters and clubs.

Among the r&b labels there is an in-house war being waged against records that contain off-color lyrics and innuendos about sex and strong drink. These "blue" records come under a full-scale attack by the powers of local and national government. It is obvious that a clean-up campaign is needed before the subject gets completely out of hand and leads to a ban on r&b from the airwaves.

In 1954 rhythm and blues artists will gross $25 million. Record sales account for $15 million and personal appearances for the remaining $10 million. The large proportion of gross revenues in personal appearances is only partly the result of an increase in the amount of money that r&b artists are beginning to demand for their performances. As always, there are a limited number of agencies that will handle personal appearance bookings for r&b artists. These include the Gale, Universal, Shaw, Associated, General Artists, and Buffalo Agencies. These agencies are hard-working and active, and while the actual number of clubs presenting live "pop" entertainment will diminish, the number of r&b clubs, theaters, and ballrooms continues to increase, eventually surpassing the total number of "pop" clubs.

Agencies rely on the well-worn path of the one-nighter trail, mixing packages of vocalists, groups, and bands. More one-nighters translates into ever-increasing record sales, so record companies co-operate with the agencies on these tours, plugging the artist in the town to be played. Agencies, on the other hand, are still very reluctant to book an untried artist, especially one without a recording contract, because club owners refuse to book artists who do not have a hit record. The end result is that booking agents are required to act as talent scouts, finding new artists in out-of-the-way clubs and recommending them to record companies. The biggest drawback to the increased action by new rhythm and blues artists lies in the lack of singers who are ready for the road. It is one thing to be lucky enough to have a hit record, and something entirely different to be able to project that song from a stage. Agencies frequently have to take up the slack in this area, training singers in stage movements, advising on clothes and arrangements, and, in general, developing a singer's "act."

This is the first big year for the "Rhythm And Blues Caravan" tours along the major circuits, and they all do well financially. The theory is to package seven to eleven artists and groups fronting one or two instrumental combos, and to send this outfit on the road playing one-night stands for a minimum of thirty days up to as long as three months. While each act might receive only a small amount of money on a daily basis, this is a trade-off against the expected increase in record sales that will in turn lead to additional tours and possibly a future job headlining on the theater circuit.

In r&b radio, the biggest stories of the year are the syndication of shows by deejays into markets far afield from their home base, and the rising popularity of White disk jockeys who play rhythm and blues. The biggest r&b deejay in the country is a White man, Alan Freed, who will switch allegiance from Cleveland to New York, and whose nightly radio show can be heard in an additional half-dozen markets in the Northeast.

The number of radio stations programming r&b, either full-time or part-time, grows as the popularity of the music grows. Deejays are required to have ingenuity to increase their audience share. They are caught in the middle as record companies vie with each other for the limited amount of airtime. Most deejays pride themselves on plugging the records that their audience wants to hear, based on industry trends, personal field surveys, or taking note of which records are actually selling. Many deejays work behind the counters of record stores to gain firsthand information. Others check the title strips of juke boxes to see which records are getting the most plays. Still others play requests telephoned in to the station.

Atlantic Records continues to be the dominant label in the field, accounting for one third of all the hits by rhythm and blues artists. Their lead is followed by Jubilee (the Orioles and Four Tunes), Federal (the Midnighters), Chess/Checker (Little Walter, Muddy Waters, and Lowell Fulson), Vee-Jay (the Spaniels), Herald (Faye Adams), RPM (B. B. King), Imperial (Fats Domino), Duke/Peacock (Johnny Ace), Rama (the Crows), DeLuxe (the Charms), and Specialty (Guitar Slim). As before, the only major record companies to consistently make inroads into the rhythm and blues market are Columbia (with affiliates Okeh and Epic) and Mercury.

The popularity of the vocal group will be firmly established by midyear. Fewer and fewer male vocalists are able to come up with hit records, so for them this is a year to reorganize their position. However, the single most important new name in the field is Roy Hamilton, a handsome young baritone, whose vocal stylings and musical arrangements are very close to "pop." New groups to capture the public's attention include the Charms and the Chords. Clyde McPhatter and the Drifters, who began in 1953, continue to dominate the field, even after McPhatter enters the Army in May. As in previous years, the established male artists continue to hold their ground: Joe Turner, Johnny Ace, Chuck Willis, Little Walter, and Fats Domino have all been around the circuit for several years or more. Guitar Slim has the biggest record of the year with "The Things That I Used To Do," and even though his name might not have been well known on a national level, he has been hard at work in the South for many years.

The best indication of the surge in popularity of rhythm and blues can be seen in the sales figures for r&b records. Looking at total record sales, r&b doubles its share of the market from five percent (where it had stood for years) to ten percent. New markets for r&b records are being opened up, and for the first time in memory, Los Angeles and southern California lead all other areas in total r&b record sales.

NATIONAL NEWS

Willie Mays is the Athlete of the Year as the New York Giants sweep the World Series in four games. On December 15th, the "Disneyland" TV show presents the first of the three-part series on the life of Davy Crockett . . . and creates a $100 million market for coonskin caps, lunch boxes, and plastic guitars. Senator McCarthy's hearings into the Army's alleged misconduct backfires as Senate Committee Attorney Joseph Welch carefully picks McCarthy apart for thirty days on national television . . . after an emotional outburst by McCarthy, he will be censured by the Senate in December. The top-selling book of fiction is "Not As A Stranger" by Morton Thompson, but the "Revised Standard Version of the Bible" outsells it 710,000 to 178,000. On the other hand, twenty million horror comics are sold each month, leading to laws in six states regulating their sale to minors. Academy Awards go to "On The Waterfront," Marlon Brando, and Grace Kelly. Television honors "Omnibus," "Dragnet," "Make Room For Daddy," and the "U.S. Steel Hour" with Emmys . . . "Your Show Of Shows" goes off the air after 160 live Saturday night performances. Among kids, the number one food is the hamburger, followed by orange juice. "Playboy" magazine premiers in June.

January 1954

"The War Is Over" refers to the end of the Korean War. A short history of the conflict: Korea split at 38th parallel after World War II; U.S. occupation forces withdrawn June 29, 1949; North Korea invades the south, June 25, 1950; massive United Nations troop landing, Inchon, September 15, 1950; armistice signed July 27, 1953. Result: 54,000 Americans died and the two countries remain divided at the 38th parallel, even today.

After the Tempo Toppers, Little Richard's famous touring band was The Upsetters. The group featured sax-man Wilbert Smith, who later recorded under the pseudonym Lee Diamond. The band backed Dee Clark in 1959 after Little Richard got religion.

Colonel Parker later managed another rock 'n roll singer, Elvis Presley. Parker's real name is Andreas Cornelius van Kuijk, and he was born June 26, 1909, in Holland. He reportedly jumped ship in 1929, entering the United States illegally.

New releases for the first week of January include "You Never Had It So Good" by the Checkers and "Midnight Lover Man" by Roy Brown, both on King; **"The War Is Over"** by Big Boy Crudup on Victor; Dinah Washington's "My Man's An Undertaker" on Mercury; John Lee Hooker's "Stuttering Blues" and Rudy Ferguson's "Everybody's Blues," both on DeLuxe; the Chords' "My Gal Sal" on Gem; the Meadowlark's "Love Only You" on RPM; and "Troubles" by Charles Brown with Johnny Moore's Three Blazers on Aladdin.

JAN 6   Amos Milburn, backed by the Paul Williams Band, starts on a tour of the South with their first one-night stop in Columbus, Georgia.
         Sarah Vaughan and the Four Aces share the stage for two weeks at the Chicago Theater.

EARLY JANUARY

Little Richard is playing his hometown of Macon, Georgia, with his new combo, the **Upsetters**.

The Fats Domino/Clovers tour heads west to California for the next two weeks.

Little Junior Parker, formerly with Sun Records, signs with Peacock Records. His future releases will be on Peacock's Memphis subsidiary, Duke Records. Also signing with Duke is Lester Williams, formerly with Specialty.

Tommy Sands and his manager, **Colonel Tom Parker**, are in New York while Sands cuts some sides for RCA Victor.

JAN 8   Johnny Otis brings his revue to the 5-4 Club in Los Angeles for three days.
         Faye Adams and Al Savage, fronting the Joe Morris Orchestra, open at the Apollo Theater in New York.

New releases for the second week of January include "Changing Partners" by the Crickets on Jay-Dee; "Quiet Whiskey" by Wynonie Harris on King; "Please Don't Go-o-o-o-oh" by Little Willie Littlefield on Federal; "Quit Pushin'" by Bill Robinson and the Quails and "I Stayed Down" by Johnny Wright, both on DeLuxe; "Santa Fe Blues" by Lightnin' Hopkins on RPM; "Chocolate Sundae" by Kid King's Combo on Excello; "Back Door Troubles" by Pete "Guitar" Lewis on Peacock; and Melvin Smith's "I Feel Like Goin' Home" and Sonny Terry's "Sonny Is Drinking," both on Victor.

JAN 15   The Orioles headline the revue at New York's Apollo Theater.

144

Also on the bill are Leslie Uggams and Sonny Stitt's Combo.

Joe Morris, Faye Adams, and Al Savage start a tour of the South.

The Howard Theater in Philadelphia hosts Ella Fitzgerald, along with Clyde McPhatter and the Drifters.

Roy Brown opens for a three-day weekend at Los Angeles' 5-4 Club.

Sugar Ray Robinson starts a week at Philadelphia's Uptown Theater.

RCA Victor announces the formation of a new subsidiary, Groove Records, which will handle all of the company's rhythm and blues artists.

Savoy Records signs Eddie Bateman, Napoleon, and the Four Hearts.

New releases for the third week of January include "Robe Of Calvary" by the Orioles on Jubilee; "I Didn't Want To Do It" by the Spiders, "Pony Tail" by T-Bone Walker, "Blue Monday" by Smiley Lewis, and "Thrill Me Baby" by **Lil Son Jackson**, all on Imperial; "Cemetery Blues" by Lightnin' Hopkins on Decca; Gladys "Glad Rags" Patrick's "Somebody's Lyin'" on Central; "The Talkedest Man In Town" by Louis Williams on Apollo; and the Flamingos' "Plan For Love" on Chance.

JAN 19   The Buddy Johnson Orchestra closes at the Savoy Ballroom in New York. They are off on a five-week tour of the South and Texas.

JAN 21   Fats Domino returns to the East Coast for an engagement at the Showboat in Philadelphia.

JAN 22   Clyde McPhatter and the Drifters open at the Royal Theater in Baltimore for a week.

Ruth Brown and the Four Tunes begin a week's engagement fronting the Sonny Stitt Combo at the Howard Theater in Washington.

Dinah Washington with Willis Jackson's band start a week's engagement at the Apollo Theater in New York.

The Wanderers open at Detroit's Flame Show Bar for a two-week layover. Also on the bill through the 30th is **Baby Washington**.

Charles Brown performs for three days at the 5-4 Ballroom in Los Angeles.

JAN 23   Peacock/Duke Records moves into its new recording studios, offices, and pressing plant in Houston, Texas. The company estimates that it sold 1.5 million records in 1953, with Willie Mae Thornton and Johnny Ace leading the company's talent roster.

JAN 24   Mabel Scott and Joe Houston entertain in Los Angeles at the Elks Ballroom for the evening.

Guitar Slim stops for the evening at the San Jacinto Club in New Orleans before embarking on a nationwide tour with Charles Brown.

New releases for the fourth week of January include "Beggin' My Baby" by Little Milton and "Come Back Baby" by Doctor Ross, both on Sun;

Melvin "Lil Son" Jackson was a Texas born and bred blues guitarist. In 1948, at age 33, he recorded for Gold Star; two years later he was picked up by Imperial. He was very religious, and started his career with the Blue Eagle Four gospel singers. From 1954, he devoted most of his time to church work and did little recording. "Lil Son" died in Dallas in 1976.

THE HEARTS

Jeanette "Baby" Washington achieved success as a member of The Hearts on Baton in 1955 with "Lonely Nights." As a solo performer, she had hits with "The Time" and "The Bells" on Neptune (1959), and "That's How Heartaches Are Made" (1963) and "Only Those In Love" (1965), both on Sue.

"I Do" by the "5" Royales on Apollo; **Howlin' Wolf's** "I Love My Baby" and Muddy Waters's "I'm Your Hootchy Cootchy Man," both on Chess; Jimmy Reed's "I Found My Baby" on Vee-Jay; Roy Brown's "Lonesome Lover," Lulu Reed's "Your Key Don't Fit It No More," and Bill Doggett's "And The Angels Sing," all on King; Tampa Red's "Big Stars Falling Blues" on Victor; "I Need You All The Time" by the Platters on Federal; "Life Of Ease" by the Imperials on Great Lakes; Ruth Brown's "Love Contest" on Atlantic; Charles Brown's "Pleading For Your Love" on Recorded In Hollywood; "Bye-Bye Baby" by the Charms on DeLuxe; and "I Can't Help Loving You" by the Bachelors on Aladdin.

JAN 29   The Four Tunes are booked for a three-day engagement at the Twin Coaches Club in Pittsburgh.

In Washington, Dinah Washington and the Swallows share the spotlight at the Howard Theater.

Arthur Prysock starts ten days at Chic's Showbar in Detroit.

In Los Angeles, **Sarah Vaughan** is on stage for a record-breaking two-week engagement at the Tiffany Club in Los Angeles. Floyd Dixon and T-Bone Walker perform for the three-day weekend at the 5-4 Ballroom, and across town, Joe Liggins and his Honeydrippers start three days at the Club Alimony.

The Orioles are headlining at Pep's Musical Bar in Philadelphia.

Ruth Brown and the Clovers take over the Uptown Theater in Philadelphia for a week.

The Ravens and Al Hibbler share the bill at the Apollo Theater for a week in New York.

JAN 31   Fats Domino starts fifteen straight one-nighters along the Eastern Seaboard.

LATE JANUARY

Dick Smith, former lead singer with the Five Keys, signs with Bruce Records.

Decca Records reaches an agreement with Recorded In Hollywood Records whereby Decca will release a portion of Hollywood's future output.

Willie Mae Thornton, Johnny Ace, and **Little Junior Parker** are currently touring Alabama and Georgia.

Bill Doggett signs to play a total of fifteen weeks at Philadelphia's Bill & Lou's Club in Philadelphia during 1954.

Billy Ward and his Dominoes are welcomed by the Colorado Contractor's Convention.

THE TOP TEN ROCK 'N' ROLL RECORDS FOR JANUARY 1954

1. Money Honey - Clyde McPhatter and the Drifters
2. I'll Be True - Faye Adams
3. Honey Hush - Joe Turner
4. Rags To Riches - Billy Ward and his Dominoes
5. You're So Fine - Little Walter
6. I Had A Notion - Joe Morris with Al Savage
7. The Things That I Used To Do - Guitar Slim
8. Marie - The Four Tunes
9. I'm Just Your Fool - Buddy Johnson
10. Something's Wrong - Fats Domino

January 1954
ARTIST OF THE MONTH

THE FOUR TUNES

THE FOUR TUNES

In 1944, Ivory "Deek" Watson, an original member of the Ink Spots, left the group to form his own Ink Spots unit. He contacted Joe King (tenor), Pat Best (baritone and guitar), and Jimmy Gordon (bass), but before they were able to proceed, a court injunction was placed against their use of the Ink Spots name. Watson decided that a new name for his group should be close in sound to the Ink Spots, and he came up with the Brown Dots. King was replaced by Jimmie Nabbie, a tenor with operatic ambitions who had sung gospel with the Orange Blossom Singers prior to being drafted in 1941. After his discharge Nabbie had auditioned for the Jimmie Lunceford band, but he was beat out of the job by the Trenier Twins.

The first recordings by the Brown Dots were made for Manor Records in 1945: "Let's Give Love Another Chance," "Just In Case You Change Your Mind," and "For Sentimental Reasons." The three newest members of the group dumped Watson in 1948 and hired Danny Owens as tenor. Owens had previously sung gospel with the Colemanaires. The new quartet called itself the Sentimentalaires until they were forced into yet another name change after band leader Tommy Dorsey claimed he owned this name. At this time the group had only four tunes left in its repertoire which had not been recorded for Manor, hence the new name for the group: the Four Tunes.

The Four Tunes stayed with Manor for another year before signing with RCA Victor in late 1949. Their success with Victor led to Manor re-releasing many of the records made by the group under the name Sentamentaires as the Four Tunes. Manor also leased recordings to the Arco, Columbia, and Kay-Ron labels. The net result was that the group had many records on the market at the same time. Lack of national success with Victor allowed them to make another label switch in mid-1953 to Jubilee, where their first release, "Marie," was a big hit. This was followed by a song written by Pat Best, "I Understand (Just How You Feel)," which was their last big seller. The group had recorded a total of eighty numbers for Manor, Victor, and Jubilee by the time they went to Crosby Records of Las Vegas in 1958. In 1963 the Four

Tunes broke up with Nabbie joining one of the Ink Spots groups in 1965. Owens joined the Silver Dollars. Best and Gordon started a new group, the Rainbeaus, before reforming the Four Tunes (+1), which still tours today with new members Lee McKay (tenor), Frank Dawes (piano), and George Gold (drums).

The group's main source of popularity over the years has rested in its constant touring. They were smooth and polished enough to be invited to play the Nevada casino circuit, including Fitzgerald's in Reno, the Last Frontier in Las Vegas, and Harvey's at Lake Tahoe. They were hits at the Park Avenue Cafe and the Paramount Theater in New York City, and they played the Apollo across town in Harlem. On stage the quartet was attractive in appearance and effective in their expert harmonies. In a word, the Four Tunes had "class."

February 1954

FEB 1   The Four Tunes start a week at the Crown Propeller Club in Chicago.

The Joe Morris Orchestra with Faye Adams, Al Savage, and the Orioles hit the road for two weeks through Alabama, Georgia, and Florida.

New releases for the first week of February include "Such A Night" by Clyde McPhatter and the Drifters on Atlantic, "Bartender Fill It Up Again!" by Otis Blackwell on Jay-Dee, "September Song" by Jimmy Ricks and the Ravens on Mercury, "All Night Long" by the Four Blazes on United, and Louis Jordan's "Whiskey Do Your Stuff" on Aladdin.

FEB 5   **Gatemouth Brown** entertains for two weeks at the New Era Club in Nashville.

B. B. King starts a three-day run at the 5-4 Club in Los Angeles.

Ruth Brown headlines at the Apollo Theater in New York for the week. Also on the bill is newcomer Roy Hamilton.

Guitar Slim appears at the Shrewsbury High School Gym near New Orleans.

Aside from being an influential blues guitarist, Clarence Brown also played a mean violin, a fact kept from the record-buying public, but which was very much in evidence when the "Gate" performed.

FEB 7   **Pee Wee Crayton** and Joe Liggins play for the Sunday night dance at the Elks Ballroom in Los Angeles.

EARLY FEBRUARY

Gladys "Glad Rags" Patrick is currently playing the Flame Club in Detroit with the Wanderers.

Varetta Dillard is set for the Royal Peacock in Atlanta.

Derby Records announces that its new subsidiary, Central Records, will issue several sides by Bette McLaurin.

Pee Wee Crayton started as a guitarist backing Ivory Joe Hunter on San Francisco-area club dates and on Hunter's sessions for 4-Star and Pacific. In 1949, Crayton had his first solo success on Modern Records with "Blues After Hours."

FEB 8   The Four Tunes appear at the Yankee Inn in Akron, Ohio, for the week.

New releases for the second week of February include "Too Late For Tears" by Lloyd Price on Specialty; "Will You Be True" by the Vocaleers on Red Robin; "Are You Looking For A Sweetheart?" by Dean Barlow and the **Crickets** on Jay-Dee; B. B. King's "Please Help Me" on RPM; "Love Is A Funny Thing" by Joe Morris (with Al Savage) on Herald; "Sister Lucy" by Bobby Mitchell and the Toppers on Imperial; "The Beating Of My Heart" by the Charmers on Central; "Secret Love" by the Moonglows on Chance; Eddie Boyd's "Picture In The Frame" on Chess; and "Darling Dear" by the Counts on Dot.

FEB 12   The Howard Theater in Washington hosts Duke Ellington
and the **Flamingos** for the week.
         Jimmy "Mister 5 By 5" Rushing starts a ten-day engagement
at Chic's in Detroit.
         Joe Houston with Christine Kittrell open for the weekend
at the 5-4 Ballroom in Los Angeles.
         Lionel Hampton's Combo headlines the revue this week at
New York's Apollo Theater.
         The Uptown Theater in Philadelphia presents the Joe Morris
Cavalcade starring Faye Adams and Al Savage.

FEB 13   Roy Brown plays a one-night stand at the Oro Ballroom
in Los Angeles.
         The music press reports that "Gee" by the Crows is a major
rhythm and blues hit in the Los Angeles area. Sales of the record
in southern California have topped 50,000 as deejays on the pop
radio stations have started plugging the disk. The record was
first issued in June 1953.

FEB 15   The Four Tunes start a month-long engagement at the Cafe
Society in New York.

New releases for the third week of February include "You Done Me
Wrong" by Fats Domino on Imperial; "Loose Lips" by **Percy Mayfield**
and "Going Away" by **Jimmy Liggins**, both on Specialty; Marie Adams's
"I'm Gonna Latch On To You" on Peacock; "Smootchie" by the
Lamplighters and "Mercy Me" by Lil Greenwood, both on Federal; "What
Do You Do" by the Topps on Red Robin; Jack Dupree's "Hard Feeling"
on King; and Bette McLaurin's "It's Easy To Remember" on Central.

MID-FEBRUARY

Following their recent tour of the South, the Orioles start a tour of
the Midwest.

Savoy Records signs Luther Bond and the Emeralds and blues singer
Little Eddie.

The B. B. King package tour has wound its way from the South through
New Mexico and is currently playing dates around Los Angeles.

FEB 16   Following two weeks of one-nighters, Fats Domino opens
at the Celebrity Club in Providence, Rhode Island.

FEB 19   Lionel Hampton brings his revue to the Howard Theater in
Washington.
         Roy Brown plays the first of three nights at the 5-4 Ballroom
in Los Angeles.
         Dinah Washington, the Checkers, and Eddie "Cleanhead" Vinson
entertain this week at Chicago's Regal Theater.
         The Flamingos appear with Duke Ellington's Band at the
Apollo Theater in New York this week.

FEB 20   Roy Hamilton is scheduled to perform in a small club in
Longbranch, New Jersey, that seats five hundred. Over two thousand

show up, attesting to the immediate local popularity of this new artist. (One account puts the fiture at 8,000.)

A group of deejays on the Eastern Seaboard announces that they are forming a club in which all members will be asked to refrain from playing records that advocate sex or drinking, or that hold the Black up to ridicule. The club, which became the Metropolitan Disk Jockey Club, is formally inaugurated on May 1st.

FEB 21   Billy Eckstine headlines a one-nighter tour with Ruth Brown, the Clovers, and Johnny Hodges' Combo. The tour will last two months and cover the South and Midwest.

Marvin Phillips, Mel Walker, Linda Hayes, the **Flairs**, and the Lamplighters entertain at the Elks Ballroom in Los Angeles.

New releases for the fourth week of February include "Do Do Do It Again" by the Four Tunes on Jubilee; "Work With Me Annie" by the Royals on Federal; "One More Time" by Buddy Johnson (with Ella Johnson) and "Feeling Mighty Lonesome" by Mel Walker, both on Mercury; Floyd Dixon's "Ooh-Eee! Ooh-Eee!" on Specialty; "I Made A Vow" by the Robins on Crown; Sonny Thompson's "Things Ain't What They Used To Be" on King; "Three Sheets In The Wind" by Peppermint Harris On Aladdin; "My Love" by the Crystals on DeLuxe; "What If You" by Luther Bond and the Emeralds on Savoy; "Tell Me" by the Five C's on United; "Stomp And Whistle" by Danny Overbea on Checker; "Joe The Grinder" by the **Hawks** on Imperial.

FEB 23   Ruth Brown, Billy Eckstine, the Clovers, and Johnny Hodges are at the Shrine Mosque in Pittsburgh. They are on a tour that will cover the Northeast down through the South for a month.

FEB 26   Sonny Thompson's Orchestra with Lulu Reed and the "5" Royales make a stopover for the week at the Howard Theater in Washington.

Bette McLaurin starts a ten-day stint at Chic's in Detroit.

In Los Angeles, Al Hibbler opens a two-week engagement at the Tiffany Club. Also in town at the Club Oasis, Roy Brown plays a one-nighter, and B. B. King starts a three-day engagement at the 5-4 Club.

The Apollo Theater in New York presents a full bill for the week's entertainment: Chuck Willis, **Sherman "Scatman" Crothers**, and the Tiny Bradshaw Orchestra.

FEB 28   Clyde McPhatter fronts the Gene Ammons band at New Orleans' Coliseum.

LATE FEBRUARY

Junior Parker is touring through the South with the Bill Johnson Combo.

B. B. King continues his tour of California.

Joe Turner is the feature of an *Ebony* magazine write-up.

THE FLAIRS
Among more famous members of the Flairs are Richard Berry (of "Louie Louie" fame), and Cornelius (Cornell) Gunter and Obediah Jessie (Young Jessie), both of whom later performed with the Coasters.

The Hawks, from New Orleans, for a time attempted to rival the popularity of the only nationally popular Crescent City group, the Spiders. Most lead vocals on their ballads were handled by "Fat Man" Matthews, although "Can't See For Lookin'" has bandleader Dave Bartholomew on lead.

Scatman Crothers (born in Terre Haute, Indiana, 1910) continued his show business career long after his popularity as a singer declined. Crothers made numerous television and movie appearances, including a part on the TV hit "Chico And The Man" in the late 1970s.

THE TOP TEN ROCK 'N' ROLL RECORDS FOR FEBRUARY 1954

1. The Things That I Used To Do - Guitar Slim
2. I'll Be True - Faye Adams
3. Money Honey - Clyde McPhatter and the Drifters
4. Saving My Love For You - Johnny Ace
5. Honey Hush - Joe Turner
6. You're Still My Baby - Chuck Willis
7. You'll Never Walk Alone - Roy Hamilton
8. Something's Wrong - Fats Domino
9. You're So Fine - Little Walter
10. I'm Just Your Fool - Buddy Johnson with Ella Johnson

February 1954
ARTIST OF THE MONTH

GUITAR SLIM
(Eddie Lee Jones, b. December 10, 1926; d. February 7, 1959)

GUITAR SLIM

Do flashy clothes and a spectacular stage act that combines the acrobatics of flips and splits make for a hit performer? In rhythm and blues, it sure can't hurt, and in the case of Guitar Slim this "style" probably gave him a longer career than he might otherwise have enjoyed.

Eddie Jones was another gospel-singing Mississippi teen-ager, from Hollendale near Greenwood, but what set him apart was his love of dancing. His nights at local clubs brought him his first wife and an invitation to join Willie Warren's troupe as a dancer/singer. By 1950 he had teamed with Huey Smith in New Orleans with the determination to make a record. A single weekend's booking at the Dew Drop Inn was all it took to make his destiny. The difference was that he played electric guitar at a time when most other blues musicians remained with the unamplified version. Legend even has it that his first guitar came from a pawn shop, and that he was self-taught. And Guitar Slim, as he named himself to set his stage persona apart from the other musicians in post-war New Orleans looking for work, turned the volume knobs on both the guitar and the amplifier all the way up to "10," creating a distorted, rattling sound later referred to as "fuzz."

Work at the local Dew Drop Inn brought recording contracts first with Imperial Records in 1951 and then J.O.B. in 1952. His first releases met with little commercial success, until he met with Johnny Vincent, a talent scout for Specialty Records. In October 1953 Slim had his first session with Specialty, which was supervised by Ray Charles-who was in New Orleans on tour - and which featured Charles on piano. It was this Guitar Slim session, and the resulting hit record, "The Things That I Used To Do," that first brought Ray Charles national attention. But what about Guitar Slim?

He flailed a low-slung guitar, sounding for all the world as though it were being played through a broken car radio speaker, which, combined with his semi-shout delivery, made the public take notice. And the record-buying public brought him work on tours, which is where Guitar

Slim really shone. He strutted, pranced, and danced. He did wild splits and deep knee-bends. He attacked his guitar as though it were a mistreatin' woman. And he continued for years in the same rut. His followup records on Specialty failed to hit the charts. As a matter of fact, he is one of the few artists whose only charted record (on the rhythm and blues sales chart) reached number one with no other record even denting the chart again. The recordings were all fine: "The Story Of My Life," "Later For You Baby," and "Sufferin' Mind" being the best. But by 1957 Specialty had to let him go, so he moved back to Imperial. Meanwhile his touring continued unabated throughout the South and Southwest.

Although likened to Gatemouth Brown, the greatest influence on Guitar Slim has to be T-Bone Walker, the prince of the dance club guitar vocalists, whose smooth style Guitar Slim tried from time to time to emulate. In turn, Slim's exaggerated use of the guitar became a role model for Jimi Hendrix in the 1960s. In Hendrix one can see the logical continuation of the wild stage antics and overamplified guitar.

It's is too bad that Guitar Slim missed seeing Jimi Hendrix in action. Eddie Jones died of pneumonia while on tour in New York City in 1959, far from his home, the result of too many days on the road. He was only thirty-two.

March 1954

New releases for the first week of March include Dinah Washington's "Short John" and Jimmy Ricks and the Ravens "Going Home," both on Mercury; "Lovey Dovey" by the Clovers on Atlantic; "All Night Long" by Rusty Bryant on Dot; "Say A Prayer" by Faye Adams on Herald; Sugar Boy's "Jock-O-Mo" and Jimmy Binkley's "Wine Wine Wine," both on Checker; "Make My Dreams Come True" by Elmore James on Flair; Joe Medlin's "Easy Come Easy Go Lover" on Decca; "Trumpet Sorrento" by **Frankie Avalon** on "X"; Jerry Wallace's "Gee, But I Hate To Go Home" on Allied; and three releases on Groove: "I Need Help" by Buddy Lucas (with Almeta Stewart), "I'd Gladly Do It Again" by Beatrice Redding, and Sam Butera's "I Don't Want To Set The World On Fire."

MAR 2   Clyde McPhatter, frustrated by the number of cover versions of "Such A Night" issues a press release making it known that he will sue any other artist who copies the musical arrangement or vocal styling that he devised for the Drifter's original recording.

MAR 5   Dinah Washington starts a one-week layover at the Broadway Capitol Theater in Detroit with Eddie Vinson and the **Cootie Williams** Orchestra.

Ray Charles and Joe Liggins entertain the patrons for three days at the 5-4 Ballroom in Los Angeles.

The Johnny Otis Revue featuring Marie Adams is the house guest at the Apollo Theater in New York for the week.

Billy Ward and his Dominoes begin their record-breaking engagement at the Uptown Theater in Philadelphia.

MAR 7   Amos Milburn performs at the CIO Hall in Stubenville, Ohio.

EARLY MARCH

Savoy Records announces the signing of the Hamilton Sisters and Dave Dixon, and Chance Records inks country blues singer Lazy Bill.

Johnny Ace and Willie Mae Thornton are currently at Pep's Musical Lounge in Philadelphia.

New releases for the second week of March include Jimmy Forrest's "Flight 3-D" on United; "That I Wanna See" by Buddy Phillips on DeLuxe; Little Junior Parker's "Can't Understand," Earl Forrest's "Out On A Party" and Long John's "Crazy Girl," all on Duke; Stick McGhee's "Wiggle Waggle Woo" and **Henry Glover's** "Lovers Only," both on King; "Wiggie" by Gene Forrest and the Four Feathers and "You're Nobody 'Til Somebody Loves You" by Maxwell Davis and the Ebonaires, both on Aladdin; "Driving Down The Highway" by the Blue Flamers on Excello; Billy 'The Kid' Emerson's "No Teasin' Around" on Sun; and Lonnie Johnson's "My Woman Is Gone" on Rama.

Fourteen-year old Frankie Avallone (born September 18, 1939, Philadelphia) would become a major teen idol in the late 1950s. A trumpet-playing child prodigy, he would be discovered on the Philadelphia TV show, "Teen Club." "Trumpet Sorrento" was the only record issued by Avalon at this time.

Charles "Cootie" Williams (born 1910, Mobile) played trumpet in the Duke Ellington Orchestra, which he first joined at age nineteen. In 1940, he shocked the jazz community by switching to Benny Goodman's band. His own big band, formed in 1944, featured Eddie Vinson, Pearl Bailey, and Eddie "Lockjaw" Davis.

Henry Glover is best remembered for his fine production work at King Records. He played trumpet in the bands of Lucky Millinder and Tiny Bradshaw during the 1940s, prior to joining King. Glover was also a prolific songwriter whose credits include "Drown In My Own Tears" (Ray Charles) and "Work With Me Annie" (the Midnighters).

MAR 10   The Ray-O-Vacs start four days at Harris' Tavern in Philadelphia.

MAR 11   Chic's Club in Detroit headlines **Jimmy Witherspoon** for a week.

MAR 12   This week the Howard Theater in Washington hosts Illinois Jacquet, Roy Hamilton and Mabel Scott.
Floyd Dixon starts a three-day weekend engagement at the 5-4 Club in Los Angeles.

MAR 13   WXYZ radio in Detroit bans all three versions of "Such A Night" by Clyde McPhatter and the Drifters, Johnnie Ray, and Bunny Paul.

MAR 14   Willie Mae Thornton and Johnny Ace are off on a series of one-night stands through Ohio and Michigan.
Billy Eckstine, Ruth Brown, the Clovers, and the **Johnny Hodges** Orchestra travel to the Coliseum Arena in New Orleans.

MAR 15   The Four Tunes begin a week-long engagement at Chubby's Club in Collingswood, New Jersey.
Louis Jordan opens for a week at the Casino Royal in Washington.
John Greer starts three days at Harris Tavern in Philadelphia. He returns on the 23rd for another three-day weekend.

New releases for the third week of March include "Goodnite, Sweetheart, Goodnite" by the Spaniels on Vee-Jay; Amos Milburn's "How Could You Hurt Me So" and Louis Jordan's "Ooo Wee," both on Aladdin; "It Should've Been Me" by Ray Charles on Atlantic; "Secret Love" by the Orioles on Jubilee; Bill Doggett's "It's A Dream" on King; Lil Son Jackson's "Big Rat," T-Bone Walker's "Vida Lee," and Little Sonny Wilson's "I Got Booted," all on Imperial; Milt Trenier's "Straighten Up Baby" on Groove; Jimmy Witherspoon's "24 Sad Hours" on Federal; and two from **John Lee Hooker**: "Women And Money" on Chess and "I'm A Young Rooster" on Checker.

MID-MARCH

Faye Adams, the Orioles, and the Joe Morris band bring in $4,000 on a one-nighter in Charleston, South Carolina, as they wind up their tour of the South, which began February 1st.

The Wanderers with **Tiny Grimes**'s Combo are touring through Ohio until the end of the month. Other artists on the road include Little Junior Parker, currently touring the Southeast, and Guitar Slim, currently booked on the one-nighter circuit through June.

MAR 19   The Apollo Theater in New York presents the Harptones and Mabel Scott for the week.
Gladys "Glad Rays" Patrick opens for a week at the Sportsman's Club in Pittsburgh.
The Ravens and Mantan Moreland play the Howard Theater in Washington for a week.

In 1949, Jimmy Witherspoon signed with Modern Records and, during the next four years, had several hits, including "Big Fine Girl" and "The Wind Is Blowin'." His full baritone voice kept him on an endless round of club and theater dates for the next thirty years.

Johnny Hodges (born Cambridge, Massachusetts, 1906) has often been referred to as the most important alto saxophonist in the history of jazz and the finest soloist ever to play in the many orchestras of Duke Ellington.

While recording simultaneously for two record companies, John Lee Hooker also used any number of pseudonyms - including Johnny Lee, John Lee, John Lee Booker, John Lee Cooker, Birmingham Sam, Texas Slim, Delta John, and The Boogie Man - during his illustrious career.

Tiny Grimes left the Art Tatum Trio in 1944 to form his own group (which featured Charlie Parker), and recorded for Savoy. In 1947, his quintet's "Nightmare Blues" was one of the earliest Atlantic releases. Within a year, he formed the Harlem Highlanders, featuring tenor saxman Red Prysock. This band also signed with Atlantic.

SAVANNAH CHURCHILL

"A Thousand Stars" was only a regional hit for the Rivileers. In 1960, Kathy Young recorded the song for the Indigo label, and her version was a million seller.

Zola Taylor had little success as a solo artist; she soon joined several friends to form the Queens ("Oop Shoop," 1954). Her greatest fame came as the female member of the Platters, beginning in 1955.

Savannah Churchill and Della Reese start a two-week run at the Flame Show Bar in Detroit.

The Orioles make their West Coast debut with a two-day stop at the 5-4 Club in Los Angeles.

MAR 20   In a report published in the music trade papers, it is reported that the nation's current high unemployment is drastically affecting the rhythm and blues record market, with record sales in certain areas of high unemployment among Blacks, such as Detroit, running as much as fifty percent behind last year's figures.

MAR 21   Fats Domino, just completing a tour of the South, heads for the West Coast and another long tour, which is booked solidly into late July.

MAR 22   In Philadelphia, Louis Jordan is this week's entertainment at the Rendezvous Club, Pep's Musical Bar hosts Bull Moose Jackson for a week, the Four Tunes open for a week at the Showboat, and Roy Hamilton begins an engagement at Emerson's Club.

New releases for the fourth week of March include "**A Thousand Stars**" by the Rivileers on Baton; "I'm Gonna Move To The Outskirts Of Town" by Billy Ward and his Dominoes and "Goofy Dust Blues" by Little Willie Littlefield, both on Federal; "Always" by the Tempo Toppers (with Little Richard) on Peacock; Junior Wells' "Junior's Wail" on States; the Sparrows "I'll Be Loving You" on Jay-Dee; the Meadowlarks' "L S M F T Blues" on RPM; and "Straight Jacket" by Billy Hale and his Comets on Essex.

MAR 23   The Orioles start three weeks at the Down Beat Club in San Francisco (through April 14).

MAR 26   The 5-4 Club in Los Angeles hosts Earl Bostic and his combo for three days, while on the other side of town, the Treniers start a ten-day engagement at the Club Oasis.

In New York, Clyde McPhatter and the Drifters and Lucky Millinder's orchestra are at the Apollo Theater this week.

MAR 28   T-Bone Walker and Tommy Ridgely headline at the Owl's Club in Shrewsbury, Louisiana.

In Biloxi, Mississippi, Joe Turner is booked into the Paradise Club.

MAR 29   Louis Jordan appears at the Celebrity Club in Providence, Rhode Island.

Guitar Slim returns to the New Orleans area to play the Sugar Bowl Club in Thibodaux.

New releases for the fifth week in March include B. B. King's "Love Me Baby" and **Zola Taylor's** "Make Love To Me," both on RPM; "Some Day Sweetheart" by the Five Keys on Alladin; "Just You" by the Crickets on Jay-Dee; Eddie Vinson's "You Can't Hve No Love No More" on Mercury; "Let's Have Some Fun" by Slim Saunders on Chess; "Rocker" by Little Walter on Checker; "Sit Back Down" by Little Esther on Decca; and "Thirteen Women" by Dickie Thompson on Herald.

156

MAR 30   Earl Bostic starts a two-week booking at the Blackhawk Club in San Francisco.

LATE MARCH

LaVern Baker returns from a successful seven-month tour of Europe that began in August 1953. During her stay in Milan she became a Countess, after being legally adopted by an Italian nobleman.

THE TOP TEN ROCK 'N' ROLL RECORDS FOR MARCH 1954

1. The Things That I Used To Do - Guitar Slim
2. You'll Never Walk Alone - Roy Hamilton
3. I Didn't Want To Do It - The Spiders
4. You're Still My Baby - Chuck Willis
5. Saving My Love For You - Johnny Ace
6. Such A Night - Clyde McPhatter and the Drifters
7. Lovey Dovey - The Clovers
8. I'll Be True - Faye Adams
9. Money Honey - Clyde McPhatter and the Drifters
10. I'm Your Hootchy Cootchy Man - Muddy Waters

March 1954
ARTIST OF THE MONTH

THE SPIDERS

THE SPIDERS

It is obvious, looking back over the history of rhythm and blues, that although New Orleans must be considered one of the home towns of this style of music, vocal groups were not its strong suit. Boogie woogie pianists - now this is where New Orleans can claim any number of native sons, starting with Fats Domino. But the vocal group sound exemplified by the Ravens and the Dominoes...sorry, not from New Orleans. Except for the Spiders.

Hayward "Chuck" Carbo (group leader and bass singer) and his brother Leonard "Chick" Carbo (baritone) were originally teamed as a gospel act. They joined with four other New Orleans hopefuls - Oliver Howard, Joe Maxon, Matthew "Max" West and Henry Wicks - and started rehearsing, never doubting that their break in show business would come. And, like so many other local New Orleans rhythm and blues performers, the Spiders were discovered at the Pelican Club by Dave Bartholomew, local band leader, entrepreneur, and musical arranger for Fats Domino. A recording contract with Imperial Records (Domino's label) followed, and in early 1954 a two-sided smash hit was the result: "I Didn't Want To Do It" and "You're The One." This led to the eventual traveling stage shows and the theater circuit along the Eastern Seaboard.

When they first played at the Apollo Theater in New York their lack of professional experience was immediately apparent. The members of the group were all young and had loads of exuberance, but they possessed only average vocal abilities. It was felt that their voices sounded too similar, no doubt because Chuck and Chick were brothers, and the Spiders alternated the two lead singers, which confused the public. Lacking a distinctive tenor in the group, their material was written for a baritone lead and their sound was based on the blues at the time when r&b vocal groups were developing a "cool" style in the North. Their singles were typical of the New Orleans productions of the time: strong rhythmic beat, saxophone break, handclapping to punctuate the beat and lead vocals far out in front of the group. In fact, on their ballads the backing vocals were frequently timid and barely audible.

The next hit for the Spiders was over a year in coming, and even then, their remake of the old standard, "Witchcraft," sold only moderately well in the face of the new music called rock 'n roll. Competing against much more polished groups, such as the Platters, Lee Andrews and the Hearts, and the Five Satins, the Spiders faded away, but not before leaving an impressive fourteen singles on Imperial.

Chick was the first to leave the group, in 1956, a year before the official split up. He recorded a few sides for Atlantic and Vee-Jay before returning to Imperial to re-record "You're The One."

Chuck Carbo also continued on, recording solo for the New Orleans-based Rex label, but before 1960 the Carbos were all back at civilian jobs. Only the memory of the Spiders remained in the rush toward rock 'n roll.

April 1954

APR 1   **Charles Brown**, Amos Milburn, Margie Day, and the Paul Williams Orchestra embark on a three-week tour of Louisiana (including Lake Charles and New Iberia), Texas, and Oklahoma (including Oklahoma City and Tulsa).

        Lynn Hope starts a tour through Pennsylvania, New Jersey, Ohio, Maryland, and West Virginia.

APR 2   Gladys "Glad Rags" Patrick opens at the New Era Club in Nashville.

        Red Prysock joins the Four Tunes on stage at the Apollo Theater in New York for the week.

        Arthur Prysock holds court in Detroit at Chic's Club.

        Roy Milton starts three days at Los Angeles' 5-4 Ballroom.

APR 3   Mercury Records becomes the first company to announce that in the future only 45 rpm records will be sent out to radio stations to promote a single release. For the past year and a half, most companies have been sending both 78 and 45 rpm records. Mercury feels that the new 45 rpm format is better for both the radio stations and the record company due to increased durability and lower shipping cost.

New releases for the first week of April include Marvin and Johnny's "Jo-Jo," Roy Milton's "A Bird In The Hand" and Frankie Lee Sims' "Rhumba My Boogie," all on Specialty; "Sentimental Journey" by Ruth Brown with the Delta Rhythm Boys on Atlantic; "Trouble At Midnight" by Roy Brown on King; "Trapped" by the Treniers on Okeh; "I Understand" by the Four Tunes on Jubilee; **Young John Watson**'s "Half-Pint Of Whiskey" on Federal; "Music Maestro Please" by the Starlings on JOZ; B. B. King's "Love You Baby" on RPM; and "Make My Dreams Come True" by Elmore James on Flair.

EARLY APRIL

The Royals, Federal recording artists, are changing their name to the Midnighters so as not to coincide with the "5" Royales, Apollo artists who are currently being wooed by King Records, the parent company of Federal Records.

Atlantic Records inaugurates a new label, **Cat Records**. The first releases for the label will be by Mike Gordon and the El Tempos, Sylvia Vanderpool (formerly Little Sylvia on Jubilee), Jimmy Lewis (formerly on Victor), and the Chords. Records should be shipped by the end of the month.

Don Robey of Peacock/Duke Records ships copies of Earl Forrest's "Out On A Party" and Little Junior Parker's "Can't Understand" to

---

Today, Charles Brown's haunting rendition of "Merry Christmas Baby" is a holiday standard. It was originally recorded with Johnny Moore's Three Blazers on the Exclusive label, and Brown has re-recorded the number many times since.

Red and Arthur Prysock are brothers; both were born in Greensboro, North Carolina. Arthur had a fine, well-trained baritone singing voice, and Red based his musical career on his raucous, honking tenor sax.

Young John Watson soon changed his moniker to Johnny "Guitar" Watson. Born on February 3, 1935, in Houston, he was young enough to help lead rhythm and blues into its metamorphosis as soul music in the 1960s.

Cat Records derived its name from a Southern expression for rhythm and blues, or cat music, and from those who "dug" it, namely, the "hep cats."

Paris following a request from a French jukebox operator, indicating a growing awareness of American r&b on the European continent. Meanwhile, the top stars of Peacock/Duke, Johnny Ace and Willie Mae Thornton, are currently playing one-nighters in New England.

James Wayne, formerly with Imperial, signs with Aladdin Records.

APR 9   **Jimmy McCracklin** and the Flairs share the spotlight for three days at the 5-4 Ballroom in Los Angeles.
The Four Tunes open for a week at the New Trinidad Club in Washington.
The Harptones are welcomed for a week at the Uptown Theater in Philadelphia.

New releases for the second week of April include "Shake, Rattle And Roll" by Joe Turner and "Oh That Will Be Joyful" by Jesse Stone, both on Atlantic; "Jungle Drums" by Earl Bostic, "Bump On A Log" by Lulu Reed, and "Rub A Little Boogie" by Jack Dupree, all on King; "I Got Loose" by Charles Edwins on Duke; "I Used To Cry Mercy Mercy" by the **Lamplighters** on Federal; Oscar McLollie's "Mama Don't Like" and Jimmy McCracklin's "Blues Blasters Boogie," both on Modern; "My Memories Of You" by the Harptones on Bruce; "I'm Not In Love With You" by the Dell-Tones on Rainbow; Lowell Fulson's "You Gotta Reap" on Aladdin; "I Know She's Gone" by Bill Robinson and the Quails on DeLuxe; and James Reed's "My Mama Told Me" on Flair.

MID-APRIL

Earl Bostic continues to remain a hot attraction on the West Coast, where he has broken through as a "pop" artist on his dance-club bookings.

The "new" Ink Spots with Charlie Fuqua are currently in the seventeenth week of their tour of the Far East.

Percy Mayfield continues to tour in the West.

Buckley's Record Shop in Nashville celebrates the eighth anniversary of its sponsorship of a one-hour show on local WLAC radio. Other major sponsors on WLAC are Randy's Record Store in Gallatin, Tennessee, owned by **Randy Wood**, founder of Dot Records, and Ernie's Record Store in Nashville owned by Ernie Young of Nashboro/Excello Records.

Atlantic Records signs George "Mr. Blues" Jackson from New Orleans.

Roy Brown is currently on a string of one-nighters through the West following an engagement at Bill and Lou's in Philadelphia. Also touring the West Coast at this time is the Johnny Otis Revue.

Lulu Reed with Sonny Thompson's Orchestra continue to tour the East and Midwest.

The Tiny Bradshaw Orchestra sets off on a tour of one-nighters in the Pacific Northwest.

After "The Walk" in 1958, Jimmy McCracklin had to wait until 1961 before another song, "Just Got To Know" on Art-Tone, sold enough in the r&b market to also cross over into the "pop" charts.

During the time that he sang with the Lamplighters, Al Frazier was recording with the Tenderfoots, also on Federal. After lead vocalist Thurston Harris left the Lamplighters in 1956 for a solo career, the group disbanded.

In 1950, Randy Wood started Dot Records out of the back of his appliance/record store. The label never had more than a few r&b acts (the Counts, the Griffin Brothers, and the Dell-Vikings), and concentrated on such "pop" talents as Billy Vaughn, Pat Boone, Gale Storm, and the Hilltoppers.

Fortune Records announces the signing of Nolan Strong and the Diablos.

APR 16   Sarah Vaughan travels to the Howard Theatre in Washington for a week.

Roy Hamilton starts a week at the Flame Show Bar in Detroit with **Della Reese**, who is a regular entertainer at the club.

Jimmy Liggins plays a three-day weekend at the 5-4 Ballroom in Los Angeles.

The Four Tunes are booked for a month-long engagement in Toronto.

The Regal Theater in Chicago presents Sugar Ray Robinson, Ruth Brown, and Clyde McPhatter and the Drifters for the week.

Louis Jordan and his Tympany Five entertain patrons this week at New York's Apollo Theater.

APR 17   Cleveland deejay **Bill Randle** is injured in an auto accident. This sidetracks his plans to start a new rock 'n roll radio program in Chicago, for which he would commute between Cleveland and Chicago on a daily basis.

Billy Wright entertains at the Dew Drop Inn indefinitely in New Orleans.

APR 18   Johnny Otis brings his revue to the Elks Ballroom in Los Angeles for a Sunday night dance.

APR 19   The Harptones play the Convention Hall in Asbury Park, New Jersey.

Tiny Bradshaw, Wynonie Harris, Big Maybelle, and Bull Moose Jackson's Orchestra entertain for the evening at the Graystone Ballroom in Detroit.

Red Prysock starts at the Celebrity Club in Philadelphia.

New releases for the third week of April include Guitar Slim's "The Story Of My Life" on Specialty; "Tears Begin To Flow" by the Spiders on Imperial; "I Cry Some More" by the "5" Royales on Apollo; "My Heart Tells Me" by the Hampton Sister on Savoy; "Hello Little Boy" by Ruth Brown and "Under A Blanket Of Blue" by the **Cardinals**, both on Atlantic; Sonny Thompson's "I Ain't No Watch Dog" on King; and Johnny Taylor's "Over The Hill" on Recorded In Hollywood.

APR 21   The "5" Royales with Tab Smith's Combo take off on a series of one-nighters that will last through June 19th.

APR 23   Johnny Ace, Willie Mae Thornton, and Hal "Cornbread" Singer's band share the spotlight for a week at the Apollo Theater in New York.

In Washington, Louis Jordan begins a week's engagement at the Howard Theater.

Al Hibbler is at Chic's in Detroit for a ten-day layover. Across town, Sugar Ray Robinson, Ruth Brown, and Clyde McPhatter and the Drifters headline a week's engagement at the Broadway Capitol Theater.

Johnny Otis and his Combo are the weekend entertainment at Los Angeles' 5-4 Ballroom. Also in town, the Treniers open at the Club Oasis.

Dellareese Taliafano was born July 6, 1932, in Detroit. Her break in show business came as backup vocalist for gospel singers Mahalia Jackson and Clara Ward.

Bill Randle never made it to Chicago, but he certainly made the big time. In 1955, he was broadcasting on WCBS in New York City, and his show rivaled that of Alan Freed in popularity.

The Cardinals issued twelve singles on Atlantic from 1951 to 1956. When Ernie Warren was drafted in 1952, his place as lead vocalist was taken by Leander Tarver. When Warren returned from the Army, Tarver remained with the group.

In Chicago, Billy Ward and his Dominoes are welcomed to the Regal Theater for a week.

APR 24   In a front-page headline article in *Billboard* titled "Teenagers Demand Music With A Beat, Spur Rhythm & Blues," it is reported that the record industry sold a total of 15 million r&b singles in 1953. There are 700 deejays programming rhythm and blues music across the country, and seventy-five companies are releasing over a thousand rhythm and blues disks each year. In a related article, the power of the independent record company in the r&b field is detailed; in the past five years, of the top fifty r&b records, forty-six were released by small record companies.

New releases for the fourth week of April include "Don't Stop Dan" by the Checkers on King; Big Maybelle's "I've Got A Feeling" on Okeh; Willie Mabon's "Would You Baby" on Chess; **Little Milton**'s "If You Love Me" on Sun; "Adios My Desert Love" by Nolan Strong and the Diablos on Fortune; Melvin Smith's "No Baby" and "I Got Drunk" by Buddy Lucas, both on Groove; "Quiet Please" by the Charms on DeLuxe; "Make Love To Me" by Joe Liggins on Specialty; "Sh-Boom" by the Chords and "Speedy Life" by Little Sylvia, both on Cat; "I Won't Tell A Soul" by the Volumes on Jaguar, and "Bus Station Blues" by Louis Brooks and his Hi-Toppers on Excello.

APR 27   The Five Keys play a date at the Odd Fellows Hall in Wilmington, Delaware.

APR 29   Roy Milton is booked into the Royal Room in Los Angeles.

APR 30   This week finds Billy Ward and his Dominoes with Pigmeat Markham at the Howard Theater in Washington.
          T-Bone Walker entertains at the Flame Show Bar in Detroit for the next two weeks.
          The 5-4 Club welcomes Red Callender and Jimmy Huff to Los Angeles for three days.
          The Apollo Theater in New York presents Sarah Vaughan for the week.

LATE APRIL

Little Richard has joined Little Junior Parker's tour of the South.

THE TOP TEN ROCK 'N' ROLL RECORDS FOR APRIL 1954

1. You'll Never Walk Alone - Roy Hamilton
2. Lovey Dovey - The Clovers
3. The Things That I Used To Do - Guitar Slim
4. I Didn't Want To Do It - The Spiders
5. Such A Night - Clyde McPhatter and the Drifters
6. Gee - The Crows
7. It Should've Been Me - Ray Charles
8. You're Still My Baby - Chuck Willis
9. Work With Me Annie - The Midnighters
10. I'm Your Hootchy Cootchy Man - Muddy Waters

"Little" Milton Campbell was born September 7, 1934, near Greenville, Mississippi. He started recording as a session guitarist for Trumpet Records in nearby Jackson. In 1953-54, he had several records released under his name on Sun Records in Memphis. Starting in 1962, he had a nine-year run of hits on Checker.

For all of the influence that T-Bone Walker had on others, he himself was most in awe of the electric guitar stylings of Les Paul. In turn, Walker led the way for Pee Wee Crayton, Johnny Watson, and Guitar Slim, among others. Walker never stopped touring or recording, up to the time of his death in March 1975.

At this time, Little Richard's career with Peacock Records was going nowhere. By February 1955 he had signed with Specialty Records. His first session for Specialty was delayed until September 1955, but it brought his first major hit record, "Tutti Frutti."

April 1954
ARTIST OF THE MONTH

ROY HAMILTON
(b. April 16, 1929; d. July 20, 1969)

ROY HAMILTON

Think about rhythm and blues. Then about the beginning of rock 'n roll. An operatic baritone wouldn't seem to have a place in either of the two forms of music. Or would he? Roy Hamilton is the exception to the rule.

Naturally enough, he started singing in church choirs at age six in his hometown of Leesburg, Georgia. The family moved to Jersey City, New Jersey, in search of a better life when Roy was fourteen. There he sang with the Central Baptist Church Choir, New Jersey's most famous Black church choir. At Lincoln High School he studied commercial art and was talented enough to place his paintings with several New York galleries. In 1947, Roy took the big step into secular music, winning talent contests at the Apollo Theater, The Baby Grand Club and the Lido Club, though nothing immediate came of it. Painting and singing did not pay the rent, so he started work in a television assembly plant during the day and became a heavyweight boxer at night, with a professional record of seven wins against only one loss.

In 1948 he joined the Searchlight Gospel Singers. He also studied light opera, but it was toward popular music that his heart was leaning. He began working the small clubs around Newark, and eventually he was heard by disk jockey and club owner Bill Cook, who became his manager and who brought him to the attention of Columbia Records. Columbia was impressed enough to sign him to their rhythm and blues subsidiary, Okeh Records. But before any records were released, the company had second thoughts and placed him with their "pop" subsidiary, Epic, in an apparent ploy to pit Hamilton against the other reigning Black baritones, Billy Eckstine and Al Hibbler, who were popular with both White and Black audiences.

His first release, "You'll Never Walk Alone," a semi-operatic inspirational song written by Rodgers and Hammerstein for the musical "Carousel," proved to be an instant smash hit, but only in the r&b market. This was followed in quick succession by other songs in a similar vein: "Unchained Melody" (the best-selling rhythm and blues record for 1955), "Hurt," and "Ebb Tide." Although his popularity was firmly established among blues audiences and was growing steadily in the "pop" field, his recordings were constantly beaten on the "pop" charts by other, more refined artists. Then, unexpectedly in 1956, he was diagnosed as having tubercular pneumonia just as he was set to play the Flame Show Bar in Detroit. His press agent announced that Roy Hamilton was retiring, but in reality he spent nine months in a hospital. It took him two years to make a comeback.

Roy Hamilton's recordings offered no gimmicks. He sang proudly and with emotion, usually fronting a large orchestra. Although an early reviewer remarked that he had a "powerful, yet undisciplined voice," it was his clean-cut appearance that made him so popular with the teen-age crowd. If he sometimes had a tendency to oversell the song, there could be no doubting his sincerity.

Hamilton's biggest success on a national scale came, ironically, with two upbeat performances, "Don't Let Go" in 1958, and "You Can Have Her" in 1961, both of which show his strong gospel influence.

Following a successful stay with Epic Records, he recorded for MGM and RCA Victor in the 1960s just as his career was fading against the strong competition of what was just being termed "soul" music. About this time he quit the "pop" music business altogether to return to his gospel roots. In 1969 he was felled by a heart attack at an age when most baritones are just reaching their full maturity.

It is difficult to say whether Hamilton was influenced by Sonny "Jackie" Wilson (lead singer with Billy Ward and his Dominoes at this time) or whether Jackie Wilson was influenced by Roy Hamilton. Certainly they were contemporary rivals even though Wilson's immense popularity was still several years away in 1954. Hamilton's influence is most readily seen in the recordings of the Righteous Brothers, who issued both "Ebb Tide" and "Unchained Melody" in the 1960s.

Roy Hamilton's phrasing and sense of timing ultimately led him away from the rhythm and blues audience. Unlike many other r&b artists, he realized that his voice contained the potential for projecting himself beyond the limitations of skin color into a new world where one's talent is judged only on its own merits.

May 1954

MAY 1   Alan Freed hosts his first dance outside of Ohio. The Coronation Ball at the Sussex Avenue Armory in Newark, New Jersey, features the Clovers, Charles Brown, the Harptones, **Sam Butera**, Muddy Waters, Buddy Johnson's Orchestra with Ella Johnson, Nolan Lewis, and Arnet Cobb. Over 10,000 people attend the show. Freed is the deejay at WJW in Cleveland and is heard via tape delay over WNJR in Newark.

Tenor-sax man Sam Butera found his musical niche leading the wild and wooly nightclub combo backing Louis Prima and Keely Smith from the late 1950s to the early 1960s.

MAY 2   Earl Bostic stops for the evening to entertain at the Elks Ballroom in Los Angeles.

MAY 3   The Four Tunes begin a month-long engagement at the Brown Derby in Toronto.

The Romaines are booked for two weeks at Chubby's in West Collingswood, New Jersey.

Red Prysock starts an engagement at Weeke's Cocktail Lounge in Atlantic City, New Jersey, following a weekend layover at Emerson's Club in Philadelphia.

New releases for the first week of May include "Shake That Thing" by Wynonie Harris on King; "Going In Your Direction" by Sonny Boy Williamson on Trumpet; John Lee Hooker's "I Wonder Little Darling" on Modern; Jimmy Witherspoon's "Highway To Happiness" on Federal; "You Got To Give" by Mike Gordon and the El Tempos and "Last Night" by Jimmy Lewis, both on Cat; Red Prysock's "Jump Red Jump" on Mercury; "Now She's Gone" by J. B. and his Hawks on Chance; "Baby" by the Crows on Rama; "I Smell A Rat" by Young Jessie on Modern; "My Baby" by **James Cotton** on Sun; "Teardrops On My Pillow" by Jimmy Wilson on Big Town; and "I Love You For Sentimental Reasons" by Smiley Lewis on Imperial.

James Cotton (born in Tunica, Mississippi, 1925) left home at age nine to go to Memphis because he greatly admired the harmonica playing of Sonny Boy Williamson. He was a good pupil, and by age thirteen he was playing harmonica alongside Little Walter in Howlin' Wolf's first band.

MAY 7   Johnny Ace, Willie Mae Thornton, and the **Harptones** are at the Howard Theater in Washington for a week.

Clyde McPhatter receives his notice to report for active duty with the U.S. Army. During his absence the Drifters will continue to record and perform without him. With the exception of a short June recording session, this marks the end of McPhatter's association with the group. David Baughn and Johnny Moore will take over the lead tenor duties until the original group disbands in 1957.

The Robins start a week at the Club Oasis in Los Angeles. Across town, Joe Turner plays the first of three days at the 5-4 Club.

THE HARPTONES

The Harptones continued to record, with various personnel changes, until 1964. However, they were never able to match the success of "Sunday Kind Of Love." In 1982, a group of Harptones featuring original member Willie Winfield recorded for Ambient Sound.

EARLY MAY

Jubilee Records inks Bette McLaurin, formerly with Coral. Also signed

Gloria Mann's cover versions of "Earth Angel" (Sound, 1955) and "Why Do Fools Fall in Love" (Decca, 1956) were big sellers.

After "Mystery Train," Junior Parker's best work included "Next Time You See Me" (1957) and "Driving Wheel" (1961), both on Duke. On the other hand, his biggest-selling record was the humorous "Annie Get Your Yo-Yo" in 1962. Parker died in Chicago November 18, 1971, during brain surgery.

Don Gardner achieved a measure of fame as half of a duo with Dee Dee Ford. Their recording of "I Need Your Loving" (1962, Fire) was influenced as much by Ike and Tina Turner's funk as by the earlier duets of Shirley and Lee or Gene and Eunice.

to Jubilee is **Gloria Mann**, who had recorded for SLS and whose cover of "Goodnite Sweetheart Goodnite" is due out this week.

On the one-nighter circuits in May, Amos Milburn is in California for most of the month, **Little Junior Parker** is booked for two months on a tour of the Midwest, while Gatemouth Brown is currently in Texas.

John "Buddy" Bailey, former lead singer with the Clovers, returns to the group following his release from the U.S. Army. The group will become a five-man unit as Billy Mitchell, who had replaced Bailey, will remain.

George "Hound Dog" Lorenz increases his r&b radio show from six to fourteen hours a week. He is heard on WJJL in Niagara Falls, New York.

Savoy Records signs Nappy Brown, of Charlotte, North Carolina, former lead singer with the Selah Jubilee Singers. Also new to the label are the Hot Shots, who have backed several vocalists on audition records, and the Dreams, a teen-age group from Philadelphia.

MAY 8   The Bihari brothers announce the expansion of their recording facilities in Culver City in the Los Angeles area. The new offices will house Saul Bihari's Modern and RPM Records, Joe Bihari's Flair Records, and Jules Bihari's Crown Records and Cadet Pressing Company.

MAY 10   Danny Overbea begins a week's engagement at the Ebony Lounge in Cleveland.
Chuck Willis stars at Emerson's in Philadelphia. Also in town, at Pep's Musical Bar, Sarah Vaughan and **Don Gardner** open for a week.

New releases for the second week of May include "Baby Please" by Fats Domino on Imperial; "I Smell A Rat" by Willie Mae Thornton on Peacock; "Jimmie Lee" by Lloyd Price on Specialty; "That Man" by Nappy Brown on Savoy; "Crazy Mixed Up World" by Faye Adams on Herald; "Just Whisper" by the Du Droppers on Groove; Amos Milburn's "Milk And Water" and Big Jay McNeely's "Real Crazy Cool," both on Aladdin; "Ain't Cha Got Me (Where You Want Me)" by Buddy Johnson (with Ella Johnson) on Mercury; Otis Blackwell's "Don't Know How I Loved You" on Jay-Dee; "Chapel Of Memories" by Sonny Woods and the Twigs on Recorded In Hollywood; "Sassy Mae" by Memphis Slim on United; "Roses Of Picardy" by the Platters on Federal; and "(We're Gonna) Rock Around The Clock" by Bill Haley and his Comets on Decca.

MAY 13   Johnny Otis starts a four-day layover at Los Angeles' Club Alimony. Otis is now a regular deejay on KFOX in Los Angeles, with a daily (except Sundays) rhythm and blues show from 7:00 to 8:00 p.m.

MAY 14   The Spiders and Guitar Slim front the Charlie Barnett Orchestra at the Apollo Theater in New York.
The Harptones perform at the Royal Theater in Baltimore for the week.

166

The "5" Royales and Tab Smith take off on a one-nighter tour through Texas.

Hadda Brooks and "Countess" LaVern Baker start a two-week layover at the Flame Show Bar in Detroit.

Amos Milburn plays the three-day weekend stint at the 5-4 Ballroom in Los Angeles.

MID-MAY

Paul Williams, formerly with Capitol Records, signs with Groove Records. Also recently signing with Groove are Big Red McHouston, Larry Dale, and Sam "Highpockets" Henderson. Other recent record company acquisitions include Delores Gibson with Aladdin, and the Four Bells with Gem.

Percy Mayfield is currently on a tour of Texas, Oklahoma, and Arkansas.

PERCY MAYFIELD

MAY 17   Louis Jordan is booked into Pep's Musical Lounge in Philadelphia.

Dinah Washington starts a week at the Club 86 in Geneva, New York.

The Orioles, the Clovers, and the Midnighters play a one-night stand at the Graystone Ballroom in Detroit.

New releases for the third week of May include "Please Forgive Me" by Johnny Ace on Duke; "Good News" by the Hawks and "School Boy Blues" by Bobby Mitchell and the Toppers, both on Imperial; "I Feel So Bad" by Chuck Willis on Okeh; "If The Sun Isn't Shining In Your Window" by Lulu Reed, "This Is My Last Goodbye" by Roy Brown, and "Overflow" by Tiny Bradshaw, all on King; "I'm Stuck" by the Five Jets on DeLuxe; and Willie Headen's "I Still Get My Kicks" on Dootone.

MAY 21   **Roy Milton** starts three evenings of entertaining at the 5-4 Ballroom in Los Angeles.

Buddy Johnson and his Orchestra featuring Ella Johnson headline the Apollo Theater revue this week in New York. Also appearing are the Counts and Nolan Lewis.

When Roy Milton signed with Specialty Records in 1947, he was required to give up his interests in the company he founded, Roy Milton Records, and soon the name of the label was changed to Miltone. Records by Roy Milton continued to be issued by Miltone (and later by DeLuxe) for several years.

MAY 22   The Tiny Bradshaw Orchestra plays a dance at the Virginia Military Institute.

The Five Keys do a one-nighter at the Elks Club in Alexandria, Virginia.

The Palace Theater in New Orleans presents the Midnighters for ticket holders tonight.

MAY 23   Charles Brown plays the Forest Hotel in Norwalk, Connecticut.

MAY 24   Dinah Washington holds court at Pep's Musical Lounge in Philadelphia for the week.

Tiny Bradshaw brings his orchestra to the Loop Lounge in Cleveland for a week.

New releases for the fourth week of May include "Maybe You'll Be There" by **Lee Andrews and The Hearts** on Rainbow; "Say Baby" by Willie Johnson on Specialty; "Cryin' Mercy" by Charles Brown on Aladdin;

Lee Andrews and the Hearts' had major hits with "Long Lonely Nights" and "Teardrops" (Chess, 1957), and "Try The Impossible" (United Artists, 1958).

Bloom In Lover's Lane" on Groove; "Darlene" by The Dreams on Savoy; "Darling I Know" by the **El Rays** on Checker; "Rock A-Beatin' Boogie" by the Treniers on Okeh; Young John Watson's "You Can't Take It With You" on Federal; and "Life I Used To Live" by Lightnin' Hopkins on Herald.

MAY 28   B. B. King and Earl Forrest make their New York debut at the Apollo Theater in New York this week backed by Lucky Millinder's Combo.

Amos Milburn starts a tour of the Pacific Northwest with a show at the Amor Ballroom in Spokane. Other shows on the tour include the Eagle Auditorium in Seattle (29), the Evergreen Ballroom in Olympia (30), and the McElroy Ballroom in Portland (31)

Buddy Johnson with sister Ella and the Counts starts a week's engagement at the Howard Theater in Washington.

In Detroit, Bill Doggett lays over for a one-week engagement at the Crystal Lounge, while **Tommy Edwards** opens for two weeks at the Flame Show Bar.

In Los Angeles, Sugar Ray Robinson opens for a ten-day run at the Club Oasis. Also in town, at the 5-4 Ballroom, Chuck Higgins starts a three-day weekend stint.

The Trianon Ballroom in Chicago admits Blacks for the first time. Featured entertainment includes the Count Basie Orchestra.

MAY 29   Floyd Dixon plays the CIO Hall in Flint, Michigan.

MAY 31   The Clovers open at Emerson's Club in Philadelphia.

Floyd Dixon is in Taunton, Massachusetts, for a one-night stand.

Count Basie and Percy Mayfield stop for the evening at Detroit's Graystone Ballroom. Mayfield is just coming off a tour through Texas, Oklahoma, and Arkansas.

New releases for the fifth week of May include "Just Make Love To Me" by Muddy Waters on Chess; "I'm Not Going Home" by Billy "The Kid" Emerson on Sun; "Only A Miracle" by the Four Bells on Gem; "You Were Untrue" by the Flairs, "Loosely" by **Ike Turner**, and "Sho Nuff I Do" by Elmore James, all on Flair; "A Dollar Down" by Louis Jordan on Aladdin; Junior Derby's "I'm Still Lonesome" on King; and **Frankie Valley**'s "Somebody Else Took Her Home" on Mercury.

THE TOP TEN ROCK 'N' ROLL RECORDS FOR MAY 1954

1. You'll Never Walk Alone - Roy Hamilton
2. Lovey Dovey - The Clovers
3. Work With Me Annie - The Midnighters
4. Shake, Rattle And Roll - Joe Turner
5. The Things That I Used To Do - Guitar Slim
6. I Didn't Want To Do It - The Spiders
7. Goodnite, Sweetheart, Goodnite - The Spaniels
8. Gee - The Crows
9. Such A Night - Clyde McPhatter and the Drifters
10. It Should've Been Me - Ray Charles

May 1954
ARTIST OF THE MONTH

THE CROWS

The only charted record by the Crows has generated as much "round table" discussion as any record ever released. Was it, as many claim, the "first" rock 'n roll record? If not, then what was the first? "Gee!"

The unit traveled a long road before becoming nationally popular. The Crows date back to 1948, when several youngsters got together, probably after school on the street corners of Harlem, to practice so they could entertain at the local teen center dances and parties. They won the Wednesday night amateur contest at the Apollo Theater, which led to a talent agent who got them several sessions as uncredited backing vocalists on other artists' records, mainly for the Jubilee label. At this time the Crows consisted on Daniel "Sonny" Norton (lead tenor), William "Bill" Davis (baritone), Harold Major (tenor), and Gerald Hamilton (bass).

They were ultimately introduced to George Goldner, owner of Tico Records, which specialized in Latin dance records. Goldner was just starting another label to concentrate on rhythm and blues. The Crows were hired by Goldner to back Lorraine Hamilton's recording of "Perfidia" on his new Gee label. The first record for the group to carry their name was "Seven Lonely Days" on Rama another Goldner label, on which they backed Viola Watkins. Their second release, named in part for that earlier label, is the record that cause all the furor: "Gee." The record was released in June 1952, but it took six months before it first caught fire on the West Coast.

The Crows were signed to the Associated Booking Agency, which sent them off to tour around Los Angeles. When they returned to New York they learned just how short the life of a "pop" star can be. The novel sound of "Gee" that made it so successful quickly led to their downfall. In an attempt to come up with another hit, the Crows recorded ballads and novelties, to no avail. They were even unable to get Associated to book them in their home area around New York. There were cries of scandal as the group complained of being cheated of its royalties ("Gee" was co-authored by Bill Davis and Viola Watkins). The Crows didn't last a full year after their only success. Davis left to join the Continentals, who also recorded for Rama, but George Goldner thought the group was too old to appeal to the teen crowd (Davis was the youngest member at twenty). Davis finally quit the business in 1963 after several years of trying to get his records released.

As the music business began to recognize that rhythm and blues tunes were the next wave in "pop" music, groups like the Crows were thrown into the limelight for only a brief moment and then just as quickly discarded. Few remained for more than one hit. It was a furious time to try to break into the music business as the public's taste in music quickly switched to the next fad. Such was the fate of the Crows.

June 1954

JUN 1   Ruth Brown goes out on an eight-week tour of California.

JUN 4   The Orioles, fronting the Erskine Hawkins Combo, headline the show at the Apollo Theater in New York for this week.
          The grand opening of Los Angeles' Savoy Ballroom features entertainment by Earl Bostic. Also in town, Ruth Brown and Johnny Moore's Three Blazers are at the 5-4 Ballroom for a three-day weekend engagement.
          In New Orleans, Tommy Ridgley opens a weekend stand at the Dew Drop Inn.

JUN 6   Johnny Otis takes his stageshow to the Lincoln Theater in Los Angeles for the evening. Across town, Sugar Ray Robinson is entertaining at the Club Oasis.

New releases for the first week of June include "Big Long Slidin' Thing" by Dinah Washington and "Tryin' To Get To You" by the Eagles, both on Mercury; **"Riot In Cell Block #9" by the Robins** on Spark; "Honey Love" by Clyde McPhatter and the Drifters and "I Can't Hold Out Any Longer" by LaVern Baker, both on Atlantic; "Sexy Ways" by the Midnighters on Federal; "Drowning Every Hope I Ever Had" by the Orioles on Jubilee; "I Was Wrong" by the Moonglows on Chance; "Darling" by the Ray-O-Vacs on JOZ; Sonny Thompson's "Single Shot" on King; "No One Else Will Do" by the Deep River Boys on Jay-Dee; and "Big Eyes" by the Majors on Original.

EARLY JUNE

Atlantic Records, following the immediate and overwhelming success of "Sh-Boom" by the Chords on its subsidiary, Cat Records, is removing the B-side, "Cross Over The Bridge," which had originally been intended as the hot side of the record. The new B-side will be "Little Maiden." **"Cross Over The Bridge"** will be held for future release, since the company still has faith that the song will be a hit. In a related story, the cover version of "Sh-Boom" by the Crew-Cuts is issued this week on Mercury.

The **Du Droppers** are booked for an eight-week engagement at Lau Lee Chai's Club in Honolulu.

The squabble between Billy Ward and the Associated Booking Corporation is still not settled. Ward claims that he and the Dominoes will no longer honor ABC bookings; the agency says otherwise. In frustration, Ward breaks off his contract with the company. In other news concerning the Dominoes, it is reported that Billy Ward is shopping for a new recording company. King Records, which releases the Dominoes' material on its subsidiary Federal as well as the parent, reports that the groups'

"Riot In Cell Block #9" by the Robins featured Richard Berry of the Flairs narrating the humorous bass lead.

The version of "Cross Over The Bridge" by the Chords was never issued as a single.

Through the years, the Du Droppers featured Julius (J.C.) Ginyard, Willie Ray, Charlie Hughes, Bob Kornegay, and Joe Van Loan (who had previously sung with the Ravens).

current contract is good through June 30, 1955, or until twelve more songs are recorded. Meanwhile, the group starts a Southern tour with the Paul Williams Orchestra this week.

Pittsburgh's WCAE radio, formerly an all-pop station, adds a daily afternoon r&b show.

Johnny Ace and Willie Mae Thornton are touring the Carolinas.

Feeling the thrill of new-found **royalties**, Guitar Slim, Amos Milburn, and Charles Brown all buy new fish-tail Cadillacs to celebrate.

This just goes to show that, contrary to the reports, at least a few rhythm and blues artists received royalties!

JUN 8   Following a successful engagement at the Royal Peacock in Atlanta, Lowell Fulson is off on a one-nighter tour of Florida (including Fort Pierce, Bellgrade, and Fort Lauderdale).

JUN 11   Johnny Otis starts three days at the 5-4 Ballroom in Los Angeles. Tonight he performs a double shift, entertaining at 6:00 p.m. at the Lincoln Theater, followed by a late show at the 5-4 Ballroom.
         The Apollo Theater in New York presents the Spaniels, in what is billed as their "initial appearance," along with Joe Turner and Arnett Cobb's Orchestra for the week.

JUN 12   In Detroit, Jimmy Witherspoon starts a ten-day layover at Chic's Club.

New releases for the second week of June include "Three Coins In The Fountain" by Billy Ward and his Dominoes and "Over The Rainbow" by the Checkers, both on King; "What Can I Do" by the Kings and "School Of Love" by Marvin and Johnny, both on Specialty; Al Savage's "Be Seein' You In My Dreams" on Herald; T-Bone Walker's "Wanderin' Heart" and Lil Son Jackson's "Blues By The Hour," both on Imperial; Big Jay McNeeley's "Let's Work" on Federal; and **Bob Crewe**'s "Cash Register Heart" on Jubilee.

Bob Crewe was a male model, interior decorator, and record producer (Freddy Cannon, the Rays, and the Four Seasons) from Bellville, New Jersey. His personal hits include 1960's "The Wiffenpoof Song," but his biggest-selling record was an instrumental, "Music To Watch Girls By," in 1967.

JUNE 15   Following his successful tour of the West Coast, Earl Bostic embarks on a tour of the Midwest.

MID-JUNE

Currently on the road are Charles Brown in North Carolina for two weeks; Amos Milburn in California; Floyd Dixon doing two weeks of one-nighters in Ohio, Indiana, Kentucky, West Virginia, and Arkansas; and Don Gardner working in Atlantic City.

Bruce Records announces the signing of the Mastertones.

Aladdin Records starts a new subsidiary, Lamp Records, which will be under the supervision of **Jesse Stone**. The label joins Aladdin's other subsidiaries, Intro, Score, and 7-11.

Jesse Stone is credited with introducing the back beat to rhythm and blues, thus adding to the development of rock 'n roll. Stone was also a prolific composer (as Charles Calhoun) with such hits as "Shake, Rattle And Roll" and "Money Honey" while with Atlantic.

In Chicago, Chess and Checker Records move into new quarters on Cottage Grove Avenue. A new recording studio is under construction which will allow the company to record all of its disks at one location.

Parrot Records has taken over the old Chess location on East 49th Street.

Record company executives on the road in search of talent include Johnny Vincent, of Specialty Records, and Ernie Young, who owns Nashboro and **Excello Records** in Nashville.

JUN 16   Guitar Slim starts a two-week tour of Texas.
          Lynn Hope is at the El Rancho in Chester, Pennsylvania, for four days.

JUN 18   Joe Turner entertains for a week at the Howard Theater in Washington.
          Count Basie brings his orchestra to the 5-4 Club for three days in Los Angeles. Also in town, Amos Milburn starts three days at the Savoy Ballroom.
          Baby Washington begins a three-day stand at New Orleans' Dew Drop Inn.

JUN 20   The "Tenth Annual Cavalcade Of Jazz" at Los Angeles' Wrigley Field features Count Basie, Ruth Brown, and the **Flairs**.

JUN 21   Roy Hamilton and Illinois Jacquet perform for the crowd at the Graystone Ballroom in Detroit.

New releases for the third week of June include "Spider Web" by Tiny Bradshaw on King; "No Place To Go" by **Howlin' Wolf** on Chess; "Nobody Met The Train" by Otis Blackwell on Jay-Dee; "You're Mine" by Danny Overbea on Checker; Eddie Clark's "Number One Baby" on J.O.B.; and "The Candy man" by Eddie "Tex" Curtis on Gee.

JUN 23   The Orioles are one of the acts featured in "Star Night" in Detroit. The short concert tour also takes in Chicago (24) and Cleveland (25).
          Lynn Hope returns to the El Rancho in Chester, Pennsylvania, for another four-day stint.

JUN 25   In Los Angeles, the 5-4 Club welcomes Sonny Thompson and Lulu Reed for a three-day layover, and at the Savoy Ballroom, Ruth Brown and Johnny Hodges entertain for the weekend.
          Baby Washington, Eddie "Cleanhead" Vinson and the Cootie Williams Orchestra start a week at New York's Apollo Theater.
          Bill Dogget is in Philadelphia at Reynolds' Hall for the evening.

JUN 26   Dinah Washington is currently on tour with Earl Bostic through the Midwest. Dates include Kansas City tonight and St. Louis on the 27th.

New releases for the fourth week of June include Earl Bostic's "Blue Skies" and Roy Brown's "Don't Let It Rain," both on King; "I'm Slippin' In" by the Spiders on Imperial; "I Cried" by the **Velvets** on Red Robin; Little Junior Parker's "Sittin' Drinkin' and Thinkin'" and the Sultans' "Good Thing Baby," both on Duke; "Love All Night" by the Platters on Federal; "Keep On" by Shirley and Lee on Aladdin; Jimmy Rogers's "Sloppy Drunk" on Chess; and "How Long Has It Been" by Tab Smith

In 1952, Excello Records was started as an offshoot of Young's successful mail-order business, Ernie's Record Mart in Nashville. Originally, the Nashboro label concentrated on gospel, while Excello issued blues records. Young's biggest hits came with the Gladiolas' original version of "Little Darlin'" (1957, Excello) and "Oh Julie" by the Crescendos (1958, Nashboro).

In 1955, the Flairs recorded for the Loma label as the Ermines. In 1961, they changed the spelling of their name to the Flares for one last hit, "Footstompin'" on Felsted. The group folded in 1964 after eleven years and innumerable personnel changes.

In 1948, when he was nearly forty years old, Howlin' Wolf had his first recording session for Chess. In 1950, he recorded at Sun studios in Memphis, and the songs were leased to both RPM and Chess Records (leading to legal hassles). Wolf moved to Chicago in 1952 and remained with Chess for twenty years.

This group of Velvets should not be confused with the group of the same name with the hit "Tonight (Could Be The Night)" on Monument in 1961. This Velvets released three singles on Red Robin (1953-54) and one on Fury in 1957.

on United.

JUN 29   Dinah Washington opens at the patio Club in Las Vegas for
          two weeks.

JUN 30   Following his short tour of Texas, Guitar Slim starts a one-
          week trek through the South including Florida.

LATE JUNE

The 45 rpm record celebrates its fifth birthday this month. RCA Victor
introduced the first 45 rpm singles in June 1949. At this time it is
estimated that there are five million 45 rpm record players in use,
and the 45 rpm format dominates the field of juke box and disk jockey
spins.

Sil Austin, former sax-man with the Cootie Williams and Tiny Bradshaw
combos, has formed his own band and signed with Jubilee Records.
He will be booked by Universal Attractions.

Sil Austin was born September 17, 1929, in Dunellon, Florida. His moody sax work led to a big instrumental hit on Mercury Records in 1956, "Slow Walk."

THE TOP TEN ROCK 'N' ROLL RECORDS FOR JUNE 1954

1. Work With Me Annie - The Midnighters
2. Shake, Rattle And Roll - Joe Turner
3. Lovey Dovey - The Clovers
4. You'll Never Walk Alone - Roy Hamilton
5. Goodnite, Sweetheart, Goodnite - The Spaniels
6. Just Make Love To Me - Muddy Waters
7. Honey Love - Clyde McPhatter and the Drifters
8. If I Loved You - Roy Hamilton
9. I Understand - The Four Tunes
10. I Didn't Want To Do It - The Spiders

June 1954
ARTIST OF THE MONTH

THE MIDNIGHTERS
(Henry Ballard, b. November 18, 1936)

Occasionally, the history of a vocal group can be written as the
history of an individual. In the case of the Midnighters, it is fair to
say that if it were not for Hank Ballard, there wouldn't have been
much of a group.

The Midnighters started out as the Royals, and they might have
stayed that way except for the politics of the music business. The
group consisted of Henry Booth (tenor), Charles Sutton (second tenor),
Lawson Smith (baritone), Sonny Woods, (bass), and Alonzo Tucker
(guitar). The group was discovered by Johnny Otis while he was in
Detroit on one of his many tours, when they filled in for the Orioles.
In May 1951, he arranged for an audition with King Records of
Cincinnati, with which he had close ties, and they in turn recorded
Otis' composition, "Every Beat Of My Heart" for Federal, a King

THE MIDNIGHTERS

in March 1952. Lawson Smith was drafted a few months later, and as a replacement, the group took another Otis discovery, Hank Ballard, born in Detroit but the product of an Atlanta childhood. By 1954, the group was creating enough of a stir to cause legal problems with the more established "5" Royales, who charged name infringement. Just as their biggest hit record to date was issued, the Royals were forced into a name change that would have been enough to destroy the career of any lesser group. They chose to call themselves the Midnighters, and the record was "Work With Me Annie." Fortunately, very few records were released bearing the Royals' name, so the transition was smooth. The road for "Work With Me Annie," on the other hand, was anything but smooth. First of all, it was an immediate and overwhelming hit. Secondly, it was resoundingly criticized for its overt sexual lyrics, which were penned by Ballard.

"Annie" went on to have a life of her own, as she spawned nearly a dozen answers to the original song. The Midnighters got on the band wagon first with "Sexy Ways" and "Annie Had A Baby," the latter creating even more criticism than the original with lyrics such as "That's what happens when the gettin' gets good." Then Johnny Otis wrote "The Wallflower" (also known as "Dance With Me Henry" and "Roll With Me Henry") (for Etta James). This was followed in quick succession by "Annie Met Henry" (the Champions), "Annie's Answer" (the El Dorados), "Annie's Aunt Fannie" (the Midnighters), "Hey Henry" (Etta James), and finally "Henry's Got Flat Feet" (the Midnighters). One would usually conclude that this form of overkill would destroy any longevity for the original group. Well, yes and no.

The "Annie" songs were just humorous enough to defray most of the criticism over the sexy lyric. And the records put out by the group had a hard, cutting edge and a rhythmic, rollicking beat all of which appealed to the teen-age audience. The Midnighters were able to work constantly throughout the South, playing college fraternity parties even though their recordings were to go through a four-year slump in sales.

By 1958, many of the original members of the Royals/Midnighters had left and been replaced, leaving Ballard's distinctive voice as the only link with their past records. Then they switched to the parent company, King Records, for what could have been their biggest hit. Issued with a medium ballad, "Teardrops On Your Letter," as the "A" side, the record started to get airplay when deejays flipped it over and started playing a song about a new dance that Ballard had written titled "The Twist." (See the related story concerning the Spaniels, July 1954.) There was enough interest in the record to convince television dance host Dick Clark to bring Ballard to Philadelphia for a guest spot on his "American Bandstand" show. This was an enormous break for any entertainer, yet Ballard was busy in Atlanta trying to patch up a failed romance, and he missed the show. Clark was reportedly so furious that he contacted Cameo/Parkway Records of Philadelphia, which had a cover record on the street within days. The hit version went to this cover by Chubby Checker, and Ballard was relegated to the role of "also ran." But he was a trooper, and in 1960 Hank Ballard and the Midnighters had two big hits with "Finger Popping Time" and "Let's Go, Let's Go, Let's Go." This was enough to keep him working steadily for the next eight years without a hit record, until he emerged, in 1968, under the guidance of James Brown. In the 1970s Ballard folded the Midnighters and recorded solo for Silver Fox and Stang, but no further hits were forthcoming. In 1974 he reportedly tried to cash in on the "streaking" fad by recording "Let's Go Streaking" in the nude.

Ballard's career may have been checkered, but the recordings he has left behind show better than most the transition that r&b music was making in the year 1954. The songs rock with a firm beat and they roll with a boogie rhythm. Ballard's gritty, slightly nasal voice is perfect for the lyrics. And, as a transitional force in creating rock 'n roll, Hank Ballard and the Midnighters are as instrumental as many other artists who got more credit.

July 1954

JUL 1   Earl Bostic is currently on tour, playing tonight in Rochester, New York. Other dates for this week include the Hotel Bradford in Boston (2), New London, Connecticut (3), Taunton, Massachusetts (4), and Bridgeport, Connecticut (5).

JUL 2   Fats Domino starts another tour of California.

The **Four Knights**, Tommy Edwards, and the Willis Jackson band entertain at the Howard Theater in Washington this week.

The Robins open for three days at the Savoy Ballroom in Los Angeles. At the 5-4 Club, T-Bone Walker and Effie Smith are the weekend's entertainment.

Lionel Hampton and the Five Flamingos open for a week at the Broadway-Capitol Theater in Detroit.

In New Orleans, Johnny Moore is booked into the Dew Drop Inn for three days.

JUL 4   Louis Jordan brings his show to the Auditorium in Oakland, California.

Alan Freed, whose taped radio broadcast is heard over WNJR, puts on a stage show featuring Roy Hamilton, the Orioles, Big Maybelle, Luther Bond and the Emeralds, **Larry Darnell**, Bull Moose Jackson, Joe Liggins, the El Tempos, the Dreams, Nappy Brown, the Orchids, Varetta Dillard, and the Four Bells. The show takes place at Patrylow's Grove Park in Kenilworth, New Jersey.

New releases for the first week of July include Roy Milton's "Gonna Leave You Baby" on Specialty; Luther Bond and the Emerald's "You Were My Love" and Johnny Otis' "Mambo Boogie," both on Savoy; "'Lizabeth" by the Thrillers on Herald; "Tryin' To Fool Me" by Leonard Lee on Lamp; and "Why Should I Love You" by the Harptones on Bruce.

EARLY JULY

The Chords are set for a West Coast tour starting in August to capitalize on the popularity of "Sh-Boom," which hit the "pop" charts a few weeks ago.

The Lark's recording of "The World Is Waiting For The Sunrise" recently issued on Lloyds, receives a big boost from their appearance on the Arthur Godfrey TV show.

Pat Boone's recording of "Loving You Madly" on Republic is covered in the "pop" field by Alan Dale.

Savoy Records signs Earl Williams and the Lee Allen combo, both from New Orleans.

The Four Knights, who began in Charlotte, North Carolina, broke into the big time in 1948 with a guest appearance on Red Skelton's radio show. They had a number of big "pop" records for Capitol, including "(It's No) Sin" (1951), and "I Get So Lonely" (1954).

Larry Darnell (born Leo Edward Donald) was born and died in Columbus, Ohio (1929-1983). His biggest hits came on Regal Records which, in 1949, released two singles simultaneously: "I'll Get Along Somehow" and "For You, My Love."

In 1954, Pat Boone could only dream of a singing career. He was enrolled as a student at North Texas State College. He was also an alumnus of both the Ted Mack and Arthur Godfrey TV talent shows. Then, lightning struck: Godfrey offered him a regular spot on his daily radio program.

Atlantic Records purchases the master recording of "Co-Operation" by Prince Partridge from Blaze Records. The single has received favorable airplay on the West Coast. The song will be released on the Cat label.

JUL 8   The **Ernie Freeman** Combo starts a four-days-per-week, four-week engagement at the New Orleans Sea Food Grotto in Los Angeles.

JUL 9   Earl Bostic continues to tour the Northeast with a show in York, Pennsylvania. Other shows this week include Saratoga Springs, New York (10), Annapolis, Maryland (11), and Cape Cod, Massachusetts (14).
New York's Apollo Theater presents the Ravens and Bette McLaurin for the week.
The "Timmie Rogers Revue" featuring Roy Hamilton opens for a week at the Howard Theater in Washington.
The Spiders make their West Coast debut with a three-day weekend performance at Los Angeles' Savoy Ballroom. Across town at the 5-4 Club, Fats Domino also entertains for the three-day weekend.
The Midnighters are booked at small clubs in the New Orleans area through July 22.

New releases for the second week in July include the Clovers' "Your Cash Ain't Nothin' But Trash" and Ray Charles' "Don't You Know," both on Atlantic; "You Don't Exist No More" by Percy Mayfield on Specialty; "Little Things Mean A Lot" by Billy Ward and his Dominoes on King; Louis Jordan's "I Seen What'cha Done" and Amos Milburn's "Glory Of Love," both on Aladdin; **Arthur "Big Boy" Crudup**'s "She's Got No Hair" and Milt Trenier's "Day Old Bread," both on Groove; and "Shake, Rattle And Roll" by Bill Haley and his Comets on Decca.

JUL 13   Billy Ward and his Dominoes start a two-week engagement in Las Vegas at the Sahara Hotel.

JUL 14   Sonny Thompson and Lulu Reed stop at the Bandbox in Covington, Louisiana, enroute to the West Coast.

MID-JULY

Recent record company acquisitions include Lamp Records' Bonnie Evans and Clarence Samuels; Columbia Records' the Wailers, **the Embers**, and Eileen Hamilton; and Checker Records' Jimmy Witherspoon.

The strength of "Sh-Boom," originally recorded by the Chords, continues to grow. The cover version by the Crew-Cuts on Mercury is a solid hit on the "pop" charts, and now there are more versions. In the "pop" field, the Billy Williams Quartet has cut it on Coral, and, for the c&w market, Bobby Williamson has a record out on RCA Victor.

Other cover records include the **McGuire Sisters'** "Goodnight Sweetheart Goodnight" on Coral, Bill Haley's "Shake, Rattle And Roll" on Decca, "Honey Love" by Vicki Young, and "I Understand (Just How You Feel)" by June Valli.

Ernie Freeman (born 1929 in Cleveland) was a popular West Coast bandleader. In 1955, his band backed the Platters on "Only You" (Mercury). Freeman had a big records with his cover versions of "Raunchy" and "Dumplin's" (both 1957, Imperial).

Arthur Crudup's hits for Victor included "So Glad Your Mine" (1946), "That's All Right" (1947), and "My Baby Left Me" (1951), all of which were later recorded by Elvis Presley.

The Embers had a sputtering career: they signed with Herald Records in 1953, which released only one single, "Paradise Hill." They went to Columbia, and again only one single, "Sweet Lips," was issued. The Embers did not reappear until "Wait For Me" and "My Dearest Darling" on Dot in 1960.

The McGuire Sisters (Chris, Dotty and Phyllis) were among the best selling of all cover artists, with million-selling versions of "Sincerely" and "Goodnight Sweetheart, Goodnight."

Willie Mae Thornton and Johnny Ace are currently on a tour of Texas, Louisiana, and New Mexico.

Apollo Records and King Records both claim rights to the "5" Royales. Apollo reports that it has a current contract with the group that is valid through October 1956. King claims to have the group currently under contract.

Okeh Records, subsidiary of Columbia Records, is the first major r&b company to start sending out copies of its records to deejays only in the 45 rpm format instead of 78 rpm. Other r&b firms are expected to follow suit.

JUL 16   In Los Angeles, Tiny Bradshaw is at the 5-4 Club and Percy Mayfield is at the Savoy Ballroom for the three-day weekend. At the Oasis Ballroom, Dinah Washington opens for two weeks.

JUL 17   The "Fifth Annual Rhythm And Blues Jubilee" at the Hollywood Shrine Auditorium features the Four Tunes, the Chords, the Robins, the Hollywood Four Flames, and Chuck Higgins and his band.
   "Riot In Cell Block #9" by the Robins is banned by CBS radio and television. The network refuses to allow the song to be aired as part of its "Juke Box Jury" show.
   Earl King plays a two-day engagement at New Orleans' Dew Drop Inn.

New releases for the third week of July include "In The Chapel In The Moonlight" by the Orioles and "The Greatest Feeling In The World" by the Four Tunes, both on Jubilee; "Any Day Now" by Buddy and Ella Johnson on King; Ruth Brown's "Oh What A Dream" on Atlantic; "Cherry Pie" by Marvin and Johnny on Modern; "One Bad Stud" by the Honey Bears on Spark; "I've Got You Under My Skin" by the Ravens on Mercury; "Goody Goody" by the Five C's on United; "Somewhere Somebody Cares" by Bill Robinson and the Quails on DeLuxe; **James Cotton**'s "Hold Me In Your Arms" and Elvis Presley's "That's All Right," both on Sun; and the Flairs' "Let's Make Love Sometime" on Flair.

JUL 22   Amos Milburn plays the Alpha Inn in Dayton, Ohio, for five days.
   The Robins are booked for an extended engagement at the Trocadero Club in Los Angeles.

JUL 23   The Midnighters front Arnett Cobb's Orchestra during their week at the Howard Theater in Washington.
   In Los Angeles, Lulu Reed with Sonny Thompson's Orchestra open for the weekend at the Savoy Ballroom. At the 5-4 Club, the Clovers team with Fats Domino to entertain nightly for the next three days.

New releases for the fourth week of July include "What's That" by the "5" Royales on Apollo; B. B. King's "Bye! Bye! Baby" on RPM; Lulu Reed's "I'll Upset You Baby" and Wynonie Harris's "I Get A Thrill," both on King; "Big Mouth Mama" by the Shadows and "Bad Things On My Mind" by **Lightnin' Hopkins**, both on Decca; "Oooh-La-La" by the Hollywood Flames on Lucky; Bobby Prince's "Too Many Keys" on Excello;

Guitarist/vocalist Earl "King" Johnson was born February 7, 1934, in New Orleans. He first recorded as Earl Johnson on Savoy backed by Huey Smith's band in 1953, and is best known for his 1955 release "Those Lonely, Lonely Nights" on Ace, which featured Smith on piano.

James Cotton remained in the Memphis area only a short while after his solo record debut on Sun. Like other Mississippi blues men, he moved to Chicago where he played harmonica in Muddy Waters band after Little Walter went solo. He stayed with Waters for twenty years before venturing out on his own.

Lightin' Hopkins never achieved widespread success, although his records sold well enough to keep him recording for over thirty years. In the 1960s, his rural blues style found a new, welcome audience among admirers of folk music. Hopkins died January 30, 1982.

"Bald Head" by the Treniers on Okeh; "Crazy With The Heat" by Clarence Samuels on Lamp; "Boogie Baby" by J. T. Brown on J.O.B.; "Can't Stop Loving You" by Smiley Lewis and "I-Yi" by the Hawks, both on Imperial; and "You Figure It Out" by Rosco Gordon and "Your Kind Of Love" by Earl Forrest, both on Duke.

ELVIS PRESLEY
Three weeks after its release, Sun Records is back-ordered 6,000 copies on Elvis Presley's "That's All right," although the record has only been issued in Memphis, New Orleans and Dallas.

JUL 27   Faye Adams, Al Savage, and Joe Morris start a one-nighter tour through the southern states.

JUL 30   The weekend entertainment bill in Los Angeles features Louis Jordan at the 5-4 Club and Floyd Dixon at the Savoy Ballroom.
          Guitar Slim, T-Bone Walker, and Joe Turner start a tour through Texas that will run through August 24th.

JUL 31   RCA Victor announces that 45 r.p.m. records are accounting for more than fifty percent of its total record volume, with long play albums far behind at twenty-three percent and 78 r.p.m. singles, twenty-one percent.
          Elvis Presley makes his first professional personal appearance as part of a country and western jamboree at the Overton Park Shell in Memphis featuring Slim Whitman.

LATE JULY

Jimmy Liggins, formerly with Specialty Records, signs with Aladdin.

Charles Brown continues on tour with dates booked in Michigan.

The Mellows sign a recording contract with Jay-Dee Records and Baby Dee signs with M-G-M Records. She is currently booked at the Cotton Club in Atlantic City through Labor Day.

THE TOP TEN ROCK 'N' ROLL RECORDS FOR JULY 1954

1. Honey Love - Clyde McPhatter and the Drifters
2. Work With Me Annie - The Midnighters
3. Sh-Boom - The Chords
4. Shake, Rattle And Roll - Joe Turner
5. Just Make Love To Me - Muddy Waters
6. If I Loved You - Roy Hamilton
7. Sexy Ways - The Midnighters
8. Goodnite, Sweetheart, Goodnite - The Spaniels
9. Lovey Dovey - The Clovers
10. I Feel So Bad - Chuck Willis

July 1954
ARTIST OF THE MONTH

THE SPANIELS

THE SPANIELS

They probably weren't the first vocal group to line up onstage with the lead tenor off to one side on his own microphone, separated from the rest of the vocalists who shared a second mike. But the Spaniels certainly started a trend among rhythm and blues groups by such a stage setup. They also simulated tap-dance routines during their songs to add excitement. This combination seems to have added at least a little confusion to their many performances. One reviewer even thought the group was trying to out-shout the lead singer.

The Spaniels were formed in Gary, Indiana, in 1952 by James "Pookie" Hudson. At first they met on the street to vocalize, eventually graduating to talent shows and church activities where they were discovered by a local deejay, Vivian Carter, who was in the middle of starting her own record company, Vee-Jay Records, with her husband, James Bracken. At this time, besides Hudson on lead tenor, the group consisted of Ernest Warren (first tenor), Opal Courtney, Jr. (baritone), Willie C. Jackson (baritone), and Gerald Gregory (bass). Their first record, "Baby It's You" was issued on Chance, before it became the first issue on Vee-Jay. The Spaniels remained with Vee-Jay for the next seven years.

"Baby It's You" sold well enough to make the r&b best-sellers charts, but follow-up material was hard to come by. Hudson wrote "Goodnite, Sweetheart, Goodnite," which was released in March 1954, and even though the song was an immediate success, it was the cover version by the McGuire Sisters that sold the most copies. The song transcended the usual life of a hit record to become one of the most requested "oldies" of all time. It is constantly used at the end of radio shows playing r&b material and by stage acts featuring rock 'n roll songs.

In 1955 Courtney was drafted and his place in the group was taken, first by Calvin Carter, then by James "Dimples" Cochran. Jerome Henderson (guitar) joined about this time, then Warren was drafted and not replaced. Eventually even Hudson and Jackson left the group, although Hudson returned to record "Stormy Weather" and "Everybody's Laughing." The Spaniels continued through all of this as a viable vocal group. Although they had few major hits, they did tour constantly with the rock 'n roll caravans. By 1960 their contract with Vee-Jay lapsed and they moved on to a succession of labels, including Neptune, Jamie, Double-L, North American, Parkway, Calla, Buddah, and Canterbury.

Pookie Hudson has claimed that they were offered a new song in 1958 that could have changed the group's history forever. They were playing the Casbah Club in Washington when the Nightingales, a gospel group, gave them the opportunity to record "The Twist," which was too secular for the Nightingales to touch. Hudson passed on it, and the song was recorded first by its author, Hank Ballard and the Midnighters, and then by Chubby Checker, who sold millions of copies of his version. So much for hindsight.

The Spaniels could easily be written off as just another r&b vocal group, a one-hit wonder. But they were much more than that. Their longevity displays their professionalism and dedication to their craft. They were immensely popular during their heyday, and they were able to exchange their instant idolatry for longevity. In 1970 they did the impossible: ten years after their last hit record, "I Know," they hit again with a completely new style in "Fairy Tales" on Calla. In the music business this amounts to a certified miracle.

August 1954

AUG 1   Dinah Washington and Tiny Bradshaw perform for the 10th Annual Disk Jockey Award Ball at the Elks Auditorium in Los Angeles. Miss Washington is booked on the West Coast through September.

AUG 2   Ruth Brown and Ray Charles kick off a short tour with a show in Cleveland.

New releases for the first week of August include "My Dear, My Darling" by the Counts on Dot; "Key To My Heart" by the Robins on Crown; Earl Bostic's "These Foolish Things" and the "5" Royales' "I'm Gonna Run It Down," both on King; The Charms' "Come To Me Baby" on DeLuxe; "Shake It Baby" by Sunnyland Slim on J.O.B.; "Lovin' On My Mind" by the Shufflers on Okeh; "Nagasaki" by the Five Chances on Chance; Red Prysock's "Blow Your Horn" on Mercury; Baby Dee's "Don't Live Like That No More" and "S'Posin'" by the Cat Men, both on M-G-M; "Say Hey" by Willie Mays with the Treniers on Okeh; and "How Sentimental Can I Be?" by the **Mellows** on Jay-Dee.

The Mellows featured a female lead vocalist, Lillian Leach. Jimmy Bailey (of the Cadillacs) and Harold Johnson (of the Crickets) were also members of the group.

AUG 6   The second annual "Biggest Rhythm And Blues Show" sets out on a month-long tour with an opening night in Cleveland. Alan "Moondog" Freed promotes this show, which brings in 9,600 fans. Other record-breaking dates for this tour include Dayton, Ohio, on the 7th (4,700 fans make this the largest audience up to that time for a non-racing event at the Dayton Speedway); and Flint, Michigan, on the 8th (6,800 reported as the biggest audience ever for the city). Dates at the Arcadia in Detroit (9th), and in Gary, Indiana (10th), have smaller crowds, but the show in Cincinnati on the 11th brings in 6,000 people. Both shows at the Lyric Theater in Indianapolis on August 12 are sellouts. In Chicago, on the 13th, over ten thousand stand in line for hours to watch the entertainers, among whom are Roy Hamilton, the Drifters, the Spaniels, the **Counts**, Faye Adams, LaVern Baker, King Pleasure, Erskine Hawkins, and **Rusty Bryant**th. The tour continues with shows in St. Louis (14) and Kansas City (15). The first eight days on the road, over 50,000 attend the shows. The tour will run through September 12th.

The Counts and Rusty Bryant were among the few Dot Records r&b acts. The Counts issued eight singles on the label from 1953-56, including "My Dear, My Darling" and "Darling, Dear." Rusty Bryant was a frantic tenor sax blower in the Red Prysock vein whose only hit was a wild version of "Night Train" titled "All Night Long."

AUG 7   Following his tour of Florida, Smiley Lewis plays the Caffin Theater in New Orleans. He follows this date with a one-nighter tour of Louisiana, Texas, and Mississippi before heading up the Atlantic Seaboard.

EARLY AUGUST

In Hollywood, the new r&b nightclub is the Riverside Rancho which previously had featured country music. The opening bill headlines Tiny

Bradshaw and the Flairs.

Decca signs the **Wanderers**, formerly with Central Records. They will be renamed the Singing Wanderers.

On separate tours of the South during August are Fats Domino and Amos Milburn.

Cat Records announces that "Sh-Boom" by the Chords is set for release in England on the EMI label. Also, the Playboys have recently signed with Cat.

The Clovers and John Greer are playing the Rainbow Ballroom in Denver.

Following the completion of a successful engagement, the Sahara Hotel in Las Vegas announces that it has signed Billy Ward and his Dominoes to a two-year pact. The contract will start in November with the group playing for two weeks at $5,000 a week. Thereafter, the Dominoes will play the hotel every four months at an increasing salary.

AUG 8   Earl Bostic takes the spotlight in Detroit at the Crystal Lounge for a week.

New **releases** for the second week of August include "Love Me" by Willie and Ruth on Spark; Fats Domino's "You Can Pack Your Suitcase" and T-Bone Walker's "Teenage Girl," both on Imperial; "The Cheater" by Jimmy McCracklin on Peacock; Roy Brown's "Girl From Kokomo" on King; "Give In" by the Five Jets on DeLuxe; "I Ain't Drunk" by Jimmy Liggins on Aladdin; "Baby, Come A Little Closer" by the Five Willows on Herald; and "Black Cat Bone" by **Peppermint Harris** on Modern.

AUG 13   Ruth Brown opens at the Apollo in New York with the Larks and the Willis Jackson band. While in Gotham, Miss Brown makes several movie shorts for use on TV to promote her latest releases.
        Jimmy Witherspoon and Percy Mayfield hold court at the Savoy Ballroom in Los Angeles for three nights. Meanwhile, at the 5-4 Club this weekend, Ray Charles and Dinah Washington are the crowd pleasers, while across town, Marvin and Johnny open at the Club Oasis.

AUG 15   *Billboard* magazine reports that rhythm and blues music is invading the "pop" market even though this is still considered a teen-age phenomena. In the Midwest, r&b has taken over the juke boxes and record stores of many middle class neighborhoods. In most locations the original rhythm and blues record is also receiving more plays on jukeboxes and over the radio than the "pop" cover versions.

MID-AUGUST

Aladdin Records opens a New York City office with Eddie Meisner in charge. Jesse Stone will continue to head Aladdin's subsidiary, Lamp Records. Aladdin has recently signed the Dodgers, a vocal quintet, and **Margie Hendricks**.

Various other groups using the name Wanderers also recorded for Savoy (1953), Onyx (1957), Orbut (1958), Cub (1958-61), Kent (1961), and M-G-M (1962). The Singing Wanderers issued two singles on Decca, including the novelty "Say Hey, Willie Mays" (1954).

Peppermint Harris' biggest hit came with "I Got Loaded," which topped the r&b charts in 1951. In addition to a long recording career, he has written songs for Bobby Bland, Junior Parker, B.B. King, and Etta James.

Marjorie "Margie" Hendricks was assigned to Lamp Records, an Aladdin subsidiary, where she was made lead singer of the Cookies. After Lamp shut down, Jesse Stone took the group with him to Atlantic, where they not only recorded under their own name, but were used extensively as a backup vocal group.

BILL DOGGETT

Shirley Gunter was the sister of Cornelius (Cornel) Gunter, who sang with the Flairs. The Queens were a group of teenage high school girls from Los Angeles. The group featured Zola Taylor, who soon left to join the Platters.

Willie Love died on August 19, 1953, at age 42, so this would have been a posthumous release. As a pianist he broke into show business with the King Biscuit Time radio program in Helena, Arkansas, in 1942. He recorded for Trumpet with the Three Aces, and with Sonny Boy Williamson.

Billy Ward and the Associated Booking Corporation settle their six-month dispute. Ward will receive a financial settlement, and their original contract, which was to run through 1958, is replaced by an agreement that will be effective only through April 1955.

AUG 16   "The Biggest Rhythm And Blues Show" moves west with tonight's performance in Tulsa. Other shows during the week are Oklahoma City (17), Dallas (18), Fort Worth (19), Corpus Christi (20), San Antonio (21), and Houston (22). (See August 6th.)

New releases for the third week of August include "Annie Had A Baby" by the Midnighters on Federal; "I Don't Hurt Anymore" by Dinah Washington on Mercury; "Hurts Me To My Heart" by Faye Adams on Herald; "Rock, Moan And Cry" by the Playboys and "Moonshine" by Floyd Dixon, both on Cat; "High Heels" by **Bill Doggett** on King; "I'm Mad" by John Lee Hooker and "Later For You Baby" by Guitar Slim, both on Specialty; and "Ain't Times Hard" by Floyd Jones on Vee-Jay.

AUG 19   B. B. King brings in a record-breaking crowd for a one-nighter at the Savoy Ballroom in Los Angeles. The room seats 2,400 and over 2,800 were turned away at the door. Also on the bill are Johnny Otis with Marie Adams, **Shirley Gunter and the Queens**, Marvin and Johnny, the Platters, and the Lamplighters. Also in Los Angeles, Louis Jordan joins the Robins at the Club Trocadera for a ten-day engagement.

AUG 20   The Orioles are booked into Weeke's in Atlantic City for a week.
       Billy Ward and his Dominoes along with the Earl "Fatha" Hines Combo are at New York's Apollo Theater for a week.
       Ivory Joe Hunter starts a week's engagement at the Flame Show Bar in Detroit.
       In Los Angeles, the three-day weekend entertainment includes Roy Milton at the Savoy Ballroom and Charles Brown with Lowell Fulson at the 5-4 Club. Brown has reformed his touring combo following a year as a solo artist.

AUG 23   "The Biggest Rhythm And Blues Show" moves into the Deep South with a show at the New Orleans Municipal Auditorium. Other dates for the remainder of the month include Mobile (24), Montgomery (25), Atlanta (26), Nashville (27), Memphis (28), Birmingham (29), Chattanooga (30), and Augusta, Georgia (31). (See August 6th.)
       Ruth Brown holds forth this week at Pep's in Philadelphia.

New releases for the fourth week in August include Roy Hamilton's "Ebb Tide" on Epic, Little Walter's "You'd Better Watch Yourself" on Checker, "Way Back" by **Willie Love** and the Three Aces on Trumpet, "Get High Everybody" by Lil Son Jackson on Imperial, and Big Jay McNeely's "Beachcomber" on Federal.

AUG 27   The Chords and Earl "Fatha" Hines start a week at the Skyliner Lounge in Washington.
       In Los Angeles, Johnny Otis and the Dreamers entertain for the weekend at the Savoy Ballroom.

The **Four Knights** headline the Apollo Theater's revue in New York.

AUG 28   Guitar Slim is booked on a California tour for three weeks.

AUG 29   Louis Jordan kicks off a three-month tour of one-night stands in Texas with a show in El Paso, tonight, Midland on the 30th, and San Antonio on the 31st. He will play fifty-two dates in twelve states through October in Texas, Oklahoma, Louisiana, Alabama, Arkansas, North Carolina, South Carolina, Mississippi, Tennessee, Florida, West Virginia, and Virginia. This is his first southern trek in two years.

Blues singer Piney Brown opens the season this week at the Club Ebony in Houston.

New releases for the fifth week of August include "Yeah Yeah Yeah" by Joe Liggins on Mercury; "Five Minutes Longer" by the Lamplighters on Federal; "Just Don't Cry" by the Strangers on King; "No There Ain't No News Today" by **Dootsie Williams**'s Orchestra on Dootone; and "Over a Cup Of Coffee" by the Castelles on Grand.

AUG 31   Fats Domino and the Clovers start a tour of the South, including Florida, through September 19th.

LATE AUGUST

Capitol Records signs the Five Keys, who have recently been recording for Apollo Records.

Decca Records announces that they have signed the popular Hollywood Four Flames, who most recently recorded for Lucky.

Jubilee Records signs Billy Ward and his Dominoes and immediately has them in the recording studio. The group started with Federal in 1951 and has recently had singles issued by both Federal and its parent company, King Records.

THE FOUR KNIGHTS

Dootsie Williams started his career in music as a violinist, but switched to trumpet when he formed his West Coast combo. The band featured the fabulous Nellie Lutcher on piano. He founded Dootone Records in 1947 after working as a talent scout for M-G-M. In 1955, he was forced to change the name from Dootone to Dooto after the Duo-Tone Needle Co. objected to the close similarity of their names. On "No There Ain't No News Today," vocals were handled by the Penguins.

THE TOP TEN ROCK 'N' ROLL RECORDS FOR AUGUST 1954

1. Honey Love - Clyde McPhatter and the Drifters
2. Work With Me Annie - The Midnighters
3. Sexy Ways - The Midnighters
4. Sh-Boom - The Chords
5. Shake, Rattle And Roll - Joe Turner
6. Oh What A Dream - Ruth Brown
7. Your Cash Ain't Nothin' But Trash - The Clovers
8. Just Make Love To Me - Muddy Waters
9. Goodnite, Sweetheart, Goodnite - The Spaniels
10. Hurts Me To My Heart - Faye Adams

MUDDY WATERS
(McKinley Morganfield, b. April 4,1915; d. April 30, 1983)

MUDDY WATERS

The name Muddy Waters is synonymous with the modern day blues. Muddy Waters's music has a much broader force for change than his record sales or audience appeal would at first indicate. Yet, by the end of his career he was billed, and rightly so, as the "Living Legend."

His father was a musician and a farmer on a small plot of land near Rolling Fork, Mississippi. His mother died when he was very young, and he was sent to live with his grandmother on the Stovall Plantation near Clarksdale. It was his grandmother who gave McKinley his nickname of "Muddy Waters" reportedly because he continualy played in the small creek near their home. He was self-taught on the guitar and harmonica, and in the 1930s he played in a string band in the Clarksdale area. He continued working on plantations, but he supplemented his income by making moonshine that he sold in his home, which was converted into a juke joint on weekends. In 1940 he was one of the musicians recorded by John Lomax for the Library of Congress series on rural folk music. By this time he was sure enough of himself to travel to St. Louis, where he found work as a musician. The next year he was hired by Silas Green's traveling tent show.

During World War II he moved to Chicago, where he worked in a paper mill by day so that he could play the blues at night. It wasn't until about 1943 that he owned his first electric guitar. In Chicago he was able to work with many of the fine country blues musicians who had migrated north. His first recording in Chicago was "Mean Red Spider" in late 1945 or early 1946, issued by 20th Century Records under the name of the pianist on the session, James "Sweet Lucy" Carter. He also recorded with Sunnyland Slim and Leroy Foster on the Aristocrat label starting in 1947. His first release under his own name, "I Can't Be Satisfied," came in 1948. He formed a band to work the clubs on the southside of Chicago that included, at one time or another, James Cotton, Willie Dixon, Little Walter, Otis Spann, Junior Wells, Jimmie Rogers, and Elgin Evans. His first national recognition came with "Louisiana Blues," issued by Chess Records in 1951. For each of the next five years, he had at least one national hit record.

His early recordings show the influence of the country blues of Son House, Robert Johnson, and Blind Lemon Jefferson. His guitar playing can best be described as crude. He sings basic twelve-bar blues, repeating the first line twice, then singing a "tag" line. In the background Little Walter wails on his harmonica, while the bass and drums are barely audible.

By 1955 there is a dramatic change in his sound: the drums keep a steady beat; the guitar is played more forcefully; the song is more structured. Little Walter's harmonica is stronger, used more as a foil against Waters's singing and guitar playing. His electrification of the blues had influenced the mainstream of rhythm and blues, helping to create rock 'n roll, and in turn, Muddy Waters had updated his style in an attempt to keep pace.

It was also in 1955 that rock 'n roll stalled his career. Straight blues, no matter how amplified, was no longer acceptable to the majority of r&b record buyers. Muddy Waters refused to compromise his music any further, and though his career slowed, it was not dead. In 1958 he made a successful tour of England, where he found an audience that was eager to hear the blues undiluted by rock 'n roll. Another career highlight for Muddy Waters at this time was his powerful appearance at the Newport Blues Festival in 1960. In 1962 it was back to England, where his influence was felt among the younger musicians like Mick Jagger, Eric Clapton, Eric Burden, Jimmy Page, and John Mayall, who would carry on the tradition started by Waters.

Muddy Water's performance at the farewell concert given by the Band in San Francisco in 1976 featured one of the most powerful renditions of "Mannish Boy" every sung. On a stage filled with luminaries in the rock field, it was the master, Muddy Waters, who stole the show from the youngsters.

He continued to record through the 1970s with Chess Records. In 1983 he passed away in his sleep at his home in Westmont, a suburb of Chicago.

September 1954

SEP 1   The "Biggest Rhythm And Blues Show" continues up the Eastern Seaboard with a show in Charleston, South Carolina. Other performances this week are Columbia, South Carolina (2), Greenville, South Carolina (3), Norfolk, Virginia (4), and Washington (5). (See August 6th.)

Bill Haley and his Comets are at the Hof Brau in Wildwood, New Jersey, for two weeks.

SEP 3   The Ink Spots featuring Charlie Fuqua headline the Labor Day Week show at the Apollo Theater in New York.

Earl "Fatha" Hines and the Chords open for a week at the Howard Theater in Washington.

In Los Angeles, the Savoy Ballroom plays host to Buddy DeFranco and the Lamplighters for three days, and the 5-4 Club welcomes Charles Brown and Stan Getz for the weekend.

SEP 6   The "Biggest Rhythm And Blues Show" winds up its tour this week with performances in Raleigh, North Carolina, tonight, Charlotte, South Carolina (7th), Richmond (8th), Philadelphia (9th), and Newark (10th). (See August 6th.)

New releases for the first week of September include "Mmm Mmm Baby" by the Spiders, "A.B.C.'s" by Smilin' Joe, and "The Things I'm Gonna Do" by Jesse Allen, all on Imperial; "Drifting" by Eddie Boyd on Chess; "Honey Baby" by the Blue Diamonds on Savoy; "Baby I Need You" by the **El Dorados** on Vee-Jay; and Louis Jordan's "If I Had Any Sense I'd Go Back Home" on Aladdin.

SEP 7   Alan "Moondog" Freed transfers from WJW in Cleveland and begins broadcasting from WINS in New York City. He is heard six nights a week from 11:00 p.m. to 2:00 a.m. His show is syndicated in a one-hour format on tape in St. Louis, Kansas City, and Columbus, Ohio, while Cleveland and Flint, Michigan, will carry the show live for three hours a day. Freed will reportedly be paid $75,000 per year. Radio station WINS also hires Bill Graham, an expert in Black marketing, to start selling the station's advertising.

SEP 10   Earl Bostic brings his combo to the Hi Hat Club in Boston.

The "new" Ink Spots, **Cootie Williams**, and Wini Brown start a week of entertaining at Washington's Howard Theater.

In Los Angeles, Shirley Gunter and the Queens play a one-night stand at the 5-4 Club. Meanwhile, Wynonie Harris makes his first Los Angeles appearance in three years during a three-day stint at the Savoy Ballroom.

SEP 11   Duke Ellington graces the 5-4 Club in Los Angeles with

Earl Hines (born 1905 near Pittsburgh) started on coronet, but when he was hired to work with Louis Armstrong in 1927, he found that was one coronet player too many and he switched to the piano. Lucky for us, because Hines has often been referred to as the greatest pianist in the entire history of jazz. He remained with "Satchmo" off and on for forty years.

THE EL DORADOS

The El Dorados were a Chicago group that started harmonizing in 1952. Shortly after "Baby I Need You" (their first release), they were hired by Vee-Jay to back Hazel McCollum on "Annie's Answer," one of the many records cashing in on the "Annie" craze started by the Midnighters.

Trumpeter Cootie Williams was a master at using the plunger mute, and is best remembered for the physical power with which he attacked each solo.

a rare two-day visit.

SEP 12   Following its successful five-week road trip, the "Biggest Rhythm & Blues Revue" opens for five days at Brooklyn's Paramount Theater. Featured performers are Roy Hamilton, the Drifters, the Counts, the Spaniels, Rusty Bryant, Erskine Hawkins, LaVern Baker, Faye Adams, and Big Maybelle.

Louis Jordan plays the New Orleans Booker T. Washington Auditorium while on a three-month trek.

SEP 13   Fats Domino comes down with tonsillitis while on tour in Baton Rouge. He is hospitalized in New Orleans. Following a tonsillectomy at the end of the month, Fats is expected to return to the tour circuit by October 10th. His place on the current tour is filled by Amos Milburn and Floyd Dixon.

New releases for the second week of September include "Zippity Zum" by the Chords on Cat; "My Heart's Crying For You" by the **Chimes** and "Oop Shoop" by Shirley Gunter and the Queens, both on Flair; "You Make Me Happy" by the Dodgers and "Foolish" by Charles Brown, both on Aladdin; "Boot 'Em Up" by the Du Droppers on Groove; "It Won't Take Long" by the Native Boys on Modern; Henry Smith's "Good Rockin' Mama" on Dot; and Ivory Joe Hunter's "Do You Miss Me?" on M-G-M.

MID-SEPTEMBER

Harlem Records, a new entry in the r&b field, releases its first records by the Kings, Brownie McGhee, the Serenaders, and Lightnin' Hopkins.

Currently on tour are Roy Brown in the South and the Ravens with Hal Singer's Combo in the Midwest.

Okeh Records signs the **Hi-Lites** to a recording contract.

SEP 16   The Midnighters make their first Los Angeles appearance fronting the Todd Rhodes Orchestra at the 5-4 Ballroom for the evening.

Bill Haley and his Comets play for three days at Andy's Log Cabin in Gloucester, New Jersey.

SEP 17   Charles Brown and the Spiders kick off a tour of the Easter Seaboard.

Dinah Washington starts in the "Tropicana Revue" this week at the Howard Theater in Washington.

The Rusty Bryant Combo backs the **Will Maston** Trio for the week at the Apollo Theater in New York.

T-Bone Walker begins a two-week layover at the Flame Show Bar in Detroit.

In Los Angeles, the Savoy Ballroom offers a "Battle Of The Blues" featuring Lowell Fulson, Jimmy Witherspoon, and Floyd Dixon for three days. The Club Oasis hosts Shirley Gunter and the Queens for the first show of a ten-day run, and the 5-4 Club presents Ray Charles and Guitar Slim for the three-day weekend.

The Chimes, with its inference to tinkling bells, has always been a popular name for r&b vocal groups. This group of Chimes recorded one single each for Flair, Dig, and Limelight, and also released three singles on Specialty (1955-56). The group is not related to the Chimes (a white group) with the 1960 hit "Once In A While" on Tag.

The Hi-Lites on Okeh recorded for Brunswick (1958), and should not be confused with the group of the same name on Record Fair (1961), who may or may not be the same as Ronnie and the Hi-Lites ("I Wish That We Were Married," 1962, Joy).

The Will Maston Trio was a song and dance act featuring Sammy Davis, Jr., nephew of Maston. They specialized in frantic, synchronized tap-dancing.

189

SEP 19   Bill Haley and his Comets are at the Sleepy Hollow Ranch in Pennsburg, Pennsylvania, for a one-night stand.

SEP 20   The Orioles are the headliners at Gleason's in Cleveland.

New releases for the third week of September include "Well All Right" by Joe Turner on Atlantic; "Never Let Me Go" by Johnny Ace on Duke; "Don't Drop It" by **Wilbert Harrison** on Savoy; "Hearts Of Stone" by the Jewels on R&B; "Give It Up" by the Hawks on Imperial; "Bye Bye" by the Dreamers on Flair; "Gonna Love You Everyday" by the Heralds and "Movin' On Out Boogie" by Lightnin' the Hopkins, both on Herald; and "Baby Be Mine" by Nolan Strong and Diablos on Fortune.

SEP 24   Bill Haley and his Comets entertain for three nights at the Armory in Painsville, Ohio. The show is sponsored by Bill Randle of WERE of Cleveland.
    Earl King spends three days in New Orleans at the Dew Drop Inn.
    At the Apollo Theater in New York this week, Dinah Washington entertains ticket holders.
    Weekend entertainment in Los Angeles leans toward the blues with Muddy Waters and Guitar Slim sharing the bill at the Savoy Ballroom and Amos Milburn playing for dancers at the 5-4 Club.

SEP 26   Buddy Johnson, Nat "King" Cole, and Ella Johnson are the featured attractions for the evening at the New Orleans Municipal Auditorium.

New releases for the fourth week of September include Marvin and Johnny's "Day In, Day Out" on Specialty; "She Couldn't Be Found" by Bobby Mitchell and the Toppers and "Jump Children" by Dave Bartholomew, both on Imperial; Varetta Dillard's "Send Me Some Money" on Savoy; "Hearts Of Stone" by the Charms and "Why Do I Wait?" by Bill Robinson and the Quails, both on DeLuxe; **Memphis Slim**'s "Four Years Of Torment" on United; Willie Mae Thornton's "Stop Hoppin' On Me" on Peacock; and "Good Rockin' Tonight" by Elvis Presley on Sun.

SEP 28   Earl Bostic returns to New York City, opening at Basin Street.

SEP 29   Bill Haley and his Comets perform for a week at the Casa Loma Ballroom in St. Louis.

LATE SEPTEMBER

Chuck Willis and Joe Turner join together for a tour of the eastern club circuit through November.

1. Oh What A Dream - Ruth Brown
2. Honey Love - Clyde McPhatter and the Drifters
3. Annie Had A Baby - The Midnighters
4. Hurts Me To My Heart - Faye Adams
5. Shake, Rattle And Roll - Bill Haley and his Comets
6. Sexy Ways - The Midnighters
7. Work With Me Annie - The Midnighters
8. Shake, Rattle And Roll - Joe Turner
9. Sh-Boom - The Chords
10. Ebb Tide - Roy Hamilton

September 1954
ARTIST OF THE MONTH

THE CHORDS

THE CHORDS

This fine rhythm and blues group had more than one strike against it almost before it began. Looking back, it is amazing, then, that their only hit record could generate such long-lasting admiration. The record was immediately covered for the "pop" audience, and this cover version went to the top of the hit parade. The song was parodied in such a harsh manner that there could be little doubt that the humorist was dead set against the original song. And their original name was dumped in favor of not one, but two alternate choices, just as it looked like they would be able to make themselves known. The group is the Chords and the song is, of course, "Sh-Boom."

The original members of the Chords included two brothers, Claude and Earl Feaster, Jimmy Keyes, Floyd McRae, and William Edwards. School pals from New York City, they were discovered by Atlantic Records, which at the time was searching for talent to head up its new subsidiary, Cat Records. The Chords' first session produced a beautiful ballad, "Cross Over The Bridge," which was a current hit for Patti Page. Needing a flip side, the group put together a quick arrangement of "Sh-Boom," a nonsensical piece of business that included one verse sung entirely in "scat": "Hey nannie ding-dong/ A lang-a-da lang-a-da lang-a-da/ Oh-whoa vip/ a-dibba-dooba-dip." Just under the saxophone break in the middle of the song, the group marked time singing over and over, "Dee ooee-oot/ Doot-doot Sh-boom." The song just as easily could have been titled "Life Could Be A Dream," since this was one of the few phrases in "Sh-Boom" that made any sense. Who knows where a song like this comes from? Certainly not the professional songwriters from Tin Pan Alley. This song had to be heard to be believed.

And the first to hear it clearly was Mercury Records, which assigned the Crew-Cuts to record a cover version for the "pop" audience. Even the Crew-Cuts were unable to do much with the lyrics, but they gave it all the gusto they could muster. Then along came humorist Stan Freberg, who recorded a parody of "Sh-Boom" that possibly came closer to the "feel" of the original recording than did the Crew-Cuts' cover version. Too close, maybe, since it appears that Freberg hit a nerve with the Chords, which led to a highly publicized feud that may or may not have been a press agent's stunt. Whatever, it certainly didn't hurt the sales of the record.

But speaking of the Chords, the group suffered its first indignity when Atlantic withdrew the original "A" side, "Cross Over The Bridge," stating that it felt the song was strong enough to be re-issued later (it never was). Then another group was discovered to have used the name "Chords" first, so a name change was in order. The Chords became the Chordcats. Close, but this certainly didn't help solidify the group's identity, especially since there were already two other versions of the song available; now it appeared as though they were competing with themselves.

To say that the Chords/Chordcats died as a result of the craze in the music industry in 1954 of pop artists covering rhythm and blues tunes may be too kind. The group itself was unable to come up with another record that was as absolutely refreshing as "Sh-Boom." They tried "Zippity-Zum," but it just wasn't the same. Onstage the group expanded to five members using the latest fad, two microphones. Although they were vigorous and exciting, had good looks, could dance well enough to excite the crowd, and had an individuality in their voices that allowed them to exchange lead vocals, the group flopped after "Sh-Boom."

Novelty records are always the hardest on which to build a lasting musical career. Just ask the Chords . . . or the Chordcats . . . or the Sh-Booms (which is how the current single from Atlantic lists the group). No wonder they failed to have a long career!

October 1954

OCT 1   Charles Brown and Ruth Brown share the bill with the Griffin Brothers Orchestra as their tour of Texas, Oklahoma, and the South kicks off today.

The Orioles with the Paul Williams Orchestra appear at the Howard Theater in Washington for a week.

The Drifters and Erskine Hawkins's Orchestra entertain for the week at the Apollo Theater in New York.

Al Hibbler, Dakota Staton, and Della Reese headline a two-week stay at the Flame Show Bar in Detroit.

In Los Angeles, the weekend finds Roy Milton and Amos Milburn at the 5-4 Club and King Perry and Joseph "Mr. Google Eyes" August at the Savoy Ballroom.

OCT 2   Less than a month after changing from Cleveland's WJW to New York's WINS radio, Alan Freed is given another hour each night and an earlier time slot to broadcast his rhythm and blues program. The show will now run from 7:00 to 11:00 p.m. nightly. The taped syndication of his show has run into opposition from Black deejays who fear that Freed's popularity will put them out of work in markets far removed from the New York area.

Elvis Presley makes his only appearance on the "Grand Ole Opry" radio broadcast from Nashville.

Smiley Lewis returns to New Orleans' Caffin Theater for the evening.

New releases for the first week of October include Ruth Brown's "Mambo Baby," the Drifters' "Bip Bam," and Tommy Ridgely's "Jam Up," all on Atlantic; "Let's Make Up" by the Spaniels on Vee-Jay; "Ain't Gonna Do It" by the Pelicans on Imperial; "Hold On" by the Peppers on Chess; "Oh Baby" by Sonny Carter on King; "Broke" by Chuck Higgins and "No One But Me" by Earl King, both on Specialty; "I Cried My Heart Out" by the Sultans on Duke; "Oh But She Did" by the Opals on Apollo; and "Tell Me, Thrill Me" by the **Chanters** on RPM.

EARLY OCTOBER

Ella Johnson's new release on Mercury, "Well Do It," is her first without her brother, bandleader Buddy Johnson.

Rhythm and blues performers currently on tour include Chuck Willis and Joe Turner, who continue to tour the Eastern Seaboard, Muddy Waters and Todd Rhodes, who are on separate tours of the West Coast, and Memphis Slim, who is on the one-night circuit in Texas.

Chess Records, a leading independent r&b company, releases its first country and western disk, "If You Don't Somebody Else Will" by Jimmy and Johnny.

On the Grand "Ole Opry," Elvis Presley is limited to only one song; he chose "Blue Moon Of Kentucky," the country-flavored side of his first release. The audience and management were not impressed, and he was not invited back.

The Chanters, who released only this one single on RPM, are not the same as the teen group on Deluxe which recorded "No, No, No" in 1958, although it is possible that they may be the same group that backed Brother Woodman on Combo in 1955.

Memphis radio station WDIA, the nation's most powerful Black station at 50,000 watts, bans all records with suggestive lyrics and double-entendres.

OCT 8   Fats Domino resumes touring with the Clovers after his tonsillectomy last month. They hit the road doing one-nighters in Texas.

LaVern Baker and the Spaniels make a week-long stopover at the Apollo Theater in New York.

Lionel Hampton travels to the Howard Theater in Washington for a week of entertaining.

The weekend finds the Midnighters with Todd Rhodes's Orchestra playing the 5-4 Club in Los Angeles, while Little Walter makes a rare West Coast appearance along with **Chuck Higgins** for the next two weekends at the Savoy Ballroom.

OCT 9   Dinah Washington headlines the talent at the "Queen Contest And Coronation Ball" at the Flint Armory in Flint, Michigan.

New releases for the second week of October include "Love Me" by Fats Domino and "Standin' At The Station" by Guitar Slim, both on Imperial; "Sufferin' Mind" by Guitar Slim on Specialty; "I'm Ready" by Muddy Waters on Chess; **Richard Berry**'s "The Big Break" on Flair; "Earth Angel" by the Penguins on Dootone; "Ubangi Stomp" by Earl Bostic and "Honey" by Bill Doggett, both on King; Big Maybelle's "I'm Getting 'Long Alright" on Okeh; "If You Believe" by the Orioles on Jubilee; "Gimmie Gimmie Gimmie" by Billy Ward and his Dominoes on Jubilee; "Such A Fool" by the Eagles on Mercury; Johnny Fuller's "Hard Times" and the Flairs' "I'll Never Let You Go," both on Flair; "God Bless You Child" by the Blue Dots on DeLuxe; and Nappy Brown's "Two-Faced Woman" on Savoy.

OCT 14   Derby Records files for bankruptcy. Started only three years previously, the label came up with only one major hit in "Wheel Of Fortune" by Eddie Wilcox and **Sunny Gale**.

OCT 15   The Apollo Theater in New York presents the Five Keys for this week.

Earl King and the Spiders front Dave Bartholomew's Combo in Shrewsbury, Louisiana.

Bill Doggett swings the crowd in Detroit at the Crystal Lounge.

In Los Angeles, Muddy Waters and Johnny "Guitar" Watson are the weekend entertainment at the 5-4 Club.

MID-OCTOBER

Billy Ward and his Dominoes are currently performing at the Latin Quarter in New York.

To add to the confusion between the Royals (now re-named the Midnighters on Federal Records) and the "5" Royales (King and Apollo Records), there is a new group from Detroit billing itself as **the Royals** on Venus Records.

Recent record company signings include the Griffin Brothers and Lowell

Chuck Higgins (born in Gary, Indiana, 1924) first studied the trumpet, but as soon as he witnessed Big Jay McNeeley in action, he switched to tenor sax. Higgins' had a West Coast hit in 1955 with "Pachuko Hop" on Combo.

After the Robins' "Riot In Cell Block #9" started selling well, Richard Berry, who was hired to sing the lead bass, came back with a self-penned answer, "The Big Break."

SUNNY GALE

Bill Doggett's biggest hit was the much-copied classic, "Honky Tonk," in 1956. His instrumental combo featured Clifford Scott on sax, Billy Butler on guitar, and himself on Hammond organ.

The Royals on Venus changed their name to the Royal Jokers. Soon, they signed with a new subsidiary of Atlantic, Atco.

194

Fulson with Chess Records.

Recorded In Hollywood Records buys the masters of five top rhythm and blues Christmas records from Swing Time. The songs are **"Merry Christmas Baby" by Charles Brown**, "Lonesome Christmas" by Lowell Fulson, "Boogie Woogie Santa Claus" by Mabel Scott, "Sleigh Ride" by Lloyd Glenn, and "How I Hate To See Christmas Come Around" by Jimmy Witherspoon.

OCT 16   Elvis Presley makes his first appearance on the "Louisiana Hayride" national radio broadcast from Shreveport. Within three weeks, he signs a long term contract to appear on the radio show every Saturday night for a year.

OCT 18   Bill Haley and his Comets starts a week's engagement at the Blue Mirror Club in Washington.

New releases for the third week of October include "Cat Fruit" by Tiny Bradshaw on King; "I Love You Madly" by Charlie and Ray on Herald; "Fool In Paradise" by the Jewels on R&B; "Ling Ting Tong" by the Five Keys on Capitol; "Standing At The Crossroads" by Elmore James on Flair; "Sweet, Soft and Really Fine" by the Five Dukes of Rhythm on Rendezvous; "Annie's Answer" by Helen McCollum and the El Dorados on Vee-Jay; "Please Bring Yourself Back Home" by the Ramblers on M-G-M; and two releases from Bill Haley and his Comets: "Dim, Dim The Lights" on Decca, and a reissue of "Jukebox Cannonball" on Essex.

OCT 19   Billy Eckstine and the Drifters, headlining the "Biggest Show Of '54," appear in Philadelphia at the Academy of Music.

OCT 22   The Clovers are scheduled for a week's run at the Apollo Theater in New York. Also on the bill are Edna McGriff and the Paul Williams Orchestra.
            Pee Wee Crayton headlines a three-day run at the Dew Drop Inn in New Orleans.
            LaVern Baker, **Big Maybelle**, the Spaniels, the Counts, Larry Darnell, and Red Prysock are the highlights of the revue at the Howard Theater in Washington.
            Arthur Prysock is on stage for a ten-day run at Chic's in Detroit.
            Percy Mayfield is at the Savoy Ballroom, Joe Morris with Al Savage is at the 5-4 Club, and the Chords are at the Club Oasis for the weekend in Los Angeles.

OCT 23   A feud has developed between the Chords and humorist **Stan Freberg**, whose parody of "Sh-Boom" is on the "pop" charts. Everything ends humorously this evening as both Freberg and the Chords appear on the CBS-TV show "Juke Box Jury" to joke with each other.
            The "Midnight Ramble" at New Orleans' Caffin Theater features Dave Bartholomew's Band and the Spiders.

New releases for the fourth week of October include a couple of answers to the Midnighters' "Annie Had A Baby, namely "Annie's Aunt Fannie"

Besides the annual hit, "Merry Christmas Baby," Charles Brown also wrote and recorded "Please Come Home For Christmas" (1961, King).

Big Maybelle's biggest-selling record was "Candy" issued on Savoy in 1956. Her only charted "pop" single was a cover of the rock number "96 Tears" in 1967.

Stan Freberg is one of the most gifted funnymen in America. His first record, "John And Marsha" (1950) was a hilarious satire on radio soap operas. From 1954 to 1956, he issued a number of parodies of rock 'n roll songs, including "Heartbreak Hotel" and "The Great Pretender."

by the Midnighters on Federal and "My Name Ain't Annie" by Linda Hayes on King. Other releases are "Yum Yum" by the Lamplighters on Federal; "Framed" by the Robins on Spark; "Monkey Hips And Rice" by the "5" Royales, "Black Diamond" by Roy Brown, and "Get It One More Time" by the Strangers, all on King; "You Upset Me Baby" by B. B. King on RPM; "Crazy Chicken" by the Five Jets on DeLuxe; "I'm A Fool To Care" by the Castelles on Grande; "Eternal Love" by the **Rivileers** on Baton; Smiley Lewis's "Too Many Drivers" on Imperial; Louis Jordan's "Put Some Money In The Pot 'Cause The Juice Is Running Low" on Aladdin; and "Ain't Got No Time" by Otis Blackwell on Jay-Dee.

OCT 28   Billy Eckstine and the Drifters with the "Biggest Show Of '54" play a one-nighter at the Peoria Mosque Theater.

OCT 29   The weekend in Los Angeles finds Linda Hayes and Prince Partridge at the Savoy. Also, Faye Adams, Johnny Ace, Memphis Slim, and Willie Mae Thornton are at the 5-4 Ballroom.
        In New York, the Apollo Theater welcomes Big Maybelle, the Regals, and Gene Ammons's Combo for the week.

OCT 30   **Pee Wee Crayton** brings his West Coast blues to Slidell, Louisiana.
        In New Orleans, the Spiders and Little Bo stop for two days at the Club Desire.

LATE OCTOBER

Lamp Records signs the **Cues** and the Mello-Fellows to recording contracts.

THE TOP TEN ROCK 'N' ROLL RECORDS FOR OCTOBER 1954

1. Hurts Me To My Heart - Faye Adams
2. Oh What A Dream - Ruth Brown
3. Annie Had A Baby - The Midnighters
4. Shake, Rattle and Roll - Bill Haley and his Comets
5. Honey Love - Clyde McPhatter and the Drifters
6. Ebb Tide - Roy Hamilton
7. Shake, Rattle And Roll - Joe Turner
8. I Don't Hurt Anymore - Dinah Washington
9. Sexy Ways - The Midnighters
10. Work With Me Annie - The Midnighters

The Rivileers featured lead singer Eugene Pearson, who would join the Drifters as a baritone from 1962 through 1966.

Pee Wee Crayton was a Texas-born and bred guitarist and vocalist, and a childhood schoolmate of Elmore James. Crayton became one of the West Coast's most popular r&b club acts. He died on June 25, 1985.

The Cues featured Ollie Jones, the original first tenor of the Ravens on Hub Records. Jones was also a fine composer, and is known for "Send For Me," a 1957 hit for Nat King Cole.

October 1954
ARTIST OF THE MONTH

LOUIS JORDAN
(Louis Thomas Jordan, b. July 8, 1908; d. February 4, 1975)

Louis Jordan did not have a charted rhythm and blues record after 1951, yet he may well have been the single most important influence on the music. By the time rock 'n roll came into being in the early 1950s, Jordan had been a musician for twenty-five years. He was easily old enough to have fathered many of the artists who had the first rock 'n roll hits. Yet he did not approach his music in a fatherly manner. No sir! Louis Jordan was born to rock.

Jordan was part of musical family in Brinkley, Arkansas. His father was a music teacher and part-time band leader. Young Louis was playing clarinet by the time he was seven. By the end of his high school years he was already proficient on the saxophone. He attended Baptist College in Little Rock, where he found time to play clarinet and dance with the Rabbit Foot Minstrels, a traveling troupe that at one time or another featured Ma Raniey, Bessie Smith, "Sleepy" John Estes, Brownie McGhee, and Big Joe Williams. In the late 1920s Jordan was a sideman with Rudy Williams's band in Hot Springs. His first recordings came with the Jungle Band on Brunswick (1929), and with Louis Armstrong on Victor and Clarence Williams on Vocallion (both 1932). For the next three years he worked with several bands in Philadelphia, including Chick Webb and Charley Gaines. He toured New York and the Midwest in 1935 with the LeRoy Smith Orchestra. In 1936 he was back with Webb for recordings on Decca. When Webb died in 1938, Jordan broke free to form his first combo, the nine-piece Elks Rendezvous Band, which recorded for Decca from 1938 to 1940. He dropped a few members and renamed the combo the Tympany Five, emphasizing a "hot" sound with horns and boogie woogie beat. The new band was booked into Chicago's Capitol Lounge in 1941 for a two-week stand. They remained for an additional thirty weeks. His first hit record came with "Knock Me A Kiss" for Decca, the label for which he would record for the next ten years.

During the war years of the early 1940s the Jordan sound captured American listeners in droves. "G.I. Jive" was perfect for 1944. "Choo Choo Ch'Boogie" sounded just like its name. "Open The Door, Richard" was based on the Dusty Fletcher comedy routine of the 1930s, and "Blue Light Boogie" proved that boogie woogie needn't be frantic to still be rhythmic. His masterpiece came in 1949 with "Saturday Night Fish Fry," a jovial parody of Black low life. In four and a half minutes the song captures the essence of a Saturday night party that got out of hand. Significantly, the vocal chorus sings about "rockin'" in the sense of having a good time. On the club circuit, the Tympany Five were a major attraction. Jordan broke the house records at the Cafe Society and the Apollo in New York, the Avalon Ballroom in Los Angeles, and the Tic Toc Club in Boston.

Most of Louis Jordan's recordings were in the novelty vein. He had the ability to walk the line of self-caricature without becoming spiteful. His comedy played to the prejudices of the White audience while having great appeal for Blacks. And, make no mistake, Louis

Jordan was immensely popular with the Black audience. No Black artist could hope to sell a million records without a significant crossover into the "pop" field, and Jordan had five gold records before 1950. In the 1940s he was the first Black vocalist to achieve nationwide popularity.

As the musical pendulum swung more toward rhythm and blues, Jordan left the relative security of Decca, one of the top five recording companies, for Aladdin Records, a much newer, smaller, and ultimately more exciting company. About this time he also broke up his big band to once again concentrate on the Tympany Five. With the smaller combo he was able to capture the fresh appeal of the music he had help found. His records never again sold in the numbers needed to reach the national charts, but Jordan was not out of work by any stretch of the imagination. On the contrary, he performed three hundred days a year, crisscrossing the country with forays to Alaska, Hawaii and Canada. He played to sold-out houses everywhere. Unlike many other artists from a jazz background, Jordan didn't just play to please himself. He always played for the audience. His songs were finely crafted to include the combo's best performances. His own saxophone breaks were at once searing and jumping, moody and tearful.

The list of rock 'n roll artists who were influenced by Louis Jordan must start with Chuck Berry. Berry's lyrics and delivery were an extension of Jordan's recordings. The sound generated by the Tympany Five was also the basis for the rock 'n roll combos of Bill Haley, Fats Domino, and Ray Charles. His stage act (and certainly with the wild music of Louis Jordan there was an even wilder act to showcase it) laid the foundation for Bo Diddley, T-Bone Walker, Amos Milburn, Roy Brown, Wynonie Harris, Roy Milton and Little Richard.

In 1957 he signed with Mercury Records as a solo artist. Here he was forced into a pseudo-rock 'n roll delivery, with terrible results. His releases lacked the humor of his days with Decca and Aladdin. His voice was strained and without authority. In 1961 he went to Warwick, singing ballads in the Tommy Edwards style. He toured England in 1962, and reformed the Tympany Five again in 1963. A year later Ray Charles hired him to record for his Tangerine label, but the singles released lacked direction. He tried conventional blues styles and even re-recorded "Saturday Night Fish Fry," with disastrous results. In 1965 he was recording for the small Pzazz label. Finally he gave up recording for good to concentrate on full-time again. It was a welcome move and he found himself a hit again in Asia, South America, Canada, and Europe. He even returned to play the Apollo. In 1974 illness forced his retirement, and he died of a heart attack in Los Angeles within a year.

Louis Jordan was a "singing, swinging, clowning maestro," whose personal tastes in music ran to light classical. He was a record collector and a amateur photographer. He loved baseball and track meets; his taste in food ran to fried chicken, gumbo, and fish of any kind. He was loved by all who came in contact with him. And he was an enormous catalyst, possibly *the* catalyst, that changed swing and boogie woogie into rhythm and blues, which led to rock 'n roll.

November 1954

NOV 1   Fats Domino and Amos Milburn start a tour that will take them from the East Coast down through the Deep South before winding up in New Orleans. This week they are playing dates in the Carolinas.

    Johnny Otis, regular deejay on KFOX radio in Los Angeles, starts a two-week engagement at the Club Oasis.

New releases for the first week of November include "Sincerely" by the Moonglows and Willie Mabon's "Poison Ivy," both on Chess; "Someday We'll Meet Again" by the Royal Jokers on Venus; "I Owe My Heart" by Faye Adams on Herald; "Baby Please" by the Chanticlaires on Dot; "Sugar" by Marvin and Johnny on Modern; Lulu Reed's "Kiss Me" on King; "Forty-Leven Dozen Ways" by the Cues and "Iddy-Biddy Baby" by the Mello-Fellows, both on Lamp; "Reconsider Baby" by Lowell Fulson on Checker; "Buick 59" by the **Medallions** on Dootone; "Something To Remember You By" by the Gentlemen on Apollo; "Shake It" by Johnny Otis on Peacock; and Johnny and Mack's "Money Money Money" on DeLuxe.

The Medallions organized in Los Angeles in late 1953, although lead singer Vernon Green was a native of Denver. The "B" side of their novelty, "Buck 59," was a beautiful ballad, "The Letter," which was a strong seller in its own right.

NOV 5   In Detroit, Earl Bostic is at the Crystal Lounge for the next two weeks, and **Nolan Strong and the Diablos** open for a three-week run at the Madison Ballroom.

    The Apollo Theater in New York presents Sonny Thompson's Orchestra featuring Lulu Reed with the Treniers.

    The weekend entertainment at Los Angeles' 5-4 Ballroom features Roy Milton and Joe Morris and his Orchestra with Al Savage on vocals.

THE DIABLOS

NOV 6   In an article in *Billboard* magazine titled "R&B Music Success Sends Major Diskers Back To The Field," it is reported that Capitol, RCA Victor, Decca, Mercury, M-G-M, and Columbia see three reasons to step up their production of rhythm and blues releases: (1) to increase the percentage of records that the major companies sell to teen-agers; (2) to continue fully utilizing their southern distributors, who are increasingly turning to independently produced r&b product; and (3) to keep from surrendering the rhythm and blues field totally to the smaller, independent record companies. Victor announces that is taking back control of Groove Records, its subsidiary, which has been run the "X" banner. Columbia is taking over the reins of Okeh, which had previously been controlled by Epic. Capitol, which had stopped r&b production in 1948, is now solidly back in the field. One reason not mentioned by the major record companies, but pointed out in the article, is that the original versions of most r&b records are selling better than the "pop" cover records issued by the majors.

Lynn Hope is entertaining at the Showboat in Philadelphia for two weeks.

On tour, T-Bone Walker, Ray Charles, and Lowell Fulson are in the Southwest, and Chuck Willis and Joe Turner are in Florida and Alabama.

Epic Records celebrates its first anniversary with a party in New York City attended by Roy Hamilton, among others.

The **Blenders** sign with R&B Records of Los Angeles, and the Chestnuts sign with Mercury.

Tiny Bradshaw is recovering from a stroke suffered last week.

Billy Ward and his Dominoes open at Basin Street in New York.

Aladdin Records signs the Regals, the Five Pearls, and the **Cookies.**

The Chords, riding the crest of a wave of popularity with their hit "Sh-Boom," are forced to change their name to the Chordcats to avoid conflict with another group that claims to have used the name first in 1953 on Gem Records.

Allied Records has initiated a r&b subsidiary, Kicks Records.

NOV 8   Dinah Washington, the Checkers, Danny Overbea, and Cootie Williams's Orchestra start a six-week tour of the South and Southwest (through December 20) before touring the Midwest.

New releases for the second week of November include "Alrighty Oh Sweetie" by the Clovers and **"White Christmas" by Clyde McPhatter and the Drifters**, both on Atlantic; "So All Alone" by Bobby Lester and the Moonlighters and Little Walter's "Mellow Down Easy," both on Checker; "Late Rising Moon" by Earl Curry and the Blenders on R&B; "Shake It Up Mambo" by the Platters on Federal; "Irene" by the Holidays on Specialty; Rusty Bryant's "House Rocker" and the Counts' "Waiting Around For You," both on Dot; "Count Your Blessings" by the Orioles on Jubilee; "I Wasn't Thinking I Was Drinking" by the Checkers on King; "Blow The Whistle" by the Sugar Tones on Benida; Guitar Slim's "Twenty Five Lies" on Specialty; and "Blues In A Letter" by the Flamingos on Chance.

NOV 12   The "Hall Of Fame Show" tour takes to the road with a performance in Kansas City. The package will be out ten days and play various locations, including Wichita and Topeka in Kansas, and Decatur, Illinois. Entertainers for the trek include Faye Adams, the Spiders, Joe Morris, Amos Milburn, and Al Savage.
The Howard Theater in Washington hosts the Timmie Rodgers Revue, featuring Roy Hamilton, for the week.
In Detroit, Wynonie Harris is the entertainer at Chic's for the week, and Bull Moose Jackson opens at the Flame Show Bar.
In Los Angeles this weekend, T-Bone Walker entertains dancers at the Savoy Ballroom and Roy Milton returns to the 5-4 Club.

The Blenders left the National label in 1950 after only one release and went to the more prestigious Decca Records, where they had eight singles in two years. After a short stay with M-G-M and Jay-Dee (1953), they signed with R&B Records and had one record issued as Earl Curry and the Blenders.

Aladdin assigned the Cookies to their Lamp subsidiary, and the group came under the tutelage of Jesse Stone, who also worked as an arranger for Atlantic. When their only Lamp release, "All Night Mambo," failed to click, Stone made certain they were signed to Atlantic. Their records were never big sellers, but the group was immediately in demand in New York as backup vocalists. Ray Charles liked them so much that he hired the group permanently, changing their name to the Raelets.

The Drifter's version of "White Christmas" was copied almost note for note from the 1948 recording by the Ravens. In turn, the Drifter's version of "White Christmas" was the basis for the controversial version by Elvis Presley in 1957.

The Apollo Theater in New York offers Louis Jordan with the Hal Singer band for the week.

New releases for the third week of November include Dinah Washington's "Teach Me Tonight," the **Chestnuts'** "Don't Go," and Buddy Johnson's "I Never Had It So Good," all on Mercury; "21" by the Spiders on Imperial; "All Night Mambo" by the Cookies on Lamp; "Tweedle Dee" by LaVern Baker on Atlantic; "Run Pretty Baby" by the Regals on Aladdin; and "My Blue Heaven" by the Hamilton Sisters on Columbia.

The Chestnuts on Mercury were not the same as the group on Davis. The Mercury Chestnuts featured Louis Heyward of the Ravens.

MID-NOVEMBER

A survey by *Billboard* magazine discloses that r&b records are aired on local radio stations an average of five hours a week, against ten hours a week for country music. There has been little change in this ratio since an earlier poll conducted in 1953.

Marvin and Johnny are currently on the road in the Midwest before opening in Cleveland at the Cotton Club later this month.

Studio Films, Inc., is producing a series of made-for-TV films titled "Apollo Varieties" that will showcase acts that appear on stage at the famed New York theater.

Decca Records begins negotiations with Spark Records of Los Angeles that would result in the Spark catalog of unreleased masters coming under the Decca banner. Decca would also acquire the services of **Jerry Leiber and Mike Stoller**, owners of Spark and major songwriters in the rhythm and blues field, and Lester Sill, sales manager for Spark.

In 1949, Jerry Leiber and Mike Stoller were just two White teen-agers. Then, they started composing rhythm and blues songs and producing record sessions in Los Angeles. The duo's first significant record came with "Hard Times," sung by Charles Brown in 1951.

Joe Davis, of Jay-Dee Records, reactivates the Beacon label, which had been in business from 1943 to 1948. The first Beacon release will be by Dean Barlow and the Crickets, who were previously on Jay-Dee Records.

Dewey Bergman, president of Benida Records, announces the start of the **Roulette** label. He will switch all of the r&b talent on Benida, including the Sugar Tones, to Roulette.

Bergman's Roulette Records has no connection with the label of the same name founded by George Goldner in 1957.

The Bihari brothers (Jules of Crown Records, Saul of Modern Records, and Joe of RPM/Flair Records) are off on another talent search through the Midwest and along the Eastern Seaboard. Last week Saul Bihari signed **Arthur Lee Maye**.

Arthur Lee Maye was seventeen years old, and a minor league player with the Milwaukee Braves baseball organization. He played in the big leagues with the Washington Senators. Maye sang lead with the Crowns starting in 1955.

NOV 19   In celebration of the second anniversary of the "Night Train" show broadcast over KEYS radio in Corpus Christi, Texas, the station airs six hours of "Night Train" (midnight to 6 a.m.), making it one of the longest r&b radio shows to date in this area.
　　　　The Five Keys headline the weekly revue at the Regal Theater in Chicago.
　　　　Roy Hamilton is welcomed for a special ten-day Thanksgiving appearance at the Apollo in New York.
　　　　In Washington, the Howard Theater offers the Drifters and Erskine Hawkins on the week's bill.
　　　　LaVern Baker is the headliner at Detroit's Flame Show Bar.

In Los Angeles, T-Bone Walker returns to the Savoy Ballroom for the weekend, while Johnny Ace and Willie Mae Thornton share the spotlight at the Savoy Ballroom.

New releases for the fourth week of November include Earl Bostic's "Song Of The Islands" and Bill Doggett's "Tara's Theme," both on King; "Look Me In The Eyes" by the Five Willows on Herald; **Arthur Gunter's** "Baby Let's Play House" and the Peacheroos' "Every Day My Love Is True," both on Excello; and "Dig That Crazy Santa Claus" by Oscar McLollie on Modern.

NOV 24   "Moondog," a blind street musician in New York City, wins a judgement in his $100,000 suit against Alan Freed for use of the "Moondog" name. The actual amount awarded is not announced, but is thought to be $5,000. Freed's new WINS radio show will be renamed "Rock And Roll Party," and will be extended. Freed will be on the air Monday through Saturday from 7:00 to 9:00 p.m (in addition to his regular late night shift of 11:00 p.m. to 1:00 a.m. Monday through Thursday, and 11:00 p.m. to 2:00 a.m. Friday and Saturday), making a total of twenty-eight hours of r&b airtime at WINS for Freed.

NOV 26   The Clovers, Joe Morris's Orchestra, and Al Savage entertain for the week at the Howard Theater in Washington.
Weekend dancers in Los Angeles have their choice between Charles Brown at the Savoy Ballroom and Johnny Otis at the 5-4 Club. Across town, Joe Houston starts a week-long engagement at the Club Oasis.

NOV 29   Earl Bostic moves into Toronto's Colonial Tavern for the week.

New releases for the fifth week of November include "Curl Up In My Arms" by the Nuggets on Capitol; "Since I Fell For You" by the Lovenotes on Riviera; and "Kiss Crazy Baby" by the Delta Rhythm Boys on Decca.

LATE NOVEMBER

The Moonglows sign with the Shaw Agency for personal appearances.

THE TOP TEN ROCK 'N' ROLL RECORDS FOR NOVEMBER 1954

1. Mambo Baby - Ruth Brown
2. Hurts Me To My Heart - Faye Adams
3. Hearts Of Stone - The Charms
4. I Don't Hurt Anymore - Dinah Washington
5. Annie Had A Baby - The Midnighters
6. You Upset Me Baby - B. B. King
7. Oh What A Dream - Ruth Brown
8. I'm Ready - Muddy Waters
9. Bip Bam - The Drifters
10. Shake, Rattle And Roll - Joe Turner (tied with)
    Shake, Rattle And Roll - Bill Haley and his Comets

Arthur Gunter was born May 23, 1926, in Nashville, and died in Port Huron, Michigan, May 16, 1976. While his biggest-selling record was "Baby Let's Play House," he admitted that his biggest payday came in 1973 when he won $50,000 in the Michigan State Lottery!

November 1954
ARTIST OF THE MONTH

DINAH WASHINGTON
(Ruth Lee Jones, b. August 29, 1924; d. December 14, 1963)

DINAH WASHINGTON

Dinah Washington was the undisputed "Queen Of The Harlem Blues." Her recordings were best sellers among the Black community for twelve years. Her stage show thrilled fans from coast to coast as she tirelessly trekked across the states performing night after night. She had a fine voice and great stage savvy. She knew her audience and she knew how to please them. Along with Ella Fitzgerald and Mahalia Jackson, she was undoubtedly one of the most popular Black female vocalist of the 1950s.

Ruth Lee Jones moved with her family from her birthplace of Tuscaloosa, Alabama, to Chicago in 1929. She had the usual church background (Baptist), and she played piano for the choir. At fifteen she won an amateur contest at the Regal Theater, which led to a few local club dates. But gospel played a stronger role in the beginning, and by 1940 she was an accompanist on tour with the Sallie Martin Singers. She auditioned for Lionel Hampton in 1943, and it was he who suggested the name change from Ruth Jones to something more sophisticated, such as Dinah Washington. She stayed with Hampton for three years, touring and recording. In 1946 she left to work solo, and she came up with a recording contract with Mercury Records the following year. Beginning in 1949 she was seldom off the top r&b hit records charts. She found stardom on both the Black theater circuit and in the posh White night clubs. When her career slowed slightly in this country, about 1956, she went to Europe and became an international star. On the outside it looked as though she had everything going her way.

But she had a fiery temper and once beat up her husband while they were on stage, using his own saxophone. Her tempestuous life paralleled that of her closest rival, Billie Holiday, and her enormous influence can also be likened to Miss Holiday's. She was a close friend of the Reverend C. L. Franklin, whose daughter, Aretha, openly admired her. Her vocal style can be heard in Aretha's earliest recordings for Columbia Records before she discovered "soul" on Atlantic. Dinah Washington also was a role model for Ruth Brown, Etta James, Esther Phillips, and another Dinah, renamed Diana Ross.

Her stage performances were honed through years of experience. She could hit hard with the blues and her rhythm songs could keep the house rocking. She could purr on a love ballad, using her perfect articulation and voice control. She knew how to handle double entendres, which was advisable, since many of her songs were about the steamier side of love affairs.

By 1955 the industry had dubbed her the "Queen Of The Juke Boxes." Her hits came in quick succession: "Baby Get Lost" and "Good Daddy Blues" in 1949; "I Only Know," "It Isn't Fair," "I Wanna Be Loved," and "I'll Never Be Free" in 1950; "I Won't Cry Anymore" and "Cold, Cold Heart" in 1951: "Wheel of Hurt" and "Trouble In Mind" in 1952; "TV Is The Thing" in 1953; "I Don't Hurt Anymore" and "Teach Me Tonight" in 1954; and "That's All I Want From You," "If It's The Last Thing I Do," "I Concentrate On You," and "I'm Lost Without You Tonight," all in 1955. "Soft Winds" went to number one in 1956, and then it took a duet with Brook Benton in 1959 on "(Baby) You've Got What It Takes" and a solo hit, "What A Difference A Day Makes," to bring her back before the American public.

Those years in between must have been hard on Dinah Washington. She died at home in 1963 of a combination of sleeping pills and alcohol. What she left behind is a remarkable legacy of fine material recorded to perfection. If she had lived, she might have been remembered as the first woman to really sing "soul." She was that much of an influence.

December 1954

DEC 1   Louis Jordan begins a two-week engagement at the Sands Hotel in Las Vegas.

DEC 2   Guitar Slim opens at the Walahuje Club in Atlanta.

DEC 3   The sixth annual WDIA (radio) "Goodwill Revue" in Memphis draws 6,700 fans to the Ellis Auditorium for a charity show that raises over $5,000. Headline attractions include the El Dorados, the Five C's, Eddie Boyd, John Greer, and Gatemouth Brown.
          The Charms, **Slim Gaillard**, and Margie Day open for a week at the Howard Theater in Washington.
          Joe Turner plays for weekend dancers at the Savoy Ballroom in Los Angeles.
          The Harptones and Buddy Johnson's Orchestra with Ella Johnson headline the show at the Apollo Theater in New York.

DEC 6   Earl Bostic is at the Surf Club in Baltimore through the 12th.
          In Providence, Rhode Island, the feature attractions are Marvin and Johnny at the Celebrity and Ivory Joe Hunter at the Downbeat.

New releases for the first week of December include Fats Domino's "I Know" and Lil Son Jackson's "My Younger Days," both on Imperial; "I've Been Away Too Long" by Chuck Willis on Okeh; **Junior Wells'** "So All Alone" on States; Dean Barlow and the Crickets' "Be Faithful" on Beacon; Memphis Slim's "Memphis Slim U.S.A." on United; "Shoo-Shoo" by the Tune Blenders on Federal; and "My Sentimental Heart" by the Cashmeres on Mercury.

EARLY DECEMBER

Sarah Vaughan starts a month-long engagement at Birdland in New York, where she shares the bill with Jimmy Rushing and Count Basie.

DEC 9   Johnny Otis plays a one-nighter at the Club Oasis in Los Angeles.

DEC 10   Savannah Churchill is the houseguest at the Flame in Detroit for two weeks.
          Chuck Willis and Faye Adams kick off a month-long tour of New Jersey and Pennsylvania with a show in Trenton. Other play dates include Newark, Pittsburgh, and Harrisburg. Joining the tour for a few dates will be the Bill Doggett Trio.
          In Los Angeles, B. B. King starts three days at the 5-4 Club, while Charles Brown plays a weekend layover at the Savoy Ballroom.

New releases for the second week of December include "Let Me Go

Guitarist Slim Gaillard's jive-talking vocals were all the rage in the 1940s. Teamed with bassist Slam Stewart, Gaillard pranced and danced through such nonsense as "Flat Foot Floogie (With The Floy-Floy)" and "Cement Mixer (Putsy-Putsy)."

Junior Wells was among the second generation of Southern blues artists who found a home in Chicago. Born in 1932 in West Memphis, his harmonica playing naturally gravitated toward the style of Sonny Boy Williamson. His first sessions were produced in Chicago in 1953 for the States label, with Muddy Waters on guitar.

Lover" by the Counts on Dot; two releases by the Charms on DeLuxe: "Ling Ting Tong" and "Mambo Sh-Mambo"; "Stingy Little Thing" by the Midnighters on Federal; "Since I Fell For You" by the **Harptones** on Bruce; "Let Me Know Tonight" by the Blue Dots on DeLuxe; Jimmy Reed's "You Don't Have To Go" on Vee-Jay; and "I'm The Child" by Buddy Milton and the Twilighters on RPM.

In 1963, Lenny Welch copied the Harptones' version of "Since I Fell For You," and had a major hit with it on Cadence Records.

DEC 15   Earl Bostic starts a week at the Markeez Club in Lowell, Mississippi.

MID-DECEMBER

The Drifters and Red Prysock wind up a Florida tour that has kept them on the road for about thirty days.

The Counts are now touring with the Gene Ammons Combo through the Midwest.

Aladdin Records, in a move of dubious legality, hires the Feathers to re-record "Johnny, Darling," which was released by the same group this week on Show Time records.

Chess Records' policy of issuing records by the Moonglows under two names, the Moonglows and the Moonlighters, has had a humorous side-effect. Promoters, eager to book the Moonlighters, are having a difficult time locating the non-existent group. The Shaw Agency, on the other hand, gets "two for the price of one" as they sign the Moonglows/Moonlighters to an exclusive personal appearance contract. On future play dates, the Moonglows and the Moonlighters will both perform.

DEC 17   Charles Brown is held over for another weekend at the Savoy Ballroom, where he is joined by Billy Ward and his Dominoes. Across town, the 5-4 Club hosts Joe Turner and Choker Campbell.

DEC 20   Tiny Bradshaw headlines the review at the Celebrity Club in Providence, Rhode Island.

Guitarist and vocalist Danny Overbea represented a blending of Billy Eckstine's vocal style and T-Bone Walker's stage antics. He is remembered today for the original version of "40 Cups of Coffee" (later covered by Bill Haley), and "Train, Train, Train."

New releases for the third week of December include **Danny Overbea's** "A Toast To Lovers" on Checker; Amos Milburn's "One-Two-Three Everybody" and Louis Jordan's "Fat Back And Corn Liquor," both on Aladdin; "I'm Tired Of Beggin'" by the Sly Fox on Spark; "For Sentimental Reasons" by the Rivileers on Baton; "Hold Me Baby" by the Chordcats on Cat; "All She Wants To Do Is Mambo" by Wynonie Harris on King; "Tell It Like It Is" by Roy Milton and "You Were Lyin' To Me" by Percy Mayfield, both on Specialty; and "With All My Heart" by the Five Scamps on Okeh.

DEC 21   Dinah Washington, the Checkers, Danny Overbea, and Cootie Williams's Orchestra start a winter tour through the Midwest. Miss Washington has taken over the management of her female backing singers, the Honey Tones, who accompany her on tour.

DEC 22   Earl Bostic, just completing a full year of tours and club dates, starts a well-deserved six-week vacation.

DEC 23   Buddy and Ella Johnson are welcomed for a three-week stay at the Savoy Ballroom in New York.

DEC 24   The Clovers and Floyd Dixon open at the 5-4 Ballroom in Los Angeles for ten days. Also in town, Johnny Otis starts an extended engagement playing weekends at the Club Alimony.

Joe Turner plays tonight in Shreveport, Louisiana, followed by a Christmas Day show in New Orleans.

In Washington, the Christmas Week show at the Howard Theater features Ivory Joe Hunter and the **Regals**.

Johnny Ace is accidentally shot backstage at the Houston Auditorium between appearances while playing Russian roulette with a loaded revolver. He dies within hours.

DEC 25   Bill Randle, deejay on WERE Cleveland, starts a weekly rhythm and blues show that will be aired every Saturday in New York over WCBS. Randle will commute between Cleveland and New York.

In California, Louis Jordan and B. B. King break the house record at the Oakland Auditorium, bringing in 12,500 patrons.

DEC 27   The Elks Ballroom in Los Angeles features B. B. King for its Christmas dance. Other performers include the Medallions, Roy Milton, Little Willie Littlefield, Johnny Otis, the Flairs, Earl Forrest, and Marie Adams.

Also in Los Angeles, the Christmas rhythm and blues benefit concert at the Shrine Auditorium features the Clovers, Big Jay McNeeley, the Robins, the Platters, the **Cheers**, and the Jewels.

New releases for the fourth week of December include "Every Day I Have The Blues" by B. B. King on RPM; "Please Help Me" by Eddie Boyd on Chess; "Annie Kicked The Bucket" by the Nu Tones on Hollywood Star; Lightnin' Hopkins's "Nothing' But The Blues" on Herald; "Doctor Velvet" by the Nite Riders on Apollo; "Ichi-Bon Tami Dachi" by the Rovers on Music City; and Mel Williams's "O-O-Wah" on Decca.

DEC 31   The New Year's Eve weekend dance at the Savoy Ballroom in Los Angeles offers Billy Ward and his Dominoes, Johnny "Guitar" Watson and Charles Brown.

Washington's Howard Theater presents the "5" Royales, the Penguins, and Tab Smith's Combo to close out the year.

LATE DECEMBER

The Phonograph Manufacturers' Association estimates that record sales in 1954 have topped $61 million.

The Regals found little success as a recording group. In three years they had three singles issued by three separate record companies, Aladdin ("Run Pretty Baby"), M-G-M ("When You're Home"), and Atlantic ("I'm So Lonely").

The Cheers were a trio of White singers hired by songwriters Jerry Leiber and Mike Stoller to make demonstration records of their songs. Their demo of "Bazoom (I Need Your Lovin')" was released by Capitol after it became an r&b hit for the Charms.

THE TOP TEN ROCK 'N ROLL RECORDS FOR DECEMBER 1954

1. Hearts Of Stone - The Charms
2. You Upset Me Baby - B. B. King
3. Mambo Baby - Ruth Brown
4. Reconsider Baby - Lowell Fulson
5. Sincerely - The Moonglows
6. Earth Angel - The Penguins
7. Teach Me Tonight - Dinah Washington
8. Hurts Me To My Heart - Faye Adams
9. I'm Ready - Muddy Waters
10. Dim, Dim The Lights - Bill Haley and his Comets
Special Category
     White Christmas - The Drifters

December 1954
ARTIST OF THE MONTH

THE CHARMS

THE CHARMS

The Charms were one of the youngest groups of the time. Even a year after their first hits, the boys were faced with overcoming their youthful appearance, and this was a hindrance. There were five of them on stage, and while they had an appealing way with a song, it was their youthfulness that left the lasting impression.

Lead tenor for the group was Otis Williams, who was born in Cincinnati on June 2, 1936. He was athletic and thought he might even work toward a baseball contract with a professional team. But his academics suffered, and he dropped out of high school at age sixteen after studying music, including piano, for a year. Richard Parker (bass) had been singing professionally since he was seventeen, while Joe Penn (baritone) had studied piano for two years although he was currently working in a car wash. The Charms were rounded out by the addition of Rolland Bradley (tenor).

Legend relates that the group was discovered while spending an afternoon playing baseball in a vacant lot across the street from the headquarters of King Records of Cincinnati. Owner Sid Nathan had just listened to a new record from the West Coast, "Hearts Of Stone," by the Jewels on the R&B label. Anxious to get his own version on the streets before the competition could ship their records this far east, he was looking out his window, pondering the situation. What he beheld was a revelation. Here was a five-man vocal group, already set to record. An immediate session was held, and the Charms' version of "Hearts Of Stone" did indeed become the more popular among the r&b audience, although both versions failed to sell as well as the cover version by the Fontane Sisters on Dot Records.

Well, its a nice story.

Truth be known, the Charms had been recording since August 1953 when they waxed "Heaven Only Knows" as the first issue on Rockin' Records. The song was re-issued on DeLuxe, a King Records subsidiary, and the Charms stayed with DeLuxe for the next eight years before switching to the parent company. "Hearts Of Stone" was their sixth issue on the label.

Their follow-up record after "Hearts Of Stone" also suffered the "cover version complex," as both Pat Boone and Frank Sinatra outsold the Charms' "Two Hearts." The same thing happened with "Ivory Tower," which was covered by Gale Storm. The Charms weren't too proud to issue their own versions of other r&b hits of the day with "Ling, Ting, Tong," which was originally issued by the Five Keys; and "Ko Ko Mo," which had been done by Gene and Eunice and was a bigger hit for Perry Como.

Musically, Williams' voice had a light vocal texture that allowed him to color his phrasing. The backing vocals on the other hand were indistinct, possibly making their records easier targets for the cover artists. Although there was a working set of Charms on Okeh as late as 1966, the group was unable to make the transition from rhythm and blues through rock 'n roll to soul. Williams finally reverted to his first love, country music, in the 1970s, with an occasional return to the spotlight with the Charms for an oldies revival show.

There is no doubt that Otis Williams and the Charms suffered from being popular in the r&b market at a time when major record companies mined this source for new material. That they were unable to capitalize for themselves is a statement on the times.

Shake Rattle & Roll

THE GOLDEN AGE
OF
AMERICAN ROCK 'N ROLL

1955

1955
A Look Ahead

"GOOD GOD A'MIGHTY THEM CATS ARE GOING' WILD"
Muddy Waters

With the great strides taken by the rhythm and blues market in 1954, the new year starts with an air of excitement and anticipation. One industry source states flatly that "r&b records are the 'pop' records of the day." Of twenty-eight awards given to BMI songs for "heavy action" in 1955, sixteen are derived from the r&b market. This insurgence of r&b into the "pop" market is not without its backlash. Fear, both real and imagined, creeps through the halls of each major record company. They are losing their stranglehold on the market and they do not know how to stop the incursion of independent labels into what had been solely their domain. The normal checks and balances within the system are on the verge of collapse.

The cottage industry of "covering" hit rhythm and blues songs reaches a fanatical climax in 1955. The majors stalk the indies like starving wolves eager for a scrap. The most minuscule r&b disk is inevitably covered by a major "pop" star, sometimes within hours after it hits the streets. Then reverse psychology sets in. By October 1955 rhythm and blues songwriters are penning tunes specifically for the "pop" audience. Those who have been most responsible for the initial excitement of the genre are diluting their own material. Serious students of r&b view this move with alarm. The blues, in many quarters, is sacred. It has grown and nurtured itself through the lives of its singers and songwriters. Now the blues is gaining acceptance as a pure strain of folk music in a world that thought of folk music as a "Whites only" genre of English ballads and Appalachian pastoral songs. But to commercialize the blues is tantamount to rewriting Shakespeare to appeal to the masses. Rhythm and blues, an offshoot of the blues, had for years also maintained this same stance. Up to now rhythm and blues artists and songwriters were less likely to place their sights on having a hit record than in setting down in words and music some deep truth about the hard times and the high times.

In 1955 rhythm and blues also starts "covering" its own hits, a strategy not seen in any abundance heretofore. "It's Love Baby" by

The Blues" by Jack Dupree is covered by Willie Dixon; "Come Back Maybellene" by John Greer is covered by Mercy Dee; "All Around The World" by Little Willie John is covered by Johnny "Guitar" Watson, "Only You" by the Platters is covered by the Cues and then re-recorded by the Platters; and "Every Day I Have The Blues," originally issued by Joe Williams in 1952, is covered by B.B. King, Lowell Fulson, and finally by Joe Williams (with Count Basie) again.

By the end of the year, country music will draw closer to r&b. Several artists, notably Marty Robbins, Elvis Presley, Bonnie Lou, and Red Foley, are building large followings by cutting country songs in the r&b manner. It is widely believed that country artists understand the blues better than the "pop" singers. Many country and blues performers do share the firsthand knowledge about the poverty and discrimination: they both have a deep sense of love for the land, and they have shared their wild Saturday nights and their deeply religious Sundays. In the South, working class Whites and Blacks share their music, too. The blues of Hank Williams cuts just as deep as the blues of B.B. King. Jimmie Rodgers was from Mississippi, just like Muddy Waters, and both men have a common bond that is reflected in their music. The blues knows no racial or musical boundary. Bob Wills and Robert Johnson both sang the blues in the 1940s, and Hank Williams and John Lee Hooker both sang the blues in the 1950s.

Rhythm and blues is also having international implications by the end of the year. Several of the more progressive independent companies have established marketing ties with European labels whereby their hits are automatically issued overseas. England in particular takes to rhythms and blues with an immediate passion that is a spin-off of the active continental jazz market.

On the airwaves, radio stations coast-to-coast are faced with the problem of which records to broadcast. Traditionally, the choice would have been easy: go with the big-name artist on the major label singing the cover version of the r&b song. But there is increased unrest among the largest segment of the listening audience, teen-agers. The average age of the typical record buyers has dropped from twenty-five in 1952 to eighteen in 1955, and the youth market wants the new sound, the original hit, the excitement of forbidden fruit. The kids want rock 'n roll, not some watered-down version sung by a performer who appealed to their parents. They want, and demand, the real thing. This leads to battle lines within the old, entrenched music establishment. In New England, deejays refuse to play the original r&b numbers, claiming that the lyrics are "dirty." Boston, as usual, leads the way in banning rock 'n roll outright. The pall of censorship spreads. In Chicago, fifteen thousand letters are sent by listeners to WGN radio demanding that the station drop all records with objectionable lyrics, including songs about drinking as a cure-all and songs about sex in any form except for "puppy love." Several other stations in Chicago set up censorship boards to review all records before airing. Some of the songs that are banned by the Chicago board included "Tweedle Dee," "Sincerely," and "Ko Ko Mo." In Sommerville, Massachusetts, the police department issues a list of tunes they may not be carried on jukeboxes: "Make Yourself Comfortable," "Teach Me Tonight," "Idle Gossip," "From The Bottom To The Top," "Honey Love," "Work With Me Annie," and all of the "Annie" answers. Rock 'n roll dances are banned by police in Bridgeport and New Haven, Connecticut, because of parents' complaints. Apparently there had been a "riot" at an August rock 'n roll dance

Apparently there had been a "riot" at an August rock 'n roll dance in New Haven. Stories from the scene are conflicting.

The role of the deejay broadens as more and more radio personalities are able to capitalize on their new-found status by staging live concerts as an adjunct to their nightly record spinning duties. In New York, Alan Freed, Tommy "Dr. Jive" Smalls, and Hal Jackson regularly schedule week-long concerts at the Apollo or the Brooklyn-Paramount or the Academy of Music. In Los Angeles, it is Dick "Huggie Boy" Hugg. In Buffalo, it is George "Hound Dog" Lorenz. In Philadelphia it is George Wood. Booking agents are afraid that the deejays will squeeze out other long-time promoters by booking the talent themselves. This would lead to gaps in the normal tour circuits that had been established twenty years previously. These booking territories are hotly contested, and the makings are present for an all-out war. On the other hand, the disk jockey is able and willing to give unlimited air time to the promotion of his own show, thereby insuring its success. The deejay finds himself in the driver's seat. If the record company or the booking agent will not provide big name talent for his promotional concert, then he won't play that artist's records. Smart deejays even have a double stranglehold because of their unique position: they can pay the talent next to nothing (top acts regularly receive $200 or less for a week's work with five to eight performances daily) in exchange for the promise of that on-the-air promotion. It is so simple it's a wonder it took so long for anyone to figure it out.

Finally, rock 'n roll has its first national "Number One" hit in 1955 with "Rock Around the Clock" by Bill Haley and his Comets. The record also tops the year-end charts, beating out such luminaries as "The Ballad of Davy Crockett" and "The Yellow Rose of Texas." Vocal groups and their records that make significant inroads into the national market are "Earth Angel" by the Penguins, "Sincerely" by the Moonglows, "Hearts Of Stone" by the Charms, and "Only You" and "The Great Pretender" by the Platters. Johnny Ace's "Pledging My Love" and Roy Hamilton's "Unchained Melody," while selling well nationally, cling to older modes. It is the new crop of male vocalists who, in 1955, cross over into the field of "pop" music that foretell of things to come: "Maybellene" by Chuck Berry, "Ain't That A Shame" by Fats Domino, and "Tutti Frutti" by Little Richard.

NATIONAL NEWS

Two deaths shake the entertainment world during the years: on January 1st, Hank Williams dies in the back seat of his Cadillac enroute to another in a string of one-nighters . . . and on September 30th, James Dean is killed when his Porsche crashes near Salinas, California. A Negro seamstress is arrested in Montgomery for refusing to give up her seat on a metropolitan bus to a White man . . . the civil rights movement is underway as Martin Luther King, Jr., organizes a boycott. Pink is the color in men's fashion in shirts, ties, and bermuda shorts . . . many haircuts resemble poodles or Mohawk Indians. The "beat generation" begins with the bohemians and beatniks in San Francisco and Greenwich Village . . . beat authors include Jack Kerouac, Allen Ginsberg, and Lawrence Ferlinghetti. The biggest-selling book of fiction is "Marjorie Morningstar" by Herman Wouk . . . "Gift From The Sea" by Anne Morrow Lindbergh is the top-selling nonfiction book. Academy awards are presented to "Marty," Ernest Borgnine, and Anna Magnani

Without A Cause" starring James Dean and "The Wild One" starring Marlin Brando. Emmys are copped by "Omnibus" and "Disneyland" . . . the best comedy series on TV is "You'll Never Get Rich," starring Phil Silvers. The number of TV sets reaches 32 million, up from 3.1 million in 1950. Floyd Patterson defeats Archie Moore for the heavyweight title, and the athlete of the year is "Hopalong" Cassidy.

January 1955

New releases for the first week of January include "I Got A Woman" by Ray Charles and "Bye Bye Young Men" by Ruth Brown, both on Atlantic; "The Girl Back Home" by the Four Speeds and "Please Love Me Baby," by the **Five Jets**, both on DeLuxe; "Hard-Headed Woman" by Big Walter on States; "School Girl" by the "5" Royales on King; and "Drinkin' Wine Spodee-O-Dee" by Malcolm Yelvington on Sun.

JAN 4   Billy Ward and his Dominoes play a two-week engagement in Los Angeles at the Macambo.

JAN 7   Billy Kenny headlines the revue at the Apollo Theater in New York for the week.
    The Bill Doggett Trio splits the bill with the Five Keys this week at Washington's Howard Theater.
    Louis Jordan plays a weekend engagement in Los Angeles at the Savoy Ballroom. Across town, Amos Milburn entertains at the 5-4 Club.
    John Lee Hooker and his Boogie Ramblers open a four-week engagement at Detroit's Town Casino.

EARLY JANUARY

Lucky Millinder signs a new contract extending his terms with King Records. Millinder heads the house band at the Apollo Theater most weeks.

Recorded In Hollywood Records leases four more sides from defunct Swing Time Records, leading to the re-release of Lowell Fulson's "Every Day I Have The Blues" and Lloyd Glenn's "Old Time Blues."

JAN 10   Bill Haley and his Comets open in Washington at the Casino Royal for one week.

New releases for the second week of January include "Upside Your Head" by Ella and Buddy Johnson on Mercury; "The Telegram" by the Medallions on Dootone; Ivory Joe Hunter's "It May Sound Silly" on Atlantic; "God Only Knows" by the Crystals on DeLuxe; "Try Holding My Hand" by the Checkers and "Waterloo" by **Boyd Bennett and his Rockets**, both on King; "Milkcow Blues Boogie" by Elvis Presley on Sun; "Jailbird" by Smiley Lewis and "How Long Must I Wait" by Smilin' Joe, both on Imperial; "Smoke From Your Cigarette" by the Mellows on Jay-Dee; "That's All Right" by Marty Robbins on Columbia; and "Gotta Go Get My Baby" by Marvin Rainwater on M-G-M.

JAN 11   Following RCA Victor's lead, M-G-M Records cuts the price of its albums. Prices for single records will remain steady at eighty-nine cents for 45 rpm and ninety-eight cents for 78 rpm disks.

The Five Jets on DeLuxe first recorded as the Thrillers (on Thriller, Big Town, and Herald), and members of the group later performed as the Five Stars on End, Columbia, and Mark-X. As the Voice Masters, they were one of Motown's first groups (one single on the Anna label).

Boyd Bennett was born December 7, 1924, in Muscle Shoals, Alabama. His band, the Rockets, was closely patterned after Bill Haley's Comets.

JAN 12   Studio Films, Inc., of Los Angeles announces a schedule of twelve thirty-six-minute shorts featuring rhythm and blues talent to be released to movie theaters following completion in early February. Entertainers to be featured include Ruth Brown, the Clovers, the Larks, Joe Turner, Dinah Washington, and the Delta Rhythm Boys.

JAN 13   Johnny Otis plays a one-nighter at the Club Alimony in Los Angeles.

JAN 14   Alan Freed produces his first "Rock And Roll Ball" in the New York area at the St. Nicholas Arena for two nights (14th and 15th). Both shows sell out a week in advance with a total of 12,000 attending to the tune of $24,000 for both days. Performers for the two nights are Joe Turner, Fats Domino, the Clovers, the Drifters, Danny Overbea, the Moonglows, the Harptones, Nolan Lewis, **Ella Johnson, the Buddy Johnson** band, and the Red Prysock Combo.

The Five Pearls open at the Madison Ballroom in Detroit for three nights.

At New York's Apollo Theater, Dinah Washington and the Penguins headline, backed by the James Moody band.

At Los Angeles' Savoy Ballroom, Roy Brown and Memphis Slim cook up a boogie woogie stew for dancers this weekend. At the 5-4 Club, the Robins join T-Bone Walker and Floyd Dixon for a three-day stand.

In Detroit, the Crystal Lounge hosts Roy Hamilton for three days, and **Nolan Strong and the Diablos** are at Dudley's Garden Theater for a week-long layover.

JAN 15   Bill Haley's "Dim, Dim The Lights" is tied to an auto safety bumper sticker campaign through a Decca Records promotion. Haley also renews his recording contract with Decca during the week.

Sonny Thompson and Lulu Reed play the weekend at the Club Desire in New Orleans.

MID-JANUARY

Roy Hamilton plays an engagement at Basin Street in New York.

Two new record labels specializing in r&b, Teenage and Dice, are formed in Lancaster, Pennsylvania.

Savoy Records announces the signing of Larry Darnell, formerly with Okeh.

Victor reports that the company will set up a recording studio in Nashville as soon as a site is located.

Dootone Records signs the Swans and the Meadowlarks. Dootsie Williams, owner of Dootone, states flatly that the Penguins, the hottest act on the label, will not be moving to a major label as has been rumored. According to Williams, he has a three-year contract with the group.

Buddy and Ella Johnson crossed over into the "pop" market in 1956 with "It's Obvious," and again in 1960 with "I Don't Want Nobody," both on Mercury. He passed away at age 62, February 9, 1977.

The Diablos from Detroit, featuring the solid tenor vocal of Nolan Strong, had their biggest hit with "The Wind," their second release on Fortune Records. Strong died on February 21, 1977, age 43.

218

JAN 17   Joe Turner is featured at the Celebrity Club in Providence, Rhode Island.

Margie Day starts an engagement at the Showboat in Philadelphia. Fats Domino stops for a week at the Hi-Hat Club in Boston.

The Crystal Lounge in Detroit hosts Tiny Bradshaw for the week.

New releases for the third week of January include "Pledging My Love" by Johnny Ace on Duke; "Ko Ko Mo" by **Gene and Eunice** on Combo; "Anything For A Friend" by Faye Adams on Herald; "I Wanna Hug Ya, Kiss Ya, Squeeze Ya" by Buddy Griffin and Claudia Swann on Chess; "Deep Freeze" by the Roamers on Savoy; "Dream Of A Lifetime" by the Flamingos on Parrot; "Rock Love" by Sonny Thompson with Lulu Reed on King; "Maggie Doesn't Work Here Anymore" by the Platters on Federal; "What A Crazy Feeling" by the Eagles on Mercury; and "Lovely Way To Spend An Evening" by the Angels on Grand.

Gene (Forrest) and Eunice (Levy) were unsuccessful in finding an even better hit to follow "Ko Ko Mo." However, they persevered and, in 1959, had another hit with "Poco Loco" on Case.

JAN 20   The Orioles start a three-day stint at the Riviera Club in St. Louis as part of their tour of the Midwest.

JAN 21   Faye Adams, the Moonglows/Moonlighters, the Bill Dogget Combo, Al Savage, and the Joe Morris Band are at the Apollo in New York for a week's stay.

In Los Angeles, the three-day weekend brings Amos Milburn, Charles Brown, and Wild Bill Davis to the Savoy Ballroom and the Four Tunes to the 5-4 Club.

JAN 22   **Joe Jones**, formerly with Roy Brown and B. B. King, is doing big business at the Dew Drop Inn in New Orleans backing the strippers and female impersonators.

Joe Jones was born in New Orleans, August 12, 1926. His one big hit came in 1960 with the million-selling "You Talk Too Much." In 1964, he was the manager for the Dixie Cups, who had a number one record with "Chapel Of Love" (Red Bird).

JAN 24   Eddie "Cleanhead" Vinson has a two-day layover in Chicago's Basin Street Club. Also in the Windy City, Muddy Waters is playing an extended engagement at the 706 Club.

New releases for the fourth week of January include "Wallflower" (also known as "Dance With Me Henry") by Etta James and the Peaches and "Shake, Holler And Run" by John Lee Hooker, both on Modern; "I'm A Natural Born Lover" by Muddy Waters on Chess; "Night And Day" by Earl Bostic on King; "Whatever Makes Me Feel This Way" by the Sultans on Duke; "Close Your Eyes" by the Five Keys on Capitol; and "She Left Me" by the Midnights on Music City.

The answering bass voice on "The Wallflower" was veteran Los Angeles singer Richard Berry, who performed similar duty on "Riot In Cell Block No. 9" for the Robins in 1954.

JAN 27   Johnny Otis performs at the Club Alimony in Los Angeles for the evening.

JAN 28   The "Top Ten Rhythm And Blues Show" booked by the Shaw Agency takes to the road for six weeks. Entertainers include the Clovers, the Charms, the Moonglows/Moonlighters, Faye Adams, Bill Doggett, Lowell Fulson, Joe Turner, and the Paul Williams Orchestra. Tonight's kickoff performance is in Norfolk, Virginia. Shows for the remainder of January are held in Richmond (29), Washington (30), and Baltimore (31). (See February 1 and March 1 for further dates.)

Oscar McLollie got his start recording for Class Records in 1953. "Convicted" (Modern, 1955) was a regional hit, and his duet with Jeannette Baker, "Hey Girl - Hey Boy" (Class, 1958) sold very well.

GENE AND EUNICE

The Ravens with Jimmy Ricks front the Arnett Cobb Band at the Apollo Theater in New York for the week.

Washington's Howard Theater hosts LaVern Baker, the Harptones, and the Counts backed by Illinois Jacquet's Combo.

In Los Angeles, the "Rock & Roll Jamboree" at the Shrine Auditorium features Billy Ward and his Dominoes, Gene and Eunice, the Medallions, the Jewels, T-Bone Walker, Shirley Gunter and the Queens, Richard Berry and the Dreamers, Marvin and Johnny, Joe Houston, Chuck Higgins, and **Oscar McLollie** for one night.

Also in Los Angeles, for the three-day weekend shows, Sonny Thompson and Lulu Reed are at the 5-4 Club and Roy Brown and the Ink Spots are at the Savoy Ballroom.

Charles Brown plays the Club Desire in New Orleans for three days.

JAN 29   Earl Bostic starts a southern tour with a show in Baltimore. The first two weeks will bring in 9,000 patrons and $13,000 with one-nighters in Salisbury, Maryland; Norfolk; Raleigh; Fayetteville, North Carolina; Columbia, South Carolina; Roanoke, Virginia; and Charleston, West Virginia.

Roy Hamilton is at Pep's Musical Bar in Philadelphia.

Decca Records announces a major coup in the signing of Billy Ward and his Dominoes. The group is one of the strongest acts currently on the rhythm and blues scene. They had recorded for King Records, and King's subsidiary Federal Records, for several years before going to Jubilee late last year.

Gene and Eunice, who are riding high with their hit "Ko Ko Mo" on Combo Records, are forced to re-record the tune for Aladdin Records, which claims prior rights to the duo, and especially to Gene Forrest's writing talents.

JAN 31   Dinah Washington is on stage for a ten-day engagement at the Crystal Lounge in Detroit.

New releases for the fifth week of January include "That's All I Want From You" by Dinah Washington on Mercury; Billy "The Kid" Emerson's "When It Rains It Pours" on Sun; Guitar Slim's "Our Only Child" and Lloyd Price's "Trying To Find Someone To Love," both on Specialty; "I Know" by the Hollywood Flames on Decca; "Earth Angel" by Gloria Mann on Sound; "Love Will Make Your Mind Go Wild" by the Penguins on Dootone; "I Wonder Why" by the Rhythm Aces on Vee-Jay; and "I Need Your Love" by Pee Wee Crayton and "Nothing Sweet As You" by Bobby Mitchell and the Toppers, both on Imperial.

1. Earth Angel - The Penguins
2. Hearts Of Stone - The Charms
3. Sincerely - The Moonglows
4. Teach Me Tonight - Dinah Washington
5. Tweedle Dee - LaVern Baker
6. Ling, Ting, Tong - The Five Keys
7. Ling, Ting, Tong - The Charms
8. Reconsider Baby - Lowell Fulson
9. You Upset Me Baby - B. B. King
10. Pledging My Love - Johnny Ace

January 1955
ARTIST OF THE MONTH

THE PENGUINS

THE PENGUINS

The Penguins could lay claim to being the first of the "garage groups." Certainly their first recording session fits that definition, as "No There Ain't No News Today" was waxed in the garage of band leader and Dootone Records owner, Dootsie Williams. The group was told that the recording was to be used as a demo disk, being sent out to other artists who would hopefully record the song. But it was released. And with another artist on the flip side. Although it had no chance in the competitive record market, the song paved the way for one of the strongest entries in the category of "first rock 'n roll record."

The Penguins were organized in 1953 when two teen-agers from Fremont High in Los Angeles got together to harmonize. Curtis Williams (no relation to Dootsie Williams) was an aspiring songwriter who sang bass. Together with his schoolmate Dexter Tisby (2nd tenor), another childhood friend Cleveland "Cleve" Duncan (first tenor), and Bruce Tate (baritone), they formed the Penguins (named after "Willie the Penguin" on a pack of Kool cigarettes). The group was discovered by Dootsie Williams at a talent show at the California Club. At the time, Dootsie was looking for local talent that was not signed to one of the area's other independent rhythm and blues labels, namely RPM/Flair/Modern, Imperial, Specialty, or Aladdin. With that kind of strong competition in his backyard, finding raw talent took determination.

As mentioned, the first session produced a less-than-successful record, but it did not dampen the spirits of either the group or the new record company owner. And, as luck would have it, lightning struck during the next session. Rarely is a record as immediately identifiable as "Earth Angel." The melody, the production, the lyrics, and the vocals all melded together perfectly to capture the moment in song. Thirty years later, "Earth Angel" is wistfully referred to as "America's favorite oldie." The song was reported to have sold an amazing two million copies for Dootone in 1955 alone.

Like all new acts with a big hit, the Penguins hit the road as soon as bookings were available. They played the Apollo Theater in

New York in January 1955, where they mistakenly reported to be from Texas. One early reviewer thought the boys were personable enough and neatly dressed, and said that they had excellent voices, though they were a bit too prone to clap their hands to generate excitement on the faster numbers. Although they had been on the road only a matter of weeks, the reviewer thought they were in need of new material! It's difficult to overcome this type of error.

Other problems were piling on the Penguins almost as fast as "Earth Angel" was selling. First of all, the group saw its record covered for the "pop" audience by the Crew-Cuts, who stole much of the thunder from the Penguins. Second, Curtis Williams was sued by songwriter/performer Jesse Belvin, who claimed to have written "Earth Angel" with Johnny Green. The suit was finally settled, giving rights jointly to Curtis and Dootsie Williams. Third, Dootsie Williams found himself with more than "Earth Angel" as a hit record, as the Medallions' "Buick 59"/"The Letter" broke nationwide. With little business background, he was swamped. Fourth, the group, finding it had to defend itself against both songwriting claims and Dootsie Williams's split loyalties, picked as its manager a local lawyer who was also dealing in split loyalties, and who was very ambitious for himself and the Penguins. This final item might not appear to be a problem except that the lawyer, Buck Ram, also had another group under contract. Admittedly the other group, even with a half-dozen releases, had failed to come up with anything close to the popularity of "Earth Angel," but with two groups to manage, Ram's duties were divided. His ambitious nature led to another lawsuit, this time from Dootsie Williams, when the Penguins signed a recording contract with a major company, Mercury Records. Ram also arranged for his second group to jump to Mercury in the same deal, and somewhere in the shuffle the Penguins got lost. The second group, as it turned out, had a major hit in both the "pop" and r&b markets with its first Mercury release, "Only You." Yes, the second group was the Platters. But what about the Penguins?

They continued to make some fine records for Mercury and its subsidiary, Wing: "Dealer In Dreams," "Peace Of Mind," "Be Mine Or A Fool." But the Penguins were unable to come up with another hit. In fact they were but another of the rhythm and blues artists that had a Number One r&b smash and not another charted record. This situation was unfair to the Penguins, and whether it reflected on Ram's lack of attention or the quickly changing tastes of the record-buying public is unclear. Certainly the group worked to overcome the many obstacles that were constantly placed in its path.

Lawsuits over royalties that Curtis Williams claimed from Dootone only antagonized the issue. The group moved on to Atlantic Records in 1957 for one release, and then finally, after two years on the road, they arrived back in Los Angeles broke. The only one willing to record them was Dootsie Williams. Three more singles were issued on Dootone before a single release on Sun State closed the book on the Penguins as a group. In 1963 lightning almost struck again with the recording of "Memories of El Monte," which was credited to the Penguins. The record featured only Cleve Duncan fronting a local studio group, the Viceroys, and it was written and produced by an aspiring Los Angeles music freak, Frank Zappa. While it failed to sell well enough to make any national charts, "Memories of El Monte" once again led to continued work for Curtis Williams and the "Penguins" in clubs and on the tour circuit. After all, on the strength of "Earth Angel" alone, the Penguins had worked steadily for eight years.

The Penguins, as a group, may not have set the world on fire, but their biggest claim to fame, "Earth Angel," certainly ranks as one of the best-loved rock 'n roll songs of all time.

February 1955

FEB 1   The "Top Ten Rhythm And Blues Show" continues touring with a performance tonight at the Court Theater in Springfield, Massachusetts. Ulysses Hicks of the Five Keys dies of a heart attack following tonight's show, and the Five Keys are forced to drop out of the tour. Hicks is quickly replaced by Rudy West, who had sung previously with the group and has just been released from active duty in the Army. Other cities played this month include Bridgeport, Connecticut; Pittsburgh; Chicago; Youngstown, Cleveland and Cincinnati, Ohio; Evansville, Indiana; Nashville and Jackson, Tennessee; St. Louis; Omaha; Kansas City; Dallas, Longview and Austin, Texas; Oklahoma City; Wichita, Kansas; Tulsa; Ft. Worth, Waco, San Antonio, Galveston, Houston and Port Arthur, Texas; New Orleans; Macon, Georgia; and Jacksonville, Florida. (See January 28th)

Louis Jordan opens at Pep's Musical Bar in Philadelphia.

FEB 4   LaVern Baker and the **Rivileers** are backed by the Illinois Jacquet Combo during their week at the Apollo Theater in New York.

The weekend in Los Angeles brings the Spiders and Chuck Willis to the Savoy Ballroom and the Orioles to the 5-4 Club.

Billy Ward and his Dominoes start a sixteen-week stay at the Saraha Hotel in Las Vegas.

FEB 5   The second annual Festival Of Negro Music is broadcast live from the Savoy Ballroom in New York and features Faye Adams, Johnny Hartman, LaVern Baker, and the **Solitaires**.

MGM Pictures announces that "Rock Around The Clock" by Bill Haley and his Comets will be featured in a new picture, "Blackboard Jungle," to be released next month.

New releases for the first week of February include "Blue Velvet" by the Clovers on Atlantic; "Ko Ko Mo" by the Charms and "Baby Let's Play House" by the Thunderbirds, both on DeLuxe; "Ko Ko Mo" by Marvin and Johnny on Specialty; "I Love You Mostly" by the Orioles on Jubilee; "Poison Ivy" by Boyd Bennett and his Rockets, "Dreams Come True" by the Strangers, and "Tweedle Dee" by **Bonnie Lou**, all on King; Rusty Bryant's "Back Street" on Dot; "Tired Of Your Sexy Ways" by Mac Burney and the Four Jacks and "Honey Sipper" by Charles Brown, both on Aladdin; and two releases by the "5" Royales: "You Didn't Learn It At Home" on King and "With All Your Heart" on Apollo. There are also several tributes to Johnny Ace released this week: Varetta Dillard's "Johnny Has Gone" on Savoy and Johnny Fuller's "Johnny Ace's Last Letter" on Aladdin. "Johnny Ace's Last Letter" is also one side of the new Recorded In Hollywood release from Johnny Moore's Three Blazers (with vocal by Frankie Irwin). The "B" side is "Why, Johnny, Why" featuring Linda Hayes.

The Rivileers formed in Jamaica, New York, in 1953 as a quintet. Other than "A Thousand Stars," the only other big hit for the group was "For Sentimental Reasons." Eugene Pearson, lead tenor of the group, later joined the Cleftones and then the Drifters.

The Solitaires hailed from Harlem, and remained on Old Town until 1963. They almost had a big hit in 1958 with "Walking Along," only to see its sales dip under the cover version by the Diamonds.

Bonnie Lou (born Sally Carson, Bloomington, IL, 1926) started as a teen-age yodeler on King Records in 1944. She was a popular member of Cincinatti's Midwestern Hayride for more than twenty years. She was the first White female vocalist to attempt to combine country with rhythm and blues into a sound resembling rockabilly. Other records by Bonnie Lou include "Daddy-O" and "No Rock And Roll Tonight" (King, 1955).

224

Alan Freed can be heard doing the introduction to the new release by Billy Williams, "I Wanna Hug Ya, Squeeze Ya, Kiss Ya," on Coral Records.

Bill Haley and his Comets play a one-night stand in Rome, New York.

Radio station WMBL in Macon, Georgia, hires its first Black deejay, Hamilton Swain, who will play r&b for two hours daily.

Rainbow Records signs guitarist Mickey Baker to the label. Other label signings include the Cookies and the Regals (both formerly with Aladdin's subsidiary, Lamp) and T-Bone Walker (previously with Imperial), all with Atlantic, and **Buddy Ace** with Duke.

The Cardinals return to the recording studios following a long period of inactivity while lead singer Ernie Warren served in the Army.

FEB 8   In a rare interview in Camden, New Jersey, Bill Kenney, former lead tenor with the Ink Spots, says that he feels "the day of group singing is passing."

FEB 11   Roy Hamilton headlines the revue at the Chicago Theater for two weeks.

    Lucky Millinder's Orchestra is the headliner at the Apollo Theater in New York for the week.

    In Washington at the Howard Theater, the week's entertainment features the Rivileers, Big Maybelle, and the Gene Ammons Band.

    The Orioles repeat at the 5-4 Club in Los Angeles for another three-day weekend. They share the bill with Charles Brown.

FEB 12   Pat Boone, previously recording for Nashville's Republic Records, signs with Dot Records of Gallatin, Tennessee. Boone is a recent winner on both "Ted Mack's Original Amateur Hour" and "Arthur Godfrey's Talent Scouts" television shows.

    Dave Bartholomew's Combo entertains dancers at New Orleans' Club Riviera for the weekend. Across town, guitarist **Roy Montrell** is playing nightly at the Hi-Hat Club.

New releases for the second week of February include Roy Hamilton's "I Believe," on Epic; "Oh! Oh!" by the Treniers and "Love Struck" by Chuck Willis, both on Okeh; Al Savage's "Dream Girl" on Herald; Big Walter's "Calling Maggie" on TNT; "Whadaya Want" by the Robins on Spark; "Mambo Rock" by Bill Haley and his Comets on Decca; "Love Of My Life" by Bill Robinson and the Quails on DeLuxe; "It's Too Late Now" by the Hawks on Imperial; "Foolishly" by the **Three Chuckles** on "X"; "Rockin' Chair" by the Five Cats on RCA Victor; and Rosco Gordon's "Three Cent Love" on Duke.

FEB 18   Willie Mae Thornton, Charlie and Ray, Danny Overbea, and the El Dorados split the bill at the Apollo Theater in New York for the week.

    In Los Angeles, the Savoy Ballroom offers patrons **Charles Brown** with the Stomp Gordon Band. At the 5-4 Club, Roy Brown

Buddy Ace was a more dynamic performer than his younger brother, Johnny Ace. Still, he had only a few minor hits on Duke in the mid-1960s. Today, he continues to draw bigger crowds than might be expected on the blues festival circuit.

Roy Montrell was a legendary r&b guitarist in New Orleans. He was born there February 27, 1928, and he worked in the bands of Lloyd Price and Roy Milton before joining Fats Domino in the early 1960s. While touring with Domino, he died of a heart attack in Holland, May 16, 1979.

The Three Chuckles were too "pop" for most of the audience that dug rock 'n roll. Somehow, they did land a spot on the roster of the classic 1956 rock 'n roll movie, "The Girl Can't Help It."

Charles Brown was responsible for the initial popularity of many of the standards which continue to make up the blues repertoire today, including "Get Yourself Another Fool," "Hard Times," "My Baby's Gone," and "Trouble Blues."

THE VALENTINES

The Valentines were named the Dreamers when they formed in New York in 1952, but they did not record under that name. As the Valentines, they are best remembered today for "Tonight Kathleen" (1954, Old Town) and "Lily Maebelle" (1955, Rama).

Bobby Relf (born Bobby Byrd in 1934) recorded hits such as "Rock-In Robin" and "Over And Over" as Bobby Day in 1958. Relf (Byrd) was also a member of the Hollywood Flames, who hit in 1957 with "Buzz-Buzz-Buzz." He is not related to the Bobby Byrd, who toured and recorded with soul-shouter James Brown.

Wynonie Harris died in 1969 at age 54. After rock 'n roll came of age, demand for humorous, uptempo blues diminished, and by the late 1950s Harris stopped recording altogether.

headlines the "Hollywood Revue," which also includes local favorites Johnny "Guitar" Watson and Linda Hayes.

FEB 19   Earl Bostic plays Columbus, Georgia, tonight and Pensacola, Florida, tomorrow.
        In Philadelphia, the Cosmopolitan Club hosts the Five Keys, Dakota Staton, and the **Valentines** for a one-night stand.
        In New Orleans, Dave Bartholomew returns to the Club Riviera for the evening. He is also scheduled to entertain at the club on Mardi Gras Tuesday. Thereafter he is booked at the Riviera for a long run of Saturday night dates.

FEB 21   The Orioles open for a week at Pep's Musical Bar in Philadelphia.
        Chuck Willis stops for a one-night stand at the Club Desire in New Orleans.
        The Savoy Ballroom in Los Angeles has an "Ookey Ook" dance (based on the song by the Penguins of the same name). The show features Johnny Otis, the Medallions, the Meadowlarks, and Marie Adams for the evening.

New releases for the third week of February include "Don't You Know" by Fats Domino on Imperial; "Lonely Nights" by the Hearts on Baton; "Truly" by Arthur Lee Maye and the Crowns on RPM; "If I Never Get To Heaven" by Billy Ward and his Dominoes on Federal; Jimmy Witherspoon's "Waiting For Your Return" on Checker; Sonny Boy Williamson's "From The Bottom" on Trumpet; Rudy Ferguson's "I'm Telling You" on DeLuxe; "Fujiyama Mama" by Annisteen Allen on Capitol; "When I Grow Too Old To Dream" by the Sandmen on Okeh; "Standin' Right There" by the Feathers on Aladdin; "Please Have Mercy" by Linda Hayes and the Platters and "Boogie At Midnight" by Boyd Bennett, both on King; and "Farewell" by **Bobby Relf** and the Laurels on Flair.

FEB 22   Charles Brown spends two days at New Orleans' Club Desire.

FEB 25   **Wynonie Harris** opens for three days at Chic's Show Bar in Detroit. Across town, Roy Hamilton plays for four days at the Crystal Lounge.
        The "5" Royales with Tab Smith's Combo entertain at the 5-4 Ballroom in Los Angeles for the three-day weekend.

FEB 26   LaVern Baker appeals to her representative, Charles Diggs (Democrat-Michigan), to have him study the possibility of authoring a bill that would revise the 1909 copyright act. Miss Baker is upset because the current copyright act does not cover duplicating the arrangements on her records, such as "Tweedle Dee." She claims she has lost $15,000 in royalties to singers Georgia Gibbs and Vicki Young, who took her record and virtually duplicated the song note for note.
        The New Orleans Municipal Auditorium presents the Clovers, the Charms, the Moonglows, Faye Adams, Joe Turner, Bill Doggett, Lowell Fulson, and the Paul Williams Orchestra for an evening concert.

FEB 28   During his one-week engagement, Earl Bostic becomes the highest-paid entertainer in the history of the Palms Supper Club in Hallendale, Florida.

New **releases** for the fourth week of February include "My Babe" by Little Walter on Checker; "The Door Is Still Open" by the Cardinals and "Flip, Flop And Fly" by Joe Turner, both on Atlantic; "Ashamed Of Myself" by the Midnighters on Federal; "My Loving Baby" by Charlie and Ray on Herald; Richard Berry's "Oh! Oh! Get Out Of The Car" on Flair; "Come Back My Love" by the Wrens on Rama; "Two Hearts" by the Charms on DeLuxe and by Pat Boone on Dot; and another tribute to Johnny Ace, "Johnny's Still Singing" by the Five Wings on King.

LATE FEBRUARY

John Greer starts a tour of New Jersey, Pennsylvania, and Delaware that will run for a month.

The **Du Droppers** are currently playing engagements in Canada.

The average age of the Du Droppers was about 40, among the oldest of the r&b groups formed from 1952-55. Their singing roots lay in gospel, with ties to the Jubilaires (Decca, King) and Dixiaires. Several members later formed the Valiants on Joy.

THE TOP TEN ROCK 'N' ROLL RECORDS FOR FEBRUARY 1955

1. Pledging My Love - Johnny Ace
2. Earth Angel - The Penguins
3. Sincerely - The Moonglows
4. I Got A Woman - Ray Charles
5. Hearts Of Stone - The Charms
6. Tweedle Dee - LaVern Baker
7. Ling, Ting, Tong - The Charms
8. Ko Ko Mo - Gene and Eunice
9. Ling, Ting, Tong - The Five Keys
10. The Wallflower - Etta James

February 1955
ARTIST OF THE MONTH

THE MOONGLOWS

By the time the Moonglows' record of "Sincerely" struck "gold," they had been together for over four years. The group was formed as a vocal quartet in Louisville, Kentucky, by two lead tenors, Bobby Lester, who previously had sung with several local groups, and Harvey Fuqua, nephew of the guitarist with the Ink Spots, Charlie Fuqua. In March 1951 they were known as the Crazy Sounds, and they were talented enough to tour the South and Midwest. By the time they were ready to audition for a recording contract, the group also included Alexander "Pete" Graves (first tenor), Prentiss (or Prentis) Barnes (bass), and Billy (or Buddy) Johnson (guitar). The lineup of three tenors was as unique as their penchant for singing in minor keys.

On a swing through the Midwest in the late summer of 1953, they auditioned for Cleveland deejay Alan Freed by long-distance telephone. Freed liked what he heard, and when an in-person meeting was arranged, he took the group on as their manager. His status in

THE MOONGLOWS

the local music scene quickly placed the Moonglows with Champagne Records, with the resulting release of "I Just Can't Tell No Lie," which was written by Fuqua and Freed (under the pseudonym of Al Lance.) Unfortunately, Champagne folded soon after the Moonglows' release; however, Freed was able to arrange for the group to move over to Chance Records of Chicago, where they released "Baby Please" in October 1953. Their recording of "Secret Love" temporarily reversed the growing trend as they covered the "pop" hit by Doris Day.

In October 1954 Chance closed shop, and the Moonglows moved downtown to the studios of Chess Records, where they recorded simultaneously as the Moonglows (on Chess) and as Bobby Lester and the Moonlighters (on Checker). "Sincerely" featured a lead vocal by Lester with the songwriter's credits going once again to Fuqua and Freed. But by this time the practice of "cover" records was rampant, and while the Moonglows sold a respectable 300,000 copies of "Sincerely," it was the McGuire Sisters who had the gold record and the "pop" hit.

From the start, the group had trouble on stage because they were booked as both the Moonglows and the Moonlighters. It was no wonder that some audiences though that the group was cut from the same fabric as other r&b quintets when it came to their vocal style and mannerisms, their gyrations and hand movements, and their song arrangements and selections. On the other hand, while they may have had trouble cutting their own niche, the Moonglows were capable of pleasing audiences with an unrestrained performance full of sexual implications that brought near hysteria from the teen-agers.

The problem with having a smash like "Sincerely" is trying to come up with a second hit. The Moonglows hit paydirt with their second Chess release, "Most Of All," but there was a year and four singles between "Most Of All" and "See Saw." "The Ten Commandments Of Love," the last hit for the group, came in late 1958, although it was recorded in December 1957.

That year the original group disbanded following an engagement at the Howard Theater in Washington. Harvey Fuqua decided to fill the remaining tour contracts by hiring another group from the Washington area, the Marquees, who featured James Knowland (or Nolan), Chester Simmons, Reese Palmer, and a young Marvin Gaye. This new group of Moonglows remained with Chess into 1960, before Fuqua met Berry Gordy of Detroit, married Gordy's sister, and changed the name of the group to the Spinners. The "new" group recorded for Tri-Phi, a joint venture between Gordy and Chess Records. Fuqua also found time to record duets with Etta James and to front the Five Quails on his own Harvey label. Eventually he became an executive for Gordy's fledgling empire, Motown Records.

In 1964 a completely new group of Moonglows, led by Alex Graves of the original group, George Thorpe and Berle Gaston of the Velvets on Red Robin, and Doc Green of the Five Crowns, re-recorded their hits for Lana Records, but the sound just wasn't the same.

The original Moonglows remained true to their rhythm and blues heritage. Their records featured an easy vocal interchange between members, and they could effectively handle both ballads and jump tunes with ease. Equally ahead of and behind their own time, they found themselves in the middle as rhythm and blues evolved rapidly into rock 'n roll. In fact, their single release of "Don't Say Goodbye" in 1956 featured a string section three years before the song usually credited with introducing violins to rock 'n roll, the Drifter's "There Goes My Baby."

March 1955

MAR 1   The "Top Ten Rhythm And Blues Show" completes its six-week tour this month with shows in the following cities: Raleigh, Fayetteville, and Kinston, North Carolina; Roanoke, Virginia; Columbia, South Carolina; Birmingham; Chattanooga; Greenville, South Carolina; Durham and Greensboro, North Carolina; Charleston, West Virginia; Knoxville, Tennessee; Bluefield, West Virginia; Atlanta; Tampa; Charleston, South Carolina; Norfolk and Richmond, Virginia; Philadelphia; New York City; and finally closing in Buffalo on the 20th. (See also January 28th and February 1st.)

Following his record-breaking engagement at the Carolyn Club in Columbus, Ohio, Rusty Bryant embarks on a tour of one-night stands.

Big Jay McNeeley brings his combo to the Crystal Lounge in Detroit.

MAR 4   The Apollo Theater in New York plays host to Ruth Brown and the Willis Jackson Orchestra for the week.

Fats Domino plays the first of two weekend engagements at Los Angeles' 5-4 Club. Also in town, LaVern Baker and Ivory Joe Hunter split the bill at the Savoy Ballroom for this weekend only. Miss Baker is just starting a three-week tour of the West Coast.

MAR 5   Earl Bostic takes to the road following his week in Hallendale, Florida, with a one-night stand in Jacksonville.

MAR 7   The **Larks** open at the Rainbow Room in York, Pennsylvania.

New releases for the first week of March include "This Is My Story" by Gene and Eunice on Combo; "Check Yourself" by Lowell Fulson on Checker; "What'cha Gonna Do" by Clyde McPhatter and the Drifters on Atlantic; "Love, Rock And Thrill" by the Lamplighters on Federal; Arthur Gunter's "She's Mine All Mine" on Excello; "I Almost Lost My Mind" by the Harptones on Bruce; Otis Blackwell's "I'm Calling Back Baby" on Jay-Dee; "One More Chance" by the El Dorados and "Tell Me Baby" by the Five Echoes, both on Vee-Jay; and "She Put The Wammee On Me" by **Jay Hawkins** on Mercury.

EARLY MARCH

Duke Records announces plans to release its first rhythm and blues album, a 10-incher containing all the hits of Johnny Ace.

Steve Gibson and his Red Caps open for a month at the Cafe Society in New York.

The rhythm and blues trend has hit its peak and is on its way out

When Allen Bunn left the Larks in 1952, he recorded under the name of Tarheel Slim, and his sessions for Red Robin were frequently backed by members of the group. The Larks also recorded gospel music under at least five different names.

Screamin' Jay Hawkins started his musical career as a pianist with the Tiny Grimes orchestra. Later, as a solo vocalist, his stage act featured shades of voodoo and witchcraft long before Alice Cooper and Ozzy Osborne made it fashionable.

230

according to an announcement from Mercury Records. Consequently, the company does not have plans for any further r&b cover records for Georgia Gibbs, Sarah Vaughan, or the Gaylords.

Coral Records and Alan Freed reach an agreement whereby Freed will become an artist, a talent scout, and an artist and repertoire representative for the company for a period of two years. The agreement is cancelled by mutual consent April 30th.

Rainbow Records launches a new subsidiary, Riviera Records, which will also specialize in r&b. First release will be by the Five Crowns.

MAR 8   Ruth Brown guests on the Steve Allen show on NBC-TV.
        Earl Bostic is the first Negro artist to play the Celtic Room in Nashville during his four-day layover.

MAR 10   **Red Prysock** and his band start a five-day engagement at the Apache Inn in Dayton, Ohio.
        On the stage of the Apollo Theater in New York, Ruth Brown receives a gold record representing sales over five million disks on Atlantic Records.

Red Pryscock started playing sax in the army while with the occupation forces in Germany after World War II. Following his discharge, he joined Cootie Williams' Band and later played in the combos of Tiny Grimes and Tiny Bradshaw.

MAR 11   Al Hibbler and Sarah Vaughan front Tito Puente's Orchestra for a week at New York's Apollo Theater.
        Bull Moose Jackson starts two weeks at the Flame Show Bar in Detroit.
        Ruth Brown moves into the Howard Theater in Washington with the Willis Jackson Orchestra for the week.

MAR 13   Roy Milton, Pee Wee Crayton, and **Chuck Higgins** share the billing for the Sunday night dance at the Elks Ballroom in Los Angeles.

Chuck Higgins' original combo featured Johnny "Guitar" Watson on piano, and it is Watson who sang the vocal on "Motorhead Baby," the flip of "Packuko Hop." Higgins later recorded for a number of labels, including Aladdin and Specialty, before becoming an instructor of music at UCLA.

New releases for the second week of March include "Most Of All" by the Moonglows on Chess; "Cat Hop" by the Dodgers and "Why Don't You Do Right" by Amos Milburn, both on Aladdin; "A Hug And A Kiss" by Bobby Lester and the Moonlighters on Checker; "How I Wonder" by the "5" Royales on King; Percy Mayfield's "The Voice Within," Roy Milton's "Baby Don't Do That To Me," and the Dukes' "Oh Kay," all on Specialty; and "I Hope" by the Four Tunes on Jubilee.

MID-MARCH

Buddy Johnson and sister Ella are currently on tour in the South and Midwest.

Alan Freed, New York deejay, hosts a meeting with Saul Bihari (RPM/Modern/Flair), Jack Angel (Herald), Bob Rolontz (Groove), and Ahmet Ertegun (Atlantic). Details are not disclosed.

MAR 16   In a rushed attempt to cover Al Hibbler's version of **"Unchained Melody,"** Epic sets up a session for Roy Hamilton. The resulting single is shipped within five days.
        Earl Bostic plays a one-nighter at the New Orleans Municipal Auditorium.

"Unchained Melody" was the theme song from the movie "Unchained," which told the story of a prison chain gang. Although Roy Hamilton's version was preferred by the rhythm and blues audience, Al Hibbler had the slightly bigger hit with help from the "pop" field.

MAR 17   Johnny Ace is posthumously awarded the first *Billboard* magazine rhythm and blues "Triple Crown" as "Pledging My Love" tops all three r&b charts: "Best Sellers in Stores," "Most Played in Juke Boxes," and "Most Played by Jockeys."

MAR 18   The Drifters team with Varetta Dillard and the Eddy Heywood Combo for a week at the Apollo Theater in New York.

Dinah Washington, Danny Overbea, and the James Moody Band thrill the crowd at the Howard Theater in Washington for the week.

Sonny Thompson and Lulu Reed play a three-day weekend engagement at the 5-4 Club in Los Angeles. Across town at the Your Room Lounge, Charles Brown with Johnny Moore's Three Blazers start an extended engagement of three-day weekends.

MAR 21   Al Hibbler is scheduled for an eight-day booking at the Crystal Lounge in Detroit.

New releases for the third week of March include Piano Red's "Jump Man Jump" and John Greer's "Lucky Lucky Me," both on Groove; Ella Johnson's "Alright Okay You Win" on Mercury; "You Ain't Been True" by Faye Adams on Herald; "Tick Tock A-Woo" by the Turbans and "Treat Me Like I Treat You" by Memphis Slim, both on Money; "I Need You Darling" by the **Falcons** on Cash; "You Came To Me" by the Five Crowns on Riviera; Nolan Strong and the Diablos' "Hold Me Until Eternity" on Fortune; "Don't Be Angry" by Nappy Brown on Savoy; and Big Mike's "Down In New Orleans" on Savoy.

MAR 23   In New England, public outcry against rhythm and blues peaks when six Boston deejays meet with press and religious leaders to form a record censorship board. Songs included on the groups' initial list of records that will not be played over local Boston stations include "Make Yourself Comfortable," "Teach Me Tonight," "Idle Gossip," "From The Bottom To The Top," "Honey Love," and all versions of the "Annie" series of songs.

MAR 25   **Jimmy Reed** entertains at the Royal Peacock in Atlanta.

The movie "Blackboard Jungle," which features Bill Haley's "Rock Around The Clock," is released to theaters.

The Apollo Theater in New York offers the Chordcats and the Charms on its weekly bill.

The "5" Royales and Tab Smith's Combo perform at the 5-4 Ballroom in Los Angeles for the weekend.

Radio station WGN in Chicago forms a record review board after receiving fifteen thousand letters, many from teen-agers, accusing the station of playing dirty records.

New releases for the fourth week of March include another tribute to Johnny Ace, "In Memory," by Johnny Otis with Marie Adams on Peacock; other releases include Mickey "Guitar" Baker's "Shake Walkin'" on Rainbow; "Bye Bye Baby Blues" by the Ravens on Jubilee; "Laugh Laugh Laugh" by Willie Mae Thornton on Peacock; "Eternally Yours" by the Barons on Imperial; "Rock Bottom" by the Rams, "Baby I Love You" by Shirley Gunter and The Queens, and "She Loves To Dance" by the Flairs, all on Flair; and "Unchained Melody" by Roy Hamilton

THE FALCONS

Joe Stubbs, one of the lead vocalists with the Falcons, joined the Contours on Motown ("Do You Love Me," 1962). In the 1970s, he sang with One Hundred Proof Aged In Soul on Hot Wax ("Somebody's Been Sleeping," 1970).

Jimmy Reed, the most successful of all the Chicago bluesmen in terms of record sales, was born in 1923 (or 1925) in Benoit (or Dunleith), Mississippi. His strongest popularity spanned six years beginning in 1955. He is best remembered for several boogie-blues numbers which have gone on to become standards: "Baby, What You Want Me To Do," "Ain't That Loving You Baby" and "Big Boss Man." Reed died Christmas Day, 1985, in his adopted hometown of Chicago.

on Epic.

MAR 29   Al Hibbler stars for the week at the Copa Casino in Buffalo, New York.

LATE MARCH

LaVern Baker opens at the Orchid Room in Kansas City for a week.

Dootone Records signs veterans Roy Milton, Mabel Scott, and Chuck Higgins.

Charlie White, formerly with the Clovers, forms a new group, the Playboys. The group will record for Cat Records.

Following Mercury's lead (see Early March above), RCA Victor decides that it will no longer cover records put out by competing companies.

THE TOP TEN ROCK 'N ROLL RECORDS FOR MARCH 1955

1. Pledging My Love - Johnny Ace
2. I Got A Woman - Ray Charles
3. The Wallflower - Etta James
4. Earth Angel - The Penguins
5. Tweedle Dee - LaVern Baker
6. Johnny Has Gone - Varetta Dillard
7. Sincerely - The Moonglows
8. My Baby - Little Walter
9. Ling, Ting, Tong - The Charms
10. Mambo Rock - Bill Haley and his Comets

March 1955
ARTIST OF THE MONTH

RAY CHARLES
(Ray Charles Robinson, b. September 23, 1930)

RAY CHARLES

Rock 'n roll has had a virtual plethora of royalty: Kings, Queens, Princes, Princesses, Dukes, Bosses, and Godfathers. Ray Charles is the only artist known as the "Genius." His tastes in music, as displayed in his varied recordings, range from basic blues to esoteric jazz to country and western. He knows no boundaries when it comes to his songs. There are no limitations to Ray Charles's genius.

Although his birthplace was Albany, Georgia, and Georgia has played an important part in his life, the Robinson family moved to Greenville, Florida, when Ray was just two months old. His early childhood in Greenville was certainly not normal. Born into a family of two children, small by the standards of the time, he learned to play boogie woogie piano at the age of three from the owner of the cafe next door. At age five he started losing his eyesight, and by seven he was completely blind, possibly from glaucoma. His parents were able to send him to the Florida State School for Deaf and Blind Children in St. Augustine, where from 1937 to 1945 he continued playing the piano as well as studying alto saxophone, trumpet, and clarinet. Following the deaths of his father when he was ten and his mother when he was fifteen, Ray quit school to follow the musician's life, playing in the small clubs in Jacksonville, Orlando, and Tampa. In 1947 he even toured with the Florida Playboys, a White country and western band. About this time, he dropped his last name to avoid confusion with boxing champion Sugar Ray Robinson. He became simply Ray Charles. By 1948 he had moved to Seattle, where he founded the McSon (also referred to as the Maxim) Trio with himself on piano accompanied by Gosady McGee (guitar) and Milt Garred (bass). His stage presence at the time was based on the "pop" vocals of Nat Cole and the silky-smooth blues stylings of Charles Brown: pleasant, evenly balanced, almost bland, and aimed at pleasing the large White population in the area. He quickly gained enough acceptance to have his own radio show and then a local television show in Seattle.

His rising popularity led to a recording contract with Los Angeles-based Swing Time Records and his first single, "Confession Blues." In 1951 he had a top ten hit in the rhythm and blues market with "Baby Let Me Hold Your Hand." He toured with another blues artist and Swing Time associate, Lowell Fulson, for two years, 1950-52. He recorded a few sides for both Sittin' In and Rockin' Records during 1952, but his career seemed stalled. In the fall of 1952 he made the biggest move of his life by signing with Atlantic Records of New York. His first session failed to produce a major hit in "Roll With Me Baby," which still had the sound of his Seattle days, but in July 1953 "Mess Around" clearly showed that Ray Charles was ready to move into the mainstream of rhythm and blues. The song was a combination of Louis Jordan and Piano Red sung in a breathless, joyous style. More releases led to more road work, and Ray found himself constantly in demand in many small night clubs from Texas through Florida to Virginia. In New Orleans in October 1953, he found time to help produce the biggest hit of the winter of 1953-54 in Guitar Slim's "The Things I Used To Do," on which he played piano. In August 1954, with his own band and singer Ruth Brown, he embarked on yet another tour, but this time he was playing clubs above the Mason-Dixon line for the first time.

His biggest break since signing with Atlantic came early in 1955 with the release of "I Got A Woman," which had been recorded with his regular band during a November stop at Georgia Tech's WGST radio station while playing in the Atlanta area. The song was closer to gospel than any popular artist had dared go up to that time. It featured a pronounced shuffle, punctuated by a three-beat brass riff under Ray's impassioned vocal. The saxophone break in mid-song led directly into a preaching-style discourse before the whole thing wound up with Ray leading the congregation on one final verse. After so many years of hard work, this song brought almost instant national fame, better club dates, and led directly to a converging of styles that was fast becoming rock 'n roll. In the mid-1950s Charles was a mainstay of many of the rock 'n roll package tours. Not content to remain a purely r&b artist, he issued his first jazz album in 1957, and he played the prestigious Newport Jazz Festival in July 1958, becoming the first entertainer invited to perform whose popularity lay almost completely outside the jazz world. It was not until 1959 that he had his first gold record with "What'd I Say." He switched to ABC-Paramount Records shortly thereafter, and his story will be picked up in Volume 3 of *The Golden*

If Ray Charles's career had ended with "I Got A Woman," he still would rate a mention in most histories of rock 'n roll. But his foresight and intuition about music were unerringly accurate. He was able to combine many of the elements of Black music into a form that was exciting and acceptable to the larger "pop" audience. This was no small accomplishment. There was a deep rift inside the Negro community over the use of religious styles and gospel overtones on records with a more down-to-earth tone. To be able to walk that fine line and to be accepted by both sides demonstrates that there definitely was a genius at work in Ray Charles' music.

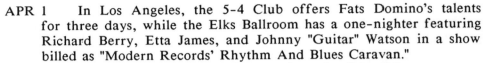

April 1955

THE CADILLACS

The Cadillacs' first release was "Gloria" on JOZ (Josie) in 1954. For this first session, the group consisted of Earl Carroll, Laverne Drake, Robert "Bobby" Phillips, John "Papa" Clark (of the Five Crowns), and Gus Willingham.

APR 1   In Los Angeles, the 5-4 Club offers Fats Domino's talents for three days, while the Elks Ballroom has a one-nighter featuring Richard Berry, Etta James, and Johnny "Guitar" Watson in a show billed as "Modern Records' Rhythm And Blues Caravan."

Ruth Brown is on stage in Detroit at the Crystal Lounge.

APR 2   The "1955 Rock And Roll Festival" is held at the St. Nicholas Arena in New York. Performers on the bill are Varetta Dillard, Red Prysock, the **Cadillacs**, the Mellows, Otis Blackwell, and the Joe Morris Combo.

Little Walter, currently touring the South, plays a one-nighter at Houma, Louisiana, followed by a performance at New Orleans' Labor Union Hall on April 3rd.

Guitar Slim plays a one-night stand at the Savoy Ballroom in Los Angeles.

All nine local radio stations in San Antonio join together to censor rhythm and blues records before allowing them to be aired.

New releases for the first week of April include Floyd Dixon's "Hey Bartender" on Cat; Willie Mabon's "Come On Baby" on Chess; "Bo Diddley" by Bo Diddley on Checker; "One Kiss" by the Robins on Spark; "That's All" by the Casanovas on Apollo; "Double Crossin' Liquor" by Stick McGhee, "Blues For Everybody" by Jack Dupree, and "Rock-A-Locka" by the Five Wings, all on King; Junior Parker's "I Wanna Ramble" on Duke; "I Need You Baby" by the Orioles on Jubilee; "5-10-15 Hours" by **Freddie Bell and the Bellboys** on Teen; and "Chop Chop Boom" by the Danderliers on States.

Freddie Bell and the Bellboys will always be remembered for their April 1956, Las Vegas booking. It was here that their romping rendition of Willie Mae Thornton's "Hound Dog" was first heard, and later adapted, by Elvis Presley.

APR 7   Earl Bostic starts a West Coast one-nighter tour that is scheduled to run through July.

The ABC radio network premiers "Rhythm And Blues On Parade," which will be broadcast live every Thursday night from prominent Black night clubs starting tonight at the Baby Grand Club in Harlem. The show will spotlight both new talent and established performers.

EARLY APRIL

Joe Van Loan joined the Ravens in 1951, and later formed the Valiants with two members of the Du Droppers, Bob Kornegay and Willie Ray. In 1956, Van Loan toured for a while with the Dominoes.

The Du Droppers are all set to record for Groove Records when it is discovered that lead tenor **Joe Van Loan** has a contract with Herald Records. The mix-up occurred in October 1954 when the contract between the Du Droppers and RCA Victor (owner of Groove) expired and the group signed with Herald. When the group took on a new lead singer, Van Loan, he signed a separate contract with Herald. RCA claimed that it had a prior arrangement to keep the group, which left Van Loan still under contract to Herald. The matter is finally resolved when a new lead tenor, Charlie Hughes, is hired for the group.

Della Reese, former gospel singer from Detroit, and now a regular performer at that city's Flame Show Bar, signs with the Jubilee label to record pop and r&b material.

Della Reese achieved success as a recording artist in 1957 with "And That Reminds Me" (Jubilee), and again in 1961 with "Don't You Know" (RCA Victor).

Juke box operators report using sixty percent more rhythm and blues records now than a year ago.

APR 8   Alan Freed's "Rock 'N Roll Easter Jubilee" opens for a one-week run at the 4,264-seat Paramount Theater in Brooklyn. Performers are LaVern Baker, the Penguins, Danny Overbea, the Moonglows/Moonlighters, the Three Chuckles, **Eddie Fontaine**, and Red Prysock's band, augmented with Sam "The Man" Taylor, Al Sears, and Mickey "Guitar" Baker. The Easter holiday show is run five times each day, and it breaks the all-time record at the Paramount set in 1932 by Russ Columbo, bringing in a total of $107,000 for the week. Freed reportedly receives $50,000 based on a percentage. The total paid out for talent comes to $11,000. News reports state that the teen-agers are exuberant but well-behaved. "There's excitement but no trouble."

Eddie Fontaine was the brother of the Fontaine Sisters. In 1955 he covered Sonny Thompson's version of "Rock Love" (as did his sisters). He had a cameo part in the movie "That Girl Can't Help It," and recorded one fine rocker, "Nothin' Shakin'" (1958, Sunbeam and Argo).

The Hearts and Louis Jordan open at New York's Apollo Theater for a week.

The 5-4 Ballroom in Los Angeles features Roy Milton for the weekend's entertainment.

Ivory Joe Hunter starts two weeks at the Flame Show Bar in Detroit.

APR 9   While in New York for the Paramount show, the Penguins sign with Mercury Records. The group had formerly been with Dootone but had recorded for Mercury in March. The contract was delayed pending court approval that their contract with Dootone was not valid, as it was signed by three members of the group who were minors. **Buck Ram**, manager of the group, also arranges for another of his acts to switch to Mercury: the Platters, formerly with Federal, who remain hitless at this time.

By 1955, Buck Ram was a lawyer in Los Angeles. Born in Chicago in 1908, he got his start in music in the 1930s, arranging for Duke Ellington and Count Basie, among others. He fronted his own combo on Savoy in 1944, which featured Earl Bostic.

APR 10   The "Dr. Jive Ball" at the Rockland Palace in New York is sponsored by WWRL radio and emceed by Dr. Jive. Entertainers include Roy Hamilton, Buddy and Ella Johnson, Charlie and Ray, and the Cadillacs. The show brings in a capacity crowd of 4,200 with over two thousand turned away at the door.

Gene and Eunice open at the Tippin Inn in Berlin, New Jersey.

The Easter Sunday dance at the Elks Ballroom in Los Angeles features the Johnny Otis Combo with Marvin and Johnny.

In New Orleans, the Easter dance at the Labor Union Hall features Jimmy Nelson, **Jesse Allen**, and the Joe Jones Combo.

Jesse Allen was a Texas blues singer who occasionally worked with the Dave Bartholomew band. Through this association, he became one of the first New Orleans artists signed in 1951 by Aladdin Records.

APR 11   The Jewels start a two-week engagement at the Midway Lounge in Pittsburgh.

New releases for the second week of April include "Bop-Ting-A-Ling" by LaVern Baker on Atlantic; Dinah Washington's "If It's The Last Thing I Do" on Mercury; "Switchie Witchie Titchie" by the Midnighters on Federal; "Heaven And Paradise" by the Meadowlarks on Dootone;

Originally, "Story Untold" by the Nutmegs was titled "Deep In My Heart There's A Story Untold," and it ran for more than three minutes. The Nutmegs re-recorded the song, and both shortened its length (to 2:20) and its title.

"Don't Ever Leave Me" by the Rivileers on Baton; Elvis Presley's "Baby Let's Play House" on Sun; Billy Ford's "Stop Lyin' On Me" on JOZ; **"Story Untold" by the Nutmegs** on Herald; "Walk That Walk" by the Shieks and "Good Golly, Miss Molly" by the Playboys, both on Cat; "Keep A-Walkin'" by Sonny Knight and "It's True" by the Twilighters, both on Specialty; Otis Blackwell's "Poor Broken Heart" on Jay-Dee; Billy Jack Wills's "Good Rocking Tonight" on M-G-M; and Tibby Edwards's "Flip, Flop and Fly" on Mercury.

APR 13   *Variety's* front-page story on the Brooklyn Paramount shows compares the opening night crowd with those of the Paramount's heyday in the 1930s and 1940s with the teens dancing in the aisles.

APR 14   Bill Haley and his Comets are off on a tour of the Eastern Seaboard with a show in Binghampton, New York. Other dates on the tour include Boston (15); Baltimore (16); Cleveland (17); Buffalo (18); Rome, New York (19); Plainville, Connecticut (20-23); and Willmington, Delaware (24).

APR 15   Louis Jordan starts a week-long engagement at the Howard Theater in Washington.
Dinah Washington is featured at the Tiffany Club in Los Angeles for two weeks. Across town, at the 5-4 Ballroom, Guitar Slim entertains for the first of two three-day weekends.

MID-APRIL

This Blind Boy Fuller is none other than Brownie McGhee using an alias. The original Blind Boy Fuller (born Wadesboro, North Carolina, 1908) recorded 135 songs before his death in 1940. It was Fuller who discovered Sonny Terry. After Fuller's death, Brownie McGhee succeeded him and teamed with Terry as Blind Boy Fuller #2.

Treat Records signs **Blind Boy Fuller** and the Five Stars.

LaVern Baker sues the Savoy Ballroom in Los Angles for $2,500 in back pay due her from previous engagements. The suit forces the ballroom to close pending settlement. The Savoy does not reopen until September 30th.

The Rivileers are currently limiting engagements to the New York area, where two of the members attend college.

Lowell Fulson is booked solid on his current tour of Texas.

APR 18   Roy Hamilton headlines at the Lord Calvert Hotel in Miami for two weeks.
Billy Eckstine starts a world-wide tour with a performance in London.
Ray Charles and Faye Adams bring in ten thousand ticket holders during their week-long stand at the Palms Club in Hallendale, Florida.

The Aladdins started as the Capris from San Diego (with no records under that name), but were renamed after their label. Lead tenor Ted Harper later recorded with the Penguins (after "Earth Angel"), and briefly with the Medallions before touring with Cornell Gunter's Coasters for many years.

New releases for the third week of April include "Talk That Talk" by the Du Droppers on Groove; "Ding Dong Ding" by Bip and Bop and "Cry, Cry Baby" by the **Aladdins**, both on Aladdin; "Jump With You Baby" by B. B. King on RPM; "Tonky Honk" by Chuck Higgins on Dootone; "Fast Life" by Lightnin' Hopkins on Harlem; "The Things I Used To Do" by Bill Robinson and the Quails on DeLuxe; and Pee Wee Crayton's "Eyes Full Of Tears," the Spiders' "Am I The One?," and Bobby Mitchell and the Toppers' "I'm In Love," all on Imperial.

238

APR 21 Following a one-nighter tour, the Penguins open at the Apache Club in Dayton, Ohio.

APR 22 Al Hibbler starts at the Kin Wah Low Club in Toledo.

Headliners this week at New York's Apollo Theater include the Clovers, Little Esther, the Paul Williams Orchestra, and teenager **Willie John**.

Louis Jordan brings his Tympany Five to the Royal Theater in Baltimore for the week.

Earl Bostic entertains at the Shrine Auditorium in Los Angeles on a one-nighter.

LaVern Baker and the Drifters join the Nat "King" Cole package tour for three weeks.

T-Bone Walker starts a two-week stay at Detroit's Flame Show Bar.

Although only seventeen years old at this time, "Little" Willie John had already toured with Paul Williams and Duke Ellington, and had recorded for Prize, Savoy, Rama, Federal, and King.

APR 24 Nat Cole, LaVern Baker, and the Drifters play a one-nighter at the National Guard Armory in Washington.

APR 25 Bull Moose Jackson starts a week-long engagement at the Creole Cabana in Philadelphia.

Bill Haley and his Comets entertain nightly for a week at the Casino Royal in Washington.

New releases for the fourth week of April include "Ain't It A Shame" by Fats Domino on Imperial; "Love Me Now Or Let Me Go" by Billy Ward and his Dominoes on Federal; "When We Get Together" by the Charms on DeLuxe; "When" by the Flamingos on Checker; Jimmy Reed's "I'm Gonna Ruin You" on Vee-Jay; "Peepin' Eyes" by **Charlie Feathers** on Flip; "Real Good Feeling" by Eddie Boyd and "I Have A Little Girl" by Howlin' Wolf, both on Chess; Charles Brown's "Walk With Me" and Johnny Fuller's "Cruel Cruel World," both on Aladdin; "Rollin' Stone" by the Marigolds on Excello; "Why Don't You Write Me" by the Feathers on Show Time, Jesse Belvin's "Gone" on Specialty; Ruth Brown's "As Long As I'm Moving" on Atlantic; "Flip, Flop and Fly" by Billy Duke and the Dukes on Casino; Wynonie Harris's "Fishtail Blues" on King; and two from the Penguins: "Kiss A Fool Goodbye" on Dootone and "Be Mine Or A Fool" on Mercury.

Charlie Feathers was another Memphis country vocalist who tried his hand at rockabilly after Elvis Presley's initial success. Flip Records was an off-shot of Sun, Elvis' first record label. Feathers also wrote "I Forgot To Remember To Forget," Elvis' last single for Sun Records.

APR 26 Curtis Williams of the Penguins sues Dootsie Williams of Dootone Records (no relation) for $100,000, claiming damage to his career because he signed a recording contract with Dootone Records when he was a minor.

APR 27 Philadelphia's Academy of Music presents the Nat Cole tour featuring LaVern Baker and the Drifters.

APR 29 The Met in Philadelphia plays host to the "Rock And Roll Show Of '55." Entertainers include Varetta Dillard, Gene and Eunice, Little Walter, the Hearts, the Roamers, Dean Barlow, and Buddy Johnson's Orchestra.

New York's Apollo Theater hosts the "5" Royales, Dakota Staton, Hal "Cornbread" Singer's Orchestra, and Memphis Slim.

Earl Bostic plays a three-day stint at the 5-4 Club in Los Angeles.

John Lee Hooker entertains at the Club Royale in Detroit.

Eddie Fontaine and the **Three Chuckles** appear with Ella Fitzgerald at the Chicago Theater for two weeks.

APR 30   The deal between Alan Freed and Coral Records, which would have resulted in Freed becoming a special artist and repertoire representative, is off due to increased demand on Freed's time following the successful run of his "Rock And Roll Easter Jubilee" at the Brooklyn Paramount Theater.

In Buffalo, New York, the Nat Cole tour with LaVern Baker and the Drifters plays to a full house.

LATE APRIL

The Harptones are on the one-nighters circuit in New England.

THE TOP TEN ROCK 'N ROLL RECORDS FOR APRIL 1955

1. Pledging My Love - Johnny Ace
2. The Wallflower - Etta James
3. My Babe - Little Woman
4. I Got A Woman - Ray Charles
5. Flip, Flop and Fly - Joe Turner
6. Close Your Eyes - The Five Keys
7. What'cha Gonna Do - The Drifters
8. Earth Angel - The Penguins
9. Don't Be Angry - Nappy Brown
10. Unchained Melody - Al Hibbler

April 1955
ARTIST OF THE MONTH

ETTA JAMES
(Etta James Hawkins, b. January 25, 1938)

ETTA JAMES

Few women were able to make a name for themselves in the early days of rock 'n roll. Of those who were popular from 1952 through 1955, only Etta James remained into the era of soul music with a viable career. Her musical influences were as diverse as her Italian/Black heritage: cool jazz to country and western, and her singing styles were just as varied.

Born in Los Angeles, she was raised by foster parents named Rogers. Following the death of her foster mother, she moved to San Francisco to be reunited with her natural mother. Her musical studies, which had started in Los Angeles, continued in the Bay Area. In the winter of 1954, as a high-school student, she formed a female vocal group, the Peaches, which was discovered in an audition for band leader and musical entrepreneur Johnny Otis during his engagement at the Fillmore Ballroom. His influence in the Los Angeles rhythm and blues scene led to an immediate recording contract for the group with Modern Records. As luck would have it, the first single, issued in January 1955, was a major hit. The song was another in the many answers to the

"Annie" songs started by the Midnighters' "Work With Me Annie."

Titled "The Wallflower," on the surface it hardly seems to be the stuff of lasting fame. First of all, the title is all wrong. When it was covered for the "pop" market by Georgia Gibbs, it was slightly rewritten and given a much better title, "Dance With Me Henry." The song's musical roots are almost identical to its predecessor's, "Work With Me Annie." It has the same melody, the same beat, and almost the same saxophone break in the middle. Miss James's vocals are adequate but not memorable. Truly, this was a hit made by promotion.

Nevertheless, "The Wallflower" was the catalyst her career needed. She was almost immediately signed to a tour of the Eastern Seaboard theaters with the "Rhythm And Blues Caravan." By June 1955 she was holding down the headliner spot for two weeks at the Flame Show Bar in Detroit. But, as is almost always the case with such a major novelty hit, the follow-up singles were not successful.

In 1956, in an attempt to change the meandering direction of her career, she recorded in New Orleans' J&M Studio under the direction of Cosimo Matassa. Still there were no hits. She returned to the Culver City studios owned by the Bihari brothers, where a few singles were issued on their new Kent label. Her career, which had started on such a promising note, now cast her as the wallflower, as rock 'n roll moved into new territory in the late 1950s. Yet she was able to secure a contract with Chess Records through her long association with Harvey Fuqua of the Moonglows, and together they waxed two successful duets in 1960. Her first solo effort for the label, "All I Could Do Was Cry," was an immediate r&b hit, and during the next three years her strong singing style brought her ten hits in the soul market on Argo Records (a subsidiary of Chess), including "Pushover," "My Dearest Darling," and "Stop The Wedding." She had another career lull in 1963 before hitting again with "Tell Mama" in 1967 on Cadet (yet another Chess subsidiary).

But her ups and downs in the music business had left their mark. She was a hefty Black woman who sported a blonde wig, and she billed herself as the female Little Richard, a title that exemplified her outrageous behavior both on and off the stage. By the 1970s she was a heavy user of street drugs, including heroin, a habit that had started ten years earlier. But Etta James had the inner strength to pull herself together, and by 1977 she was rehabilitated and back on the scene with several finely-crafted blues albums that received widespread critical acclaim, although little in the way of sales. In 1978 she opened a tour for the Rolling Stones, and again received acclaim in the music press, and her 1986 album "Blues In The Night" brought Etta James a Grammy nomination for "best female jazz performance." Today she remains popular on the concert circuit both as a holdover from the earlier age of rhythm and blues as well as a powerful soul songstress.

May 1955

Hank Snow was a business partner with country booking agent Colonel Tom Parker. At this time, Parker had his eyes on Presley, having booked him in Carlsbad, New Mexico, in February 1955.

THE JACKS
"Why Don't You Write Me," with lead vocal by Willie Davis, was the biggest hit for the Jacks. The same group also recorded novelties and jump tunes as the Cadets on Modern ("Stranded In The Jungle," 1956).

MAY 1 Ray Charles and Fats Domino perform at the New Orleans Municipal Auditorium.

Elvis Presley joins "Hank Snow's All Star Jamboree" tour in New Orleans. This is his first major trek, covering twenty cities in twenty-one days through Louisiana, Alabama, Florida, Georgia, North Carolina, and Virginia.

MAY 2 The Jewels are at the Creole Cabana and Ivory Joe Hunter is opening at the Club Zelmar, both in Philadelphia.

Bill Haley and his Comets start a four-week engagement at Andy's Log Cabin in Glouchester, New Jersey. Also in New Jersey, Red Prysock brings his combo to the Cadillac Club in Trenton.

Guitar Slim is in Cleveland at the Ebony Lounge for a week.

MAY 3 Roy Milton brings rock 'n roll to Alaska with a series of one-nighters in and around Anchorage.

New releases for the first week of May include "Love Bug" by the Clovers, "Got The Water Boiling" by the Regals and "Precious Love" by the Cookies, all on Atlantic; "Dearest One" by Charlie and Ray on Herald; Muddy Waters's "I Want To Be Loved" on Chess; "Why Don't You Write Me" by the Jacks on RPM; Sam "The Man" Taylor's "Harlem Nocturne" on M-G-M; "Don'cha Go" by the Spaniels on Vee-Jay; "Daddy Rockin' Strong" by Nolan Strong and the Diablos on Fortune; "I'll Be Faithful" by the Dreams on Savoy; and "Chop Chop Ching A Ling" by the Roamers on Savoy.

MAY 4 Chuck Willis starts a four-day run at the Crown Propeller Lounge in Chicago.

MAY 6 Bill Doggett and his trio perform for three days at the 5-4 Ballroom in Los Angeles.

At the Apollo Theater in New York City, the Cardinals share the headline with Sister Rosetta Tharpe for the week.

This week, the Penguins move into the State Theater in Hartford.

The Howard Theater in Washington features the talents of Sarah Vaughan and Al Hibbler for the week.

Sonny Thompson and Lulu Reed open in Detroit at the Crystal Lounge.

EARLY MAY

Star Maid Records of Chicago, formerly specializing exclusively in country and western releases, has started a rhythm and blues department.

A two-year-old recording by the Embers on Ember Records, "Paradise Hill," has been revived in Los Angeles and is re-released on Herald Records.

Dean Barlow, lead singer with the Crickets, records "Forever" on Jay-Dee Records. The song is the first with both words and music by Alan Freed.

New releases for the second week of May include "The Verdict" by the Five Keys on Capitol; Etta James's "Hey! Henry" on Modern; Red Prysock's "Zonked" and the Cashmere's "Don't Let It Happen To You," both on Mercury; "Ain't No Use" by Big Maybelle on Okeh; Joe Houston's "Candy Rock" on RPM; "Send Me Some Kisses" by the Tenderfoots on Federal; Roy Milton's "Fools Are Getting Scarcer" on Dootone; "I Cross My Fingers" by Bennie Woods and the Five Dukes on Atlas; "Goddess Of Love" by the Nu-Tones on Recorded In Hollywood; and "Seventeen" by **Boyd Bennett** and his Rockets on King.

MAY 11   The motion picture "Harlem Variety Revue" opens across the country. The film stars Faye Adams, Amos Milburn, and the Larks, among others.

MAY 13   In Los Angeles, Joe Houston and his band entertain the dancers at the 5-4 Ballroom for the weekend.
          The Apollo Theater in New York hosts Wynonie Harris and the **Regals** for the week.
          Al Hibbler starts a five-day appearance at the Royal Peacock Club in Atlanta.
          "The Biggest Show of 1955," featuring Roy Hamilton, LaVern Baker, the Drifters, Willie Mabon, the Hearts, the Spaniels, Jimmy Reed, and the combos of Little Walkin' Willie and Erskine Hawkins, starts a six-week tour with a show in Oklahoma City. The package will play dates throughout the Southwest, South (including New Orleans on the 18th), and East Coast before winding up with a show in western New York on June 26th.
          The "Rhythm & Blues Caravan" plays the Howard Theater in Washington for a week. Featured performers include the Moonglows, Etta James, and Memphis Slim.
          At the Chicago Theater, Pat Boone shares the stage with the Mariners for two weeks.
          In Los Angeles, Dootone Records sues Mercury Records for allegedly inducing the Penguins to breach their three-year contract with Dootone. In a related matter, Jesse Belvin and Johnny Green file a suit in Los Angeles claiming that they wrote "Earth Angel," the big hit for the Penguins ascribed to Curtis Williams, a member of the group. The court places an injunction against Dootone Records, requiring that all monies generated from the sale of "Earth Angel" be placed in trust. (See April also 9th)

MAY 14   Alan Freed emcees the "Command Performance Concert" at the Olympia Arena in Detroit. Performers for the benefit show include the Charms, the Penguins, Dinah Washington, and the **Count Basie** Combo.

MAY 15   Ruth Brown travels to the Crown Propeller Lounge in Chicago.

Boyd Bennett was a protege of Moon Mulligan, a country and western pianist in the boogie style who also recorded for the King label. Bennett had been a deejay in Kentucky before becoming a performer. "Seventeen" was Bennett's biggest record.

Harold Wright of the Regals, who recorded for Atlantic, started with the Diamonds (also on Atlantic). Later, four of the Regals joined Sonny Til as a new group of Orioles. Wright went on to form the Metronomes.

COUNT BASIE

243

Baton Records announces that it has found a name for its previously unnamed vocal group. Through popular consent, the group will be called the **Miracles**. A new release should be out shortly.

After all the ballyhoo, the Miracles issued only one record on Baton and one on Cash before disbanding. This group had no connection with the famous soul group on Tamla, or with Carl Hogan and the Miracles on Fury.

T-Bone Walker is currently playing a series of dates around his home town of Chicago while he recuperates from an operation.

MAY 16   Fats Domino is welcomed for a short stay at the Showboat in Philadelphia.

New releases for the third week of May include "Henry's Got Flat Feet" by the Midnighters and "Sitting On The Curbstone" by Little Willie Littlefield, both on Federal; "Forever" by Dean Barlow on Jay-Dee; Memphis Slim's "She's All Right" on United; John Lee Hooker's "Taxi Driver" on Modern; **Bobby Bland**'s "It's My Life Baby" on Duke; Richard Berry's "Don'cha Go" and Elmore James's "No Love In My Heart," both on Flair; Earl Bostic's "Cherry Bean," Jack Dupree's "Let The Doorbell Ring," and Stick McGhee's "Get Your Mind Out Of The Gutter," all on King; "Come Back To Me" by the Dappers on Peacock; "You're The Answer To My Prayer" by Varetta Dillard on Savoy; "Make Me Or Break Me" by the Empires on Harlem; and "I Like Moonshine" by the Five Owls on Vulcan.

Bobby "Blue" Bland was born Robert Calvin Bland, January 27, 1930, Rosemark, Tennessee. "It's My Life Baby" was his first successful single.

MAY 18   Earl Bostic takes his combo into the Blackhawk Cafe in San Francisco for two weeks.

MAY 20   Alan Freed brings his "Rock 'N Roll Show" to Boston's Lowes State Theater for a seven-day run. Entertainment includes Dinah Washington, Al Hibbler, Dakota Staton, Little Walter, the Moonglows, the Five Keys, Bo Diddley, Nappy Brown, Ella Johnson, and the Buddy Johnson Orchestra. (See also May 27th.)
　　　　Roy Milton plays the 5-4 Ballroom in Los Angeles for the three-day weekend.
　　　　Arthur Prysock and Della Reese share the bill for two weeks at Detroit's Flame Show Bar.
　　　　Charlie and Ray open for two weeks at the Royal Peacock in Atlanta.

MAY 21   "Shake, Rattle and Roll," the ten-inch long-play album by Bill Haley and his Comets, is released by Decca Records.

MAY 22   The owner of the Otis Ballroom in Bridgeport, Connecticut, cancels a scheduled dance when he learns that Fats Domino will be playing rock 'n roll music. The local police have banned all rock 'n roll dances following reports of a riot at the New Haven Arena during a rock 'n roll concert.

This group of Four Buddies should not be confused with the group of the same name that recorded on Savoy in the early 1950s. This Four Buddies was a Chicago-based quintet that also recorded on Club 51 in 1956, but had no hits.

MAY 23   The **Four Buddies** and Rudy Greene entertain at Chicago's first rock 'n roll dance at the City Bowl Park.

New releases for the fourth week of May include B. B. King's "I'm In Love" on RPM; "Finally" by the Heartbeats on Jubilee; "Whisper To Me" by the Rhythm Aces on Vee-Jay; "I Gotta Go Now" by the

Starlings on Dawn; and **Johnny Olenn's** "Sally Let Your Bangs Hang" on TNT.

MAY 27   Alan Freed takes his "Rock 'N Roll Show" to Providence, Rhode Island, for three days. (See May 20th.)
    The Bill Doggett Trio entertains at the 5-4 Ballroom in Los Angeles for the weekend.
    Lionel Hampton and his band headline the Apollo Theater revue for the week in New York.
    In Washington, the Howard Theater hosts the Orioles, Gene and Eunice, and Jimmy Witherspoon for the week.
    The Dew Drop Inn in New Orleans features Floyd Dixon for three days.

MAY 29   Joe Turner, Smiley Lewis, and the Joe Morris Orchestra hold forth for the evening at New Orleans' Labor Union Hall.

New releases for the fifth week of May include "Boppin' The Rock" by **Clifton Chenier** and "I Got Sumpin' For You" by Guitar Slim, both on Specialty; "Roller Coaster" by Little Walter on Checker; Mister Ruffin's "A Touch Of Heaven" on Spark; "One More Break" by Chuck Willis on Okeh; and Boyd Bennett's "Tennessee Rock And Roll" on King.

MAY 30   Bill Haley and his Comets start a week-long stint at the Colonial Tavern in Toronto. The group makes its first major television appearance as guests on the Milton Berle show on the 31st.

MAY 31   Roy Milton, on a tour of one-nighters, makes a stop in Denver.

LATE MAY

The Clovers are booked into the Palm Club in Hallendale, Florida.

Johnny Olenn, an early White rock 'n roll artist, lacked any real feel for the music. He was a roly-poly, blond-haired leader of a quasi-r&b combo. He did make an appearance with his band of lunatics in the film "That Girl Can't Help It." He also signed with Liberty Records, and issued an outrageous album.

Louisiana-born (June 25, 1925) and Cajun-bred Clifton Chenier, an exponent of accordian-led zydeco music, also recorded in a quasi-rockabilly style such tunes as "Boppin' The Rock." Chenier died December 12, 1987.

THE TOP TEN ROCK 'N ROLL RECORDS FOR MAY 1955

1. Unchained Melody - Roy Hamilton
2. Don't Be Angry - Nappy Brown
3. My Babe - Little Walter
4. What'cha Gonna Do - The Drifters
5. The Wallflower - Etta James
6. Unchained Melody - Al Hibbler
7. Flip, Flop and Fly - Joe Turner
8. Bo Diddley - Bo Diddley
9. I Got A Woman - Ray Charles
10. Rock Around The Clock - Bill Haley and his Comets

NAPPY BROWN
(Napoleon Brown, b. October 12, 1929)

NAPPY BROWN

For a rock 'n roller, Nappy Brown was a fine gospel singer, but as a gospel singer he had a strange beginning. Born in Charlotte, North Carolina, he was the son of one of the area's finest bootleggers. It is probable that to make sure Nappy did not follow in his father's footsteps, his mother was overly religious, to the point that her son found himself a member of the Heavenly Lights, singing gospel and not shouting the blues down at the local speakeasy. Brown also preformed with the Selah Jubilee Singers, a famous gospel group that recorded from 1939 to 1951 before dissolving, only to be reformed in Charlotte in 1954. Both groups recorded for Savoy Records of Newark, New Jersey, a label famous for both gospel and blues songs, so it was natural that Brown would be tempted to make the switch to the blues once he saw the inside of the music business in 1954. This may also have been Brown's way of rebelling against the strict religious upbringing imposed by his mother.

Savoy Records was owned by Herman Lubinsky, an opportunistic man who reportedly did not have much personal respect for his stable of artists. In March 1954, when he asked Brown if he wanted to sing the blues, Lubinsky offered a seven-year contract, but paid an advance of only $500. Later, Brown constantly complained that he never received any royalties.

Nappy Brown's first non-gospel session resulted in two singles, "That Man" and "Is It True, Is It True," but it was not until the second session, in February 1955, that he was able to come up with "Don't Be Angry," which would be the biggest record of his career. He was immediately snapped up for the rapidly expanding rhythm and blues circuit, appearing on an Alan Freed show in Boston in May 1955, and at the Apollo Theater in New York City the next month. His follow-up single, "Piddily Patter" also sold well, insuring a lasting round of personal appearances. Beginning with a two-month tour that hit the road in July, Brown was part of the "Pop R&B Show," which featured Sarah Vaughan and Al Hibbler. In September it was back with Freed's biggest extravaganza to date, the week-long Paramount Theater bash in New York. And then the balloon burst. After "Piddily Patter" there were no more hits, and there was little in the way of bookings.

Brown was just another victim of the cover record craze, which by mid-1955 was running rampant in the "pop" market. "Don't Be Angry" was covered by the Crew-Cuts, from whom Lubinsky received $6,500 for the publishing rights. "Piddily Patter" was covered by Patti Page. Both covers outsold the originals by a wide margin. Nappy Brown finally had another hit in 1957 with "Little By Little," which was reminiscent of "Don't Be Angry." In 1958 Brown got the chance to cover someone else's record by recording Hank Snow's country hit, "I Don't Hurt Anymore," as "It Don't Hurt Anymore," which made a respectable showing on the r&b charts. That same year, he watched as Ray Charles recorded his song "The Right Time" and took it into the "pop" r&b charts for another hit. Through it all, he remained with Savoy Records.

In 1961, out of frustration and embittered over his years without proper royalties, he committed armed robbery. He was caught and sent to prison for seven years. Once out, he returned to Charlotte and gospel music with records released on Jewel and Savoy.

Nappy Brown was a large man with a forceful delivery and it was said that he had a fierce countenance, and no less than Etta James remarked that he was "a heck of a singer." His offbeat blending of gospel and rhythm tunes gave his performance a revivalist quality. Although best remembered for his catchy tunes, it was on the slow ballads that his broad baritone showed his best work.

June 1955

JUN 1   Bo Diddley is the inaugural act at the new Figueroa Ballroom in Los Angeles. He performs for five days.

Steve Gibson and his Red Caps with Damita Jo return to New York's Cafe Society for a month.

JUN 3   The weekend entertainment at the 5-4 Ballroom in Los Angeles features the Jewels for three days.

The Apollo Theater in New York offers Linda Hayes and Nappy Brown fronting the Perez Prado Combo for this week's entertainment.

In Lubbock, Texas, in the middle of a month-long tour Elvis Presley gives a free performance at a Pontiac dealership along with local country performers, **Buddy and Bob.**

JUN 5   "The Big Show," featuring Roy Hamilton, LaVern Baker, the Drifters, the Spaniels, Jimmy Reed, and the Hearts, plays a one-night stand at Washington's National Guard Armory.

JUN 6   Lowell Fulson and Choker Campbell's Orchestra open at the Palm Club in Hallendale, Florida.

New releases for the first week of June include "Feel So Good" by Shirley and Lee and "My Love" by the Five Keys, both on Aladdin; Arthur Lee Maye and the Crowns' "Love Me Always" and B. B. King's "Shut Your Mouth," both on RPM; "Soldier Boy" by the Four Fellows on Glory; Marvin and Johnny's "Butter Ball" and the **Cadets'** "Fine Lookin' Baby," both on Modern; "Only You" by the Cues on Jubilee; the first E.P. from the Penguins on Dootone; and Sunnyland Slim's "That Woman" on J.O.B.

EARLY JUNE

The Du Droppers are playing dates in Canada. Also on the tour circuit, Amos Milburn, the Clovers, and the Paul Williams Orchestra are currently in Texas.

Charlie Hughes, lead singer on the Du Droppers' latest release, signs as solo artist with Groove.

The first release from Atlantic's Twin Tones has stirred up trade action as inquisitive deejays are guessing who the members are.

M-G-M Records signs eighteen-year old **Connie Francis**, who had previously appeared on the Horn and Hardhardt children's show.

Following the demise of Bruce Records, the Harptones sign with Old Town Records.

Buddy and Bob were two local boys, Charles "Buddy" Holley and Bob Montgomery, who were yearning for a career in music. They recorded a few demo tapes in their hillybilly style before witnessing the power of Elvis' rockabilly performance.

The Cadets (who also recorded ballads as the Jacks on RPM) were made up of Aaron Collins, Willie Davis, Ted Taylor, Dub Jones, and Lloyd McGraw. Taylor had a successful soul career in the 1960s, and Jones joined the Coasters in 1956.

Connie Francis (born Constance Franconero, December 12, 1938, Newark, New Jersey) was among the all-time top-selling female vocalists, beginning with "Who's Sorry Now" (1958, M-G-M). Her popularity continued into early 1960s.

Mercury Records establishes a new subsidiary, Wing Records. New r&b talent assigned to the label includes Jay Hawkins and Titus Turner.

JUN 8   Earl Bostic starts two weeks at the 1042 Club in Anchorage, Alaska.

The Charms open for a five-day run at the Figueroa Ballroom in Los Angeles.

JUN 9   The Five Keys are the house guests of the Copa Ballroom in Pittsburgh.

JUN 10   "Dr. Jive's Rhythm And Blues Show" fills New York's Apollo Theater with music for the week. Featured entertainers include Gene and Eunice, the **Four Fellows**, Delores Ware, the Nutmegs, Bo Diddley, Etta Jones, Charlie and Ray, the Moonglows, and the Buddy Johnson Band featuring Ella Johnson.

Rusty Bryant blows for patrons at Weeke's Tavern in Atlantic City.

JUN 13   The Graystone Gardens and Ballroom in Detroit offers "The Big Show" with Roy Hamilton, LaVern Baker, the Drifters, the Spaniels, Willie Mabon, Jimmy Reed, the Hearts, and Della Reese for the evening's entertainment.

New releases for the second week of June include "Close The Door" by **Jim Lowe** on Dot; "Freddy" by Connie Francis on M-G-M; "Song Of The Dreamer" by Billy Brooks on Duke; "A Fool For You" by Ray Charles on Atlantic; Bo Diddley's "Diddley Daddy" on Checker; Ella Johnson's "Someday" on Mercury; "Gum Drop" by Otis Williams on DeLuxe; "All My Heart Belongs To You" by the Hearts and "A Lover's Chant" by the Miracles, both on Baton; "I Must Be Dreamin'" by the Robins on Spark; "Hey Pretty Girl" by the Twin Tones on Atlantic; "For A Thrill" by the Spiders on Imperial; "Speedin'" by the Medallions on Dootone; "Sittin' Here Drinkin'" by Johnny Otis on Peacock; "It's Been A Long Time" by the Casanovas on Apollo; "You Yakity Yak Too Much" by the Flippers on Flip; "Everyday (I Have The Blues)" by Count Basie's Orchestra featuring Joe Williams on Clef; and two releases by Lightnin' Hopkins: "Grieving Blues" on Lightning and "Untrue" on Harlem.

JUN 15   Lowell Fulson starts a five-day layover at Los Angeles' Figueroa Ballroom.

JUN 17   The Nutmegs, T-Bone Walker, and **Buddy Johnson**'s Combo featuring Ella Johnson are booked for a week at the Howard Theater in Washington.

Sam "The Man" Taylor has his first major booking at the Apollo Theater in New York. Also on the bill are the Orioles, Etta James and the Peaches, and Baby Washington.

Ruth Brown, Bo Diddley, Dean Barlow, the Dreams, Screamin' Jay Hawkins, Charlie and Ray, and the Diamonds entertain for two shows at the Philadelphia Town Hall.

The Ernie Fields Combo plays for dancers at the 5-4 Ballroom in Los Angeles this weekend.

New releases for the third week of June include "Piddily Patter" by

The Four Fellows had their only major hit with "Soldier Boy" on Glory Records. The group hailed from New York city and featured Hal Miller and David Jones, who later recorded "Silhouettes" with the Rays (1957, Cameo).

Jim Lowe was a twenty-eight year old deejay from Missouri working in New York. He had previously composed "Gambler's Guitar," a 1950 hit for Rusty Draper. Lowe's biggest personal success came with his recording of "Green Door" (1956, Dot).

ELLA & BUDDY JOHNSON

The Cochran Brothers weren't brothers at all. Eddie Ray Cochran (born October 3, 1938, Oklahoma City) had several major rock 'n roll hits from 1957-59, including "Summertime Blues." Hank Cochran (born August 2, 1935, Greenville, Mississippi) was much more successful as a songwriter ("I Fall To Pieces," "Make The World Go Away") than as a country singer.

Johnny Fuller was a West Coast vocalist who achieved his greatest recording success in New Orleans. His bouncy, shuffle, "All Night Long" (1958, Checker), is his best known recording.

Members of the Tenderfoots later recorded as the Sharps backing Duane Eddy, and later had a big hit as the Rivingtons ("Papa-Oom-Mow-Mow," 1962). Lead vocalist Al Frazier also sang with the Lamplighters while recording with the Tenderfoots.

Nappy Brown on Savoy; "Foolish Me" by the Moonglows on Chess; Frankie Marshall's "No One Else Will Ever Know" on Spark; Pat Boone's "Ain't That A Shame" on Dot; "Two Blue Singing Stars" by the **Cochran Brothers** on Ekko; "Red Rover" by Dean Beard on Fox; "Fool's Paradise" by Charles Brown on Aladdin; "Teller Of Fortune" by the Dootones and "Only For You" by the Cameos, both on Dootone; Titus Turner's "All Around The World" and Jay Hawkins' "Well I Tried," both on Wing; "My Baby Is Fine" by the Fortunes on Checker; Shirley Gunter's "That's The Way I Like It" on Flair; and the Jewels' "Angel In My Life" on Imperial.

JUN 21   Joe Liggins and the Honeydrippers open in Los Angeles at the Sirocco Club.

JUN 24   The second edition of the "Rock 'N Roll Show" plays the Philadelphia Arena. Featured on the bill are Bill Haley and his Comets, the Cardinals, Gloria Mann, Jimmy Ricks and the Ravens, Varetta Dillard, the Nutmegs, and the Buddy Johnson Orchestra.
Etta James opens her two-week engagement at the Flame Show Bar in Detroit.
At the 5-4 Ballroom in Los Angeles, the headliners for this weekend are the Medallions and the **Johnny Fuller** Band.
Bo Diddley and Faye Adams split the bill for a week at the Howard Theater in Washington.
The Apollo Theater in New York plays host to Big Maybelle, the Harptones, and Gene Ammons's Combo.

JUN 25   It is reported in the music press that Bill Haley and his Comets have sold an astounding three million singles in their first thirteen months with Decca Records. "Shake, Rattle And Roll" and "Rock Around The Clock" have each sold more than a million copies.

JUN 27   LaVern Baker moves into the Showboat Lounge in Philadelphia.

New releases for the fourth week of June include "Razzle-Dazzle" by Bill Haley and his Comets on Decca; "Those Golden Bells" by the **Tenderfoots** on Federal; "Truly Truly" by Bobby Relf the Laurels and "Need Your Lovin'" by Peppermint Harris, both on "X"; Bill Doggett's "True Blue" and Wynonie Harris's "Git With The Grits," both on King; "Hey Bop De Bow" by Bert Convy and the Thunderbirds on Era; and "So Near And Yet So Far" by the Four Students on Groove.

THE TOP TEN ROCK 'N ROLL RECORDS FOR JUNE 1955

1. Ain't It A Shame - Fats Domino
2. Unchained Melody - Roy Hamilton
3. Bo Diddley - Bo Diddley
4. Rock Around The Clock - Bill Haley and his Comets
5. Don't Be Angry - Nappy Brown
6. Bop-Ting-A-Ling - LaVern Baker
7. Unchained Melody - Al Hibbler
8. My Babe -Little Walter
9. As Long As I'm Moving - Ruth Brown
10. What'cha Gonna Do - The Drifters

June 1955
ARTIST OF THE MONTH

BO DIDDLEY
(Otha Ellas Bates, b. December 30, 1928)

BO DIDDLEY

Within a year after the summer of 1955, self-righteous people would be railing against rock 'n roll in the vilest of terms. One of the most frequently heard was "jungle music." If any early star of this emerging musical form could be accused of playing "jungle music," it was Bo Diddley. His recordings had a wild abandon and an infectious rhythm base previously unheard in the musical mainstream of either rhythm and blues or, especially, "pop" music.

Ellas Bates was born in Magnolia, Mississippi, near McComb, in the heart of the cotton-growing region. Soon after the death of his father he was adopted by Gussie McDaniel, and he took her last name as his own. The Great Depression was felt nowhere as strongly as the Deep South. Negro farm workers were among the poorest of all the country's citizens before the market fell, and in the early 1930s many were absolutely destitute. The McDaniels, following a time-honored tradition, moved north to Chicago when Ellas was four or five. He wanted to study music, but the family was obviously too poor to afford an instrument. The local Baptist church stepped in with a violin; later Ellas would become self-taught on the guitar. At thirteen he helped form the Langley Avenue Jive Cats, with Earl Hooker also on guitar, Jerome Green (maracas), and Roosevelt Jackson (washtub bass). They played the area around Chicago's Maxwell Street Market, passing the hat for pennies. Following graduation from Foster Vocational School, Ellas tried his hand at semi-pro boxing. It was about this time that he acquired the nickname "Bo Diddley." There are several stories concerning the origin of this colorful moniker: that it referred to a one-stringed African guitar, that it was a childhood name referring to a bully-boy, or that it meant storyteller. Whatever. The name stuck. When not boxing, he still was trying to break into the musical scene on the south side of Chicago. The washboard trio started hustling the small clubs, but it was impossible to make a living. By 1951 he was broke and on relief.

By 1954 he had quit boxing but not music. He drove a truck during the day and played at the south side clubs in the evening. He worked the local tour circuit around Chicago whenever possible. By now the trio consisted of Bo on guitar, with Green still shaking the maracas, and Frank Kirkland playing drums. They auditioned for Chess Records, which had offices around the corner from Bo's apartment. Leonard Chess was impressed enough to schedule a recording session, and in February 1955 Bo Diddley was in the studio pounding out four songs. The usual trio was supplemented by Billy Boy Arnold (harmonica) and Otis Spaan (piano). The first release, on Chess's subsidiary Checker Records, was the semi-autobiographical "Bo Diddley" backed by the self-serving "I'm A Man." While vastly different from each other, the two sides were complimentary. "Bo Diddley" relied on a heavy, chunk chunk-chunk a-chunk-chunk rhythm that would become a mainstay of rock 'n roll. The song took this rhythm and several lines from the 1952 single "Hambone" by Red Saunders and his orchestra. "I'm a Man," while much more in the blues vein, was strutting in its pride and heavily influenced Muddy Waters' "Manish Boy." The record was a sensation

251

in the r&b field as soon as it hit the stores in April 1955.

New York deejay Alan Freed, who had strong ties with Chess Records, pushed both the record and Diddley by hiring him to play a rock 'n roll package in Boston in May 1955. He was booked into the Apollo Theater in New York in June, followed by theaters in Philadelphia and Washington the same month. He was back at the Apollo in August, immediately followed by two months on the road with another package unit. He was a guest on the Ed Sullivan television show in November, where he was supposed to sing the bland "16 Tons," and shocked the host by belting out his hit instead.

Diddley issued a string of wild, pounding, rhythmic records from 1955 into the late 1960s. He never again had a hit the size of "Bo Diddley," but that didn't seem to matter much as far as he was concerned. Each record found a ready audience of aficionados who were eager to hear the latest from an artist who would come to be billed as "the Black Gladiator." His songs were uncompromising. They spoke completely from the male point of view. He often shouted, screamed, and moaned unabashedly. His stage act, by comparison, was tame. He stood, almost cemented to the stage, fronting the faithful duo on drums and maracas, augmented from time to time by piano, bass, and harmonica. His only show business trapping took the form of a large number of strangely constructed guitars with which he performed.

He remained with Chess/Checker Records until 1971. As mentioned, his success, as measured purely by the record charts, would appear small. "Diddley Daddy" followed "Bo Diddley" in 1955, but wasn't nearly as successful. It was four years before he made the charts again. "I'm Sorry," "Crackin' Up," and the hilarious "Say Man" were followed in 1960 by "Say Man, Back Again" and "Road Runner." His last charted record was possibly his only message song, "You Can't Judge A Book By Looking At The Cover," in 1962. He didn't break into the "pop" charts until "Crackin' Up" in 1959. Not that he was unknown to White teen-agers. Far from it.

Diddley has said that his greatest influences were Louis Jordan and Muddy Waters. This may be so, but his contribution to the legacy of rock 'n roll is so unique that specific influential identities are hard to pinpoint. On the other hand, his influence on the generation of musicians that followed can be easily traced. Eric Burdon and the Animals, the Beatles, Buddy Holly, Elvis Presley, the Yardbirds (especially guitarists Jimmy Page and Eric Clapton), and the Rolling Stones all bear testimony to the powerful influence of Bo Diddley.

July 1955

JUL 1   Ivory Joe Hunter opens at the New Era Club in Nashville.
At the Apollo Theater in New York, the Drifters and Illinois Jacquet entertain for the week.
The Charms and Marvin and Johnny start a three-day run at Los Angeles' 5-4 Ballroom.

JUL 3   Rusty Bryant is booked into the Hollywood Club in Akron, Ohio.
The Jaguars and the **Savoys** play a one-nighter at the Will Rogers Auditorium in Los Angeles.

JUL 4   Bull Moose Jackson starts a two-week engagement at the Zanzibar Club in Buffalo, New York.

New releases for the first week of July include "Rock Around The Clock" by the M-G-M Studio Orchestra on M-G-M; "Mannish Boy" by Muddy Waters and "Are You Out There" by Percy Mayfield, both on Chess; Ivory Joe Hunter's "Heaven Came Down To Earth" and T-Bone Walker's "Papa Ain't Salty," both on Atlantic; "It's Love Baby" by the Midnighters and "Sindy" by the Tenderfoots, both on Federal; "Since My Baby's Gone" by the Jacks and "Don't Touch Me" by **Johnny "Guitar" Watson**, both on RPM; "Rock It, Davy, Rock It" by the Jaguars on Aardell; "Always And Always" by Don Julian and the Meadowlarks on Dootone; "Don't Know Why I Cry" by the Chromatics on Million; "From The Bee" by the Larks on Apollo; and "Death Of An Angel" by Donald Woods and the Vel-Aires on Flip.

JUL 5   Gleason's in Cleveland welcomes Big Maybelle for a two-week stay.
Also in Cleveland, radio station WINS sues Alan Freed after it was sued, in turn, by "Moondog," the New York street performer, for allowing Freed to use the "Moondog" name on the air. The station claims that Freed told them the "Moondog" name was fully protected.

JUL 7   Dinah Washington holds court at Basin Street in New York for two weeks.

EARLY JULY

Mercury Records, in a move designed to help rhythm and blues and country and western records cross over into the mainstream of "pop" music, consolidates the color scheme for all of its single releases. Previously, rhythm and blues singles were issued with a pink label, country and western singles were issued with a green label, and "pop" came with a maroon label. All singles will be released with a black label as soon as the colored labels are phased out.

Naturally, the Savoys recorded for Savoy Records, but the group soon changed labels and names, becoming the Sparks Of Rhythm on Apollo. Lead singer of both groups was Jimmy Jones, who went on to have major hits with "Handy Man" and "Good Timin'" (1959-60, Cub).

Johnny "Guitar" Watson is remembered for his classic 1957 blues number, "Gangster Of Love," originally issued on the Keen label. His first charted single came with "Cuttin' In" on King in 1962.

Mercury Records was started in 1947 as an independent company, but early successes in "pop" and country music pushed it into head-to-head competition with the major labels. The r&b division was headed by Clyde Otis, the first Black artist and repertoire man to work for a major company.

THE SOLITAIRES

Red Prysock's name first came to the attention of record buyers when he was blowing tenor sax with Tiny Bradshaw's Orchestra on King. In 1953, he formed his own combo and signed with Red Robin, before moving to Mercury and a series of honking instrumentals including "Hand Clappin,'" "Foot Stompin','" and "Rock 'N Roll Party."

The Los Angeles-based Squires featured Don "Sugarcane" Harris and Dewey Terry, who recorded as Don and Dewey on Specialty (1957-59), and had the original versions of such rock 'n roll standards as "Justine," "I'm Leaving It Up To You," "Big Boy Pete," and "Farmer John."

The Meadowlarks issued two singles on RPM before moving to Dootone, where their six singles included the hit "Heaven And Paradise." In the 1960s, leader of the group, Don Julian, altered the name of the group, and the Larks came up with a top ten dance tune, "Cool Jerk" (1964, Money).

JUL 8   The Drifters open at Weeke's Tavern in Atlantic City.
The "Hal Jackson Rhythm And Blues Show," featuring Willie Mabon, Titus Turner, the **Solitaires**, the Cadillacs, and Arnett Cobb's Band, plays the Apollo Theater in New York for the week.
Los Angeles' 5-4 Ballroom offers the Penguins and Percy Mayfield for three days.
The Harptones spend the weekend in Pennsylvania performing a series of one-nighters in Harrisburg, Altoona, and Johnson.

JUL 9   Fats Domino becomes only the second rhythm and blues artist to be awarded *Billboard* magazine's "Triple Crown" as "Ain't That A Shame" tops all three r&b charts.

JUL 10   The "Pop R&B Show" starts a two-month tour with this evening's show at Chicago's Trianon Ballroom. The tour features Sarah Vaughan, Al Hibbler, **Red Prysock**, Nappy Brown, Muddy Waters, the Moonglows, the Cardinals, among many other headliners. The tour winds up August 6th after traveling through Texas and the South.
Lowell Fulson plays for Sunday night dancers at the Elks Ballroom in Los Angeles.

New releases for the second week of July include a reissue of "Rock The Joint" by Bill Haley and his Comets on Essex; Charlie Gracie and his Wildcats' "Honey Honey" on 20th Century-Fox; "Life Is But A Dream" by the Harptones on Paradise; "Very Truly Yours" by Jimmy Scott on Savoy; "Only You" by the Platters on Mercury; "Rockin' With Red" by Piano Red, "Bumble Bee" by the Sonics, and "Worried Life Blues" by Big Maceo, all on Groove; "Ding Dong Baby" by Marvin Phillips on Specialty; "My Baby Left Town" by the Dixie Blues Boys and "Romp And Stomp Blues" by Mercy Dee, both on Flair; "Sindy" by the **Squires** on Combo; "Schemin'" by the Griffin Brothers on Mercury; and "Blues In The Closet" by the Tri-Tones on Grand.

JUL 15   The Shrine Auditorium in Los Angeles hosts the "Annual Rhythm And Blues Jubilee," featuring Earl Bostic, the **Meadowlarks**, Chuck Higgins, the Clovers, Marvin and Johnny, the Voices, and the Jewels.
The Clovers do double duty this evening as they also open for three days with the Paul Williams Combo at the 5-4 Club in Los Angeles.

MID-JULY

Clyde McPhatter formally announces that he is leaving the Drifters and will continue to record as a solo artist with Atlantic. He has been a member of the Army since May 1954 and has recorded with the group only once since that time.

Groove Records recently inked the Cherokees. Other recent signings include the Sparks of Rhythm with Apollo, and blues singer Irene Reed with Savoy.

The Du Droppers open a four-week engagement at the Surf Club in Wildwood, New Jersey.

Ruth Brown is at the Patio Club in Philadelphia.

Bill Haley and his Comets, following their successful booking at the Regal Theater in Chicago, are booked on an extensive tour of one-night stands starting in Maryland and continuing through Virginia, North and South Carolina, Georgia, Florida, Alabama, Louisiana, Kentucky, Iowa, Michigan, Minnesota, Montana, Ohio, Nebraska, and Kansas. Also scheduled are stops in Canada.

Guitar Slim and T-Bone Walker are touring night spots in Texas.

JUL 22   Earl Bostic starts a three-day layover at the 5-4 Ballroom in Los Angeles.
          In Baltimore, the Royal Theater offers the talents of the Orioles for the week.

New releases for the third week of July include "Anymore" by Johnny Ace on Duke; "Don't You Know I Love You So" by the Five Keys on Capitol; "Sho-wop" by the Danderliers on States; **Wilbert Harrison's** "Darling Listen To This" on Savoy; "Learnin' The Blues" by Billy Ward and his Dominoes on King; Buddy Johnson's "Bitter Sweet" on Mercury; B. B. King's "Talkin' The Blues" on RPM; "Little Did I Dream" by the Twilighters on M-G-M; and the Medallions E.P. on Dootone.

Besides his enormous 1959 hit, "Kansas City," Wilbert Harrison also did well ten years later with the hypnotic "Let's Work Together" on Sue Records, which he recorded as a one-man band.

JUL 23   Atlantic Records reports that the company will be starting a new subsidiary to be named Atlas Records. Talent signed to the new label includes the Royal Jokers, New Orleans blues shouter Billy Nightingale, and Jesse Stone. (See August 6th.)
          It is reported that "Shake, Rattle And Roll" by Bill Haley and his Comets is set to be included in the motion picture "**How To Be Very, Very Popular**," starring Sheree North, following the success of Haley's "Rock Around The Clock" in "Blackboard Jungle." In addition, Haley's "Razzle-Dazzle" is to be featured in "**Running Wild**," starring Mamie Van Doren.

"How To Be Very, Very Popular" was released in July 1955, and "Running Wild" came out that November. As might be inferred from the careers of the leading ladies in these films, neither received much critical notice, although both had rock 'n roll music in their soundtracks.

JUL 24   LaVern Baker graces the stage at the Lord Calvert Hotel in Miami for one week.

New releases for the fourth week of July include "Maybellene" by Chuck Berry on Chess; Lowell Fulson's "Lonely Hours," a reissue of Joe Williams's "Every Day I Have The Blues," and the Flamingos' "I Want To Love You," all on Checker; **Young Jessie's** "Mary Lou" on Modern; Dean Barlow's "True Love" on Jay-Dee's; "Daybreak Rock" by Jack Dupree, "All Around The World" by "Little" Willie John, "Shake 'Em Baby" by Roy Brown, and "Pistol Packin' Mama" by the Hurricanes, all on King; Roy Milton's "You Got Me Reeling And Rocking" on Dootone; "My Dream My Love" by the Barons and "I Hear You Knocking" by Smiley Lewis, both on Imperial; "Heavenly Ruby" by the Californians and "Give It Up" by the Midnighters, both on Federal; "I'm So Glad" by **Mickey and Sylvia** on Rainbow; "It Only Happens With You" by the Penguins on Mercury; "Hide And Seek" by Joe Turner on Atlantic; and "Flim Flam" by Gene and Eunice on Aladdin.

"Mary Lou" by Young Jessie featured the Jacks/Cadets on backing vocals; the song was a 1959 hit for Ronnie Hawkins.

Mickey and Sylvia were guitarist Mickey Baker and "Little" Sylvia Vanderpool. They reportedly met when she hired him to teach her how to play guitar.

JUL 29   Faye Adams starts a week's engagement at the Flame Show Bar in Detroit.

Gene and Eunice front the Gene Ammons Combo for two three-day weekends at the 5-4 Club in Los Angeles. Also in town for three days, Pee Wee Crayton headlines the show at the Harlem Club.

JUL 30   Bill Haley is awarded the *Billboard* "Triple Crown" as "Rock Around The Clock" tops all three "pop" record charts.

LATE JULY

Despite their earlier proclamation that rhythm and blues music was declining in popularity, "pop" record companies continue to heavily cover r&b tunes. Recent cover versions include "Gum Drop," originally by Otis Williams, covered by the Crew-Cuts; "Seventeen," originally by Boyd Bennett, covered by Rusty Draper, the Fontane Sisters, and Ella Mae Morse; "Razzle-Dazzle," by Bill Haley, covered by Ella Mae Morse; "Story Untold," originally by the Nutmegs, covered by the Crew-Cuts; "The Wallflower," originally by Etta James, covered by Georgia Gibbs; "Ain't It A Shame," originally by Fats Domino, covered by Pat Boone as "Ain't That A Shame"; "Piddily Patter," originally by Nappy Brown, covered by Patti Page; and "Song Of The Dreamer," originally by Billy Brooks, covered by Johnnie Ray and Eddie Fisher.

As cover artists went, the most enthusiastic performer was Ella Mae Morse. She got her first break with the Jimmy Dorsey Orchestra at age fifteen. At age seventeen, in 1942, she fronted Freddy Slack's band on "Cow Cow Boogie," the record that launched the Capitol label, and her career was ensured.

TOP TEN ROCK 'N ROLL RECORDS FOR JULY 1955

1. Rock Around The Clock - Bill Haley and his Comets
2. Ain't It A Shame - Fats Domino
3. Story Untold - The Nutmegs
4. Fool For You - Ray Charles
5. Bo Diddley - Bo Diddley
6. Every Day (I Have The Blues) - Count Basie with Joe Williams
7. Soldier Boy - The Four Fellows
8. Unchained Melody - Roy Hamilton
9. It's Love Baby - Louis Brooks
10. Unchained Melody - Al Hibbler

July 1955
ARTIST OF THE MONTH

BILL HALEY AND HIS COMETS
(William John Clifton Haley, Jr., b. July 6, 1925; d. February 9, 1981)

BILL HALEY AND HIS COMETS

Bill Haley was either the "Father of Rock 'n Roll" or the greatest "cover" artist of all time. There can be little doubt that his popularity on a nationwide scale in 1955 paved the way for the floodgates to open in 1956 with the coming of Elvis Presley's enormous impact on the course of music. Haley, on the other hand, seemed genuinely baffled by the reaction that his own music was having on the teen-aged audience. After all, he had been playing the same music for four years, and no one had taken much notice before.

Haley was born in Highland Park, Michigan, to parents who had fled the harsh poverty of Kentucky for the chance of work in the Detroit area. There was little work to be found, so during the Depression of the early 1930s the family moved again, to Chester, Pennsylvania. Bill's father played banjo for his son's amusement, and his mother was a classically-trained pianist. Sometime during his early childhood, Bill was blinded in his left eye as the result of a mastoid operation, and this led to his extreme shyness as a young boy. At age thirteen he found work in a local farmer's market, and at the owner's insistence Bill accompanied himself on guitar and sang for the patrons for $1.00 a night. By the time he was fifteen he was singing at local amusement parks. He joined a western band led by Cousin Lee, who had a popular radio show on a Wilmington, Delaware, station. Because of his blindness, Haley was ineligible for the draft during World War II, so he was hired to take the place of yodeler Kenny Roberts in the Downhomers, a Hartford, Connecticut, western combo in 1944. In 1946 he suddenly left the Downhomers in mid-tour with two other members of the band to form his own unit. Shortly thereafter he was deserted by his new band, and he returned to Chester to take a job as a radio deejay.

He formed another band and recorded for Cowboy Records in 1948, under the name Bill Haley and the Four Aces of Western Swing. The band moved on to Center Records a year and three releases later. After only one record on Center, the group disbanded and Haley formed the Saddlemen to play dates in and around Philadelphia. Two records were issued on Keystone in 1949-50 before he recorded one single for the newly-formed Atlantic Records. There were five releases on Holiday Records, including a cover of Jackie Brenston's "Rocket 88," from 1951-52. Most of the above recordings were in the western swing vein that featured Haley's fine yodeling vocals.

The Saddlemen moved on to Philadelphia's Essex Records in 1952. As the flip side of "Icy Heart," Haley had to be convinced to record the up-tempo number, "Rock The Joint." This was the first release in Haley's four-year career as a recording artist to actually sell in even moderate numbers (75,000 reported), and it got his band bookings far afield from the local Chester area. One of the first of these play dates was in Chicago, where he entertained in a Black nightclub. Haley was in the middle of a career decision: he felt that he was on the verge of becoming a nationally-known and respected cowboy singer, and now here he was with his first small hit singing an unfamiliar type of music based on the blues. Haley's business sense won out. The band changed their ten-gallon hats, high heel boots, and western-cut shirts for formal stage suits. After another release as the Saddlemen, Haley changed the group's name to the Comets, befitting their new image. Only now was Bill Haley ready to take on the musical world.

"Crazy Man, Crazy" in 1953 was his first national hit, and it led to more regional work and an important audition with a major New York record company, Decca. In April 1954 the Comets were in a makeshift studio belting out a number that had been part of their repertoire for over a year, "Rock Around The Clock." Upon its release the record again sold only moderately well (another 75,000 copies), but the band was on the move. Club engagements were steady now, and the group's second Decca record, "Shake, Rattle And Roll," took off like a rocket (or comet!), eventually selling over a million copies. This was followed in quick succession by "Dim, Dim The Lights" and "Mambo Rock." In February 1955 it was announced that "Rock Around The Clock" would be used in a pivotal scene in a new motion picture currently in production. A month later the release of "Blackboard Jungle" immediately made the connection in many minds between rock 'n roll (a musical form so new that most Americans did not understand it, and therefore feared it) and juvenile delinquency (which was all too easy to understand). "Rock Around The Clock" became a rallying point for teen-agers in the summer of 1955. It quickly topped the "pop" charts. Those floodgates were beginning to open.

At this time Haley suffered through another internal problem with his combo. The original Comets were Johnny Grande (accordion), Billy Williamson (steel guitar), Joe D'Ambrosia (bass), Dick Richards (drums), and Marshall Lytell (tenor sax). In September 1955, D'Ambrosia, Richards, and Lytell quit the band to form the Jodimars. Their places were immediately filled by Rudy Pompelli (sax), Dan Raymond (drum), and Al Rex (bass). With the addition of Francis Beecher on guitar, this was the lineup that most fans remember.

By now, all of the Comets' releases were big sellers: "Razzle-Dazzle," "Burn That Candle," "Rock A-Beatin' Boogie," "See You Later Alligator." Haley and the Comets appeared on numerous television shows, including those hosted by Sammy Kaye, Milton Berle, and Ed Sullivan. In early 1956 he and his Comets received $40,000 for six days work, to appear as themselves in the "quickie" movie titled after "Rock Around The Clock" and based loosely on their own rising popularity. This film was followed quickly by "Don't Knock The Rock" which spawned another hit single. By now those floodgates had opened wide, but it was Haley who was swept aside in favor of newer artists who were not so rooted in the country sound, who were younger (Haley was now thirty-one), and who were more exciting. For all of his hits, Haley's sound rarely varied. It was "professional rock 'n roll" at a time when teens wanted wild abandon. After "See You Later, Alligator," Haley never had another top ten hit record.

He found a new audience in Europe during his first English tour in February 1957. He returned again in October 1958 and included West Germany in the itinerary. Back in the United States, his career troubles that had started in 1956 seemed small compared with his rejection as the 1950s came to a close. His fan club, which in early 1957 rivaled Elvis' for circulation, had dwindled to only a few faithful followers. Hits had stopped coming automatically long ago. A change of record companies, to Warner Brothers, did nothing to boost his career. For the next twenty years, Haley would be relegated to the role of "has-been," "star of the oldies show," "musical lame duck." He continued to tour, expanding his reach to Japan, Australia, and South America. But back home he was almost forgotten. In 1981, he was reportedly a lonely, embittered man when he died at his home in Harlingen, Texas.

"Rock Around The Clock" is ranked as the largest-selling record in the history of rock 'n roll, with the total number sold reaching six million by the end of 1956, fifteen million by 1960, and thirty million today. The record even had a revival of sorts in 1974, following a resurgence in interest in early rock 'n roll that briefly brought new life to Haley's career. Once again he was in demand on the circuit that catered to the children of the 1950s.

The musical forces in 1954-55 needed a bridge between the rhythm and blues of the Blacks and the "pop" music of the Whites. Bill Haley and his Comets certainly provided that bridge. More important, they were the catalyst that fused two divergent musical styles in a way that none of the regular "cover" artists could approach. And, make

258

no mistake, Haley was certainly a "cover" artist. Of all his early hits, over half were originally recorded by rhythm and blues artists, even though, at this late date, many people would attribute the songs first to the Comets. Such was the breadth of his popularity. This is not meant to detract from Haley's achievements: it was standard practice for the times. Looking back at the career of Bill Haley and the Comets, one sees a western band playing up-tempo jump numbers. His song style was repetitive, and one number blended into the next. The longevity of his recording career was doomed from the beginning because he did not change the formula achieved with "Rock Around The Clock." It was impossible for him to stay on the crest of popular music when the audience was constantly searching for the next new sound. In the end, maybe he was more like the "Grandfather of Rock 'N Roll."

August 1955

New releases for the first week of August include "Maybellene" by Jim Lowe on Dot; "What'd I Say" by Ruth Brown and "Everyone's Laughing" by Clyde McPhatter, both on Atlantic; "Good Rockin' Daddy" by Etta James on Modern; **Ray Agee**'s "Wobble Lou" on Spark; "He's A Jelly Roll Baker" by Lonnie Johnson on Groove; Floyd Dixon's "A Long Time Ago" on Aladdin; Elvis Presley's "Mystery Train" on Sun; and three on JOZ: "Come Back To Me" by the Clicks, "I Still Love You" by the Ray-O-Vacs, and "Down The Road" by the Cadillacs.

AUG 2   LaVern Baker spends five days at Gleason's in Cleveland.

AUG 3   As an example of the speed with which one record company could cover another artist's record, at a 2:00 p.m. session in New York, Georgia Gibbs, Mercury recording star, waxes a version of Lillian Briggs's "I Want You To Be My Baby." By the next morning, deejays in the area are already airing acetate copies of Gibbs's version, and on August 5th regular copies are in the stores.

AUG 5   The Nutmegs start a three-day stand at the Copa Casino in Youngstown, Ohio.
The Four Fellows play a one-nighter at the Royal Peacock in Atlanta.
Arthur Prysock is booked for a three-week run at the Club Ebony in Houston.
Roy Hamilton opens in Washington at the Casino Royal for three days.
"Rock 'N' Roll Revue" opens across the country. The motion picture features Nat Cole, Lionel Hampton, Joe Turner, Duke Ellington, Dinah Washington, Ruth Brown, the Clovers, and the **Delta Rhythm Boys**.

AUG 6   The Trinidad Club in Cleveland hosts the Four Fellows for a three-day weekend stint.
The "Pop R&B Show" plays a one-nighter at the Watergate Theater in Washington to close out its four-week tour. (See July 10th.)
Bill Haley files a lawsuit in Philadelphia against his former label, Essex Records, in an attempt to stop them from reissuing his older recordings, which Haley feels are "of inferior quality" to his recent Decca releases.
In New Orleans, Larry Darnell is the featured performer for the grand opening of the Club Caravan.
Atlantic Records launches its new subsidiary, Atco Records. The new company had originally been planned to be named Atlas Records. (See July 23rd.)

Raymond Clinton "Ray" Agee was one of the most prolific West Coast r&b artists, although he never had a record that sold well nationally. Born April 10, 1930, in Dixon Mills, Alabama, he contracted polio at age four, and his family moved to Los Angeles shortly thereafter. Ray first recorded in 1952 for Modern, and thereafter for Aladdin, Recorded In Hollywood, RK, Elko, Rhythm And Blues, Spark, Ebb, Cash, and on and on into the 1970s.

When the Delta Rhythm Boys signed with Atlantic in 1949, they were still under contract to Musicraft. "Don't Ask Me Why" was released by both labels, with Atlantic naming the group The Four Sharps. The Delta Rhythm Boys also backed Ruth Brown on two of her early Atlantic releases.

AUG 7   The Penguins and Big Jay McNeeley's Band entertain at the Elks Ballroom in Los Angeles.

EARLY AUGUST

The Drifters, following a four-day engagement at the Farm Dell Club in Dayton, Ohio, are off on a series of one-nighters that will take them to California.

Gene and Eunice play a one-night stand in El Paso on their current swing through the Southwest.

AUG 8   The Casino Royal Club in Philadelphia plays host to Della Reese.
         LaVern Baker is booked into Weeke's Tavern in Atlantic City for a week.
         Bill Haley and his Comets play the Broadway-Capitol Theater in Detroit for three days.

New releases for the second week of August include "Ship Of Love" by the Nutmegs on Herald; "Two Strangers" by the Marigolds on Excello; "I Don't Want You To Go" by the Casanovas on Apollo; "W-P-L-J" by the 4 Deuces and "Tell Me Darling" by the Gaylarks, both on Music City; "Without A Friend" by the Strangers and "Women About To Make Me Go Crazy" by the "5" Royales, both on King; "Walkin' The Blues" by **Willie Dixon** on Checker; "Traveling Mood" by Wee Willie Wayne on Imperial; and "When You Dance" by the Turbans on Herald.

WILLIE DIXON

Willie Dixon (born April 1, 1915, Vicksburg, Mississippi) is the best known bass player of the rhythm and blues era. He was also a noted record producer and songwriter ("My Babe," "Seventh Son," "Little Red Rooster" and "I'm Your Hootchy Cootchy Man").

AUG 9   Rusty Bryant stops over for a week's engagement at the Club Zanzibar in Buffalo, New York.
         Bill Doggett returns to his hometown of Philadelphia to play a gig at Pep's Musical Bar.

AUG 11   Roy Hamilton fronts the Buddy Johnson Orchestra featuring Ella Johnson at Basin Street in New York for two weeks.
         In New Orleans, Dave Bartholomew's Combo is featured at the Lincoln Beach midway for the evening.

AUG 12   Ruth Brown, the Clovers, Little Willie John, and the Paul Williams Orchestra entertain at New York's Apollo Theater for the week.
         Charlie Fuqua's Ink Spots are continuing a Canadian tour with a two-week engagement in Hull, Quebec.
         T-Bone Walker is welcomed for a two-week engagement at the Flame Show Bar in Detroit.
         The Platters start an eight-week run at the Show Bar of the Flamingo Hotel in Las Vegas.

AUG 15   Chuck Berry makes his initial booking at Gleason's in Cleveland. Following this engagement, he travels to the Copa Casino in Youngstown, Ohio, and the Paramount Theater in New York.
         Al Hibbler holds court for a week at the Hollywood Club in Akron, Ohio.
         Earl Bostic plays at Sealer's House of Jazz in Milwaukee.

AL HIBBLER

After the hits stopped coming and the national tours dried up, Piano Red returned to his hometown of Atlanta, where he became a renowned fixture in the area known as Underground Atlanta. He passed away on August 1, 1985.

New releases for the third week of August include "Paradise Princess" by Al Savage on Herald; "Come Back Maybellene" by John Greer and "Six O'Clock Bounce" by **Piano Red**, both on Groove; Johnny "Guitar" Watson's "Those Lonely Lonely Nights" on RPM; "Done Got Over" by the Blasers on United; "The Shape I'm In" by Marie Adams on Peacock; "Front Page Blues" by the Solotones on Excello; and "Smokey Joe's Cafe" by the Robins on Spark.

MID-AUGUST

Roy Brown is booked into the Palms in Hallendale, Florida.

The "5" Royales are currently on tour in the South and Southwest. In a related story, Lowman Pauling, leader of the "5" Royales, files a lawsuit in New York City against his former label, Apollo Records. He asks the court to require an accounting of all royalties and rights to songs that he wrote while with the company.

Recent signings include the Cavaliers, a new Philadelphia group, with Atlantic; and the Empires, previously on Harlem, with Wing.

Sonny Thompson, Lulu Reed, and the Champions are booked solid through the end of the year. They play the South and Southwest into September and the West Coast through Christmas.

Atlantic, Savoy, Decca, Capitol, Mercury, and Dootone announce that they will soon be releasing r&b material on 12-inch long-play records. They will also greatly increase the output of rhythm and blues 45 rpm extended-play (E.P.) records.

AUG 19   "Dr. Jive's Rhythm And Blues Show" returns to the Apollo Theater in New York for a one-week run. Extra performances have to be added each day to accommodate the overflow crowd. Featured performers include the Spaniels, Charlie and Ray, the **Hearts**, Joe Turner, the Five Keys, Bo Diddley, the Moonglows, and the Griffin Brothers' Orchestra. Following the week's run, many of the performers join the "Top Ten Review" tour.

      At Lincoln Beach in New Orleans, Dinah Washington performs for the midway crowd.

      Pee Wee Crayton plays the blues during his three-day stand at the 5-4 Ballroom in Los Angeles.

The Hearts are not to be confused with Lee Andrews and the Hearts. They were a New York group featuring the odd combination of a female lead (Baby Washington) fronting two females and a male. The group had two minor hits, "Lonely Nights" (1955, Baton) and "Dear Abby" (1963, Tuff).

New releases for the fourth week of August include Fats Domino's "All By Myself" on Imperial; "Nip Sip" by the Clovers on Atlantic; Nappy Brown's "Well Well Well Baby-La" on Savoy; John Lee Hooker's "The Syndicator" and **Jimmy McCracklin**'s "Gonna Tell Your Mother," both on Modern; "Deep In My Heart For You" by the Pyramids on Federal; and "Sweethearts On Parade" by Billy Ward and his Dominoes on Jubilee.

Jimmy McCracklin continued to have regional hits after "The Walk" and "Just Got To Know." In 1962 he signed with Imperial, and by 1966 he was the only blues artist still recording regularly for the label.

AUG 22   The Four Fellows headline for a week at the Copa in Pittsburgh.

AUG 26   "The Top Ten Review" takes to the road with a show in St. Louis. The tour will be a 60-day trek through the East, Midwest, Southwest, and the South. Performers include the Clovers, Gene and Eunice, the Five Keys, Joe Turner, Bo Diddley, Etta James, Jimmy Reed, Charlie and Ray, Faye Adams, Bill Doggett, the Charms, and the Paul Williams Orchestra. Other dates for the tour include Memphis (27) and New Orleans (28). (See October 29th.)

Roy Hamilton kicks off two weeks at the Cat and Fiddle Club in Nassau, the Bahamas.

The "Big Blues-O-Rama" starts rolling on a six-week tour. Featured entertainers include the Cardinals, Little Walkin' Willie, Jimmy Reed, and Little "Junior" Lewis.

The Apollo Theater in New York offers up the Moonglows, Baby Dee, and the Jimmy Smith Trio for patrons this week.

Pat Boone is the headliner at the Chicago Theater this week.

AUG 28   In New Orleans, Arthur Prysock and Earl King share the spotlight at the Labor Union Hall this evening.

AUG 29   The Charlie Fuqua Ink Spots start a week in Toronto.

New releases for the fifth week of August include Amos Milburn's "All Is Well" on Aladdin; "I'm Good To You Baby" by the Gypsies on Groove; Shirley Gunter's "How Can I Tell You" and **Richard Berry** and the Dreamers' "Together," both on Flair; "Bad Feeling Blues" by Lightnin' Hopkins and "Those Lonely Lonely Nights" by Earl King, both on Ace; "Love" by the Sheppards on Theron; and "I Ain't Got Room To Rock" by Glenn Reeves on TNT. Also, Dootone Records releases a twelve-inch long-play album, "The Best Of The Vocal Groups," featuring the Penguins, the Meadowlarks, the Medallions, and the Dootones.

Richard Berry sang with the Flairs from 1953-55, and lent his distinctive bass voice to both "Riot In Call Block No. 9" and "The Wallflower." But his biggest hit came under his own name came in 1956, when he recorded the original version of "Louie Louie" for Flip Records.

LATE AUGUST

The Ravens are touring the Carolinas, Georgia, Alabama, and Florida into next month.

Fortune Records signs the **Five Dollars**.

The Five Dollars from Detroit featured Andre Williams on lead. When Williams went solo, the group continued to back him as the Don Juans. Williams' had a couple of lesser hits as a solo artist, including "Bacon Fat" (1957, Epic) and "Cadillac Jack" (1958, Checker).

THE TOP TEN ROCK 'N ROLL RECORDS FOR AUGUST 1955

1. Rock Around The Clock - Bill Haley and his Comets
2. Maybellene - Chuck Berry
3. Ain't It A Shame - Fats Domino
4. Every Day (I Have The Blues) - Count Basie with Joe Williams
5. Fool For You - Ray Charles
6. It's Love Baby - Louis Brooks
7. Soldier Boy - The Four Fellows
8. Story Untold - The Nutmegs
9. Seventeen - Boyd Bennett and his Rockets
10. Razzle-Dazzle - Bill Haley and his Comets

August 1955
ARTIST OF THE MONTH

CHUCK BERRY
(Charles Edward Anderson Berry, b. October 18, 1926)

CHUCK BERRY

Chuck Berry. Even the name has a humorous ring to it. Buchannan and Goodman, in their 1956 novelty record "Flying Saucer," called him "Chuckleberry," which is even closer to the man than the two humorists probably imagined. He was the Clown Prince of Rock n' Roll. His stage antics punctuated his wildly imaginative music. He was bound to happen. In the summer of 1955, there was need for a Chuck Berry to bridge the gap opened by the many earlier rhythm and blues artists. Chuck Berry was quick of wit, teen-oriented, and musically astute. And he was a Negro - a "colored." The new music needed a Black man who could overcome this, the most basic prejudice of the time. Chuck Berry happened along at just the right time. But it almost wasn't so.

You see, he loved to sing the blues.

The early days of Chuck Berry were somewhat different from those of millions of other Black families. His father, an East St. Louis carpenter, was a part-time minister, and his mother sang in the church choir. Although Chuck started singing in the local Antioch Baptist Church choir at an early age, he had graduated to a gospel quartet by the time he was six. The family's middle-class life style smoothed the edges of his early years. He learned to play guitar, piano, saxophone, and drums. By 1942, while a student at Sumner High School, he was proficient enough to perform as a sideman in the Ray Band Orchestra. But something went wrong following graduation. He was involved in an armed robbery and he spent the better part of three years (1944-47) in a Missouri reform school. Upon his release he found work at a General Motors assembly plant while attending the Poro School of Beauty Culture, where he studied hairdressing and cosmetology. All the while he continued to practice guitar and play in small, local clubs.

The influences on Chuck Berry's music were varied: Charlie Christian, one of the first jazz artists to use an electric guitar; Louis Jordan's zany stage antics and down-to-earth lyrics; the recordings of T-Bone Walker and Guitar Slim; Nat Cole's enunciation; and Hank Williams's sing-from-the-heart style. Consequently, Chuck's music was a fusion of big band, jazz, pop, country, and blues.

In 1951 Berry joined the Johnny Johnson Trio in St. Louis. Johnson, a locally renowned pianist, was in need of a guitarist. He got more than he bargained for: within a year, the combo was known as the Chuck Berry Trio. They worked most of the Black bars and ballrooms, including Huff Gardens and the Moonlight Bar, playing a set composed mainly of slow blues numbers. In 1954, for reasons unknown, Berry played guitar on a local recording session for the Ballad label. One single, "Oh Maria," was issued with Joe Alexander doing vocals and Berry on guitar as a member of the Cubans.

That same year he auditioned for Vee-Jay Records of Gary, Indiana. Although he was rejected, he constantly sent out demonstration tapes to record companies, including Capitol (Nat Cole's label) and Mercury, trying to interest them in his talent. By 1955 he was considering a move to Houston (home of Peacock Records) or Memphis (home of Sun Records), but a chance meeting with Muddy Waters, who was playing a date in St. Louis, convinced him to try Chicago. Berry never moved to the Windy City, but he did make a pilgrimage in the spring of 1955. True to his word, Muddy Waters introduced Berry to Leonard Chess of Chess Records in May 1955.

For his audition session, Chuck decided to record several of his favorite blues numbers as well as a semi-country ditty titled "Ida Red." Chess was impressed with the last item and suggest a title change that would make it less country and more appealing to the Black market. The exact origin of "Maybellene" is not clear, although Berry has stated that it had nothing to do with his cosmetology background. His first real session followed immediately, with Johnson on piano, as well as Chess regulars Willie Dixon (bass), Jasper Thomas (drums), and Jerome Green of Bo Diddley's band on maracas. At the time, Berry thought that the blues number "Wee Hours" would be on the "A" side. Chess knew better. In order to insure airplay for "Maybellene," a third of the writer's royalties were signed over to New York deejay Alan Freed, who started plugging the number over WINS radio. The other third of the royalties went to Russ Frato, Chicago jukebox entrepreneur and Chess's landlord. Such was the music business in 1955.

"Maybellene" was a beautifully crafted novelty song aimed directly at the teen market. In a little over two minutes, the listener was presented with a high-speed race between a Cadillac Coupe De Ville and a V-8 Ford, a story of lost love with a happy ending, and an eternal question ("Maybellene, why can't you be true?"). The record was sung at breakneck speed, but Berry's enunciation was perfectly clear. Not a word was slurred. Even such Berry-isms as "moto-vating" were clearly understood. The song was broken into two parts, tied together with a guitar break that is both complimentary to the lyrics (it is reminiscent of an auto horn flashing through a rainy night), and full of its own tension (the first verse is composed almost entirely of the same short riff repeated again and again). The record easily sold a million copies by the end of the year, and "Maybellene" was only a precursor of things to come.

By the end of 1956 Berry had released "Thirty Days," "No Money Down," "Roll Over Beethoven," "Too Much Monkey Business," and "Brown Eyed Handsome Man." Each song was a complete, humorous slice of American life presented rapid-fire in a style similar to, but at the same time different from, "Maybellene." This was Berry's secret of success. Each new release was a fresh contribution to the growing legacy of rock 'n roll, and each one built upon its predecessors. Lyrics covered the gamut of subjects near and dear to the hearts of teen-agers no matter what their backgrounds might be: cars, dates, jukeboxes, part-time jobs, music, school.

Along with Fats Domino and Little Richard, Chuck Berry was at the forefront of those Black artists whose popularity broke through the color lines while they remained true to the essence of their heritage. At the same time, Chuck and these other rock 'n roll pioneers refused to emasculate their music in the same way Nat Cole or Louis Armstrong had done. Of the three mentioned above, it was only Chuck Berry who clearly had a "White" sound in his recordings.

While a discussion of his music must certainly cover his lyrics and melodies, his prowess with a guitar must not be dismissed. Along with only one other person, Scotty Moore (the premier guitarist on the recordings of Elvis Presley), Chuck Berry clearly defined the sound of rock 'n roll. Each song featured a stinging instrumental break midway through, and just as the songs were similar and yet different, so it was with these guitar pieces. Each was matched to the song. The lyrics, the melody, and the guitar riff were a troika, a perfect three-sound team, each complementing the other. In the emerging hierarchy of rock 'n roll, Chuck Berry was certainly a prince, even a clown prince, as this was the role he chose to play.

(The Chuck Berry story will continue in Volume 2 of *The Golden Age of American Rock 'N Roll*.)

September 1955

SEP 2   Alan Freed's "Big Rock 'N Roll Show" spends the week at the Paramount Theater in Brooklyn. The show features Tony Bennett, the Harptones, the Moonglows, Chuck Berry, the Cardinals, the **Nutmegs**, Lillian Briggs, Sam "The Man" Taylor, Nappy Brown, and Red Prysock's Orchestra. Bennett becomes ill and only plays the first day.

Roy Hamilton plays a weekend engagement at Michigan State University.

The Larks and Bette McLaurin backed by Tito Puente's mambo orchestra start a week at the Apollo Theater in New York.

The Regal Theater in Chicago hosts the "Rhythm In Blue Revue," featuring the Buddy Johnson Band with Ella Johnson and Al Savage, LaVern Baker, the Spaniels, the Orchids, and the Four Fellows.

Willie Mabon is at the Blue Flame in East St. Louis, Illinois.

Al Hibbler heads the show at the Flame Show Bar in Detroit.

The 5-4 Club in Los Angeles presents the Penguins with the Chuck Higgins Combo for the three-day weekend.

Boyd Bennett and his Rockets are part of the revue for two weeks at the Chicago Theater with Patti Page.

SEP 5   **Sil Austin** entertains for a week at the Zanzibar Club in Buffalo, New York.

New releases for the first week of September include "Black Denim Trousers" by the **Cheers** on Capitol; Red Prysock's "Hand Clappin'" on Mercury; Charlie and Ray's "Oh Gee-Oo-Wee" on Herald; B. B. King's "Ten Long Years" on RPM; Stomp Gordon's "The Grind" on Chess; "Doctor Baby" by the Five Dollars on Fortune; "You Tickle Me Baby" by the Royal Jokers on Atco; "Come Back Maybellene" by Mercy Dee on Flair; "It's Hot" by Gene and Billy on Spark; "Natural Natural Ditty" by the Jewels on Imperial; "I Wanna Love You" by the Du Droppers on Groove; and "Tabarin" by the Tangiers on Decca.

EARLY SEPTEMBER

Fats Domino is currently playing "pop" clubs in New London, Connecticut, and Hyannis, Massachusetts, as well as the usual r&b locations on his East Coast tour.

SEP 8   Roy Hamilton is the houseguest at St. Louis' Riviera Club.

Billy Ward and his Dominoes open at New York's Copacabana for six weeks following three weeks at Harrah's Club at Lake Tahoe. The group is currently negotiating for a weekly half-hour television show.

SEP 9   Buddy Johnson's "Big Rock & Roll Show" starts a two-month

The Nutmegs' "Ship Of Love" was first recorded by the group in 1953 when they were called the Lyres on J&G Records. The Herald version is a re-recording by the group.

SIL AUSTIN

The Cheers were a trio of studio vocalists including Bert Convy (currently an actor and TV game show host). As fate would have it, "Black Denim Trousers," the tale of a wild "rebel of the road," was released the same week that actor/rebel James Dean was killed in an auto accident.

tour. Featured performers include Chuck Berry, the Nutmegs, the Cardinals, the Spaniels and the Four Fellows. (See September 25th and November 4th.)

Ruth Brown, the Moonglows, and Guitar Slim share top billing for the week at Washington's Howard Theater.

In Los Angeles, Roy Milton headlines at the 5-4 Ballroom for the weekend.

SEP 10   Chuck Berry becomes the third rhythm and blues artist to be awarded *Billboard* magazine's "R&B Triple Crown" for "Maybellene."

SEP 12   The Buddy Johnson package tour plays a one-nighter at the Graystone Ballroom in Detroit. Featured in tonight's lineup are Chuck Berry, the Nutmegs, the Four Fellows, the Spaniels, Ella Johnson, and Al Savage.

The Brass Rail in London, Ontario, hosts Sil Austin's show for a week.

New releases for the second week of September include "Maybellene" by **Marty Robbins** on Columbia; "Painted Picture" by the Spaniels on Vee-Jay; Earl King's "I Get So Happy" and Bubber Johnson's "There'll Be No One," both on King; "Starlite" by the Moonglows on Chess; "Shame On Old Me" by Faye Adams on Herald; "I Want To Know" by the Empires on Wing; "Tears On My Pillow" by the Chimes on Specialty; "Love Only You" by the Feathers on Show Time; "So Fine" by the Sheiks on Federal; "Wetback Hop" by Chuck Higgins on Dootone; and "Hey Bartender" by the Red Saunders Orchestra on Okeh.

SEP 14   Steve Gibson and his Red Caps are booked for a month at the Cafe Society in New York.

MID-SEPTEMBER

Imperial Records starts a new affiliate, Post Records. Talent already signed to the new label includes T-Bone Walker, the Kidds, and the Hawks, all previously recording for the parent company.

Ivory Joe Hunter is currently touring through Texas.

Grand Records announces the signing of the Dreamers to a contract.

The music press reports that Bill Haley will probably earn $300,000 to $500,000 this year from tours alone. By way of comparison, B. B. King will only bring in $30,000 from over 300 days on the road.

Am-Par Records officially changes its name to ABC-Paramount Records.

SEP 16   Al Hibbler takes over the Copa Casino in Youngstown, Ohio, for the week.

Billie Holiday graces the stage of the Apollo Theater in New York for a week.

The Drifters, backed by Joe Houston's band, entertain for three days at the 5-4 Ballroom in Los Angeles.

Marty Robbins started his long career in 1948 at age twenty-three. He ventured briefly into rock 'n roll in 1955, issuing several excellent records, before returning to the country fold with "Singing The Blues" (1956) and "A White Sport Coat" (1957).

After "Since I Met You Baby" in 1956, Ivory Joe Hunter drifted from label to label with little success. In the 1970s he joined the Grand Ole Opry, searching for a renewed career in the Ray Charles vein. Hunter died on November 8, 1974.

She was called "Lady Day." Miss Holiday was arguably the finest of all the jazz singers, male or female, and she influenced virtually every female rhythm and blues vocalist from the 1940s and 1950s. Traces of her style can be detected in the recordings of artists as seemingly disparate as Dinah Washington and Ruth Brown.

SEP 17 Alan Freed expands his time on the air as WINS radio schedules his show from 6:00 to 9:00 p.m. and 11:00 p.m. to 1:00 a.m. weeknights, and from 11:00 p.m. until 2:00 a.m. on Friday and Saturday nights.

SEP 19 Sil Austin begins a week-long stint at Darrow's Lounge in Cleveland.

New releases for the third week of September include Boyd Bennett's "My Boy Flat-Top" and Wynonie Harris's "Man's Best Friend" both on King; "Black Denim Trousers" by the Diamonds on Coral; "Adorable" by the Colts on Vita; Varetta Dillard's "I'll Never Forget You" on Savoy; "I Don't Go For That" by Jimmy Reed and **"At My Front Door" by the El Dorados**, both on Vee-Jay; "It's You, You, You" by the Charms on DeLuxe; Bobby Tuggle's "The $64,000 Question" on Checker; Smokey Hogg's "I Declare" on Meteor; "Hey Now" by the Voices on Cash; "Foolish Dreams" by the Fi-Tones on Atlas; and "There's A Rumor" by the Cashmeres on Mercury.

"At My Front Door" is even more well known by its' first line, "Crazy Little Mama, Come Knock, Knock, Knocking." The El Dorados never had another charted record following this smash hit.

SEP 23 T-Bone Walker starts a two-week layover at Detroit's Flame Show Bar.

At the 5-4 Club in Los Angeles, Lowell Fulson entertains patrons for the weekend.

SEP 24 Bill Haley hires a new group of Comets to replace three members who have left the group. The new Comets are Francis Beecher (guitar), Rudy Pompelli (sax), Al Rex (bass), and Don Raymond (drums).

In a related story, the departing Comets are joining Capitol Records. The ex-Comets are Joe D'Ambrosia (sax); Dick Reynolds (drums), and Marshall Lytell (bass). The group will be called the **Jodimars** (arrived at by combining the first portions of their first names). Joining the group are Charles Hess (guitar), Jim Buffington (drums), and Bob Simpson (piano).

The Jodimars had a very brief stay in the limelight. They signed a recording contract with Capitol, but saw their place as the company's rock 'n roll act quickly disappear when Gene Vincent had a major hit in 1956 with "Be-Bop-A-Lulu."

SEP 25 "The Big Rock & Roll Show" plays the New Orleans Municipal Auditorium. Featured performers are Buddy Johnson's Band, the Chuck Berry Trio, the Spaniels, the Nutmegs, the Four Fellows, Al Savage, Ella Johnson, and Arthur Prysock. Also in town, Ray Charles entertains at the Labor Union Hall for the evening.

New releases for the fourth week of September include Pat Boone's "At My Front Door," Gale Storm's "I Hear You Knocking," and the Counts' "I Need You Tonight," all on Dot; LaVern Baker's "Play It Fair" on Atlantic; "The Wedding" by the **Solitaires** on Old Town; "Dear Angels Above" by the Belvederes on Baton; "Tears in My Eyes" by the Dreamers on Grand; "Devil That I See" by the Penguins on Mercury; Sonny Boy Williamson's "Don't Start Me Talkin'," Little Walter's "Too Late," and the Flamingos' "Please Come Back Home," all on Checker; "Give Me You" by Billy Ward and his Dominoes on King; Eddie Boyd's "I'm A Prisoner" on Chess; "I Wonder" by the Striders and "Don't Love You Anymore" by the Sparks of Rhythm, both on Apollo; and "Don't Take Your Love From Me" by the Calvanes on Dootone.

The early Solitaires were made up of Herman Curtis (from the Vocaleers), Bobby Baylor (from the Mello-Moods), and Cecil Holmes (from the Cavaliers and Fi-Tones). Rounding out the quintet, Pat Gaston and Buzzy Willis had appeared, but not recorded, with the Crows. Curtis was replaced by Milton Love (from the Concords).

SEP 30 Al Hibbler, LaVern Baker, the El Dorados, the Hearts, and the Red Prysock Combo perform for a week at the Howard Theater in Washington.

The Apollo Theater in New York hosts the Royal Jokers backed by the Lucky Millinder Orchestra for the week.

The Savoy Ballroom in Los Angeles reopens following some legal problems. Louis Jordan headlines for two three-day weekend engagements. Also in Los Angeles, Savannah Churchill and Oscar McLollie perform at the 5-4 Club for the weekend.

THE TOP TEN ROCK 'N ROLL RECORDS FOR SEPTEMBER 1955

1. Rock Around The Clock - Bill Haley and his Comets
2. Maybellene - Chuck Berry
3. Ain't It A Shame - Fats Domino
4. It's Love Baby - Louis Brooks
5. Seventeen - Boyd Bennett and his Rockets
6. Why Don't Your Write Me - The Jacks
7. Only You - Platters
8. Every Day (I Have The Blues) - Count Basie with Joe Williams
9. Soldier Boy - The Four Fellows
10. Feel So Good - Shirley and Lee

September 1955
ARTIST OF THE MONTH

ALAN FREED
(b. December 15, 1922; d. January 20, 1965)

ALAN FREED

Alan Freed was the most important rock 'n roll disk jockey in the middle 1950s. In that context, he was also one of the most powerful men in the music business. He constantly promoted the music that he called rock 'n roll, and he certainly loved the music as much as any of the fans or performers. Yet his own vocal abilities were so limited that he couldn't carry a tune in the shower.

Freed was born in Johnstown, Pennsylvania, and raised by his Russian mother and Welsh/Jewish father in Salem, Ohio. He wanted to front his own band, and one report has him playing trombone with Claude Thornhill until an ear infection caused a loss of musical ability. He studied electrical engineering at Ohio University before landing a job at a radio station in New Castle, Pennsylvania. Other radio jobs as a sports announcer and program director followed in Youngstown and Akron, Ohio. It was in Akron, around 1945, that he first got the chance to spin records over the air. In 1950 he moved on to WXEL in Cleveland before landing a job at WJW across town in 1951.

At WJW he started mixing in a few rhythm and blues records with the "pop" hits of the day. Acceptance by the primarily White audience was favorable, especially among teen-agers who up to that time had no radio programming aimed directly at them. In August of that year he started his "Moondog" radio show, which featured mostly r&b records. In 1952 he staged several rhythm and blues dances promoted via his radio show. Such names as the Swallows, the Buddy Johnson Orchestra, and Charles Brown were the featured entertainers who played regularly to standing-room only audiences. In 1953 he added the title of manager to his growing list of achievements, as he represented the up-and-coming Moonglows. By the end of the year his "Moondog" show was being heard over several radio stations, including WNJR in Newark, via tape syndication. He presented his biggest live promotion up to that time in Newark in May 1954, with a show featuring the Clovers, the Harptones, Charles Brown, and Muddy Waters, among others. This was followed by a July 4th extravaganza in New Jersey with Roy Hamilton, the Orioles, Bull Moose Jackson, and Varetta Dillard.

In September 1954, he transferred his base of operations to WINS in New York City. His radical broadcasting style quickly made WINS the top station in the nation's largest radio market. Freed's name became a household word. Within a month he was holding down the early evening spot as well as a midnight weekend show. His syndicated broadcast became so popular that Black deejays organized in opposition, fearing that many of them would lose work in their home markets to a personality broadcasting from hundreds of miles away.

The bigger he became, the more enemies he found waiting to knock him off his perch. The first was the original Moondog, a New York street musician, who successfully blocked Freed's use of the term in the New York area. But there would be more to come.

In January 1955, he booked his first New York promotion, featuring Joe Turner, the Drifters, the Clovers, the Moonglows, Fats Domino, and the Harptones. He was courted by record companies eager to have him play their latest releases. He was offered an endless smorgasbord of enticements. Record companies wanted to hire him to develop new talent. He was given partial writer's credit on several new releases in exchange for his promotion over the air. He was presented with every imaginable inducement to play a specific record. The temptation must have been unbearable.

His New York shows on Easter and Labor Day 1955 each ran for a week at the Brooklyn Paramount Theater, and they broke all attendance records. In December 1955 he was presented with several awards at the annual Broadcast Music, Incorporated (BMI) dinner. This was followed immediately by a twelve-day run of his "Holiday Rock 'N Roll Show" at New York's Academy of Music. Certainly, Freed was a force to be reckoned with.

In 1956 he expanded his horizons by appearing in the first of four motion pictures that paralleled the emergence of rock 'n roll: "Rock Around The Clock" and "Don't Knock The Rock," with Bill Haley and his Comets; "Rock, Rock, Rock," which featured two artists with which he had close ties, Chuck Berry and the Moonglows; and "Mister Rock And Roll," with LaVern Baker and Frankie Lymon and the Teenagers. These movies were shot on the cheap, but they accomplished two things, one expected and one a surprise. As expected, the movies broadened the acceptance of rock 'n roll at a time when the music was greatly feared as an evil manifestation of the Devil. The surprise was Freed in the flesh. In his mid-thirties at the time, he looked at least ten years older. He was klutzy. He had no stage presence to speak of. He came off looking very out of place, overbearing, tired, old. To many teens, he looked like the ultimate adult. For Freed, it was the beginning of the end.

He was arrested for inciting a riot in Boston in 1958, following the collapse of one of his rock 'n roll promotions. In 1959, amid growing concern over the methods used to coerce deejays into playing certain records, Freed openly refused to sign an affidavit against accepting money to play records. He was fired from his current job at WABC radio. On February 8, 1960, a House of Representatives subcommittee started hearings on "payola," as it came to be known. On May 19, 1960, a New York Grand Jury formally charged Freed with taking payola. He was the only deejay mentioned by name. He was tried in December 1962 on two counts of bribery and fined $300. In the meantime, he had left New York for sunnier climes, accepting radio jobs in Los Angeles (KDAY) and Miami (WQAM) before returning to the Big Apple to host the Twist Revue at the Camelot Club. On March 16, 1964, he was indicted by a federal grand jury on income tax evasion stemming from his receipt of payola. The Internal Revenue claimed $37,920 in taxes on unreported income of $56,652 for the period 1957-59. Freed never met the charges. He died of uremic poisoning at his home in Palm Springs, California, in 1965.

Freed was a radio personality. That was obvious to everyone but himself. For teen-agers, his "Moondog" show and later his "Rock 'N Roll Party" were required listening wherever they could be picked up. Freed's quick banter, freely spliced with the jive expressions of the day, made him an accepted part of the adolescent world. He sang along with the records though he couldn't hold a note. He pounded out the beat by banging on a telephone book. He howled at the moon and barked like a dog to show his approval of the latest disk. And he refused to play any cover versions, holding out for the original rhythm and blues sound. Teens loved him - on the radio. Adults feared the music and therefore feared his existence. Certainly, he was a scapegoat for the hundreds of deejays who freely partook of the money being offered for playing records. But he had the chance to play the game straight and he chose the high road. It's not easy to turn down a quarter of a million dollars (his earnings for 1957). The best records would have still been hits. Rhythm and blues music would have still evolved into rock 'n roll. And Alan Freed would have still been the king of radio disk jockeys. It just didn't turn out that way.

October 1955

OCT 3   Boyd Bennett and his Rockets open at the Town Casino in Buffalo following their engagement at the Chicago Theater.

New releases for the first week of October include "Greenbacks" by Ray Charles on Atlantic; "Why Oh Why" by the Hawks on Post; "My Heart Belongs To You" by Pat Boone on Republic; **Arthur Lee Maye and the Crowns'** "Please Don't Leave Me" and Ray Hawkins's "If I Had Listened," both on RPM; Carl Van Moon's "Why Does It Have To Be" on Duke; Irene Reed's "I'm So Glad" on Savoy; and two by T-Bone Walker: "Why Not?" on Atlantic and "I Get So Worried" on Post.

Other than Maye, the Crowns consisted of Richard Berry (of the Flairs), Johnny Morris, Johnny Coleman, and Charles Holm. Thomas Fox (who sang with the Penguins, Flairs, Dodgers, and Jacks/Cadets) also appeared frequently with the group.

OCT 6   **Connie Francis** opens for a week at the LaVie Club in New York.

OCT 7   LaVern Baker, Al Hibbler, the El Dorados, and the Red Prysock Combo share the stage for a week at the Apollo Theater in New York.

The second annual "Rock And Roll Dance" is held at the Moose Auditorium in Trenton, New Jersey. Featured performers included the Moonglows/Moonlighters with Arnett Cobb's band.

The Jodimars are booked for a week at the Palace Theater in New York as part of the revue.

Sonny Thompson and the Champions start a three-day stint at the 5-4 Club in Los Angeles.

OCT 8   In Los Angeles, the Medallions, the Gaylarks, and the Calvanes entertain at the Masonic Ballroom for the evening.

The Palace Theater in New Orleans presents the "Big Blues-O-Rama" show, featuring the Cardinals, Little "Junior" Lewis, Jimmy Reed, and Little "Walking" Willie, as the tour winds down. (See August 26th.)

CONNIE FRANCIS

OCT 9   John Lee Hooker and the **Turbans** play a one-nighter at the Stan Pan Bar in Detroit.

OCT 10   Bill Haley joins country music star Hank Snow on a tour with tonight's opening performance in Omaha. Over six thousand attend the show. During the next three days with shows in Lincoln (11) and Topeka (12), almost seventeen thousand will attend. On the 13th, Elvis Presley joins the troupe for a show in Oklahoma City.

The Turbans (who actually did wear turbans on stage) formed in Philadelphia, with Al Banks on lead vocals. Their recording of "When You Dance" was originally released by Herald Records in August 1955. Then another version of the song by the same group showed up as the flip-side of "Emily" by the Turks on Money Records in October 1955.

New releases for the second week of October include "Whole Lotta Shakin' Goin' On" by Roy Hall on Decca; "Ring Dang Doo" by Chuck Willis on Okeh; "Miss The Love" by Otis Williams on DeLuxe; "Love Has Joined Us Together" by Clyde McPhatter and Ruth Brown on Atlantic; "If I Can't Have The One I Love" by the Four Pals on Royal Roost;

MICKEY AND SYLVIA

Mickey and Sylvia's million-selling hit came in 1956 with "Love Is Strange" on Groove. Sylvia Vanderpool went on to record as Sylvia ("Pillow Talk," 1973) on Vibration records, her own label.

Tiny Bradshaw continued to work all over the country out of his Chicago home base until he suffered a series of strokes. He died in Cincinatti in January 1959.

"I Don't Care No More" by the Cats and "Don't Change Your Pretty Ways" by the Midnighters, both on Federal; "Baby Baby What's Wrong" by Earl Gaines and "Calling All Cows" by the Blues Rockers, both on Excello; "Witchcraft" by the Spiders and "Mercy Mercy" by Johnny Fuller, both on Imperial; "Burn That Candle" by the Cues on Capitol; Rusty Bryant's "The Honeydripper" on Dot; "Angels Say" by the Four Fellows on Glory; and "Beyond The Blue Horizon" by Earl Bostic and "Daddy-O" by Bonnie Lou, both on King.

OCT 14   Sonny Til and the newly reformed Orioles share the bill with Joni James at the Chicago Theater for two weeks.

The Apollo Theater in New York hosts Roy Hamilton, the Cardinals, and the Eddie Heywood Combo for the week.

Al Hibbler, Red Prysock, Lillian Briggs, the Moonglows, **Mickey and Sylvia**, and Screamin' Jay Hawkins are at Philadelphia's Academy of Music performing two shows that draw a total of five thousand fans.

In Detroit, Otis Williams and the Charms open at the Roosevelt Lounge for five days.

The 5-4 Ballroom in Los Angeles presents Lowell Fulson and Dakota Staton for the weekend. Also in town, Louis Jordan stops for a night to perform for dancers at the Elks Ballroom before starting a lengthy engagement at the Sands Hotel in Las Vegas.

George Woods, popular rhythm and blues deejay on WHAT radio and successful promoter of local r&b stage shows, is fired. His spot is filled by a man the station manager terms "very sweet and cooperative."

MID-OCTOBER

Performers currently on tour include Fats Domino and Ray Charles playing dates in the Texas-Oklahoma area, Percy Mayfield traveling through the Southwest, **Tiny Bradshaw** working the Midwest, the Midnighters performing for a series of one-nighter dances in the South, and Billy Ward and his Dominoes at Pep's in Philadelphia.

Atlantic Records purchases the small independent label Spark Records of Los Angeles. Atlantic acquires all the master recordings as well as the talents of Spark owners Jerry Leiber and Mike Stoller, well-known songwriters in the rhythm and blues field. The top recording group for Spark Records has been the Robins, but the group has recently split up. A new group will be formed that will feature the lead tenor and bass singers from the Robins.

OCT 16   Pee Wee Crayton plays a one-night stand at the Club Harlem in Los Angeles.

OCT 17   The "Top Ten Revue" plays the Madison Ballroom in Detroit on its one-nighter trek across the country. (See August 26th and October 29th.)

New releases for the third week of October include Chuck Berry's "Thirty Days" and Howlin' Wolf's "Don't Mess With My Baby," both on Chess; Charles Brown's "Trees Trees" on Aladdin; Tony Allen and the Champs' "Nite Owl" and Jesse Belvin's "Love, Love Of My Life," both on Specialty; Rosco Gordon's "Weeping Blues" on Flip; "On Chapel Hill" by the Orioles on Jubilee; Jack Dupree's "Stumbling Block" and the "5" Royales' "Someone Made You For Me," both on King; "Burn That Candle" b/w "Rock A-Beatin' Boogie" by Bill Haley and his Comets on Decca; "Gone Gone Gone" by **Carl Perkins** on Sun; "How Come My Dog Don't Bark (When You Come 'Round)" by Prince Partridge on Crest; and Little Junior Parker's "Driving Me Mad" on Duke. "Smokey Joe's Cafe" by the Robins is released by Atco following an August release on Spark.

CARL PERKINS

Carl Lee Perkins (born Jackson, Tennessee, April 9, 1932) was Elvis Presley's successor at Sun Records in Memphis, and he recorded a string of fine rockabilly classics, the most popular being the 1956 million selling "Blue Suede Shoes."

OCT 20   Roy Milton opens for four days at the Savoy Ballroom in Los Angeles.

OCT 21   The Platters make their New York debut at the Apollo Theater this week. The group just finished eight weeks at the Flamingo Hotel in Las Vegas. Also on the bill is Varetta Dillard.
        Roy Hamilton heads the show in Washington at the Howard Theater for a week.
        The Turks, Johnny "Guitar" Watson, and the Chuck Higgins Combo share the billing for a weekend engagement at the 5-4 Club in Los Angeles.

OCT 27   Roy Milton is back by popular demand at the Savoy Ballroom in Los Angeles for another four-day weekend.

New releases for the fourth week of October include "Adorable" by the Drifters on Atlantic; "Hands Off" by Jay McShann with Priscilla Bowman on Vee-Jay; "Lee's Dream" by **Shirley and Lee** and "Home On Alcatraz" by the Rollin' Crew, both on Aladdin; Titus Turner's "Big John" on Wing; "This Must Be Paradise" by Don Julian and the Meadowlarks on Dootone; "Blues For My Cookie" by Lightnin' Hopkins on Herald; and "She's Gone Too Long" by Roy Brown and "Come In The House" by Joe Tex, both on King.

Shirley and Lee's biggest hit came in 1956 with "Let The Good Times Roll." Shirley Goodman went on to have an early disco hit, 1975's "Shame, Shame, Shame," as Shirley (And Company) on Vibration Records.

OCT 28   The "Lucky Eleven Blues Show" embarks on a three-month tour with a week at the Apollo Theater in New York. The revue features Jack Dupree, Earl King, Little Willie John, Otis Williams, Marie Knight, and Hal "Cornbread" Singer's Band. The tour will make its way through the South and Midwest before finishing about New Year's on the West Coast. (See November 4th.)
        Fats Domino performs for three days at the 5-4 Ballroom in Los Angeles.

OCT 29   The "Top Ten Revue" closes out two months on the road with a triumphant show at Carnegie Hall in New York. This is the first exclusively r&b show to play this venue. Featured performers include Faye Adams, Bo Diddley, the Five Keys, the Clovers, Joe Turner, Bill Doggett, the Charms, Charlie and Ray, Etta James, Gene and Eunice, and the Paul Williams Orchestra. (See August 26th and November 11th.)

New releases for the fifth week of October include Piano Red's "Gordy's Rock" on Groove; **"Speedoo" by the Cadillacs** on JOZ, "Emily" by the Turks on Money; "Please Sing My Blues Tonight" by the Orioles on

"Speedo" by the Cadillacs has an "inside" joke in the opening line: "They often call me Speedo, but my real name is Mister Earl." The lead singer of the group and composer of the song was Earl Carroll, who later joined the Coasters.

275

Jubilee; "Pretty Mama" by Marty Robbins on Columbia; "Jump, Shake And Move" by Nolan Strong and the Diablos on Fortune; "Could It Be" by the Sh-Booms on Cat; "Donna" by Billy Brooks on Duke; and "Tutti Frutti" by Little Richard on Specialty.

THE TOP TEN ROCK 'N ROLL RECORDS FOR OCTOBER 1955

1. Maybellene - Chuck Berry
2. Only You - The Platters
3. Rock Around The Clock - Bill Haley and his Comets
4. All By Myself - Fats Domino
5. I Hear You Knocking - Smiley Lewis
6. Ain't It A Shame - Fats Domino
7. At My Front Door - The El Dorados
8. Why Don't You Write Me - The Jacks
9. All Around The World - Little Willie John
10. It's Love Baby - Louis Brooks

October 1955
ARTIST OF THE MONTH

SMILEY LEWIS

SMILEY LEWIS

(Overton Amos Lemons, b. July 5, 1913; d. October 7, 1966)

In the fall of 1955, just as the steady movement from rhythm and blues to rock 'n roll was becoming a panic-stricken, headlong rout, along comes an artist from another era to remind us of our roots. Smiley Lewis was a pleasant blues artist in the Fats Domino vein; a veritable workhorse of an artist who enjoyed his craft but received almost no recognition for it. He was a crowd pleaser, always welcomed back to the one-room clubs that he frequently played from Texas to the Carolinas. A happy man, jovial and jolly - a tan Santa Claus. Forever smiling and smiling. A bright, round face with an ear-to-ear grin punctuated by a quarter-inch gap between his two front teeth. "Smiley." His nickname described him perfectly.

According to his wife, Overton Lemons was born in DeQuincy, Louisiana, the second of three sons. His mother died when he was young and his father remarried. The family moved to West Lake, Louisiana. By the age of eleven he had either run away or been sent away from home, and he found himself in New Orleans, where he was raised by a White family. Following high school, he joined the Thomas Jefferson Dixieland Band to work nights while he searched for a job during the day. In the early 1940s he worked the Boogie Woogie Club in Bunkie, Louisiana, until the other members of the combo were drafted. He returned to New Orleans, once again in search of a "day job."

After the war, he formed a trio that was an immediate success on the local scene. As "Smiling" Lewis, he was discovered by DeLuxe Records of Cincinnati in 1947, during one of the company's talent scouting expeditions into the Deep South. His recordings only sold well enough to secure work in the south Louisiana area at clubs such as the Dew Drop Inn and the Hideaway. New Orleans' resident rhythm and blues talent scout, Dave Bartholomew, was able to secure a recording contract for Lewis with Imperial Records in 1950. Imperial was looking for another artist from the area who might be developed into another Fats Domino.

In May 1950, "Tee-Nah-Nah" was popular enough to put him on the road for two hundred miles around New Orleans. In 1952 he had his first national hit with "The Bells Are Ringing." His tours expanded to cover Tennessee, Ohio, and the Gulf States, but he regularly returned to New Orleans. His biggest hit came in 1955 with the release of "I Hear You Knocking." The recording features New Orleans veteran Huey Smith on piano playing in the rock 'n roll style of Fats Domino. The song was a best-seller for three months in the late fall of 1955, but only in the narrow rhythm and blues field. Unfortunately for Lewis, "I Hear You Knocking" was immediately covered for the "pop" audience by Gale Storm, who easily sold a million copies.

By 1960 Lewis's contract with Imperial lapsed. After ten years and only two hits he was expendable. He continued to perform in his beloved New Orleans, and he picked up an occasional record deal with Okah, Loma, or Dot. His ascending star had passed him by. While Fats Domino's popularity continued to climb into the 1960s, Lewis remained at home. When he died of stomach cancer in 1966, he was broke and forgotten. Ironically, ten years later he was "rediscovered" during the worldwide resurgence of interest in rhythm and blues.

During his heyday, Smiley Lewis was often referred to as one of the most enjoyable new Orleans artists of the 1950s. The easiest comparison is with Fats Domino, another New Orleans artist and stable-mate of Lewis at Imperial Records. But they displayed differing styles. Lewis was more strident in his delivery. His voice was higher than Domino's and his singing was more forced. Domino represented the easy life in the Crescent City, Lewis the hard life.

November 1955

The Colts were four students from Los Angeles City College, and were discovered by Buck Ram, the manager of the Platters. Their first release, "Adorable" on Vita, was written by Ram, but a cover version by the Drifters outsold that of the Colts by a wide margin.

THE HEARTBEATS

Success for the Heartbeats came with "A Thousand Miles Away" in 1957. Lead vocalist James Sheppard formed Shep and the Limelites a few years later, and hit again in 1961 with "Daddy's Home," an answer to the earlier record.

After one release on Atlas, their name was amended to read The Fi-Tones Quintet. Still later, they recorded as the Fi-Tones on Old Town (1957) and Angeltone (1958-59).

NOV 2   The "Rock 'N Roll Revue" at the Paramount Theater in Los Angeles features Dinah Washington, Big Jay McNeeley, Joe Houston, the Platters, the Penguins, and the **Colts**.

NOV 3   In Los Angeles, Fats Domino is held over for four days at the 5-4 Club, and Johnny Otis and Marie Adams entertain at the Savoy Ballroom for the weekend.

NOV 4   Buddy Johnson's "Big Rock & Roll Show" winds up its two-month-long road trip with a week's stay at Washington's Howard Theater. (See September 9th, 12th, and 25th)
        Joe Turner heads the show for six days at the Flame Show Bar in Detroit.
        Following a successful week at the Apollo Theater in New York, the "Lucky Eleven Blues Show" takes to the road with a performance in Pittsburgh tonight. Other scheduled dates include Cleveland (6); Detroit (7-8); Indianapolis (9); Evansville, Indiana (10); Davenport, Iowa (11); Saginaw, Michigan (12); Toledo (13); Cincinnati (14); Chattanooga (15); Atlanta (16); Tuskeegee, Alabama (17); Jacksonville, Florida (18); Tampa (19); Miami (20); Durham, North Carolina (22); Roanoke (23); and Raleigh (24), before stopping for a week at the Howard Theater in Washington (25). (See October 28th)

New releases for the first week of November include Fats Domino's "Poor Me" on Imperial; "Little" Willie John's "Need Your Love So Bad" and Wynonie Harris's "Shotgun Wedding," both on King; "Gee Whittakers!" by the Five Keys on Capitol; "Lily Maebelle" by the Valentines on Rama; Mercy Dee's "Stubborn Woman" and Elmore James's "Blues Before Sunrise," both on Flair; "Shadows Of Love" by the Pearls; "Yes Sir That's My Baby" by the Sensations, and "Always Look Up" by Nolan Lewis, all on Atco; "Crazy For You" by the **Heartbeats** on Hull; and "Gotta Go" by Louis Jordan on Aladdin.

EARLY NOVEMBER

The **Fi-Tones**, formerly the Cavaliers on Atlas Records, sign with Mercury, and Little Jimmy Scott signs with Savoy.

Screamin' Jay Hawkins is currently playing Spider Kelly's in Philadelphia.

NOV 10   The Savoy Ballroom in Los Angeles presents Dinah Washington for four days. She is also held over for the next weekend.

NOV 11   The "Top Ten Revue" stops for a week at Washington's Howard Theater. Featured performers are the Clovers, the Solitaires, Joe Turner, and the Five Keys. (See October 29th.)

B. B. King performs for the first of two three-day weekends at the 5-4 Club in Los Angeles.

Gene and Eunice share top billing with a mambo revue this week at New York's Apollo Theater.

NOV 12   **Pat Boone** is voted "The Most Promising Male Vocalist" in pop music in *Billboard* magazine's annual disk jockey poll. Elvis Presley is voted the "Most Promising Male Vocalist" in country and western music, while Chuck Berry garners the same award for r&b music. This week, *Billboard* also awards the Platters a "Triple Crown" in rhythm and blues music for topping all three r&b charts with "Only You."

NOV 13   Ray Charles, the Moonglows, Cadillacs, Five Crowns, and Charlie and Ray entertain a large crowd at the Rockland (NY) Palace.

NOV 14   Buddy Johnson and sister Ella open for three days at the Copa in Pittsburgh.

PAT BOONE

New releases for the second week of November include "Let's All Rock Together" by the Jodimars on Capitol; Willie Mabon's "The Seventh Son" on Chess; Oscar McLollie's "Convicted" on Modern; Jimmy Witherspoon's "It Ain't No Secret" on Checker; "We Two" by the Belvederes on Baton; "My Clumsy Heart" by the Jacks on RPM; and "Double Duty Lovin'" by **Eddie Bond** on Ekko.

MID-NOVEMBER

Jules Bihari of Modern Records purchases the California Record Manufacturing Company in Los Angeles, which expands his pressing output to 30,000 singles a day.

Eddie Bond, from Memphis, released several other fine rockabilly singles, including "Love Makes A Fool" (also on Ekko), "Boppin' Bonnie," "Rockin' Daddy," and "Flip, Flop Mama" (all for Mercury).

NOV 16   Ruth Brown, Count Basie, Joe Williams, George Shearing, the Orioles, T-Bone Walker, and the Jacks set off on a tour with a show in Lake Charles, Louisiana.

NOV 17   Ray Charles and the Sensations entertain on a one-night stand at the Town Hall in Philadelphia.

NOV 18   "Hal Jackson's Rhythm And Blues Revue" plays the Apollo Theater in New York for a week. Featured performers include the Valentines, Screamin' Jay Hawkins, the Four Fellows, Arthur Prysock, the Solitaires, the Chuck Berry Trio, and Buddy Johnson's Orchestra featuring Ella Johnson.

Detroit's Flame Show Bar presents Al Hibbler and the Royal Jokers for a week.

NOV 20   **Elvis Presley** signs a three-year contract with RCA Victor Records. His previous recording contract is purchased from Sun Records for $35,000, with Presley receiving an additional $5,000 in back royalties.

"The Ed Sullivan Show" on CBS-TV presents a special fifteen-minute segment hosted by Dr. Jive (Tommy Smalls) that features LaVern Baker, Bo Diddley, and the Five Keys.

Hill and Range Songs put up $15,000 of the $35,000 for Presley's contract in order to obtain the publishing rights to his songs. In later years, this resulted in limitations on the types of material Presley was offered to record.

Lead singer of the Cadets was Aaron Collins. His sisters, Betty and Rose, had a hit with "Eddie My Love" as the Teen Queens in 1956.

Little Willie John's career peaked in 1956 with "Fever" and "Talk To Me." He continued to have hits into 1961. He died May 26, 1968, of pneumonia at age thirty, while serving time at Washington State Prison for manslaughter.

BOBBY CHARLES

"Later Aligator" by Bobby Charles (last name Guidry) was covered by Bill Haley as "See You Later Alligator." Charles wrote several hits for other artists: "But I Do" (Clarence Henry), and "Walking To New Orleans" (Fats Domino).

NOV 21　Bubber Johnson starts a week-long engagement at the New Marinas Club in Washington.

New releases for the third week of November include "Pretty Thing" by Bo Diddley on Checker; "Rock And Roll Wedding" by the Midnighters on Federal; "Will You Love Me" by Marvin and Johnny and "Do You Wanna Rock" by the **Cadets**, both on Modern; "Heavenly Angel" by the Squires on Vita; "Short Circuit" by Red Prysock on Mercury; "I'd Love To Love You" by Brownie McGhee, "Imagination" by Little Jimmy Scott, and "Sittin' In The Dark" by Nappy Brown, all on Savoy; and "Until The Real Thing Comes Along" by the Hearts on Baton.

NOV 23　Bill Haley and his Comets, Johnnie Ray, and LaVern Baker are booked for five days at the Paramount Theater in Brooklyn. Gate receipts exceed $65,000.

NOV 24　Sonny Thompson and Lulu Reed entertain at the Savoy Ballroom in Los Angeles for the weekend.

NOV 25　Chuck Berry, Nappy Brown, Big Maybelle, the Cardinals, the Nutmegs, and the Red Prysock Band share the stage at the Regal Theater in Chicago for the next two weeks.
　　　　The Howard Theater in Washington offers a full bill for the Thanksgiving weekend patrons in the form of the "Lucky Eleven Blues Show": Earl King, Jack Dupree, **Little Willie John**, the Charms, Marie Knight, and the Hal Singer Orchestra. Following this week, the caravan takes off for shows in the South and on the West Coast through January.
　　　　Charlie and Ray entertain nightly at the Flame Show Bar in Detroit for the week.
　　　　In Los Angeles, Guitar Slim, Johnny "Guitar" Watson, and Young Jessie share the weekend bill at the 5-4 Club.

NOV 26　A film short starring Cleveland deejay Bill Randle is cancelled in mid-production because of a dispute between Universal Films, producer of the short, and CBS-TV in New York, where part of the short was to be filmed. Artists scheduled to make an appearance in the short were Bill Haley and his Comets, LaVern Baker, Johnnie Ray, Roy Hamilton, Gloria Mann, the Chordettes, the Crew-Cuts, the McGuire Sisters, and Elvis Presley.
　　　　In New Orleans, the Dew Drop Inn schedules Paul Monday to back the continuous run of strippers.

NOV 27　Fats Domino opens in Los Angeles at the Club Harlem.

New releases for the fourth week of November include "Gee Whittakers!" by Pat Boone on Dot; "Dungaree Doll" by the Rock Brothers and Boyd Bennett's "The Most," both on King; "I Gotta Go Home" by Gene and Eunice and "House Party" by Amos Milburn, both on Aladdin; Etta James' "W-O-M-A-N" on Modern; "Don't Make It So Good" by the Lamplighters on Federal; "Woke Up Screaming" by Bobby Bland on Duke; Willie Dixon's "Crazy For My Baby" on Checker; "I Can't Refuse" by the Orchids on Parrot; "Later Alligator" by **Bobby Charles** on Chess; Johnny "Guitar" Watson's "Oh Baby" on RPM; "Jivin' Around" by the Ernie Freeman Combo on Cash; "Dear Darling" by the Medallions on Dootone; and

"Beetle-Bug Bop" by the Collins Kids on Columbia.

LATE NOVEMBER

Federal Records sues Mercury Records claiming prior rights to the song "Only You" by the Platters. The group had recorded it for Federal in May 1954, but the company thought it was so poorly handled that they refused to release it at the time.

Savoy Records signs bandleaders Hal "Cornbread" Singer and Buddy Lucas to recording contracts.

Earl Bostic is currently on tour along the East Coast.

THE TOP TEN ROCK 'N ROLL RECORDS FOR NOVEMBER 1955

1. Only You - The Platters
2. At My Front Door - The El Dorados
3. I Hear You Knocking - Smiley Lewis
4. Rock Around The Clock - Bill Haley and his Comets
5. Hands Off - Jay McShann with Priscilla Bowman
6. Play It Fair - LaVern Baker
7. All Around The World - Little Willie John
8. All By Myself - Fats Domino
9. Maybellene - Chuck Berry
10. Feel So Good - Shirley and Lee

November 1955
ARTIST OF THE MONTH

THE PLATTERS

Certainly no other vocal group of the early rock 'n roll era had the longevity or commercial success enjoyed by the Platters. But were they singing rock 'n roll in the first place? Their delivery was almost "pop." Almost, but not quite. "Pop" meant controlled, refined, schmaltz. By definition, rock 'n roll was the antithesis of all three. Somewhere in the middle, straddling both worlds, was the Platters, a vocal group that could be enjoyed equally, but for different reasons, by teens and adults, Blacks and Whites.

The nucleus of the Platters was formed in a Los Angeles high school by Cornell Gunter, who left shortly thereafter to join the Flairs and later the Coasters. He was joined by Herbert Reed (bass from Kansas City), David Lynch (second tenor from St. Louis), and Alex Hodge. About this time, Linda Hayes had a hit with "Yes, I Know." When she decided to further her singing career by moving from New Jersey to Hollywood, she brought along her brother, Tony Williams. He had studied music at the Essex Conservatory and had won a few talent contests in theaters like the Apollo in New York. In Los Angeles he found work at the Douglas Aircraft factory, and he continued singing, winning another contest at the Club Alabam. It was here that he met the members of the Platters, who urged him to join the group after Gunter left.

THE PLATTERS

Through his sister he had already made the acquaintance of a talent manager and local lawyer, Buck Ram. Ram, on the other hand, was only interested in Williams if he was as a member of a group, not as a solo artist. The stage was set.

In late 1953 the Platters signed with Federal Records. For the next eighteen months, the group worked diligently with little recognizable success. Record after record was released, each failing to attract the public's attention. By this time the group had added a female voice, Zola Taylor, formerly with Shirley Gunter and the Queens. This novel lineup also fell short of winning popular approval. Alex Hodge decided to call it quits, and his baritone position was filled by Paul Robi from New Orleans. It was time for the manager to earn his ten percent.

In the winter of 1954-55, Buck Ram also represented the Penguins, who were having a major hit with "Earth Angel." At his insistence, the Penguins switched record labels from Dootone, a small independent company, to Mercury, one of the five major record corporations. To sweeten the deal, Ram threw in the Platters' contract. For their first release, the Platters chose a song they had recorded during their days with Federal, but which had been so poorly handled that Federal refused to release it. The song was "Only You."

Released in July 1955, it started building slowly. Disk jockeys on both sides of the music spectrum had difficulty pinning a label on the sound. It certainly wasn't the usual rhythm and blues vocal group record. It also wasn't exactly "pop," but it sure was catchy. Williams's tenor soared and then dropped whole octaves, slid from one note to the other in a graceful ballet of notes. Radio listeners continued to request "Only You" over and over again. Records were being sold for the first time in the group's existence. And what about those personal appearance offers? No more Club Alabam for the Platters. Now it was a four-week engagement in the cabaret of the Flamingo Hotel in Las Vegas, followed by a week headlining the Apollo Theater revue. Television, movies, more hit records, more smash personal appearances, including worldwide tours. It was every vocal group's dream come true, and the dream wasn't over after "Only You." There was "The Great Pretender," "The Magic Touch," "Twilight Time," "Smoke Gets In Your Eyes," "Harbor Lights," and a dozen more hits. From 1955 to the end of the decade, the Platters were the most popular vocal group of the day.

If only it could have lasted forever.

The Platters enjoyed sixteen gold records, a record in itself. They were the first rhythm and blues group to win wide recognition and commercial success in the highly competitive world of popular music. Their stage act was a model for other groups to follow. They never lost their tight grip on the audience, building steadily and surely to an exciting climax singing their current hit song. There is a single word that describes the Platters, and it is "class." They had it in abundance.

(The Platters' story will be continued in Volume 2 of *The Golden Age of American Rock 'N Roll.*)

December 1955

DEC 1   Bubber Johnson starts a four-day engagement at the Veterans Club in Sewickley, Pennsylvania.

The Savoy Ballroom in Los Angeles offers a four-day run featuring Nappy Brown and **Percy Mayfield**.

DEC 2   Fats Domino headlines the three-day weekend show at the 5-4 Club in Los Angeles before leaving on a tour of Texas and the East Coast.

The Apollo Theater in New York features the Cadillacs, the **Pearls**, and the Sil Austin Combo for the week.

DEC 3   Bill Haley and his Comets pack the Keith Theater in Baltimore, with over four thousand showing up for two shows.

DEC 5   Alan Freed receives several awards at the annual Broadcast Music, Incorporated (BMI) dinner in New York for his assistance in getting BMI records played on the radio. Performers during the evening include LaVern Baker.

The Chatterbox Club in Cleveland plays host for a week to the Bubber Johnson Orchestra.

New releases for the first week of December include Ruth Brown's "I Wanna Do More" and Joe Turner's "The Chicken And The Hawk," both on Atlantic; The Great Pretender" by the Platters on Mercury; B. B. King's "I'm Cracking Up Over You" and Richard Berry's "Big John," both on RPM; **Young Jessie**'s "Do You Love Me?" and the Sounds' "So Unnecessary," both on Modern; Johnny Fuller's "Black Cat" on Recorded In Hollywood; and "In My Diary" by the Moonglows on Chess. "Mystery Train" by Elvis Presley is reissued by RCA Victor following his recent label switch.

EARLY DECEMBER

Lloyd Price returns to civilian life after twenty-one months with the U.S. Army.

At the Magnolia Ballroom in Atlanta, the Drifters beat the El Dorados in a mock "Battle Of The Quartets."

Dootone Records signs the Four Pipes and the Cool Notes.

Groove Records announces the signing of a new group from Detroit, the Nitecaps.

Chuck Berry opens for two weeks at the Stage Club in Chicago.

DEC 8   B. B. King begins a four-day stand at the Savoy Ballroom

Percy Mayfield had only one record that made the crossover into the "pop" field: "River's Invitation" on the Tangerine label in 1963. Tangerine was owned by Ray Charles, for whom Mayfield composed "Hit The Road Jack" in 1961.

The Pearls featured Dave Cortez Clowney, who sang with the Valentines in 1956. In 1959, Dave dropped his last name, stopped singing, and recorded a series of popular instrumentals on organ as Dave "Baby" Cortez ("The Happy Organ" on Clock).

Obediah "Young" Jessie (also known as Jessie Obe) was a mainstay in the Los Angeles group scene, recording and/or appearing alternately with the Robins, Flairs, and Coasters.

Jack Dupree was a boxer during the 1930s, hence his nickname, "Champion." His influence on other rhythm and blues pianists extended to Fats Domino and Huey Smith.

in Los Angeles. Also in town, Johnny Otis entertains at the Rutland Inn for the evening, while the Ernie Freeman Combo is playing the Backstage Bar for an extended engagement.

DEC 9   The Flame Show Bar in Detroit presents Willie Mabon for the week. Across town, **Jack Dupree** entertains patrons at the Roosevelt Lounge.
          In New Orleans, the Dew Drop Inn books Larry Darnell for three-day weekends through the end of the year.
          The Turbans and Nolan Strong and the Diablos headline the show at the Apollo Theater in New York.

DEC 11   The Drifters start an engagement at the Lord Calvert Club in Miami.

DEC 12   LaVern Baker headlines the week-long show at the Mastbaum Theater in Philadelphia. Other entertainers include the Valentines, the El Dorados, Screamin' Jay Hawkins, Gloria Mann, Red Prysock, and Bubber Johnson's Orchestra.

New releases for the second week of December include "Here Goes My Heart To You" by the Cardinals on Atlantic; Smiley Lewis's "Come On By" on Imperial; "Whispering Sorrows" by the **Nutmegs** on Herald; "Sugar Sweet" by Muddy Waters on Chess; "I'll Be Forever Loving You" by the El Dorados and "Mambo Chillun'" by John Lee Hooker, both on Vee-Jay; "Sing Sing Sing" by Dean Beard on Fox; "A Christmas Prayer" by the Penguins on Mercury; Joe Turner's "Piney Brown Blues" on Decca; "Searching For You" by the Barons on Imperial; and "Chicken Back" by Louis Jordan on "X."

DEC 15   Joe Houston and Oscar Peterson entertain patrons of the Savoy Ballroom in Los Angeles for four days.

THE NUTMEGS

MID-DECEMBER

Ekko Recording artist Eddie Bond returns to his hometown of Memphis after several play dates in the Louisville, Kentucky, area. His latest release is "Double Duty Lovin'." Ekko's other rockabilly outfit, the Cochran Brothers (Eddie and Hank), have just completed an extended tour that started on the West Coast and wound up in Kansas and Arizona.

In a reverse move, rhythm and blues giant Chess Records starts a "pop" subsidiary, Marterry Records.

Neshui Ertegun joins his brother Ahmet as a partner in Atlantic Records.

DEC 16   Bull Moose Jackson brings his orchestra to the Flame Show Bar in Detroit for a week.
          Joe Turner and Floyd Dixon are appearing at the 5-4 Ballroom in Los Angeles for three days. Also in town, Johnny "Guitar" Watson, Tony Allen and the Champs, the Voices, and the Sounds perform for three days at Bard's Theater in Los Angeles.

DEC 17   Bill Haley and his Comets play the first of two days at the Court Square Theater in Springfield, Massachusetts. They break the house record with a two-day take of $5,500.

Elvis Presley signs for four consecutive appearances on Jackie Gleason's "Stage Show" program that will be broadcast nationally over CBS-TV beginning January 28, 1956. He will be paid $1,250 per show.

New releases for the third week of December include "I Was Dreaming" by the **Cleftones** on Gee; Clyde McPhatter's "Seven Days" on Atlantic; "Love's Our Inspiration" by the Charms on Chart; "That's Your Mistake" by Otis Williams on DeLuxe; Jack Dupree's "Silent Partner" and Earl King's "Time Will Tell," both on King; "I Don't Know" by the Keynotes, "When I'm All Alone" by Solomon Burke, and "My Baby's Love" by the Casanovas, all on Apollo; Lowell Fulson's "I Still Love You Baby" on Checker; "Charlie Brown" by the Cues on Capitol; "Hot Rod" by Hal Singer on Savoy; "Dance With A Rock" by the Esquire Boys on Dot; "Yes My Baby" by the Scamps on Peacock; and "Tippity Top" by the **Rays** on Chess.

The Cleftones' biggest hits came in 1961 with revivals of the standards "Heart And Soul" and "For Sentimental Reasons."

DEC 20   Shirley and Lee with the Joe Jones Orchestra embark on a tour of the South.

DEC 22   LaVern Baker headlines the twelve-day "Rock 'N Roll Holiday" show presented by Alan Freed at the Academy of Music in New York. Also on the bill are the Three Chuckles, the Cadillacs, the **Valentines**, Gloria Mann, the Heartbeats, the Wrens, Boyd Bennett and his Rockets, the Al Sears Orchestra with Sam "The Man" Taylor, and the Count Basie Band with Joe Williams.

The Savoy Ballroom in Los Angeles offers Big Jay McNeeley, the Gaylarks, and Shirley Gunter for a four-day run.

The Rays (which included two former members of the Four Fellows) sold a million copies of "Silhouettes" (1957, Cameo) and had a minor hit with "Magic Moon" (1961, XYZ).

DEC 23   Chuck Berry takes to the road for a two-week tour of one-nighters.

At the Brooklyn Paramount, Dr. Jive opens his holiday revue featuring Pat Boone, Ruth Brown, the Cheers, Bo Diddley, the Five Keys, the Turbans, and Willis Jackson's Orchestra.

Willie Dixon is booked at the Blue Flame in East St. Louis, Illinois, for twelve days.

The Orioles, Sonny Boy Williamson, and Nolan Strong and the Diablos entertain for the week at the Howard Theater in Washington.

Percy Mayfield is scheduled through Christmas at the Rutland Inn in Los Angeles. Also in town, Ray Charles opens for the three-day weekend at the 5-4 Ballroom in Los Angeles.

The Clovers headline the revue at the Apollo Theater for the week.

The Valentines featured Richard Barrett, a proficient songwriter and producer. He discovered Frankie Lymon and the Teenagers, and produced the Chantels, Little Anthony and the Imperials, and the Isley Brothers. Also a member of the Valentines was Ronnie Bright, who sang bass on Johnny Cymbal's "Mr. Bass Man" (1963, Kapp).

DEC 26   Della Reese, the El Dorados, Big Maybelle, the Royal Jokers, and James Moody's Combo entertain at the Graystone Gardens and Ballroom in Detroit.

New releases for the fourth week of December include "See You Later Alligator" by Bill Haley and his Comets on Decca; "Anyway" by the Three Chuckles on "X"; "Forever And A Day" by Mickey and Sylvia on Rainbow; "A Kiss And A Vow" by the Nitecaps on Groove; **Billy Bland's** "Chicken In A Blanket" on Old Town; "Double Date" by the

Billy Bland went on to fame in 1960 with "Let The Little Girl Dance," also on Old Town. "Chicken In The Basket" featured blues harmonica by Sonny Terry.

Five Encores on Rama; "I Want To Be Ready" by the Voices on Cash; "Tennessee Toddy" by Marty Robbins on Columbia; "Move It Or Lose It" by Johnny Janis on Coral; "One Kiss" by the Calvanes on Dootone; and "Tarzan And The Dignified Monkey" by Willie Mae Thornton on Peacock. RCA Victor reissues the remaining four singles by Elvis Presley picked up in his trade from Sun: "That's All Right," "Good Rockin' Tonight," "Milkcow Blues Boogie," and "Baby Let's Play House."

DEC 29   The Drifters return to Atlanta's Magnolia Gardens, the site of their success in the recent "Battle Of The Quartets."

Johnny Otis plays a one-nighter at the Rutland Inn in Los Angeles.

DEC 30   Lloyd Price, the Turbans, Bubber Johnson's Band, and the Cardinals are featured in the "Happy New Year Revue" at the Howard Theater in Washington.

Faye Adams starts a week's engagement at the Flame Show Bar in Detroit.

In Los Angeles, Louis Jordan plays for two nights at the Savoy Ballroom, Joe Turner and Floyd Dixon open for the three-day weekend at the 5-4 Club, and Chuck Higgins and his band are at the Rutland Inn through New Year's Eve.

DEC 31   The Plaza Theater in Buffalo, New York, boasts a fine New Year's Eve lineup with Clyde McPhatter headlining the show.

Screamin' Jay Hawkins plays the Mandy Lounge in Buffalo, New York.

The New Year's Eve party at the Shrine Auditorium in Los Angeles features the newly re-formed **Robins**, Joe Turner, Oscar McLollie, Gene and Eunice, and the Calvanes.

LATE DECEMBER

Bull Moose Jackson, formerly with King Records, and Savannah Churchill, previously with Decca and Victor, sign with Chess Records.

The music press reports that 1955 record sales are up more than forty percent over 1954.

The "new" Robins were comprised of original members Bobby Nunn and Carl Gardner, who joined Billy Guy (of Bip and Bop), Leon Hughes (from the Lamplighters), and guitarist Adolph Jacobs. Only one single was issued on Atco by the Robins before they changed their name to the Coasters.

THE TOP TEN ROCK 'N ROLL RECORDS FOR DECEMBER 1955

1. Only You - The Platters
2. Hands Off - Jay McShann and Priscilla Bowman
3. Poor Me - Fats Domino
4. Adorable - The Drifters
5. Tutti Frutti - Little Richard
6. Play It Fair - LaVern Baker
7. Feel So Good - Shirley and Lee
8. The Great Pretender - The Platters
9. All Around The World - Little Willie John
10. At My Front Door - The El Dorados

December 1955
SPECIAL RECOGNITION

AHMET ERTEGUN AND ATLANTIC RECORDS

It is safe to say that without Atlantic Records, the changes that took place in music during the years 1952 through 1955 would have been vastly different. Not that the change would have been averted altogether, it is just that the sound of rock 'n roll after 1955 would not have been the same. Looking back over those four years, the importance of this single record company is astounding in its breadth. From January 1952 until September 1955, Atlantic Records has at least one record (and often as many as three) on the monthly top ten charts in this book. No other company can boast such continuous popularity. In all, Atlantic placed thirty-three songs on the charts for those four years. And it all started with a smallish man, his brother, their friend, and their collection of jazz records.

AHMET ERTEGUN

Ahmet and Neshui Ertegun were the sons of the Turkish ambassador to the United States in the late 1930s. As teen-agers they amassed one of the largest collections of jazz records in this country, which reached a total number in excess of fifteen thousand. Together with their friend, Herb Abramson, a government employee in Washington, they staged frequent jazz jam sessions and recitals at the Turkish embassy, which led to the production of several well-received concerts in halls around Washington. The structure of these concerts was unique in that the musicians were chosen solely on their popularity among the trio, with little other regard. This led to some exciting music as the performers played off each other, trying new techniques, new tonal forms. World War II and college split up the trio. Abramson joined the Army and studied dentistry. Ahmet attended several colleges, finally studying for his Ph.D. in philosophy at Georgetown University in Washington. Neshui traveled to the West Coast, where he started a small record company specializing in jazz. He also began teaching courses in folk and jazz at UCLA.

After the war, Abramson continued to study dentistry in Baltimore while acting as a talent scout and recording director for National Records, the label of the Orioles, the Ravens, Joe Turner, and Billy Eckstine. He left National to start his own gospel record company, Jubilee, but he sold it within a year. Ahmet was a frequenter of the Quality Record Shop near the Howard Theater when he was not studying at nearby Georgetown. Here, he patiently watched to see which records appealed to the buyers. He talked to customers to glean their tastes, and in October 1947 he and Abramson incorporated Atlantic Records. Almost immediately they, and all other record companies, were hit with a musician's union ban on recording that would commence on January 1, 1948. The two partners spent every dime they could muster during the last two months of 1947 recording any artist or band who would sit still for their microphone. By the deadline they had amassed over two hundred titles. Not all were choice pieces, but there was enough material to sustain the label. The men moved to New York and set up a small office in a two-room suite in the Jefferson Hotel. Ahmet slept in the bedroom; the living room was the first office of Atlantic Records.

Their first releases were by trumpet-playing bandleader Joe Morris ("The Spider") and guitarist Tiny Grimes ("That Old Black Magic" and

"Blue Harlem"). During the first year, Atlantic stayed with the jazz music that the owners knew so well. Sales were slow but not stagnant. Distributors were taking a few copies of each title, but the label desperately needed a hit. In early 1949 Ahmet was tipped by one of his Southern distributors about a record that was stirring local play action. Originally recorded on the Harlem label, "Drinkin' Wine Spo-Dee-O-Dee" by Stick McGhee had been around for a few years. Ahmet found McGhee and had him re-record the song for Atlantic. The record took off in the Deep South, and even though the Harlem master was purchased and released by Decca Records, one of the five major record companies, it was the Atlantic release that garnered the sales. This was just the boost the new owners needed to steady their confidence.

Another tip, from the owner of the Quality Record Shop back in Washington, led to Ruth Brown, who was singing in a local club. She was to be Atlantic's first star. In 1949 her "So Long" was the first Atlantic release to make the national rhythm and blues sales charts. Almost yearly after that, the company was fortunate enough to add another best-selling artist to its stable: the Clovers and Joe Turner (1951), Ray Charles (1952), and LaVern Baker and Clyde McPhatter and the Drifters (1953).

In 1953, Abramson was called away to finish his tour with the Army, and Ahmet hired Jerry Wexler away from Big Three Music to be his co-producer. In late 1955, Neshui returned from Los Angeles to run Atlantic's album and jazz departments. With the return of Abramson shortly thereafter, the management of Atlantic Records was set.

There are several reasons Atlantic rapidly became a major force in the new rhythm and blues field. First, being naive businessmen, the men took risks that more experienced entrepreneurs would have shunned. Atlantic tried many musical styles, starting with jazz and blues, but they branched into country (including one very early single by Bill Haley and his Saddlemen), spoken word, and virtually any other project that took their fancy. Secondly, they had the unshakable reputation of being honest with their artists. In a time when Black artists were frequently paid a stipend for the actual session and then nothing for royalties on record sales, Atlantic made sure that each artist had a contract and that both sides lived up to it. While most rhythm and blues artists shifted company loyalties on a daily basis, the roster of Atlantic artists remained solid. Third, Atlantic prided itself on obtaining the finest New York jazz and blues musicians to back the vocalists, and the best songwriters to provide fresh material. Too many record companies fell into the trap of trying to repeat their past hit sounds. Atlantic built on each previous record while not duplicating it. Finally, Atlantic perfected an advanced recording technique under the supervision of engineer Tom Dowd, who started with the company as a teen-ager. While they did not use expensive equipment in the beginning (recordings were made in the same room that served as the office), Dowd was able to achieve a sound that was clean enough that each instrument could be heard clearly.

Songwriter, talent coordinator, and record producer Jesse Stone, one of the major contributors at Atlantic, feels that the key to Atlantic's early success was the ability to write r&b music that had previously been spontaneous. Everyone agrees that Atlantic's emphasis on "the beat" was equally important. Also, Atlantic never had the strong ties to the blues community which other independent companies found made

288

it difficult to combine gospel feelings with r&b words. Finally, Atlantic always conscientiously attempted to release records with a commercial sound.

In mid-1954, the rhythm and blues assault on the "pop" music world was led by Atlantic. The records by Joe Turner, the Drifters, and Ruth Brown sold equally well on both sides of the racial line. The Chords' "Sh-Boom" became one of the first records to actually compete sale-for-sale with a "pop" cover version. Atlantic felt the squeeze from cover versions more than most other r&b companies for the very reason that their records were so tightly arranged, and therefore easy to duplicate. As mentioned above, the first month since January 1952 that Atlantic did not have a top ten record on the charts was September 1955, which came in the middle of the dramatic crossover of rhythm and blues into the "pop" market. Why, after years as the top r&b company, would Atlantic suddenly falter?

The answer again lies in the methods that Atlantic used to record their songs. Most r&b artists wrote and produced their own records, while Atlantic's artists were more often than not given songs written for them by Stone (often using the pen name Charles Calhoun), Ahmet Ertegun (writing as A. Nugetre), and, starting in 1955, Jerry Leiber and Mike Stoller. Also, Atlantic at this crucial time did not have an r&b artist with the same appeal for the rock 'n roll audience as Fats Domino (Imperial), Little Richard (Specialty), or Chuck Berry (Chess).

Atlantic, of course, was able to change with the times. They immediately bounced back, and from 1956 to the early 1960s they had major rock 'n roll hits with the Coasters, the Bobettes, Bobby Darin, Chuck Willis, Ivory Joe Hunter, and the re-formed Drifters. Their affiliation with the Memphis/Muscle Shoals studio labels, Stax and Volt, led to a major presence in the soul revolution of the 1960s, with Aretha Franklin, Wilson Pickett, Otis Redding, Joe Tex, Sam and Dave, Carla Thomas, Solomon Burke, King Curtis, Barbara Lewis, Booker T. and the MG's, Percy Sledge, Johnny Taylor, the Dramatics, and Ben E. King. From the late 1960s through the 1980s Atlantic was a leader in rock music with Led Zeppelin, Iron Butterfly, Cream, the Rascals, Sonny and Cher, Eric Clapton, AC/DC, Twisted Sister, Phil Collins and Genesis, Laura Branagan, the Rolling Stones, and Crosby, Stills, and Nash.

This longevity is amazing. From the earliest releases in 1948 to the most current rock music of today, Atlantic has continued to be a major force in the music of rock 'n roll. The reason, simply put, is that Ahmet, Neshui, Herb, and Jerry never lost sight of their reason for starting Atlantic Records in the first place: they loved the music.

Shake Rattle & Roll

THE GOLDEN AGE
OF
AMERICAN ROCK 'N ROLL

INDEXES

Performer Index

In order to make the contents of this book more fully accessible, I have instituted a method of citation based on references to the dates mentioned herein:

KEY TO CITATIONS

By day: 1/15/52 = January 15, 1952

By week: F/1/52 = First week of January 1952; F = 1st week, S = 2nd week, T = 3rd week, Fo = 4th week, Fi = 5th week

Also: E/1/52 = Early January 1952; E = Early, M = Mid, L = Late

Date in boldface: Refers to sidebar

Date in italics: Refers to photo (possibly with sidebar as well)

SINGERS, SAXMEN AND GUITAR SLINGERS

A

Ace, Buddy **E/2/55**

Ace, Johnny S/8/52, M/8/52, L/8/52, 10/3/52, E/11/52, 11/18/52, T/1/53, E/3/53, 3/14/53, Fi/6/53, 8/9/53, 8/21/53, T/9/53, 10/23/53, 12/2/53, T/12/53, 1/23/54, L/1/54, E/3/54, 3/14/54, E/4/54, 4/23/54, 5/7/54, T/5/54, E/6/54, M/7/54, T/9/54, 11/19/54, 12/24/54, T/1/55, F/2/55, E/2/55, Fo/2/55, E/3/55, 3/16/55, T/7/55

Adams, Alberta E/7/53

Adams, Faye **Fo/1/53**, L/7/53, S/9/53, M/10/53, 10/16/53, 11/13/53, 11/18/53, Fi/11/53, 1/8/54, 1/15/54, 2/1/54, 2/12/54, F/3/54, M/3/54, S/5/54, T/7/54, 8/6/54, 9/12/54, F/11/54, 11/12/54, 12/10/54, 1/21/55, T/1/55, 1/28/55, 2/25/55, 2/26/55, T/3/55, 4/18/55, 5/11/55, 6/24/55, 7/29/55, 8/26/55, S/9/55, 10/29/55, 12/30/55

Adams, Marie **2/17/52**, S/8/52, **L/8/52**, F/9/52, 2/14/53, M/3/53, 7/5/53, 8/30/53, L/10/53, 11/24/53, T/2/54, 3/5/54, 8/19/54, 10/29/54, 12/27/54, 2/21/55, Fo/3/55, T/8/55, 11/3/55

Agee, Ray Fo/9/52, **F/8/55**

Alladins **T/4/55**

Allen, Annisteen **T/2/53**, S/5/53, 10/2/53, 12/25/53, T/2/55

Allen, James M/4/53

Allen, Jesse 2/9/52, Fo/4/52, F/9/54, **4/10/55**

Allen, Lee **2/2/52**, 6/5/53, F/7/54

Allen, Tony and the Champs T/10/55, 12/16/55

Ammons, Gene 2/1/52, **6/22/52**, 1/1/53, 1/16/53, T/5/53, **11/20/53**, 2/28/54, 10/29/54, M/12/54, 2/11/55, 6/24/55, 7/29/55

Andrews, Debbie E/2/53

Andrews, Lee and the Hearts **Fo/5/54**

Angels T/1/55

Archibald F/12/52

Armstrong, Louis 2/20/53, M/3/53

August, Joseph "Mr. Google Eyes" **L/10/53**, T/12/53, 10/1/54

Austin, Sil **L/6/54**, 9/5/55, 9/19/55, 12/2/55

Avalon, Frankie **F/3/54**

B

Bachelors Fo/1/54

Bailey, Joe L/5/52

Bailey, John "Buddy" E/5/54

Bailey, Pearl 4/11/52, 4/18/52, 5/16/52, 5/1/53

Baker, LaVern **1/1/52**, 3/15/52, Fo/7/52, E/8/52, 8/17/52, 9/12/52, 12/12/52, 1/1/53, 1/9/53, 1/16/53, **Fo/2/53**, 4/6/53, 5/15/53, 5/29/53, 6/12/53, 7/24/53, *E/8/53*, Fo/8/53, L/3/54, 5/14/54, F/6/54, 8/6/54, 9/12/54, 10/8/54, 10/22/54, T/11/54, 11/19/54, 1/28/55, 2/4/55, 2/5/55, 2/26/55, 3/4/55, L/3/55, 4/8/55, S/4/55, M/4/55, 4/22/55, 4/24/55, 4/27/55, 4/30/55, 5/13/55, 6/13/55, 6/27/55, 7/24/55, 8/2/55, 8/8/55, 9/2/55, 9/30/55, Fo/9/55, 10/7/55, 11/20/55, 11/23/55, 11/26/55, 12/5/55, 12/12/55, 12/22/55

Baker, Mickey S/10/52, F/12/52, E/2/55, Fo/3/55, 4/8/55

Barlow, Dean (See also Crickets) 4/29/55, E/5/55, T/5/55, 6/17/55, Fo/7/55

Barnett, Charlie 12/24/52, 5/14/54

Barons F/11/53, Fo/3/55, Fo/7/55, S/12/55

Bartholomew, Dave **2/24/52**, Fo/2/52, 3/7/52, 3/20/52, 4/14/52, F/5/52, **5/25/52**, **9/21/52**, F/12/52, 4/24/53, Fo/9/54, 10/15/54, 10/23/54, 2/12/55, 8/11/55

Bascomb, Paul S/6/52

Basie, Count 2/8/52, 2/20/52, 5/9/52,
    5/16/52, 6/20/52, 2/27/53, 4/8/53,
    4/17/53, 10/23/53, **11/15/53**, 1/28/54,
    5/28/54, 5/31/54, 6/18/54, 6/20/54,
    E/12/54, *5/14/55*, S/6/55, 11/15/55,
    12/22/55
Bateman, Eddie M/1/54
Baughn, David 5/7/54
Bayou, Duke Fo/7/52
Bayou Boys S/12/52
Beard, Dean T/6/55, S/12/55
Beard, Herbert S/7/53
Beecher, Francis 9/24/55
Bell, Freddie and the Bellboys **F/4/55**
Belvederes Fo/9/55, S/11/55
Belvin, Jesse (See also Jesse and Marvin)
    T/7/52, L/1/53, Fo/4/55, 5/13/55,
    T/10/55
Bennett, Boyd and his Rockets **S/1/55**,
    F/2/55, T/2/55, **S/5/55**, Fi/5/55, L/7/55,
    9/2/55, T/9/55, 10/3/55, Fo/11/55,
    12/22/55
Bennett, Tony 9/2/55
Berry, Chuck Fo/7/55, 8/15/55, 9/2/55,
    9/9/55, 9/10/55, 9/12/55, 9/25/55,
    T/10/55, 11/12/55, 11/18/55, 11/25/55,
    E/12/55, 12/23/55
Berry, Richard S/10/53, F/6/54, **S/10/54**,
    1/28/55, Fo/2/55, 4/1/55, T/5/55,
    Fi/8/55, F/12/55
Big, Little Billy M/4/52
Big Maybelle *M/10/52*, F/12/52, 1/1/53,
    1/8/53, 1/16/53, 1/26/53, 2/20/53,
    3/6/53, 3/13/53, 4/3/53, Fo/4/53,
    5/15/53, S/8/53, 4/19/54, Fo/4/54,
    7/4/54, 9/12/54, S/10/54, **10/22/54**,
    10/29/54, 2/11/55, S/5/55, 6/24/55,
    7/5/55, 11/25/55, 12/26/55
Big Mike T/3/55
Big Walter F/1/55, S/2/55
Billy Williams Quartet S/1/52, 2/2/52,
    3/1/52, 3/21/52, 10/14/54
Binkley, Jimmy F/3/54
Bip and Bop T/4/55
Black, Oscar "Big Blues" L/1/52, F/2/55
Blackwell, Bumps **8/10/52**, 11/2/52, **4/5/53**
Blackwell, Otis **T/3/53**, Fo/10/53, E/11/53,
    F/2/54, S/5/54, T/6/54, Fo/10/54,
    F/3/55, 4/2/55, S/4/55
Blanchard, Edgar 2/14/53
Bland, Billy **Fo/12/55**
Bland, Bobby "Blue" Fo/11/5, S/10/53,
    T/5/55, Fo/11/55
Blasers T/8/55
Blazer Boy S/8/53

Blenders 3/21/52, T/4/52, M/4/53, T/5/53,
    F/7/53, T/9/53, **E/11/54**, S/11/54
Blue Diamonds F/9/54
Blue Dots S/10/54, S/12/54
Blue Flamers S/3/54
Blue Jays S/10/53
Blues Chasers F/1/53
Blues Rockers S/10/55
Boines, Houston Fo/8/52
Bond, Eddie S/11/55, M/12/55
Bond, Luther and the Emeralds M/2/54,
    Fo/2/54, 7/4/54, F/7/54
Bonnie Lou **F/2/55**, S/10/55
Boone, Pat E/7/54, 2/12/55, Fo/2/55,
    5/13/55, T/6/55, L/7/55, 8/26/55,
    Fo/9/55, F/10/55, *11/12/55*, Fo/11/55,
    12/23/55
Bostic, Earl 1/1/52, 5/25/52, 5/26/52,
    6/9/52, 7/13/52, 7/29/52, 8/24/52,
    Fo/8/52, 9/29/52, 10/17/52, 10/31/52,
    S/12/52, 12/19/52, 12/24/52, 1/8/53,
    1/9/53, 2/20/53, F/13/53, 3/15/53,
    4/24/53, 5/10/53, S/5/53, F/7/53,
    8/17/53, M/9/53, 3/26/54, 3/30/54,
    S/4/54, M/4/54, 5/2/54, 6/4/54,
    6/15/54, 6/26/54, Fo/6/54, 7/1/54,
    7/9/54, F/8/54, 8/8/54, 9/10/54,
    9/28/54, S/10/54, 11/5/54, Fo/11/54,
    11/29/54, 12/6/54, 12/15/54, 12/22/54,
    1/29/55, Fo/1/55, 2/19/55, 2/28/55,
    3/7/55, 3/8/55, 3/16/55, 4/7/55,
    4/22/55, 4/29/55, T/5/55, 5/18/55,
    6/8/55, 7/15/55, 7/22/55, 8/15/55,
    S/10/55, L/11/55
Bowman, Priscilla Fo/10/55
Boyd, Eddie Fo/7/52, M/8/52, 2/1/53,
    S/3/53, 3/20/53, 4/3/53, F/6/53,
    M/9/53, T/11/53, S/2/54, F/9/54,
    12/3/54, Fo/12/54, Fo/4/55, Fo/9/55
Bradshaw, Tiny 1/1/52, 1/28/52, **T/2/52**,
    3/7/52, 4/14/52, 4/21/52, Fo/4/52,
    5/2/52, 5/12/52, 5/29/52, 6/23/52,
    6/27/52, Fi/6/52, 7/8/52, E/8/52,
    9/4/52, 9/20/52, T/11/52, 1/23/53,
    2/20/53, T/5/53, **7/3/53**, 7/27/53,
    10/4/53, 11/6/53, 12/7/53, 2/26/54,
    M/4/54, 4/19/54, T/5/54, 5/22/54,
    5/24/54, T/6/54, L/6/54, 7/16/54,
    8/1/54, E/8/54, T/10/54, E/11/54,
    12/20/54, 1/17/55, **M/10/55**
Brenston, Jackie **5/11/52**
Briggs, Lillian 8/3/55, 9/2/55, 10/14/55
Brooks, Billy S/6/55, L/7/55, Fi/10/55
Brooks, Hadda M/2/52, L/8/52, 12/12/52,
    5/14/54

Brooks, Louis Fo/4/54, T/4/55
Brown, Bennie Fo/3/53
Brown, Boots and his Blockbusters F/1/53,
    2/21/53
Brown, Charles **T/1/52**, S/2/52, 2/17/52,
    2/22/52, 3/14/52, 4/2/52, 4/17/52,
    4/27/52, 4/28/52, Fo/4/52, 5/1/52,
    E/5/52, 7/11/52, 8/2/52, F/8/52,
    8/11/52, M/8/52, 8/16/52, 8/29/52,
    9/26/52, 9/30/52, 10/19/52, 10/25/52,
    L/10/52, 11/1/52, 11/15/52, F/11/52,
    12/31/52, E/1/53, **2/13/53**, 2/27/53,
    3/20/53, 3/26/53, 3/26/53, 3/30/53,
    4/19/53, 4/25/53, T/6/53, 7/18/53,
    8/28/53, 9/27/53, 9/30/53, 10/18/53,
    T/10/53, 11/2/53, 11/4/53, Fo/11/53,
    E/12/53, 1/22/54, 1/24/54, Fo/1/54,
    4/1/54, 5/1/54, 5/23/54, Fo/5/54,
    E/6/54, M/6/54, L/7/54, 8/20/54,
    9/3/54, S/9/54, 9/17/54, 10/1/54,
    M/10/54, 11/26/54, 12/10/54, 12/17/54,
    12/31/54, 1/21/55, 1/28/55, F/2/55,
    2/11/55, **2/18/55**, 3/18/55, Fo/4/55,
    T/6/55, T/10/55
Brown, Clarence "Gatemouth" 2/17/52,
    4/13/52, 4/20/52, **4/25/52**, E/5/52,
    6/22/52, **T/7/52**, 8/12/52, E/11/52,
    11/27/52, E/12/52, **12/28/52**, L/1/53,
    4/5/53, Fo/7/53, S/12/53, **M/12/53**,
    2/5/54, E/5/54, 12/3/54
Brown, Earl T/9/52
Brown, Gabriel F/1/53
Brown, J. T. Fo/7/54
Brown, Nappy E/5/54, S/5/54, S/10/54,
    T/3/55, 5/20/55, 6/3/55, T/6/55,
    7/10/55, L/7/55, Fo/8/55, 9/2/55,
    T/11/55, 11/25/55, 12/1/55
Brown, Nature Boy T/7/52
Brown, Piney 7/4/52, S/9/52, Fo/6/53,
    8/29/54
Brown, Roy 1/19/52, 1/28/52, 2/2/52,
    S/3/52, 5/25/52, 6/1/52, *E/6/52*,
    6/19/52, 7/3/52, 7/6/52, 7/26/52,
    E/8/52, M/8/52, **8/16/52**, 9/5/52,
    10/10/52, 12/7/52, F/2/53, **Fi/3/53**,
    T/4/53, 5/25/53, 6/14/53, Fi/6/53,
    7/12/53, 7/17/53, S/11/53, F/1/54,
    1/15/54, Fo/1/54, 2/13/54, **2/19/54**,
    2/26/54, F/4/54, M/4/54, T/5/54,
    Fo/6/54, S/8/54, M/9/54, Fo/10/54,
    M/12/54, 1/14/55, 1/28/55, Fo/7/55,
    M/8/55, Fo/10/55
Brown, Ruth 1/1/52, 1/18/52, 1/28/52,
    2/1/52, 2/4/52, S/3/52, 3/17/52, E/5/52,
    L/5/52, 6/6/52, 6/13/52, 7/4/52,

7/11/52, 7/18/52, F/8/52, 8/9/52,
    Fo/8/52, 8/31/52, 9/23/52, F/10/52,
    10/31/52, 11/29/52, 1/23/53, Fo/1/53,
    2/6/53, 2/27/53, 3/2/53, 3/9/53,
    3/16/53, 3/23/53, 4/3/53, 4/5/53,
    4/16/53, T/4/53, 4/26/53, M/5/53,
    5/18/53, 5/20/53, Fo/5/53, 5/28/53,
    6/9/53, 6/15/53, 6/22/53, 7/3/53,
    8/9/53, 9/11/53, S/9/53, 9/20/53,
    9/25/53, 9/26/53, 10/3/53, 10/9/53,
    10/18/53, 10/23/53, 11/1/53, 11/2/53,
    11/24/53, 12/14/53, 1/22/54, Fo/1/54,
    1/29/54, 2/5/54, 2/19/54, 2/23/54,
    3/14/55, F/4/54, 4/16/54, T/4/54,
    4/23/54, 6/1/54, 6/4/54, 6/20/54,
    6/25/54, T/7/54, 8/2/54, 8/13/54,
    8/23/54, 10/1/54, F/10/54, F/1/55,
    1/12/55, 3/4/55, 3/8/55, 3/10/55,
    3/11/55, 4/1/55, Fo/4/55, 5/15/55,
    6/17/55, M/7/55, F/8/55, 8/5/55,
    8/12/55, 9/9/55, S/10/55, 11/16/55,
    F/12/55, 12/23/55
Brown, ("Little") Tommy S/10/53
Brown, Wini 4/4/52, 5/23/52, 6/2/52,
    7/4/52, **E/8/52**, 10/10/52, 11/2/52,
    F/2/53, 5/16/53, 7/3/53, 9/10/54
Bryant, Beula E/1/53
Bryant, Rusty F/3/54, **8/6/54**, 9/13/54,
    9/17/54, S/11/54, F/2/55, 3/1/55,
    6/10/55, 7/3/55, 8/9/55, S/10/55
Buccaneers E/12/52, F/2/53, M/4/53
Buckner, Milt 11/4/53, 11/24/53
Buddy and Bob **6/3/55**
Buffington, Jim 9/24/55
Bumble Bee Slim F/2/52
Bunn, Allen L/1/52, T/3/52, T/6/52, **F/6/53**
Bunn, Billy and his Buddies F/2/52,
    2/22/52, Fo/4/52
Burke, Solomon T/12/55
Burney, Mac and the Four Jacks F/2/55
Butera, Sam F/3/54, **5/1/54**
Butler, Cliff and the Doves Fo/8/53
Butters, Sam E/10/53
Byrd, Roy (See also Professor Longhair)
    S/5/52

C
Cabineers 1/11/52, Fo/1/52
Cadillacs *4/2/55*, 4/10/55, 7/8/55, F/8/55,
    Fi/10/55, 12/2/55, 12/22/55
Cadets *F/5/55*, **F/6/55**, **T/11/55**
Californians Fo/7/55
Callender, Red 4/30/54
Calloway, Cab 1/4/52
Calvanes Fo/9/55, 10/8/55, Fo/12/55,

12/31/55
Cameos T/6/55
Campbell, Choker 3/13/53, E/12/53,
    12/17/54, 6/6/55
Cardinals **F/2/52**, *3/14/52, 3/21/52,* 5/17/52,
    F/8/52, **Fo/5/53**, **T/4/54**, E/2/55,
    Fo/2/55, S/6/55, 6/24/55, 7/10/55,
    8/26/55, 9/2/55, 9/9/55, 10/8/55,
    10/14/55, 11/25/55, S/12/55, 12/30/55
Carols M/5/53, F/6/53
Carpenter, Ike T/2/53, T/4/53, Fo/6/53
Carpenter, Thelma 9/6/52, 10/10/52
Carter, Betty 9/26/52, 2/13/53, 4/17/53
Carter, Sonny F/10/54
Casanovas F/4/55, S/6/55, S/8/55, T/12/55
Cashmeres F/12/54, S/5/55, T/9/55
Castelles Fi/8/54, Fo/10/54
Cat Men F/8/54
Cats S/10/55
Cats and a Fiddle M/6/52
Cavaliers M/8/55, E/11/55
Champion, Mickey F/7/52
Champions M/8/55, 10/7/55
Chanters **F/10/54**
Chanticlaires F/11/54
Chapters S/5/53
Charioteers 5/2/52, F/6/52, M/7/53, E/8/53
Charles, Bobby *Fo/11/55*
Charles, Ray T/2/52, 5/31/52, 6/23/52,
    S/7/52, M/8/52, Fo/8/52, 8/30/52,
    9/12/52, F/10/52, S/10/52, 12/12/52,
    12/19/52, Fi/12/52, Fo/1/53, Fo/2/53,
    F/7/53, 8/9/53, 8/21/53, Fo/9/53,
    10/23/53, 3/5/54, T/3/54, S/7/54,
    8/2/54, 8/13/54, E/11/54, 4/18/55,
    5/1/55, S/6/55, 9/25/55, F/10/55,
    M/10/55, 11/17/55, 12,23/55
Charlie and Ray T/10/54, 2/18/55, Fo/2/55,
    4/10/55, F/5/55, 5/20/55, 6/10/55,
    8/19/55, 8/26/55, F/9/55, 10/29/55,
    11/25/55
Charmers S/2/54
Charms T/8/53, L/10/53, Fo/1/54, Fo/4/54,
    F/8/54, Fo/9/54, 12/3/54, S/12/54,
    1/28/55, F/2/55, 2/26/55, Fo/2/55,
    3/24/55, Fo/4/55, 5/14/55, 6/8/55,
    S/6/55, 7/1/55, L/7/55, 8/26/55, T/9/55,
    10/14/55, 10/29/55, 11/25/55, T/12/55
Checkers **S/9/52**, T/11/52, 12/5/52,
    12/26/52, T/5/53, F/11/53, F/1/54,
    2/19/54, Fo/4/54, S/6/54, 11/8/54,
    S/11/54, 12/21/54, S/1/55
Cheers S/9/54, **12/27/54, F/9/55**, 12/23/55
Chenier, Clifton **Fi/5/55**
Cherokees M/7/55

Chestnuts E/11/54, **T/11/54**
Chimes S/9/54, S/9/55
Chordcats (See also Chords, Sh-Booms)
    E/11/54, T/12/54, 3/25/55
Chordettes **F/10/53**, 11/26/55
Chords (on Cat; see also Chordcats, Sh-
    Booms) E/4/54, Fo/4/54, **E/6/54**,
    E/7/54, M/7/54, 7/17/54, E/8/54,
    8/27/54, 9/3/54, S/9/65, 10/22/54,
    10/23/54, E/11/54
Chords (on Gem) F/1/54, E/11/54
Chromatics F/7/55
Chuckles (See Three Chuckles)
Churchill, Savannah 1/18/52, 4/25/52,
    6/13/52, **L/7/52**, 10/6/52, 1/1/53,
    2/26/53, 3/5/53, 4/10/53, **5/1/53**,
    E/8/53, F/9/53, 10/9/53, 10/22/53,
    Fo/10/53, *3/19/54*, 12/10/54, 9/30/55,
    L/12/55
Cincinatians M/4/53
Clark, Eddie T/6/54
Cleftones **T/12/55**
Clicks F/8/55
Clovers 2/9/52, S/3/52, 3/28/52, 4/18/52,
    4/19/52, L/5/52, 6/15/52, F/7/52,
    8/2/52, M/8/52, 8/29/52, 9/5/52,
    9/26/52, 9/30/52, F/10/52, 11/6/52,
    1/15/53, 2/1/53, 2/6/53, 2/13/53,
    T/2/53, 3/13/53, M/5/53, 6/21/53,
    Fi/6/53, 7/3/53, 7/13/53, 7/14/53,
    8/9/53, 9/11/53, 10/1/53, F/11/53,
    12/7/53, 12/21/53, E/1/54, 1/29/54,
    2/23/54, F/3/54, 3/14/54, 5/1/54,
    E/5/54, 5/17/54, 5/31/54, S/7/54,
    7/23/54, E/8/54, 8/31/54, 10/8/54,
    10/22/54, S/11/54, 11/26/54, 12/24/54,
    12/27/54, 1/12/55, 1/14/55, 1/8/55,
    F/2/55, 2/26/55, L/3/55, 4/22/55,
    F/5/55, L/5/55, E/6/55, 7/15/55,
    8/5/55, 8/12/55, 8/26/55, Fo/8/55,
    10/29/55, 11/11/55, 12/23/55
Cobb, Arnett 2/15/52, 4/11/52, 5/30/52,
    2/6/53, **4/24/53**, 5/1/54, 6/11/54,
    7/23/54, 1/28/55, 7/8/55, 10/7/55
Cobb, Danny 8/30/52
Cochran Brothers **T/6/55**, M/12/55
Cochran, Eddie (See Cochran Brothers)
Cochran, Hank (See Cochran Brothers)
Coe, Jimmy T/6/53
Cole, Bonita M/3/52
Cole, Cozy **E/11/53**
Cole, Nat "King" 9/26/54, 4/22/55, 4/24/55,
    4/27/55, 4/30/55, 8/5/55
Coleman, Carlton L/8/52
Collins, Big Tim F/1/52

Collins Kids Fo/11/55
Colts T/9/55, **11/2/55**
Columbo, Russ 4/8/55
Convy, Bert and the Thunderbirds Fo/6/55
Cook, Jimmy S/3/52
Cookies **E/11/54**, T/11/54, F/5/55
Cool Notes F/12/55
Cooper, Dolly L/8/52, F/4/53, Fo/6/53
Coronets T/8/53
Cotton, James **F/5/54, T/7/54**
Cotton, Sammy Fo/10/52
Country Paul T/9/52, S/11/52
Country Slim S/12/53
Counts S/2/54, 5/21/54, 5/28/54, F/8/54,
    8/6/54, 9/12/54, 10/22/54, S/11/54,
    S/12/54, M/12/54, 1/28/55, Fo/9/55
Crayton, Pee Wee 1/20/52, 2/15/52, 3/15/52,
    3/30/52, 6/22/52, 9/7/52, 11/14/52,
    3/8/53, 4/26/53, 7/3/53, 9/27/53,
    11/22/53, 12/24/53, **2/7/54**, 10/22/54,
    10/30/54, F/1/55, 3/13/55, T/4/55,
    7/29/55, 8/19/55, 10/16/55
Crew-Cuts E/6/54, M/7/54, L/7/55, 11/26/55
Crewe, Bob S/6/54
Crickets (See also Dean Barlow) **E/1/53**,
    Fo/2/53, F/6/53, **6/21/53**, 7/3/53,
    F/8/53, F/10/53, S/1/54, S/2/54,
    Fi/3/54, M/11/54, F/12/54, E/5/55
Crothers, Sherman "Scatman" F/4/53,
    2/26/54
Crowns, (See also Maye, Arthur Lee)
    M/11/54
Crows S/5/53, Fi/6/53, 2/13/54, F/5/54
Crudup, Arthur "Big Boy" **Fo/3/52**, S/6/52,
    T/12/52, T/2/53, **S/7/54**
Crystals Fo/2/54, S/1/55
Cues **L/10/54**, F/11/54, F/6/55, S/10/55,
    T/12/55
Culley, Frank 6/26/52
Cummings, Larry and the Rhythm Aces
    E/5/52
Curtis, Eddie "Tex" T/6/54
Curtis, Peck 2/9/52

D
Dale, Alan E/7/54
Dale, Larry M/5/54
D'Ambrosia, Joe 9/24/55
Danderliers F/4/55, T/7/55
Dappers T/5/55
Darnell, Larry E/2/52, 3/22/52, E/5/52,
    7/4/52, 9/15/52, 10/10/52, Fo/10/52,
    2/27/53, 3/7/53, 3/28/53, S/4/53,
    4/17/53, **7/4/54**, 10/22/54, M/1/55,
    8/6/55, 12/9/55

Davis, ("Wild") Bill 7/25/52, M/7/53,
    12/31/53, 1/21/55
Davis, Maxwell Fo/11/52 (and the
    Ebonaires) **F/12/53**, S/3/54
Davis, (Little) Sam Fo/5/53
Davis, Sammy, Jr. 9/17/54
Day, Bobby (See Relf, Bobby)
Day, Doris 1/18/52
Day, Margie 4/25/52, 10/26/52, 2/13/53,
    3/21/53, 4/12/53, 4/25/53, 5/20/53,
    S/8/53, 8/17/53, 9/17/53, 9/25/53,
    10/18/53, Fo/10/53, 11/24/53, 4/1/54,
    12/3/54, 1/17/55
DeBerry, Jimmy **Fo/9/53**
Dee, Baby L/7/54, F/8/54, 8/26/55
Dee, Mercy Fo/3/53, **4/19/53**, Fo/5/53,
    Fo/7/53, S/12/53, S/7/55, F/9/55,
    F/11/55
Deep River Boys Fo/4/53, F/6/54
DeFranco, Buddy 9/3/54
Dell-Tones S/4/54
Delta Rhythm Boys **M/1/53**, F/4/54,
    Fi/11/54, 1/12/55, **8/5/55**
Denby, Junior Fi/5/54
Diablos (See Strong, Nolan and the Diablos)
Diamonds (r&b group) T/12/52, S/5/53,
    T/8/53, T/12/53, 6/17/55
Diamonds (pop group) T/9/55
Diddley, Bo F/4/55, 5/20/55, 6/1/55,
    6/10/55, S/6/55, 6/17/55, 6/24/55,
    8/19/55, 8/26/55, 10/29/55, 11/20/55,
    T/11/55
Dillard, Varetta L/1/52, T/2/52, 4/18/52,
    T/5/52, 7/11/52, 7/28/52, 8/29/52,
    9/19/52, F/11/52, M/12/52, 1/16/53,
    1/23/53, F/2/53, 2/9/53, 3/7/53,
    3/28/53, 4/17/53, 5/4/53, 5/22/53,
    9/4/53, 10/16/53, Fi/11/53, E/2/54,
    7/4/54, Fo/9/54, F/2/55, 3/18/55,
    4/2/55, 4/29/55, T/5/55, 6/24/55,
    T/9/55, 10/21/55
Dixie Blues Boys S/7/55
Dixon, Dave E/3/54
Dixon, Floyd Fo/2/52, 3/30/52, **L/3/52**,
    4/20/52, T/6/52, 7/26/52, T/8/52,
    9/22/52, **10/26/52**, T/2/53, 3/13/53,
    3/21/53, 4/12/53, 5/1/53, F/5/53,
    6/12/53, Fo/7/53, 7/31/53, T/8/53,
    T/11/53, 1/29/54, Fo/2/54, 3/12/54,
    5/29/54, 5/31/54, M/6/54, 7/30/54,
    T/8/54, 9/13/54, 9/17/54, 12/24/54,
    1/13/55, 5/27/55, F/8/55, Fo/11/55,
    12/16/55, 12/23/55, 12/30/55
Dixon, Willie *S/8/55*, Fo/11/55
Dodgers M/8/54, S/9/54, S/3/55

Doggett, Bill S/5/52, **6/13/52**, 6/23/52,
    L/8/52, F/1/53, M/2/53, **7/11/53**,
    F/9/53, Fo/1/54, L/1/54, T/3/54,
    5/28/54, 6/25/54, *T/8/54*, S/10/54,
    10/15/54, Fo/11/54, 12/10/54, 1/7/55,
    1/21/55, 1/28/55, 2/26,55, 5/6/55,
    Fo/6/55, 8/9/55, 8/26/55, 10/29/55
Domino, Fats F/1/52, 1/12/52, 3/30/52,
    T/4/52, 5/25/52, 11/11/52, 12/29/52,
    1/15/53, Fo/1/53, 2/1/53, 3/20/53,
    S/4/53, 4/17/53, 5/1/53, Fi/6/53, 7/6/53,
    7/31/53, 8/12/53, 8/18/53, 8/30/53,
    S/9/53, 9/17/53, 9/26/53, 10/11/53,
    10/18/53, M/11/53, Fi/11/53, E/12/53,
    12/21/53, E/1/54, 1/21/54, 1/31/54,
    T/2/54, 2/16/54, 3/21/54, S/5/54,
    7/2/54, 7/9/54, 7/23/54, E/8/54, S/8/54,
    8/31/54, 9/13/54, 10/8/54, S/10/54,
    11/1/54, F/12/54, 1/14/55, 1/17/55,
    T/2/55, 3/4/55, 4/1/55, Fo/4/55, 5/1/55,
    5/16/55, 5/22/55, 7/9/55, L/7/55,
    Fo/8/55, E/9/55, M/10/55, 10/28/55,
    11/3/55, F/11/55, 11/27/55, 12/2/55
Dominoes (see Ward, Billy and his Dominoes)
Dootones T/6/55
Doves (See Butler, Cliff)
Dozier Boys E/2/53, Fo/12/53
Draper, Rusty L/7/55
Dream Man T/3/52
Dreamers (See also Berry, Richard) M/4/52,
    8/15/52, 8/22/52, 8/27/54, T/9/54,
    Fi/8/55, M/9/55, Fo/9/55
Dreams E/5/54, Fo/5/54, F/5/55, 6/17/55
Drifters (See also McPhatter, Clyde and the
    Drifters) 8/6/54, 9/12/54, 10/1/54,
    F/10/54, 10/19/54, 10/28/54, 11/19/54,
    M/12/54, 1/14/55, F/3/55, 3/18/55,
    4/22/55, 4/24/55, 4/27/55, 4/30/55,
    5/13/55, 6/5/55, 6/13/55, 7/1/55, 7/8/55,
    M/7/55, E/8/55, 9/16/55, Fo/10/55,
    E/12/55, 12/11/55, 12/29/55
Drifting Sam F/11/52
Du Droppers *Fo/3/53*, 4/3/53, Fo/5/53,
    T/6/53, F/7/53, 8/15/53, S/11/53,
    S/5/54, **E/6/54**, S/9/54, **L/2/55**, E/4/55,
    T/4/55, E/6/55, M/7/55, F/9/55
Duce of Rhythm M/3/53, T/6/53, 11/28/53
Duke, Billy and the Dukes Fo/4/55
Dukes S/3/55
Dupree, "Champion" Jack **7/30/53**, 8/2/53,
    8/7/53, Fo/9/53, S/4/54, F/4/55, T/5/55,
    Fo/7/55, T/10/55, 10/28/55, 11/25/55,
    12/9/55, T/12/55
Duram, Eddie E/5/52

E

Eagles F/6/54, T/1/55
Earls 9/26/52
Ebonaires (See also Davis, Maxwell)
    F/11/53, 11/20/53
Eckstine, Billy 1/12/52, 2/8/52, 4/19/52,
    L/4/52, 5/7/52, 7/4/52, 8/29/52,
    9/12/52, M/9/52, 11/1/52, 11/22/52,
    12/26/52, 2/14/53, 2/27/53, 3/2/53,
    3/9/53, 3/16/53, 3/23/53, 4/8/53,
    4/26/53, 7/15/53, **9/11/53**, 9/20/53,
    2/21/54, 2/23/54, 3/14/54, 10/19/54,
    4/18/55
Edwards, Tibby S/4/55
Edwards, Tommy *5/18/52*, 5/21/52, **5/28/54**,
    7/2/54
Edwins, Charles S/2/54
El Dorados *F/9/54*, T/10/54, 12/3/54,
    2/18/55, F/3/55, **T/9/55**, 9/30/55,
    10/7/55, E/12/55, S/12/55, 12/12/55,
    12/26/55
El Rays **Fo/5/54**
El Tempos (See Gordon, Mike)
Ellington, Duke 9/26/52, 10/22/52, 8/14/53,
    9/14/53, 12/25/53, 2/12/54,
    2/19/54,y9/11/54, 8/5/55
Embers L/5/53, E/7/53, **M/7/54**, E/5/55
Emerson, Billy "The Kid" S/3/54, Fi/5/54,
    Fi/1/55
Empires T/5/55, M/8/55, S/9/55
Enchanters E/1/52, T/4/52, 12/12/52
Esquire Boys T/12/55
Evans, Bonnie M/7/54
Evans, Melvin M/2/52

F

Falcons **M/5/53**, T/5/53, *T/3/55*
Feathers M/12/54, T/2/55, Fo/4/55, S/9/55
Feathers, Charlie **Fo/4/55**
Ferguson, Charlie E/7/53, 8/13/53
Ferguson, H-Bomb S/1/52, Fo/1/52, S/2/52,
    5/8/52, E/8/52, S/11/52, M/5/53
Ferguson, Rudy F/1/54, T/2/55
Fields, Ernie **1/19/52**, 6/17/55
Fisher, Eddie L/7/55
Fisher, Herb S/8/53
Fi-Tones **E/11/55**
Fitzgerald, Ella 2/1/52, 3/12/52, 6/16/52,
    2/6/53, **11/27/53**, 1/15/54, 4/29/55
Five Barons M/7/52
Five Bills S/2/53
Five Blue Notes F/12/53
Five Buds F/3/53, T/4/53, S/5/53
Five C's Fo/2/54, T/7/54, 12/3/54

Five Cats S/2/55
Five Chances F/8/54
Five Crowns *E/7/52*, Fo/10/52, E/11/52,
    T/1/53, F/4/53, M/3/55, T/3/55
Five Dollars **L/8/55**, F/9/55
Five Dukes (See Woods, Bennie)
Five Dukes of Rhythm T/10/54
Five Echoes T/9/53, F/3/55
Five Encores Fo/12/55
Five Flamingos (See Flamingos)
Five Jets T/5/54, S/8/54, Fo/10/54, **F/1/55**
Five Keys T/1/52, S/4/52, **4/18/52**, 4/19/52,
    5/9/52, S/5/52, 5/16/52, **7/4/52**, F/7/52,
    8/9/52, 8/23/52, 8/29/52, 9/19/52,
    10/16/52, F/11/52, 11/14/52, 11/24/52,
    11/28/52, 12/24/52, 1/16/53, S/2/53,
    4/10/53, T/4/53, M/5/53, M/7/53,
    Fo/9/53, 10/23/53, 11/1/53, 11/24/53,
    S/12/53, L/1/54, Fi/3/54, 4/27/54,
    5/22/54, L/8/54, T/10/54, 11/19/54,
    1/7/55, Fo/1/55, 2/1/55, 2/19/55,
    S/5/55, 5/20/55, F/6/55, 6/8/55, T/7/55,
    8/19/55, 8/26/55, 10/29/55, F/11/55,
    11/11/55, 11/20/55, 12/23/55
Five Owls T/5/55
Five Pearls E/11/54, 1/14/55
"5" Royales Fo/8/52, 12/5/52, Fi/12/52,
    1/7/53, 1/16/53, 1/23/53, Fo/1/53,
    S/4/53, 4/24/53, 5/11/53, E/7/53,
    T/7/53, 8/13/53, 10/12/53, Fo/10/53,
    Fo/1/54, 2/26/54, E/4/54, T/4/54,
    4/21/54, 5/14/54, M/7/54, Fo/7/54,
    F/8/54, M/10/54, Fo/10/54, 12/31/54,
    F/1/55, F/2/55, 2/25/55, S/3/55,
    3/25/55, 4/29/55, S/8/55, M/8/55,
    T/10/55
Five Satins **8/14/53**
Five Scamps T/12/54
Five Stars M/4/55
Five Willows Fi/6/53, S/8/54, Fo/11/54
Five Wings Fo/2/55, F/4/55
Flairs **8/15/53**, 10/16/53, T/11/53, *2/21/54*,
    4/9/54, Fi/5/54, **6/20/54**, T/7/54,
    E/8/54, S/10/54, 12/27/54, Fo/3/55
Flamingos **L/1/52**, *L/2/53*, S/3/53, 6/15/53,
    Fo/7/53, 10/12/53, **T/10/53**, 12/25/53,
    T/1/54, **2/12/54**, 2/19/54, T/4/54,
    7/2/54, S/11/54, T/1/55, Fo/4/55,
    Fo/7/55, Fo/9/55
Flippers S/6/55
Fontaine, Eddie **4/8/55**, 4/29/55
Fontane Sisters L/7/55
Ford, Billy 4/18/52, 6/15/52, 9/30/52,
    11/1/52, E/2/53, M/7/53, S/4/55
Ford, Ernie 1/1/53

Ford Brothers E/12/52
Forrest, Earl **Fo/11/52**, Fi/6/53, S/3/54,
    E/4/54, 5/28/54, Fo/7/54, 12/27/54
Forrest, Gene and the Four Feathers (See
    also Gene and Eunice) S/3/54
Forrest, Jimmy F/3/52, S/5/52, E/6/52,
    9/5/52, 12/12/52, 12/21/52, T/3/53,
    5/1/53, S/3/54
Fortunes T/6/55
Foster, Eva F/7/53
Four Aces 1/6/54
Four Bells F/7/53, M/5/54, Fi/5/54, 7/4/54
Four Blazes T/5/52, F/8/52, F/10/52,
    10/10/52, 10/17/52, **10/24/52**, 12/31/52,
    1/18/53, T/3/53, 6/6/53, L/8/53,
    F/9/53, **M/9/53**, F/2/54
Four Buddies 1/11/52, S/5/52, **5/23/52**,
    F/11/52, **5/23/55**
Four Clefs Fo/2/52
Four Deuces S/8/55
Four Fellows Fo/7/53, F/6/55, **6/10/55**,
    8/5/55, 8/6/55, 8/22/55, 9/2/55, 9/9/55,
    9/12/55, 9/25/55, S/10/55, 11/18/55
Four Flames (see also Hollywood Four
    Flames) **F/3/52**, 8/8/52, **9/12/52**
Four Friends T/9/53
Four Jacks (see also Burney, Mac) Fo/5/52,
    T/7/52, F/9/52
Four Knights **7/2/54**, *8/27/54*
Four Lads 2/2/52, T/8/52
Four Pals S/10/55
Four Pipes E/12/55
Four Plaid Throats 5/15/53, F/6/53
Four Speeds F/1/55
Four Students Fo/6/55
Four Tunes 1/4/52, S/1/52, 1/17/52,
    T/2/52, F/5/52, 5/16/52, 6/16/52,
    6/26/52, T/7/52, 10/10/52, 10/24/52,
    1/2/53, E/6/53, 7/1/53, M/7/53,
    T/11/53, 12/28/53, 1/22/54, 1/29/54,
    2/1/54, 2/8/54, Fo/2/54, 3/15/54,
    3/22/54, 4/2/54, F/4/54, 4/9/54,
    4/16/54, 5/2/54, 7/17/54, T/7/54,
    1/21/55, S/3/55
Foxx, Redd **7/11/52**
Francis, Connie **E/6/55**, S/6/55, *10/6/55*
Franks, Jay M/5/52, Fo/5/52
Frazier, Calvin L/8/52
Freberg, Stan **10/23/54**
Freeman, Ernie **7/8/54**, Fo/11/55, 12/8/55
Fuller, Blind Boy **M/4/55**
Fuller, Johnny S/10/54, F/2/55, Fo/4/55,
    6/24/55, S/10/55, F/12/55
Fulson, Lowell **F/1/52**, T/2/52, 2/22/52,
    2/29/52, 4/11/52, 5/17/52, 6/22/52,

S/8/52, 9/1/52, 9/14/52, M/10/52,
11/10/52, 11/19/52, 11/20/52, Fo/11/52,
11/28/52, 12/19/52, F/3/53, 4/5/53,
4/30/53, **5/23/53**, 10/3/53, S/4/54,
6/8/54, 8/20/54, 9/17/54, M/10/54,
F/11/54, E/11/54, E/1/55, 1/28/55,
2/26/55, F/3/55, M/4/55, 6/6/55,
6/15/55, 7/10/55, Fo/7/55, 9/23/55,
10/14/55, T/12/55
Fuqua, Charlie (see Ink Spots, "new"
group)

G
Gaillard, Slim 8/31/53, **12/3/54**
Gaines, Earl S/10/55
Gale, Sunny (See Wilcox, Eddie) *10/15/54*
Gant, Cecil S/7/52
Gardner, Don **5/10/54**, M/6/54
Garlow, Clarence "Bon Ton" **S/12/53**
Garner, Erroll 1/1/52, 1/11/52, 9/12/52,
3/4/53, 4/13/53
Gaylarks S/8/55, 10/8/55
Gaylords (r&b group) F/7/52
Gaylords (pop group) E/3/55
Gayton, Paul 1/28/52
Gene and Billy F/9/55
Gene And Eunice (see also Forrest, Gene)
T/1/55, 1/28/55, *1/29/55*, F/3/55,
4/10/55, 4/29/55, 5/27/55, 6/10/55,
7/29/55, Fo/7/55, E/8/55, 8/26/55,
10/29/55, 11/11/55, Fo/11/55, 12/31/55
Gentlemen F/11/54
Getz, Stan 9/3/54
Gibbs, Georgia 2/26/55, E/3/55, L/7/55,
8/3/55
Gibson, Delores M/5/54
Gibson, Steve and his Red Caps E/1/52,
4/1/52, 4/14/52, F/5/52, 5/6/52, M/7/52,
Fo/7/52, **M/8/52**, E/9/52, 10/3/52,
11/17/52, E/12/52, 4/12/53, F/3/55,
6/1/55, 9/14/55
Giles, Johnny T/9/52
Gillespie, Dizzy 6/13/52, 12/31/53
Glenn, Lloyd 4/13/52, 5/18/52, 8/8/52,
9/12/52, Fo/10/52, 11/14/52, F/3/53,
4/30/53, 5/34/53, M/10/54, E/1/55
Glover, Henry **S/3/54**
Gonzales, Babs M/10/53
Gordon, Mike and the El Tempos E/4/54,
F/5/54
Gordon, Rosco S/3/52, M/3/53, 5/11/52,
L/5/52, M/6/52, 8/29/52, F/9/52,
9/5/52, 9/26/52, 9/30/52, F/11/52,
Fo/11/52, Fo/1/53, T/5/53, T/10/53,
Fo/7/54, S/2/55, T/10/55

Gordon, Stomp T/10/52, S/12/52, S/4/53,
6/13/53, S/11/53, 2/18/55, F/9/55
Gracie, Charlie and his Wildcats S/7/55
Green, Boote E/1/53
Green, Carl S/3/53
Green, George Fo/4/53
Green, Johnny 5/13/55
Green, Lil 3/21/52, 4/11/52, **M/11/52**
Greene, Rudy T/8/53, Fo/11/53, L/11/53,
5/23/53
Greenwood, Lil 6/22/52, Fo/6/52, 11/22/53
Greer, John T/2/52, 4/21/52, S/5/52,
T/8/52, T/11/52, S/2/53, Fo/4/53,
Fo/8/53, 3/15/54, Fo/5/54, E/8/54,
12/3/54, L/2/55, T/3/55, T/8/55
Grey, Al E/11/52, L/1/53, M/12/53
Griffin, Buddy T/1/55
Griffin Brothers 1/8/52, M/2/52, 4/25/52,
5/26/62, 6/16/52, **6/25/52**, 8/12/52,
8/23/52, 9/27/52, 1/16/53, 7/31/53,
L/11/53, 10/1/54, M/10/54, S/7/55,
8/19/55
Grimes, Tiny F/3/52, 4/7/52, 5/2/52,
L/8/52, 9/9/52, 5/15/53, **5/31/53**,
L/5/53, **M/3/54**
Gross, Felix S/7/52
Guitar Slim 8/3/52, 8/4/52, 2/6/53,
2/14/53, 4/25/53, 6/14/53, 11/13/53,
S/12/53, 1/24/54, 2/5/54, M/3/54,
3/29/54, T/4/54, 5/14/54, E/6/54,
6/16/54, 6/30/54, 7/30/54, T/8/54,
8/28/54, 9/24/54, S/10/54, S/11/54,
Fi/1/55, 4/2/55, 4/15/55, 5/2/55,
Fi/5/55, M/7/55, 9/9/55, 11/25/55
Gunter, Arthur **Fo/11/54**, F/3/55
Gunter, Shirley and the Queens **8/19/54**,
9/10/54, S/9/54, 9/17/54, 1/28/55,
Fo/3/55, T/6/55, Fi/8/55
Guy, Browley and the Skyscrapers S/11/52,
S/7/53
Guy Brothers T/6/52
Gypsies Fi/8/55

H
Haley, Bill and his Comets S/2/52, F/4/52,
S/8/52, S/11/52, Fo/4/53, 6/5/53,
T/7/53, T/10/53, Fo/12/53, Fo/3/54,
S/5/54, S/7/54, M/7/54, 9/1/54,
9/16/54, 9/19/54, 9/24/54, 9/28/54,
10/18/54, T/10/54, 1/10/55, 1/15/55,
2/5/55, E/2/55, S/2/55, 3/25/55,
4/14/55, 4/2/55, 5/21/55, 5/30/55,
6/24/55, 6/25/55, Fo/6/55, S/7/55,
M/7/55, 7/23/55, 7/30/55, L/7/55,
8/6/55, 8/8/55, M/9/55, 9/24/55,

10/10/55, T/10/55, 11/23/55, 11/26/55,
  12/3/55, 12/17/55, Fo/12/55
Hall, Freddie Fi/6/52
Hall, Rene 8/14/53
Hall, Roy S/10/55
Hamilton, Eileen M/7/54
Hamilton, Roy E/11/53, 2/5/54, 2/20/54,
  3/12/54, 3/22/54, 4/16/54, 6/21/54,
  7/4/54, 7/8/54, 8/6/54, Fo/8/54,
  9/12/54, E/11/54, 11/12/54, 11/19/54,
  1/14/55, M/1/55, 1/29/55, 2/11/55,
  S/2/55, 2/25/55, 3/16/55, Fo/3/55,
  4/10/55, 4/18/55, 5/13/55, 6/5/55,
  6/13/55, 8/5/55, 8/11/55, 8/26/55,
  9/1/55, 9/8/55, 10/14/55, 10/14/55,
  10/21/55
Hamilton Sisters E/3/54, T/4/54, T/11/54
Hampton, Lionel 1/1/52, 4/19/52, 4/24/52,
  5/10/52, 5/30/52, 12/26/52, 1/11/53,
  1/23/53, 5/21/53, 5/29/53, 6/12/53,
  M/7/53, 2/12/54, 2/19/54, 7/2/54,
  10/8/54, 5/27/55, 8/5/55
Hardison, Bernie S/12/53
Harmonica Frank T/8/52
Harptones F/12/53, **3/19/54**, 4/9/54,
  S/14/54, 4/19/54, 5/1/544, 5/7/54,
  5/14/54, *F/7/54*, 12/3/54, S/12/54,
  1/14/55, 1/28/55, F/3/55, L/4/55,
  E/6/55, 6/24/55, S/7/55, 7/15/55, 9/2/55
Harris, Bill 6/20/52
Harris, "Dimples" **L/1/52**
Harris, Peppermint 1/1/52, T/1/52, **2/8/52**,
  M/2/52, S/5/52, 7/26/52, **F/8/52**,
  8/10/52, 9/19/52, Fo/11/52, **F/5/53**,
  Fo/2/54, **S/8/54**, Fo/6/55
Harris, Thurston **8/29/53**, 12/11/53
Harris, Wynonie **E/2/52**, F/3/52, T/4/52,
  E/5/52, L/5/52, 7/4/52, Fo/7/52, 8/1/52,
  8/9/52, 10/6/52, S/1/53, 2/27/53,
  3/7/53, **3/28/53**, S/4/53, 4/17/53,
  M/5/53, 6/1/53, Fo/6/53, 7/9/53,
  F/8/53, 8/9/53, M/9/53, 10/16/53,
  S/11/53, S/1/54, 4/18/54, F/5/54,
  Fo/7/54, 9/10/54, 11/12/54, T/12/54,
  2/25/55, Fo/4/55, 5/13/55, Fo/6/55,
  T/9/55, F/11/55
Harrison, Wilbert **T/9/54, T/7/55**
Hartman, Johnny 2/5/55
Harvey, Bill M/3/52, L/1/53, E/5/53,
  10/19/53
Haven, Shirley Fo/5/52, F/9/52, 9/30/52,
  10/25/52
Hawkins, Delores T/8/52
Hawkins, Erskine 1/16/52, 6/6/52, 10/3/52,
  4/24/53, M/5/53, 6/4/54, 8/6/54,

9/12/54, 10/1/54, 11/19/54, 4/30/55,
  5/13/55
Hawkins, Roy F/10/55
Hawkins, Screamin' Jay *5/15/53*, L/5/53,
  F/3/55, E/6/55, 6/17/55, T/6/55,
  10/14/55, E/11/55, 11/18/55, 12/12/55,
  12/31/55
Hawks (See J. B. and his Hawks on
  Chance)
Hawks (on Imperial) **Fo/2/54**, T/5/54,
  T/9/54, S/2/55, M/9/55, Fo/10/55
Hayes, Linda Fo/1/53, 2/23/53, F/3/53,
  3/13/53, 4/3/53, 4/5/53, 4/11/53,
  4/16/53, 10/30/53, 12/24/53, 2/21/54,
  Fo/10/54, 10/29/54, 2/18/55, T/2/55,
  6/3/55
Headen, Willie T/5/54
Heartbeats Fo/5/55, *F/11/55*, 12/22/55
Heartbreakers 1/25/52, **Fo/2/52**, S/5/52,
  F/8/52, 11/21/52
Hearts (see also Andrews, Lee) T/2/55,
  4/8/55, 4/29/55, 5/13/55, 6/5/55,
  6/13/55, S/6/55, **8/19/55**, 9/30/55,
  T/11/55
Henderson, Sam "High Pockets" M/5/54
Hendricks, Margie **M/8/54**
Heralds T/9/54
Herman, Woody 6/9/53, 10/12/53, 10/23/53,
  11/1/53
Hess, Charles 9/24/55
Heywood, Eddie 3/28/52, 3/18/55, 10/14/55
Hibbler, Al 1/1/52, **4/11/52**, 4/17/52,
  5/23/52, 7/26/52, 8/3/52, L/8/52,
  12/24/52, 12/25/54, 1/23/53, 5/1/53,
  6/19/53, 10/13/53, 11/20/53, 1/29/54,
  2/26/54, 4/23/54, 10/1/54, 3/11/55,
  3/16/55, 3/18/55, 3/29/55, 4/22/55,
  5/6/55, 5/13/55, 5/20/55, 7/10/55,
  8/15/55, 9/2/55, 9/26/55, 9/30/55,
  10/7/55, 10/14/55, 11/18/55
Hicks, Ulysses 2/1/55
Higgins, Chuck 8/7/53, 8/15/53, 5/28/54,
  7/17/54, F/10/54, **10/8/54**, 1/28/55,
  3/13/55, L/3/55, 7/15/55, 9/2/55,
  S/9/55, 10/21/55, 12/30/55
Hightower, "Little" Donna T/3/52, S/6/52,
  7/4/53
Hi-Lites M/9/54
Hill, Gladys 10/19/53
Hill, Jesse **4/12/52**
Hines, Earl "Fatha" 5/18/53, 8/20/54,
  8/27/54, **9/3/54**
Hobson, Emmett L/10/53
Hodges, Johnny 5/12/52, 4/26/53, 2/21/54,
  2/23/54, **3/14/54**, 6/25/54

Hogg, Smokey Fi/3/52, Fi/9/52, 12/5/52,
    Fo/12/52, Fo/1/53, Fo/2/54, S/5/53,
    T/9/55
Holiday, Billie 7/25/52, *12/5/52*, 7/27/53,
    8/14/53, **9/25/53**, **9/16/55**
Holiday, Joe 6/20/52
Holidays S/11/54
Holly, Buddy **6/3/55**
Hollywood Flames (see also below) Fo/7/54,
    Fi/1/55
Hollywood Four Flames (see also Four
    Flames) Fo/10/52, 7/17/54, L/8/54
Holmes, LeRoy and his Darktown Boys
    2/9/52
Holmes, Sonny Boy Fi/6/52
Honey Bears T/7/54
Honey Tones 12/21/54
Hooker, John Lee *T/6/52*, S/7/52, S/12/52,
    T/5/53, T/7/53, S/10/53, F/1/54,
    T/3/54, F/5/54, 1/7/55, Fo/1/55,
    4/29/55, T/5/55, Fo/8/55, 10/9/55,
    S/12/55
Hope, Lynn 2/9/52, 6/27/52, 7/12/52,
    8/16/52, 9/11/52, S/11/52, 11/17/52,
    1/26/53, **F/2/53**, 5/1/53, E/6/53,
    8/21/53, T/10/53, M/11/53, 4/1/54,
    6/16/54, 6/23/54, E/11/54
Hopkins, Lightnin' F/2/52, L/3/52, Fo/1/53,
    T/7/53, E/8/53, T/8/53, S/11/53, S/1/54,
    T/1/54, Fo/5/54, **Fo/7/54**, E/9/54,
    T/9/54, Fo/12/54, T/4/55, S/6/55,
    Fi/8/55, Fo/10/55
Hornets T/12/53
Hot Shots E/5/54
Houston, Joe E/4/52, F/5/52, 7/26/52,
    7/27/52, 4/19/53, Fo/5/53, 9/6/53,
    M/11/53, Fi/11/53, 1/24/54, 2/12/54,
    11/26/54, 1/28/55, 5/13/55, 8/5/55,
    9/16/55, 11/2/55, 12/15/55
Houston, Soldier Boy F/8/52
Howard, Camille T/7/52
Howlin' Wolf **Fo/1/54**, **T/6/54**, Fo/4/55,
    T/10/55
Huchins, Bill "88" 9/19/52
Huff, Jimmy S/9/52, 4/30/54
Hughes, Charlie E/4/55, E/6/55
Humes, Helen Fo/4/52, 8/15/53
Humphries, Frank "Fat Man" and the Four
    Seasons F/7/52, 3/7/53
Hunter, Ivory Joe 1/1/52, F/1/52, **1/13/52**,
    1/19/52, *1/23/52*, 1/25/52, 2/22/52,
    2/28/52, 3/6/52, 3/22/52, T/6/52,
    7/11/52, 7/21/52, M/8/52, 9/19/52,
    10/10/52, 10/24/52, F/12/52, L/12/52,
    1/19/53, 1/31/53, **F/4/53**, M/9/53,

10/16/53, 8/20/54, S/9/54, 12/24/54,
    S/1/55, 3/4/55, 4/8/55, 5/2/55, 7/1/55,
    F/7/55, **M/9/55**
Hunters S/10/53
Hurricanes Fo/7/55

I

Imperials Fo/1/54
Ink Spots (the "new" Charlie Fuqua group)
    8/9/52, **E/11/52**, 1/9/53, 1/16/53,
    1/23/53, 4/24/53, M/11/53, M/4/54,
    9/3/54, 9/10/54, 8/12/55, 8/19/55
Ink Spots (Bill Kenny group) **9/18/52**,
    9/25/52, 12/12/52, 12/25/52, 1/9/53,
    2/6/53, 2/13/53, 5/22/53, 5/30/53,
    9/20/53, 10/22/53, 1/28/55, 2/8/55
Inspirators T/4/55
Irving, Gloria Fo/3/53, 5/16/53
Irwin, Frankie F/2/55

J

J. B. and his Hawks F/5/54
Jacks (See also Burney, Mac) *F/5/55*,
    F/7/55, S/11/55
Jackson, Bull Moose 2/22/52, 3/4/52,
    3/14/52, F/5/52, M/7/52, 7/24/52,
    F/8/52, **M/8/52**, 8/29/52, M/9/52,
    10/10/52, 11/24/52, **1/26/53**, 2/19/53,
    S/6/53, **9/4/53**, Fo/9/53, 12/4/53,
    3/22/54, 4/19/54, 7/4/54, 11/12/54,
    3/11/55, 4/25/55, 7/4/55, 11/16/55,
    12/17/55, L/12/55
Jackson, George "Mr. Blues" M/4/54
Jackson, Lil Son **F/11/52**, Fo/9/53,
    S/11/53, **T/1/54**, T/3/54, S/6/54,
    Fo/8/54, F/12/54
Jackson, Willis 1/1/52, 1/18/52, F/7/52,
    7/18/52, 8/31/52, 9/23/52, 11/29/52,
    1/22/54, 7/2/54, 8/13/54, 3/4/55,
    3/11/55, 12/23/55
Jackson Brothers F/11/52, 7/3/53, E/1/53
Jacquet, Illinois 5/23/52, 8/16/52, 9/19/52,
    9/27/52, 11/21/52, 12/24/52, 1/30/53,
    5/30/53, 9/4/53, 3/12/54, 6/21/54,
    1/28/55, 2/4/55, 7/1/55
Jaguars 7/3/55, F/7/55
James, Elmore T/12/52, F/1/53, F/5/53,
    S/6/53, **S/8/53**, T/8/53, S/12/53,
    F/3/54, Fi/5/54, T/10/54, T/5/55,
    F/11/55
James, Etta Fo/1/55, 4/1/55, 5/13/55,
    S/5/55, 6/17/55, 6/24/55, L/7/55,
    F/8/55, 8/26/55, 10/29/55, Fo/11/55
Janis, Johnny Fo/12/55
Jesse and Marvin **Fo/12/52**

302

Jets T/3/53

Jewels T/9/54, T/10/54, 12/27/54, 1/28/55,
    5/2/55, 6/3/55, T/6/55, F/9/55

Jimmy and Johnny E/10/54

Jimmy and Walter F/4/53

Jive Bombers (see also Palmer, Clarence)
    M/7/52

Jive Five **T/9/52**

Jo, Damita T/4/52, **5/6/52**, M/7/52, Fo/7/52,
    E/9/52, 4/12/53, 6/1/55

Jodimars **9/24/55**, 10/7/55, S/11/55

John, "Little" Willie (see Little Willie)
    T/11/52, S/12/53, **4/22/55**, Fo/7/55,
    8/12/55, 10/28/55, F/11/55, **11/25/55**

Johnny and Mack F/11/54

Johnson, Bill L/2/54

Johnson, Bubber Fo/7/52, 11/21/55, 12/1/55,
    12/5/55, 12/12/55, 12/30/55

Johnson, Buddy (and Ella) **2/11/52**, S/2/52,
    3/9/52, M/3/52, E/4/52, 5/23/52,
    M/6/52, 7/11/52, 9/12/52, 10/2/52,
    10/19/52, 10/31/52, 2/12/53, 3/20/53,
    4/3/53, T/4/53, **E/6/53**, S/6/53, 7/9/53,
    8/9/53, 9/25/53, 11/2/53, S/11/53,
    12/4/53, 1/19/54, Fo/2/54, 5/1/54,
    S/5/54, 5/21/54, 5/28/54, T/7/54,
    9/26/54, E/10/54, T/11/54, 12/3/54,
    12/23/54, **1/14/55**, S/1/55, M/3/55,
    4/10/55, 4/29/55, 5/20/55, 6/10/55,
    6/17/55, 6/24/55, T/7/55, 8/11/55,
    9/2/55, 9/9/55, S/9/55, 9/25/55,
    11/4/55, 11/14/55, 11/18/55

Johnson, Ella (see also Johnson, Buddy)
    E/10/54, T/3/55, S/6/55

Johnson, Earl S/7/53

Johnson, Eddie T/7/53

Johnson, Lem S/4/53

Johnson, Lonnie S/3/54, F/8/55

Johnson, Rock Heart T/10/52

Johnson, Willie M/11/52, M/6/53, Fo/5/54

Jones, Doctor Willie M/10/52

Jones, Etta 5/8/53, 6/10/55

Jones, Floyd T/8/54

Jones, Joe **1/22/55**, 4/10/55, 12/20/55

Jones, Spike 1/12/52

Jones, Willie S/5/53

Jordan, Louis M/1/52, 4/7/52, 4/22/52,
    5/2/52, 5/9/52, 5/16/52, 5/24/52, 6/1/52,
    6/8/52, M/6/52, 6/20/52, 6/24/52,
    7/2/52, 7/9/52, 7/16/52, 8/12/52,
    8/31/52, 9/27/52, 10/2/52, 10/18/52,
    12/28/52, 1/16/53, 1/23/53, 2/1/53,
    4/4/53, 4/12/53, 4/23/53, 5/7/53,
    5/29/53, 6/19/53, 8/2/53, 9/8/53,
    9/11/53, 9/16/53, 9/30/53, 10/2/53,

    11/7/53, 11/17/53, 11/27/53, F/2/54,
    3/15/54, T/3/54, 3/22/54, 3/26/54,
    4/16/54, 4/23/54, 5/17/54, Fi/5/54,
    7/4/54, S/7/54, 7/30/54, 8/19/54,
    8/29/54, F/9/54, 9/12/54, Fo/10/54,
    11/12/54, 12/1/54, T/12/54, 12/24/54,
    1/7/55, 2/1/55, 4/8/55, 4/15/55,
    4/22/55, 9/30/55, 10/14/55, F/11/55,
    S/12/55, 12/30/55

Julian, Don (See Meadowlarks)

K

Kari, Sax Fo/3/53, 5/15/53

Kenny, Bill (see also Ink Spots, Bill Kenny
    group) 1/7/55, 2/8/55

Keynotes T/12/55

Kidds M/9/55

King, Al E/1/53

King, B. B. M/3/52, 4/4/52, 5/8/52,
    Fo/8/52, 11/27/52, S/12/52, L/1/53,
    F/3/53, E/5/53, S/6/53, M/9/53,
    Fo/9/53, 10/19/53, T/11/53, 11/28/53,
    2/5/54, S/2/54, M/2/54, 2/26/54,
    L/2/54, Fi/3/54, F/4/54, 5/28/54,
    Fo/7/54, 8/19/54, Fo/10/54, 12/10/54,
    M/12/54, 12/24/54, 12/27/54, Fo/12/54,
    T/4/55, Fo/5/55, T/7/55, F/9/55,
    M/9/55, 11/11/55, F/12/55, 12/18/55

King, Earl **7/17/54**, 9/24/54, F/10/54,
    10/15/54, Fi/8/55, S/9/55, 10/28/55,
    11/25/55, T/12/55

King, Jewel **1/12/52**

King, Johnny E/4/52, F/6/52

King, Kid S/1/54

King, Maurice F/4/52

King Curtis **T/5/53**

King Pleasure **5/20/52**, 1/1/53, 4/17/53,
    8/6/54

Kings S/6/54, E/9/54

Kirkland, "Little" Eddie S/7/**52**, S/9/52,
    T/10/53

Kittrell, Christine F/8/52, 9/21/52,
    S/10/53, 2/12/54

Knight, Gladys **7/15/52**

Knight, Marie 10/28/55, 11/25/55

Knight, Sonny **F/11/53**, S/4/55

L

Laine, Frankie 10/31/52

Lamplighters 8/29/53, F/9/53, S/11/53,
    12/1/53, T/2/54, 2/21/54, **S/4/54**,
    8/19/54, Fi/8/54, 9/3/54, Fo/10/54,
    F/3/55, Fo/11/55

Lane, Georgia L/10/53, S/12/53

Larks T/1/52, L/1/52, **Fo/7/52**, E/7/54,

8/13/54, 1/12/55, **3/7/55**, 5/11/55,
F/7/55, 9/2/55
Laurels (See Relf, Bobby)
Laurie, Annie E/5/52, 7/4/52, 8/9/52,
5/10/53
Lazy Bill E/3/54
Lazy Boy Slim S/11/52
Lazy Slim Jim Fo/7/52, Fi/3/53
Lee, John Fi/3/52
Lee, Leonard (See also Shirley and Lee)
F/7/54
Lenoir, J. B. Fo/8/52, T/8/53
Lester, Bobby and the Moonlighters
S/11/54, M/12/54, 1/21/55, 1/28/55,
S/3/55, 4/8/55, 10/7/55
Lewis, Bobby **F/9/52**
Lewis, Jimmy 1/4/52, Fo/9/52, E/4/54,
F/5/54
Lewis, Junior 8/26/55, 10/8/55
Lewis, Nolan 5/1/54, 5/21/54, 1/14/55,
11/1/55
Lewis, Pete "Guitar" S/4/52, T/5/52,
Fo/10/52, S/1/54
Lewis, Smiley 2/24/52, F/7/52, Fo/10/52,
4/24/53, 6/14/53, Fo/7/53, Fo/9/53,
T/1/54, 10/2/54, Fo/10/54, S/1/55,
5/29/55, Fo/7/55, S/12/55
Liggins, Jimmy Fo/3/52, T/7/52, **2/15/53**,
T/2/54, 4/16/54, S/8/54
Liggins, Joe 1/1/52, 1/17/52, **Fi/3/52**,
T/4/52, 6/19/52, 6/26/52, S/10/52,
12/7/52, T/1/53, **2/15/53**, E/5/53,
Fi/6/53, Fo/8/53, 9/20/53, Fo/9/53,
1/29/54, 2/7/54, 3/5/54, Fo/4/54,
L/7/54, Fi/8/54, 6/17/55
Lightfoot, Papa 11/30/52, T/3/53
Lil Miss Cornshucks F/2/52, 2/9/52, S/4/52,
S/6/52
Little Bo 10/30/54
Little Caesar **S/8/52**, S/9/52, 9/4/52,
L/10/52, 11/21/52, F/3/53, 4/5/53,
Fo/7/53, Fo/10/53, T/11/53
Little David F/8/52
Little Eddie M/2/54
Little Esther **1/4/52**, 1/27/52, 2/17/52,
F/3/52, S/4/52, 4/18/52, 4/25/52,
Fo/5/52, E/6/52, 6/15/52, S/8/52,
8/21/52, 9/1/52, 10/6/52, T/11/52,
11/28/52, **S/2/53**, Fi/4/53, 4/24/53,
5/11/52, F/9/53, 10/1/53, **S/11/53**,
4/22/55
Little Hudson T/10/53
Little Junior's Blue Flames (See also Parker,
Little Junior) S/8/53, F/12/53
Little Milton Fo/1/54, **Fo/4/54**

Little Miss Sharecropper (See Baker,
Lavern)
Little Mr. Blues F/4/53
Little Richard (See also Tempo Toppers)
M/1/52, Fo/3/52, T/7/52, T/11/52,
1/2/53, M/3/53, *T/6/53*, 10/30/53,
11/28/53, **E/1/54**, Fo/3/54, **L/4/54**,
Fi/10/55
Little Sylvia **E/9/52**, S/11/52, E/4/54,
Fo/4/54
Little Walking Willie F/13/55, 8/26/55,
10/8/55
Little Walter F/6/52, F/8/52, E/10/52,
F/12/52, 2/11/53, 3/20/53, T/4/53,
5/8/53, 7/21/53, 8/4/53, S/9/53,
T/12/53, Fi/3/54, T/4/54, Fo/8/54,
10/8/54, S/11/54, Fo/2/55, 4/2/55,
4/29/55, 5/20/55, Fi/5/55, Fo/9/55
Little Willie (see also John, Little Willie)
Fo/6/52
Littlefield, Little Willie 2/3/52, **4/20/52**,
7/27/52, 9/4/52, 10/24/52, **F/1/53**,
F/7/53, 10/9/53, 12/24/53, S/1/54,
Fo/3/54, 12/27/54, T/5/55
Long John S/3/54
Louis, Joe **9/19/52**, 4/10/53, 5/1/53,
M/5/53, 5/29/53, 6/5/53, 6/12/63,
6/26/53, 7/9/53, 8/9/53, 9/25/53
Louis, Joe Hill T/2/52, Fi/3/53
Love, Clayton Fi/9/52
Love, Preston S/7/52
Love, Willie and his Three Aces S/5/52,
T/10/52, T/12/53, **Fo/8/54**
Lovenotes F/10/53, Fi/11/54
Lowe, Jim **S/6/55**, F/8/55
Lucas, Buddy E/6/52, 6/13/52, 6/19/52,
T/9/52, 10/31/52, 11/30/52, M/12/52,
L/12/52, Fo/2/53, L/7/53, 8/17/53,
F/3/54, Fo/4/54, L/11/55
Lutcher, Joe 12/5/52
Lutcher, Nellie L/11/53
Lytell, Marshall 9/24/55

M
M-G-M Studio Orchestra F/7/55
Mabon, Willie F/12/52, 1/1/53, 1/9/53,
1/16/53, Fo/1/53, 1/30/53, 2/7/53,
T/2/53, F/3/53, T/4/53, 6/5/53,
7/20/53, 9/4/53, T/9/53, 10/12/53,
10/17/53, T/12/53, Fo/4/54, F/11/54,
F/4/55, 5/13/55, 6/13/55, 7/8/55,
9/2/55, S/11/55, 12/9/55
McCollom, Hazel T/10/54
McCracklin, Jimmy T/2/52, **7/20/52**,
T/8/52, *9/7/52*, E/12/52, 12/25/52,

304

T/4/53, **4/9/54**, S/4/54, **Fo/8/55**

McGhee, Brownie Fo/1/52, S/10/52, **F/12/52**, S/7/53, E/9/54

McGhee, Stick F/2/52, **E/5/52**, T/4/53, T/5/53, Fo/11/53, S/3/54

McGriff, Edna F/4/52, 5/2/52, E/6/52, 6/13/52, 6/19/52, F/7/52, 7/12/52, *9/12/52*, L/9/52, 10/31/52, F/11/52, 11/30/52, M/12/52, L/12/52, Fo/2/53, 6/21/53, 8/17/53, 9/11/53, 10/9/54, 10/22/54

McGuire Sisters E/12/52, **M/7/54**, 11/26/55

McHouston, Big Red M/5/54

Mack, Eddie M/4/52, Fo/7/52

McKinney, Peter **M/4/52**

McLaurin, Bette 1/11/52, 7/27/52, 10/3/52, *L/10/52*, 11/21/52, 12/12/52, 1/30/53, 2/7/53, 3/6/53, 4/20/53, 9/4/53, E/2/54, T/2/54, 2/26/54, E/5/54, 7/9/54, 9/2/55

McLawler, Sarah 7/3/53

McLollie, Oscar F/3/53, 4/26/53, 5/15/53, Fi/11/53, S/4/54, Fo/11/54, **1/28/55**, 9/30/55, S/11/55, 12/31/55

McNeeley, Big Jay 4/13/52, **7/5/52**, 7/26/52, S/1/53, 2/13/53, 3/4/53, **7/24/53**, S/8/53, S/11/53, S/5/54, S/6/54, Fo/8/54, 12/27/54, 3/1/55, 8/7/55, 11/2/55

McPhail, Jimmy 4/1/52

McPhatter, Clyde (See also McPhatter, Clyde and the Drifters) M/3/53, 5/7/53, 2/28/54, 3/2/54, 5/7/54, M/7/55, F/8/55, S/10/55, T/12/55, 12/31/55

McPhatter, Clyde and the Drifters 5/7/53, S/9/53, 10/9/53, 12/4/53, 1/15/54, 1/22/54, F/2/54, 3/2/54, 3/13/54, 3/26/54, 4/16/54, 4/23/54 5/7/54, F/6/54, S/11/54, F/3/55

McShann, Jay Fo/10/52, **S/1/53**, Fo/10/55

Magic-Tones S/12/53

Majors S/1/52, F/6/54

Mann, Gloria **E/5/54**, Fi/1/55, 6/24/55, 11/26/55, 12/12/55, 12/22/55

Manse, Henry M/11/52

Marchan, Bobby **2/6/53, S/6/53**

Marigolds Fo/4/55, S/8/55

Mariners 5/13/55

Mars, Mitzi T/5/53

Marshall, Frankie T/6/55

Marveltones S/4/52

Marvin and Johnny Fi/11/53, F/4/54, S/6/54, T/7/54, 8/13/54, 8/19/54, Fo/9/54, F/11/54, M/11/54, 12/6/54, 1/28/55, F/2/55, 4/10/55, F/6/55, 7/1/55, 7/15/55, T/11/55

Marylanders M/4/52, T/4/52, F/9/52, L/3/53, F/4/53

Mastertones M/6/54

Maye, Arthur Lee and the Crowns **M/11/54**, T/2/55, F/6/55, **F/10/55**

Mayfield, Percy 2/24/52, F/3/52, Fo/5/52, 6/9/52, **Fo/9/52**, 12/31/52, T/1/53, 4/19/53, F/5/53, 7/26/53, 9/4/53, Fo/9/53, 12/18/53, **T/2/54**, M/4/54, *M/5/54*, 5/31/54, S/7/54, 7/16/54, 8/13/54, 10/22/54, T/12/54, S/3/55, F/7/55, 7/8/55, M/10/55, **12/1/55**, 12/22/55

Mays, Willie F/8/54

Meadowlarks F/1/54, Fo/3/54, M/1/55, 2/21/55, S/4/55, F/7/55, **7/15/55**, T/7/55, Fi/8/55, Fo/10/55

Medallions **F/11/54**, 12/27/54, S/1/55, 1/28/55, 2/21/55, S/6/55, 6/24/55, T/7/55, Fi/8/55, 10/8/55, Fo/11/55

Medlin, Joe 3/22/52, F/3/54

Mello-Fellows L/10/54, F/11/54

Mello-Moods T/1/52

Mellows L/7/54, **F/8/54**, S/1/55, 4/2/55

Memphis Minnie T/5/53, **T/11/53**

Memphis Slim F/2/52, *Fi/6/52*, S/10/52, M/11/52, S/2/53, Fo/7/53, **Fo/12/53**, S/5/54, **Fo/9/54**, E/10/54, 10/29/54, F/12/54, 1/14/55, T/3/55, 4/29/55, 5/13/55, T/5/55

Mickey and Sylvia **Fo/7/55**, *10/14/55*, Fo/12/55

Middleton, Velma S/1/55

Midnighters (Formerly the Royals) E/4/54, 5/17/54, 5/22/54, F/6/54, 7/9/54, 7/23/54, T/8/54, 9/16/54, 10/8/54, M/10/54, Fo/10/54, S/12/54, Fo/2/55, S/4/55, Fo/4/55, T/5/55, F/7/55, Fo/7/55, S/10/55, M/10/55, T/11/55

Midnights Fo/1/55

Milburn, Amos 2/10/52, F/3/52, L/3/52, 4/27/52, 4/29/52, 5/1/52, F/5/52, F/6/52, 6/27/52, 7/14/52, 8/9/52, 8/11/52, 8/31/52, Fi/9/52, 10/13/52, L/10/52, 11/27/52, 12/1/52, F/12/52, 12/12/52, 12/14/52, 12/31/52, Fo/1/53, L/1/53, 2/22/53, 3/23/53, 4/11/53, 4/16/53, 4/25/53, 5/15/53, Fo/5/53, 7/27/53, T/8/53, T/9/53, 10/18/53, E/11/53, E/12/53, S/12/53, 1/6/54, 3/7/54, T/3/54, 4/1/54, E/5/54, S/5/54, 5/14/54, 5/28/54, E/6/54, M/6/54, 6/18/54, S/7/54, 7/22/54, E/8/54, 9/13/54, 9/24/54, 10/1/54, 11/1/54, 11/12/54, T/12/54, 1/7/55, 1/21/55,

T/7/54, 8/20/54, 9/20/54, S/10/54,
S/11/54, 1/20/55, 2/4/55, F/2/55,
2/11/55, 2/21/55, F/4/55, 5/27/55,
6/17/55, 7/22/55, 10/14/55, T/10/55,
Fi/10/55, 11/16/55, 12/23/55
Otis, Johnny 1/4/52, T/1/52, 1/27/52,
2/17/52, 4/18/52, 4/25/52, Fo/4/55,
E/6/52, 6/15/52, T/7/52, Fo/7/52,
8/21/52, 9/1/52, 10/6/52, 11/28/52,
Fo/12/52, 1/9/53, S/1/53, 1/23/53,
3/6/53, M/3/53, 7/5/53, 8/30/53,
S/10/53, L/10/53, **M/11/53**, 11/25/53,
1/8/54, 3/5/54, M/4/54, 4/18/54,
4/23/54, 5/13/54, 6/4/54, 6/11/54,
F/7/54, 8/19/54, 8/27/54, 11/1/54,
F/11/54, 11/26/64, 12/9/54, 12/24/54,
12/27/54, 1/13/55, 1/27/55, 2/21/55,
Fo/3/55, 4/10/55, S/6/55, 11/3/55,
12/8/55, 12/29/55
Overbea, Danny Fo/1/53, S/6/53, Fo/2/54,
5/10/54, T/6/54, 11/8/54, **T/12/54**,
2/18/55, 3/18/55, 4/8/55

P
Paige, Hal M/5/53
Page, Hot Lips L/5/52
Page, Patti 1/18/52, L/7/55, 9/2/55
Palmer, Clarence and the Jive Bombers
T/1/52
Palmer, Earl **E/12/52**
Parker, Charlie 3/21/52, 4/18/52
Parker, Leo "Mad Lad" L/7/52
Parker, Little Junior (See also Little
Junior's Blue Flames) **10/23/53**,
12/2/53, E/1/54, **L/1/54**, L/2/54, S/3/54,
M/3/54, E/4/54, L/4/54, **E/5/54**,
Fo/6/54, F/4/55, T/10/55
Parker, Sonny S/5/52
Parrish, Gene S/4/52
Partridge, Prince E/7/54, 10/29/54, T/10/55
Patrick, Gladys "Glad Rags" T/1/54, E/2/54,
3/19/54, 4/2/54
Patty Anne T/8/52
Paul, Billy M/4/52, F/7/52
Paul, Bunny 3/13/54
Pauling, Lowman M/8/55
Peacheroos Fo/11/54
Peacock, Burnie 1/1/52
Pearls F/11/55, **12/2/55**
Pelicans F/10/54
Penguins Fi/8/54, S/10/54, 12/31/54,
1/14/55, M/1/55, Fi/1/55, 2/21/55,
4/8/55, 4/9/55, 4/21/55, 4/26/55,
Fo/4/55, 5/6/55, 5/13/55, 5/14/55,
F/6/55, 7/8/55, Fo/7/55, 8/7/55,

Fi/8/55, 9/2/55, Fo/9/55, 11/2/55,
S/12/55
Peppers F/10/54
Perkins, Carl *T/10/55*
Perry, Columbus L/1/52
Perry, King 10/1/54
Peterson, Oscar 12/15/55
Phillip, Buddy S/3/54
Phillips, Esther (see Little Esther)
Phillips, Joe 5/25/52
Phillips, Marvin (See also Jesse and
Marvin, Marvin and Johnny) T/11/52,
6/21/53, 10/16/53, 2/21/54, S/7/55
Piano Red **T/3/52**, F/7/52, S/10/52, T/3/53,
Fi/6/53, T/12/53, T/3/55, S/7/55,
T/8/55, Fi/10/55
Pierce, Henry F/5/53
Platters Fo/11/53, Fo/1/54, S/5/54,
Fo/6/54, 8/19/54, S/11/54, 12/27/54,
T/1/55, T/2/55, 4/9/55, S/7/55,
8/12/55, 10/21/55, 11/2/55, 11/12/55,
F/12/55, E/12/55
Playboys E/8/54, T/8/54, L/3/55, S/4/55
Pompelli, Rudy 9/24/55
Poppa Treetop T/8/52
Porter, John "Schoolboy" F/6/52, S/8/52,
T/5/53
Porter, King T/10/52
Powell, Austin M/6/52
Powell, Chris and his Five Blue Flames
1/1/52, 4/8/52, S/5/52, 5/16/52,
5/23/52, T/9/52
Prado, Perez 6/3/55
Presley, Elvis (for a complete day-by-day
chronology of Elvis's life, see *All
Shook Up* by the author) T/7/54,
7/31/54, Fo/9/54, **10/2/54**, 10/16/54,
S/1/55, S/4/55, 5/1/55, 6/3/55, F/8/55,
10/10/55, 11/12/55, **11/20/55**, 11/26/55,
F/12/55, 12/17/55, Fo/12/55
Price, Lloyd M/4/52, T/4/52, 5/31/52,
6/13/52, S/9/52, 9/21/52, 10/28/52,
10/31/52, 11/7/42, 11/14/52, 12/28/52,
T/1/53, 2/14/53, 2/20/53, 3/6/53,
S/3/53, Fo/5/53, 6/26/53, Fo/8/53,
10/2/53, S/2/54, S/5/54, E/12/55,
12/30/55
Prince, Bobby Fo/7/54
Prisonaires **L/7/53**, S/12/53
Professor Longhair (See also Roy Byrd)
1/1/52, 2/15/52, 5/25/52, 9/20/52,
4/10/53
Prysock, Arthur 3/9/52, 5/23/52, M/6/52,
Fo/6/52, 7/7/52, 7/18/52, 9/19/52,
12/5/52, L/1/53, 2/14/53, M/3/53,

Samuels, Clarence M/7/54, Fo/7/54
Sandmen T/2/55
Sands, Tommy E/1/54
Saunders, Red F/3/52, 2/13/53, 2/27/53,
    S/9/55
Saunders, Slim Fi/3/55
Savage, Al S/9/53, 10/16/53, 1/8/54, 2/1/54,
    S/2/54, 2/12/54, S/6/54, 7/27/54,
    10/22/54, 11/5/54, 11/12/54, 11/26/54,
    1/21/55, S/2/55, T/8/55, 9/2/55,
    9/12/55, 9/25/55
Savoys **7/3/55**
Scott, Jimmy S/5/52, T/9/52, E/11/55,
    T/11/55
Scott, Mabel 9/4/52, 9/20/52, 10/24/52,
    11/21/52, 2/20/53, 3/20/53, 5/8/53,
    9/17/53, 10/16/53, 10/31/53, 12/31/53,
    1/24/54, 3/12/54, 3/19/54, M/10/54,
    L/3/55
Scruggs, Fay (See Adams, Faye)
Sears, Al S/2/52, S/6/52, 4/8/55, 12/22/55
Selah Jubilee Singers E/5/54
Sellers, Johnny S/8/52, 6/12/53
Sensations F/11/55, 11/17/55
Serenaders F/5/52, T/6/53, E/9/54
Sh-Booms (See also Chords, Chordcats)
    Fi/10/55
Sha-Weez F/4/53
Shadows 7/4/53, T/7/53, Fi/11/53, Fo/7/54
Shaw, Joan 9/19/52, 10/3/52
Shearing, George 10/9/53, 11/16/55
Sheiks S/4/55, S/9/55
Shepherds Fi/8/55
Shirley and Lee (See also Lee, Leonard)
    T/10/52, *1/18/53*, T/3/53, 6/13/53,
    Fi/6/53, Fo/6/54, F/6/55, **Fo/10/55**,
    12/20/55
Shufflers Fi/8/54
Simms, Sonny F/8/52
Simpson, Bob 9/24/55
Sims, Frankie Lee F/5/53, F/4/54
Singer, Hal "Cornbread" 2/22/52, 2/29/52,
    4/11/52, M/4/52, 5/31/52, 6/23/52,
    7/3/52, 7/25/52, 7/26/52, L/8/52,
    Fi/9/52, F/4/53, 4/10/53, 5/16/53,
    5/29/53, 6/12/53, 4/23/54, M/9/54,
    11/12/54, 4/29/55, 10/28/55, 11/25/55,
    L/11/55, T/12/55
Singing Wanderers E/8/54
Slay, Emitt, Trio **E/2/53**, S/2/53, 4/27/53,
    Fo/4/53
Sly Fox T/12/54
Smilin' Joe F/9/54, S/1/55
Smith, Bessie M/4/52
Smith, Bobby Fo/7/52

Smith, Dick L/1/54
Smith, Dottie 8/12/52
Smith, Effie 4/26/53, 7/2/54
Smith, Henry S/9/54
Smith, Huey **M/6/53**
Smith, Jimmy 8/26/55
Smith, Lloyd "The Fat Man" T/5/52
Smith, Melvin S/1/54, Fo/4/54
Smith, Maybelle (see Big Maybelle)
Smith, Tab 1/25/52, 3/7/52, 4/16/52,
    7/12/52, T/7/52, E/8/52, Fo/7/53,
    10/23/53, Mi/11/53, 4/21/54, 5/14/54,
    Fo/6/54, 12/31/54, 3/25/55
Snow, Hank **5/1/55**, 10/10/55
Solid Senders (see Milton, Roy)
Solitaires **2/5/55**, *7/8/55*, **Fo/9/55**,
    11/11/55, 11/18/55
Solotones T/8/55
Sonics S/7/55
Sounds F/12/55, 12/16/55
Spaniels M/7/53, Fo/7/53, Fo/10/53,
    T/3/54, 6/11/54, 8/6/54, 9/12/54,
    F/10/54, 10/8/54, 10/22/54, F/5/55,
    5/13/55, 6/5/55, 6/13/55, 8/19/55,
    9/2/55, 9/9/55, S/9/55, 9/25/55
Sparks of Rhythm M/7/55, Fo/9/55
Sparrow, Johnny and his Bows and Arrows
    S/9/52, L/5/53
Sparrows Fo/3/54
Spiders T/9/53, T/1/54, T/4/54, 5/14/54,
    Fo/6/54, 7/9/54, F/9/54, 9/17/54,
    10/15/54, 11/12/54, T/11/54, 2/4/55,
    T/4/55, S/6/55, S/10/55
Squires **S/7/55**, T/11/55
Starlings F/4/55, Fo/5/55
Staton, Dakota 10/1/54, 2/19/55, 4/29/55,
    10/14/55
Stewart, Almeta F/3/54
Stidham, Arbee S/10/52
Stitt, Sonny 1/11/52, 5/11/53, 5/28/53,
    7/3/53, 1/15/54, 1/22/54
Stone, Jesse S/4/54, **M/6/54**, 7/23/55
Stone, Red and his Grave Diggers T/3/52
Storm, Gale Fo/9/55
Strangers Fi/8/54, Fo/10/54, F/2/55,
    S/8/55
Street Singers F/4/52
Striders 1/18/52, 6/13/52, Fo/9/55
Strong, Nolan and the Diablos M/4/54,
    Fo/4/54, T/9/54, *11/5/54*, **1/14/55**,
    T/3/55, F/5/55, Fi/10/55, 12/9/55,
    12/23/55
Sugar Boy T/10/53
Sugar Tones S/11/54, M/11/54
Sullivan, Maxine 3/14/52

Sultans Fo/6/54, F/10/54, Fo/1/54
Sunnyland Slim **Fo/1/52**, F/8/54, F/6/55
Sutton, Danny S/7/52
Swallows F/1/52, 3/20/52, 4/11/52, **T/4/52**,
    T/5/52, **5/31/52**, E/6/52, 6/11/52,
    6/19/52, E/8/52, 8/17/52, T/11/52,
    12/12/52, 12/26/52, 3/13/53, Fi/3/53,
    S/6/53, Fo/9/53, T/11/53, 1/29/54
Swann, Claudia T/1/55
Swans, M/1/55

T
Tampa Red Fo/5/52, T/9/52, S/2/53,
    Fo/4/53, Fo/11/53, Fo/1/54
Tangiers F/9/55
Tate, Blind Billy S/5/53
Tate, Laurie 4/27/52, **M/8/52**, 8/30/52,
    11/28/52, 1/1/53
Taylor, Danny Fo/12/53
Taylor, Dudlow (See Duce of Rhythm)
Taylor, Johnny T/4/54
Taylor, Sam "The Man" 4/8/55, F/5/55,
    7/17/55, 9/2/55, 12/22/55
Taylor, Zola **Fi/3/54**
Tenderfoots S/5/55, **Fo/6/55**, F/7/55
Tempo Toppers (See also Little Richard)
    M/3/53, **T/6/53**, 10/30/53, 11/28/53,
    Fo/3/54
Terry, Dossie T/8/52
Terry, Sonny Fo/1/52, **E/10/53**, S/11/53,
    S/1/54
Tex, Joe Fo/10/55
Tharpe, Sister Rosetta 5/6/55
Thomas, Al "Fat Man" F/8/52
Thomas, Lafayette **M/2/52**
Thomas, Rufus, Jr. Fo/3/53, F/4/53, L/8/53,
    Fo/9/53
Thompson, Dickie Fi/3/55
Thompson, Sonny (and Lulu Reed) T/1/52,
    2/15/52, 3/2/52, 3/7/52, T/4/52, M/5/52,
    5/28/52, **6/12/52**, T/6/52, 8/8/52,
    M/11/52, F/4/53, F/7/53, 8/28/53,
    10/11/53, S/10/53, Fo/2/54, 2/26/54,
    M/4/54, T/4/54, F/6/54, 6/25/54,
    7/14/54, 7/23/54, 11/5/54, 1/15/55,
    T/1/55, 1/28/55, 3/18/55, 5/6/55,
    M/8/55, 10/7/55, 11/24/55
Thornton, Willie Mae "Big Mama" 1/11/52,
    2/17/52, 4/25/52, E/6/52, 6/15/52,
    F/10/52, S/10/52, 11/28/52, S/3/53,
    E/3/53, 3/14/53, T/4/53, 8/9/53,
    8/21/53, F/9/53, 10/23/53, 11/28/53,
    12/2/53, 1/23/54, L/1/54, E/3/54,
    E/4/54, 4/23/54, 5/7/54, S/5/54, E/6/54,
    M/7/54, Fo/9/54, 10/29/54, 11/19/54,
    2/18/55, Fo/3/55, Fo/12/55
Three Baritones T/4/52
Three Chuckles *Fo/10/53*, **S/2/55**, 4/8/55,
    4/29/55, 12/22/55, Fo/12/55
Thrillers S/9/53, F/7/54
Thunderbirds F/2/55
Tibbs, Andrew Fo/6/52
Til, Sonny (See also Orioles) S/5/52,
    M/5/52, F/11/52, Fo/2/53, S/5/53,
    10/14/55
Topps T/2/54
Trenier, Milt 2/21/53, Fo/4/53, T/3/54,
    S/7/54
Treniers 2/14/52, T/2/52, S/5/52, M/7/52,
    Fo/9/52, F/1/53, 1/17/53, 2/21/53,
    T/5/53, M/6/53, **M/7/53**, F/8/53,
    E/11/53, 3/26/54, F/4/54, 4/23/54,
    Fo/5/54, Fo/7/54, F/8/54, 11/5/54,
    S/2/55
Tribble, TNT T/1/52, 1/25/52, E/12/52,
    M/5/53, 11/20/53
Tri-Tones S/7/55
Tuggles T/9/55
Tune Blenders F/12/54
Turbans T/3/55, S/8/55, **10/9/55**, 12/23/55
Turks 10/21/55, Fi/10/55
Turner, "Baby Face" Fi/9/52
Turner, Bonnie Fo/8/52
Turner, Ike **M/5/52**, Fo/5/52, **Fo/8/52**,
    10/11/52, **Fi/5/54**
Turner, Joe 2/14/52, S/3/52, 4/13/52,
    4/17/52, 4/20/52, 4/28/52, 5/9/52,
    5/16/52, Fo/5/52, 5/30/52, 5/31/52,
    6/23/52, 6/27/52, 7/3/52, F/7/52,
    7/25/52, 8/3/52, 8/4/52, 9/1/52,
    9/23/52, Fo/12/52, 2/16/53, S/8/53,
    10/10/53, **T/12/53**, L/2/54, 3/28/54,
    S/4/54, 5/7/54, 6/11/65, 6/18/54,
    7/30/54, T/9/54, L/9/54, E/10/54,
    E/11/54, 12/3/54, 12/17/54, 12/24/54,
    1/12/54, 1/14/55, 1/28/55, Fo/2/55,
    2/26/55, 5/29/55, Fo/7/55, 8/5/55,
    8/19/55, 8/26/55, 10/29/55, 11/4/55,
    11/11/55, F/12/55, S/12/55, 12/16/55,
    12/30/55, 12/31/55
Turner, Odelle L/1/52, 3/21/52, E/4/52
Turner, Titus T/6/52, T/12/52, Fo/2/53,
    F/6/53, E/6/55, T/6/55, 7/8/55,
    Fo/10/55
Twilighters S/4/55, T/7/55
Twin Tones E/6/55, S/6/55, Fo/10/55
Tyler, Jimmy M/7/53

U
Uggams, Leslie 8/21/53, 1/15/54

310

Upsetters E/1/54

V

Valdeler, Pat S/8/53
Valentines *2/19/55*, F/11/55, 11/18/55,
 12/12/55, 12/22/55
Valley, Frankie (Valli) **Fi/5/54**
Valli, June M/7/54
Van Loan, Joe **E/4/55**
Van Walls, Harry (See Rockets)
Vanderpool, Sylvia (See Little Sylvia)
Vaughan, Sarah 1/1/52, 1/16/52, 1/18/52,
 2/22/52, *L/2/52*, 3/12/52, 6/13/52,
 6/20/52, M/7/52, 7/26/52, 9/5/52,
 12/24/52, **1/2/53**, 2/28/53, 4/24/53,
 7/3/53, 1/6/54, **1/29/54**, 4/16/54,
 4/30/54, 5/10/54, E/12/54, E/3/55,
 3/11/55, 5/6/55, 7/10/55
Vel-Aires (See Woods, Donald)
Velvets **Fo/6/54**
Victorians F/2/52
Vinson, Eddie "Cleanhead" 1/13/52, **3/16/52**,
 S/12/52, 2/13/53, 2/27/53, 2/19/54,
 3/5/54, Fi/3/54, 6/25/54, 1/24/55
Vocaleers 6/26/53, S/2/54
Voices 7/15/55, T/9/55, 12/16/55, Fo/12/55
Volumes Fo/4/55

W

Wailers M/7/54
Walker, Mel 2/17/52, 4/25/52, F/6/52,
 8/21/52, 9/1/52, 10/6/52, 11/28/52
Walker, T-Bone **1/10/52**, 1/18/52, 1/25/52,
 3/2/52, T/4/52, 6/16/52, 7/18/52,
 7/26/52, 8/17/52, F/10/52, 11/16/52,
 3/8/53, 4/5/53, 4/30/53, 5/23/53,
 5/29/53, S/6/53, 6/19/53, 7/31/53,
 8/17/53, 8/24/53, M/9/53, 9/17/53,
 10/23/53, S/11/53, 12/25/53, 12/27/53,
 T/1/54, 1/29/54, T/3/54, 3/28/54,
 4/30/54, S/6/54, 7/2/54, 7/30/54,
 S/8/54, 9/17/54, E/11/54, 11/12/54,
 11/19/54, 1/14/55, 1/28/55, E/2/55,
 4/22/55, M/5/55, 6/17/55, F/7/55,
 M/7/55, 8/12/55, M/9/55, 9/23/55,
 F/10/55, 11/16/55
Wallace, Jerry F/3/54
Walton, Square E/10/53, S/11/53
Wanderers M/10/53, Fo/10/53, 11/27/53,
 1/22/54, E/2/54, T/3/54, **E/8/54**
Ward, Billy and his Dominoes 1/1/52,
 1/28/52, S/3/52, 4/19/52, T/4/52,
 4/20/52, 5/1/52, 6/14/52, 8/15/52,
 8/29/52, 9/19/52, 9/20/52, 10/4/52,
 T/10/52, E/11/52, 11/11/52, Fo/12/52,

12/25/52, 2/6/53, 2/13/53, 2/20/53,
 2/27/53, M/3/53, F/5/53, 5/7/53,
 5/21/53, 6/5/53, S/7/53, E/8/53,
 M/8/53, 9/14/53, 9/17/53, 9/25/53,
 9/29/53, 10/23/53, F/11/53, E/11/53,
 11/15/53, S/11/53, 11/28/53, T/12/53,
 12/31/53, L/1/54, 3/5/54, Fo/3/54,
 4/23/54, 4/30/54, E/6/54, S/6/54,
 S/7/54, 7/13/54, E/8/54, M/8/54,
 8/20/54, L/8/54, S/10/54, M/10/54,
 E/11/54, 12/17/54, 12/31/54, 1/4/55,
 1/28/55, 1/29/55, 2/4/55, T/2/55,
 Fo/4/55, T/7/55, Fo/8/55, 9/8/55,
 Fo/9/55, M/10/55
Warren, Ernie E/2/55
Washington, Baby **1/22/54**, 6/18/54,
 6/25/54, 6/17/55
Washington, Dinah 1/1/52, 1/13/52, F/2/52,
 2/14/52, 3/21/52, 4/11/52, 4/20/52,
 5/21/52, 5/30/52, 6/20/52, L/6/52,
 7/4/52, 7/11/52, 7/21/52, 8/2/52,
 L/8/52, T/9/52, 10/23/52, 11/21/52,
 S/12/52, 12/12/52, 12/26/52, 1/11/53,
 3/27/53, S/4/53, S/6/53, 6/21/53,
 7/10/53, 8/17/53, 9/25/53, F/10/53,
 11/23/53, 12/28/53, F/1/54, 1/22/54,
 1/29/54, 2/19/54, F/3/54, 3/5/54,
 5/17/54, 5/24/54, F/6/54, 6/26/54,
 6/29/54, 7/16/54, 8/1/54, 8/13/54,
 T/8/54, 9/17/54, 9/24/54, 10/9/54,
 11/8/54, T/11/54, 12/21/54, 1/12/55,
 1/14/55, 1/31/55, Fi/1/55, 3/18/55,
 4/15/55, T/4/55, 5/14/55, 5/20/55,
 7/7/55, 8/5/55, 8/19/55, 11/2/55,
 11/10/55
Waters, Muddy S/11/52, Fo/10/53, L/11/54,
 Fo/1/54, 5/1/54, Fi/5/54, 9/24/54,
 E/10/54, S/10/54, 10/15/54, 1/24/55,
 Fo/1/55, F/5/55, F/7/55, 7/10/55,
 S/12/55
Watson, Johnny "Guitar" **F/4/54**, Fo/5/54,
 10/15/54, 12/31/54, 2/18/55, 4/1/55,
 F/7/55, T/8/55, 10/21/55, 11/25/55,
 Fo/11/55, 12/16/55
Watson, Paula E/1/53, S/4/53
Watson, Young John (see Watson Johnny
 "Guitar") F/4/54
Wayne, James E/4/54
Wayne, Wee Willie S/8/55
Wells, Junior F/8/53, Fo/3/54, **F/12/54**
West, Rudy 2/1/55
Westbrook, Chauncy E/10/53
White, Clarence F/3/55
White, Edward Gate Fo/8/53
Whitman, Slim 7/31/54

Wick, Johnny F/9/52
Wideman, Andrew M/4/53
Wilcox, Eddie S/1/52, 2/2/52, 3/1/52,
    3/21/52, 10/14/54
Will Maston Trio **9/17/54**
Williams, Cootie 1/1/52, 3/21/52, 8/22/52,
    12/12/52, 12/26/52, **3/5/54**, 6/25/54,
    L/6/54, **9/10/54**, 11/8/54, 12/21/54
Williams, Curtis 4/26/55, 5/13/55
Williams, Dootsie 8/29/53, **Fi/8/54**, M/1/55,
    4/26/55
Williams, Earl E/7/54
Williams, Florence 8/29/52
Williams, James S/8/52
Williams, Joe (on Trumpet) Fo/2/52, **F/6/52**
Williams, Joe (Joseph Goreed) Fo/9/52,
    S/6/55, Fo/7/55, 11/16/55, 12/22/55
Williams, L. C. 2/3/52
Williams, Lester Fi/3/52, E/1/54
Willaims, Lloyd L/5/52
Williams, Louise T/1/54
Williams, Mel 9/26/52, Fo/12/54
Williams, Otis (See also Charms) S/10/55,
    10/28/55
Williams, Paul S/1/52, 2/8/52, E/7/52,
    7/18/52, 8/12/52, **8/30/52**, 9/12/52,
    2/6/53, 4/25/53, 5/20/53, 7/3/53,
    8/17/53, 9/17/53, 9/25/53, 10/18/53,
    11/24/53, 1/6/54, 4/1/54, M/5/54,
    E/6/54, 10/1/54, 10/22/54, 1/28/55,
    2/26/55, 4/22/55, E/6/55, 7/15/55,
    8/26/55, 10/29/55
Williams, Teddy E/1/53
Williamson, Bobby M/7/54
Williamson, Sonny Boy Fo/8/52, T/12/52,
    5/16/53, T/12/53, F/4/54, Fo/9/55,
    12/23/55
Willie and Ruth T/4/54, S/8/54

Willis, Chuck F/5/52, Fo/9/52, 11/30/52,
    Fi/12/52, 1/5/53, S/5/53, 4/25/53,
    Fi/6/53, 7/31/53, 9/26/53, 10/1/53,
    11/4/53, 11/24/53, S/12/53, 2/26/54,
    5/10/54, T/5/54, L/9/54, E/10/54,
    E/11/54, F/12/54, 12/10/54, 2/4/55,
    S/2/55, 2/21/55, 5/4/55, Fi/5/55,
    S/10/55
Willis, Little Son S/8/52, F/9/52, Fo/1/53
Wills, Billy Jack S/4/55
Wilson, Jimmy Fo/5/53, Fi/6/53, 9/27/53,
    10/30/53, F/5/54
Wilson, Little Sonny T/3/54
Wilson, Sonny "Jackie" **E/11/53**
Winley, Harold 6/12/53
Witherspoon, Jimmy 1/1/52, 1/17/52,
    2/14/52, T/2/52, 4/11/52, 4/16/52,
    6/1/52, 7/3/52, 7/20/52, 7/26/52,
    Fo/7/52, Fo/11/52, F/12/52, Fo/1/53,
    F/3/53, F/6/53, S/7/53, 8/15/53,
    9/27/53, Fo/11/53, **3/11/54**, T/3/54,
    F/5/54, 6/12/54, M/7/54, 8/13/54,
    9/17/54, M/10/54, T/2/55, 5/27/55,
    S/11/55
Woods, Bennie and the Five Dukes S/5/55
Woods, Donald and the Vel-Aires F/7/55
Woods, Sonny and the Twigs S/5/54
Wrens Fo/2/55, 12/22/55
Wright, Billy T/2/52, **5/16/52**, 5/30/52,
    4/5/52, M/6/53, S/7/53, 4/17/54
Wright, Johnny S/1/54

Y

Yelvington, Malcolm F/1/55
Young, Lester 7/9/53, 8/9/53
Young, Vicki 2/26/55
Young Jessie F/5/54, **Fo/7/55**, 11/25/55,
    F/12/55

Song Index

Only original release date or first mention of a given song is noted.

A

"A.B.C.'s" - Smilin' Joe F/9/54
"Adios My Desert Love" - Nolan Strong and Diablos Fo/4/54
"Adorable" - Colts T/9/55
"Adorable" - Drifters Fo/10/55
"After Hours Joint" - Jimmy Coe T/6/53
"After 'While You'll Be Sorry" - Joe Turner Fo/5/52
"Aged And Mellow" - Little Esther Fo/5/52
"Ain't Cha Got Me (Where You Want Me)" - Buddy Johnson S/5/54
"Ain't Gonna Do It" - Pelicans Fo/10/54
"Ain't Got No Time" - Bumps Blackwell Fo/10/54
"Ain't It A Shame" - Lloyd Price T/1/53
"Ain't No Meat On De Bone" - Champion Jack Dupree Fo/9/53
"Ain't No Use" - Big Maybelle S/5/55
"Ain't No Use" - Rosco Gordon T/1/53
"Ain't Nothin' Baby" - Ike Carpenter Fo/6/53
"Ain't Nothin' Happenin'" - Little Richard T/7/52
"Ain't That A Shame" - Fats Domino Fo/4/55
"Ain't That A Shame" - Pat Boone T/6/55
"Ain't Times Hard" - Floyd Jones T/8/54
"All Around The World" - Little Willie John Fo/7/55
"All Around The World" - Titus Turner T/6/55
"All By Myself" - Fats Domino Fo/8/55
"All Is Well" - Amos Milburn Fi/8/55
"All My Heart Belongs To You" - Hearts S/6/55
"All Night Baby" - Robins Fo/4/53
"All Night Long" - Rusty Bryant F/3/54
"All Night Long" - Bull Moose Jackson F/5/52
"All Night Mambo" - Cookies T/11/54
"All Righty!" - "5" Royales Fo/10/53
"All She Wants To Do Is Mambo" - Wynonie Harris T/12/54
"Alley Cat" - Dolly Cooper Fo/6/53
"Alone Again" - Five Crowns F/4/55

"Alright, Okay, You Win" - Ella Johnson T/3/55
"Alrighty Oh Sweetie" - Clovers S/11/54
"Always" - Little Richard and the Tempo Toppers Fo/3/54
"Always And Always" - Don Julian and Meadowlarks F/7/55
"Always Look Up" - Nolan Lewis F/11/55
"Am I The One?" - Spiders T/4/55
"And The Angels Sing" - Bill Doggett Fo/1/54
"Angels Say" - Four Fellows S/10/55
"Annie Had A Baby" - Midnighters T/8/54
"Annie Kicked The Bucket" - Nu Tones Fo/12/54
"Annie's Answer" - Hazel McCallum and El Dorados T/10/54
"Annie's Aunt Fannie" - Midnighters Fo/10/54
"Another Fool In Town" - Lightnin' Hopkins Fo/1/53
"Any Day Now" - Buddy Johnson T/7/54
"Anymore" - Johnny Ace T/7/55
"Anything For A Friend" - Faye Adams T/1/55
"Anyway" - Three Chuckles Fo/12/55
"Are You Forgetting" - Royals T/12/52
"Are You Lonesome Tonight?" - Dream Man T/3/52
"Are You Looking For 'A Sweetheart" - Dean Barlow and Crickets S/2/54
"Are You Out There" - Percy Mayfield F/7/55
"As Long As I'm Moving" - Ruth Brown Fo/4/55
"Ashamed Of Myself" - Midnighters Fo/2/55
"At My Front Door" - Pat Boone Fo/9/55
"At My Front Door" - El Dorados T/9/55
"Atomic Baby" - Linda Hayes F/3/53

B

"Baby" - Crows F/5/54
"Baby, Baby All The Time" - Amos Milburn T/9/53
"Baby, Baby What's Wrong" - Earl Gaines S/10/55
"Baby Be Mine" - Nolan Strong and Diablos T/9/54
"Baby, Come A Little Closer" - Five Willows S/8/55
"Baby Come Back To Me" - Five Echoes T/9/55
"Baby Doll" - Marvin and Johnny Fi/11/53
"Baby Don't Do It" - "5" Royales Fi/12/53

"Baby Don't Do That To Me" - Roy Milton
S/3/55

"Baby Don't Go" - Jesse Belvin T/7/52

"Baby, Don't Turn Your Back On Me" -
Lloyd Price Fo/5/53

"Baby Don't You Tear My Clothes" - Smokey
Hogg Fi/9/52

"Baby I Love You" - Shirley Gunter and
Queens Fo/3/55

"Baby I Need You" - El Dorados F/9/55

"Baby I'm Gonna Throw You Out" - Allen
Bunn F/6/53

"Baby I'm Losing You" - Cecil Gant S/7/52

"Baby It's You" - Spaniels Fo/7/53

"Baby Let Me Hear You Call My Name" -
Ray Charles S/7/52

"Baby Let's Play House" - Arthur Gunter
Fo/11/54

"Baby Let's Play House" - Elvis Presley
S/4/55, Fo/12/55

"Baby Let's Play House" - Thunderbirds
F/2/55

"Baby Mine" - Cabineers Fo/1/52

"Baby Please" - Chanticlaires F/11/54

"Baby Please" - Fats Domino S/5/54

"Baby Please No No" - Al "Fat Man" Thomas
F/7/52

"Baby, Rock Me" - Pat Valdeler S/8/53

"Baby What's Wrong" - Elmore James F/5/53

"Baby You're The One" - Ebonaires F/11/53

"Back Door Troubles" - Pete "Guitar" Lewis
S/1/54

"Back Street" - Rusty Bryant F/2/55

"Bad Feeling Blues" - Lightnin' Hopkins
Fi/8/55

"Bad Heart Blues" - Joe Williams F/6/52

"Bad Neighborhood" - Floyd Dixon with
Johnny Moore's Three Blazers Fo/2/52

"Bad News" - Brownie McGhee F/12/52

"Bad News Baby" - Wynonie Harris S/1/53

"Bald Head" - Treniers Fo/7/54

"Bambalya" - Bayou Boys S/12/52

"Barfly" - Orioles F/7/52

"Bartender Fill It Up Again" - Otis Blackwell
F/1/54

"Be Bop Wino" - Lamplighters S/11/53

"Be Faithful" - Dean Barlow and Crickets
F/12/54

"Be Mine Or Be A Fool" - Penguins Fo/4/55

"Be Seeing You In My Dreams" - Al Savage
S/6/54

"Beachcomber" - Big Jay McNeeley Fo/8/54

"Bear Cat" - Rufus Thomas, Jr. Fo/3/53

"Beating Of My Heart" - Charmers S/2/54

"Beetle Bug Bop" - Collins Kids Fo/11/55

"Beggar For Your Kisses" - Diamonds
T/12/52

"Beggin' For Your Mercy" - Earl Johnson
S/7/53

"Beggin' My Baby" - Little Milton Fo/1/54

"Beginning To Miss You" - John Greer
Fo/8/53

"Beginning To Miss You" - Patty Anne
Fo/8/53

"Believe Me Baby" - Roy Milton Fo/12/52

"Bells, The" - Dominoes Fo/12/52

"Bells Are Ringing, The" - Smiley Lewis
F/7/52

"Bells Ring Out, The" - Spaniels Fo/10/53

"Beside You" - Swallows T/4/52

"Best Wishes" - Lowell Fulson E/1/52

"Better Beware" - Little Esther S/4/52

"Beyond The Blue Horizon" - Earl Bostic
S/10/55

"Big Break" - Richard Berry S/10/54

"Big Dip" - Jimmy Forrest S/5/52

"Big Dipper, The" - Joe Liggins Fo/9/53

"Big Dog" - Bill Doggett S/5/52

"Big Eyes" - Little Caesar Fo/7/53

"Big Eyes" - Majors F/6/54

"Big John" - Richard Berry F/12/55

"Big John" - Titus Turner Fo/10/55

"Big Leg Mama" - Rockets T/4/53

"Big Long Slidin' Thing" - Dinah
Washington F/6/54

"Big Mamou" - Smiley Lewis Fi/3/53

"Big Mouth" - Jimmy Nelson T/9/53

"Big Mouth Mama" - Shadows Fo/7/54

"Big Question, The" - Percy Mayfield
F/3/52

"Big Rat" - Lil Son Jackson T/3/54

"Big Stars Falling Blues" - Tampa Red
Fo/1/54

"Big Things On My Mind" - Lightin'
Hopkins Fo/7/54

"Bip Bam" - Drifters F/10/54

"Bird In The Hand, A" - Roy Milton
F/4/54

"Bitter Sweet" - Buddy Johnson T/7/55

"Black Cat" - Johnny Fuller F/12/55

"Black Cat Bone" - Peppermint Harris
S/8/54

"Black Denim Trousers" - Cheers F/9/55

"Black Denim Trousers" - Diamonds T/9/55

"Black Diamond" - Roy Brown Fo/10/54

"Black Diamond" - Mr. Sad Head F/8/52

"Blackout" - Paul Bascomb S/6/52

"Blind Love" - B. B. King T/11/53

"Block Buster" - Boots Brown F/1/53

"Blow The Whistle" - Sugar Tones S/11/54

"Blow Your Horn" - Red Prysock F/8/54
"Blowin' Crazy" - Joe Houston Fi/11/53
"Blowin' The Blues" - Paul Williams S/1/52
"Blue Boy" - Chris Powell T/9/52
"Blue Monday" - Smiley Lewis T/1/54
"Blue Moon" - Ivory Joe Hunter F/1/52
"Blue Serenade" - Baby Face Turner Fi/9/52
"Blue Skies" - Earl Bostic Fo/6/54
"Blue Skies" - Four Friends T/9/53
"Blue Velvet" - Clovers F/2/55
"Blues Before Sunrise" - Elmore James
     F/11/55
"Blues Blasters Boogie" - Jimmy McCracklin
     S/4/54
"Blues By The Hour" - Lil Son Jackson
     S/6/54
"Blues Came Pouring Down, The" - Tiny
     Bradshaw T/5/53
"Blues For Anna Bacoa" - Lynn Hope F/2/53
"Blues For Everybody" - Jack Dupree F/4/55
"Blues For My Cookie" - Lightnin' Hopkins
     Fo/10/55
"Blues In A Closet" - Tri-Tones S/7/55
"Blues In A Letter" - Flamingos S/11/54
"Blues Is A Woman" - T-Bone Walker
     F/10/52
"Blues Train" - Browley Guy S/11/52
"Blues With A Feeling" - Little Walter
     S/9/53
"Bo Diddley" - Bo Diddley F/4/55
"Boogie At Midnight" - Boyd Bennett and his
     Rockets T/2/55
"Boogie Baby" - J. T. Brown Fo/7/54
"Boogie Woogie Lou" - Joe Liggins Fi/3/52
"Boogie Woogie On St. Louis" - Lloyd Glenn
     F/10/52
"Boogie Woogie Santa Claus" - Mabel Scott
     M/10/54
"Boogie's Blues" - H-Bomb Ferguson S/2/52
"Boot 'Em Up" - Du Droppers S/9/54
"Bop-Ting-A-Ling" - LaVern Baker S/4/55
"Boppin' The Rock" - Clifton Chenier
     Fi/5/55
"Born On The 13th" - Smokey Hogg Fi/3/52
"Boudoir Boogie" - Johnny Sparrow and Bows
     and Arrows T/9/52
"Break My Bones" - Four Fellows Fo/7/53
"Break Thru" - John "Schoolboy" Porter
     F/6/52
"Broke" - Chuck Higgins F/10/54
"Broken Hearted Traveler" - Floyd Dixon
     w/Johnny Moore's Three Blazers
     T/2/53
"Brown Boy" - Clarence Palmer and the Jive
     Bombers T/1/52

"Brown Skin Girl" - Jimmy Liggins T/7/52
"Buick 59" - Medallions F/11/54
"Bumble Bee" - Sonics S/7/55
"Bump, The" - Cardinals F/8/52
"Bump On A Log" - Lulu Reed S/4/54
"Burn That Candle" - Cues S/10/55
"Burn That Candle" - Bill Haley and his
     Comets T/10/55
"Bus Station Blues" - Louis Brooks Fo/4/54
"Butter Ball" - Marvin and Johnny F/6/55
"Bye Bye" - Dreamers T/9/54
"Bye-Bye Baby" - Charms Fo/1/54
"Bye! Bye! Baby" - B. B. King Fo/7/54
"Bye Bye Baby Blues" - Johnny Giles and
     the Jive Five T/9/52
"Bye Bye Baby Blues" - Ravens Fo/3/55
"Bye Bye Young Men" - Ruth Brown
     F/1/55

C
"Caldonia's Wedding Day" - Roy Brown
     S/11/53
"Call Before You Go Home" - Memphis Slim
     Fo/12/53
"Call Me A Hound Dog" - Jimmy Wilson
     Fo/5/53
"Call Operator 210" - Floyd Dixon T/6/52
"Call Operator 210" - Johnny Otis T/7/52
"Calling All Cows" - Blues Rockers S/10/55
"Calling Maggie" - Big Walter S/2/55
"Can't Stand No More" - Wini Brown
     F/2/53
"Can't Stop Lovin'" - Elmore James T/8/53
"Can't Stop Loving You" - Smiley Lewis
     Fo/7/54
"Can't Understand" - Little Junior Parker
     S/3/54
"Candy Man, The" - Eddie "Tex" Curtis
     T/6/54
"Candy Rock" - Joe Houston S/5/55
"Careless Love" - Fats Domino F/1/52
"Carolina Blues" - Brownie McGhee and
     Sonny Terry Fo/1/52
"Cash Register Heart" - Bob Crewe S/6/54
"Cat Hop" - Tiny Bradshaw T/10/54
"Cat Hop" - Dodgers S/3/55
"Cat Hop" - Sonny Boy Williamson T/12/53
"'Cause I Lost My Helping Hand" - Lil Miss
     Cornshucks F/2/52
"Cemetery Blues" - Lightnin' Hopkins
     T/1/54
"Chained To Your Love" - Clayton Love
     Fi/9/52
"Chains Of Love Have Disappeared" - Little
     Caesar Fo/10/53

315

"Changing Partners" - Crickets S/1/54
"Chapel Of Memories" - Sonny Woods and
    the Twigs S/5/54
"Charlie Brown" - Cues T/12/55
"Cheater, The" - Jimmy McCracklin S/8/54
"Check Yourself" - Lowell Fulson F/3/55
"Cherokee" - Earl Bostic S/5/53
"Cherry" - Tab Smith Fo/7/53
"Cherry Bean" - Earl Bostic T/5/55
"Cherry Pie" - Marvin and Johnny T/7/54
"Cherry Red" - Little Caesar F/9/53
"Cherry Wine" - Little Esther F/9/53
"Chicken And The Hawk" - Joe Turner
    F/12/55
"Chicken Back" - Louis Jordan S/12/55
"Chicken In A Blanket" - Billy Bland
    Fo/12/55
"Chocolate Blonde" - Joe Hill Louis T/2/52
"Chocolate Sundae" - Kid King's Combo
    S/1/54
"Chop Chop Boom" - Danderliers F/4/55
"Chop Chop Ching A Ling" - Roamers
    F/5/55
"Christmas In Heaven" - Billy Ward and his
    Dominoes S/11/53
"Christmas Morning" - Titus Turner T/12/52
"Christmas Prayer, A" - Penguins S/12/55
"Clock, The" - Johnny Ace Fi/6/53
"Close The Door" - Jim Lowe S/6/55
"Close Your Eyes" - Five Keys F0/1/55
"Co-Operation" - Prince Partridge E/7/54
"Cold Mama" - Gabriel Brown F/1/53
"Come A Little Bit Closer" - Ravens S/4/53
"Comeback, The" - Memphis Slim Fo/7/53
"Come Back Baby" - Doctor Ross Fo/1/54
"Come Back Baby" - Roosevelt Sykes F/8/53
"Come Back Maybellene" - Mercy Dee
    F/9/55
"Come Back Maybellene" - John Greer
    T/8/55
"Come Back My Love" - Wrens Fo/2/55
"Come Back To Me" - Clicks F/8/55
"Come Back To Me" - Dappers T/5/55
"Come Go My Bail Louise" - Five Keys
    S/2/53
"Come In The House" - Joe Tex Fo/10/55
"Come On And Love Me" - Du Droppers
    T/6/53
"Come On Baby" - Willie Mabon F/4/55
"Come On Back Home" Sonny Boy Williamson
    Fo/3/52
"Come On By" - Smiley Lewis S/12/55
"Come To Me Baby" - Charms F/8/54
"Come What May" - Four Tunes T/2/52
"Confession" - Lil Son Jackson Fo/9/53

"Convicted" - Oscar McLollie S/11/55
"Cool, Cool Baby" - Magic-Tones S/12/53
"Corn Whiskey" - Jimmy Witherspoon
    F/12/52
"Cornbread And Cabbage" - Joe Houston
    Fo/5/53
"Could It Be" - Sh-Booms Fi/10/55
"Count The Days I'm Gone" - Piano Red
    T/3/52
"Country Boy" - Elmore James S/8/53
"Courage To Love" - "5" Royales Fo/8/52
"Crawlin'" - Clovers T/2/53
"Crazy Chicken" - Five Jets Fo/10/54
"Crazy Crazy" - Ike Carpenter T/4/53
"Crazy For My Baby" - Willie Dixon
    Fo/11/55
"Crazy For You" - Heartbeats F/11/55
"Crazy Girl" - Long John S/3/54
"Crazy Man, Crazy" - Bill Haley with
    Haley's Comets Fo/4/52
"Crazy Mixed Up World" - Faye Adams
    S/5/54
"Crazy She Calls Me" - Larry Darnell
    S/4/53
"Crazy With The Heat" - Clarence Samuels
    Fo/7/54
"Cross My Heart" - Johnny Ace T/1/53
"Cross Over The Bridge" - Chords E/6/54
"Cross Over The Bridge" - Flamingos
    T/4/54
"Cruel Cruel World" - Johnny Fuller
    Fo/4/55
"Cry" - Johnnie Ray 1/11/52
"Cry, Cry Baby" - Aladdins T/4/55
"Cry Some More" - "5" Royales T/4/54
"Cryin' And Driftin'" - Charles Brown
    T/10/53
"Cryin' In My Sleep" - Herb Fisher S/8/53
"Cryin' Mercy" - Charles Brown T/10/53
"Crying In The Chapel" - Four Dukes
    F/9/53
"Crying In The Chapel" - Orioles T/7/53
"Curl Up In My Arms" - Nuggets Fi/11/54
"Cut That Out" - Junior Wells F/8/53

D

"Daddy, Daddy" - Ruth Brown F/8/52
"Daddy-O" - Bonnie Lou S/10/55
"Daddy Rockin' Strong" - Nolan Strong and
    Diablos F/5/55
"Daddy Rolling Stone" - Otis Blackwell
    Fo/11/53
"Damp Rag" - Stomp Gordon T/10/52
"Dance With A Rock" - Esquire Boys
    T/12/55

"Dance With Me Henry" (See also
     "Wallflower, The") - Georgia Gibbs
     L/7/55
"(Danger) Soft Shoulders" - Sonny Til
     S/5/53
"Dark and Lonely Room" - Jimmy Lewis
     Fo/9/52
"Darlene" - Dreams Fo/5/54
"Darling" - Ray-O-Vacs F/6/54
"Darling Dear" - Counts S/2/54
"Darling I Know" - El Rays Fo/5/54
"Darling Listen To This" - Wilbert Harrison
     T/7/55
"Daughter (That's Your Red Wagon)" - Sax
     Kari and Gloria Irving Fo/3/53
"Day In, Day Out" - Marvin and Johnny
     Fo/9/54
"Day Old Bread" - Milt Trenier S/7/54
"Daybreak Rock" - Jack Dupree Fo/7/55
"Deacon Don't Like It, The" - Wynonie
     Harris Fo/6/53
"Dealin' From The Bottom" - Stick McGhee
     Fo/11/53
"Dear Angels Above" - Belvederes Fo/9/55
"Dear Darling" - Medallions Fo/11/55
"Dear Wonderful God" - Sonny Knight
     F/1/53
"Dearest One" - Charlie and Ray F/5/55
"Death Of An Angel" - Donald Woods and
     Vel-Aires F/7/55
"Decatur Street" - Piano Red Fi/6/53
"Deep Freeze" - Roamers T/1/55
"Deep In My Heart For You" - Pyramids
     Fo/8/55
"Delta Blues" - Joe Williams Fo/2/52
"Dem Days" - Orioles T/4/53
"Devil That I See" - Penguins Fo/9/55
"Devil's Daughter" - Stomp Gordon S/4/53
"Diddley Daddy" - Bo Diddley S/6/55
"Dig That Crazy Santa Claus" - Oscar
     McLollie Fo/11/54
"Dig These Blues" - Four Clefs Fo/2/52
"Dim, Dim The Lights" - Bill Haley and
     Comets T/10/54
"Ding Dong Baby" - Marvin Phillips S/7/55
"Ding Dong Ding" - Bip and Bop T/4/55
"Discouraged" - Allen Bunn T/6/52
"Do Do Do It Again" - Four Tunes Fo/2/54
"Do It No More" - Smokey Hogg Fo/12/52
"Do Right Blues" - Little Caesar F/3/53
"Do You Love Me?" - Young Jesse F/12/55
"Do You Miss Me?" - Ivory Joe Hunter
     S/9/54
"Do You Wanna Rock" - Cadets T/11/55
"Doctor Baby" - Five Dollars F/9/55

"Doctor Velvet" - Nite Riders Fo/12/54
"Dollar Down, A" - Louis Jordan Fi/5/54
"Don'cha Go" - Richard Berry T/5/55
"Don'cha Go" - Spaniels F/5/55
"Don't Be Angry" - Nappy Brown T/3/55
"Don't Be Bashful" - Shadows Fi/11/53
"Don't Blame Her" - Lonnie Johnson S/4/52
"Don't Change Your Pretty Ways" -
     Midnighters S/10/55
"Don't Cry Baby" - Orioles F/9/52
"Don't Deceive Me" - Chuck Willis Fi/6/53
"Don't Drop It" - Wilbert Harrison T/9/54
"Don't Ever Leave Me" - Rivileers S/4/55
"Don't Go" - Chestnuts T/11/54
"Don't Know How I Loved You" - Otis
     Blackwell S/5/54
"Don't Know Why I Cry" - Chromatics
     F/7/55
"Don't Let It Happen To You" - Cashmeres
     S/5/55
"Don't Let It Rain" - Roy Brown Fo/6/54
"Don't Live Like That No More" - Baby Dee
     F/8/54
"Don't Love You Anymore" - Sparks of
     Rhythm Fo/9/55
"Don't Make It So Good" - Lamplighters
     Fo/11/55
"Don't Make Me Love You" - Lulu Reed
     F/9/53
"Don't Marry Too Soon" - Lil Miss
     Cornshucks S/6/52
"Don't Mention My Name" - Ravens S/2/53
"Don't Mess With My Baby" - Howlin' Wolf
     T/10/55
"Don't Pass Me By" - Du Droppers S/11/53
"Don't Start Me Talkin'" - Sonny Boy
     Williamson Fo/9/55
"Don't Stop Dan" - Checkers Fo/4/54
"Don't Take Your Love From Me" -
     Calvanes Fo/9/55
"Don't Touch Me" - Johnny "Guitar" Watson
     F/7/55
"Don't You Know" - Ray Charles S/7/54
"Don't You Know" - Fats Domino T/2/55
"Don't You Know I Love You So" - Five
     Keys T/7/55
"Don't You Remember Baby?" - Roy Milton
     S/3/53
"Don't You Think I Ought To Know" -
     Little Donna Hightower 5/6/52
"Done Got Over You" - Blasers T/8/55
"Donna" - Billy Brooks Fi/10/55
"Door Is Still Open, The" - Cardinals
     Fo/2/55
"Double Crossin' Liquor" - Stick McGhee

F/4/55

"Double Date" - Five Encores Fo/12/55

"Double Dealing Daddy" - Dinah Washington T/9/52

"Double Duty Lovin'" - Eddie Bond S/11/55

"Down At Haydens" - Hunters S/10/53

"Down At The Depot" - John Lee Fi/3/52

"Down In New Orleans" - Big Mike T/3/55

"Down The Road" - Cadillacs F/8/55

"Dragnet Blues" - Johnny Moore's Three Blazers Fo/7/53

"Dream Baby" - Roscoe Gordon F/11/52

"Dream Girl" - Jesse And Marvin Fo/12/52

"Dream Girl" - Al Savage S/2/55

"Dream Of A Lifetime" - Flamingos T/1/55

"Dreams Come True" - Strangers F/2/55

"Driftin'" - Eddie Boyd F/9/54

"Drinkin' Wine Spodee-O-Dee" - Malcolm Yelvington F/1/55

"Dripper's Boggie" - Joe Liggins T/4/52

"Driving Down The Highway" - Blue Flamers S/3/54

"Drivin' Me Mad" - Memphis Slim S/2/53

"Driving Me Mad" - Little Junior Parker T/10/55

"Drowning Every Hope I Ever Had" - Orioles F/6/54

"Drunk" - Jimmy Liggins Fo/8/53

"Drunkard, The" - Thrillers S/9/54

"Dungaree Doll" - Rock Brothers Fo/11/55

"Dust My Broom" - Earl Brown T/9/52

E

"Each Time" - Delores Hawkins and the Four Lads T/8/52

"Early In The Morning" - Elmore James E/6/53

"Early Morning Blues" - Archibald F/12/52

"Early Morning Blues" - Dozier Boys Fo/12/53

"Earth Angel" - Gloria Mann Fi/1/55

"Earth Angel" - Penguins S/10/54

"Easy" - Jimmy and Walter F/4/53

"Easy Come Easy Go Lover" - Joe Medlin F/3/54

"Easy, Easy Baby" - Varetta Dillard T/5/52

"Ebb Tide" - Roy Hamilton Fo/8/54

"Emily" - Turks Fi/10/55

"Eternal Love" - Rivileers Fo/10/54

"Eternally Yours" - Barons Fo/3/55

"Every Beat Of My Heart" - Royals S/4/52

"Every Day (I Have The Blues)" - Count Basie with Joe Williams S/6/55

"Every Day I Have The Blues" - Lowell Fulson E/1/55

"Every Day I Have The Blues" - B. B. King Fo/12/54

"Every Day I Have The Blues" - Joe Williams Fo/9/52

"Every Day My Love Is True" - Peacharoos Fo/11/54

"Every Day Of The Week" - Christine Kitterell S/10/53

"Everyone's Laughing" - Clyde McPhatter F/8/55

"Evilest Woman In Town" - Rock Heart T/10/52

"Eyes Full Of Tears" - Pee Wee Crayton T/4/55

F

"Farewell" - Bobby Relf and Laurels T/2/55

"Farewell" - Willie and Ruth T/4/54

"Farewell Blues" - Joe Liggins Fi/6/53

"Farewell, So Long, Goodbye" - Bill Haley and his Comets T/10/53

"Fast Life" - Lightnin' Hopkins T/3/55

"Fat Back And Corn Liquor" - Louis Jordan T/12/54

"Feed My Body To The Fishes" - Willie Love S/5/52

"Feel Like I Do" - H-Bomb Ferguson Fo/1/52

"Feel So Good" - Shirley and Lee F/6/55

"Feelin' Good" - Little Junior's Blue Flames S/8/53

"Feeling Is So Good, The" - Clovers F/1/53

"Feeling Mighty Lonesome" - Mel Walker Fo/2/54

"Fifty Million Women" - Carols F/6/53

"Finally" - Heartbeats Fo/5/55

"Finance Man" - George Green Fo/4/53

"Fine Brown Frame" -Buccaneers F/2/53

"Fine Lookin' Baby" - Cadets F/6/55

"Fire Dome" - School Boy Porter S/8/52

"Fishtail Blues" - Wynonie Harris Fo/4/55

"Five Long Years" - Eddie Boyd Fo/7/52

"Five Minutes Longer" - Lamplighters Fi/8/54

"5-10-15 Hours" - Freddy Bell and Bellboys F/4/55

"5-10-15 Hours" - Ruth Brown S/3/52

"Flame In My Heart - Checkers S/9/52

"Flight 3-D" - Jimmy Forrest S/3/54

"Flim Flam" - Gene and Eunice Fo/7/55

"Flip, Flop And Fly" - Billy Duke and Dukes Fo/4/55

"Flip, Flop And Fly" - Tibby Edwards S/4/55

"Flip, Flop And Fly" - Joe Turner Fo/2/55
"Flirtin' Blues" - Ray Agee Fo/9/52
"Flying Home" - Amos Milburn F/5/52
"Flying Saucer" - Solid Senders Fo/8/52
"Fool At The Wheel" - Duce Of Rhythm and
   Tempo Toppers T/6/53
"Fool For You, A" - Ray Charles S/6/55
"Fool In Paradise" - Jewels T/10/54
"Fool's Paradise" - Charles Brown T/6/55
"Foolish" - Charles Brown S/9/54
"Foolish Dreams" - Fi-Tones T/9/55
"Foolish Me" - Moonglows T/6/55
"Foolish One" - Rockateers F/7/53
"Foolishly" - Three Chuckles S/2/55
"Fools Are Getting Scarcer" - Roy Milton
   S/5/55
"For A Thrill" - Spiders S/6/55
"For Sentimental Reasons" - Rivileers
   T/12/54
"For You I Have Eyes" - Crickets F/6/53
"'Fore Day Train" - Little Tommy Brown
   S/10/53
"Forever" - Dean Barlow E/5/55
"Forever And A Day" - Mickey and Sylvia
   Fo/12/55
"Forget If You Can" - Bubber Johnson
   Fo/7/52
"Forty Cups Of Coffee" - Danny Overbea
   S/6/53
"Forty-Leven Dozen Ways" - Cues F/11/54
"Found Me A Sugar Daddy" - Nic Nacs
   T/12/52
"Four Cold, Cold Walls" - Billy Wright
   S/7/53
"4-11-44" - Bobby Mitchell and Toppers
   S/9/52
"Four O'Clock In The Morning" - Brownie
   McGhee S/7/53
"Four Years Of Torment" - Memphis Slim
   Fo/9/54
"Fractured" - Bill Haley and Haley's Comets
   T/7/53
"Framed" - Robins Fo/10/54
"Freddy" - Connie Francis S/6/55
"Freight Train Blues" - Joe Liggins T/1/54
"Frog Hop" - Hal Singer Fi/9/52
"From The Bee" - Larks F/7/55
"From The Bottom" - Sonny Boy Williamson
   T/2/55
"Front Page Blues" - Solotones T/8/55
"Fujiyama Mama" - Annisteen Allen T/2/55

G
"Gabbin' Blues" - Big Maybelle F/12/52
"Gal! You Need A Good Whippin'" - Herbert

Beard S/7/53
"Gamblers Blues" - Dinah Washington
   S/12/52
"Gate Walks The Board" - Clarence
"Gatemouth" Brown" S/12/53
"Gee" - Crows Fi/6/53
"Gee But I Hate To Go Home" - Jerry
   Wallace F/3/54
"Gee Whittakers" - Pat Boone Fo/11/55
"Gee Whittakers" - Five Keys F/11/55
"Georgia Woman" - Lazy Slim Jim Fo/7/52
"Get High Everybody" - Lil Son Jackson
   Fo/8/54
"Get It" - Royals Fo/6/53
"Get It One More Time" - Strangers
   Fo/10/54
"Get Mad Baby" - Gaylords F/7/52
"Get On My Train" - Lovenotes F/10/53
"Get Rich Quick" - Little Richard Fo/3/52
"Get To Gettin'" - Mercy Dee S/12/53
"Get Your Mind Out Of The Gutter" - Stick
   McGhee T/5/55
"Getting Ready For Daddy" - Varetta
   Dillard F/2/53
"Ghost Of My Baby" - Checkers T/5/53
"Ghost Train" - Joe Morris Fo/8/52
"Gimmie Gimmie Gimmie" - Billy Ward and
   Dominoes S/10/54
"Girl Back Home, The" - Four Speeds
   F/1/55
"Girl From Kokomo" - Roy Brown S/8/54
"Git With The Grits" - Wynonie Harris
   Fo/6/55
"Give In" - Five Jets S/8/54
"Give It Up" - Hawks T/9/54
"Give Me You" - Billy Ward and Dominoes
   Fo/9/55
"Give Thanks" - Platters Fo/11/53
"Glasgow Kentucky Blues" - Johnny Wick's
Orchestra F/9/52
"Glory Of Love" - Amos Milburn S/7/54
"God Bless You Child" - Blue Dots S/10/54
"God Only Knows" - Crystals S/1/55
"Goddess Of Love" - Nu Tones S/5/55
"Goin' Back To Georgia" - Big Boy Crudup
   Fo/3/52
"(Goin' Down To) The River - Little Caesar
   S/18/52
"Goin' Home" - Fats Domino T/5/52
"Going Away" - Jimmy Liggins T/2/54
"Going Away Walking" - Harmonica Frank
   T/8/52
"Going Back To New Orleans" - Joe Liggins
   S/10/52
"Going Home" - Ravens F/3/54

"Going In Your Direction" - Sonny Boy
    Williamson F/5/54
"Going To The River" - Fats Domino S/4/53
"Going To The River" - Chuck Willis S/4/53
"Golden Teardrops" - Flamingos T/10/53
"Gone" - Jesse Belvin Fo/4/55
"Gone, Gone, Gone" - Smokey Hogg S/5/53
"Gone Gone Gone" - Carl Perkins T/10/55
"Gone So Long" - Roy "Bald Head" Byrd
    S/5/52
"Gonna Find My Baby" - Elmore James
    T/12/52
"Gonna Leave You Baby" - Roy Milton
    F/7/54
"Gonna Love You Everyday" - Heralds
    T/9/54
"Gonna Need My Help Someday" - Memphis
    Slim F/2/52
"Gonna Take A Train" - Johnny Otis
    Fo/7/52
"Gonna Tell Your Mother" - Jimmy
    McCracklin Fo/8/55
"Good" - Edna McGriff and Sonny Til
    F/11/52
"Good Golly, Miss Molly" - Playboys S/4/55
"Good, Good Whiskey" - Amos Milburn
    S/12/53
"Good Lovin'" - Clovers Fi/6/53
"Good News" - Hawks T/5/54
"Good Old 99" - Marylanders F/4/53
"Good Rockin' Daddy" - Etta James F/8/55
"Good Rockin' Mama" - Henry Smith S/9/54
"Good Rockin' Tonight" - Elvis Presley
    Fo/9/54, Fo/12/55
"Good Rockin' Tonight" - Billy Jack Wills
    S/4/55
"Good Thing Baby" - Sultans Fo/6/54
"Goodbye Baby" - Little Caesar S/9/52
"Goodbye My Love" - Chapters S/5/53
"Goodnite, Sweetheart, Goodnite" - Gloria
    Mann E/5/54
"Goodnite, Sweetheart, Goodnite" - Spaniels
    T/3/54
"Goodnight Sweetheart Goodnight" - McGuire
    Sisters M/7/54
"Goody Goody" - Five C's T/7/54
"Goofy Dust Blues" - Little Willie Littlefield
    Fo/3/54
"Goomp Blues" - Johnny Otis Fo/4/52
"Gordy's Rock" - Piano Red Fi/10/55
"Got A Mind To Leave This Town" - Tampa
    Red Fo/4/53
"Got The Water Boiling" - Regals F/5/55
"Gotta Go" - Louis Jordan F/11/55
"Gotta Go Get My Baby" - Marvin Rainwater
    S/1/55

"Grandpa Stole My Baby" - Roy Brown
    Fi/3/53
"Great Pretender, The" - Platters F/12/55
"Greatest Feeling In The World, The" -
    Four Tunes T/7/54
"Greedy Pig" - Buddy Lucas L/7/53
"Greenbacks" - Ray Charles F/10/55
"Greyhound" - Amos Milburn Fi/9/52
"Grieving Blues" - Lightnin' Hopkins
    S/6/55
"Grind, The" - Stomp Gordon F/9/55
"Groove Station" - Al Sears Orchestra
    S/2/52
"Gum Drop" - Otis Williams S/6/55
"Gum Drop" - Crew-Cuts L/7/55
"Guy With the '45', The" - Allen Bunn
    L/1/52

H

"Hadacol, That's All" - Treniers S/5/52
"Half-Pint Of Whiskey" - Young John
    Watson F/4/54
"Hambone" - Red Saunders F/3/52
"Hand Clappin'" - Red Prysock F/9/55
"Hands Off" - Jay McShann and Priscilla
    Bowman Fo/10/55
"Hard Feeling" - Jack Dupree T/2/54
"Hard Headed Woman" - Big Walter F/1/55
"Hard Times" - Charles Brown T/1/52
"Hard Times" - Johnny Fuller S/10/54
"Harlem Blues" - Little Son Willis S/8/52
"Harlem Nocturne" - Sam "The Man" Taylor
    F/5/55
"Harmonica Boogie" - Pete "Guitar" Lewis
    T/5/52
"Have A Good Time" - Ruth Brown F/8/52
"Have Mercy Baby" - Dominoes T/4/52
"Have You Heard" - Sonny Til Fo/2/53
"He's A Jelly Roll Baker" - Lonnie Johnson
    F/8/55
"He's My Man" - Marie Adams S/8/52
"Heartache Blues" - Big Tom Collins
    F/1/55
"Heartbreaker" - Ray Charles Fo/9/53
"Hearts Of Stone" - Charms Fo/9/54
"Hearts Of Stone" - Jewels T/9/54
"Heaven And Paradise" - Meadowlarks
    S/4/55
"Heaven Came Down To Earth" - Ivory Joe
    Hunter F/7/55
"Heaven Only Knows" - Charms T/8/53
"Heavenly Father" - Edna McGriff F/4/52
"Heavenly Father" - Squires T/11/55
"Heavenly Ruby" - Californians Fo/7/55

"Hello Little Boy" - Ruth Brown T/4/54
"Help Me Blues" - Mel Walker F/6/52
"Help Me Somebody" - "5" Royales S/4/53
"Henry's Got Flat Feet" - Midnighters
   T/5/55
"Here Goes My Heart To You" - Cardinals
   S/12/55
"Hey Bartender" - Floyd Dixon F/4/55
"Hey Bartender" - Red Saunders S/9/55
"Hey Bop De Bow" - Bert Convy and the
   Thunderbirds Fo/6/55
"Hey Fine Mama" - Five Notes Fo/4/53
"Hey Fine Mama" - Henry Pierce F/5/53
"Hey Henry" - Etta James S/5/55
"Hey, Little School Girl" - Peppermint Harris
   and Maxwell Davis Fo/11/52
"Hey Miss Fannie" - Clovers F/10/52
"Hey Miss Fine" - Royals Fo/10/53
"Hey Now" - Ray Charles Fo/8/52
"Hey Now" - Voices T/9/55
"Hey Pretty Girl" - Twin Tones S/6/55
"Hey Santa Claus" - Moonglows S/12/53
"Hey! There" - Red Prysock S/10/53
"Hide And Seek" - Joe Turner Fo/7/55
"High Flying Woman" - Dave Bartholomew
   F/12/52
"High Heels" - Bill Dogett T/8/54
"Highway Is My Home" - Lowell Fulson
   S/8/52
"Highway To Happiness" - Jimmy Witherspoon
   F/5/54
"Hit The Road Again" - Sunnyland Slim
   Fo/1/52
"Hittin' On Me" - Buddy Johnson T/4/53
"Hodge Podge" - Bull Moose Jackson
   Fo/9/53
"Hold Me" - Larks Fo/7/52
"Hold Me Baby" - Chordcats T/12/54
"Hold Me In Your Arms" - James Cotton
   T/7/54
"Hold Me Til Eternity" - Nolan Strong and
   Diablos T/3/55
"Hold On" - Peppers F/10/54
"Hole In The Wall" - Floyd Dixon T/11/53
"Hollerin' And Screamin'" - Little Esther
   S/2/53
"Home On Alcatraz" - Rollin' Crew
   Fo/10/55
"Honey" - Bill Doggett S/10/54
"Honey Honey" - Charlie Gracie and Wildcats
   S/7/55
"Honey Hush" - Joe Turner S/8/53
"Honey Love" - Clyde McPhatter and the
   Drifters F/6/54
"Honey Love" - June Valli M/7/54

"Honey Love" - Vicki Young M/7/54
"Honey Slipper" - Charles Brown F/2/55
"Honey's Lovin' Arms" - Bobby Smith
   Fo/7/52
"Honeydripper" - Rusty Bryant S/10/55
"Hootin' And Jumpin'" - Sonny Terry
   S/11/53
"Hot Rod" - Hal Singer T/12/55
"Hound Dog" - Little Esther S/4/53
"Hound Dog" - Willie Mae Thornton S/3/53
"House Party" - Amos Milburn Fo/11/55
"House Rocker" - Rusty Bryant S/1/54
"How Can I Tell You" - Shirley Gunter
   Fi/8/55
"How Can You Leave A Man Like This" -
   LaVern Baker Fo/8/53
"How Come My Dog Don't Bark" - Prince
   Partridge T/10/55
"How Could You Be So Mean" - Johnny
   Moore's Three Blazers F/8/52
"How Could You Hurt Me So" - Amos
   Milburn T/3/54
"How Deep Is The Well?" - Percy Mayfield
   Fo/9/53
"How I Hate To See Christmas Come
   Around" - Jimmy Witherspoon
   Fo/11/52
"How I Wonder" - "5" Royales S/3/55
"How Long Has It Been" - Tab Smith
   Fo/6/54
"How Long Must I Wait" - Smilin' Joe
   S/1/55
"How Sentimental Can I Be?" - Mellows
   F/8/54
"Hug And A Kiss, A" - Bobby Lester and
   the Moonlighters S/3/55
"Hurry Baby" - Roy Brown F/2/53
"Hurry Back Good News" - Clarence
   "Gatemouth" Brown Fo/7/53
"Hurts Me To My Heart" - Faye Adams
   T/8/54
"Hustlin' Family Blues" - Buddy Lucas
   F/7/52

I
"I Ain't Drunk" - Jimmy Liggins T/8/54
"I Ain't Gonna Tell" - Varetta Dillard
   Fi/11/53
"I Ain't Got Room To Rock" - Glenn Reeves
   Fi/8/55
"I Ain't No Fool Either" - Willie Mae
   Thornton F/12/53
"I Ain't No Watchdog" - Sonny Thompson
   T/4/54
"I Almost Lost My Mind" - Harptones

F/3/55
"I Believe" - Roy Hamilton S/2/55
"I Believe" - Elmore James F/1/53
"I Can't Do No More" - Ray Charles
    S/10/52
"I Can't Get Started With You" - Frank
    Humphries and the Four Notes F/7/52
"I Can't Help Loving You" - Bachelors
    Fo/1/54
"I Can't Hold Out Any Longer" - LaVern
    Baker F/6/54
"I Can't Lose With The Stuff I Use" - Lester
    Williams Fi/3/52
"I Can't Refuse" - Orchids Fo/11/55
"I Cried" - Velvets Fo/6/54
"I Cried For You" - Five Keys F/11/52
"I Cross My Fingers" - Bennie Woods and
    Five Dukes S/5/55
"I Declare" - Smokey Hogg T/9/55
"I Didn't Want To Do It" - Spiders T/1/54
"I Do" - "5" Royales Fo/1/54
"I Don't Care No More" - Cats S/10/55
"I Don't Go For That" - Jimmy Reed T/9/55
"I Don't Hurt Anymore" - Dinah Washington
    T/8/54
"I Don't Know" - Keynotes T/12/55
"I Don't Know" - Willie Mabon F/12/52
"I Don't Know Any Better" - Patty Anne
    T/8/52
"I Don't Know, Yes I Know" - Johnny
    Moore's Three Blazers F/3/53
"I Don't Miss You Anymore" - Blenders
    T/5/53
"I Don't Want To Set The World On Fire" -
    Sam Butera F/3/54
"I Don't Want You To Go" - Casanovas
    S/8/55
"I Feel Like Goin' Home" - Melvin Smith
    S/1/54
"I Feel So Bad" - Chuck Willis T/5/54
"I Feel So Blue" - Royals T/3/53
"I Found A New Love" - Little Donna
    Hightower T/3/52
"I Found My Baby" - Jimmy Reed Fo/1/54
"I Found Out" - Du Droppers Fo/5/53
"I Get A Thrill" - Wynonie Harris Fo/7/54
"I Get My Kicks In The Country" - TNT
    Tribble T/1/52
"I Get So Happy" - Earl King S/9/55
"I Get So Worried" - T-Bone Walker F/1/55
"I Get That Lonesome Feeling" - Ivory Joe
    Hunter T/6/52
"I Got A Letter" - Lem Johnson S/4/53
"I Got A Woman" - Ray Charles F/1/55
"I Got Booted" - Little Sonny Wilson T/3/54

"I Got Drunk" - Buddy Lucas Fo/4/54
"I Got Loose" - Charles Edwin S/4/54
"I Got Sumpin' For You" - Guitar Slim
    Fi/5/55
"I Got The Blues Again" - T-Bone Walker
    T/4/52
"I Got To Go" - Willie Mabon T/12/53
"I Gotta Go Home" - Gene and Eunice
    Fo/11/55
"I Gotta Go Now" - Starlings Fo/5/55
"I Guess It's All Over Now" - Five Budds
    S/5/53
"I Had A Notion" - Joe Morris with Al
    Savage S/9/53
"I Hadn't Anyone 'Til You" - Five Keys
    F/7/52
"I Have A Little Girl" - Howlin' Wolf
    Fo/4/55
"I Hear You Knocking" - Smiley Lewis
    Fo/7/55
"I Hear You Knocking" - Gale Storm
    Fo/9/55
"I Hope" - Four Tunes S/3/55
"I Know" - Fats Domino F/12/54
"I Know" - Hollywood Flames Fi/1/55
"I Know" - Prisonaires S/12/53
"I Know She's Gone" - Bill Robinson and
    the Quails S/4/54
"I Know You Will" - Big Bill Broonzy
    Fo/7/52
"I Like Barbeque" - Guy Brothers T/6/52
"I Like Moonshine" - Five Owls T/5/55
"I Lost Everything" - Charles Brown
    T/6/53
"I Love My Baby" - Howling Wolf Fo/1/54
"I Love To Ride" - Paula Watson S/4/53
"I Love You For Sentimental Reasons" -
    Smiley Lewis F/5/54
"I Love You Madly" - Charlie and Ray
    T/10/54
"I Love You Mostly" - Orioles F/2/55
"I Made A Vow" - Robins Fo/2/54
"I May Hate Myself In The Morning" -
    Steve Gibson F/2/52
"I Miss You So" - Orioles S/2/53
"I Must Be Dreamin'" - Robins S/6/55
"I Need A Shoulder To Cry On" - Billy
    Bunn and his Buddies F/2/52
"I Need Help" - Buddy Lucas with Amelia
    Stewart F/3/54
"I Need You All The Time" - Platters
    Fo/1/54
"I Need You Baby" - Orioles F/4/55
"I Need You Darling" - Falcons T/3/55
"I Need You Tonight" - Counts Fo/9/55

"I Need Your Love" - Pee Wee Crayton
Fi/1/55
"I Never Had It So Good" - Buddy Johnson
T/11/54
"I Only Have Eyes For You" - Four Blazes
T/5/52
"I Owe My Heart" - Faye Adams F/11/54
"I Played The Fool" - Clovers F/10/52
"I Seen What'cha Done" - Louis Jordan
S/7/54
"I Smell A Rat" - Willie Mae Thornton
S/5/54
"I Smell A Rat" - Young Jesse F/5/54
"I Stayed Down" - Johnny Wright S/1/54
"I Still Get My Kicks" - Willie Headen
T/5/54
"I Still Love You" - Ray-O-Vacs F/8/55
"I Still Love You Baby" - Lowell Fulson
T/12/55
"I Stood By" - Roy Milton Fo/12/53
"I Understand" - Four Tunes F/4/54
"I Used To Cry Mercy, Mercy" -
Lamplighters S/4/54
"I Wanna Do No More" - Ruth Brown
F/12/55
"I Wanna Hug Ya, Squeeze Ya, Kiss Ya" -
Buddy Griffin and Claudia Swann
T/1/55
"I Wanna Know" - Dolly Cooper with Hal
Singer F/4/53
"I Wanna Know" - Du Droppers Fo/3/53
"I Wanna Love You" - Du Droppers F/9/55
"I Wanna Ramble" - Junior Parker F/4/55
"I Want To Be Loved" - Muddy Waters
F/5/55
"I Want To Be Ready" - Voices Fo/12/55
"I Want To Know" - Empires S/9/55
"I Want To Love You" - Flamingos F/7/55
"I Want To Love You Baby" - Serenaders
T/6/53
"I Want You To Be My Baby" - Lillian Briggs
8/3/55
"I Want You To Be My Baby" - Louis Jordan
Fo/10/53
"I Was Dreaming" - Cleftones T/12/55
"I Was Such A Fool" - Five Budds F/3/53
"I Was Wrong" - Moonglows F/6/54
"I Wasn't Thinking, I Was Drinking" -
Checkers S/11/54
"I Went To Your Wedding" - Little Sylvia
E/9/52
"I Went To Your Wedding" - Steve Gibson
with Damita Jo Fo/7/52
"I Wish Your Picture Was You" - Lloyd Price
Fo/8/53

"I Wonder" - Four Tunes F/5/52
"I Wonder" - Striders Fo/9/55
"I Wonder Little Darling" - John Lee
Hooker F/5/54
"I Wonder Why" Rhythm Aces Fi/1/55
"I Won't Tell A Soul" - Volumes Fo/4/54
"I'd Be A Fool Again" - Blenders T/4/52
"I'd Gladly Do It Again" - Bernice Redding
F/3/54
"I'd Love To Love You" - Brownie McGhee
T/11/55
"I'll Be Faithful" - Dreams F/5/55
"I'll Be Forever Loving You" - El Dorados
S/12/55
"I'll Be Home Again" - Four Jacks T/7/52
"I'll Be Loving You" - Sparrows Fo/3/54
"I'll Be There" - Chuck Higgins F/10/54
"I'll Be True" - Faye Adams Fi/11/53
"I'll Be True" - Bill Haley and Comets
Fo/12/53
"I'll Die Trying" - J. B. Lenoir T/8/53
"I'll Drown In My Tears" - Sonny Thompson
and Lulu Reed T/4/52
"I'll Never Forget You" - Varetta Dillard
T/9/55
"I'll Never Let You Go" - Flairs S/10/54
"I'll Never Walk In Your Door" - Country
Paul T/9/52
"I'll See You In My Dreams" - Four Tunes
S/1/52
"I'll Upset You Baby" - Lulu Reed Fo/7/54
"I'm A Fool To Care" - Castelles Fo/10/54
"I'm A Natural Born Lover" - Muddy Waters
Fo/1/55
"I'm A Prisoner" - Eddie Boyd Fo/9/55
"I'm A Sentimental Fool" - Marylanders
T/4/52
"I'm A Young Rooster" - John Lee Hooker
T/3/54
"I'm About To Lose My Mind" - T-Bone
Walker S/11/53
"I'm Coming Back Baby" - Otis Blackwell
F/3/55
"I'm Cracking Up Over You" - B. B. King
F/12/55
"I'm Getting 'Long Alright" - Big Maybelle
S/10/54
"I'm Gone" - Shirley And Lee T/10/52
"I'm Gonna Cross That River" - Tommy
Ridgely Fo/9/55
"I'm Gonna Jump In The River" - Buddy
Johnson S/2/52
"I'm Gonna Latch On To You" - Marie
Adams T/2/54
"I'm Gonna Move To The Outskirts Of

Town" - Billy Ward and his Dominos
Fo/3/54

"I'm Gonna Put You Down" - Tampa Red
Fo/5/52

"I'm Gonna Ruin You" - Jimmy Reed
Fo/4/55

"I'm Gonna Run It Down" - "5" Royales
F/8/54

"I'm Gonna Tell Everybody" - Piano Red
T/3/53

"I'm Good To You Baby" - Gypsies Fi/8/55

"I'm In Love" - B. B. King Fo/5/55

"I'm In Love" - Bobby Mitchell and Toppers
T/4/55

"I'm Just Your Fool" - Buddy Johnson with
Ella Johnson S/1/53

"I'm Mad" - John Lee Hooker T/8/54

"I'm Mad" - Willie Mabon T/4/53

"I'm Not Going Home" - Billy "The Kid"
Emerson Fi/5/54

"I'm Not In Love With You" - Dell-Tones
S/4/54

"I'm Not The One You Love" - Crickets
F/10/53

"I'm Only Fooling My Heart" - Heartbreakers
Fo/2/52

"I'm Ready" - Muddy Waters S/10/54

"I'm Slippin' In" - Spiders Fo/6/54

"I'm So Glad" - Mickey and Sylvia Fo/7/55

"I'm So Glad" - Irene Reed F/10/55

"I'm Still In Love With You" - Richard Berry
S/10/53

"I'm Still Lonesome" - Junior Denby Fi/5/54

"I'm Stuck" - Five Jets T/5/54

"I'm Telling You" - Rudy Ferguson T/2/55

"I'm The Child" - Buddy Milton and the
Twilights S/12/54

"I'm The Fat Man" - John Greer T/11/52

"I'm Tired Of Beggin'" - Sly Fox T/12/54

"I'm Your Hootchy Cootchy Man" - Muddy
Waters Fo/1/54

"I've Been A Fool From The Start" - Orchids
T/9/53

"I've Been Away Too Long" - Chuck Willis
F/12/54

"I've Got A Feeling" - Big Maybelle Fo/4/54

"I Wonder Little Darling" - John Lee Hooker
F/5/54

"I've Got My Eyes On You" - John Lee
Hooker and Little Edie Kirkland S/7/52

"I've Got News For You" - Blind Billy Tate
S/5/53

"I've Got The Last Laugh Now" - Roy Brown
S/3/52

"I've Got You Under My Skin" - Ravens
T/7/54

"I've Learned My Lesson" - Emitt Slay Trio
Fo/4/53

"I've Lost" - Enchanters T/4/52

"I've Tried" - King Porter T/10/52

"I-Yi" - Hawks Fo/7/54

"Ichi-Bon Tami Dachi" - Rovers Fo/12/54

"Ida Red" - Bumble Bee Slim F/2/52

"Ida Red" - Chris Powell and his Five Blue
Flames S/5/52

"Iddy-Biddy Baby" - Mello Fellows F/11/54

"If I Can't Have The One I Love" - Four
Pals S/10/55

"If I Had Any Sense I'd Go Back Home" -
Louis Jordan F/9/54

"If I Had Listened" - Roy Hawkins F/10/55

"If I Never Get To Heaven" - Billy Ward
and his Dominoes T/2/55

"If It's The Last Thing I Do" - Dinah
Washington S/4/55

"If Loving You Is Wrong" - Inspirations
T/4/55

"If The Sun Isn't Shining In My Window" -
Lulu Reed T/5/54

"If You Believe" - Orioles S/10/54

"If You Don't Somebody Else Will" - Jimmy
and Johnny E/10/54

"If You Love Me" - Little Milton Fo/4/54

"If You See My Baby" - Ivory Joe Hunter
F/4/53

"Imagination" - Little Jimmy Scott T/11/55

"In Memory" - Johnny Otis with Marie
Adams Fo/3/55

"In My Diary" - Moonglows F/12/55

"In The Alley" - Dave Bartholomew F/5/52

"In The Chapel In The Moonlight" - Orioles
T/7/54

"In The Mission Of St. Augustine" - Orioles
F/10/53

"Insulated Sugar" - Sonny Thompson with
Rufus Thomas, Jr. F/4/53

"Irene" - Holidays S/11/54

"It Ain't No Secret" - Jimmy Witherspoon
S/11/55

"It May Sound Silly" - Ivory Joe Hunter
S/1/55

"It Moves Me" - Lloyd Glenn F/3/53

"It Only Happens With You" - Penguins
Fo/7/55

"It Rocks! It Rolls! It Swings!" - Treniers
T/2/52

"It Should Have Been Me" - Ray Charles
T/3/54

"It Won't Take Long" - Native Boys S/9/54

"It's A Dream" - Bill Dogget T/3/54

"It's Because We're Through" - Orioles
S/5/52
"It's Been A Long Time" - Casanovas S/6/55
"It's Easy To Remember" - Bette McLaurin
T/2/54
"It's Funny" - Serenaders F/5/52
"It's Hot" - Gene and BIlly F/9/55
"It's Love Baby" - Louis Brooks T/4/55
"It's Love Baby" - Midnighters F/7/55
"It's My Life Baby" - Bobby Bland T/5/55
"It's Raining" - Edna McGriff F/7/52
"It's So Peaceful" - Smiley Lewis Fo/10/52
"It's Too Late Now" - Hawks S/2/55
"It's True" - Twilighters S/4/55
"It's You, You, You" - Charms T/9/55

J
"Jailbird" - Smiley Lewis S/1/55
"Jam Up" - Tommy Ridgely F/10/54
"Jay's Blues" - Jimmy Witherspoon F/3/53
"Jeronimo" - Jay McShan Fo/10/52
"Jimmie Lee" - Lloyd Price S/5/54
"Jivin' Around" - Ernie Freeman Fo/11/55
"Jo-Jo" - Marvin and Johnny F/4/54
"Jock-O-Mo" - Sugar Boy F/3/54
"Jockey Jump" - Willie Jones S/5/53
"Joe Louis Story Theme, The" - Maxwell
Davis F/12/53
"Joe The Grinder" - Hawks Fo/2/54
"Johnny Ace's Last Letter" - Johnny Fuller
F/2/55
"Johnny Ace's Last Letter" - Johnny Moore's
Three Blazes F/2/55
"Johnny, Darling" - Feathers M/12/54
"Johnny Has Gone" - Varetta Dillard F/2/55
"Josie Jones" - Johnny Sellers S/8/52
"Juke" - Little Walter F/8/52
"Juke Box Cannonball" - Red Stone and the
Grave Diggers T/3/52
"Jukebox Cannonball" - Bill Haley and his
Comets T/10/53
"Jump Children" - Dave Bartholomew
Fo/9/54
"Jump Shake And Move" - Nolan Strong and
the Diablos Fi/10/55
"Jump Man Jump" - Piano Red T/3/55
"Jump Red Jump" - Red Prysock F/5/54
"Jump The Blues" - Joe Houston F/5/52
"Jump With You Baby" - B. B. King T/4/55
"Jumpin' In The Morning" - Ray Charles
Fo/1/53
"Jungle Drums" - Earl Bostic S/4/54
"Junior's Wail" - Junior Wells Fo/3/54
"Just A Little Walk" - Bobby Marchan
S/6/53

"Just Can't Stay" - Willie Nix F/12/53
"Just Crazy" - Big Jay McNeeley S/1/53
"Just Don't Cry" - Strangers Fi/8/54
"Just Got Lucky" - Clarence "Gatemouth"
Brown T/7/52
"Just In From Texas" - Rosco Gordon
Fo/1/53
"Just Make Love To Me" - Muddy Waters
Fi/5/54
"Just Want Your Love" - Big Maybelle
Fo/4/53
"Just Whisper" - Du Droppers S/5/54
"Just You" - Crickets Fi/3/54

K
"K. C. Lovin'" - Little Willie Littlefield
F/1/53
"Keep A-Walkin'" - Sonny Knight S/4/55
"Keep It A Secret" - Five Crowns T/1/53
"Keep On" - Shirley and Lee Fo/6/54
"Keep On Churnin'" - Wynonie Harris
T/4/52
"Keep On Drinkin'" - Big Boy Crudup
T/2/53
"Key Hole Blues" - Eddie Mark Fo/7/52
"Key To My Heart" - Robins F/8/54
"Key To The Highway" - Brownie McGhee
S/10/52
"Kiss A Fool Goodbye" - Penguins Fo/4/55
"Kiss And A Vow, A" - Nitecaps Fo/12/55
"Kiss Crazy Baby" - Delta Rhythm Boys
Fi/11/54
"Kiss Me" - Lulu Reed F/1/54
"Kissa Me Baby" - Ray Charles T/2/52
"Kissing In The Dark" - Memphis Minnie
T/11/53
"Knock Him Down Whiskey" - Sugar Ray
Robinson Fo/6/53
"Ko Ko Mo" - Charms F/2/55
"Ko Ko Mo" - Gene and Eunice T/1/54
"Ko Ko Mo" - Marvin and Johnny F/2/55

L
"L S M F T Blues" - Meadowlarks Fo/3/54
"L'Amour, Tjour, L'Amour" - Four Tunes
T/11/53
"Last Laugh Blues" - Little Esther and
Little Willie T/11/52
"Last Night" - Jimmy Lewis F/5/54
"Last Night's Dream" - Earl Forrest
Fi/6/53
"Late Rising Moon" - Earl Curry and
Blenders S/11/54
"Later Alligator" - Bobby Charles Fo/11/55
"Later For You Baby" - Guitar Slim T/8/54

"Laugh Laugh Laugh" - Willie Mae Thornton
    Fo/3/55
"Laugh (Though You Want To Cry)" -
    Swallows Fi/3/53
"Laughing On The Outside, Crying On The
    Inside" - Majors S/1/52
"Lawdy, Lawdy Lord" - Dave Bartholomew
    Fo/2/52
"Lawdy Miss Clawdy" - Lloyd Price T/4/52
"Lay It On The Line" - Tiny Bradshaw
    Fi/6/52
"Learnin' The Blues" - Billy Ward and his
    Dominoes T/7/55
"Lee's Dream" - Shirley and Lee Fo/10/55
"Left With A Broken Heart" - Jimmy Rogers
    T/7/53
"Let Me Give You All My Love" - Roy
    Milton Fi/6/53
"Let Me Go Home Whiskey" - Amos Milburn
    Fo/1/53
"Let Me Go Lover" - Counts S/12/54
"Let Me Know Tonight" - Blue Dots S/12/54
"Let Me Ride" - Lowell Fulson F/3/53
"Let The Doorbell Ring" - Jack Dupree
    T/5/55
"Let's All Rock Together" - Jodimars
    S/11/55
"Let's Call It A Day" - Sonny Thompson and
    Lulu Reed T/6/52
"Let's Have Some Fun" - Slim Saunders
    Fi/3/54
"Let's Make Love Sometime" - Flairs T/7/54
"Let's Make Up" - Spaniels F/10/54
"Let's Roll" - J. B. Lenoir Fo/8/52
"Let's Work" - Big Jay McNeeley S/6/54
"Letter, The" - Rudy Greene Fo/11/53
"Life I Used To Live" - Lightin' Hopkins
    Fo/5/54
"Life Is But A Dream" - Harptones S/7/55
"Life Of Ease" - Imperials Fo/1/54
"Lightnin's Jump" - Lightnin' Hopkins
    S/11/53
"Lily Maebelle" - Valentines F/11/55
"Ling Ting Tong" - Charms S/12/54
"Ling Ting Tong" - Five Keys T/10/54
"Little Did I Dream" - Twiliters T/7/55
"Little Fernandez" - Smiley Lewis Fo/9/53
"Little Girl" - Lil Son Jackson S/11/53
"Little Maiden" - Chords E/6/54
"Little Things Mean A Lot" - Billy Ward and
    his Dominoes S/7/54
"Livin' In Misery" - Titus Turner F/5/53
"'Lizbeth" - Thrillers F/7/54
"Lollipop" - Oscar McLollie Fi/11/53
"Lonely Hours" - Lowell Fulson Fo/7/55

"Lonely Nights" - Hearts T/2/55
"Lonely One, The" - Percy Mayfield F/5/53
"Lonely Wall" - Schoolboy Porter T/5/53
"Lonesome And Blue" - John Greer S/5/52
"Lonesome Baby" - Hornets T/12/53
"Lonesome Christmas" - Lowell Fulson
    Fo/11/52
"Lonesome Highway" - Percy Mayfield
    FO/9/52
"Lonesome Lover" - Roy Brown Fo/1/54
"Lonesome Old Train" - James Williams Trio
    S/8/52
"Long, Long Day" - Amos Milburn Fo/3/53
"Long Time Ago, A" - Floyd Dixon F/8/55
"Look A There, Look A There" - Tampa Red
    T/9/52
"Look Me In The Eyes" - Five Willows
    Fo/11/54
"Lookin' For My Baby" - Big Boy Crudup
    T/12/52
"Looking For My Baby" - Bonnie and Ike
Turner Fo/8/52
"Loose Lips" - Percy Mayfield T/2/54
"Loosely" - Ike Turner Fi/5/54
"Lost Child" - Todd Rhodes Fo/2/54
"Lost My Child" - Dossie Terry T/8/52
"Loud Mouth Lucy" - Chuck Willis F/5/52
"Louisiana" - Percy Mayfield Fo/5/52
"Louisiana Hop" - Pete "Guitar" Lewis
    S/4/52
"Love" - Shepherds Fi/8/55
"Love All Night" - Platters Fo/6/54
"Love Bug" - Clovers F/5/55
"Love Bug Boogie" - Johnny Otis S/1/53
"Love Contest" - Ruth Brown Fo/1/54
"Love Has Joined Us Together" - Clyde
    McPhatter and Ruth Brown S/10/55
"Love In My Heart" - Royals Fi/9/52
"Love Is A Funny Thing" - Joe Morris with
    Al Savage S/2/54
"Love Is A Pain" - Rudy Greene F/8/53
"Love Me" - Fats Domino S/10/54
"Love Me" - Willie and Ruth S/8/54
"Love Me Always" - Arthur Lee Maye and
    the Crowns F/6/55
"Love Me Baby" - B. B. King Fi/3/54
"Love, Love Of My Life" - Jesse Belvin
    T/10/55
"Love Me Baby" - Bernie Hardison S/12/53
"Love Me Or Let Me Go" - Billy Ward and
    his Dominoes Fo/4/55
"Love Me 'Til Dawn" - Willie Johnson
    Fo/5/53
"Love Of My Life" - Bill Robinson and the
    Quails S/2/55

"Love Only You" - Feathers S/9/55
"Love Only You" - Meadowlarks F/1/54
"Love, Rock And Thrill" - Lamplighters
	F/3/55
"Love Struck" - Chuck Willis S/2/55
"Love Will Make Your Mind Go Wild" -
	Penguins Fi/1/55
"Love You Baby" - B. B. King F/4/54
"Love's Our Inspiration" - Charms T/12/55
"Lovely Way To Spend An Evening" - Angels
	T/1/55
"Lovey Dovey" - Clovers F/3/54
"Lover's Chant" - Miracles S/6/55
"Lovin' Blues" - Bobby "Blue" Bland
	Fo/11/52
"Lovin' On My Mind" - Shufflers F/8/54
"Loving You Madly" - Pat Boone E/7/54
"Low Flame" - Sonny Thompson F/7/53
"Lucky Lucky Me" - John Green T/3/55
"Lucy Mae Blues" - Frankie Lee Simms
	F/5/53

M
"Mad Love" - Muddy Waters Fo/10/53
"Maggie Doesn't Work Here Anymore" -
	Platters T/1/55
"Mailman's Sack" - Tiny Bradshaw Fo/4/52
"Make Love To Me" - Joe Liggins Fo/4/54
"Make Love To Me" - Zola Taylor Fi/3/54
"Make Me Or Break Me" - Empires T/5/55
"Make Me Thrill Again" - Marylanders
	F/8/52
"Make My Dreams Come True" - Elmore
	James F/3/54
"Mam'selle" - Ravens Fi/6/52
"Mama Don't Like" - Oscar McLollie S/4/54
"Mama (He Treats Your Daughter Mean)" -
	Ruth Brown Fo/1/53
"Mama, What Happened To Our Christmas
	Tree?" - Willie John S/12/53
"Mama, Your Daughter Plays It Cool" - Little
	Mr. Blues F/4/53
"Mama, Your Daughter Told A Lie On Me" -
	Five Keys T/4/53
"Mama, Your Daughter's Done Lied On Me" -
	Wynonie Harris S/4/53
"Mambo Baby" - Ruth Brown F/10/54
"Mambo Baby" - Johnny Otis F/7/54
"Mambo Chillun'" - John Lee Hooker
	S/12/55
"Mambo Rock" - Bill Haley and his Comets
	S/2/55
"Mambo Sh-Mambo" - Charms S/12/54
"Mambola" - Mickey Baker S/10/52
"Man's Best Friend" - Wynonie Harris

T/9/55
"Mannish Boy" - Muddy Waters F/7/55
"Married Men Like Sport" - Jimmy Nelson
	S/5/53
"Married Woman's Boogie" - Billy Wright
	T/2/52
"Married Women" - Floyd Dixon Fo/7/53
"Mary Jo" - Four Blazes T/5/52
"Mary Lou" - Young Jesse Fo/7/55
"Maybe You'll Be There" - Lee Andrews and
	Hearts Fo/5/54
"Maybellene" - Chuck Berry Fo/7/55
"Maybellene" - Jim Lowe F/8/55
"Maybellene" - Marty Robbins S/9/55
"Me And My Chauffeur" - Memphis Minnie
	T/5/53
"Mean Poor Girl" - Jimmy Nelson T/11/53
"Meet Me With Your Black Dress On" - Bull
	Moose Jackson S/6/53
"Meet You In The Morning" - Stick McGhee
	T/4/53
"Melancholy Serenade" - Earl Bostic F/7/53
"Mellow Blues" - Sonny Thompson S/1/52
"Mellow Down Easy" - Little Walter
	S/11/54
"Memphis Slim U.S.A." - Memphis Slim
	F/12/54
"Mercy Me" - Lil Greenwood T/2/54
"Mercy Mercy" - Johnny Fuller S/10/55
"Mercy, Mr. Percy" - Varetta Dillard
	Fo/5/53
"Merry Christmas Baby" - Charles Brown
	M/10/54
"Mess Around" - Ray Charles F/7/53
"Middle Of The Night" - Clovers S/3/52
"Midnight Hour Was Shining, The" - Little
	Willie Littlefield F/7/53
"Midnight Hours Journey" - Johnny Ace
	T/9/53
"Million Tears, A" - Little Sylvia S/11/52
"Milk And Water" - Amos Milburn S/5/54
"Milkcow Blues Boogie" - Elvis Presley
	S/1/54, Fo/12/55
"Mischievous Boogie" - Willie Mae Thornton
	S/10/52
"Misery In My Heart" - Ray Charles
	Fo/2/53
"Miss The Love" - Otis Williams S/10/55
"Mistakes" - Five Keys S/5/52
"Mr. Hound Dog's Back In Town" - Roy
	Brown T/4/53
"Mr. Sandman" - Chordettes F/10/53
"Mrs. Jones' Daughter" - Jimmy Forrest
	T/3/53
"Mistreated Blues" - Lightnin' Hopkins

T/7/53
"Mistreater" - Bill Doggett F/1/53
"Monday Morning" - Lil Greenwood and
    Little Willie Fo/6/52
"Money Ain't Everything" - Sonny Parker
    S/5/52
"Money Honey" - Clyde McPhatter and the
    Drifters S/9/53
"Money Money Money" - Johnny and Mack
    F/11/54
"Monkey Hips and Rice" - "5" Royales
    Fo/10/54
"Monkey Motion" - Houston Boines Fo/8/52
"Moon Dog" - Treniers 1/17/53
"Moonglow" - Earl Bostic Fo/8/52
"Moonrise" - Royals Fo/7/52
"Moonshine" - Floyd Dixon T/8/54
"Most, The" - Boyd Bennett Fo/11/55
"Most Of All" - Moonglows S/3/55
"Mother-In-Law" - Edward Gates White
    Fo/8/53
"Mother's Letter" - Andrew Tibbs Fo/6/52
"Move It" - Lynn Hope S/11/52
"Move It Or Lose It" - Johnny Janis
    Fo/12/55
"Move Me, Baby" - Jimmy Witherspoon
    Fo/11/53
"Movin' On Down The Line" - Jimmy
    McCracklin T/2/52
"Movin' Out Boogie" - Lightnin' Hopkins
    T/9/54
"Mumbles' Blues" - Bobby Lewis F/9/52
"Music Maestro Please" - Starlings F/4/54
"My Babe" - Little Walter Fo/2/55
"My Baby" - James Cotton F/5/54
"My Baby Is Fine" - Fortunes T/6/55
"My Baby Left Town" - Dixie Blues Boys
    S/7/55
"My Baby's Love" - Casanovas T/12/55
"My Best Friend" - Carl Green S/3/53
"My Blue Heaven" - Hamilton Sisters
    T/11/54
"My Boy Flat-Top" - Boyd Bennett T/9/55
"My Clumsy Heart" - Jacks S/11/55
"My Days Are Limited" - Jimmy McCracklin
    T/8/52
"My Dear, Dearest Darling" - Five Willows
    Fi/6/53
"My Dear My Darling" - Counts F/8/54
"My Dream Of Love" - Barons Fo/7/55
"My Gal Is Gone" - Five Blue Notes
    F/12/53
"My Gal Sal" - Chords F/1/54
"My Hat's On The Side Of My Head" - Four
    Blazes T/3/53

"My Heart Belongs To You" - Pat Boone
    F/10/55
"My Heart Belongs To You" - Arbee
    Stidham S/10/52
"My Heart Is Yours" - Marveltones S/4/52
"My Heart Needs Someone" - Sonny
    Thompson S/10/53
"My Heart Tells Me" - Hampton Sisters
    T/4/54
"My Heart's Crying For You" - Chimes
    S/9/54
"My Inspiration" - Four Plaid Throats
    F/6/53
"My Kind Of Woman" - Emitt Slay Trio
    S/2/53
"My Last Affair" - Charles Brown Fo/4/52
"My Lean Baby" - Dinah Washington
    S/6/53
"My Lost Love" - Larks F/1/52
"My Love" - Crystals Fo/2/54
"My Love" - Five Keys F/6/55
"My Loving Baby" - Charlie and Ray
    Fo/2/55
"My Mama Told Me" - Lightnin' Hopkins
    T/8/53
"My Mama Told Me" - James Reed S/4/54
"My Man's An Undertaker" - Dinah
    Washington F/1/54
"My Memories Of You" - Harptones S/4/54
"My Name Ain't Annie" - Linda Hayes
    Fo/10/54
"My Playful Baby's Gone" - Wynonie Harris
    F/3/52
"My Plea" - Titus Turner Fo/2/53
"My Song" - Johnny Ace L/8/52
"My Song" - Johnny Moore's Three Blazers
    Fo/8/52
"My Story" - Chuck Willis Fo/9/52
"My Sweet Woman" - Drifting Sam F/11/52
"My Woman Is Gone" - Lonnie Johnson
    S/3/54
"My Younger Days" - Lil Son Jackson
    F/12/54
"Mystery Train" - Little Junior's Blue
    Flames F/12/53
"Mystery Train" - Elvis Presley F/8/55,
    F/12/55

N
"Nadine" - Coronets T/8/53
"Nagasaki" - Five Chances F/8/54
"Naggin' Woman Blues" - Poppa Treetop
    T/8/52
"Natural Natural Ditty" - Jewels F/9/55
"Naturally Too Weak For You" - Victorians

F/2/52
"Need Your Love So Bad" - Little Willie John
   F/11/55
"Need Your Lovin'" - Peppermint Harris
   Fo/6/55
"Nelson Street Blues" - Willie Love T/10/52
"Nervous, Man Nervous" - Big Jay McNeeley
   S/8/53
"Never Let Me Go" - Johnny Ace T/9/54
"New Boogie Chillen'" - John Lee Hooker
   S/12/52
"Night And Day" - Earl Bostic Fo/1/55
"Night And Day" - Roy Milton Fo/8/52
"Night Curtains" - Checkers T/11/52
"Night Train" - Jimmy Forrest F/3/52
"Night Train" - Four Blazes F/8/52
"Night Train" - Wynonie Harris Fo/7/52
"Nine Below Zero" - Sonny Boy Williamson
   T/2/53
"1958 Blues" - Little Sam Davis Fo/5/53
"Nip Sip" - Clovers Fo/8/55
"Nite Owl" - Tony Allen and the Champs
   T/10/55
"No Baby" - Melvin Smith Fo/4/54
"No Blow, No Show" - Bobby "Blue" Bland
   Fo/10/53
"No Help Wanted" - Crows S/5/53
"No Love In My Heart" - Elmore James
   T/5/55
"No More Doggin'" Rosco Gordon S/3/52
"No More In My Life" - Bill Doggett F/9/53
"No One But Me" - Earl King F/10/54
"No One Else Will Do" - Deep River Boys
   F/6/54
"No One Else Will Ever Know" - Frankie
   Marshall T/6/55
"No One To Love Me" - Sha-Weez F/4/53
"No Place To Go" - Howlin' Wolf T/6/54
"No Room" - Billy Ward and his Dominoes
   T/10/52
"No Teasin' Around" - Billy "The Kid"
   Emerson S/3/54
"No There Ain't No News Today" - Penguins
   Fi/8/54
"No Time At All" - Larry Darnell Fo/10/52
"No Use" - Shadows T/7/53
"Nobody Loves Me" - Fats Domino Fo/1/53
"Nobody's Lovin' Me" - Swallows S/6/53
"Nothin' But The Blues" - Lightnin' Hopkins
   Fo/12/54
"Nothing Sweet As You" - Bobby Mitchell
   and Toppers Fi/1/55
"Now She's Gone" - J. B. and the Hawks
   F/5/54
"Number 000" - Otis Blackwell T/3/53

"Number One Baby" - Eddie Clark T/6/54

O

"O-O-Wah" - Mel Williams Fo/12/54
"O What A Fool" - Joseph "Mr. Google
   Eyes" August T/12/53
"Off The Wall" - Little Walter T/4/53
"Oh Babe" - Five Keys S/12/53
"Oh Baby" - Sonny Carter F/10/54
"Oh Baby" - Smiley Lewis Fo/7/53
"Oh Baby" - Johnny "Guitar" Watson
   Fo/11/55
"Oh But She Did" - Opals F/10/54
"Oh Gee-Oo-Wee" - Charlie and Ray
F/9/55
"Oh Happy Day" - Mickey Baker F/12/52
"Oh Kay" - Dukes S/3/55
"Oh Little Baby" - Little Walter T/4/54
"Oh Mother, Dear Mother" - Jimmy
   Witherspoon S/7/53
"Oh! Oh!" - Treniers S/2/55
"Oh! Oh! Get Out Of The Car" - Richard
   Berry Fo/2/55
"Oh That Will Be Joyful" - Jesse Stone
   S/4/54
"Oh What A Dream" - Ruth Brown T/7/54
"Oh Why?" - Orchids F/9/53
"Old Age Boogie" - Roy Brown Fi/6/53
"Old Baldy Boogie" - Camille Howard
   T/7/52
"Old Fashioned Blues" - Blues Chasers
   F/1/53
"Old Man's Blues" - Marvin Phillips
   T/11/52
"Old Spice" - Lucky Millinder S/1/53
"Old Time Blues" - Lloyd Glenn E/1/55
"Old Chapel Hill" - Orioles T/10/55
"One Bad Stud" - Honey Tones T/7/54
"One Fine Gal" - Jimmy Witherspoon
   F/6/53
"One Kiss" - Robins F/4/55
"One Mint Julep" - Clovers S/3/52
"One More Break" - Chuck Willis Fi/5/55
"One More Chance" - El Dorados F/3/55
"One More Drink" - Lazy Slim Jim Fi/3/53
"One More Kiss" - Calvanes Fo/12/55
"One More Time" - Buddy Johnson Fo/2/54
"One More Time" - Orioles Fi/6/53
"One Room Country Shack" - Mercy Dee
   Fo/3/53
"One Scotch, One Bourbon, One Beer" -
   Amos Milburn T/8/53
"One Two Three Everybody" - Amos Milburn
   T/12/54
"Only A Miracle" - Four Bells Fi/5/54

"Only For You" - Cameos T/6/55
"Only You" - Cues F/6/55
"Only You" - Platters S/7/55
"Oo-Shoo-Be-Do-Be" - Deep River Boys
    Fo/4/53
"Ooh-Eee! Ooh-Eee!" - Floyd Dixon FO/2/54
"Ooh Yes" - Stomp Gordon S/12/52
"Ookey Ook" - Penguins 2/21/55
"Ooo Wee" - Louis Jordan T/3/54
"Oooh-La-La" - Hollywood Flames Fo/7/54
"Oooh, Oooh, Oooh" - Lloyd Price S/9/52
"Oop Shoop" - Shirley Gunter and the
    Queens S/9/54
"Oopy Doo" - Johnny Otis T/1/52
"Operator Blues" - Little Son WIllis Fo/1/53
"Our Only Child" - Guitar Slim Fi/1/55
"Over A Cup Of Coffee" - Castelles Fi/8/54
"Over The Hill" - Johnny Taylor T/4/54
"Over The Rainbow" - Checkers S/6/54
"Overboard" - Sugar Boy T/10/53
"Overflow" - Tiny Bradshaw T/5/54
"Out On A Party" - Earl Forrest S/3/54

P

"P. H. Blues" - Peppermint Harris T/1/52
"P. L. Blues" - Pappa Lightfoot T/3/53
"Pachuko Hop" Ike Carpenter T/2/53
"Papa Ain't Salty" - T-Bone Walker F/7/55
"Papa (I Don't Treat That Little Girl Mean)
    - Scatman Crothers F/4/53
"Papa (She Treats Your Son So Mean)" -
    Benny Brown Fo/3/53
"Painted Picture" - Spaniels S/9/55
"Paradise Hill" - Embers E/7/53, E/5/55
"Paradise Princess" - Al Savage T/8/55
"Party Girl" - T-Bone Walker S/6/53
"Peace Of Mind" - Savannah Churchill
    Fo/10/53
"Peepin' Eyes" - Charlie Feathers Fo/4/55
"Perfect Woman" - Four Blazes F/9/53
"Picture In The Frame" - Eddie Boyd S/2/54
"Piddily Patter" - Nappy Brown T/6/55,
    L/7/55
"Piddily Patter" - Patti Page L/7/55
"Pillow Blues" - Dinah Washington T/9/52
"Piney Brown Blues" - Joe Turner S/12/55
"Pistol Packin' Mama" - Hurricanes Fo/7/55
"Plan For Love" - Flamingos T/1/54
"Play It Fair" - LaVern Baker Fo/9/55
"Playboy Blues" - Elmore Nixon S/2/53
"Pleading For Your Love" - Charles Brown
    Fo/1/54
"Please Be Careful" - Lucky Millinder
    Fo/10/52
"Please Bring Yourself Back Home" -

Ramblers T/10/54
"Please Come Back Home" - Flamingos
    Fo/9/54
"Please Don't Go" - Floyd Dixon T/8/53
"Please Don't Leave Me" - Fats Domino
    Fi/6/53
"Please Don't Leave Me" - Arthur Lee Maye
    and Crowns F/10/55
"Please Don't Go-O-O-Oh" - Little Willie
    Littlefield S/1/54
"Please Forgive Me" - Johnny Ace T/5/54
"Please Have Mercy" - Linda Hayes and the
    Platters T/2/55
"Please Have Mercy On Me" - Little
    Richard T/11/52
"Please Help Me" - Eddie Boyd Fo/12/54
"Please Help Me" - B. B. King S/2/54
"Please Hurry Home" - B. B. King Fo/9/53
"Please Louise" - Wynonie Harris S/11/53
"Please Love Me" - B. B. King Fo/9/53
"Please Love Me Baby" - Five Jets F/1/55
"Please Open Your Heart" - Danny Sutton
    S/7/52
"Please Send Her Back To Me" - Four
Blazes F/10/52
"Please Sing My Blues Tonight" - Orioles
    Fi/10/55
"Please Take Me Back" - Blenders F/7/53
"Please Take Me Back" - John Lee Hooker
    T/7/53
"Please Tell It To Me" - Four Bells F/7/53
"Please Understand" - Mercy Dee Fo/5/53
"Pledging My Love" - Johnny Ace T/1/55
"Poison Ivy" - Boyd Bennett and his
    Rockets F/2/55
"Poison Ivy" - Willie Mabon F/1/54
"Pony Tail" - T-Bone Walker T/1/54
"Poon-Tang" - Treniers F/1/53
"Poor Broken Heart" - Otis Blackwell
    S/4/55
"Poor Me" - Fats Domino F/11/55
"Port Of Rico" - Illinois Jacquet 1/30/53
"Precious Love" - Cookies F/5/55
"Pretty Mama" - Marty Robbins Fi/10/55
"Pretty Thing" - Bo Diddley T/11/55
"Proud Of You" - Sonny Til S/5/52
"Puddin' Head Jones" - Freddie Hill
    Fi/6/52
"Put Some Money In The Pot 'Cause The
    Juice Is Running Low" - Louis Jordan
    Fo/10/54

Q

"Question, The" - Memphis Slim Fi/6/52
"Quiet Please" - Charms Fo/4/54

"Quit Pushin'" - Bill Robinson and the Quails S/1/54

R

"Rags To Riches" - Billy Ward and his Dominoes F/11/53
"Ram-Bunk-Shush" - Lucky Millinder Fo/4/52
"Ramblin' Blues" - Little Esther S/8/52
"Razzle-Dazzle" - Bill Haley and his Comets Fo/6/55
"Razzle-Dazzle" - Ella Mae Morse L/7/55
"Reach" - Jay McShan S/1/53
"Real Crazy Fool" - Big Jay McNeeley S/5/53
"Real Good Feeling" - Eddie Boyd Fo/4/55
"Real Rock Drive" - Bill Haley and Haley's Comets S/11/52
"Real Thing, The" - Spiders T/9/53
"Reconsider Baby" - Lowell Fulson F/11/54
"Red Cherries" - Floyd Dixon T/8/52
"Red Rover" - Dean Beard T/6/55
"Red Sails In The Sunset" - Five Keys S/4/52
"Red Top" - Gene Ammons T/5/53
"Rent Man Blues" - Mercy Dee Fo/7/53
"Rhumba My Boogie" - Frankie Lee Sims F/4/54
"Ride Daddy Ride" - Fats Noel F/1/52
"Ride Pretty Baby" - John Greer Fo/4/53
"Ride 'Til I Die" - John Lee Hooker T/5/53
"Right Back On" - Peppermint Harris S/5/52
"Ring Dang Doo" - Chuck Willis S/10/55
"Riot In Cell Block #9" - Robins F/6/54
"River, The, (Goin' Down To)" - Little Caesar S/8/52
"River Hip Mama" - Smokey Hogg Fo/1/53
"River's Invitation, The" - Percy Mayfield T/1/53
"Robe Of Calvary" - Orioles T/1/54
"Rock A-Beatin' Boogie" - Bill Haley and his Comets T/10/55
"Rock A-Beatin' Boogie" - Treniers Fo/5/54
"Rock And Roll Wedding" - Midnighters T/11/55
"Rock Around The Clock" - Bill Haley and his Comets S/5/54
"Rock Around The Clock" - M-G-M Studio Orchestra F/7/55
"Rock Bottom" - Rams Fo/3/55
"Rock Bottom" - Milt Trenier Fo/4/53
"Rock H-Bomb, Rock" - H-Bomb Ferguson Fo/1/52
"Rock It, Davy, Rock It" - Jaguars F/7/55
"Rock Love" - Sonny Thompson with Lulu Reed T/1/55
"Rock Me All Night Long" - Ravens F/10/52
"Rock Me Baby" - Johnny Otis S/10/53
"Rock, Moan And Cry" - Playboys T/8/54
"Rock 'N Roll Blues" - Anita O'Day S/4/52
"Rock, Rock, Rock" - Willis Jackson F/7/52
"Rock, Rock, Rock" - Amos Milburn F/12/52
"Rock The Joint" - Bill Haley and the Saddlemen F/4/52
"Rock This Morning" - Jesse Allen Fo/6/52
"Rock-A-Locka" - Five Wings F/4/55
"Rocker" - Little Walter Fi/3/54
"Rocket 69" - Todd Rhodes F/5/52
"Rockin' And Rollin' #2" - Lil Son Jackson F/11/52
"Rockin' Chair" - Five Cats S/2/55
"Rockin' Chair Boogie" - Ivory Joe Hunter F/12/52
"Rockin' Is Our Bizness" - Treniers T/5/53
"Rockin' On Sunday Night" - Treniers Fo/9/52
"Rockin' With Red" - Piano Red S/7/55
"Rocking Chair On The Moon" - Bill Haley and the Saddlemen S/8/52
"Roll and Rhumba" - Jimmy Reed T/8/53
"Roll 'Em" - Mitzi Mars T/5/53
"Roll Mr. Jelly" - Amos Milburn F/6/52
"Roll With My Baby" - Ray Charles F/10/52
"Roller Coaster" - Little Walter Fi/5/55
"Rollin' Like A Pebble In Sand" - Charles Brown F/11/52
"Rollin' Stone" - Marigolds Fo/4/55
"Romance In The Dark" - Diamonds T/12/53
"Romp And Stomp Blues" - Mercy Dee S/7/55
"Rose Mary" - Fats Domino S/9/53
"Roses Of Picardy" - Platters S/5/54
"Rot Gut" - Wynonie Harris F/8/53
"Rough Rider" - Ravens F/10/53
"Rough Treatment" - Little Hudson T/10/53
"Route 90" - Clarence Garlow S/12/53
"Rub A Little Boogie" - Duke Bayou Fo/7/52
"Rub A Little Boogie" - Jack Dupree S/4/54
"Run Pretty Baby" - Regals T/11/54
"Runaround" - Three Chuckles Fo/10/53

S

"Sabre Jet" - Joe Houston Fo/5/53
"Sad Hour" - Little Walter F/12/52

"Sales Tax Boogie, The" - Piano Red F/7/52
"Sally Let Your Bangs Hang" - Johnny Olenn
    Fo/5/55
"Salty Tears" - Chuck Willis Fi/12/52
"Santa Fe Blues" - Lightnin' Hopkins S/1/54
"Sassy Mae" - Memphis Slim S/5/54
"Saturday Night" - Timmie Rogers Fi/3/53
"Saving My Love For You" - Johnny Ace
    T/12/53
"Say A Prayer" - Faye Adams F/3/54
"Say Baby" - Willie Johnson Fo/5/54
"Say Hey" - Willie Mays with the Treniers
    F/8/54
"Schemin'" - Griffin Brothers S/7/55
"School Boy Blues" - Bobby Mitchell and the
    Toppers T/5/54
"School Girl" - "5" Royales F/1/55
"School Of Love" - Marvin and Johnny
    S/6/54
"Scratchin' Boogie" - Pete "Guitar" Lewis
    Fo/10/52
"Screamin' In My Sleep" - Gene Parrish
    S/4/52
"Searching For You" - Barons S/12/55
"Secret Love" - Moonglows S/2/54
"Secret Love" - Orioles T/3/54
"See You Later Alligator" - Bill Haley and
    his Comets Fo/12/55
"Send For Me" - Big Maybelle S/8/53
"Send Me Some Kisses" - Tenderfoots
    S/5/55
"Send Me Some Money" - Varetta Dillard
    Fo/9/54
"Sentimental Fool" - Arthur Prysock
    Fo/6/52
"Sentimental Journey" - Ruth Brown and the
    Delta Rhythm Boys F/4/54
"September Song" - Ravens F/2/54
"Seven Days" - Clyde McPhatter T/12/55
"Seventeen" - Boyd Bennett and his Rockets
    S/5/55
"Seventeen" - Rusty Draper L/7/55
"Seventeen" - Fontane Sisters L/7/55
"Seventeen" - Ella Mae Morse L/7/55
"Seventh Son" - Willie Mabon S/11/55
"Sexy Ways" - Midnighters F/6/54
"Sh-Boom" - Chords Fo/4/54
"Sh-Boom" - Crew Cuts E/6/54, M/7/54
"Sh-Boom" - Billy Williams Quartet M/7/54
"Sh-Boom" - Bobby Williamson M/7/54
"Shadows Of Love" - Pearls F/11/55
"Shake A Hand" - Faye Adams L/7/53
"Shake A Hand" - Savannah Churchill
    F/9/53
"Shake 'Em Baby" - Roy Brown Fo/7/55

"Shake, Holler and Run" - John Lee Hooker
    Fo/1/55
"Shake It" - Johnny Otis F/11/54
"Shake It Baby" - Sunnyland Slim F/8/54
"Shake It Up Mambo" - Platters S/11/54
"Shake, Rattle And Roll" - Bill Haley and
    Comets S/7/54
"Shake, Rattle And Roll" - Joe Turner
    S/4/54
"Shake That Thing" - Wynonie Harris
    F/5/54
"Shake Walkin'" - Mickey Baker Fo/3/55
"Shame On Old Me" - Faye Adams S/9/55
"Shape I'm In" - Marie Adams T/8/55
"She Couldn't Be Found" - Bobby Mitchell
    and the Toppers Fo/9/54
"She Felt Good to Me" - Jimmy McCracklin
    T/4/53
"She Left Me" - Midnights Fo/1/55
"She Loves To Dance" - Flairs Fo/3/55
"She May Be Yours" - Joe Hill Louis
    Fi/3/53
"She Put The Wammee On Me" - Jay
    Hawkins F/3/55
"She's All Right" - Memphis Slim T/5/55
"She's Gone Too Long" - Roy Brown
    Fo/10/55
"She's Got No Hair" - Arthur Crudup
    S/7/54
"She's Gotta Go" - Jimmy Ricks S/5/53
"She's Mine All Mine" - Arthur Gunter
    F/3/55
"She's My Baby" - Jimmy Huff S/9/52
"Ship Of Love" - Nutmegs S/8/55
"Shirley, Come Back To Me" - Shirley And
    Lee T/3/53
"Shirley's Back" - Shirley And Lee Fi/6/53
"Sho Nuff I Do" - Elmore James Fi/5/54
"Sho-Wop" - Danderliers T/7/55
"Short Circuit" - Red Prysock T/11/55
"Short John" - Dinah Washington F/3/54
"Shotgun Wedding" - Wynonie Harris
    F/11/55
"Shut Your Mouth" - B. B. King F/6/55
"Sidewalk Boogie" - Country Paul S/11/52
"Silent Partner" - Jack Dupree T/12/55
"Since I Fell For You" - Harptones S/12/54
"Since I Fell For You" - Lovenotes
    Fi/11/54
"Since My Baby's Gone" - Jacks F/7/55
"Sincerely" - Moonglows F/11/54
"Sindy" - Squires S/7/55
"Sindy" - Tenderfoots F/7/55
"Sing, Sing, Sing" - Dean Beard S/12/55
"Single Shot" - Sonny Thompson F/6/54

"Sister Lucy" - Bobby Mitchell and the
Toppers S/2/54
"Sit Back Down" - Little Esther Fi/3/54
"Sittin' And Thinkin'" - Memphis Slim
"Sittin', Drinkin' And Thinkin'" - Little
Junior Parker Fo/6/54
"Sittin' Here Drinkin'" - Chirstine Kittrell
F/8/52
"Sittin' Here Drinkin'" - Johnny Otis S/6/55
"Sittin' In The Dark" - Nappy Brown
T/11/55
"Sitting On The Curbstone" - Little Willie
Littlefield T/5/55
"Six O'Clock Bounce" - Piano Red T/8/55
"$64,000 Question, The" - Bobby Tuggle
T/9/55
"Skin And Bones" - Little Son Willis F/9/52
"Sleigh Ride" - Lloyd Glenn M/10/54
"Sloppy Drunk" - Jimmy Rogers Fo/6/54
"Slow Your Speed" - Jimmy Witherspoon
Fo/1/53
"Slowly Goin' Crazy" - H-Bomb Ferguson
S/1/52
"Smoke From Your Cigarette" - Mellows
S/1/55
"Smokey Joe's Cafe" - Robins T/8/55
"Smokin' And Dreamin'" - Streetsingers
F/4/52
"Smootchie" - Lamplighters T/2/54
"Snatchin' It Back" - Margie Day Fo/10/53
"So All Alone" - Bobby Lester and the
Moonlighters S/11/54
"So All Alone" - Junior Wells F/12/54
"So Crazy 'Bout You Baby" - Tampa Red
Fo/11/53
"So Fine" - Sheiks S/9/55
"So Long" - Lloyd Price S/3/53
"So Near And Yet So Far" - Four Students
Fo/6/55
"So Tired" - Roy Milton T/4/52
"So Unnecessary" - Sounds F/12/55
"Soft" - Tiny Bradshaw T/11/52
"(Danger) Soft Shoulders" - Sonny Til
S/5/53
"Soldier Boy" - Four Fellows F/6/55
"Solitude" - Tiny Grimes F/3/52
"Some Day Sweetheart" - Five Keys Fi/3/54
"Someday" - Ella Johnson S/6/55
"Someday, Someway" - Flamingos S/3/53
"Someday We'll Meet Again" - Royal Jokers
F/11/54
"Somebody Else Took Her Home" - Frankie
Valley (Valli) Fi/5/54
"Somebody's Lyin'" - Gladys Patrick T/1/54
"Someone Made For You And Me" - "5"

Royales T/10/55
"Something To Remember You By" -
Gentlemen F/11/54
"Something's Wrong" - Fats Domino
Fi/11/53
"Something's Wrong" - Woo Woo Moore
F/8/53
"Somewhere Somebody Cares" - Bill
Robinson and the Quails T/7/54
"Song Of The Dreamer" - Billy Brooks
S/6/55, L/7/55
"Song Of The Dreamer" - Eddie Fisher
L/7/55
"Song Of The Dreamer" - Johnny Ray
L/7/55
"Song Of The Islands" - Earl Bostic
Fo/11/54
"Sonny Boy's Christmas Blues" - Sonny Boy
Williamson T/12/52
"Sonny Is Drinking" - Sonny Terry S/1/54
"Sowing Love And Reaping Tears" - Three
Baritones T/4/52
"Speedin'" - Medallions S/6/55
"Speedo" - Cadillacs Fi/10/55
"Speedy Life" - Little Sylvia Fo/4/54
"Spider Web" - Tiny Bradshaw T/6/54
"S'Posin" - Cat Man F/8/54
"Sposin'" - Charioteers F/6/52
"Sposin'" - Velma Middleton S/1/52
"Standin' At The Station" - Guitar Slim
S/10/54
"Standin' Right There" - Feathers T/2/55
"Standing Around Crying" - Muddy Waters
S/11/52
"Standing At The Crossroads" - Elmore
James T/10/54
"Starlite" - Moonglows S/9/55
"Starting From Tonight" - Royals Fo/6/52
"Steady Eddie" - Al Sears S/6/52
"Stripped Gears" - Jay Francis Fo/5/52
"Steamwhistle Jump" - Earl Bostic F/3/53
"Still In Love" - Joe Turner Fo/12/52
"Stingy Little Thing" - Midnighters S/12/54
"Stolen Love" - Jimmy Liggins Fo/3/52
"Stomp And Whistle" - Danny Overbea
Fo/2/54
"Stop Cryin'" - Little Esther S/11/53
"Stop Hoppin' On Me" - Willie Mae
Thornton Fo/9/54
"Stop Lyin' On Me" - Billy Ford S/4/55
"Stop Now Baby" - Sonny Boy Williamson
Fo/8/52
"Story From My Heart And Soul" - B. B.
King S/12/52
"Story Of My Life" - Guitar Slim T/4/54

"Story Untold" - Crew-Cuts L/7/55
"Story Untold" - Nutmegs S/4/55
"Straight Jacket" - Bill Haley and his Comets
    Fo/3/54
"Straighten Up Baby" - Milt Trenier T/3/54
"Strange Kinda Feeling" - Elmore James
    S/12/53
"Street Lights" - Little Esther F/4/53
"Strickly Gone" - Nature Boy Brown T/7/52
"Strictly Cash" - Preston Love S/7/52
"String Bean" - Margie Day S/8/53
"Strong Red Whiskey" - John Greer T/2/52
"Stumblin' Block" - Jack Dupree T/10/55
"Stubborn Woman" - Mercy Dee F/11/55
"Stuttering Blues" - John Lee Hooker
    F/1/54
"Such A Fool" - Eagles S/10/54
"Such A Night" - Clyde McPhatter and
    Drifters F/2/54
"Sufferin' Mind" - Guitar Slim S/10/54
"Sugar" - Marvin and Johnny F/11/54
"Sugar Sweet" - Muddy Waters S/12/55
"Sugaree" - Lazy Boy Slim S/11/52
"Summertime" - Little Esther F/3/52
"Sunday Kind Of Love" - Harptones F/12/53
"Sure Cure For The Blues" - Shirley Haven
    and Four Jacks Fo/5/52
"Sweet Sixteen" - Joe Turner S/3/52
"Sweet, Soft And Really Fine" - Five Dukes
    of Rhythm T/10/54
"Sweet Talk" - Joe Morris with Faye Adams
    S/9/53, M/10/53
"Sweet Talking Daddy" - Marie Adams
    F/9/52
"Sweethearts On Parade" - Billy Ward and
    his Dominoes Fo/8/55
"Swing Train" - Lynn Hope T/10/53
"Switchie Witchie Titchie" - Midnighters
    Fo/4/55
"Syndicator, The" - John Lee Hooker
    Fo/8/55

T
"T.V. Is The Thing" - Dinah Washington
    F/10/53
"TV Mama" - Joe Turner T/12/53
"Tab's Purple Heart" - Tab Smith T/7/52
"Tabarin" - Tangiers F/9/55
"Take Me" - Charles Brown S/5/53
"Talk That Talk" - Du Droppers T/4/55
"Talkedest Man In Town" - Louise Williams
    T/1/54
"Talking The Blues" - B. B. King T/7/5
"Tara's Theme" - Bill Doggett Fo/11/54
"Tarzan And The Dignified Monkey" - Willie

Mae Thornton Fo/12/55
"Taxi Driver" - John Lee Hooker T/5/55
"Taxi Taxi 6963" - Piano Red T/12/53
"Teach Me Tonight" - Dinah Washington
    T/11/54
"Teachin' And Preachin'" - Royal Kings
    T/11/52
"Teardrops From My Eyes" - Five Keys
    Fo/9/53
"Teardrops On My Pillow" - Orioles T/1/53
"Teardrops On My Pillow" - Jimmy Wilson
    T/1/54
"Tears Began To Flow" - Spiders T/4/54
"Tears In My Eyes" - Dreamers Fo/9/55
"Tears Keep Tumbling Down, The" - Ruth
    Brown S/9/53
"Tears On My Pillow" - Chimes S/9/55
"Teenage Girl" - T-Bone Walker S/8/54
"Telegram, The" - Medallions S/1/55
"Tell It Like It Is" - Roy Milton T/12/54
"Tell Me" - Five C's Fo/2/54
"Tell Me" - Jimmy Wilson Fi/6/53
"Tell Me Baby" - Five Echoes F/3/55
"Tell Me Darling" - Gaylarks S/8/55
"Tell Me So" - John Greer T/8/52
"Tell Me Thrill Me" - Chanters F/10/54
"Tell Me Why" - Swallows F/1/52
"Tell Me You Love Me" - Flairs T/11/53
"Teller Of Fortune" - Dootones T/6/55
"Ten Days In Jail" - Robins Fo/10/53
"Ten Long Years" - B. B. King F/9/55
"Tender Heart" - Charles Brown S/2/52
"Tennessee Rock And Roll" - Boyd Bennett
    and his Rockets Fi/5/55
"Tennessee Toddy" - Marty Robbins
    Fo/12/55
"That I Wanna See" - Buddy Phillips
    S/3/54
"That Man" - Nappy Brown S/5/54
"That Woman" - Sunnyland Slim F/6/55
"That's All" - Casanovas F/4/55
"That's All I Want From You" - Dinah
    Washington Fi/1/55
"That's All Right" - Little Eddie Kirkland
    S/9/52
"That's All Right" - Little Walter F/6/52
"That's All Right" - Elvis Presley T/7/54,
    Fo/12/55
"That's All Right" - Marty Robbins S/1/55
"That's How I Feel About You" - Buddy
    Johnson S/6/53
"That's My Desire" - Flamingos Fo/7/53
"That's The Way I Like It" - Shirley Gunter
    T/6/55
"That's What Makes My Baby Fat" - Joe

Morris with Fay Scruggs Fo/1/53
"That's Where Your Heartaches Begin" - Billy
    Bunn and his Buddies Fo/4/52
"That's Your Mistake" - Otis Williams and
    Charms T/12/55
"Them There Eyes" - Varetta Dillard
    F/11/52
"There Is A Time" - Heartbreakers F/8/52
"There Is No Greater Love" - Bull Moose
    Jackson F/8/52
"There'll Be No One" - Bubber Johnson
    S/9/55
"There's A Dead Cat On The Line" -
    Peppermint Harris F/8/52
"There's A Rumor" - Cashmeres T/9/55
"These Foolish Things" - Earl Bostic F/8/54
"These Foolish Things Remind Me Of You" -
    Billy Ward and his Dominoes F/5/53
"They Call Me Big Mama" - Willie Mae
    Thornton Fo/9/53
"They Don't Understand" - Four Tunes
    T/7/52
"They Raided The Joint" - Helen Humes
    Fo/4/52
"Things Ain't What They Used To Be" -
    Sonny Thompson Fo/2/54
"Things I'm Gonna Do, The" - Jesse Allen
    F/9/54
"Things That I Used To Do, The" - Guitar
    Slim S/12/53
"Things She Used To Do, The" - Bill
    Robinson and Quails T/4/55
"Thinkin' And Drinkin'" - Amos Milburn
    F/3/52
"Third Degree" - Eddie Boyd F/6/53
"Thirteen Women" - Dickie Thompson
    Fi/3/54
"Thirty Days" - Chuck Berry T/10/55
"This Is It" - Treniers F/8/53
"This Is My Last Goodbye" - Roy Brown
    T/5/54
"This Is My Story" - Gene and Eunice
    F/3/55
"This Must Be Paradise" - Don Julian and
    Meadowlarks Fo/10/55
"Those Golden Bells" - Tenderfoots Fo/6/55
"Those Lonely Lonely Nights" - Earl King
    Fi/8/55
"Those Lonely Lonely Nights" - Johnny
    "Guitar" Watson T/8/55
"Thousand Stars, A" - Rivileers Fo/3/54
"Three Cent Love" - Rosco Gordon S/2/55
"Three Coins In The Fountain" - Billy Ward
    and his Dominoes S/6/54
"3-D" - Big Jay McNeeley S/11/53

"Three Letters" - Ruth Brown F/10/52
"Three O'Clock In The Morning" - Lowell
    Fulson T/2/52
"Three Sheets In The Wind" - Peppermint
    Harris Fo/2/54
"Thrill Me Baby" - Lil Son Jackson T/1/54
"Tick Tock A-Woo" Turbans T/3/55
"Tiger Man" - Rufus Thomas, Jr. Fo/9/53
"Til I Waltz Again With You" - Five Bills
    S/2/53
"Till Dawn And Tomorrow" - Five Bills
    S/2/53
"Time For Lovin' To Be Done" - Eddie
    Kirkland T/10/53
"Time Will Tell" - Earl King T/12/55
"Ting-A-Ling" - Clovers F/7/52
"Tip Toe" - Eddie Johnson T/7/53
"Tippity Top" - Rays T/12/55
"Tired Of Your Sexy Ways" - Mac Burney
    and Four Jacks F/2/55
"Toast To Lovers" - Danny Overbea
    T/12/54
"Today Is My Birthday" - Enchanters
    E/1/52
"Together" - Richard Berry and the
    Dreamers Fi/8/55
"Too Late" - Little Walter Fo/9/55
"Too Late For Tears" - Lloyd Price S/2/54
"Too Late Too Long" - Tampa Red S/2/53
"Too Many Drivers" - Smiley Lewis
    Fo/10/54
"Too Many Keys" - Bobby Prince Fo/7/54
"Too Many Women" - Rosco Gordon
    Fo/11/52
"Too Much Boogie" - John Lee Hooker
    S/10/53
"Too Much Jellyroll" - Floyd Dixon F/5/53
"Too Much Lovin'" - "5" Royales T/7/53
"Tortured Love" - H-Bomb Ferguson
    S/11/52
"Tortured Soul" - Eddie Boyd T/11/53
"Touch Of Heaven, A" - Mister Ruffin
    Fi/5/55
"Train Kept A-Rollin'" - Tiny Bradshaw
    T/2/52
"Train, Train, Train" - Danny Overbea
    Fo/1/53
"Trapped" - Treniers F/4/54
"Traveling Mood" - Wee Willie Wayne
    S/8/55
"Treat Me Like I Treat You" - Memphis
    Slim T/3/55
"Trees Trees" - Charles Brown T/10/55
"Trouble At Midnight" - Roy Brown F/4/54
"Troubled Mind Blues" - Oscar "Big" Black

F/2/52
"Troubles" - Charles Brown with Johnny Moore's Three Blazers F/1/54
"True Blue" - Bill Doggett Fo/6/55
"True Love" - Dean Barlow Fo/7/55
"Truly" - Arthur Lee Maye and the Crowns T/2/55
"Truly Truly" - Bobby Relf and the Laurels Fo/6/55
"Trumpet Sorrento" - Frankie Avalon F/3/54
"Trust Me" - Swallows Fo/9/53
"Try Holding My Hand" - Checkers S/1/55
"Tryin' To Fool Me" - Leonard Lee F/7/54
"Tryin' To Get To You" - Eagles F/6/54
"Trying" - Todd Rhodes with LaVern Baker Fo/7/52
"Trying To Find Someone To Love" - Lloyd Price Fi/1/55
"Trying To Live My Life Without You" - Annisteen Allen S/5/53
"Turn Me Loose" - Lamplighters F/9/53
"Tutti Frutti" - Little Richard Fi/10/55
"Tweedle Dee" - LaVern Baker T/11/54, 2/26/55
"Tweedle Dee" - Bonnie Lou F/2/55
"21" - Spiders T/11/54
"24 Hours" - Eddie Boyd S/3/53
"24 Sad Hours" - Jimmy Witherspoon T/3/54
"Twenty Five Lies" - Guitar Slim S/11/54
"Two Blue Singing Stars" - Cochran Brothers T/6/55
"Two Faced Daddy" - Mickey Champion F/7/52
"Two Faced Woman" - Nappy Brown S/10/54
"Two Hearts" - Pat Boone Fo/2/55
"Two Hearts" - Charms Fo/2/55
"Two Little Girls" - Jimmy Witherspoon Fo/7/52
"Two Lovers Have I" - Diamonds T/8/53
"Two Strangers" - Marigolds S/8/55

U
"Ubangi Stomp" - Earl Bostic S/10/54
"Unchained Melody" - Roy Hamilton 3/16/55, Fo/3/55
"Unchained Melody" - Al Hibbler 3/16/55
"Under A Blanket Of Blue" - Cardinals T/4/54
"Until The Real Thing Comes Along" - Hearts T/11/55
"Until The Real Thing Comes Along" - Billy Ward and his Dominoes T/12/53
"Untrue" - Lightnin' Hopkins S/6/55
"Upside Your Head" - Buddy Johnson with Ella Johnson S/1/55

V
"Vanity Dresser Blues" - Willie Love T/12/53
"Verdict, The" - Five Keys S/5/55
"Very Truly Yours" - Jimmy Scott S/7/55
"Vida Lee" - T-Bone Walker T/3/54
"Voice Within, The" - Percy Mayfield S/3/55
"Volcano" - Jets T/3/53
"Voo Doopee Do" - Piano Red S/10/52
"Voodoo Magic" - Jimmy Cook S/3/52

W
"W-O-M-A-N" - Etta Jones Fo/11/55
"W-P-L-J" - 4 Deuces S/8/55
"Wait Down At The Bottom Of The Hill" - Johnny King F/6/52
"Waiting Around For You" - Counts S/11/54
"Waiting For My Baby" - Blazer Boy S/8/53
"Waiting For Your Return" - Jimmy Witherspoon T/2/55
"Waiting In Vain" - Lil Miss Cornshucks S/4/52
"Wake Up Baby" - Felix Gross S/7/52
"Walk That Walk" - Sheiks S/4/55
"Walk With Me" - Charles Brown Fo/4/55
"Walkin' And Talkin' To Myself" - Ray Charles Fi/12/52
"Walkin' The Blues" - Willie Dixon 5/8/55
"Walkin' The Boogie" - John Lee Hooker T/6/52
"Walking And Crying" - Sonny Boy Holmes Fi/6/52
"Wallflower, The" - Etta James and Peaches Fo/1/55, L/7/55 (See also "Dance With Me Henry")
"Wanderin' Heart" - T-Bone Walker S/6/54
"War Is Over, The" - Big Boy Crudup F/1/54
"Wasted Love" - Peppermint Harris F/5/53
"Waterloo" - Boyd Bennett and hid Rockets S/1/55
"Way Back" - Willie Love and the Three Aces Fo/8/54
"We Could Find Happiness" - Wanderers Fo/10/53
"We Two" - Belvederes S/11/55
"We'll Do It" - Ella Johnson E/10/54
"We're All Loaded" - Rosco Gordon T/5/53
"We're Gonna Rock This Joint" - Jackson Brothers F/11/52
"Wedding, The" - Solitaires Fo/9/55

"Wedding Boogie" - Johnny Otis Fo/12/52
"Wee Wee Hours" - Stick McGhee F/2/52
"Weeping Blues" - Rosco Gordon T/10/55
"Well All Right" - Joe Turner T/9/54
"Well I Tried" - Jay Hawkins T/6/55
"Well Well Well Baby-La" - Nappy Brown
    Fo/8/55
"Western Rider Blues" - Soldier Boy Houston
    F/8/52
"Wetback Hop" - Chuck Higgins S/9/55
"Whadaya Want" - Robins S/2/55
"What A Crazy Feeling" - Eagles T/1/55
"What Can I Say" - Ray-O-Vacs F/11/52
"What Can I Do" - Kings S/6/54
"What Do You Do" - Topps T/2/54
"What If You" - Luther Bond and Emeralds
    Fo/2/54
"What Kind Of Fool Is He?" - Little Caesar
    T/11/53
"What Makes Me Feel This Way" - Sultans
    Fo/1/55
"What Wrong Have I Done" - Country Slim
    S/12/53
"What You Got On Your Mind?" - Rosco
    Gordon F/9/52
"What'cha Gonna Do" - Clyde McPhatter and
    the Drifters F/3/55
"What'cha Gonna Do For Me" - Titus Turner
    T/6/52
"What'd I Say" - Ruth Brown F/8/55
"What's Her Whimsey, Dr. Kinsey?" - Stomp
    Gordon S/11/53
"What's That" - "5" Royales Fo/7/54
"What's The Matter With Me?" - Four
    Buddies F/11/52
"Wheel Of Fortune" - Cardinals F/2/52
"Wheel Of Fortune" - Four Flames F/3/52
"Wheel Of Fortune" - Maurice King F/4/52
"Wheel Of Fortune" - Dinah Washington
    F/2/52, 5/21/52
"Wheel Of Fortune" - Eddie Wilcox and
    Sunny Gale S/1/52
"When" - Flamingos Fo/4/55
"When I Grow Too Old To Dream" - Sandmen
    T/2/55
"When I Met You" - Crickets Fo/7/53
"When I'm All Alone" - Solomon Burke
    T/12/55
"When It Rains It Pours" - Billy "The Kid"
    Emerson Fi/1/55
"When The Roses Bloom In Lover's Lane" -
    John Greer Fo/5/54
"When The Swallows Come Back To
    Capistrano" - Ray-O-Vacs T/1/52
"When The Swallows Come Back To

Capistrano" - Billy Ward and his
    Dominoes S/3/52
"When We Get Together" - Charms Fo/4/55
"When You Dance" - Turbans S/8/55
"When You Surrender" - Jimmy Scott
    S/4/52
"When You Talk" - Cliff Butler and the
    Doves Fo/8/53
"Where Are You" - Mello-Moods T/1/52
"Where Do I Go From Here" - Swallows
    T/11/52
"Whiskey Do Your Stuff" - Louis Jordan
    F/2/54
"Whiskey Drinkin' Women" - St. Louis
    Jimmy S/5/53
"Whiskey, Women And Loaded Dice" - Stick
    McGhee T/5/53
"Whisper To Me" - Rhythm Aces Fo/5/55
"Whispering Blues" - Piney Brown Fo/6/53
"Whispering Sorrows" - Nutmegs S/11/55
"Whistle My Love" - Moonglows Fo/10/53
"White Christmas" - Clyde McPhatter and
    the Drifters S/11/54
"White Cliffs Of Dover" - Blue Jays
    S/10/53
"White Cliffs Of Dover" - Checkers
    F/11/53
"Who Drank The Beer While I Was In The
    Rear" - Dave Bartholomew F/12/52
"Whole Lotta Shakin' Goin' On" - Roy Hall
    S/10/55
"Whoopin' And Hollerin'" - Earl Forest
    Fo/11/52
"Why Did You Leave Me?" - Ravens S/6/52
"Why Do I Wait?" - Bill Robinson and the
    Quails Fo/9/54
"Why Does It Have To Be" - Carl Van Moon
    F/10/55
"Why Don't I?" - Heartbreakers S/5/52
"Why Don't You Do Right" - Amos Milburn
    S/3/55
"Why Don't You Write Me" - Feathers
    Fo/4/55
"Why Don't You Write Me" - Jacks F/5/55
"Why, Johnny, Why" - Linda Hayes with
    Johnny Moore's Three Blazers F/2/55
"Why Not?" - T-Bone Walker F/10/55
"Why, Oh Why" - Edna McGriff Fo/2/53
"Why, Oh Why" - Lloyd "The Fat Man"
    Smith T/5/52
"Why Should I Love You" - Harptones
    F/7/54
"Wiggie" - Gene Forrest and the Four
    Feathers S/3/54
"Wiggle Waggle Woo" - Stick McGhee

S/3/54
"Wild, Wild Young Men" - Ruth Brown
    Fo/5/53
"Will You Love Me" - Marvin and Johnny
    T/11/55
"Wind Keeps Blowin'" - Jimmy Witherspoon
    T/2/52
"Wine Head" - King Curtis T/5/53
"Wine-O-Wine" - Willis Jackson F/2/52
"Wine Wine Wine" - Jimmy Binkley F/3/54
"Witchcraft" - Spiders S/10/55
"With All My Heart" - Five Scamps T/12/54
"With All Your Heart" - "5" Royales F/2/55
"Without A Friend" - Strangers S/8/55
"Without A Song" - Ravens T/10/53
"Without Your Love" - Charles Brown
    F/8/52
"Wobble Lou" - Ray Agee F/8/55
"Woke Up Screaming" - Bobby Bland
    Fo/11/55
"Woke Up This Morning" - B. B. King
    F/3/53
"Women About To Make Me Go Crazy" - "5"
    Royales S/8/55
"Women And Money" - John Lee Hooker
    T/3/54
"Work With Me Annie" - Royals Fo/2/54
"World Is Waiting For The Sunrise, The" -
    Larks E/7/54
"Worried 'Bout You Baby" - Big Boy Crudup
    5/6/52
"Worried Life Blues" - Big Maceo S/7/55
"Would You Baby" - Willie Mabon Fo/4/54

Y
"Yeah, Yeah, Yeah" - Joe Liggins Fi/8/54
"Yes, I Know" - Annisteen Allen T/2/53
"Yes, I Know" - Linda Hayes Fo/1/53,
    F/3/53
"Yes My Baby" - Scamps T/12/55
"Yes Sir That's My Baby" - Five Keys
    T/1/52
"Yes Sir That's My Baby" - Sensations
    F/11/55
"You Ain't Been True" - Faye Adams T/3/55
"You Are My Only Love" - Cardinals
    Fo/5/53
"You Belong To Me" - Buddy Lucas T/9/52
"You Belong To Me" - Orioles T/11/52
"You Came To Me" - Five Crowns T/3/55
"You Can Pack Your Suitcase" - Fats Domino
    S/8/54
"You Can't Bring Me Down" - Oscar McLollie
    F/3/53
"You Can't Have No Love No More" - Eddie

"Cleanhead" Vinson Fi/3/54
"You Can't Keep A Good Man Down" - Billy
    Ward and his Dominoes S/7/53
"You Can't Take It With You" - Young
    Johnny Watson Fo/5/54
"You Didn't Know" - Billy Paul F/7/52
"You Didn't Learn It At Home" - "5"
    Royales F/2/55
"You Done Me Wrong" - Fats Domino
    T/2/54
"You Don't Exist No More" - Percy
    Mayfield S/2/55
"You Don't Have To Go" - Jimmy Reed
    S/12/54
"You Figure It Out" - Rosco Gordon
    Fo/8/54
"You Got Me Reeling And Rocking" - Roy
    Milton Fo/7/55
"You Got To Give" - Mike Gordon and the
    El Tempos F/5/54
"You Gotta Reap" - Lowell Fulson S/4/54
"You Know I Love You" - B. B. King
    Fo/8/52
"You Let My Love Grow Cold" - Dinah
    Washington S/4/53
"You Look Bad" - Danny Taylor Fo/12/53
"You Look Good To Me" - Browler Guy
    S/7/53
"You Made Me This Way" - Piney Brown
    S/9/52
"You Make Me Happy" - Dodgers S/9/54
"You Never Had It So Good" - Checkers
    F/1/54
"You Never Miss Your Water" - Jimmy Scott
    T/9/52
"You Played On My Piano" - John Greer
    S/2/53
"You Played Your Part In Breaking My
    Heart" - Little David F/8/52
"You Tickle Me Baby" - Royal Jokers
    F/9/55
"You Took My Heart" - Damita Jo T/4/52
"You Upset Me Baby" - B. B. King
    Fo/10/54
"You Were Lyin' To Me" - Percy Mayfield
    T/12/54
"You Were My Baby" - Luther Bond and the
    Emeralds F/7/54
"You Were Untrue" - Flairs Fi/5/54
"You Yakity Yak Too Much" - Flippers
    S/6/55
"You'd Better Watch Yourself" - Little
    Walter Fo/8/54
"You'll Never Be Mine" - Blenders T/9/53
"You'll Never Know" - Eva Foster F/7/53

"You're A Fool" - Willie Mabon T/9/53
"You're A Part Of Me" - Four Buddies
    S/5/52
"You're Driving Me Insane" - Ike Turner
    Fo/5/52
"You're Mine" - Crickets Fo/2/53
"You're Mine" - Danny Overbea T/6/54
"You're My Inspiration" - Five Crowns
    Fo/10/52
"You're Nobody 'Till Somebody Loves You" -
    Maxwell Davis and the Ebonaires
    S/3/54
"You're Not To Worry My Life Anymore" -
    Lightnin' Hopkins F/2/52
"You're So Fine" - Little Walter T/12/53
"You're Still My Baby" - Chuck Willis
    S/12/53
"You're The Answer To My Prayer" - Varetta
    Dillard T/5/55

"You're The Beating Of My Heart" -
    Falcons T/5/53
"Your Cash Ain't Nothin' But Trash" -
    Clovers S/7/54
"Your Daddy's Doggin' Around" - Todd
    Rhodes F/3/52
"Your Key Don't Fit It No More" - Lulu
    Reed Fo/1/54
"Your Kind Of Love" - Earl Forrest
    Fo/7/54
"Your Mouth Got A Hole In It" - Todd
    Rhodes T/7/53
"Yours Forever" - Billy Ward and his
    Dominoes T/10/52
"Yum Yum" - Lamplighters Fo/10/54

Z
"Zippity Zum" - Chords S/9/54
"Zonked" - Red Prysock S/5/55

Record Company Index

(Company news other than record release dates.)

A

ABC Paramount M/9/55
Ace **4/3/53**
Aladdin **3/1/52**, M/8/52, E/11/52, 11/14/52,
    E/1/53, E/4/54, M/5/54, M/6/54,
    E/11/54, M/12/54, 1/29/55, E/2/55,
    E/11/55
Allied E/11/54
Am-Par M/9/55
Apollo L/1/52, M/3/52, E/4/54, M/7/54,
    M/8/54, L/8/54, M/7/55, M/8/55
Atlantic L/1/52, E/4/52, M/4/52, M/6/52,
    M/8/52, L/9/52, M/10/52, 10/31/52,
    5/7/53, M/5/53, L/5/53, L/7/53, E/8/53,
    L/8/53, M/10/53, M/12/53, 12/26/53,
    E/4/54, M/4/54, E/7/54, E/2/55,
    3/10/55, M/3/55, 7/23/55, 8/6/55,
    M/8/55
Atlas 7/23/55, 8/6/55, E/11/55
Atco 8/6/55, M/10/55, E/11/55

B

Baton M/5/55
Beacon M/11/54
Benida M/11/54
Big Town E/5/53
Bruce E/11/53, L/1/54, M/6/54, E/6/55
Brunswick 11/22/52, M/4/53

C

Cadence **12/20/52**
Capitol **6/7/52**, M/5/54, L/8/54, 11/6/54,
    M/8/55, 9/24/55
Cat **E/4/54**, E/7/54
Central L/10/53, E/2/54
Champion L/3/53
Chance L/2/53, L/10/53
Checker 5/10/52, M/6/54, M/7/54
Chess 5/10/52, **L/10/53**, M/6/54, E/10/54,
    M/12/54, M/12/55, L/12/55
Columbia L/2/52, M/6/52, E/7/52, M/3/53,
    E/11/53, M/7/54, 11/6/54
Combo 1/29/55
Coral 11/22/52, E/12/52, M/4/53, E/5/54,
    E/3/55, 4/30/55
Crown M/11/53, E/5/54

D

Decca E/5/52, E/9/52, M/3/53, 7/4/53,
    E/8/53, L/1/54, L/8/54, 11/6/54,
    M/11/54, 1/15/55, 1/29/55, 5/21/55,
    M/8/55, Fo/12/55
Deluxe L/10/53
Derby 2/2/52, M/8/52, E/2/54, 10/4/54
Diamond 2/9/52
Dice M/1/55
Dootone M/1/55, L/3/55, 4/9/55, M/4/55,
    4/26/55, 5/13/55, M/8/55, E/12/55
Dot M/**4**/54, 2/12/55
Duke M/6/52, 7/26/52, M/8/52, L/8/53,
    1/10/53, E/1/54, 1/23/54, E/4/54,
    E/2/55, E/3/55

E

Ecco M/12/55
Ember E/5/55
Epic E/11/53, 11/6/54, E/11/54, 3/16/55
Essex 8/6/55
Excello M/**6**/54

F

Federal E/4/54, E/6/54, L/8/54, 1/29/55,
    E/12/55
Flair 12/13/52, E/6/53, E/8/53, E/5/54,
    M/3/55
Fortune M/4/54
Four Star **E/5/53**

G

Gem M/5/54
Grand M/9/55
Groove M/1/54, M/5/54, 11/6/54, M/3/55,
    E/4/55, E/6/55

H

Harlem E/9/54, M/8/55
Herald L/5/53, E/7/53, L/7/53, M/10/53,
    M/3/55, E/4/55, E/5/55

I

Imperial 3/1/52, **E/4/52**, M/8/52, 8/23/52,
    9/26/53, E/4/54, M/9/55
Intro M/6/54

J

J.O.B. L/10/53
Jay-Dee M/11/54, E/5/55
Jubilee E/1/52, 3/1/52, E/3/52, M/4/53,
    E/9/52, M/4/53, L/7/53, E/4/54,
    E/5/54, L/6/54, L/8/54, 1/29/55,
    E/4/55

340

K

Kicks E/11/54
King 3/1/52, **M/11/52**, E/8/53, L/10/53,
    M/11/53, 12/26/53, E/4/54, E/6/54,
    M/7/54, L/8/54, 1/29/55, L/12/55

L

Lamp M/6/54, M/7/54, L/10/54

M

M-G-M E/4/52, 5/17/52, **M/8/52**, 12/13/52,
    E/1/53, M/3/53, M/4/53, 11/6/54,
    1/11/55, E/6/55
Marterry M/12/55
Mercury L/3/52, M/6/52, 9/26/52, M/11/52,
    M/3/53, M/11/53, 4/3/54, 11/6/54,
    E/11/54, E/3/55, L/3/55, 4/9/55,
    5/13/55, E/6/55, ·E/7/55, 8/3/55,
    M/8/55, E/11/55, E/12/55
Meteor 12/13/52
Modern 1/15/52, 2/9/52, M/2/52, 3/1/52,
    M/8/52, 10/11/52, 12/13/52, L/1/53,
    E/2/53, E/5/54, M/3/55, M/11/55
Music Makers E/2/53

N

National M/6/52

O

Okeh M/2/52, L/2/52, 3/1/52, E/7/52,
    M/10/52, E/11/53, M/7/54, M/9/54,
    11/6/54, M/1/55
Old Town E/6/55

P

Parrot M/6/54
Peacock 1/12/52, M/2/52, M/3/52, M/5/52,
    7/26/52, M/8/52, M/11/52, E/12/52,
    M/3/53, M/11/53, E/1/54, 1/23/54,
    E/4/54
Post M/9/55

R

R & B E/11/54
RCA Victor (see Victor)
RPM 2/9/52, 3/1/52, M/6/52, M/8/52,
    10/11/52, 12/13/52, L/1/53, E/2/53,
    E/6/53, E/5/54, M/3/55
Rainbow L/5/52, E/7/52, E/2/55, M/3/55
Republic 2/12/55
Recorded In Hollywood L/1/54, M/10/54,

E/1/55
Regent L/1/52
Rhythm And Blues 2/9/52, 10/11/52
Riviera M/3/55
Rockin' L/10/53
Roulette **M/11/54**

S

SLS E/5/54
Savoy L/1/52, M/2/52, M/4/52, M/8/52,
    L/8/52, 9/26/52, M/11/52, E/2/53,
    M/5/53, M/6/53, M/10/53, L/10/53,
    M/1/54, M/2/54, E/3/54, E/5/54,
    E/7/54, E/11/55, L/11/55
Score E/1/53, M/6/54, M/1/55
    7-11 E/11/52, M/6/54
Show Time M/12/54
Sittin' In With M/8/52
Southern E/12/52
Spark M/11/54, M/10/55
Specialty M/4/52, **M/6/52**, M/8/52, L/3/53,
    M/6/54, M/4/55
Star Maid E/5/55
Starmaker M/11/53
States M/8/52
Sun L/7/53, E/1/54, 11/20/55
Swing Time E/1/52, M/10/54, M/1/55

T

Teenage M/1/55
Tempo M/4/52
Treat M/4/55
Tuxedo E/8/53

U

United M/8/52, E/2/53

V

Vee-Jay **M/7/53**
Victor M/2/52, 6/7/52, M/8/52, M/11/52,
    E/2/53, 2/21/53, M/3/53, L/7/53,
    E/9/53, E/10/53, E/1/54, M/1/54,
    2/8/54, E/4/54, L/6/54, 7/31/54,
    11/6/54, 1/11/55, M/1/55, L/3/55, .
    E/4/55, 11/20/55, F/12/55

W

Wing E/6/55, M/8/55

X

"X" 11/6/54

341

Industry Personnel Index

OWNERS, WRITERS, DEEJAYS

A
Abramson, Herb L/5/53
Allen, Steve 3/8/55
Angel, Jack M/3/55

B
Bergman M/11/54
Berle, Milton 12/12/52
Beyer, Archie 12/20/52
Bihari Brothers M/6/52, 10/11/52, L/1/53,
    E/2/53, E/8/53, E/5/54, M/11/54
Bihari, Joe 1/15/52, M/10/52, E/5/54,
    M/11/54
Bihari, Jules 1/15/52, 2/9/52, M/11/53,
    E/5/54, M/11/54, M/11/55
Bihari, Lester 12/13/52, L/1/53
Bihari, Saul L/1/53, E/5/54, M/11/54,
    M/3/55
Bracken, Jimmy M/7/53
Brown, Joe L/10/53
Bruce, Money E/11/53
Bryant, Willie 4/21/52

C
Calhoun, Charles 7/23/55
Carroll, Ray 4/21/52
Carter, Vivian M/7/53
Charles, Ezzard 9/19/52
Chess, Leonard L/10/53
Chudd, Lou 8/23/52

D
Davis, Joe M/11/54
Dr. Daddy-O E/2/52
Dr. Jive 8/19/55, 11/20/55, 12/23/55

E
Ertegun, Ahmet M/5/53, L/5/53, L/8/53,
    M/12/53, M/3/55, M/12/55
Ertegun, Neshui M/12/55

F
Freed, Alan 3/21/52, E/6/52, M/8/52,
    E/6/53, 8/14/53, L/10/53, M/12/53,
    5/1/54, 7/4/54, 8/6/54, 9/7/54, 10/2/54,
    11/24/54, 1/14/55, E/2/55, E/3/55,
    M/3/55, 4/8/55, 4/30/55, E/5/55,
    5/14/55, 5/20/55, 5/27/55, 7/5/55,
    9/2/55, 9/17/55, 12/5/55, 12/22/55

G
Glover, Henry M/11/52
Godfrey, Arthur 12/20/52, E/7/54, 2/12/55
Graham, Bill 9/7/54

H
Henderson, Douglas "Jocko" M/4/53,
    M/11/53
Horn, Bob 10/6/52

J
Jackson, Hal 7/8/55, 11/18/55

K
Kessler, Danny E/9/53, E/10/53
Kirby, George 2/20/53
Krefitz, Lou M/5/53

L
Leiber, Jerry **M/11/54**, M/10/55
Lorenz, George "Hound Dog" E/5/54

M
Mabley, Jackie "Moms" 5/15/53
Mack, Ted M/7/52, 2/12/55
Magdid, Lee M/6/53, L/10/53
Markham, Pigmeat 2/22/52, 4/30/54
Marks, Rose 9/19/52
Meisner, Eddie E/11/52, M/8/54
Meisner, Lou E/11/52
Moondog 11/24/54, 7/5/55
Morelan, Mantan 3/19/54

N
Nathan, Sydney M/11/5
North, Sheree 7/23/55

P
Parker, Colonel Tom **E/1/54**
Phillips, Sam L/7/53

R
Ram, Buck **4/9/55**
Randle, Bill 6/5/53, **4/17/54**, 9/24/54,
    12/24/54
Roby, Don L/8/53, E/4/54
Rolontz, Bob M/3/55
Rupe, Art M/4/52

S
Shaw, Billy M/1/52

342

Sill, Lester M/11/54
Smalls, Tommy **Fi/9/52**, 4/10/55
Stewart, Lee 10/6/52
Stoller, Mike **M/11/54**, M/10/55
Stone, Jesse M/4/52, M/8/54
Sullivan, Ed M/3/53, 11/20/55

V

Van Doren, Mamie **7/23/55**
Vincent, John L/3/53, M/6/54

W

Wexler, Jerry L/5/53, L/8/53
White, Slappy 7/11/52
Wiggles 2/26/53
Williams, Dootsie (listed under Singers)
Wood, Randy M/4/54
Woods, George 4/21/52, 10/14/55

Y

Young, Ernie M/6/54

Broadcast Media Index

ABC Radio Network 4/7/55
CBS Radio and Television Network 10/23/54,
     11/26/55
KDET, Center, TX L/9/52
KEYS, Corpus Christi, TX M/11/54
KFOX, Los Angeles, CA 5/13/54, 11/1/54
WCAE, Pittsburgh, PA E/6/54
WCBS, New York, NY 12/24/54
WDAS, Philadelphia, PA M/11/53
WDIA, Memphis, TN L/8/53, M/11/53,
     E/10/54, 12/3/54
WERE, Cleveland, OH 9/24/54, 12/24/54
WFIL-TV, Philadelphia, PA **10/6/52**

WGN, Chicago, IL 3/25/55
WGRY, Gary, IN M/7/53
WHAT, Philadelphia, PA M/4/53, 10/14/55
WINS, New York, NY 9/7/54, 10/2/54,
     11/24/54, 7/5/55
WJJL, Niagara Falls, NY E/5/54
WJMR, New Orleans, LA M/7/52
WJW, Cleveland, OH E/6/53, 9/7/54,
10/2/54
WLAC, Nashville, TN M/4/54
WLIP, New York, NY M/4/53
WMBL, Macon, GA E/2/55
WNJR, Newark, NJ M/12/53, 5/1/54, 7/4/54
WOV, New York, NY 4/21/52
WPIX-TV, New York, NY 8/31/53
WWRL, New York, NY 4/21/52, 4/10/55
WXYZ, Detroit, MI 3/13/54

Shake Rattle & Roll

THE GOLDEN AGE
OF
AMERICAN ROCK 'N ROLL

APPENDIXES
&
BIBLIOGRAPHY

Appendix A

1952-1955 ADDRESSES OF
RHYTHM & BLUES RECORD COMPANIES

Aardell
6130 Selma Avenue
Hollywood, CA

Aladdin
451 North Cannon Drive
Beverly Hills, CA

Apollo
457 West 45th Street
New York, NY

Aristocrat
5249 South Cottage Grove
Chicago, IL

Atlantic
234 West 56th Street
New York, NY

Atco
234 West 125th Street
New York, NY

Atlas
271 West 125th Street
New York, NY

Baton
108 West 44th Street
New York, NY

Big Town
305 South Fair Oaks
Pasadena, CA

Bruce
1650 Broadway
New York, NY

Brunswick
50 West 57th Street
New York, NY

Capitol
1507 North Vine
Hollywood, CA

Cash
2610 South Crenshaw
Los Angeles, CA

Cat
234 West 56th Street
New York, NY

Central
520 West 50th Street
New York, NY

Chance
1151 East 47th Street
Chicago, IL

Chart
1214 South West 8th Street
Miami, FL

Checker
4858 South Cottage Grove
   Avenue (1952)
750 East 49th Street (1954)
4750 Cottage Grove (1955)
Chicago, IL

Chess
750 East 49th Street (1954)
4750 Cottage Grove (1955)
Chicago, IL

Co-Ed
12 West 177th Street
New York, NY

Columbia
799 Seventh Avenue
New York, NY

Combo
1107 El Centro
Hollywood, CA

Coral
50 West 57th Street
New York, NY

Crest
1248 South Berendo
Los Angeles, CA

Crown
6365 Selma Avenue
Hollywood, CA

Crystalette
601 East 4th
Santa Ana, CA

Decca
50 West 57th Street
New York, NY

Dee Jay
324 Sunrise Highway
Rockville Centre, NY

DeLuxe
1540 Brewster Avenue
Cincinnati, OH

Derby
767 Tenth Avenue
New York, NY

Dootone
9514 South Central
Los Angeles, CA

Dot
Gallatin, TN

Duke
4104 Lyons Avenue (1952)
2809 Erastus Street (1953)
Houston, TX

Ember
1697 Broadway
New York, NY

Epic
799 Seventh Avenue
New York, NY

Essex
8406 Lyons (1953)
3208 South 34th Street (1954)
Philadelphia, PA

Excello
177 Third Avenue North
Nashville, TN

Federal
1540 Brewster Avenue
Cincinnati, OH

Fidelity
8508 Sunset Boulevard
Hollywood, CA

Flair
686 North Robertson Boulevard
Beverly Hills, CA (1954)
9317 West Washington Boulevard
Culver City, CA (1955)

Flip
706 Union Avenue
Memphis, TN

Fortune
11629 Linwood
Detroit, MI

Gee
220 West 42nd Street
New York, NY

Glory
2 West 47th Street
New York, NY

Gotham
1626 Federal Street (1952)
1416 Wood Street (1954)
Philadelphia, PA

Grand
109 West 49th Street
New York, NY

Groove
630 West Fifth Avenue (1954)
153 East 24th Street (1955)
New York, NY

Harlem
103 East 125th Street
New York, NY

Herald
469 West Broadway (1953)
236 West 55th Street (1954)
1697 Broadway (1955)
New York, NY

Imperial
6425 Hollywood Boulevard
Hollywood, CA

Intro
451 North Cannon Drive
Beverly Hills, CA

Jaguar
1650 Broadway
New York, NY

Jay-Dee
1519 Broadway (1954)
441 West 49th Street (1955)
New York, NY

J.O.B.
4008 South Ellis Avenue
Chicago, IL

Josie (JOZ)
315 West 47th Street (1954)
1650 Broadway (1955)
New York, NY

Jubilee
315 West 47th Street (1954)
1650 Broadway (1955)
New York, NY

King
1540 Brewster Avenue
Cincinnati, OH

Lamp
451 North Cannon Drive
Beverly Hills, CA

M & M
701 Seventh Avenue
New York, NY

Magnet
104 Mitchell Avenue
Ashville, NC

Mambo
1486 North Fair Oaks
Pasadena, CA

Mercury
35 East Wacker Drive
Chicago, IL (1954)
745 Fifth Avenue
New York, NY (1955)

Meteor
1914 Chelsea Avenue
Memphis, TN

M-G-M
701 Seventh Avenue
New York, NY

Modern
686 North Robertson Boulevard
Beverly Hills, CA (1954)
9317 West Washington Boulevard
Culver City, CA (1955)

Money
1248 South Berendo Street
Los Angeles, CA

Music City
1815 Alcatraz Avenue
Berkeley, CA

Nashboro
177 Third Avenue North
Nashville, TN

Okeh
799 Seventh Avenue
New York, NY

Old Town
701 Seventh Avenue
New York, NY

Paradise
701 Seventh Avenue
New York, NY

Parrot
4858 Cottage Grove Avenue
Chicago, IL

Peacock
    4104 Lyons Avenue (1952)
    2809 Erastus Street (1953)
    Houston, TX

Rainbow
    767 Tenth Avenue
    New York, NY

Rama
    220 West 42nd Street
    New York, NY

RCA Victor
    630 Fifth Avenue
    New York, NY

Recorded in Hollywood
    2528 West Pico Boulevard (1954)
    1248 South Berendo Street (1955)
    Los Angeles, CA

Red Robin
    301 West 125th Street
    New York, NY

Regent
    58 Market Street
    Newark, NJ

Republic
    535 Fourth Avenue South (1952)
    714 Allison Street (1953)
    Nashville, TN

Rhythm and Blues
    240 North Cannon Drive
    Beverly Hills, CA

Robin
    315 West 47th Street
    New York, NY

Roost
    625 Tenth Avenue
    New York, NY

RPM
    257 North Robertson Boulevard
    Beverly Hills, CA (1954)
    9317 West Washington Boulevard
    Culver City, CA (1955)

Savoy
    58 Market Street
    Newark, NJ

Score
    451 North Cannon Drive
    Beverly Hills, CA

7-11
    451 North Cannon Drive
    Beverly Hills, CA

Show Time
    1248 South Berendo Street
    Los Angeles, CA

Sittin' In With
    733 11th Avenue
    New York, NY

Spark
    1119 South Crenshaw Boulevard
    Los Angeles, CA

Specialty
    8508 Sunset Boulevard
    Los Angeles, CA

States
    5052 South Cottage Grove Avenue
    Chicago, IL

Sun
    706 Union Avenue
    Memphis, TN

Swing Time
    3427 South San Pedro Street
    Los Angeles, CA

Tempo
    8540 Sunset Boulevard
    Hollywood, CA

Trumpet
    309 North Farrish
    Jackson, MS

Tuxedo
    132 Nassau Street
    New York, NY

United
    5052 South Cottage Grove Avenue
    Chicago, IL

Vee-Jay
Gary, IN (1953)
412 East 47th Street (1954)
4747 Cottage Court (1955)
Chicago, IL

"X"
630 Fifth Avenue
New York, NY

Appendix B

RECORD COMPANY AFFILIATES

Atlantic	Aladdin	Chess	Columbia	Decca	Jubilee
Atco	Lamp	Checker	Epic	Brunswick	JOZ
Cat	Score		Okeh	Coral	Robin
	7-11				

King	Modern	Money	Nashboro	Peacock	RCA Victor
DeLuxe	Crown	Cash	Excello	Duke	Groove
Federal	Flair				"X"
	Rhythm & Blues				
	RPM				

Sun	Tico	United
Flip	Gee	States
	Rama	

Bibliography

BOOKS

Author	Title
ASCAP editors	ASCAP Biographical Dictionary
BMI editors	BMI: Meet The Artist
Belz, Carl	The Story of Rock
Berman, Jay	The Fifties Book
Berry, Peter E.	. . . And The Hits Just Keep On Comin'
Broven, John	Rhythm And Blues In New Orleans
Busnar, Gene	It's Rock 'N Roll
Case, Brian & Britt, Stan	The Illustrated Encyclopedia Of Jazz
Chipman, Bruce L.	Hardening Rock
Chapple, Steve & Garofalo, Reebee	Rock 'N Roll Is Here To Pay
Chilton, John	Who's Who Of Jazz
Clark, Dick & Robinson, Richard	Rock, Roll And Remember
Clifford, Mike (ed.)	Illustrated Encyclopedia Of Black Music
Cohn, Nik	AWopBopaLooBopALopBamBoom
Cohn, Nik	Rock From The Beginning
Coleman, Stuart	They Kept On Rockin'
Cooper, B. Lee	The Literature of Rock, II, 1979-1983
Cotten, Lee	All Shook Up: Elvis, Day-By-Day, 1954-1977
Cottrill, Les	45 Label Lists, Volumes 1-4
Dalton, David & Kaye, Lenny	Rock 100
DeWitt, Howard A.	Chuck Berry: Rock 'N Roll Music
Eisen, Jonathan (ed.)	The Age Of Rock
Escott, Colin & Hawkins, Martin	Sun Records: The Brief History Of The Legendary Record Label
Fong-Tores, Ben (ed.)	The Rolling Stone Rock and Roll Reader
Gillett, Charlie	Making Tracks (The History Of Atlantic Records)
Gillett, Charlie	The Sound Of The City
Goldstein, Stewart & Jacobson Alan	Oldies But Goodies
Guralnick, Peter	Feel Like Going Home: Portraits In Blues And Rock 'N Roll
Guralnick, Peter	Listener's Guide To The Blues
Guralnick, Peter	Lost Highway: Journeys And Arrivals Of American Musicians
Guralnick, Peter	Sweet Soul Music
Hannusch, Jeff	I Hear You Knockin'
Haralambos, Michael	Right On: From Blues To Soul In Black America
Hardy, Phil & Laing, Dave (ed.)	Encyclopedia Of Rock, Vol 1
Harris, Sheldon	Blues Who's Who
Helander, Brock	The Rock Who's Who
Hendler, Herb	Year By Year In The Rock Era
Hill, Randal C.	Collectable Rock Records

Hoffman, Frank   The Cash Box Singles, 1950-1981
Hoffman, Frank   The Literature Of Rock, 1954-1978
Hughes, Penassie & Gauthier, Madeline   Guide To Jazz

Jahn, Mike   Rock From Elvis Presley To The Rolling Stones

Jenkinson, Phillip & Warner, Alan   Celluloid Rock
Jones, Leroi   Blues People

Leadbetter, Mike & Slaven, Neil   Blues Records, 1943-1966
Lyndon, Michael   Boogie Lightning
Lyndon, Michael   Rock Folk

McCutcheon, Lynn   Rhythm And Blues
McKee, Margaret & Chisenhull, Fred   Beale, Black & Blue
Marcus, Greil   Mystery Train
Marcus, Greil   Rock And Roll Will Stand
Meltzer, R.   The Esthetics Of Rock
Millar, Bill   The Drifters
Miller, Jim (ed.)   The Rolling Stone Illustrated History Of Rock & Roll

Murrells, Joseph   The Book Of Golden Discs

Nite, Norman   Rock On
Norman, Phillip   The Road Goes On Forever
Nugent, Steven & Gillett, Charlie   Rock Almanac

Oakley, Giles   The Devil's Music: A History Of The Blues
Oliver, Paul & Osborne, Jerry   The Story Of The Blues
Osborne, Jerry & Hamilton, Bruce   Blues, Rhythm & Blues, Soul

Palmer, Robert   Deep Blues
Palmer, Robert   A Tale Of Two Cities: Memphis Rock And New Orleans Roll

Parales, Jon & Romanowski, Patricia (ed.)   The Rolling Stone Encyclopedia Of Rock & Roll

Pascall, Jeremy (ed.)   The Stars And Superstars Of Rock
Pascall, Jeremy (ed.)   The Story Of Rock (Vol. 103)
Pollock, Bruce   When Rock Was Young
Propes, Steve   Those Oldies But Goodies

Redmond, Mike & Gonzales, Fernando   Disco-File
Reed, Bill & Ehrenstein, David   Rock On Film
Rhode, H. Kandy   The Gold Of Rock & Roll: 1955-1967
Rolling Stones editors   Rolling Stone Rock Review
Rolling Stones editors   Rolling Stone Rock Almanac
Rowe, Mike   Chicago Breakdown
Roxon, Lillian   Rock Encyclopedia
Ruppli, Michael   The Atlantic Labels, A Discography
Ruppli, Michael   The Chess Labels, A Discography
Ruppli, Michael   The Savoy Labels, A Discography

Salisbury, Harrison E.   The Shook Up Generation
Sawyer, Charles   The Arrival Of B. B. King
Shaw, Arnold   Honkers And Shouters

Shaw, Arnold	The Rock Revolution
Shaw, Arnold	The Rockin' '50s
Shaw, Arnold	The World Of Soul
Southern, Eileen	Biographical Dictionary Of Afro-American And African Musicians
Stambler, Irwin	Encyclopedia Of Pop, Rock & Soul
Stambler, Irwin & Landon, Grelun	Encyclopedia of Folk, Country And Western Music
Swenson, John	Bill Haley
Toches, Nick	Country: The Biggest Music In America
Toches, Nick	Unsung Heroes Of Rock 'N Roll
Whitburn, Joel	Top Pop Records 1940-1955
Whitburn, Joel	Top Rhythm & Blues Records, 1949-1971
Worth, Fred	Rock Facts
Yorke, Ritchie	The History Of Rock 'N Roll

MAGAZINES

Audio Trader
Bay Area Magazine (BAM)
Big Town Review
Billboard
Bim, Bam, Boom
Blast From The Past
Blues 'N Rhythm
Blues Unlimited
Crawdaddy
Goldmine
Juke Blues
Living Blues
Music Bible
Music World
Nostalgia Monthly
Nostalgia World
Now Dig This
Paul's Record Magazine
Pickin' The Blues
Pop Top
Pulse
R&B Magazine
Record Auction Monthly (RAM)
Record Collector's Journal
Record Collector's Monthly
Record Digest

Record Exchanger
Record Finder
Record Profile Magazine (RPM)
Record Spinner
Rock & Roll
Rollin' Rock
Rolling Stone
Stormy Weather
Variety
Who Put The Bomp
Yesterday's Memories

NEWSPAPERS

Baltimore Afro-American
Las Vegas Record
Los Angeles Sentinel
Los Angeles Times
Louisiana Weekly (New Orleans)
Michigan Chronicle (Detroit)
New York Times
Philadelphia Tribune
Sacramento Bee
Sacramento Union
San Francisco Chronicle
Washington Post

About the Author

Lee Cotten has enjoyed a lifelong involvement with rock 'n roll music. Although he was born in Philadelphia, he grew up in small towns in Mississippi and Georgia. He received his initiation in the blues listening late at night to WLAC radio, a clear-channel station broadcasting from Nashville. He vividly remembers hearing "Maybellene" in the fall of 1955 as it played on the jukebox at the back of the local soda shop on those waning evenings after his Boy Scout meetings. He readily recalls the reaction when "Tutti Frutti" and "Long Tall Sally" were sneaked onto the turntable at summer church camp dances in North Carolina. He also recollects the first time Elvis's voice came blasting out of a jukebox near the public pool in the small town of Monroe, Georgia. He has ordered records from Randy's Record Shop in Gallatin, Tennessee (the home of Dot Records). As a teen-ager, he was the kid who brought the latest records to the parties. He always knew what artist recorded for which label, and he could regale about musical influences, styles, and backgrounds. He played piano in a high school rock 'n roll band, flat-top guitar in a college folk trio, and electric guitar in a long-forgotten rock 'n roll/ rhythm and blues band. In the years since, his interest in rock 'n roll music has never diminished. It grew as he grew, first as a collector, then as a mail-order dealer, finally for fifteen years as owner of Golden Oldies in Sacramento, California, a specialty shop dealing almost exclusively in 45 rpm records, which at one time boasted an inventory hovering around 250,000 singles.

Lee is the co-author of *Jailhouse Rock: The Bootleg Recordings of Elvis Presley, 1970-1983* (Popular Culture, Ink.), and the author of *All Shook Up: Elvis Day-By-Day, 1954-1977* (Popular Culture, Ink.). Both books have received overwhelming acclaim from the fans of Elvis Presley and the critics in the rock music press alike. In October 1986, he closed his retail store to concentrate on writing about rock 'n roll full time. In August 1987, Doubleday published his next book, *The Elvis Catalog: The Authorized Edition*. Lee is currently hard at work on Volume 2 of *The Golden Age of American Rock 'N Roll*, which will cover the years 1956-1959.